Effective Physical Education Content and Instruction

Phillip Ward, PhD

Harry Lehwald, EdD

The Ohio State University

SHAPE America SOCIETY OF HEALTH AND PHYSICAL EDUCATORS®

health. moves. minds.

HUMAN KINETICS

Library of Congress Cataloging-in-Publication Data

Names: Ward, Phillip, 1957- | SHAPE America (Organization)
Title: Effective physical education content and instruction : an
  evidence-based and teacher-tested approach / [edited by] Phillip Ward,
  PhD, Harry Lehwald, EdD.
Description: Champaign, IL : Human Kinetics, Inc., [2018] | "SHAPE America
  Society of Health and Physical Educators." | Includes bibliographical
  references.
Identifiers: LCCN 2017019784 (print) | LCCN 2017040607 (ebook) | ISBN
  9781492543664 (e-book) | ISBN 9781492543541 (print)
Subjects: LCSH: Physical education and training--Study and teaching--United
  States. | Physical fitness--Study and teaching--United States.
Classification: LCC GV365 (ebook) | LCC GV365 .E45 2018 (print) | DDC
  372.86--dc23
LC record available at https://lccn.loc.gov/2017019784

ISBN: 978-1-4925-4354-1 (print)

The web addresses cited in this text were current as of July 2017, unless otherwise noted.

Acquisitions Editor: Scott Wikgren
SHAPE America Editor: Joe McGavin
Senior Developmental Editor: Bethany J. Bentley
Senior Managing Editor: Amy Stahl
Graphic Designer: Julie L. Denzer
Cover Designer: Keith Blomberg
Photograph (cover): © Human Kinetics
Senior Art Manager: Kelly Hendren
Illustrations: © Human Kinetics
Printer: Sheridan Books

SHAPE America – Society of Health and Physical Educators
1900 Association Drive
Reston, VA 20191
800-213-7193
www.shapeamerica.org

Printed in the United States of America   10 9 8 7 6 5 4 3 2 1

The paper in this book is certified under a sustainable forestry program.

Human Kinetics
P.O. Box 5076
Champaign, IL 61825-5076
Website: www.HumanKinetics.com

In the United States, email info@hkusa.com or call 800-747-4457.
In Canada, email info@hkcanada.com.
In the United Kingdom/Europe, email hk@hkeurope.com.

For information about Human Kinetics' coverage in other areas of the world,
please visit our website: **www.HumanKinetics.com**

E6933

To Daryl Siedentop and Alan Launder, who led the way.
To my father, Phillip Ward Sr., who provided me with
the opportunity and encouragement to pursue my work,
and to my sons, Robert and Trevor, who provided
me with the motivation.

-Phillip Ward

To my wife, LeAnn, and my sons, Kyle, Bryce, and Brett,
who supported and inspired this book, and to the memory
of my parents, Herman and Lola Mae Lehwald,
who believed in education and supported me
throughout my teaching career.

-Harry Lehwald

Contents

Preface

A few years ago, we asked more than 3,000 preservice and in-service physical education teachers in 14 different states 24 fundamental questions about teaching basketball in elementary and secondary schools. The questions focused on rules of the game, techniques (such as the layup and the chest pass), common errors, and instructional progressions to teach the sport skills. The results were startling. Approximately 85 percent of the respondents got fewer than 50 percent of the answers correct for these basic questions (Kim et al., 2010; Li et al., 2013). This is striking because basketball is the most frequently taught activity in grades 3 through 12 and is one of the most popular sports in the United States. Similar findings have been reported for teacher knowledge of health-related fitness, volleyball, and soccer (Castelli & Williams, 2007; Stuhr et al., 2007). It is increasingly recognized that teachers in preservice and in-service settings need more assistance in understanding physical education content.

Why is content knowledge such a significant problem? It seems obvious that you cannot teach what you do not know. If you were asked to teach slideball, you would not be able to because you do not know anything about our invented game. The rules, techniques, tactics, and demands on the players are all unknown. If you attempted to teach slideball, you would need to understand the common errors students might make in learning this sport so you could anticipate student challenges, know what feedback to provide, and know how to tailor the feedback to your students of different ages and abilities. It often takes many years to acquire this knowledge.

The challenges we describe for new teachers of slideball are the same challenges that confront teachers of most subjects. We have repeatedly found that physical education teachers are often very knowledgeable about only one or two sports or activities. For the other activities, the teachers typically know the skills to be taught, how to perform the techniques, and a little about the tactics, but their knowledge of task progressions, how to organize and adapt the tasks, and the types of errors students make is often limited.

Imagine working with a master teacher who describes what can be taught at each grade level and who shares ways to organize lessons and units so students can engage in skillful play relative to their ability levels. The master teacher provides you with game-like teaching progressions. As you teach the game to your students, the master teacher points out common errors that could occur and tells you how to correct these common errors with cues and task modifications. This book serves as a master teacher.

We have designed this book as a primary resource for practicing teachers, preservice teachers, and teacher education faculty. The content we included, although it is based on common content taught in K-12 physical education, is not meant to be inclusive. Our goal is to provide you with an understanding of physical education content and how to present and sequence that content.

We hope the instructional tasks and their techniques and tactics, the common errors and their corrections, and the content maps and sample block plans provided in this book will help you gain an understanding of teaching that you can apply to content that is not included in this book. In addition, you should adapt the content in this book to your students' ability levels, the context in which it is taught, and the duration of the unit. We hope that this model will also improve your teaching as you continue to use it.

You should feel confident that the material in this book is tried and tested. This book has been developed in collaboration with master teachers who know their content and know how to teach it. They have used the content in this book in their own teaching. In addition, we used the content of this book in our teacher education program at The Ohio State University to educate preservice teachers. The content has also been taught to teachers in professional development workshops and evaluated in research studies. What we provide in this book is truly teacher tested.

In designing the chapter content, we drew on the play practice teaching model (Launder & Piltz, 2013) and on instructional approaches developed at Ohio State. We also focused on developing content that requires the fewest organizational and transitional changes in any one lesson. Most importantly, we designed the instructional tasks in this book such that they can be used by teachers who are not experienced with the particular sports and activities addressed. The resulting chapters in this book are a special blend of what works for teachers.

The strongest and most powerful testimony for the content and teaching approaches used in the book comes from research. Beginning in 2011, experimental studies have consistently demonstrated that this approach is effective. The differences between students taught in typical instruction and those taught using our approach and content are staggering. The average student taught using the approach we discuss in this book performed better than the majority of students during their typical physical education instruction. Put another way, this equates to moving a child from the 50th percentile to the 84th percentile in performance on a skill test. This occurred regardless of ability level or gender. In short, all students were more competent performers when taught using the approach presented in this book. A list of the studies that support our approach appears at the end of this preface.

For seven years we have experimented with the best way to present the information in chapters 4 through 12 so you can quickly learn it. Initially, we sought feedback from pedagogy and content experts. When we used the chapters in our preservice teacher education program and with practicing teachers, we received feedback that shaped the organization and presentation of the content.

In this book, we use two terms for content related to movement. The first, *common content knowledge*, includes the understanding of safety and etiquette in the sport, the rules of playing it, and general techniques and tactics used. The second, *specialized content knowledge*, includes knowledge about how to teach the techniques, tactics, and game sense as well as what errors are common and how to correct them. In fact, the 2017 SHAPE America Initial Physical Education Teacher Education Standards now differentiate between common and specialized content knowledge:

- **Standard 1–Content and Foundational Knowledge:** Physical education candidates demonstrate an understanding of common and specialized content, and scientific and

theoretical foundations for the delivery of an effective PreK-12 physical education program.

The standards require beginning teachers to

- **1.a** Describe and apply common content knowledge for teaching PreK-12 physical education.
- **1.b** Describe and apply specialized content knowledge for teaching PreK-12 physical education.

This book is one of the few to present both common and specialized content knowledge for physical education teachers, and it is the only one that is evidenced based. This is one of the reasons that SHAPE America copublishes this book with Human Kinetics.

The following studies demonstrate the effectiveness of our instructional approach and content:

- Asma, M., Akarçeşme, C., Ward, P., Çamliyer, H., & Yildiran, I. (2016). *The investigation of the effects of volleyball content knowledge workshop on middle school physical education teachers.* Oral presentation at the 14th International Sport Science Congress in Papillon Ayscha-Belek, Antalya, Turkey.
- Dervent, F., Devrilmez, E., Tsuda, E., & Ward, P. (2016). *Examining content development of preservice teachers.* Oral presentation at the 14th International Sport Science Congress in Papillon Ayscha-Belek, Antalya, Turkey.
- Iserbyt, P., Ward, P., & Li, W. (2016). Effects of improved content knowledge on pedagogical content knowledge and student performance in physical education. *Physical Education and Sport Pedagogy, 21,* 539-556.
- Iserbyt, P., Ward, P., & Martens, L. (2016). The influence of content knowledge on teaching and learning in traditional and sport educa-

tion contexts: An exploratory study. *Physical Education and Sport Pedagogy, 21,* 539-556.

- Iserbyt, P. Theys, L., Ward, P., & Charlier, N. (2017). The effect of a specialized content knowledge workshop on teaching and learning Basic Life Support in elementary school: A cluster randomized controlled trial. *Resuscitation, 112,* 17-21.

- Sinelnikov, O., Kim, I., Ward, P., Curtner-Smith, M., & Li, W. (2016). Changing beginning teachers' content knowledge and its effect on student learning. *Physical Education and Sport Pedagogy, 21,* 425-440.

- Stefanou, L., Tsangaridou, N., Charalambous, C. Y., & Kyriakides, L. (2015). *Assessing subject matter knowledge of in-service generalist teachers: The case of basketball.* Paper presented at the 1st National Conference of Physical Education and Physical Activity, Nicosia, Cyprus.

- Stefanou, L., Tsangaridou, N., Charalambous, C. Y., & Kyriakides, L. (2016). *Examining the impact of a professional development program on generalist teachers' content knowledge in basketball.* Paper presented at the 14th Conference of the Cyprus Pedagogical Association, Nicosia, Cyprus.

- Ward, P. Kim, I., Ko, B., & Li, W. (2015). Effects of improving teachers' content knowledge on teaching and student learning in physical education. *Research Quarterly for Exercise and Sport, 86,* 130-139.

- Zhang, P., Ward, P., Li, W., Sutherland, S., & Goodway, J. (2012). Effects of play practice on teaching table tennis skills. *Journal of Teaching Physical Education, 31,* 71-85.

The following studies examine the presentation of content as used in this book:

- Ward, P., Dervent, F., Lee, Y. S., Ko, B., Kim, I., & Tao, W. (2017). Using content maps to measure content development in physical education: Validation and application. *Journal of Teaching in Physical Education, 36,* 20-31.

- Ward, P., Ayvazo, S., & Lehwald, H. (2014). Using knowledge packets in teacher education to develop pedagogical content knowledge. *Journal of Physical Education, Health, Recreation and Dance, 85*(6), 38-43.

- Ward, P., Lehwald, H., & Lee, Y. S. (2015). Content maps: A teaching and assessment tool for content knowledge. *Journal of Physical Education, Health, Recreation and Dance, 86*(5), 46-54.

50 MILLION STRONG BY 2029

Approximately 50 million students are currently enrolled in America's elementary and secondary schools (grades pre-K to 12). SHAPE America is leading the effort to ensure that by the time today's preschoolers graduate from high school in 2029, all of America's students will have developed the skills, knowledge and confidence to enjoy healthy, meaningful physical activity.

Acknowledgments

Much of the content in this book has been validated by researchers in the Learning to Teach Physical Education Research program at The Ohio State University (http://u.osu.edu/ltpe/). In addition, we are grateful to Dr. Justin Haegele, who provided the sections in the content chapters that address modifications for students with disabilities. We also thank Yilin Li for her modeling in figure 1.2 and Dena Deglau for her working technique example in chapter 3.

The contributors of this book's chapters share much in common with each other. In addition to knowing their content very well, they are master teachers and each has worked to improve the professional development of teachers in physical education. As such, they represent a level of expertise and experience that has informed the content of this book. Our thanks to Shiri Ayvazo, Chris Bell, Ali Brian, Insook Kim, Yun Soo Lee, Kevin Lorson, Jim Ressler, Debra Sazama, Bobbie Siedentop, and Adrian Turner for their significant contributions to making this book credible, practical, and meaningful for teachers.

How to Access the Web Resource

Throughout *Effective Physical Education Content and Instruction*, you will find references to materials that can be found in the web resource. This online content is available to you free of charge when you purchase a new print or electronic version of the book. The web resource offers printable content maps, student awards, and more. To access the online content, simply register with the Human Kinetics website.

1. Visit www.humankinetics.com/Effective PhysicalEducationContentAndInstruction.

2. Click the First Edition link next to the corresponding first-edition book cover.

3. Click the Sign In link on the left or at the top of the page. If you do not have an account with Human Kinetics, you will be prompted to create one.

4. Once you have registered, if the online product does not appear in the Ancillary Items box at the left, click the Enter Pass Code option in that box. Enter the following pass code exactly as it is printed here, including any capitalization and hyphens: **WARD-PR49-WR**.

5. Click the Submit button to unlock your online product.

6. After you have entered your pass code for the first time, you will never have to enter it again to access this online product. Once you have unlocked your product, a link to the product will appear permanently in the menu on the left. All you need to do to access your online content on subsequent visits is sign in to www.human kinetics.com/EffectivePhysicalEducation ContentAndInstruction.

If you need assistance, click the Need Help? button on the book's website.

Key to Diagrams

Symbol	Description
✗	Offensive player
O	Defensive player
⊗	Possession of ball
———————⟶	Movement of people
∼∼∼∼∼⟶	Dribble
– – – – – –⟶	Pass
·············⟶	Shooting
🛆	Cone
⌒	Dome
●	Poly spot
UH/OH	Underhand/overhead

PART

I

Preparing for Successful Teaching

Chapter 1

Understanding and Acquiring Content Knowledge

What do terms such as *effective teaching* and *quality teaching* mean? There is no single way to teach effectively, and there are certainly ineffective ways to teach (e.g., poor use of time, low levels of student engagement, tasks that are not developmentally appropriate). The outcomes of teaching are often very closely tied to the decisions that teachers make, and decision-making may be one of the most challenging aspects of teaching.

As a teacher, the decisions you make are only as good as the extent of your knowledge and the quality of your experiences. In this chapter, we introduce you to essential knowledge for teaching physical education content that will allow you to learn from your practice and make good decisions when teaching physical education.

PEDAGOGICAL CONTENT KNOWLEDGE

Researchers have defined the following as the most common and most useful types of knowledge you need to teach effectively (Shulman, 1987; Ward, 2009):

- **Knowledge of students.** Know students' personalities and culture and how they learn.
- **Knowledge of curriculum.** Know the large-scale scope of the content and pedagogies that you will teach.
- **Knowledge of context.** Know the social milieu of the class and the school, the school demographics, and the organizational structure of the school (e.g., schedules, teaching arrangements) as well as the equipment and space that is available for teaching.
- **Knowledge of pedagogy.** Know the different instructional strategies and models you can use.
- **Knowledge of content.** Know what will be taught and how it will be presented to students.

When you make a content-related teaching decision based on your understanding of these knowledge bases, you are using *pedagogical content knowledge* (PCK) (Ward, 2009; Ward, Kim, Ko, & Li, 2015). There are several definitions of PCK, but the one we use in this book was developed specifically for physical education at the Learning to Teach Physical Education Research Program at The Ohio State University. This program uses institutional research teams across the United States and in Belgium, China, Israel, Korea, and Turkey to investigate pedagogical content knowledge and content knowledge in physical education. Our definition of PCK is a focal point, a locus, defined as such, as an event in time (and therefore specific contextually) where teachers make decisions in terms of content based on their understandings of a number of knowledge bases [e.g., pedagogy, content, students, contexts, and curriculum]) (Ward, Kim, Ko & Li, 2015).

Applying PCK means that each decision you make about what and how to teach draws on your experiences and knowledge and addresses your particular students and the situations in which you are teaching. The use of PCK will not look the same for every teacher, even within the same school, because all teachers have different experiences, knowledge, and students. Students vary in their abilities, knowledge, and experiences, so you need to be purposeful in your decision-making.

Let's look at Zoey, who has been a middle school teacher for six years. She has good familiarity with her students, the school, and the content she teaches, and she is competent in class management and instructional skills. Consider how Zoey's PCK would be affected in the following scenarios:

- **Zoey decides to try a new instructional strategy.** In the short term, learning a new instructional strategy would likely change the routine of her lessons. Using a new instructional strategy, such as peer tutoring (Ward & Lee, 2005) or sport education (Siedentop, Hastie, & van der Mars, 2011), would initially involve increased time devoted to management and teaching students the new system. In the long term, however, management time would likely decrease and students would understand the new routines as they engage more frequently with the instructional strategy.

- **At the urging of her students, Zoey decides to teach team handball, a sport she knows little about and has never played.** This would present significant challenges. Zoey would first need to learn the rules, techniques, and tactics of team handball. Then she would need to learn the instructional progressions to teach these rules, techniques, and tactics.

- **Zoey receives a letter from the district indicating that she is being moved from middle school to elementary school.** This would be a big change for her. She would have to teach new content and a new curriculum in a new school, in a gymnasium that is much smaller, and with different equipment than she has used before. She would also be teaching students who are quite different from those she is familiar with. The biggest challenge would be accommodating the developmental differences of elementary school students.

In these scenarios, Zoey's PCK would change as a function of her changing knowledge or the changing contexts in which she is adapting the knowledge. Though it would take time to learn an instructional strategy or get to know new students and a new school setting, one of Zoey's greatest challenges would be developing content knowledge.

CONTENT KNOWLEDGE

Content knowledge refers to knowledge of movement, such as fundamental motor skills (e.g., throwing, catching, kicking) and movements used in individual and team sports, dance, and other movement activities (e.g., yoga); knowledge of health-related fitness and wellness; and knowledge of social skills. Movement is central to SHAPE America's Grade-Level Outcomes for K-12 Physical Education (SHAPE America – Society of Health and Physical Educators, 2013) and the physical education standards of many countries. In the National Standards and Grade-Level Outcomes for K-12 Physical Education, movement is represented in the first two standards:

Standard 1. The physically literate individual demonstrates competency in a variety of motor skills and movement patterns.

Standard 2. The physically literate individual applies knowledge of concepts, principles, strategies and tactics related to movement and performance.

In China, elementary and middle school standards require students to (a) demonstrate knowledge of physical education and health, basic skills, and fitness and (b) demonstrate the ability to practice sports productively and to be creative participants in sport and physical activities (Wang, Housner, Ji, Torsney, & Mao, 2011). In the United Kingdom (Gov. UK, 2013), the initial stage, called key stage 1, focuses on developing fundamental movement skills. Key stage 2 requires students to apply and develop a broader range of skills, learn how to use them in different ways, and link them to make actions and sequences of movement. As students progress, they are asked to build on and embed the physical development and skills learned in key stages 1 and 2; become more competent, confident, and expert in their techniques; and apply them across different sports and physical activities in key stage 3. In key stage 4, students are asked to tackle complex and demanding physical activities. Although there are other dimensions to these standards, including knowledge, social skills, and fitness outcomes, the central focus is movement; therefore, you must know the movement content you are to teach.

Management and instructional strategies are important prerequisites for effective teaching, but you must also know *what* to teach (Ward, & Ayvazo, 2016). For example, as a beginning teacher, Phillip was organized and was familiar with class management techniques and instructional strategies. One of his favorite types of instruction was to use a circuit in which students move through stations and complete instructional tasks based on the task cards at each station. Phillip felt that he could teach most things if he was organized ahead of time. When he knew the content deeply, he did a good job; however, when he did not know the content well (which was a lot of the time), he relied very heavily on the task cards to do the teaching for him. Though he explained what to do when students didn't understand the tasks, he didn't teach the tasks in ways that resulted in students learning the content well. In addition, the tasks he used for teaching were not particularly challenging. However, his students' time on task was very high, and the students behaved and enjoyed his lessons. Over time, Phillip has benefited from the tutelage of some master teachers, and his teaching has improved. His initial experiences, however, highlight the important idea that you can't teach what you don't know.

Acquiring adequate content knowledge presents unique challenges. The following sections discuss three important aspects of content knowledge.

Content Knowledge Is Activity Specific

You may be skilled at teaching soccer but not as skilled at teaching tennis or gymnastics. Teachers have different levels of knowledge and thus have strengths in different content areas. Figure 1.1*a* and *b* shows the content knowledge profiles of two teachers using a scale of 0 to 100 to indicate the level of expertise in a sport. As you look at the figures, you should be able to determine each teacher's content knowledge strengths and weaknesses.

Teacher A (see figure 1.1*a*) has strengths in flag football, volleyball, and basketball and good knowledge of dance, tennis and soccer. He has less knowledge of badminton, gymnastics, and orienteering. Teacher B (see figure 1.1*b*) has strengths in soccer, dance, and gymnastics and good knowledge of orienteering and tennis. She has less knowledge of badminton, flag football, volleyball, and basketball.

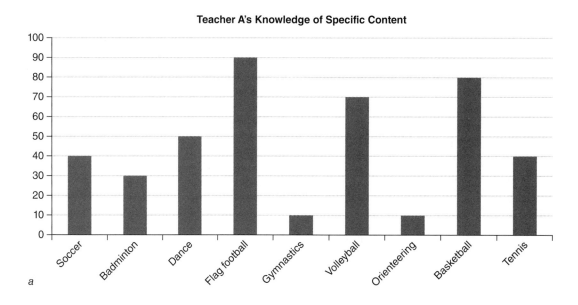

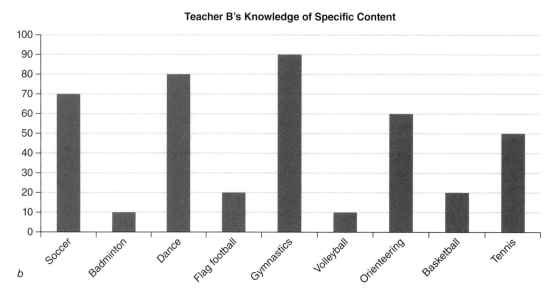

Figure 1.1 Two profiles of content knowledge: *(a)* Teacher A; *(b)* Teacher B.

All teachers have unique profiles due to their experiences with specific content (or lack thereof). You acquire content knowledge in four ways. The first is through experiences in school physical education. Surprisingly, participating in physical education appears to be the least effective way to acquire content knowledge (Ward, 2009). In fact, it is recognized that a typical physical education teacher's content knowledge is not likely to be strong across multiple content areas (Kim, Lee, Ward, & Li, 2015; Siedentop, 2002). It is challenging to produce student learning in content you know little about.

The second way you acquire content knowledge is through your sporting and movement history, such as extracurricular engagement in recreational and competitive activities (e.g., intramurals, clubs). Most physical education teachers have strong positive experiences with a few activities, and often their involvement in these activities has been ongoing since childhood. Performing an activity is one of the strongest ways to learn specific content (Siedentop, 2002). Most teachers, however, do not have in-depth experiences in numerous activities, which results in content knowledge that is limited to a few areas.

Teacher education programs are a third way you can acquire content knowledge, but often movement content is a small part of the curriculum (Kim, Lee, Ward, & Li, 2015; Siedentop, 2002; Ward, Li, Kim, & Lee, 2012). There is simply not enough time to learn all the movement content you will be expected to teach (Kim, Lee, Ward, & Li, 2015).

Finally, you can acquire content knowledge through professional development over the course of your career, but this takes a special kind of effort that we discuss later in the chapter. Having experience is *not* the same as having expertise (Schempp, Manross, Tan, & Fincher, 1998). There is a large body of research that shows time spent teaching does not result in improvement of content knowledge (Schempp, Manross, Tan, & Fincher, 1998; Siedentop & Eldar, 1989; Ward & O'Sullivan, 2006). Table 1.1 provides a summary of the pros and cons of these ways of acquiring content knowledge.

Earlier in this chapter, we asked you to think about the content knowledge strengths and weaknesses of two teachers (figure 1.1). If you look at the profiles in the figure, teacher A's strengths include flag football, volleyball, and basketball. This teacher has a history of playing, coaching, and teaching these sports and teaching others how to teach them. As a result, he has studied these sports in detail. His weaker areas of content knowledge are soccer, badminton, gymnastics, and orienteering. He has never played these sports, and he has only taught soccer and badminton.

Teacher B's strengths include soccer, dance, and gymnastics. She has a long history performing, teaching, and coaching gymnastics, and she has written manuals and books on gymnastics. She also has a strong background in dance because she was taught to teach dance by experts. Similarly, her soccer experience comes from her teaching experience and her connection to master coaches. Teacher B's weaker areas include badminton, flag football, volleyball, and basketball. She has not played these sports, and she has seldom taught them. The experiences of these teachers demonstrate the different ways content knowledge can be acquired and provide an explanation for stronger and weaker understandings of specific content areas.

Content Knowledge Is Developmentally Specific

Content knowledge differs across grade and skill levels. An elementary school teacher might be skilled at teaching first graders to throw but might not be able to teach a baseball pitch to eighth graders. Studies have shown that the more familiar you are with students' characteristics and developmental levels, the better you will be able to select appropriate tasks and provide corrections to common errors (Hill, Ball, & Schilling, 2008). Similarly, your ability to select appropriate tasks is based on your knowledge of instructional tasks. Again, put simply, you cannot teach what you do not know.

Imagine you are assigned to teach swimming to a class of new students. It's the first day, and the students are lined up in their swimwear alongside the pool. It would be dangerous if you said, "Okay, go ahead and jump in." You would first

Table 1.1 Pros and Cons of Common Ways to Acquire Content Knowledge

Type of content knowledge experience	Pro	Con
K-12 physical education classes	Many years of physical education experiences	Frequency and duration of lessons and minimal evidence that students learn content well in physical education classes
Extracurricular experiences (intramurals, clubs)	In-depth learning of content over many years	Involvement in a limited number of activities (perhaps one or two)
College teacher education training	By design, universities are a key location for teachers to learn content knowledge from experts.	Too little time spent training teachers on movement content.
Professional development	Perhaps the best way to learn content as teachers; actively pursue content specific professional development.	Too little physical education-specific professional development

want to assess the swimming skills of the students to determine the appropriate instructional tasks. You would provide different instruction to students who cannot hold their breath underwater and those who can swim several laps using different strokes.

Acquiring Content Knowledge Requires a Specific Kind of Experience

Experience in teaching an activity does not necessarily result in quality content knowledge (Ericsson, 2008; Siedentop & Eldar, 1989). Quality content knowledge requires learning from experience (Ball, Thames, & Phelps, 2008; Ericsson, 2008; Ward, 2009). Our experience working with teachers over many decades and our research on this topic have taught us that professional development opportunities and deliberate practice and reflection are necessary for you to learn from experience.

Active Pursuit of Professional Development

In their study of expert teachers, Siedentop and Eldar (1989) described the following three elementary teachers who actively pursued professional development:

1. Chris had a long performance and coaching history with gymnastics.
2. Bobbie studied with four prominent movement educators and tried the formula approaches to movement education, but she discarded them when she developed her own unique orientation.
3. Gary showed expertise in teaching adventure skills such as climbing and rappelling. He worked on these skills himself and also visited Project Adventure to train in adventure education.

These teachers have strong content knowledge. Because content knowledge is hard to acquire, you must actively engage in learning it through formal professional development, such as workshops, and informal professional development, such as this book.

Deliberate Practice and Reflection

Professional development can provide you with opportunities to learn new pedagogies, content, and curricula, but, like experience, it is insufficient to ensure content learning. You must also learn from deliberate practice. We argue that teaching should be intentional, and learning from practice is a critical element of this.

Ericsson (2008) describes deliberate practice as "deliberate efforts to improve one's performance." He notes that "experts deliberately construct and seek out . . . situations to attain desired goals that exceed their current level of reliable performance" (p. 991). Deliberate practice requires you to "attend to the critical aspects of the situation and incrementally improve [your] performance in response to knowledge of results, feedback, or both" (Ericsson, Krampe, & Tesch-Römer, 1993, p. 368).

Teacher reflection is tied to the notion of deliberate practice. Though there are many definitions, many forms, and different foci of reflection (Tsangaridou, 2009), we define it in the context of PCK as the purposeful act of inquiry into your own behavior and students' behaviors. This reflection can occur at the moment of PCK when a decision is enacted by the teacher or during or after the lesson. It can also take place long after the event (e.g., reflecting on how you taught something last year). You have many thoughts that you do not act on, so in the context of PCK, your reflection should be purposeful. That purpose is to maintain or change your behavior or student behavior when a situation occurs. You are engaged in a process of self-observation and self-evaluation.

We use the term *tinkering* to refer to the idea that teaching requires exploration, experimentation, and reflection. As teachers, you are intentional decision-makers who create PCK of their knowledge and experiences; fundamental to this view is that as the teacher as you do this, you are learning from your practice through the act of tinkering. In this case, you are tinkering with the PCK of the lesson.

THEORY OF CONTENT KNOWLEDGE

The challenges of acquiring content knowledge are similar for teachers in all subject areas. Ball and her colleagues (2008), who focus on mathematics education at the University of Michigan, classified content knowledge into two categories. First, *common content knowledge* (CCK) refers to the knowledge and skills needed to perform a task, such as solving a math problem or performing a layup. Second, *specialized content knowledge* (SCK) refers to the knowledge and skills required to determine the correct instructional task sequence you will use to teach and how to represent it to students. These categories form a theory of content knowledge that distinguishes each type of knowledge and defines its relationship to PCK.

Ball et al. (2008) argue that CCK can be acquired by learning how to perform and by performing the specific task (e.g., playing basketball, dancing, throwing). In contrast, SCK is typically only acquired by being taught how to teach the content.

SCK is often confused with PCK. PCK involves the transformation of different types of knowledge, of which SCK is one, into an instructional decision. For example, if you were asked to list the instructional tasks and progression you would use to teach the handstand, your list might begin with weight-bearing activities and progress toward the kick up to a handstand. This is SCK. If you were asked how you would teach the handstand to first graders, you would likely select tasks that are appropriate for beginners. If you were asked how you would teach the task to high school students, all of whom have previous gymnastics lessons, you would likely select more advanced tasks. In both cases, to make decision about what to teach, you would draw on knowledge such as your understanding of your students' abilities and learning characteristics, the space and equipment, and the pedagogy to be used (e.g., whole group, self-directed, or partner instruction). The SCK (i.e., the instructional progressions you select) will be different depending on what you know about your students and the equipment you have available. This is an example of PCK.

Figure 1.2 shows the relationship between CCK, SCK, and PCK for the sit-up. The first column presents CCK with a text description of the sit-up technique. The second column presents SCK with instructional tasks to teach the technique in a progression of increasing difficulty. The final column shows the PCK that teachers select to help different students according to their need. The take home message is that the more SCK you have, the better you can match tasks to the ability of your students.

Another important conceptualization of content knowledge was developed by Ward (2009). He categorized movement content into the following four domains:

1. **Knowledge of the rules, etiquette, and safety.** Knowledge of rules refers to primary rules that define the fundamental character of the game, secondary rules that can be changed to make the game more developmentally appropriate, and general rules of an activity (e.g., where the line of scrimmage is in football). Examples of the etiquette used in an activity are thanking your partner after a dance or rolling the ball under the net to give it to the other team in volleyball. This domain also includes knowledge of safety issues and knowing how to set up equipment.

2. **Knowledge of technique and tactics.** Knowledge of technique refers to the skills required to perform an activity, such as the basic stance in table tennis or the sequence of steps in a dance. In some activities, this knowledge will include basic tactics such as knowing how to draw your opponent away from the baseline in tennis or knowing how to make a fake just outside the defender's tackling range to beat the defender in soccer.

3. **Knowledge of errors.** This refers to the ability to discriminate between errors of technique and tactical performance. In basketball, for example, you should know that a common shooting error is having the elbow positioned sideways instead of vertically under the wrist. As another example, in tennis, getting pulled away from the baseline to return a shot but not returning to the baseline is an error.

4. **Knowledge of instructional representations and tasks.** Knowledge of instructional representations refers to how a task is presented to students. The most common examples are seen in cues, such as in tennis for both the forehand and backhand. The teacher may say "imagine you have a table with cups on it. Swipe all cups off the table as you contact and follow through." Or during the follow through, "As you follow through, finish the strike in a position where you could read the watch on your wrist." Instructional tasks are used to teach the activity (Griffey & Housner, 2007). In basketball, an example is teaching the game to beginners as a passing game, while developing student skillfulness in dribbling the ball over time. In table tennis and badminton, an example is focusing on targets early in the instruction to teach the placement of the ball or shuttle.

FITNESS EXERCISE CONTENT KNOWLEDGE

Common Content Knowledge (CCK)	Specialized Content Knowledge (SCK)	Pedagogical Content Knowledge (PCK)
Lie on your back on the floor, bend your knees 90 degrees, and plant your feet flat. Tuck your chin slightly toward your chest. Arms as directed by the teacher (e.g., extended in front, on the floor, across chest, near ears, or behind head) and sit up toward your knees and then lower yourself back down again.		For use with students being introduced to the sit-up for the first time.
		For use with students with experience performing sit-ups and who can perform the simplest version easily and correctly.

		For use with students who can perform the intermediate versions of the sit-up easily and correctly.

Figure 1.2 The distinctions among CCK, SCK, and PCK.

If we integrate the work of Ball et al. (2008) and Ward (2009), we can situate knowledge of the rules, etiquette, and safety and knowledge of technique and tactics in CCK. This is knowledge that can be acquired from performance. We can situate knowledge of errors and knowledge of instructional representations and tasks in SCK. This is knowledge that is often hard to obtain unless it has been specifically taught to you.

Does SCK make a difference? Our research in physical education indicates that it does. One of the largest studies of teaching effectiveness in physical education was conducted by a group of researchers at The Ohio State University, the University of Alabama, East Carolina University, and Kent State University between 2011 and 2013. The study was conducted during middle school badminton units (Sinelnikov et al., 2016; Ward et al., 2015). First, teachers (who had various levels of experience) taught badminton units as they typically would. The teachers then participated in a workshop that provided SCK for badminton. After this training, the teachers taught a new set of students using what they had learned. The results were staggering: 84 percent of the students who were taught before the workshop scored below the average of the students taught after the workshop. The effects were similar for beginning teachers who had never taught or played badminton and for experienced teachers who had taught badminton their entire careers.

These findings are so important that the SHAPE America Initial Physical Education Teacher Education Standards (2017) differentiate between CCK and SCK and require all beginning teachers to know them.

Standard 1: Content and Foundational Knowledge. Physical education candidates demonstrate an understanding of common and specialized content, and scientific and theoretical foundations for the delivery of an effective preK-12 physical education program.

Components – Candidates will:

- 1.a Describe and apply common content knowledge for teaching preK-12 physical education.
- 1.b Describe and apply specialized content knowledge for teaching preK-12 physical education.
- 1.c Describe and apply physiological and biomechanical concepts related to skillful movement, physical activity and fitness for preK-12 students.
- 1.d Describe and apply motor learning and behavior-change/psychological principles related to skillful movement, physical activity and fitness for preK-12 students.
- 1.e Describe and apply motor development theory and principles related to fundamental motor skills, skillful movement, physical activity and fitness for preK-12 students.
- 1.f Describe historical, philosophical and social perspectives of physical education issues and legislation.

Key Points

- You must have content knowledge to teach.

- Acquiring content knowledge is a significant challenge.

- Experience does not necessarily result in improved in content knowledge. You must actively pursue professional development and engage in tinkering and reflection.

- You will have strengths in some content areas and limitations in others.

- Specialized content knowledge is critical to improving pedagogical content knowledge.

- If you have specialized content knowledge, you can produce significant learning gains in students.

Chapter 2

Conceptualizing Content for Teaching

In chapter 1, we mentioned that decision-making is one of the most difficult aspects of teaching. Among the decisions you must make are what content you will teach and how you will teach it. As discussed, PCK factors into how you represent content to students and what instructional tasks you select to teach this content.

REPRESENTING CONTENT TO STUDENTS

What students come to understand about content depends on how it is presented to them. For example, the following are two ways of teaching a log roll in gymnastics:

Example 1. I want you to stay straight and roll on your side.

Example 2. Have you seen a log? It is straight, firm, and long. Look at Trevor; he is lying like a log on the mat. His body is stretched, and his arms and legs are together and straight. He is now going to roll like a log. . . .

Researchers use a continuum of less mature to more mature to differentiate content representations (Ayvazo & Ward, 2011; Chen, 2004; Ward Kim, Ko, & Li, 2015). Example 2 is more mature because it connects the characteristics of a log to the performance of a log roll. This is precise and relatable for students. Although example 2 provides more information than example 1, this is not always better. A longer explanation might not aid student understanding if it provides too much information or the wrong kinds of information.

You need a repertoire of content representations that you can use to describe tasks, respond to student questions for clarification, and provide alternative explanations for students who don't understand (Brophy, 1991). Representations of content are typically verbal or visual.

Verbal Representations of Content

Verbal representations are instructions on how to perform a task. They can be enhanced through analogies, cues, and specific feedback.

Analogies

An analogy can connect a new concept to a student's prior knowledge by drawing a comparison. The following are some examples you can use:

- For both the forehand and backhand swings, imagine you have a table with cups on it. When you swing, swipe all cups off the table as you contact and follow through.
- As you follow through, you should be able to read the watch on your wrist.
- Pretend you're dipping your racquet in a can of paint behind you before you serve.

- Imagine you are putting a nail through the ball when you hit your volleys.

These examples connect actions to things the students can visualize, which supports student understanding.

Cues

An instructional cue is a word, phrase, or sentence that is used to focus student attention on an element of a technique or tactic. The following are some examples of cues:

- *Elbow:* prompts students to keep their elbows under their hands in set shots
- *Get open:* prompts students to move away from the defender in a soccer game
- *Baseline:* prompts students to return to the baseline in a game of tennis
- *Look through the diamond:* prompts students to look at the incoming volleyball and have the hands in the ready position for an overhead pass

Cues should be aligned with the focus of the instructional task. When a new task is being taught, the cues should relate to the critical elements of that task. As the instruction progresses, cues can be used to prompt elements that have already been taught.

Specific Feedback

Specific feedback is precise information that is provided to help the student maintain or improve performance of a task. A feedback statement is specific if describes the technique or tactic you are teaching, as in the following examples:

- Nice way to follow through across your body (throwing a ball).
- I really like that you returned to baseline after that hit (tennis).
- Excellent ground ball catch; you placed yourself in front of the ball (softball).
- Good decision drawing the defender (soccer).
- Keep the forearm vertical when you make that set shot (basketball).

Visual Representations of Content

Visual representations of content include demonstrations, task cards, pictures, diagrams, videos, and other methods. Visual representations deepen and extend student understanding of

Resources for Technology in Physical Education

Martin, M., & Zimmerman, R. (2014). Technology in action: Developing school-wide activity programs. *Journal of Physical Education, Recreation and Dance, 85*(7), 44-47.

Roth, K. (2014). Technology for tomorrow's teachers. *Journal of Physical Education, Recreation and Dance, 85*(4), 3-5.

Trout, J. (2013). Digital movement analysis in physical education. *Journal of Physical Education, Recreation and Dance, 84*(7), 47-50.

the task by providing a model or highlighting specific aspects of the task. Advances in technology provide additional ways to find and present visual representations. For example, you can use a smartphone or tablet to access instructional videos on YouTube or other internet sites. You can digitally record student performances to use as models or to provide feedback. You can also use specific apps that are available on Google Play or the App Store (Trout, 2013). To find out more about the use of technology for physical education, refer to articles such as those listed in the Resources for Technology in Physical Education sidebar.

Principles for Verbal and Visual Representations of Content

We believe the following four critical principles are necessary in all content representations because they increase student understanding:

1. **Clarity.** Present precise and unambiguous descriptions of what to do and how to do it.

2. **Incremental presentations.** Present the content in very small chunks.

3. **Accuracy.** If you are using a demonstration, make sure it is a complete demonstration of what you want students to do. Avoid partial or incomplete demonstrations. Similarly, use accurate pictures and recordings.

4. **Short presentations**. Although there are occasions, such as at the beginning of an instructional unit, when you might take more time to introduce content, we believe that most content representations should be

delivered quickly. We teach a very simple rule devised by Chris Bell, one of our master teachers. She calls this principle *show and go*: Show (and tell) students what you want them to do, and then send them to practice it quickly.

If you are unsure whether students understand a task, you should

- ask them to demonstrate,
- present correct and incorrect examples and ask them to discriminate between them,
- ask them to restate the purpose or the focus of the task, and
- ask them questions about the task.

DEVELOPING INSTRUCTIONAL TASKS

The instructional task is how the curriculum is enacted; without an instructional task, there is nothing to teach. The task might focus on motor skills, knowledge, affective skills, health-related fitness outcomes, or combinations of these. Each task should be related to previous tasks and should be meaningful, relational, progressive, and modifiable.

Instructional Tasks are Meaningful

When we say that instructional tasks are *meaningful*, we are referring to instruction that is connected to the past learning experiences and knowledge of the student, relevant to the context in which the activity occurs in the real world, and focused on developing skillfulness in students. Students perform modified versions of the activity that are consistent with how it is performed in the real world, and they value and enjoy the movement experiences. These outcomes are accomplished through the selection and arrangement of instructional tasks and the use of effective instructional strategies.

Consider the way we have observed volleyball being taught in many middle and high schools in the United States. Teachers often begin by teaching the basic skills of the serve, the overhead and forearm passes, the block, and the spike. Typically, there is discrete skill practice and followed by a full-sided volleyball game. The following are some criticisms of this traditional approach to teaching physical education:

- There is little attempt to connect past learning with new learning,
- There is little, if any, connection with the real context of the sport or activity as it is played or performed.
- Students do not have many opportunities to practice skills.
- There is little requirement for skillfulness in technique performance.
- There is little effort to help students transition to playing games.
- Students are engaged in moderate to vigorous physical activity for less than 30 percent of the lesson.

Similar observations for physical education in general have been reported by researchers (Launder & Piltz, 2013; Siedentop, Hastie, & van der Mars, 2011).

In contrast, we have also observed the following examples of meaningful instruction in volleyball in middle and high school settings:

- Teachers making connections with what students have learned previously
- Instruction that is organized in ways that create affiliation among students and with the sport, such as using the sport education curriculum to organize students in teams and connecting them to ranked men's and women's NCAA volleyball teams or the top eight ranked Olympic teams
- Students playing in small-sided, 3v3 games designed to create more opportunities to touch the ball and use a tactic
- Competition that is organized not as a round-robin tournament but as a series of developmental games that focus on an aspect of game play and lead to a culminating activity that resembles a World Cup or NCAA championship
- Students engaging in moderate to vigorous physical activity for more than 50 percent of the lesson

Students in these settings come to understand volleyball very differently. They develop better skill performance and have a different understanding of and experience in playing the game.

Instructional Tasks Are Relational

When we use the term *relational*, we mean that the instructional tasks are interrelated and organized around a set of conceptual principles. Conceptual principles describe the connectivity of the content and how it should be developed. In this book, we frame our principles around the work of Ward and his colleagues (Ward, Ayvazo, & Lehwald, 2014; Ward, et al., 2015; Ward, Lehwald, & Lee, 2015), who have contributed conceptual perspectives to understanding content knowledge in physical education, and Launder and Piltz's (2013) instructional model called *play practice*.

Central to our conceptual principles is the relationship among tasks. We first consider the sequence of tasks for teaching a fundamental skill. The following is a sequence of tasks for teaching the lay-up in basketball:

Task 1: walking without the ball. From a starting position 10 feet (3 meters) from the basket and at a 45-degree angle, walk toward the basket without a basketball. On the last step, raise your right knee to a 90-degree angle and extend the right arm upward.

Task 2: walking with the ball. Carry the ball and extend the arm without taking a shot.

Task 3: walking dribble with a shot. Dribble while walking toward the basket and execute a lay-up shot. As an extension, increase the distance and the speed of the dribble (once you get to this point, a second line of rebounds can be added).

Task 4: dribbling to layup. Starting 30 feet (9.1 meters) from the basket and at a 45-degree angle, dribble toward the basket with the outside hand and execute a lay-up. A defender moves alongside you as you dribble in for the lay-up. The defender does not attempt to disrupt the shot. As an extension, the defender can begin 8 feet (2.4 meters) behind the dribbler and attempt to catch the dribbler and disrupt the lay-up.

In this example, each task teaches a little more and builds on the previous one. We call this a *vertical development* of the content. The sequence is typically used to teach fundamental skills that are critical for performance.

Skills and tactics also need to be combined to be used in a game or performance. We call this combination a *relational development* of the content. For example, a relational connection occurs in volleyball when the forearm pass is combined with the overhead pass or in basketball when shooting is added to a passing task.

One way to conceptualize vertical and relational tasks is through content maps. A content map is a visual representation of the content of a unit that includes tasks to be taught, the order in which they are taught, and their relationship to other tasks (Ward, Lehwald, et al., 2015). It emphasizes specialized content knowledge by organizing and sequencing the instructional tasks to be taught. It can be grade specific, school-level specific, or a representation of a curricular unit across school grades. Figure 2.1 is a content map that illustrates how volleyball skills could be developed. This volleyball content map is divided into secondary and elementary levels, and the elementary section is divided into grade levels.

You must begin your instruction with the first level of tasks; the grades shown in the figure are only an example. For example, if you begin volleyball in the fourth grade, you would not begin with the fourth-grade tasks in this figure. You would begin with the first level of tasks (the third-grade tasks in the figure) and progress from there. Even at the secondary level, if your students have not had previous volleyball instruction, you would start with the first-level tasks. (Be sure you know about students' previous experiences.) However, instead of starting with balloons and beach balls (as you should in early grades), you can begin with volleyball trainers. In addition, the rate at which you progress through the tasks might be faster with secondary students. Your SCK and PCK for volleyball will be major factors in making these types of decisions.

Why are content maps important? Content maps define the scope of the content to be taught and when we have used these with teachers one of the most common responses is that for the first time they get the big picture of what is to be taught in a specific unit or units of instruction. A content map provides a clear overview of the skills and learning tasks that will increase the development of skillful play in a particular activity. Using a content map, you can determine the performance levels of your students, decide where to start, and edit the map to fit your students and classroom contexts. The content map shows the relationship between skills and tasks in a logical and progressive manner. It also allows you to see how prior learning lays the foundation for subsequent tasks, and it provides a blueprint for how students will progress through a lesson.

Instructional Tasks Are Progressive

You should use incremental task progressions to lead students from beginning levels to more advanced levels of content. Progressions should be established based on the instructional objectives for the lesson, your knowledge of the content, your ability to analyze that content, and your assessment of students' needs in relation to the content. Instructional tasks must be sequenced in a manner that facilitates learning.

An instructional task should result in increasing competencies in motoric, affective, cognitive, and health-related fitness content. Students' written, oral, or movement products should demonstrate these competencies. You will determine instructional task progressions based on lesson or unit objectives. Figure 2.2 illustrates this. The horizontal sequence of tasks in the figure represents task development within the lesson. The vertical development in the figure shows how tasks are developed across lessons.

One way to consider the progression of instructional tasks is to use Judy Rink's (2014) content development framework. In this framework, the initial task in teaching a specific objective is the informing task. Tasks can then be extended by increasing the complexity or difficulty relative to a previous task, or they can be refined by focusing on the quality of the performance (e.g., improving the technique). A student's performance can be assessed using specific tasks. If the informing task is a modified game (e.g., a 1v1 or keep-away game), it can still be extended (e.g., reduce the size of the play area) and refined (e.g., set targets for passes to develop accuracy). We call these extending-applying tasks and refining-applying tasks. Table 2.1 presents a summary of these tasks.

Figure 2.3 shows a content map for volleyball in grades 3 through 5. Each task has been labeled using the categories defined in table 2.1. There is no magic number or arrangement of tasks that is desirable.

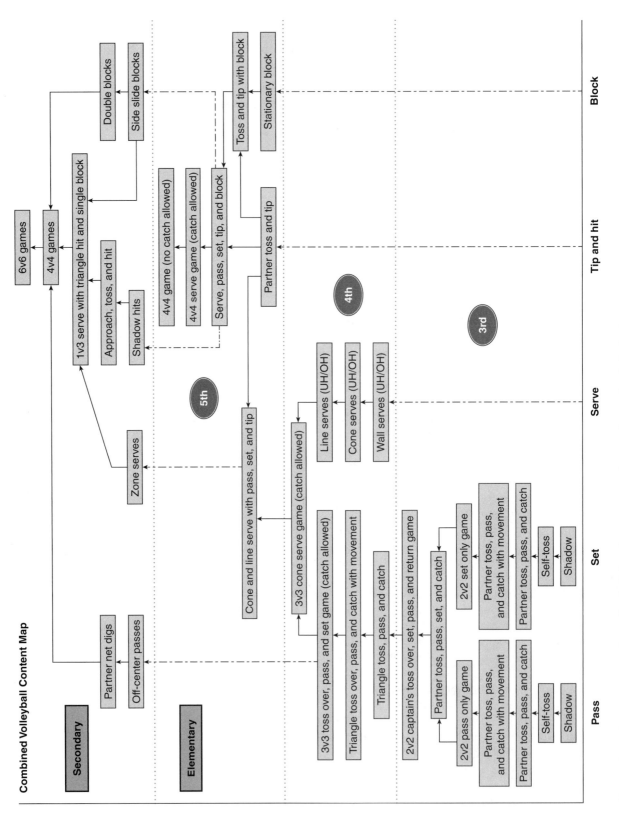

Figure 2.1 A content map for volleyball for elementary and secondary school students.

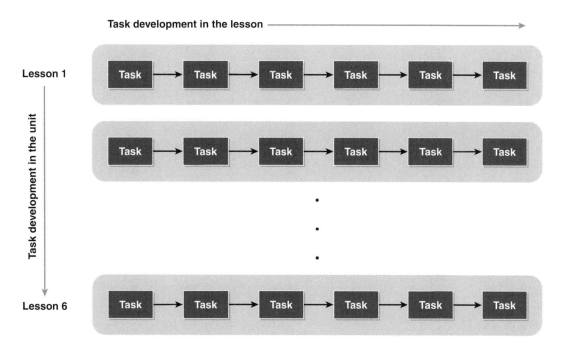

Figure 2.2   Tasks in lesson and unit development.

Table 2.1   Task Categories

Informing task (I; can be designated 1 or 2 such as I1)	The initial task for a skill.
	Example: Let's start with rolling the ball and trapping it by. . . .
Extending task (E)	A task that increases the level of difficulty of a previous task by adding elements (e.g., part to whole), changing or adding a dimensions (e.g., distance, space, speed, target area), or adding variety (e.g., asking students to move in a different way).
	Example: Let's make this more difficult by moving the cones closer.
Extending-applying task (EA)	A task that is extended in a game-like environment.
	Example: In this 3v3 keep away game, let's turn the defense from passive to active.
Refining task (R)	A task that requires focus on the quality of the technique or tactical performance.
	Example: In trapping, you need to keep your hips open. Imagine that the side of your hip is smiling away from the ball.
Refining-applying tasks (RA)	A task that is refined in a game-like environment.
	Example: In this 3v3 game, get open by moving away from the defender.
Applying task (A) game	A task that uses the content of the lesson in a game but a focus is not specified.
	Example: Let's play a 4v4 game.

Source: Adapted from Rink (2014).

Figure 2.4 shows the categorization of tasks in a common plan for teaching volleyball as a content map

Figure 2.4 shows much less development of SCK than Figure 2.3. The students taught using the content map in figure 2.3 will experience a different kind of volleyball experience than those taught using the content in figure 2.4. Moreover, it is very likely that the student taught with the content in figure 2.3 will be more skillful. The difference between the two content maps lies in the use of extension and extension-applying tasks.

Level 3 Volleyball Content Map

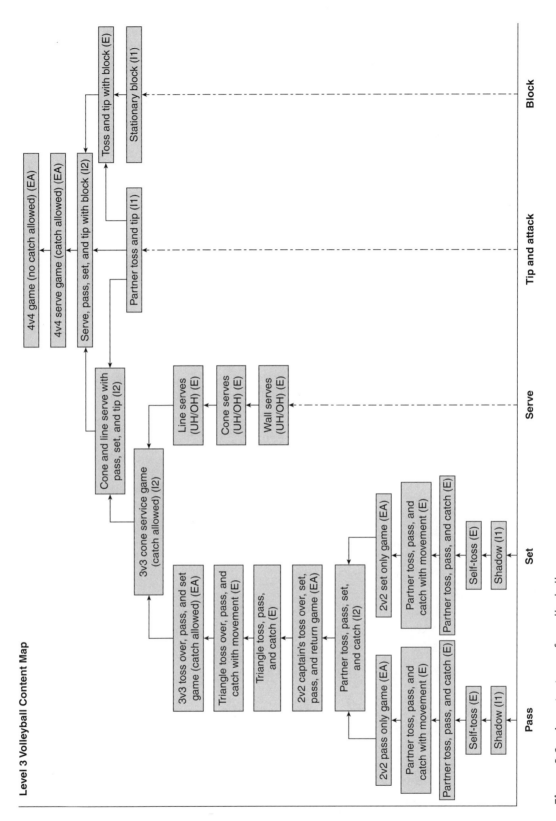

Figure 2.3 A content map for volleyball.

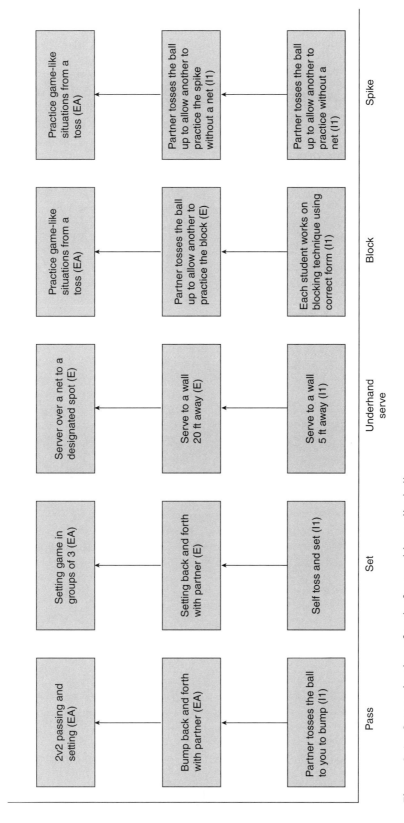

Figure 2.4 Categorization of tasks for teaching volleyball.

Instructional Tasks Are Modifiable

The sequence of tasks you decide to use might not be carried out as planned. When you make in-the-moment decisions while teaching a task, you are using what Alexander (1982) calls a *contingency developed task* (see figure 2.5). When you describe a task, students are expected to perform it. They might perform a more difficult version of the task, perform it as stated, or perform it incorrectly (Siedentop & Tannehill, 2000). (In this discussion, we will ignore occasions when students are off task.) In response, you can intentionally or unintentionally ignore the students' performances, correct errors, or reinforce the positive aspects of the performances. These decisions are complex because you are dealing with many students at once.

Doyle (1986) has found that teachers use a reference or steering group to decide when to move on and when to stop and provide further explanation. Research has found that teachers tend to avoid the most competent and the least competent students when they are making instructional decisions; instead, they look at a middle group (Doyle, 1986). The steering group often drives instructional decisions.

When a student performs a task incorrectly, you might provide a new task to that student or to a small group of students who also struggled with it. You might make the task easier with an extending task, such as moving the students closer together to facilitate catching a ball or making a pass, or you might refine the task and focus on the technical performance. If you decide to make the task more demanding, you might add an extending task such as moving students farther apart.

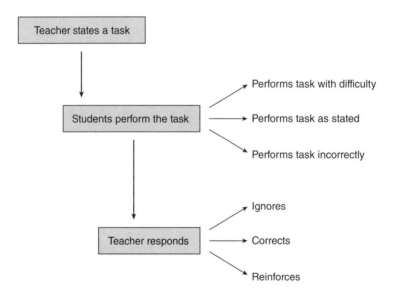

Figure 2.5 Teacher and student actions relative to a task.

Key Points

- How content is represented to students influences their understanding of it.
- Content representations can be verbal or visual.
- Content representations should be clear, incremental, accurate, and short.
- Instructional tasks must be meaningful, relational, and progressive.
- A content map is an important tool to conceptualize the scope of and the relationship among tasks.

Chapter 3

Organizing Content for Teaching

One of the truisms in teaching is that you must understand what you teach. Your deep understanding of content leads to deeper content learning by students (Ward, 2013; Ward, Ayvazo, & Lehwald, 2014). In addition, the quality of the tasks is critical, because students acquire better knowledge and perform better if you use high-quality tasks. Your capacity to improve student learning is grounded in the professional knowledge that informs PCK. As discussed in chapter 1, PCK is influenced by your knowledge of students, the curriculum, the context in which you teach, the pedagogical strategies you use, and the content you teach.

What does it mean to know content deeply? In the following two examples, much of the teachers' decision-making and many of their instructional behaviors, content representations, and task selections depend on the extent of their SCK. In chapter 2, we argued that SCK is meaningful, relational, and progressive. It is reflective of deeper content knowledge. When you compare the following two examples, you will see that the second teacher shows a deeper and more explicit knowledge of basketball.

Consider a simple 4v1 keep-away basketball game. The first teacher introduces the game with a demonstration and an explanation. There is an off-the-ball focus of moving away from the defender to receive a pass, and there is a rule that the ball carrier must pass to the open players. The defensive rule is that the ball can be intercepted, but there cannot be any physical contact between players. Students are sent to practice in groups. During the practice, the teacher provides feedback to students. Once the task is completed, the teacher moves the students to the more difficult 3v1 keep-away game.

The second teacher also provides an explanation and demonstration of the 4v1 keep-away game. The focus is the same as in the previous example. However, this teacher begins by requiring the defender to walk and not intercept the ball; this gives students learning the offense time to make decisions relative to the defender (i.e., a passive defense). The teacher prompts students to get open. Next, the teacher asks the defender to move more quickly and indicates that no interceptions are allowed (i.e., an active defense). As the practice progresses, the defender can intercept the ball (i.e., a competitive defense). The teacher pauses game play to emphasize moving deep or wide or to refine the technique. The advantages of this process include the following:

- Small progressive incremental changes allow for student understanding, refinement, and extension.
- Keeping the same instructional format as new concepts are introduced allowing students to build on the original task, which builds competence.
- The creation of high numbers of repetitions that occur as task complexity or difficulty increase, without major changes to the pedagogical conditions of game.

The teacher in the second example uses extension and applying tasks, and the task progression is more incremental and systematic than in the first example. As these two examples show, teaching a skill demands in-depth and detailed knowledge that goes beyond the critical elements and the ability to demonstrate the skill. You must have extensive SCK (Ayvazo & Ward, 2011;

Ward, 2009), including knowledge of errors that students could make in performing the task and knowledge of the instructional representations and tasks. The deeper your knowledge, the more choices you will have in adapting instruction for students (Ayvazo & Ward, 2011; Griffey & Housner, 2007; Ward, 2013).

DEFINING THE SCOPE OF CONTENT KNOWLEDGE IN K-12 TEACHING

Deep understanding of content does not mean you must know everything about a sport or activity to teach it. Figure 3.1 illustrates the broad scope of knowledge for tennis. The large box represents all that is known about tennis. The smaller circle represents the tennis knowledge students in K-12 settings need. It includes CCK such as rules of the game, safety rules, techniques, and tactics. If you are using an instructional strategy in which one student is teaching another (e.g., peer tutoring), students will also need the SCK required to provide feedback. The larger circle represents what you need to know: the SCK for teaching the CCK in the small circle and the SCK required for adaptations for students with disabilities or more skilled students.

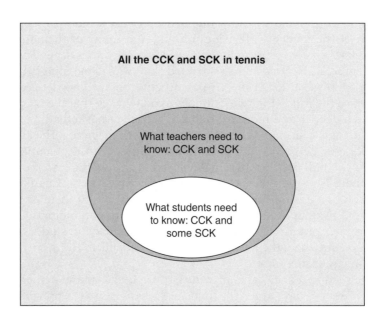

Figure 3.1 The scope of K-12 content knowledge in tennis.

PRINCIPLES BEHIND
OUR APPROACH

This book is based on several principles for teaching physical education that are derived from our research and practice over the past 30 years. Here we list these principles and discuss how they influence the contents of the book.

- **Teachers are decision makers.** You should neither blindly follow a plan nor teach without one; rather, you should adapt instruction from an existing plan that you create or that comes from another source. If you have to create plans for content you know little about, you are likely to experience frustration in your teaching. In addition, student learning will suffer. In this book, we provide models for teaching content. Contexts and students differ, however, so we expect you to adapt these models as needed. It is our firm belief that it is better to operate from a good plan that needs to be adapted than to create a weak plan that is ineffective.

- **Experts teach content differently from nonexperts.** If you are learning to teach content as a nonexpert, you will probably learn differently than an expert because you have less SCK and less experience teaching this content. The models in this book were not created for experts. They allow teachers who do not know the content well to teach their students successfully and learn from that teaching as they develop increasingly better PCK.

- **In middle school and high school, longer instructional units are preferred over shorter ones because longer instructional units allow more time for skillful performance to be developed, deeper understanding of the game, and for game sense to be developed.** Longer instructional units serve students better if they are organized around meaningful, relational, and progressive content. There are many arguments for teaching short units in the multiactivity curriculum format. Two common ones are that short units maintain student interest by providing variety and that some students might not like a particular sport but do like another. Students get bored with the typical instruction in most schools (i.e., short units, limited skill development, little development of game sense) because the tasks used in these short units are not meaningful, relational, or progressive. Our goal in this book is to change that to create more engaging units.

Similarly, the argument that students will like one sport over another is misleading. A much better indicator of student enjoyment in physical education is not the sport or activity being taught but rather the way it is taught. In our own teaching experiences, training of preservice teachers, and work with in-service teachers, we have consistently found that content that is meaningful, relational, and progressive engages students and creates learning and enjoyment.

- **In elementary school, instructional units should be related to each other in ways that cumulatively build content**. Elementary school teachers have fewer lessons per year than their secondary school counterparts; therefore, we present elementary school instructional units as 5-7 lesson blocks. Our assumption is that many skills transfer across units, such as the ready position (e.g., basketball, volleyball, football), the concept of having fast feet to move into a position to receive the ball (e.g., tennis, volleyball, badminton, softball, baseball), calling for the ball, person-to-person defense, and moving (invasion games). Elementary instruction units should be sequenced to develop complexity and refinement of movements introduced in previous units and to extend and refine movements in later units.

- **Small-sided games rather than full-sided games should be taught first in physical education.** The question of whether a full-sided game (or a doubles game in a racket sport) should be played is a function of the time it takes to teach students to play the game. In this book, the end goal is to play full-sided games, but to get there you must progress from small-sided games to ensure that students have the skills and the game sense to be successful. The modified games we provide represent the main features of full-sided games. If longer instructional units are used, students in middle school and high school might be able to progress toward full-sided games.

- **Skillful performance in sports is a function of technique and game sense.** We use the term *technique* to describe the critical elements of the performance of a movement such as how to hold a bat in softball, assume the starting position, swing, and follow through. The term *game sense* refers to "the ability to use an understanding of the rules, tactics, strategy and of oneself (and of one's teammates) to overcome the problems posed by the sport or by one's opponents" (Launder & Piltz, 2013, p. 16). Game sense is represented by what players do in the game to demonstrate their understanding, such as reading the play and making decisions. When players apply the rules in the game, they are demonstrating game sense. Technique development and game sense are highly interdependent. This interdependence has been described by Launder and Piltz (2013, p. 59) as "what is tactically desirable must be technically possible." In short, if the goal is to play the game, then technique and games sense must be developed synchronously.

Develop Working Technique

In her article "It's OK to Be a Beginner," Rink (2004) observed that being good or not good at motor skills is not a permanent condition for children and youth. That is why we have teachers. The variety of abilities found in physical education classes means that at any given time, students are at different places in their learning of motor skills, knowledge, and understanding and use of affective skills. Rink's point is that your goal is to move all students forward, and it is important for students to understand that they will get better with practice. Given that students arrive in class at different places in their learning, Launder and Piltz (2013) have suggested the need to develop a *working technique*. Using a working technique, a student moves from A to B, in which A represents the student's current level and B is where you would like the student to be at the end of instruction. The student should travel the most effective and efficient road between these two points. In this example, the road represents technique. Even beginners should have a working technique that places them on the road to improved learning.

In the Working Technique in Volleyball sidebar, Dr. Dena Deglau, a professor of physical education and an expert volleyball teacher, describes the development of a working technique.

Dr. Deglau clearly has deep content knowledge of volleyball. Her example highlights the developmental nature of working technique. Our point is that *teachers must determine what are the essential elements of a working technique* that they want to develop as they teach their students. A teacher's understanding of a working technique and their expectations for students will likely change over time as they reflect and tinker with their instruction.

Implement a Sport Education Curriculum

We used the term *meaningful* in chapter 2 to refer to instruction that is connected to students' past learning experiences and knowledge and the real-world context of the activity. The focus is on developing skillfulness in the students so that they can perform modified versions of the activity that are consistent with how it is performed in the real world while valuing and enjoying the movement experience. Though there are many ways to achieve this, we think one of the best is the use of the sport education curriculum and instructional model (Siedentop, Hastie, & van der Mars, 2011) in combination with content knowledge. You do not have to use the sport education model with the content in this book, but we recommend it.

Sport education has several pedagogical features that allow you to present content in meaningful ways. In this section, we discuss the key features of sport education. A more complete description of sport education can be found in the *Complete Guide to Sport Education* by Siedentop, Hastie, and van der Mars (2011).

Seasons

Creating seasons provide a similar structure to that used in sports. There is often a practice season followed by a competition season. In our secondary block plans, we provide 5-, 10-, 15-, and 20-day plans. Three-quarters of the unit is typically the practice season, and simple games take place each day. The tournament season lasts 2 to 5 days, and the primary focus is competition. Several games are played each day against different opponents.

Team Affiliation

Sport education assumes that you will make every effort to create mixed-ability teams, because this is the most equitable strategy to ensure that students perceive the game play as fair. Affiliation is created in sport education by placing students in the same teams for the duration of a unit and providing a team identity (e.g., team colors, team name, team cheer, home field or court, team mascot). We recommend that teams be named after college or professional sports teams, depending on the sport. Teams can adopt the colors, icons, or cheers of these teams (e.g., "Go Bucks" is an Ohio State cheer).

Lesson Management

A central feature of sport education is that students share in the management of and responsibility for the lesson because each person has a role. There are many possible roles to be filled. With groups of four (either one team of four students or two teams of two for racquet sports), we

Working Technique in Volleyball: Example of Development

Beginners

To begin to understand how the game is played, young children need to learn how angles affect where the ball will go. They will have some experience with this from the use of paddles and racquets in other activities. However, the force production demands are different in volleyball than in racquet sports. In racquet sports students learn that more force is generated by swinging the paddle faster. In volleyball, students must not think of their arms as having this function. In volleyball, students must learn that force production is generated differently. Students will often exclusively focus on the forearm pass as beginners, which is the most used skill in the game.

1. Students will move and receive the ball in the center of their body at thigh height (young children can move and let the ball bounce between their legs and then move and catch).

2. Student should learn to change the degree of bend at the waist and recognize how this affects the trajectory of the ball regardless of what they do with their arms. Students learn to place their arms forward and locked as they try to forearm pass in ready position, then straightening the torso a little. They will learn that this is required if you are bumping repeatedly to yourself and that in a game, the closer you are to the net, the straighter your torso should be.

3. Students should learn that force production occurs from the legs and not from swinging their arms.

Beyond the Initial Performance of the Forearm Pass

To approximate the game, students at this level would build from the forearm pass to understand the spatial relationship of the ball relative to body position and target. Here students must understand the three performance characteristics that afford or constrain one's ability to play a modified game

1. Move and receive a high ball in front of the forehead. Most students cannot position their bodies appropriately in relation to the ball, and thus the set or volley looks like a throw or hit off the hands. They contact the ball behind or on top of the head, and this constrains the ability to correctly volley the ball.

2. Move and volley the ball to someone in front of you. This is truly a volley. Students receive the ball in front of them, and then volley it to someone in front of them. This would lead to continuous passing back and forth with a partner.

3. Move and set a ball in a different direction. For example, if a free ball comes over the net to team A, the back-row person would volley or bump the ball to the setter. The setter is standing sideways at the net and must move behind and around the ball to set it to the hitter. Students can't execute a set in the game because they can't move sideways from the net and position themselves correctly to pass to a hitter. If the setter faces the teammates while waiting for the pass to the front row instead of standing sideways, the task of moving around the ball to face the hitter is even more difficult.

I intentionally make a distinction between volleying and setting. The difference is the orientation of the body to the ball and the target. Volleying occurs when the ball is coming directly at you and you are passing directly back (continuous passing back and forth). Setting occurs when the ball is coming at you from the side and you must set in front of you (setter to hitter).

This understanding extends to the hitter who will set the ball over the net instead of hitting or tipping it over in grade 6. The ball is coming from the setter, so the person getting the ball over the net must see the ball coming from the side, move around and behind the pass, and then set it forward over the net.

More Advanced Performance of the Forearm Pass

At this level of performance students need to understand the spatial relationship of the ball with the body, the target, and the net (height above and distance from). This allows the hitter to learn how to do more than set or bump the ball over the net. Students will also need to develop the ability to execute the cycle of the game. Here students must learn and understand the three new performance characteristics that afford or constrain one's ability to play in a game.

1. Students who understand how to tip a ball relative to the height and distance from the net can jump and catch a ball above the forehead. This develops the timing of the jump for the spike. Students need to understand how their movement must be adapted to account for differing sets. Often they are forced to bump the ball over instead of setting or tipping because their movement is too slow relative to the set.

2. To learn to play the game, students must inherently learn how to move from the passing position to hitting, setting, or defensive positions. These patterns need to be built into tasks.

have used the roles of captain, trainer, equipment manager, and statistician. Descriptions of these roles can be found in the Common Team Roles in Sport Education sidebar. To introduce these roles, you must explain the tasks that a student will do in each role. We typically introduce the roles at the beginning of the unit and leave students in the same roles for the duration. If we have additional students, we create new roles or co-roles.

Common Team Roles in Sport Education

Team Roster

Captain
Captain's assistant
Equipment manager
Trainer
Statistician

Roles

Captain

Start the game (rock, paper, scissors).
Act as a referee during game play.
Call wall (a defensive strategy) for the team.
Keep the team on task.
Line up the team to shake hands at the end of the game.

Captain's assistant

Hand out and turn in team quizzes.
Hand out and collect pedometers.

Equipment manager

Keep equipment neat and organized.
Set up equipment when needed.
Return equipment to the proper location at the end of class.

Trainer

Lead the warm-up activity.
Keep the team on task during the warm-up.
Encourage teammates to accumulate pedometer steps.

Statistician

Record fair play points.
Record pedometer steps.
Record game points.

Records

Records are kept in sport education. We find that the easiest method is to use a team chart (see table 3.1). On this chart we record wins and losses, pedometer steps (a goal is set each day), completion of daily roles, fair play (see the web resource for a printable fair play form), and bonus points for good behavior (e.g., extra effort in performance, starting quickly after warm-up, the entire team starting the warm-up on time, excellence performance).

Fair play guidelines are as follows:

- Be respectful to yourself, other players, officials, and equipment.
- Know and play by the rules.
- Practice self-control prior to, during, and after class.
- Give full effort, and appreciate others' efforts.
- Smile and have fun.

You assign the points. The statistician is responsible for recording the points each day at the end of class. These points can be accrued during the unit and totaled at the end to identify the teams with best win-loss and fair play records and to allow the teams to play for a championship on the final day of the unit (see next section).

Culminating Event

The last day of the unit is reserved for a culminating event. Such an event can take many forms, but we typically have pairs of teams (ranked by win-loss records) play championship games. Then we have an awards ceremony in which the teams march onto the field and line up. We award teams and individuals based on specific categories. Some examples of these awards are provided in the web resource. You can print and use these awards or adapt them to suit your needs.

PEDAGOGICAL FEATURES IN KNOWLEDGE PACKETS

Our goal is to provide you with an organizational framework that will allow you to not only understand the content but also to make instructional decisions about the content as you select and use it in your teaching practice. Central to this goal is understanding why we have not provided

Table 3.1   Sample Sport Education Records Chart

Goals and points awarded	DAY									
	1	2	3	4	5	6	7	8	9	10
Win a game										
Win (3 points)										
Draw (2 points)										
Loss (1 point)										
Pedometer steps										
Everyone exceeds goal (3 points)										
At least half of students meet goal (2 points)										
Majority of students do not meet goal (1 point)										
Completion of roles										
Role is completed (1 point for each, 5 points max)										
Fair play										
Exceeds goal (3 points)										
Meets goal (2 points)										
Does not meet goal (1 point)										
Bonus (up to 3 points per day)										
Total points										

specific lesson plans in this book (other than our examples of lesson plan organization and block plans). One of the great contributions of the late Alan Launder (Launder & Piltz, 2013) was his insistence that physical education teachers need to observe student performance relative to the assigned task and then introduce the next task that will further develop student performance. Although you need a plan to guide you, the overall goal you are trying to accomplish (e.g., skillfully playing a 4v4 game) and knowing the steps (i.e., the instructional tasks and the sequencing of tasks toward the major goals) are a critical element of teaching. You must observe the performances and make the best decision on the basis of your knowledge and what you see as the performance needs of your students. This book provides you with the knowledge about the big picture in terms of the content to be taught. Knowing all of the content to be taught allows the teacher to make informed instructional decisions

about which content to use in particular learning contexts. We organized chapters 4 through 12 as knowledge packets (Ward et al., 2014) that present what (i.e., the big picture) you need to know to teach the content (as shown in figure 3.1 earlier in the chapter).

Each chapter begins with a description of the pedagogical approach we recommend for teaching the content. Subsections discuss task modifications to address the needs of students with disabilities, organization of students for instruction, and space and equipment needs.

Next, we provide content maps. These provide an overview of the instructional tasks and the relationship among them and a broad recommendation about when content might be introduced in the K-12 curriculum. With this information, you can decide where your students are in their performances and then select instructional tasks to advance them. There is a combined content map that illustrates the flow of the tasks used to develop sport-specific techniques and tactics starting with beginners and ending with advanced players (in school settings). The combined content maps for chapters 6 through 12 are divided into three levels, and each level has its own separate content map that includes the application games (outline of box is dashed) used to refine the techniques and tactics in that level (outline of box is solid).

Then we provide our recommendations for lesson structure based on the content. An important feature of our lesson structure is a belief, common to many games pedagogies, that students should play games that teach them to use what they have learned in past lessons at the start of the current lesson and to use what they have learned in the current lesson at the end of the lessons. We call these *application games*. Many of our instructional tasks are presented as games (e.g., overload games in invasion sports, target games in volleyball and badminton) to emphasize a particular outcome. However, application games allow new techniques and game sense elements to be added to previous outcomes to strengthen student performance. Application games are important pedagogical tools that allow you to determine the performance of the students; as such, they can drive the selection of instructional tasks to meet the needs of students.

The lesson plan organization examples include sample warm-up activities that have been used for elementary and secondary classes.

In chapters 4 and 5 we provide sample 5- and 7-day block plans, and in chapters 6 through 12 we provide 5-, 10-, 15-, and 20-day block plans for each content area. These block plans are organized according to the lesson format we just described and provide examples of the content that could be used depending on the duration of the unit and the experiences and abilities of the students.

Next, we identify key grade-level outcomes for K-12 physical education and match them with instructional tasks in the content map. This allows you to choose which tasks you will use to meet specific standards.

The remainder of each chapter is devoted to presenting the instructional tasks. Each instructional task is organized using the following headings:

- Purpose
- Description
- Equipment
- Critical elements and cues
- Common errors, causes, and corrections

Key Points

- Effective teaching requires deep content knowledge, which enables you to adapt instruction to meet the needs of your students.

- You need to look at the performance of your students and determine the instructional tasks that will best improve their performance.

- Longer instructional units provide you with time to develop students' skillfulness.

- Skillful performance in sports is a function of technique and game sense.

- Given the time available to teach physical education, progressing to full-sided games might be unrealistic and developmentally inappropriate.

- Students should acquire a working technique, regardless of their ability level, to progress.

- Sport education is a curriculum model that allows content to be meaningfully presented to students.

PART

II

Teaching Primary Movement Content

Chapter 4

Early Elementary Locomotion

Locomotion skills include movements such as walking, running, skipping, hopping, jumping, leaping, and side sliding. These movements are *fundamental motor skills,* which are the building blocks for many other movements. For example, the application of side sliding can be seen in dance movements and in the screening skills of the defense in basketball. Children's competence in these skills is an important component of their success in physical education and in maintaining lifelong active lifestyles (Gallahue, Ozman, & Goodway, 2012). Research has shown that many children do not acquire fundamental motor skills without instruction (Gallahue et al., 2012). Therefore, you have a critical role in supporting children's early movement skills. In this chapter, our focus is on kindergarten through second grade, which is when these locomotion skills are typically taught.

OUR PEDAGOGICAL APPROACH TO LOCOMOTION SKILLS

In this chapter, we address eight locomotion skills: walking, running, side sliding, galloping, hopping, jumping, skipping, and leaping. Our primary focus is to develop movement competency; and then to refine this using movement education themes such as force production (e.g., hard or soft stepping), moving in different directions (which we call *pathways*), and speed (e.g., fast or slow); and then apply these skills in rhythmic contexts (e.g., set to music) and in movement routines.

Although there are many ways to teach locomotion skills, we focus on instructional task progressions that are similar across skills to strengthen teacher and student understanding of instruction procedures. A key element of our pedagogy is the use of demonstration and follow the leader (typically the teacher and sometimes a peer).

Music and drum beats are important pedagogical tools to teach locomotion. The beat motivates students, and it provides a rhythm that students can follow and controls the pace of movement.

We have designed many of the tasks to build on these eight skills. For example, once students learn to use walk in different pathways (e.g., curved and diagonal), they then travel these paths while moving slowly and quickly or softly and heavily. In this way, prior movement elements become embedded in current movements.

We draw on *Understanding Motor Development* by Gallahue et al. (2012) for the techniques of the locomotion skills. We think it is important that you have a reference for fundamental motor skills, because there are many variations of how locomotion skills are performed. The Gallahue text is an excellent reference.

Modifications to Address Individual Needs of Students

For students with disabilities, appropriate modifications to activities depend on the nature of the disability. For example, to modify activities such as walking, skipping, hopping, or jumping for students with visual impairments, you can use tactile modeling (i.e., demonstration by touch rather than sight) or physical guidance (i.e., moving the student's body into positions) to demonstrate the proper form. Children with visual impairments, particularly those with congenital vision loss, tend not to demonstrate proper arm actions associated with locomotion movements (e.g., running) because they do not have visual examples to follow. Therefore, it is essential to explicitly teach these students the proper upper-body movements. One way to do this is to have the student stand to your left while you both face the same direction. Hold one end of a long-handled implement (e.g., a hockey stick) in your left hand and have the student hold the other end in the right hand. Move your arms while you both do the locomotion movement. As your arms move, the long-handled implement will also move, which demonstrates the motion by moving the student's right arm.

You may need to make additional modifications for students with physical disabilities. Children with cerebral palsy may present locomotion skills differently than children without disabilities. Children who use wheelchairs cannot engage in activities that involve lower limb movement, but they can participate in pathway, speed, and game activities in these units. Be aware of potential limitations and plan accordingly to ensure that all students can be successfully included in activities.

For students with cognitive disabilities such as autism spectrum disorder, learning disabilities, or attention deficit disorder, few modifications to locomotion activities are needed. Your primary concern will be appropriately communicating what locomotion activity you expect the students to perform (e.g., by using picture symbols for children with autism spectrum disorder) and establishing effective stop and start signals (e.g., a whistle).

Organization

Place students in small groups to allow for more efficient organization of the lesson. Placing students in small groups allows students to observe peers easier than in the whole group. It also allows the teacher to designate areas for groups to practice, creating safe spaces between groups. If the task requires a larger area than the group area, then you can combine two or more areas and groups.

Space

Ensure that home court areas have sufficient space for students to move. Use the same home court area for each group to ensure that students do not move into each other.

Equipment Needed

Equipment includes mats, hoops, polyspots, cones, and rope.

CONTENT MAP STRUCTURE

Figure 4.1 is a content map that shows the flow of all of the tasks used to develop locomotion skills. This content map is not divided into levels, as is done in later chapters.

STRUCTURE OF THE LESSONS

The following is a sample daily lesson structure for a 40-minute locomotion lesson.

Warm-up (6 minutes)

Review task (from the previous lesson): run at varying speeds, such as to fast, medium, and slow drum beats (3 to 4 minutes)

Review task: run varying pathways (3 minutes)

Informing task: side slide in general space (3 minutes)

Extension task: side slide using varying speeds (4 minutes)

Extension task: side slide using varying forces (4 minutes)

Application task: side slide mirroring (4 minutes)

Informing task: galloping in general space (3 minutes)

Extension task: galloping using varying forces (3 minutes)

Application task—follow the leader: leaders uses side sliding and galloping; follower copies (3 minutes)

Closure (3 minutes)

Warm-up

The warm-up is approximately six minutes long. Students warm up in their groups in the group areas. Using music or drum beats, count about eight beats to time each activity. You will have to demonstrate until students know the warm-up; then they can be led by a student in each group or perform without leaders.

Walking and Standing

- Walk in general space.
- Walk tall like a giant in general space and stretch your hands overhead.
- Walk on your hands and feet in general space like a mouse.
- Walk and clap with the beat.
- Walk and lift the knees high.
- Stand still and tap your head, shoulders, chest, abdomen, knees, and toes with your hands. It's okay to bend your knees to touch your toes.

Sitting

- Butterfly stretch: Sit with your legs bent and the soles of your feet touching, and then gently move your knees toward the floor.
- Lift one foot, clap over it in the air, clap under your knee, and then clap back and forth over and under the knee. Repeat with the other leg.
- Do sit-ups or crunches.
- Sit with your legs apart and straight. Walk your hands toward your knees and back again.
- Sit with your knees tucked closely to your chest, and then straighten your legs.

Moving on Hands and Knees

- Sad cat: Arch your back downward.
- Happy cat: Arch your back upward.
- Shake your tail: Wiggle your buttocks.
- Sea lion: Straighten your legs and push your chest upward to stretch.

BLOCK PLANS

The first block plan (see table 4.1) introduces locomotor skills that might be taught to kindergarten students, and the second (see table 4.2) introduces skills that might be taught to second grade students. There is overlap between the two plans. Although longer units are always preferred, we recognize that there are time limitations at the elementary level; therefore, we have limited each block plan to seven days. You can modify these plans with regard to duration and grades taught.

K-2 Locomotion Content Map

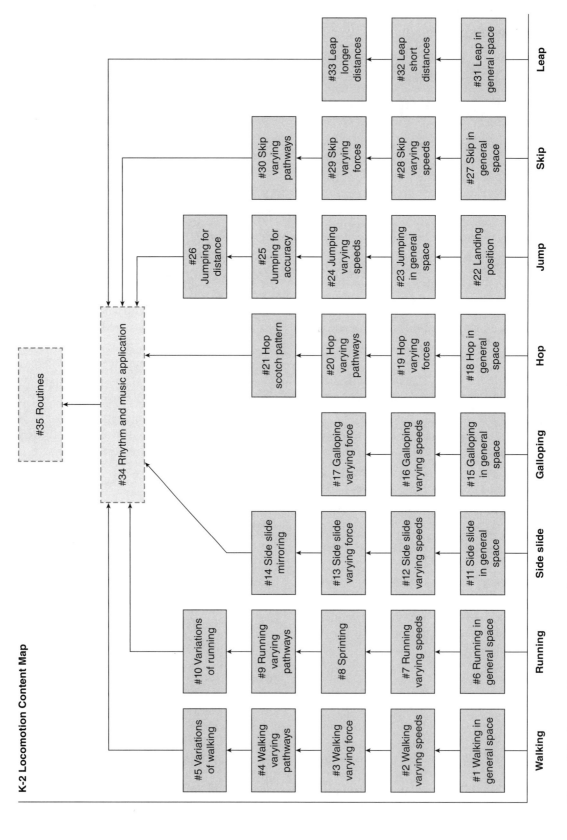

Figure 4.1 Locomotion content map for kindergarten through second grade.

Table 4.1 Kindergarten Locomotion Block Plan: Seven-Day Unit

This is an example of a beginning block plan for kindergarten students. It is based on an initial seven-day unit and, as such, it does not include all of the tasks on the content map. You can use this as a template for developing an appropriate initial block plan for kindergarten students.

Lesson 1	Lesson 2	Lesson 3	Lesson 4	Lesson 5
Warm-up	Warm-up	Warm-up	Warm-up	Warm-up
Content development	Content development	Content development	Content development	Content development
(1) Walk in general space	(1) Walk in general space	(22) Land from jump	(18) Hop in general space	(11) Side slide in general space
(2) Walk at varying speeds	(2) Walk at varying speeds	(23) Jump in general space	(19) Hop using varying force	(12) Side slide at varying speeds
(6) Run in general space	(6) Run in general space	(24) Jump at varying speeds	(20) Hop along varying pathways	(13) Side slide using varying force
(8) Sprint	(7) Run at varying speeds		(27) Skip in general space	(31) Leap in general space
(15) Gallop in general space	(8) Sprint		(28) Skip at varying speeds	(32) Leap short distances
(16) Gallop at varying speeds	(15) Gallop in general space			(33) Leap longer distances
	(16) Gallop at varying speeds			
Application	Application	Application	Application	Application
(34) Sequences: rhythm and music application	(34) Sequences: rhythm and music application	(34) Sequences: rhythm and music application, longer time than usual, applying the skills of lessons 1 and 2	(34) Sequences: rhythm and music application	(34) Sequences: rhythm and music application

Lesson 6	Lesson 7
Warm-up	Warm-up
Content development	Content development
(34) Sequences: rhythm and music application	(35) Routines: present
(35) Routines: designing and practicing	
Application	Application
(35) Routines: practice	(35) Routines: present

Table 4.2 Second Grade Locomotion Block Plan: Seven-Day Unit

This is an example of a beginning block plan for grade 2 students. It is based on an initial seven-day unit and, as such, it does not include all of the tasks on the content map. You can use this as a template for developing an appropriate initial block plan for grade 2 students.

Lesson 1	Lesson 2	Lesson 3	Lesson 4	Lesson 5
Warm-up	Warm-up	Warm-up	Warm-up	Warm-up
Content development **(1)** Walk in general space **(2)** Walk at varying speeds **(3)** Walk using varying force **(4)** Walk along varying pathways **(5)** Variations of walking **(6)** Run in general space **(7)** Run at varying speeds **(8)** Sprint **(9)** Run along varying pathways **(10)** Variations of running	**Content development** **(11)** Side slide in general space **(12)** Side slide at varying speeds **(13)** Side slide using varying force **(14)** Side slide mirroring **(15)** Gallop in general space **(16)** Gallop at varying speeds **(17)** Gallop using varying force	**Content development** **(22)** Land from jump **(23)** Jump in general space **(24)** Jump at varying speeds **(25)** Jump for accuracy **(26)** Jump for distance **(10)** Variations of running (combine with jumping)	**Content development** **(18)** Hop in general space **(19)** Hop using varying force **(20)** Hop along varying pathways **(21)** Hop in hopscotch pattern **(27)** Skip in general space **(28)** Skip at varying speeds **(29)** Skip using varying force **(30)** Skip along varying pathways	**Content development** **(31)** Leap in general space **(32)** Leap short distances **(33)** Leap longer distances **(10)** Variations of running (combine with leaping)
Application **(34)** Sequences: rhythm and music application	**Application** **(34)** Sequences: rhythm and music application	**Application** **(34)** Sequences: rhythm and music application, longer time than usual, applying the skills of lessons 1 and 2	**Application** **(34)** Sequences: rhythm and music application	**Application** **(34)** Sequences: rhythm and music application

Lesson 6	Lesson 7
Warm-up	Warm-up
Content development **(34)** Sequences: rhythm and music **(35)** Routines: designing and practicing	**Content development** **(35)** Routines: present
Application **(35)** Routines: practice	**Application** **(35)** Routines: present

SHAPE AMERICA'S GRADE-LEVEL OUTCOMES FOR K-12 PHYSICAL EDUCATION

In table 4.3, we identify key grade-level outcomes for locomotion for kindergarten through second grade. These are linked to specific tasks on the content map that are appropriate for teaching the skill and assessing the outcome.

Table 4.3   Grade-Level Outcomes for Locomotion

Outcome	Description	Content map focus and tasks
S1.E1.K	Performs locomotor skills (hopping, galloping, running, sliding, skipping) while maintaining balance.	Tasks 18-19 (hopping); 15 (galloping); 6, 8-9 (running); 11-12 (sliding); 27 (skipping)
S1.E1.1	Hops, gallops, jogs and slides using a mature pattern.	Tasks 20-21 (hopping); 16-17 (galloping); 13-14 (sliding)
S1.E1.2	Skips using a mature pattern.	Tasks 29-30
S1.E2.2a	Runs with a mature pattern.	Task 7
S1.E2.2b	Travels showing differentiation between jogging and sprinting.	Task 34
S1.E3.K	Performs jumping & landing actions with balance.	Task 22
S1.E3.1	Demonstrates 2 of the 5 critical elements for jumping & landing in a horizontal plane using 2-foot take-offs and landings.	Task 23
S1.E3.2	Demonstrates 4 of the 5 critical elements for jumping & landing in a horizontal plane using a variety of 1- and 2-foot take-offs and landings.	Tasks 24, 26, 32-33
S1.E4.1	Demonstrates 2 of the 5 critical elements for jumping & landing in a vertical plane.	Task 25
S1.E4.2	Demonstrates 4 of the 5 critical elements for jumping & landing in a vertical plane.	Task 25
S1.E5.K	Performs locomotor skills in response to teacher-led creative dance.	Task 34
S1.E5.1	Combines locomotor and nonlocomotor skills in a teacher-designed dance.	Task 34
S1.E5.2	Performs a teacher- and/or student-designed rhythmic activity with correct response to simple rhythms.	Task 35

TASK 1: WALK IN GENERAL SPACE

PURPOSE

Following is the purpose of the task as related to aspects of skilled performance.

Technique: Walking involves the transfer of weight from one foot to the other while moving forward or backward. One foot is always in contact with the ground, and the arms swing freely in opposition. Being able to walk fluently is a fundamental motor skill and it is a prerequisite for locomotion skills.

DESCRIPTION

Students walk in general space and do not touch each other. The task can be modified so students follow the leader in groups or in pairs. This task can be accomplished and evaluated as part of the warm-up and does not need to be taught as a separate task.

EQUIPMENT

Define group court areas with cones

CRITICAL ELEMENTS

Technique

- Hold the body straight with good posture (walk tall).
- Keep the head up and look straight ahead.
- Swing the arms freely and in opposition to the feet.
- Use a heel-toe action.

COMMON ERRORS, CAUSES, AND CORRECTIONS

- The student's walking pattern is bouncy or jerky. *Cause:* Movement fluency. *Correction:* Have the student practice more. This is a very unlikely pattern in kindergarten.
- The student's arms swing excessively away from the sides. *Cause:* Movement fluency. *Correction:* Ask the student to relax the arms.
- The student's feet are too close together. *Cause:* Movement fluency. *Correction:* Ask the student to move the feet farther apart.
- The student's feet are too far apart. *Cause:* Movement fluency. *Correction:* Ask the student to walk a little faster and move the feet closer together.
- The student's toes are turned in or turned out. *Cause:* Movement fluency. *Correction:* Ask the student to point the toes forward.
- The student's head is too far forward. *Cause:* Movement fluency. *Correction:* Ask the student to look forward.

TASK 2: WALK AT VARYING SPEEDS

PURPOSE

Following is the purpose of the task as related to aspects of skilled performance.

Technique: Students demonstrate and identify different speeds of walking.

DESCRIPTION

Students move at different paces to even or uneven drum beats or music.

EQUIPMENT

Define group court areas with cones to mark court boundaries

CRITICAL ELEMENTS

Technique

- Hold the body straight with good posture (walk tall).
- Keep the head up and look straight ahead.
- Swing the arms freely and in opposition to the feet.
- Use a heel-toe action.
- Move slowly in time with the music or drum beat.
- Move quickly in time with the music or drum beat.

COMMON ERRORS, CAUSES, AND CORRECTIONS

- The student struggles to control the speed. *Cause:* Movement fluency. *Correction:* For slow movement, say "move slowly like a snail"; for quick movement, say "move quickly like a rabbit being chased by a dog."
- The student runs instead of walking. *Cause:* Student is too enthusiastic. *Correction:* Remind the student to walk instead of run.

TASK 3: WALK USING VARYING FORCE

PURPOSE

Following is the purpose of the task as related to aspects of skilled performance.

Technique: Students demonstrate and identify different force productions while walking. Being able to modify force production is an important ability in sports games.

DESCRIPTION

Students walk softly and lightly and then loudly and heavily. To accomplish this, ask them to move like the following animals:

- Duck: Walk low to the ground with the knees bent.
- Monkey: Walk with the knees bent, let the arms hang and sway, and move faster than a duck.
- Rooster: Stick the chest up, use the arms as wings, and step slowly using a toe-heel motion.
- Elephant: Stomp the feet, use the arms to make a trunk, and move slowly and heavily.
- Giraffe: Walk on the toes and stretch.

EQUIPMENT

Group court areas and cones to mark boundaries

CRITICAL ELEMENTS

Technique

- Hold the body straight with good posture (walk tall).
- Keep the head up and look straight ahead.
- Swing the arms freely and in opposition to the feet.
- Use a heel-toe action.
- Walk softly and lightly.
- Walk loudly and heavily.

COMMON ERRORS, CAUSES, AND CORRECTIONS

The student struggles to control the force production. *Cause:* Movement fluency. *Correction:* For soft and light movement, say "step on the leaves in the water but don't step so hard that they sink"; for loud and heavy movement, say "step on imaginary balloons and burst them."

TASK 4: WALK ALONG VARYING PATHWAYS

PURPOSE

Following is the purpose of the task as related to aspects of skilled performance.

Technique: Students identify and walk along different pathways. Changing direction is an important ability in sports, dance, and various movement forms.

DESCRIPTION

Students walk along a straight path by following a line on the floor and then following an imaginary straight line. For the task extensions, provide students with verbal directions and use cues such as lines on the ground, cones, or other markers. Students can perform these tasks individually in general space in the group area.

- *Extension 1.* Walk along a diagonal path between two cones or following a line on the floor.
- *Extension 2.* Walk along a zigzag path.
- *Extension 3.* Walk along a curved path.
- *Extension 4.* Walk along an imaginary circle.

EQUIPMENT

Define group court areas with cones

CRITICAL ELEMENTS

Technique

- Hold the body straight with good posture (walk tall).
- Keep the head up and look straight ahead.
- Swing the arms freely and in opposition to the feet.
- Use a heel-toe action.

COMMON ERRORS, CAUSES, AND CORRECTIONS

The student struggles to stay on the path. *Cause:* Movement fluency. *Correction:* Make the pathway wider or reduce sharpness of turns or corners.

TASK 5: VARIATIONS OF WALKING

PURPOSE

Following is the purpose of the task as related to aspects of skilled performance.

Technique: Students demonstrate variations on walking. In many sports, dances, and movement forms, the arms are often used in combination with locomotion such as shooting in basketball, or bending down to retrieve a ground ball in softball. In addition, walking using different parts of the foot is also used. As such these variations are important prerequisites to more advanced forms of locomotion.

DESCRIPTION

Students walk in general space until you direct them to change positions and directions.

- *Extension 1.* Walk with your hands over your head.
- *Extension 2.* Walk with your knees bent and your hands close to floor.
- *Extension 3.* Walk on your toes.
- *Extension 4.* Walk on your heels.
- *Extension 5.* Walk and lift your knees high (march).
- *Extension 6.* Walk backward.
- *Extension 7.* Walk in a way we have not practiced.

Students can also walk in these ways along the pathways presented in task 4: straight, diagonal, zigzag, curved, and imaginary.

EQUIPMENT

Group court areas and cones to mark boundaries

CRITICAL ELEMENTS

Technique

- Hold the body straight with good posture (walk tall).
- Keep the head up and look straight ahead.
- Swing the arms freely and in opposition to the feet.
- Use a heel-toe action.

COMMON ERRORS, CAUSES, AND CORRECTIONS

The student struggles to follow directions. *Cause:* The student does not understand from the directions what to do. *Correction:* Pair the student with a partner who can model the movement.

TASK 6: RUN IN GENERAL SPACE

PURPOSE

Following is the purpose of the task as related to aspects of skilled performance.

Technique: Running is characterized by a period of flight where neither foot is touching the ground. Students demonstrate their ability to run by jogging and changing directions. Running is a foundational movement form for many sports and games.

DESCRIPTION

Students jog in general space and cover as much of the specified area as possible. They should change directions to avoid bumping into others. Once students can do this, they can play nonexclusionary tag games (i.e., once tagged you stand still or walk for five seconds before rejoining the game). To develop students' running skills increase the area of the tag game. We recommend that students play the tag games in their group spaces to limit the number of students in any one area and decrease the likelihood of them running into each other.

EQUIPMENT

Group court areas and cones to mark boundaries

CRITICAL ELEMENTS

Technique

- Keep the torso straight and vertical.
- Hold the head still and relax the face, neck, and shoulders.
- Bend the elbows 90 degrees.
- Lightly clench the hands as if holding a rolled-up towel.
- Pump the arms from hip to lip, and keep them close to the sides.
- With each stride, lift the front knee high and straighten the back leg.

COMMON ERRORS, CAUSES, AND CORRECTIONS

- The student has short or limited leg swings. *Cause:* Poor movement competency. *Correction:* Remind the student to take larger steps.
- The student has stiff, uneven strides. *Cause:* Poor movement competency. *Correction:* Have the student practice for longer distances.

- The student has no observable flight phase. *Cause:* Poor movement competency. *Correction:* Ask the student to run faster.
- The student's arms are straight. *Cause:* Poor understanding of arm position. *Correction:* Tell the student to make an open *L* with the arm.
- The student's arms have little swing. *Cause:* Poor understanding of arm position. *Correction:* Tell the student to pump the arms from hip to lip.
- The student's arms are too far from the body. *Cause:* Poor understanding of arm position. *Correction:* Remind the student to keep the arms close to the body.

TASK 7: RUN AT VARYING SPEEDS

PURPOSE
Following is the purpose of the task as related to aspects of skilled performance.

Technique: Students run at varying speeds. Being able to run and vary your speed is an essential requirement in many sports, games, and dances.

DESCRIPTION
Students demonstrate running at varying speeds by performing the following activities:
- Students run at speeds that are dictated by the rhythm of music or drum beats.
- Tell students they are being chased through the forest by different animals. The type of animal determines how fast they will run: tiger (fastest), elephant (fast), chimpanzee (slower), koala (very slow).

EQUIPMENT
Group court areas and cones to mark boundaries

CRITICAL ELEMENTS

Technique
- Keep the torso straight and vertical.
- Hold the head still and relax the face, neck, and shoulders.
- Bend the elbows 90 degrees.
- Lightly clench the hands as if holding a rolled-up towel.
- Pump the arms from hip to lip, and keep them close to the sides.
- With each stride, lift the front knee high and straighten the back leg.

COMMON ERRORS, CAUSES, AND CORRECTIONS
- The student has short or limited leg swings. *Cause:* Poor movement competency. *Correction:* Remind the student to take larger steps.
- The student has stiff, uneven strides. *Cause:* Poor movement competency. *Correction:* Have the student practice for longer distances.
- The student has no observable flight phase. *Cause:* Poor movement competency. *Correction:* Ask the student to run faster.
- The student's arms are straight. *Cause:* Poor understanding of arm position. *Correction:* Tell the student to make an open *L* with the arm.
- The student's arms have little swing. *Cause:* Poor understanding of arm position. *Correction:* Tell the student to pump the arms from hip to lip.
- The student's arms are too far from the body. *Cause:* Poor understanding of arm position. *Correction:* Remind the student to keep the arms close to the body.

- The student does not lift the knees high. *Cause:* Poor understanding of knee position. *Correction:* Have the student jog in place and the teacher, facing them holds both hands horizontal. The student jogs in place lifting their knees to hip level. Facing a partner and holding hands often provides stability for the performance.

TASK 8: SPRINT

PURPOSE

Following is the purpose of the task as related to aspects of skilled performance.

Technique: Students sprint. Sprinting is a requirement for many sports and games. Being able to perform proficiently is an important locomotion outcome.

DESCRIPTION

Students sprint from different locations. Set up cones 10, 20, and 30 yards (9.1, 18.3, and 27.4 meters) apart. Students sprint to the 10-yard cone and wait. When you say *go,* students sprint to the 20-yard marker, wait, and then sprint to the 30-yard marker when you say *go* again. After resting, students can sprint 20 yards without stopping and then 30 yards without stopping. Encourage students to run past the markers to maximize the sprint over the distance. Be sure to give students time to recover between sprints, but they should not sit down. A good strategy for recovery is giving students a task to perform at each marker, such as walking a pathway, before sprinting again.

EQUIPMENT

Group court areas and cones to mark boundaries

CRITICAL ELEMENTS

Technique

- Keep the torso straight and vertical.
- Hold the head still and relax the face, neck, and shoulders.
- Bend the elbows 90 degrees.
- Lightly clench the hands as if holding a rolled-up towel.
- Pump the arms from hip to lip, and keep them close to the sides.
- With each stride, lift the front knee high and straighten the back leg.
- At the start the sprint, strides are short and quick. Lengthen the strides as you gain speed and momentum.

COMMON ERRORS, CAUSES, AND CORRECTIONS

- The student has short or limited leg swings. *Cause:* Poor movement competency. *Correction:* Remind the student to take larger steps.
- The student has stiff, uneven strides. *Cause:* Poor movement competency. *Correction:* Have the student practice for longer distances.
- The student has no observable flight phase. *Cause:* Poor movement competency. *Correction:* Ask the student to run faster.
- The student's arms are straight. *Cause:* Poor understanding of arm position. *Correction:* Tell the student to make an open *L* with the arm.
- The student's arms have little swing. *Cause:* Poor understanding of arm position. *Correction:* Tell the student to pump the arms from hip to lip.
- The student's arms are too far from the body. *Cause:* Poor understanding of arm position. *Correction:* Remind the student to keep the arms close to the body.

- The student does not lift the knees high. *Cause:* Poor understanding of knee position. *Correction:* Have the student jog in place and the teacher, facing them, holds both hands horizontal. The student jogs in place lifting their knees to hip level. Holding hands often provides stability for the performance.

TASK 9: RUN ALONG VARYING PATHWAYS

PURPOSE

Following is the purpose of the task as related to aspects of skilled performance.

Technique: Students run along different pathways. Many sports, and games require that students move away from defenders. Being able to run along pathways is a prerequisite for avoiding defenders and other similar demands in more advanced activities.

DESCRIPTION

This task is similar to task 4 except students are running instead of walking. The critical difference is the increased space needed for moving due to the distance covered by running. Set up pathways along which students can run with their groups. Create straight, zigzag, curved, and circular paths. Any pathway is appropriate for students to demonstrate their ability to run along a pathway.

EQUIPMENT

Define group court areas with cones; rope markers

CRITICAL ELEMENTS

Technique

- Keep the torso straight and vertical.
- Hold the head still and relax the face, neck, and shoulders.
- Bend the elbows 90 degrees.
- Lightly clench the hands as if holding a rolled-up towel.
- Pump the arms from hip to lip, and keep them close to the sides.
- With each stride, lift the front knee high and straighten the back leg.

COMMON ERRORS, CAUSES, AND CORRECTIONS

- The student has short or limited leg swings. *Cause:* Poor movement competency. *Correction:* Remind the student to take larger steps.
- The student has stiff, uneven strides. *Cause:* Poor movement competency. *Correction:* Have the student practice for longer distances.
- The student has no observable flight phase. *Cause:* Poor movement competency. *Correction:* Ask the student to run faster.
- The student's arms are straight. *Cause:* Poor understanding of arm position. *Correction:* Tell the student to make an open *L* with the arm.
- The student's arms have little swing. *Cause:* Poor understanding of arm position. *Correction:* Tell the student to pump the arms from hip to lip.
- The student's arms are too far from the body. *Cause:* Poor understanding of arm position. *Correction:* Remind the student to keep the arms close to the body.
- The student does not lift the knees high. *Cause:* Poor understanding of knee position. *Correction:* Have the student jog in place and the teacher, facing them, holds both hands horizontal. The student jogs in place lifting their knees to hip level. Holding hands often provides stability for the performance.

TASK 10: VARIATIONS OF RUNNING

PURPOSE

Following is the purpose of the task as related to aspects of skilled performance.

Technique: Students run using different variations. In sports and games, students often bend low while running to scoop something from the ground such as in lacrosse. They often catch a ball or throw on the run, such as in softball. Being able to run, balance, and engage in movement tasks demanded in sports is important for success in performing the sport or game.

DESCRIPTION

Students imagine they are running through the jungle. They encounter obstacles such as logs they need to leap over, branches they need to duck under, snakes they need to tiptoe around, and mud they must walk through with high knees so they don't get stuck.

EQUIPMENT

Define group court areas with cones; ropes or foam equipment (to simulate jungle obstacles)

CRITICAL ELEMENTS

Technique

- Keep the torso straight and vertical.
- Hold the head still and relax the face, neck, and shoulders.
- Bend the elbows 90 degrees.
- Lightly clench the hands as if holding a rolled-up towel.
- Pump the arms from hip to lip, and keep them close to the sides.
- With each stride, lift the front knee high and straighten the back leg.

COMMON ERRORS, CAUSES, AND CORRECTIONS

- The student has short or limited leg swings. *Cause:* Poor movement competency. *Correction:* Remind the student to take larger steps.
- The student has stiff, uneven strides. *Cause:* Poor movement competency. *Correction:* Have the student practice for longer distances.
- The student has no observable flight phase. *Cause:* Poor movement competency. *Correction:* Ask the student to run faster.
- The student's arms are straight. *Cause:* Poor understanding of arm position. *Correction:* Tell the student to make an open *L* with the arm.
- The student's arms have little swing. *Cause:* Poor understanding of arm position. *Correction:* Tell the student to pump the arms from hip to lip.
- The student's arms are too far from the body. *Cause:* Poor understanding of arm position. *Correction:* Remind the student to keep the arms close to the body.
- The student does not lift the knees high. *Cause:* Poor understanding of knee position. *Correction:* Have the student jog in place and the teacher, facing them, holds both hands horizontal. The student jogs in place lifting their knees to hip level. Holding hands often provides stability for the performance.

TASK 11: SIDE SLIDE IN GENERAL SPACE

PURPOSE

Following is the purpose of the task as related to aspects of skilled performance.

Technique: Side sliding involves moving sideways with one foot leading; this is sometimes called a sideways gallop. This task introduces side sliding. Side sliding is used in many sports, games, and dances.

DESCRIPTION

Demonstrate the slide, and ask students to slide first in one direction and then in the other. Once students can perform the slide, ask them to slide sideways along different pathways such as straight, zigzag, or curved.

EQUIPMENT

Define group court areas with cones

CRITICAL ELEMENTS

Technique

- The right or left leg steps sideways.
- The trailing leg lands next to the leg that stepped off.
- Bend both legs at the knees.
- Make contact with the ground in front of the feet.

COMMON ERRORS, CAUSES, AND CORRECTIONS

- The student has difficulty coordinating the sliding movement. *Cause:* Movement fluency. *Correction:* Say "step together, step together."
- The student has difficulty sliding smoothly. *Cause:* Movement fluency. *Correction:* Have the student slide for longer durations or longer distances.
- The student does not lift the feet when sliding. *Cause:* Movement fluency. *Correction:* Have the student practice springing off the front foot.

TASK 12: SIDE SLIDE AT VARYING SPEEDS

PURPOSE

Following is the purpose of the task as related to aspects of skilled performance.

Technique: Changing speeds while side sliding is an important movement in many sports and in dance. In this task, students learn to perform this fluently.

DESCRIPTION

Students demonstrate side sliding at different speeds. They can side slide freely in general space or slide along zigzag and curved pathways. Music and drum beats are useful to control the pace of the movement.

EQUIPMENT

Define group court areas with cones

CRITICAL ELEMENTS

Technique

- The right or left leg steps sideways.
- The trailing leg lands next to the leg that stepped off.
- Bend both legs at the knees.
- Make contact with the ground in front of the feet.

COMMON ERRORS, CAUSES, AND CORRECTIONS

- The student has difficulty coordinating the sliding movement. *Cause:* Movement fluency. *Correction:* Say "step together, step together."
- The student has difficulty sliding smoothly. *Cause:* Movement fluency. *Correction:* Have the student slide for longer durations or longer distances.
- The student does not lift the feet when sliding. *Cause:* Movement fluency. *Correction:* Have the student practice springing off the front foot.

TASK 13: SIDE SLIDE USING VARYING FORCE

PURPOSE

Following is the purpose of the task as related to aspects of skilled performance.

Technique: This task introduces force production while side sliding.

DESCRIPTION

Students demonstrate side sliding at different speeds. Changing speed while sliding occurs in many sports, games, and dances.

EQUIPMENT

Define group court areas with cones

CRITICAL ELEMENTS

Technique

- The right or left leg steps sideways.
- The trailing leg lands next to the leg that stepped off.
- Bend both legs at the knees.
- Make contact with the ground in front of the feet.

COMMON ERRORS, CAUSES, AND CORRECTIONS

- The student has difficulty coordinating the sliding movement. *Cause:* Movement fluency. *Correction:* Say "step together, step together."
- The student has difficulty sliding smoothly. *Cause:* Movement fluency. *Correction:* Have the student slide for longer durations or longer distances.
- The student does not lift the feet when sliding. *Cause:* Movement fluency. *Correction:* Have the student practice springing off the front foot.

TASK 14: SIDE SLIDE MIRRORING

PURPOSE

Following is the purpose of the task as related to aspects of skilled performance.

Technique: Mirroring another performer while side sliding is an important movement in many sports because it is a foundation in defending such as person to person defense in basketball. In this task, students learn to perform this fluently.

DESCRIPTION

Place students in pairs. The task here is for one student to mirror the movement of the other. One student, the person being mirrored, holds a ball and side slides in different directions. The student mirroring uses their hand to track the ball while side sliding to match the movement of the student they are mirroring. Encourage students with the ball to start slowly and then move faster and to move from left to right.

EQUIPMENT

Define group court areas with cones

CRITICAL ELEMENTS

Technique

- The right or left leg steps sideways.
- The trailing leg lands next to the leg that stepped off.
- Bend both legs at the knees.
- Make contact with the ground in front of the feet.

COMMON ERRORS, CAUSES, AND CORRECTIONS

- The student has difficulty coordinating the sliding movement. *Cause:* Movement fluency. *Correction:* Say "step together, step together."
- The student has difficulty sliding smoothly. *Cause:* Movement fluency. *Correction:* Have the student slide for longer durations or longer distances.
- The student does not lift the feet when sliding. *Cause:* Movement fluency. *Correction:* Have the student practice springing off the front foot.

TASK 15: GALLOP IN GENERAL SPACE

PURPOSE

Following is the purpose of the task as related to aspects of skilled performance.

Technique: Galloping is an exaggerated slide step combined with a leap. It is an important fundamental motor skill that is a precursor to many sports and types of dance. In this task, students learn to perform this fluently.

DESCRIPTION

Demonstrate the gallop, and then have students practice galloping in general space. Practice is important. Drum beats or country music can be used to encourage children to gallop like horses. Be sure to cue students to switch the lead foot so they are able to lead on each side.

EQUIPMENT

Define group court areas with cones

CRITICAL ELEMENTS

Technique

- The front foot makes a forward slide and spring movement.
- Transfer your weight to the back foot. (Teachers often say "the front foot leads and the back foot catches up.")
- The back leg lands behind the front leg.
- Make contact with the ground in a heel-toe pattern.

COMMON ERRORS, CAUSES, AND CORRECTIONS

- The student's back leg comes in front of the lead leg. *Cause:* Movement fluency. *Correction:* Remind the student that the back leg follows; it doesn't lead.
- The student's lead leg takes off only after the back leg has landed. *Cause:* Movement fluency. *Correction:* Ask the student to gallop a little faster and move the lead leg sooner.
- The student's gallop is not rhythmic. *Cause:* Movement fluency. *Correction:* Use a drum beat or wording (e.g., tick tock, tick tock) to create a pace of movement.

TASK 16: GALLOP AT VARYING SPEEDS

PURPOSE

Following is the purpose of the task as related to aspects of skilled performance.

Technique: Being able to change speeds is an important galloping skill. In this task, students learn to perform this fluently.

DESCRIPTION

Students demonstrate galloping at varying speeds by performing the following activities:

- Students gallop at speeds that are dictated by the rhythm of music or drum beats.
- Tell students they are being chased through the forest by different animals. The type of animal determines how fast they will gallop: tiger (fastest), elephant (fast), chimpanzee (slower), koala (very slow).
- Students gallop along different pathways (e.g., curved, circle, diagonal).

EQUIPMENT

Define group court areas with cones

CRITICAL ELEMENTS

Technique

- The front foot makes a forward slide and spring movement.
- Transfer your weight to the back foot. (Teachers often say "the front foot leads and the back foot catches up.")
- The back leg lands behind the front leg.
- Make contact with the ground in a heel-toe pattern.

COMMON ERRORS, CAUSES, AND CORRECTIONS

- The student's back leg comes in front of the lead leg. *Cause:* Movement fluency. *Correction:* Remind the student that the back leg follows; it doesn't lead.
- The student's lead leg takes off only after the back leg has landed. *Cause:* Movement fluency. *Correction:* Ask the student to gallop a little faster and move the lead leg sooner.
- The student's gallop is not rhythmic. *Cause:* Movement fluency. *Correction:* Use a drum beat or wording (e.g., tick tock, tick tock) to create a pace of movement.

TASK 17: GALLOP USING VARYING FORCE

PURPOSE

Following is the purpose of the task as related to aspects of skilled performance.

Technique: This task introduces the use of varying force while galloping. The use of galloping with varying force occurs in many dances and in some children's playground games.

DESCRIPTION

Students demonstrate galloping using varying force or effort by performing the following activities:

- Tell students they are runaway horses and they must gallop hard to get away from a wolf.
- Tell students they are horses galloping across a very old bridge and they must move softly.
- Students gallop over rope logs, rope ponds, and the like to create opportunities for force production.

EQUIPMENT

Define group court areas with cones

CRITICAL ELEMENTS

Technique

- The front foot makes a forward slide and spring movement.
- Transfer your weight to the back foot. (Teachers often say "the front foot leads and the back foot catches up.")
- The back leg lands behind the front leg.
- Make contact with the ground in a heel-toe pattern.

COMMON ERRORS, CAUSES, AND CORRECTIONS

- The student's back leg comes in front of the lead leg. *Cause:* Movement fluency. *Correction:* Remind the student that the back leg follows; it doesn't lead.
- The student's lead leg takes off only after the back leg has landed. *Cause:* Movement fluency. *Correction:* Ask the student to gallop a little faster and move the lead leg sooner.
- The student's gallop is not rhythmic. *Cause:* Movement fluency. *Correction:* Use a drum beat or wording (e.g., tick tock, tick tock) to create a pace of movement.

TASK 18: HOP IN GENERAL SPACE

PURPOSE

Following is the purpose of the task as related to aspects of skilled performance.

Technique: Hopping is a springing action that involves taking off on one foot and landing on the same foot. It is used in sports as well as in track and field events and dance. This task introduces hopping on each leg.

DESCRIPTION

Demonstrate the hop, and then ask students to practice hopping in general space. Ask students to do the following on each leg:

- Hop on one spot.
- Hop three times in a row before changing to the other leg. Then try to hop five times on each leg.
- Hop once for each letter in your name.

EQUIPMENT

Define group court areas with cones

CRITICAL ELEMENTS

Technique

- Swing both arms back and then quickly swing them forward and upward.
- Push off using the toes.
- Land on the toes and then on the balls of the feet, and then bend the knees.
- Use a heel-toe action.

COMMON ERRORS, CAUSES, AND CORRECTIONS

- The student doesn't move forward on the hop. *Cause:* The body is too upright. *Correction:* Tell the student to lean forward a little on the foot before hopping.
- The student achieves little height or distance. *Cause:* The arms may not be moving correctly. *Correction:* Have the student practice more and tell the student to swing the arms forward.
- The student's hopping is not rhythmical. *Cause:* Movement fluency. *Correction:* Have the student practice over more distance with short hops.

TASK 19: HOP USING VARYING FORCE

PURPOSE

Following is the purpose of the task as related to aspects of skilled performance.

Technique: This task introduces varying force production in hopping using both legs. This movement is used in sports and in children's games.

DESCRIPTION

Ask students to do the following on each leg:

- Hop softly so you don't make a sound.
- Hop loudly so we can hear you coming.
- Hop over a rope log (height).
- Hop across a rope river (distance).
- Hop on alternating feet.
- Hop slowly.
- Hop quickly.
- Hop in a pattern.

EQUIPMENT

Define group court areas with cones

CRITICAL ELEMENTS

Technique

- Swing both arms back and then quickly swing them forward and upward.
- Push off using the toes.
- Land on the toes and then on the balls of the feet, and then bend the knees.
- Use a heel-toe action.

COMMON ERRORS, CAUSES, AND CORRECTIONS

- The student doesn't move forward on the hop. *Cause:* The body is too upright. *Correction:* Tell the student to lean forward a little on the foot before hopping.
- The student achieves little height or distance. *Cause:* The arms may not be moving correctly. *Correction:* Have the student practice more and tell the student to swing the arms forward.
- The student's hopping is not rhythmical. *Cause:* Movement fluency. *Correction:* Have the student practice over more distance with short hops.

TASK 20: HOP ALONG VARYING PATHWAYS

PURPOSE

Following is the purpose of the task as related to aspects of skilled performance.

Technique: This task focuses on hopping along various pathways. This is a fundamental movement competency used in children's games.

DESCRIPTION

Students hop along a straight path by following a line on the floor and then following an imaginary straight line. For the task extensions, provide students with verbal directions and use cues such as lines on the ground, cones, or other markers. Students can perform these tasks individually in general space in the group court area. Each task should be performed on each leg.

- *Extension 1.* Hop along a diagonal path between two cones or following a line on the floor.
- *Extension 2.* Hop along a zigzag path.
- *Extension 3.* Hop along a curved path.
- *Extension 4.* Hop along an imaginary circle.
- *Extension 5.* Hop backward, then forward, then backward.
- *Extension 6.* Hop, then jump, then hop.
- *Extension 7.* Hop into and out of squares or hoops.

EQUIPMENT

Define group court areas with cones

CRITICAL ELEMENTS

Technique

- Swing both arms back and then quickly swing them forward and upward.
- Push off using the toes.
- Land on the toes and then on the balls of the feet, and then bend the knees.
- Use a heel-toe action.

COMMON ERRORS, CAUSES, AND CORRECTIONS

- The student doesn't move forward on the hop. *Cause:* The body is too upright. *Correction:* Tell the student to lean forward a little on the foot before hopping.
- The student achieves little height or distance. *Cause:* The arms may not be moving correctly. *Correction:* Have the student practice more and tell the student to swing the arms forward.
- The student's hopping is not rhythmical. *Cause:* Movement fluency. *Correction:* Have the student practice over more distance with short hops.

TASK 21: HOP IN HOPSCOTCH PATTERN

PURPOSE

Following is the purpose of the task as related to aspects of skilled performance.

Technique: This task introduces hopscotch games. These games are common children's games and being able to perform them is important not only for movement competency, but also for social engagement.

DESCRIPTION

Introduce two hopscotch games. Each game can be drawn in chalk or with tape on the floor. Create many stations for a given lesson so there are not more than 3 to 5 students at one station. Have students perform the games on each leg.

Simple hopscotch

Following the number sequence, each player hops on one foot on the numbers and places both feet on the empty spaces (see figure 4.2).

Traditional hopscotch

Each player throws a beanbag onto square 1 and hops over square 1 to square 2 (see figure 4.3). The player continues through the sequence of numbers and lands with two feet on home. Then the player hops back down the sequence and collects the beanbag. Then, the player repeats the process of hopping over a square by throwing the beanbag to square 2 and so on.

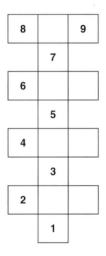

Figure 4.2 Simple hopscotch.

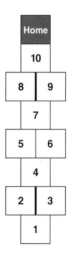

Figure 4.3 Traditional hopscotch.

EQUIPMENT

Define group court areas with cones, chalk, or tape; beanbags

CRITICAL ELEMENTS

Technique

- Swing both arms back and then quickly swing them forward and upward.
- Push off using the toes.
- Land on the toes and then on the balls of the feet, and then bend the knees.
- Use a heel-toe action.

COMMON ERRORS, CAUSES, AND CORRECTIONS

- The student doesn't move forward on the hop. *Cause:* The body is too upright. *Correction:* Tell the student to lean forward a little on the foot before hopping.
- The student achieves little height or distance. *Cause:* The arms may not be moving correctly. *Correction:* Have the student practice more and tell the student to swing the arms forward.
- The student's hopping is not rhythmical. *Cause:* Movement fluency. *Correction:* Have the student practice over more distance with short hops.

TASK 22: LAND FROM JUMP

PURPOSE

Following is the purpose of the task as related to aspects of skilled performance.

Technique: Being able to land from a jump is a critical safety skill for children. This task introduces landing safely.

DESCRIPTION

Have students stand with their knees bent, their feet shoulder-width apart, and their arms out in front of them and slightly to the side (see figure 4.4). Tell the students that this is the landing position. Ask students to do a little jump from this position and land back in the position. Ask the students to jump higher and higher while still landing in the position. This task is accomplished when students can consistently land in this position.

EQUIPMENT

Define group court areas with cones

CRITICAL ELEMENTS

Technique

- Bend the knees.
- Keep the feet shoulder-width apart.
- Keep the arms in front of the body and slightly to the side.
- Cushion with the legs on landing.

Figure 4.4 Technique for landing from a jump.

COMMON ERRORS, CAUSES, AND CORRECTIONS

- The student's landing is jarred (i.e., landing with straight legs). *Cause:* The knees are not bent. *Correction:* Tell the student to bend the knees more.
- The student's landing is unstable. *Cause:* The arms are not stretched out. *Correction:* Tell the student to lift the arms.

TASK 23: JUMP IN GENERAL SPACE

PURPOSE

Following is the purpose of the task as related to aspects of skilled performance.

Technique: Jumping is a skill that involves pushing off the ground with both legs and landing on both legs. It is a common movement used in sports and dance. This task introduces jumping.

DESCRIPTION

Begin this task only after students have mastered the landing task. In the group court areas or in another designated area, ask students to jump around as much of the space as possible. Each time, emphasize the landing position. You can also read the following for jumping rhythms:

- *Anna Banana: 101 Jump Rope Rhymes* by Joanna Cole
- *Five Little Monkeys Jumping on the Bed* by Eileen Christelow

EQUIPMENT

Define group court areas with cones

CRITICAL ELEMENTS

Technique

- Bend the knees.
- Keep the feet shoulder-width apart.
- Begin with the arms at the sides.
- Time the forceful upward swing of the arms with the leg push.
- The leg push is strong.
- Cushion with the legs on landing.
- There are no steps on landing.
- The arms are in front of the body and slightly to the side on landing.

COMMON ERRORS, CAUSES, AND CORRECTIONS

- The student achieves little height. *Cause:* Poor extension of the legs. *Correction:* Tell the student to push harder and swing the arms upward.
- The student jumps with little force. *Cause:* Shallow starting position. *Correction:* Tell the student to bend the knees more before the jump.
- The student's landing is jarred (i.e., landing with straight legs). *Cause:* The knees are not bent. *Correction:* Tell the student to bend the knees more.
- The student's landing is unstable. *Cause:* The arms are not stretched out. *Correction:* Tell the student to lift the arms.

TASK 24: JUMP AT VARYING SPEEDS

PURPOSE

Following is the purpose of the task as related to aspects of skilled performance.

Technique: This task teaches jumping at varying speeds. This movement is used in many children's games.

DESCRIPTION

Tell students that they are going to jump like the following different animals:

- Bunnies use short, fast jumps that don't stop.
- Kangaroos use longer jumps that don't stop (emphasize that jumps should not be too long).
- Grasshoppers jump from a low position.
- Frogs jump from place to place and cover a little more distance.

EQUIPMENT

Define group court areas with cones

CRITICAL ELEMENTS

Technique

- Bend the knees.
- Keep the feet shoulder-width apart.
- Begin with the arms at the sides.
- Time the forceful upward swing of the arms with the leg push.
- The leg push is strong.
- Cushion with the legs on landing.

- There are no steps on landing.
- The arms are in front of the body and slightly to the side on landing.

COMMON ERRORS, CAUSES, AND CORRECTIONS

- The student achieves little height. *Cause:* Poor extension of the legs. *Correction:* Tell the student to push harder and swing the arms upward.
- The student jumps with little force. *Cause:* Shallow starting position. *Correction:* Tell the student to bend the knees more before the jump.
- The student's landing is jarred (i.e., landing with straight legs). *Cause:* The knees are not bent. *Correction:* Tell the student to bend the knees more.
- The student's landing is unstable. *Cause:* The arms are not stretched out. *Correction:* Tell the student to lift the arms.

TASK 25: JUMP FOR ACCURACY

PURPOSE

Following is the purpose of the task as related to aspects of skilled performance.

Technique: This task teaches jumping for accuracy. This is an important movement competency for some children's games

DESCRIPTION

This task is a game that teaches jumping for accuracy. Place at least double the number of hoops or poly spots on the floor as there are students. They should be close enough that students can jump from one spot to another but far enough apart that they cannot just walk from spot to spot. Tell the students to stand in a poly spot or hoop. Explain that these are islands, and the space between the islands is full of hungry sharks. If a student touches the shark-infested water or lands with a step, that student must go to the boundary (side) of the playing area and begin from there. Only one student can be in each poly spot or hoop. You can make the task harder by reducing the number of islands and increasing the distance between them.

EQUIPMENT

Cones to mark the game area and poly spots or hoops

CRITICAL ELEMENTS

Technique

- Bend the knees.
- Keep the feet shoulder-width apart.
- Begin with the arms at the sides.
- Time the forceful upward swing of the arms with the leg push.
- The leg push is strong.
- Cushion with the legs on landing.
- There are no steps on landing.
- The arms are in front of the body and slightly to the side on landing.

COMMON ERRORS, CAUSES, AND CORRECTIONS

- The student achieves little height. *Cause:* Poor extension of the legs. *Correction:* Tell the student to push harder and swing the arms upward.
- The student jumps with little force. *Cause:* Shallow starting position. *Correction:* Tell the student to bend the knees more before the jump.

- The student's landing is jarred (i.e., landing with straight legs). *Cause:* The knees are not bent. *Correction:* Tell the student to bend the knees more.
- The student's landing is unstable. *Cause:* The arms are not stretched out. *Correction:* Tell the student to lift the arms.

TASK 26: JUMP FOR DISTANCE

PURPOSE
Following is the purpose of the task as related to aspects of skilled performance.

Technique: The task teaches jumping for distance. This is used in children's games, fitness activities, and some sports.

DESCRIPTION
Tell students they are in the 1912 Olympic Games and they will be performing the standing long jump. In our rules, students will land on their feet in a crouch. To control the jump, use ropes to indicate the starting line and the target line. Start with the lines about 1 foot (0.3 meters) apart, and then gradually increase the distance. Don't move the ropes so far apart that students will fall forward onto their hands. Students can jump for distance on a mat or beside the ropes.

- *Extension 1.* A rule of thumb is that students should be able to jump their height. Have students lie on the mat and place a rope at the feet and a rope at the head to measure height. Students can use a third rope (or chalk) to measure how far they jump each time toward the goal of their height.
- *Extension 2.* Play swamp jump. Create lily pads using mats, hoops, poly spots, or circles made with chalk, and place them in a fixed area bound by four cones. Have students jump from lily pad to lily pad without landing in the swamp.

EQUIPMENT
Define group court areas with cones, ropes, and mats

CRITICAL ELEMENTS
Technique
- Bend the knees.
- Keep the feet shoulder-width apart.
- Begin with the arms at the sides.
- Time the forceful upward swing of the arms with the leg push.
- The leg push is strong.
- Cushion with the legs on landing.
- There are no steps on landing.
- The arms are in front of the body and slightly to the side on landing.

COMMON ERRORS, CAUSES, AND CORRECTIONS
- The student achieves little height. *Cause:* Poor extension of the legs. *Correction:* Tell the student to push harder and swing the arms upward.
- The student jumps with little force. *Cause:* Shallow starting position. *Correction:* Tell the student to bend the knees more before the jump.
- The student's landing is jarred (i.e., landing with straight legs). *Cause:* The knees are not bent. *Correction:* Tell the student to bend the knees more.
- The student's landing is unstable. *Cause:* The arms are not stretched out. *Correction:* Tell the student to lift the arms.

TASK 27: SKIP IN GENERAL SPACE

PURPOSE

Following is the purpose of the task as related to aspects of skilled performance.

Technique: This task introduces skipping. Skipping is a rhythmical skill that is fundamental to many games played by children.

DESCRIPTION

Demonstrate skipping. Then ask the students to skip in their areas and cover as much space as possible.

EQUIPMENT

Define group court areas with cones

CRITICAL ELEMENTS

Technique

- Demonstrate a rhythmical step hop.
- Land on the balls of the feet.
- Bend the knee of the support leg to prepare for the hop.
- The head and trunk are upright and slightly forward.
- The arms swing in opposition to the takeoff leg.

COMMON ERRORS, CAUSES, AND CORRECTIONS

- The student does not use the skip pattern. *Cause:* Lack of student understanding. *Correction:* Tell the student to push harder and swing the arms upward. For the step hop, have the student hold a beach ball at waist height and take a step so the knee touches the ball.
- The student's skip pattern is not rhythmical. *Cause:* Poor movement competency. *Correction:* Have the student practice skipping for longer distances.

TASK 28: SKIP AT VARYING SPEEDS

PURPOSE

Following is the purpose of the task as related to aspects of skilled performance.

Technique: This task introduces skipping at varying speeds. Being able to change speeds is often a component of children's games.

DESCRIPTION

Students can demonstrate skipping at varying speeds by performing the following activities:

- Students skip at speeds that are dictated by the rhythm of music or drum beats.
- Tell students they are being chased through the forest by different animals. The type of animal determines how fast they will skip: tiger (fastest), elephant (fast), chimpanzee (slower), koala (very slow).

EQUIPMENT

Define group court areas with cones

CRITICAL ELEMENTS

Technique

- Demonstrate a rhythmical step hop.
- Land on the balls of the feet.
- Bend the knee of the support leg to prepare for the hop.
- The head and trunk are upright and slightly forward.
- The arms swing in opposition to the leg.

COMMON ERRORS, CAUSES, AND CORRECTIONS

- The student does not use the skip pattern. *Cause:* Lack of student understanding. *Correction:* Tell the student to push harder and swing the arms upward. For the step hop, have the student hold a beach ball at waist height and take a step so the knee touches the ball.
- The student's skip pattern is not rhythmical. *Cause:* Poor movement competency. *Correction:* Have the student practice skipping for longer distances.

TASK 29: SKIP USING VARYING FORCE

PURPOSE

Following is the purpose of the task as related to aspects of skilled performance.

Technique: This task introduces skipping using varying force. This movement is used in many children's games.

DESCRIPTION

Students can demonstrate skipping using varying force by performing the following activities:

- Tell students to push off hard from their legs and skip very high into the air.
- Tell students to skip softly.
- Have students skip over rope logs, rope ponds, and the like to create opportunities for force production.

EQUIPMENT

Define group court areas with cones

CRITICAL ELEMENTS

Technique

- Demonstrate a rhythmical step hop.
- Land on the balls of the feet.
- Bend the knee of the support leg to prepare for the hop.
- The head and trunk are upright and slightly forward.
- The arms swing in opposition to the leg.

COMMON ERRORS, CAUSES, AND CORRECTIONS

- The student does not use the skip pattern. *Cause:* Lack of student understanding. *Correction:* Tell the student to push harder and swing the arms upward. For the step hop, have the student hold a beach ball at waist height and take a step so the knee touches the ball.
- The student's skip pattern is not rhythmical. *Cause:* Poor movement competency. *Correction:* Have the student practice skipping for longer distances.

TASK 30: SKIP ALONG VARYING PATHWAYS

PURPOSE

Following is the purpose of the task as related to aspects of skilled performance.

Technique: This task introduces skipping along varying pathways. This movement is used in many children's games.

DESCRIPTION

First, have students skip along the following paths:

- A straight path between two cones or following a line on the floor
- A zigzag path
- A curved path
- An imaginary circle

Next, have them play the garbage collectors game as a timed game (e.g., 3 or 5 minutes). Scatter as many beanbags or rolled up paper balls onto the floor. In their groups, students stand behind a hoop (one per team) that is placed outside the skipping area. Students skip and collect beanbags or paper balls one at a time and skip back to place the item in the hoop. All students in the group can collect at the same time. The team with the most items wins. Another version of this game allows students to collect items from the hoops of opposing teams.

EQUIPMENT

Define group court areas with cones; beanbags or paper balls and hoops

CRITICAL ELEMENTS

Technique

- Demonstrate a rhythmical step hop.
- Land on the balls of the feet.
- Bend the knee of the support leg to prepare for the hop.
- The head and trunk are upright and slightly forward.
- The arms swing in opposition to the takeoff leg.

COMMON ERRORS, CAUSES, AND CORRECTIONS

- The student does not use the skip pattern. *Cause:* Lack of student understanding. *Correction:* Tell the student to push harder and swing the arms upward. For the step hop, have the student hold a beach ball at waist height and take a step so the knee touches the ball.
- The student's skip pattern is not rhythmical. *Cause:* Poor movement competency. *Correction:* Have the student practice skipping for longer distances.

TASK 31: LEAP IN GENERAL SPACE

PURPOSE

Following is the purpose of the task as related to aspects of skilled performance.

Technique: Leaping is a skill that involves taking off from one foot, having a long flight path with both feet in the air, and landing on the other foot. Leaping is a prerequisite to hurdling, and it is used in many children's games.

DESCRIPTION

Demonstrate the leap, and then ask students to practice leaping in general space. Ask students to do the following on each leg:

- Leap from a walk.
- Leap from a short jog.
- Leap over obstacles such as milk crates, foam logs, mats, and ropes.

EQUIPMENT

Define group court areas with cones and use beanbags, paper balls, and hoops to create obstacles for students to leap over.

CRITICAL ELEMENTS

Technique

- Focus the eyes forward during the leap.
- Bend the knee of the take-off leg.
- Keep both legs straight in flight.
- Keep the head and trunk slightly forward.
- Land on the other foot on toes first, then lowering to the foot and bend the knee to absorb force.

COMMON ERRORS, CAUSES, AND CORRECTIONS

- The student's legs are not straight in the flight phase. *Cause:* Lack of student awareness. *Correction:* Tell the student to straighten the legs in the air.
- The student achieves little height in flight. *Cause:* Leg power is weak. *Correction:* Tell the student to bend the legs more at the start and push off hard.
- The student's leap is not rhythmical. *Cause:* Poor movement competency. *Correction:* Have the student practice more.

TASK 32: LEAP SHORT DISTANCES

PURPOSE

Following is the purpose of the task as related to aspects of skilled performance.

Technique: This task introduces leaping short distances. This is a prerequisite for more advanced forms of leaping.

DESCRIPTION

Set up obstacles for students to leap over. The leaping distances should be marked with ropes or tape and should not be more than 1 to 2 feet (0.3 to 0.6 meters) apart. Students practice leaping using both feet.

EQUIPMENT

Define group court areas with cones and use beanbags, paper balls, and hoops to create obstacles for students to leap over.

CRITICAL ELEMENTS

Technique

- Focus the eyes forward during the leap.
- Bend the knee of the take-off leg.
- Keep both legs straight in flight.
- Keep the head and trunk slightly forward.
- Land on the other foot, toes first, then lowering to the foot and then bend the knee to absorb force.

COMMON ERRORS, CAUSES, AND CORRECTIONS

- The student's legs are not straight in the flight phase. *Cause:* Lack of student awareness. *Correction:* Tell the student to straighten the legs in the air.
- The student achieves little height in flight. *Cause:* Leg power is weak. *Correction:* Tell the student to bend the legs more at the start and push off hard.
- The student's leap is not rhythmical. *Cause:* Poor movement competency. *Correction:* Have the student practice more.

TASK 33: LEAP LONGER DISTANCES

PURPOSE

Following is the purpose of the task as related to aspects of skilled performance.

Technique: This task introduces leaping long distances. Being able to leap is important to avoid obstacles when running, and it is a prerequisite for hurdling.

DESCRIPTION

Set up obstacles for students to leap over. The leaping distances should be marked with ropes or tape and should range between 2 to 4 feet (0.6 meters to 1.2 meters) apart. Students practice leaping using both feet.

EQUIPMENT

Define group court areas with cones and use beanbags, paper balls, and hoops to create obstacles for students to leap over.

CRITICAL ELEMENTS

Technique

- Focus the eyes forward during the leap.
- Bend the knee of the take-off leg.
- Keep both legs straight in flight.
- Keep the head and trunk slightly forward.
- Land on the other foot, toes first, then lowering to the foot and then bend the knee to absorb force.

COMMON ERRORS, CAUSES, AND CORRECTIONS

- The student's legs are not straight in the flight phase. *Cause:* Lack of student awareness. *Correction:* Tell the student to straighten the legs in the air.
- The student achieves little height in flight. *Cause:* Leg power is weak. *Correction:* Tell the student to bend the legs more at the start and push off hard.
- The student's leap is not rhythmical. *Cause:* Poor movement competency. *Correction:* Have the student practice more.

TASK 34: SEQUENCES: RHYTHM AND MUSIC APPLICATION

PURPOSE

Following is the purpose of the task as related to aspects of skilled performance.

Technique: This task combines locomotion movements into a sequence with a rhythm.

DESCRIPTION

This application occurs for lessons 1-5 for each block plan as the culminating activity of the lesson. In lessons 1-5 this is directed by the teacher; ask students to combine in a sequence particular content taught that day or in previous lessons. This task is an opportunity for students to combine short sequences of different locomotion activities. This prepares students for the routines they will *present* in lesson 7 and is tied to task 35 (routines). You will need to determine how much time to spend on these activities and how often you will revisit specific tasks. In the group court area, students progress through the following activities:

- *Initial task in lessons 1-5.* The first time students participate in this task in lesson 1, teach them to recognize a rhythmic, 8-beat pattern on a drum. Have students clap their hands to the beat. You can also use children's movement music that has easily definable beats. Many of the tasks in this knowledge packet use a beat or music.
- *Extension 1.* Play music or beats on a drum. Have students choose a locomotion movement they learned that day or in a previous lesson that best matches the rhythm. As you change the rhythm students should change the movement.

EQUIPMENT

Define group court areas with cones; music or drum

CRITICAL ELEMENTS

Technique

- The movement chosen by the students should match the rhythm of the music or the drum or the animal characteristic.
- The change from one movement to another should flow smoothly without stops and stumbles.

COMMON ERRORS, CAUSES, AND CORRECTIONS

- The student's movement does not match the music or drum or the animal characteristic. *Cause:* The student might not be aware of rhythm. *Correction:* Revisit the initial task and progress more slowly. Provide the student with a partner to mimic.
- The student's transition is not smooth and it has stops or stumbles. *Cause:* The student is not moving fluently because the task is too fast. *Correction:* Slow down the rhythm to provide the student with more time to transition.

TASK 35: ROUTINES

PURPOSE

Following is the purpose of the task as related to aspects of skilled performance.

Technique: This task teaches students to combine several locomotion movements into a routine. The skills required to do this include designing the sequence, practicing the sequence, and presenting the sequence.

DESCRIPTION

This task used in lessons 6 and 7. Day 6 is devoted to designing and practicing the routine, and day 7 can involve more practice and then the presentation, or it can be devoted to just presentation depending on the student's progress on day 6. The complexity and difficulty of the routines are different for each grade. Provide students with instructions for designing a routine. The instructions can be written on cards, provided as pictures that students can use to a create picture boards of the sequence, or placed on a board for the class to see. Following are some sample sequences in order of increasing difficulty. Choose the task relative to the grade level you are teaching and your students. The sequences begin without music accompaniment, and music is added in the later tasks. These are only examples; any order of movements is appropriate. Students should practice these patterns several times to improve their proficiency.

- *Initial task.* Practice the following sequence: walk, jog, run, walk, jump (without music).
- *Extension 1.* Hop, jump, run, gallop, side slide (without music).

- *Extension 2.* Hop, jump, run, gallop, side slide (without music).
- *Extension 3.* Side slide, hop, gallop, sprint, stop moving, jump, and skip.
- *Extension 4.* Gallop, skip, gallop, hop, jump.
- *Extension 5.* Provide groups with different music and have each student in the group create his or her own sequence of movements.
- *Extension 6.* Students design a sequence with any combination of the locomotor movements listed by the teacher. This is the sequence that students will practice on lesson 6 and if need be part of lesson 7 and then present to their peers on day 7.
- *Extension 7.* Determine how much time you will allow for students to present their routines. An important decision for you to make is whether the students will present to their group only (i.e., within group), or to the whole class. It is important to teach students how to behave during a performance if they are observing (e.g., not to whisper, talk, or move), to applaud at the end, and to appreciate the effort that members of the class put into their performances.

EQUIPMENT

Define group court areas with cones; music and a drum

CRITICAL ELEMENTS

Technique

- The movements chosen by the students should match the rhythm of the music or drum.
- The transitions from one movement to another should flow smoothly without stops and stumbles.

COMMON ERRORS, CAUSES, AND CORRECTIONS

- The student's movement does not match the music or drum. *Cause:* The student might not be aware of rhythm. *Correction:* Revisit the initial task and progress more slowly. Provide the student with a partner to mimic.
- The student's transition is not smooth, and it has stops or stumbles. *Cause:* The student is not moving fluently because the task is too fast. *Correction:* Slow down the rhythm to provide the student with more time to transition.

Chapter 5

Elementary Gymnastics

Gymnastics is a foundational content area in physical education that teaches body awareness. Performing gymnastics movements supports children's general movement competency in other activities and increases their strength and flexibility in the lower, upper, and core regions of the body. In this chapter, we focus on gymnastics that can be performed in most elementary schools, which is typically called *tumbling*. We categorize tumbling skills into four general groups: (1) rolling, (2) jumping and landing, (3) transfer of weight from and to hands and feet, and (4) static balances. These gymnastic skills are used in routines that students will perform. We present the tasks to teach these skills and the tasks to teach students to combine movements in creative ways and perform them. Our focus is on students in kindergarten through fifth grade.

OUR PEDAGOGICAL APPROACH TO GYMNASTICS SKILLS

When teaching gymnastics, you must first consider safety. The pedagogies used and the skills taught in this chapter reflect safety considerations. For example, teaching students how to land and how to fall are important gymnastics and sport skills, and these are emphasized and revisited throughout the chapter. We excluded the backward roll and its associated skills because, in our experience, teachers who do not have prior gymnastics experience struggle with these skills.

Most skills in this chapter do not require spotting and assistance; however, some students will need assistance performing the initial forward roll, the headstand, and the handstand. Whenever spotting is used, we recommend the use of a circuit (see the Organization section for more details).

In the movie *What About Bob?*, Richard Dreyfuss gives advice to the slightly neurotic Bill Murray: Deal with life as a series of baby steps. This is consistent with our teaching approach throughout this book, and it is a critical pedagogical principle in teaching gymnastics. Go slow, and don't advance until the easier skills are accomplished.

Not all students will be able to perform advanced skills such as the handstand. A key pedagogical decision is matching task progressions to students' abilities and successes in previous tasks. Take care not to advance students too far along the task sequence. Different students will progress at different rates and accomplish different versions of the skills.

Another important pedagogical principle is to provide adequate time for practice. Students need enough repetitions of the tasks to acquire some proficiency. We suggest that weight bearing on the hands be interspersed with other skills in a lesson to allow the wrists to recover.

Modifications to Address Individual Needs of Students

For students with disabilities, gymnastics units provide excellent opportunities to learn about and enhance skills in tumbling and balances. For many students with physical disabilities or visual impairments, delays in balance activities are common. Activity modifications might not be needed, but you must provide enough practice time so students can demonstrate improvements. In addition, you can assign physical education homework so students can practice the activities at home with their families.

When modifications are needed, they depend on the nature of the student's disability. For example, to modify tumbling activities for children with visual impairments, you can use tactile modeling (i.e., demonstration by touch rather than sight) or physical guidance (i.e., moving the student's body into positions) to demonstrate proper body positioning.

Tumbling activities may be unsafe for individuals with certain disabilities. For example, individuals with Down syndrome tend to experience atlantoaxial instability (i.e., excessive movement between the C1 and C2 vertebrae), and students with visual impairments caused by retinal detachment should not participate in activities that put excessive pressure on the head or neck. You must be aware of disability characteristics and plan accordingly to safely include students in classes.

For children with cognitive disabilities such as autism spectrum disorder, an essential accommodation might be providing visual examples of each movement by using video modeling. You can record a same-age peer correctly performing each tumbling movement and then display the video on repeat for students to observe and replicate.

Organization

Equipment should be set up so there is space for students to work safely without touching each other. Although there are many ways to teach gymnastic skills, we focus on two fundamental arrangements for teachers who have limited experience teaching gymnastics.

In the first pedagogical arrangement, groups of 3 to 4 students work on a mat (the lower the student-to-mat ratio the better). We call this the *home mat* or *home area*. The group does not leave the home area. The mats are typically placed in a circle with enough space between them to ensure that students will not come near each other as they perform. When mats are set up in a circle, you can walk the perimeter and monitor all students. You must assign tasks to be done on each mat and consider safety in determining when students should take their turns.

The second pedagogical arrangement uses the same mat arrangement, but a different skill or task is performed at each mat station, and students rotate from mat to mat in a circuit. If you are supervising a challenging skill (e.g., the forward roll or handstand), you should place yourself such that you can see the rest of the class but provide feedback or assistance to students performing at that station.

Space

Gymnastics requires space: space between mats, space around raised platforms, and space around benches that might be used. You must judge the amount of space needed for each activity relative to the configuration of your gym or instructional setting.

Equipment Needed

Mats are important in teaching gymnastics. One mat for every 3 to 4 students is a good ratio. A triangular mat, often called a *wedge,* is a valuable tool for teaching rolls. If you don't have one, consider building up mats, placing solid objects under a mat, or using two panels on a folding mat to create the incline. You might also use benches (be sure they are stable), hoops, ropes, solid boxes, foam logs, and the walls of the gym as equipment. To show the placement for hands and feet, tape cutouts of hands and feet or carpet squares to mats, or use computer mouse pads (they tend not to slip).

CONTENT MAP STRUCTURE

Figure 5.1 is a content map that shows the flow of all the tasks used to develop gymnastics skills. Because there is considerable overlap and repetition, this content map is not divided into levels (as is done in later chapters). A dashed line separates basic skills (those for kindergarten through second grade) from the more advanced skills (those for third through fifth grades).

STRUCTURE OF THE LESSONS

The following is a sample daily lesson structure for a 40-minute gymnastics lesson.

Warm-up (6 minutes)

Review task: over and under game (3 to 4 minutes)

Review task: landing shape (2 minutes)

Informing task: jump and land on the floor (4 minutes)

Extension task: jump and make shapes in the air (8 minutes)

Extension task: jump and land from a height (3 to 5 minutes)

Application task: routine practice (5 to 8 minutes)

Closure (3 minutes)

Warm-up

The warm-up is approximately six minutes long. Students warm up in their groups in their home areas. Using music or drum beats, count about eight beats to time each activity. You will have to demonstrate until students know the warm-up; then they can be led by a student in each group or perform without leaders.

Walking and Standing

- Walk in general space.
- Walk tall like a giant in general space and stretch your hands overhead.
- Walk on your hands and feet in general space like a mouse.
- Walk and clap with the beat.
- Walk and lift the knees high.
- Stand still and tap your head, shoulders, chest, abdomen, knees, and toes with your hands. It's okay to bend your knees to touch your toes.

Sitting

- Butterfly stretch: Sit with your legs bent and the soles of your feet touching, and then gently move your knees toward the floor.
- Lift one foot, clap over it in the air, clap under your knee, and then clap back and forth over and under the knee. Repeat with the other leg.
- Do sit-ups or crunches.
- Sit with your legs apart and straight. Walk your hands toward your knees and back again.
- Sit with your knees tucked closely to your chest, and then straighten your legs.

K-5 Gymnastics Content Map

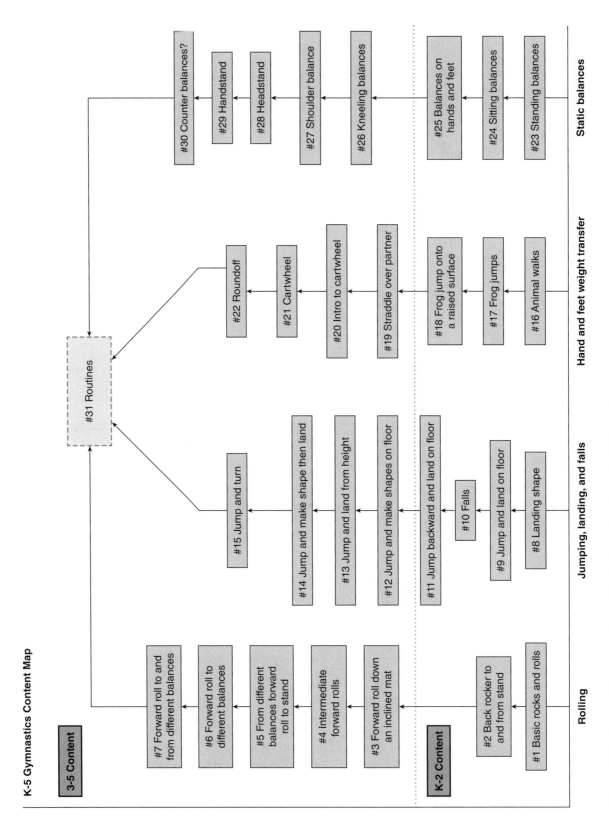

Figure 5.1 Gymnastics content map for kindergarten through fifth grade.

Moving on Hands and Knees

- Sad cat: Arch your back downward.
- Happy cat: Arch your back upward.
- Shake your tail: Wiggle your buttocks.
- Sea lion: Straighten your legs and push your chest upward to stretch.

BLOCK PLANS

The first block plan introduces gymnastic skills for kindergarten and first grade (table 5.1). The second block plan is for second and third grades (table 5.2), and the third is for fourth and fifth grades (table 5.3). Although longer units are always preferred, we recognize that there are time limitations at the elementary level; therefore, we have limited each block plan to seven days. You can modify these plans with regard to duration and grades taught. There is overlap in the plans because students will need to revisit tasks they learned in previous units.

Table 5.1 Kindergarten and First Grade Gymnastics Block Plan: Seven-Day Unit

This is an example of a beginning block plan for kindergarten and grade 1 students. It is based on an initial seven-day unit and, as such, it does not include all of the tasks on the content map. You can use this as a template for developing an appropriate initial block plan for kindergarten and grade 1 students.

Lesson 1	Lesson 2	Lesson 3	Lesson 4	Lesson 5
Warm-up	Warm-up	Warm-up	Warm-up	Warm-up
Content development • **(8)** Falls • **(1)** Basic rocks and rolls • **(15)** Animal walks • **(21)** Standing balance • **(9)** Landing shape	**Content development** • **(8)** Falls • **(9)** Landing shape • **(1)** Basic rocks and rolls • **(2)** Rock to and from standing • **(15)** Animal walks • **(21)** Standing balance	**Content development** • **(8)** Falls • **(9)** Landing shape • **(1)** Basic rocks and rolls • **(2)** Rock to and from standing • **(15)** Animal walks • **(21)** Standing balance	**Content development** • **(8)** Falls • **(9)** Landing shape • **(2)** Rock to and from standing • **(15)** Animal walks • **(21)** Standing balance	**Content development** • **(8)** Falls • **(9)** Landing shape • **(2)** Rock to and from standing • **(15)** Animal walks • **(21)** Standing balance • **(22)** Sitting balance
Application • **(28)** Routines	**Application** • **(28)** Routines	**Application** • **(28)** Routines	**Application** • **(28)** Routines	**Application** • **(28)** Routines

Lesson 6	Lesson 7
Warm-up	Warm-up
Content development • **(28)** Routines: practice	**Content development** • **(28)** Routines: present
Application • **(28)** Routines: practice	**Application** • **(28)** Routines: present

Table 5.2 Second and Third Grade Gymnastics Block Plan: Seven-Day Unit

This is an example of a beginning block plan for grade 2 and grade 3 students. It is based on an initial seven-day unit and, as such, it does not include all of the tasks on the content map. You can use this as a template for developing an appropriate initial block plan for grade 2 and grade 3 students.

Lesson 1	Lesson 2	Lesson 3	Lesson 4	Lesson 5
Warm-up	Warm-up	Warm-up	Warm-up	Warm-up
Content development • **(8)** Falls • **(1)** Basic rocks and rolls • **(15)** Animal walks • **(21)** Standing balance • **(9)** Landing shape	**Content development** • **(8)** Falls • **(9)** Landing shape • **(15)** Animal walks • **(10)** Jump and land on the floor • **(11)** Jump and make shapes on the floor • **(12)** Jump and land from a height • **(16)** Frog jump	**Content development** • **(8)** Falls • **(9)** Landing shape • **(11)** Jump and make shapes on the floor • **(12)** Jump and land from a height • **(16)** Frog jump • **(17)** Frog jump onto a raised surface	**Content development** • **(8)** Falls • **(23)** Balance on hands and feet • **(2)** Rock to and from standing • **(3)** Forward roll down an inclined mat • **(17)** Frog jump onto a raised surface • **(24)** Balances on knees	**Content development** • **(8)** Falls • **(23)** Balance on hands and feet • **(2)** Rock to and from standing • **(3)** Forward roll down an inclined mat • **(4)** Intermediate forward rolls • **(17)** Frog jump onto a raised surface • **(24)** Balances on knees
Application • **(28)** Routines	**Application** • **(28)** Routines	**Application** • **(28)** Routines	**Application** • **(28)** Routines	**Application** • **(28)** Routines

Lesson 6	Lesson 7
Warm-up	Warm-up
Content development • **(28)** Routines: practice	**Content development** • **(28)** Routines: present
Application • **(28)** Routines: practice	**Application** • **(28)** Routines: present

Table 5.3 Fourth and Fifth Grade Gymnastics Block Plan: Seven-Day Unit

This is an example of a beginning block plan for grade 4 and grade 5 students. It is based on an initial seven-day unit and, as such, it does not include all of the tasks on the content map. You can use this as a template for developing an appropriate initial block plan for grade 4 and grade 5 students.

Lesson 1	Lesson 2	Lesson 3	Lesson 4	Lesson 5
Warm-up	Warm-up	Warm-up	Warm-up	Warm-up
Content development • **(8)** Falls • **(9)** Landing shape • **(23)** Balance on hands and feet • **(24)** Balances on knees • **(25)** Balance on shoulders • **(16)** Frog jump	Content development • **(8)** Falls • **(9)** Landing shape • **(10)** Jump and land on the floor • **(11)** Jump and make shapes on the floor • **(12)** Jump and land from a height • **(16)** Frog jump • **(17)** Frog jump onto a raised surface • **(18)** Straddle over a partner	Content development • **(8)** Falls • **(2)** Rock to and from standing • **(23)** Balance on hands and feet • **(3)** Forward roll down an inclined mat • **(4)** Intermediate forward rolls • **(6)** Forward roll to different balances	Content development • **(8)** Falls • **(23)** Balance on hands and feet • **(4)** Intermediate forward rolls • **(5)** Forward roll to stand from different balances • **(6)** Forward roll to different balances • **(26)** Headstand • **(27)** Handstand • **(20)** Cartwheel	Content development • **(8)** Falls • **(7)** Forward roll to and from different balances • **(26)** Headstand • **(27)** Handstand • **(20)** Cartwheel
Application • **(28)** Routines	Application • **(28)** Routines	Application • **(28)** Routines	Application • **(28)** Routines	Application • **(28)** Routines

Lesson 6	Lesson 7
Warm-up	Warm-up
Content development • **(28)** Routines: practice	Content development • **(28)** Routines: present
Application • **(28)** Routines: practice	Application • **(28)** Routines: present

SHAPE AMERICA'S GRADE-LEVEL OUTCOMES FOR K-12 PHYSICAL EDUCATION

In table 5.4, we identify key grade-level outcomes for gymnastics for kindergarten through fifth grade. These are linked to specific tasks on the content map that are appropriate for teaching the skill and assessing the outcome.

Table 5.4 Grade-Level Outcomes for Gymnastics

Outcome	Description	Content map focus and tasks
S1.E7.Ka	Maintains momentary stillness on different bases of support.	Task 21-22
S1.E7.Kb	Forms wide, narrow, curled & twisted body shapes.	Tasks 21-24
S1.E7.1	Maintains stillness on different bases of support with different body shapes.	Tasks 21-25
S1.E7.2a	Balances on different bases of support, combining levels and shapes.	Tasks 21-25
S1.E7.2b	Balances in an inverted position with stillness and supportive base.	Tasks 25-27
S1.E7.3	Balances on different bases of support, demonstrating muscular tension and extensions of free body parts.	Tasks 21, 27
S1.E7.5	Combines balance and transferring weight in a gymnastics sequence or dance with a partner.	Task 28
S1.E8.1	Transfers weight from one body part to another in self-space in dance and gymnastics environments.	Tasks 15-17
S1.E8.2	Transfers weight from feet to different body parts/bases of support for balance and/or travel.	Tasks 15-18
S1.E8.3	Transfers weight from feet to hands for momentary weight support.	Tasks 15-19
S1.E8.4	Transfers weight from feet to hands, varying speed and using large extensions (e.g., kick, handstand, cartwheel).	Tasks 17-20
S1.E8.5	Transfers weight in gymnastics and dance environments.	Task 28
S1.E9.K	Rolls sideways in a narrow body shape.	Task 1
S1.E9.1	Rolls with either a narrow or curled body shape.	Tasks 1-2
S1.E9.2	Rolls in different directions with either a narrow or curled body shape.	Tasks 1-2
S1.E10.K	Contrasts the actions of curling & stretching.	Tasks 1-3
S1.E10.1	Demonstrates twisting, curling, bending & stretching actions.	Tasks 1-3
S1.E10.2	Differentiates among twisting, curling, bending & stretching actions.	Task 28
S1.E10.3	Moves into and out of gymnastics balances with curling, twisting & stretching actions.	Tasks 5-7, 28
S1.E10.5	Performs curling, twisting & stretching actions with correct application in dance, gymnastics, small-sided practice tasks in games environments.	Task 28
S1.E11.2	Combines balances and transfers into 3-part sequence (i.e., dance, gymnastics).	Task 28
S1.E12.3	Combines balance and weight transfers with movement concepts to create and perform a dance.	Task 28
S1.E12.4	Combines traveling with balance and weight transfers to create a gymnastics sequence with and without equipment or apparatus.	Task 28
S1.E12.5	Combines actions, balances and weight transfers to create a gymnastics sequence with a partner on equipment or apparatus.	Task 28

TASK 1: BASIC ROCKS AND ROLLS

PURPOSE

Following is the purpose of the task as related to aspects of skilled performance.

Technique: This task introduces the fundamental rocking and rolling movements that serve as foundations for more advanced skills that follow.

DESCRIPTION

Rocking refers to movements that mimic a rocking chair. *Rolling* refers to movements that resemble a ball rolling in one direction (there is no reversal). Students should perform the following rock and roll movements on mats. We recommend teaching these tasks the first time with the class placed in small groups assigned to mats. But when these rocks and rolls are used in later classes they can be used in a circuit where students in their small groups move from station to station.

EQUIPMENT

Rocks

CRITICAL ELEMENTS

Technique: Rocks

Rocker (see figure)

- Students sit on the mats in a tucked sitting position with chin to chest palms on the mat.
- The back should be rounded, the knees should be bent, and the toes should touch the floor.
- Holding this shape, students lean backward and rock backward and forward on their backs for an increasing number of rocks (i.e., 1, 2, 3, 4, 5).
- *Extension 1:* Repeat the activity from a squat position.

Side rocker

- Students lie on their backs with their knees to the chest.
- They rock side to side for an increasing number of rocks.

Stomach rocker

- Students lie on their bellies and arch their backs slightly.
- They stretch the legs and arms lengthwise.
- Then rock from front to back for an increasing number of rocks.

Sit and spin

- Students start in a tucked position with their hands on the floor on either side of the hips.
- The spin is initiated when the legs lift off and the hands push the body.
- Stay tightly tucked with the hands on the knees; the feet should not touch the floor.

Technique: Rolls

Pencil roll

- Students start by lying on their backs.
- The body is stretched and tight, and the legs are straight and together.
- The arms are together, stretched overhead, and touching the mat.
- Roll onto the belly, and continue in the same direction to roll onto the back.
- Students should practice rolling in both directions.

Log roll

- Students start by lying on their backs.
- The body is stretched, and the legs are straight and together.
- Hold the arms close to the sides of the body.
- Roll onto the belly, and continue in the same direction to roll onto the back.
- Students should practice rolling in both directions.

Puppy roll (see figure)

- The students start on all fours on the floor with their hands and knees on the mat.
- They bend the arm on one side and then pull both arms to their chest, then lean into the direction of the bent arm, they then roll over their shoulder, then hip and back to return the starting position on all knees with straight arms.
- This should be practiced in both directions.

COMMON ERRORS, CAUSES, AND CORRECTIONS

Rocker

- The student is not in a tucked position. *Cause:* Weak abdominal strength. *Correction:* Tell the student to use the hands to hold the knees onto the chest and to tuck the chin. Encourage students to do sit-ups outside of class.
- The student is rocking in a jerky manner. *Cause:* The back is not rounded enough. *Correction:* Tell the student to rock like a ball and stay curved like a ball.

Side rocker

- The student is not in a tucked position. *Cause:* Weak abdominal strength. *Correction:* Tell the student to use the hands to hold the knees. Encourage students to do sit-ups outside of class. Use hands to pull legs to chest.

Stomach rocker

- The student is arching the back too much. *Cause:* Misunderstanding how much arch is needed. *Correction:* Tell the student to just lift the legs and arms a little. Have the student hold a beanbag under the chin. Encourage students to do sit-ups outside of class.

Sit and spin

- The student is not in a tucked position. *Cause:* Weak abdominal strength. *Correction:* Tell the student to use the hands to hold the knees. Encourage students to do sit-ups outside of class.

Pencil roll

- The student's body is loose during the roll. *Cause:* Lack of strength or lack of understanding about how tight the body should be. *Correction:* Remind the student that pencils are firm and to keep the hands and feet together and tighten the belly.

Log roll

- The student's body is loose during the roll. *Cause:* Lack of strength or lack of understanding about how tight the body should be. *Correction:* Remind the student that logs are firm and to keep the hands and feet together and tighten the belly.

Puppy roll

- The collapse from support to shoulder is too much of a drop. *Cause:* The student does not bend the arm on the side they are rolling; lower the body down with the arms more slowly and in control. *Correction:* Tell the student to bend the arms slowly.
- The student is not in a tucked position during the roll. *Cause:* Weak abdominal strength. *Correction:* Tell the student to use the hands to hold the knees. Encourage students to do sit-ups outside of class.

TASK 2: ROCK TO AND FROM STANDING

PURPOSE

Following is the purpose of the task as related to aspects of skilled performance.

Technique: This task introduces students to rolls. Being able to rock to and from standing is the prerequisite for many rolls and for combinations using more advanced skills that are used in sequences.

DESCRIPTION

Students perform the following three movements: The rock to stand, moving from standing to rocking, and then combining the two, starting in a stand and then rocking backward and forward, and returning to stand.

EQUIPMENT

Mats

CRITICAL ELEMENTS

Technique

Rock to stand

- Start in a tucked sitting position.
- Round the back.
- Bend the knees.
- Rock forward quickly to get your hands in front of your feet.
- Push off hard with the hands as you stand up.
- Finish in a standing position with arms stretched overhead.

From stand to rock

- Start in a standing position with the arms stretched overhead.
- Squat down.
- Stay tucked throughout the rock.

From stand to rock and back to stand

- Start in a standing position with the arms stretched overhead.
- Squat down.
- Stay tucked throughout the rock.
- Rock forward quickly to get your hands in front of your feet as you rock.
- Push off hard with the hands as you stand up.

COMMON ERRORS, CAUSES, AND CORRECTIONS

Rock to stand

- The student is unable to stand up. *Cause:* Not rocking fast enough to move the center of gravity over the feet. *Correction:* Tell the student to rock faster and lift the arms forward on standing. Have the student work with a partner who can grab the hands to help the student stand up.

From stand to rock

- The student falls to the floor as the rock begins. *Cause:* Not squatting from the stand. *Correction:* Tell the student to squat down before rocking.
- The student falls to the floor as the rock begins. *Cause:* Not using the hands to provide support while rocking backward. *Correction:* Tell the student to use the hands and be sure the fingers point forward.

TASK 3: FORWARD ROLL DOWN AN INCLINED MAT

PURPOSE

Following is the purpose of the task as related to aspects of skilled performance.

Technique: This is the first task in a progression to teach the forward roll. The forward roll is the basic roll in gymnastics, and it is a component of most routines students will perform.

DESCRIPTION

Prior to performing this roll, students should have completed animal walks and balancing on the hands and feet, which teach them to bear weight on their hands and to place their bottoms above their heads. Students should be comfortable in the straddle balance position. We recommend that this skill be taught at one of several stations; good choices for the stations are animal walks, balances, and basic jumps.

For many students this is a challenging and uncommon movement. To aid students in performing this task we have them perform the forward roll down an inclined mat. Students begin this roll from the straddle stand rather than the squat for several reasons, the most important of which is that it places the hips above the hands, thus shifting the center of gravity forward and allowing the roll to begin more easily. You must ensure that students tuck their heads as the roll begins. To assist them, you can gently place your hand on the back of the neck to move students into position as they roll. The top of the head should *not* touch the mat.

EQUIPMENT

Inclined mats

CRITICAL ELEMENTS

Technique

- Stand at the top of the inclined mat in a straddle stand.
- Place the hands in front of the feet and tuck the head.
- Roll down the mat and stand up from a squat.
- During the roll, tuck the legs to prepare for the squat.
- As the feet contact the mat, lean forward and stand up.
- Extension: Start in squat (see figure).

COMMON ERRORS, CAUSES, AND CORRECTIONS

- The student is unable to begin the roll. *Cause:* The hands are too far forward and the center of gravity is not far enough forward to begin the roll. *Correction:* Tell the student to place the hands closer to the feet.
- The student is worried about beginning the roll too soon. *Cause:* Lack of experience with a new skill. *Correction:* Once the student's hands are on the mat, hold the shoulder and gently remove the support as the student rolls.
- The student rolls on the top of the head. *Cause:* The student is not tucking the head under. *Correction:* Tell the student to tuck the chin to the chest. Place a bean bag under the chin and ask the student to keep it there during the roll. Gently support the student by placing your hand on the back of the neck during the roll.

TASK 4: INTERMEDIATE FORWARD ROLLS

PURPOSE

Following is the purpose of the task as related to aspects of skilled performance.

Technique: In this task, students learn to transition from the inclined mat to the flat mat. The forward roll is the basic roll in gymnastics, and it is a component of most routines the students will perform.

DESCRIPTION

This skill uses a number of tasks that can be presented in different orders. Again, we suggest that this skill be taught at one of several stations. Students should first be proficient at rolling down the inclined mat on their own. Then students can perform the straddle roll to squat and then stand and the tucked forward roll off the floor mat. The safety considerations introduced in the previous tasks apply here. There should be no need to spot students on the flat mat if they can successfully roll down the incline unassisted. You may have students at different levels; students who need assistance can stay on the inclined mat and others can move to the floor mats and practice. Students can also start lower down on the incline as an intermediate progression.

EQUIPMENT

Inclined mats and flat mats

CRITICAL ELEMENTS

Technique

Tucked forward roll down the inclined mat

- Start in a squat and push hard against the mat to generate force for the roll. Straighten the legs into a pike position, which will lift the bottom over the head.
- Place the hands in front of the body and tuck the head.
- Roll down the mat and stand up through a squat with the arms overhead.

Tucked forward roll on the floor mat

- Start in a squat and strongly straighten the legs and lift the bottom over the head. Push hard against the mat to generate force for the roll.
- Place the hands in front of the body and tuck the head.
- Roll down the mat and stand up through a squat to stand with the arms overhead.

Forward straddle roll on the floor mat

- Start in a straddle stand.
- Place the hands in front the body and tuck the head.
- Roll on the mat and stand up to a straddle stand.
- During the roll, keep the legs straight.
- Place hands between legs to push up to stand.

COMMON ERRORS, CAUSES, AND CORRECTIONS

- The student is unable to begin the roll. *Cause:* The hands are too far forward and the center of gravity is not far enough forward to begin the roll. *Correction:* Tell the student to place the hands closer to the feet.
- The student is worried about beginning the roll too soon. *Cause:* Lack of experience with a new skill. *Correction:* Once the student's hands are on the mat, hold the shoulder and gently remove the support as the student rolls.
- The student rolls on the top of the head. *Cause:* The student is not tucking the head under. *Correction:* Tell the student to tuck the chin to the chest. Gently support the student by pushing the head downward during the roll.
- The student is unable to stand in the tucked forward roll on the floor mat. *Cause:* The student does not roll fast enough to stand. *Correction:* Instruct the student to push off harder with the feet.

TASK 5: FORWARD ROLL TO STAND FROM DIFFERENT BALANCES

PURPOSE

Following is the purpose of the task as related to aspects of skilled performance.

Technique: In this task, the forward roll is connected to balances. Because routines involve sequences of movements that transition to and from each other, transition movements are important for both movement competency and safety.

DESCRIPTION

This skill requires students to begin a balance and finish it by rolling forward in a tucked position and then finish the roll with standing arms overhead. This is done on a mat. It is useful to first review standing balances and balances on hands and feet, knees, and toes before performing this task. Students perform forward rolls from a balance. The balance choices are the stork stand, lunge, bent-knee stand, one-foot toe stand, knee scale, or forward scale with front support. Students can also select their own starting positions, but they should get your permission before performance. The headstand and handstand balances should not be used here. Students should also practice as many of these balances as they feel comfortable with.

EQUIPMENT

Mats

CRITICAL ELEMENTS

Technique

- The student starts in the balance shape they have chosen and then performs a forward roll.
- As students move from the balance they should consider weight bearing by the hands and arms. This differs according to the balance they are in, but the common feature is that weight-bearing is controlled.
- Place the hands in front of the body and tuck the head.
- Roll on the mat and stand up through a squat to stand with the arms overhead.

COMMON ERRORS, CAUSES, AND CORRECTIONS

- The student's transition from balance to roll is jerky. *Cause:* The student is not transferring weight smoothly. *Correction:* Tell the student to bend the knees and arms more slowly and to bear weight as the roll begins.
- The student is worried about the roll and hesitates. *Cause:* Lack of confidence. *Correction:* Choose an easier balance.

TASK 6: FORWARD ROLL TO DIFFERENT BALANCES

PURPOSE

Following is the purpose of the task as related to aspects of skilled performance.

Technique: In this task, students learn to begin a forward roll by standing with the arms overhead and to finish the roll in a balance. As in the previous task this performance emphasizes a transition in preparation for routines.

DESCRIPTION

This should be done after task 5 so students will have practiced the balances. From standing, students perform a forward roll and finish in a balance. This is done on a mat. The balance choices are the stork stand, bent-knee stand, one-foot toe stand, knee scale, or forward scale with front support. Students can also select their own starting positions, but they should get your permission before performance. The headstand and handstand balances should not be used here. Students should also practice as many of these balances as they feel comfortable with.

EQUIPMENT

Mats

CRITICAL ELEMENTS

Technique (see figure)

- Start in a standing position with the arms overhead. Perform the forward roll and finish in the balance.
- Place the hands in front of the body, and tuck the head.
- Push off hard with the feet.
- Roll on the mat and move into the balance that is chosen.

COMMON ERRORS, CAUSES, AND CORRECTIONS

The student's transition from roll to balance is jerky. *Cause:* The student is not transferring weight smoothly. *Correction:* Depending on the balance, tell the student to bend or straighten the knees and arms more slowly and to bear weight when assuming the balance.

TASK 7: FORWARD ROLL TO AND FROM DIFFERENT BALANCES

PURPOSE

Following is the purpose of the task as related to aspects of skilled performance.

Technique: In this task transition to and from balances using the forward roll is taught. Being able to successfully make these transitions is essential for performing a routine fluently.

DESCRIPTION

This is a combination of tasks 5 and 6. From a balance, students perform a forward roll and finish in a balance. Students should now be skilled in performing balances and rolls, and we encourage you to allow students to choose from the available balances they have learned and to experiment with different combinations. The balance choices are the stork stand, lunge, bent-knee stand, one-foot toe stand, knee scale, or forward scale with front support. Students can also select their own starting positions, but they should get your permission before performance. The headstand and handstand balances should not be used here. Students should practice a variety of balances to start and finish in.

EQUIPMENT

Mats

CRITICAL ELEMENTS

Technique

- As students move from the balance, they should consider weight bearing by the hands and arms. This will differ according the balance they are in, but the common feature is that weight bearing is controlled.
- Place the hands in front of the body and tuck the head.
- Push off hard with the feet.
- Roll on the mat and move into the balance that is chosen.

COMMON ERRORS, CAUSES, AND CORRECTIONS

- The student's transition to or from the balance is jerky. *Cause:* The student is not transferring weight smoothly. *Correction:* Depending on the balance, tell the student to bend or straighten the knees and arms more slowly and to bear weight when assuming or leaving the balance.

TASK 8: FALLS

PURPOSE

Following is the purpose of the task as related to aspects of skilled performance.

Technique: Falling safely is a critical skill for children. The movements in this task teach students to fall safely from a variety of positions.

DESCRIPTION

Falls occur from movements, and in this task, we draw on previous movements to emphasize what to do if a fall occurs. We begin by revisiting the puppy roll where we emphasize the bending of the arm in the direction of the roll to create control in the roll. This would be used if a student were to fall off balance to their hands and knees. We then introduce a modification of the rocker with the arms held across the chest. This would be used if the student were to fall backwards out of control. Have students perform each fall after a standing jump. Students will practice using these falls from the floor and from a height of approximately 1 foot (0.3 meters). In every fall, emphasize that students must land on their feet before performing the roll.

EQUIPMENT

Mats and small raised platforms (e.g., benches, other mats)

CRITICAL ELEMENTS

Technique

Puppy roll

- The students start on all fours on the floor with their hands and knees on the mat.
- They bend the arm on one side and then pull both arms to their chest, then lean into the direction of the bent arm, they then roll over their shoulder, then hip and back to return the starting position on all knees with straight arms.
- This should be practiced in both directions.

Modified rocker (see figure)

- Start in a squat position.
- Round the back.
- Bend the knees.
- Fold the arms across the chest.

COMMON ERRORS, CAUSES, AND CORRECTIONS

Modified rocker

- The student falls backward with the hands outstretched. *Cause:* Not absorbing force on landing and not using the legs to cushion. *Correction:* Tell the student to bend the knees more to cushion the fall and to keep the hands across the chest during the rock backward.

Puppy roll

- The student falls with the hands outstretched. *Cause:* Not absorbing force on landing and not using the legs to cushion. *Correction:* Tell the student to bend the knees more to cushion the fall and to keep the hands across the chest during the roll.

TASK 9: LANDING SHAPE

PURPOSE

Following is the purpose of the task as related to aspects of skilled performance.

Technique: In this task the landing shape is introduced. The landing shape is the primary strategy for maintaining control at the end of movements such as jumping or landing from heights. It is the most basic safety position in gymnastics, and it is a component of most routines the students will perform.

DESCRIPTION

This task should be introduced in the first lesson and revisited in every subsequent lesson. Have students stand with their knees bent, their feet shoulder-width apart, and their arms out in front of them and slightly to the side. Tell the students that this is the landing position. Ask students to do a little jump from this position and land back in the position. Ask the students to jump higher and higher while still landing in the position. This task is accomplished when students can consistently land in this position.

EQUIPMENT

Mats

CRITICAL ELEMENTS

Technique (see figure)

- Look at a spot on the wall that is at eye level. (Looking down could cause a forward fall.)
- Bend the knees as though you are sitting in a chair.
- Lean forward slightly to ensure that weight is distributed over the whole foot.
- Hold the arms in front of the body and slightly to the side for balance.
- The feet should be shoulder-width apart and should stick to the mat on landing (i.e., no steps).

COMMON ERRORS, CAUSES, AND CORRECTIONS

- The student's knees are not bent. *Cause:* The student is unaware that their knees are straight. *Correction:* Tell the student to bend the knees.
- The student's arms are not up. *Cause:* The student is unaware that their arms are down. *Correction:* Tell the student to lift the arms to the correct position.
- The student is rocking. *Cause:* The feet are too close together. *Correction:* Tell the student place the feet shoulder-width apart.

TASK 10: JUMP AND LAND ON THE FLOOR

PURPOSE

Following is the purpose of the task as related to aspects of skilled performance.

Technique: Jumping is a fundamental motor skill used in many gymnastics routines. Landing safely from a jump is a critical safety skill for children. In this task, students apply the landing position from task 8 to a jump.

DESCRIPTION

First, review the landing position in task 8. Next, ask students to do a little jump from this position and land back in the same position. Students use a straight jump, in which the body stretches upward at takeoff to create a straight line from the top of the hands to the toes. Ask the students to jump higher and higher while landing in the position. This task is accomplished when students can consistently land in this position.

EQUIPMENT

Mats

CRITICAL ELEMENTS

Technique

- Bend the knees.
- Keep the feet shoulder-width apart.
- Swing the arms upward from the hips as the legs push forcefully off the floor and straighten.
- Cushion with the legs by landing on the balls of the feet, then the foot, assuming the landing position.

COMMON ERRORS, CAUSES, AND CORRECTIONS

- The student's landing is jarred (i.e., landing with straight legs). *Cause:* The knees are not bent. *Correction:* Tell the student to land on the balls of the feet and to bend the knees more on landing.
- The student's landing is unstable. *Cause:* The arms are not stretched out. *Correction:* Tell the student to lift the arms.

TASK 11: JUMP AND MAKE SHAPES ON THE FLOOR

PURPOSE

Following is the purpose of the task as related to aspects of skilled performance.

Technique: Jumping is a fundamental motor skill used in many gymnastics routines. Landing safely from a jump is a critical safety skill for children. In this task, students learn to make shapes with their bodies when they are in the air and then land safely on the floor.

DESCRIPTION

This task can be performed with or without a mat. We recommend the following shapes, but students can invent their own after these are mastered.

- *Star.* The students spread their legs apart after leaving the floor and bring them together before landing.
- *Tuck.* The students tuck (lift) their legs to the hips or to the chest after leaving the floor and then straighten the legs before landing.
- *One knee bent and clap.* After jumping off the floor, the students lift one leg with the knee bent and clap under it. Repeat with the other leg.

- *Twist to the left and back before landing.* After jumping, the students twist quickly to the left and back to center.
- *Twist to the right and back before landing.* After jumping, the students twist quickly to the right and back to center.

EQUIPMENT

Mats or floor area

CRITICAL ELEMENTS

Technique

- Bend the knees.
- Keep the feet shoulder-width apart.
- Swing the arms upward from the hips as the legs push forcefully off the floor and straighten.
- Cushion with the legs by landing on the balls of the feet and assuming the landing position.

COMMON ERRORS, CAUSES, AND CORRECTIONS

- The student's landing is jarred (i.e., landing with straight legs). *Cause:* The knees are not bent. *Correction:* Tell the student to land on the balls of the feet and to bend the knees more on landing.
- The student's landing is unstable. *Cause:* The arms are not stretched out. *Correction:* Tell the student to lift the arms and to look at a spot the wall level to where they are during the jump.
- The student's jump is uncoordinated. *Cause:* The timing of the arm swing and leg movement is not in sync. *Correction:* The student should practice bending and straightening the legs; as the legs straighten, the arms should move upward. After a few trials, add the jump.

TASK 12: JUMP AND LAND FROM A HEIGHT

PURPOSE

Following is the purpose of the task as related to aspects of skilled performance.

Technique: Jumping is a fundamental motor skill used in many gymnastics routines. Landing safely from a jump is a critical safety skill for children. This task applies the landing position learned in task 8 with a jump from 1 foot (0.3 meters) for students in kindergarten through grade 2 or from 2 feet (0.6 meters) for students in grades 3 through 5.

DESCRIPTION

First, review the landing position in task 8. Next, tell the students that you want them to practice jumping and landing. All landings should be on a mat. Students should not jump from a height that exceeds the height of their chest. This task is accomplished when students can consistently land in the correct position.

EQUIPMENT

Mats and raised platforms

CRITICAL ELEMENTS

Technique

- Jump down from a 1- or 2-foot height.
- Land with the feet shoulder-width apart.
- Hold the arms in front of the body and slightly to the side for balance.
- Cushion with the legs on landing.

COMMON ERRORS, CAUSES, AND CORRECTIONS

- The student's landing is jarred (i.e., landing with straight legs). *Cause:* The knees are not bent. *Correction:* Tell the student to bend the knees more and land on the balls of the feet.
- The student's landing is unstable. *Cause:* The arms are not stretched out. *Correction:* Tell the student to lift the arms.
- The student's jump is uncoordinated. *Cause:* The timing of the arm swing and leg movement is not in sync. *Correction:* The student should practice bending and straightening the legs; as the legs straighten, the arms should move upward. After a few trials, add the jump.

TASK 13: JUMP AND MAKE SHAPES IN THE AIR

PURPOSE

Following is the purpose of the task as related to aspects of skilled performance.

Technique: Jumping is a fundamental motor skill used in many gymnastics routines. Landing safely from a jump is a critical safety skill for children. This is the same as task 11, but it is performed from a low height. In this task, students learn to make shapes with their bodies when they are in the air and then land safely on the floor.

DESCRIPTION

We suggest that students jump from heights of 1 or 2 feet (0.3 or 0.6 meters), but slightly higher heights are appropriate if you and your students are comfortable. All landings should be on a mat. We recommend the following shapes:

- *Star.* The students spread their legs apart after leaving the floor and bring them together before landing.
- *Tuck.* The students tuck (lift) their legs to the hips or to the chest after leaving the floor and then straighten the legs before landing.
- *One knee bent and clap.* After jumping off the floor, the students lift one leg with the knee bent and clap under it. Repeat with the other leg.
- *Twist to the left and back before landing.* After jumping, the students twist quickly to the left and back to center.
- *Twist to the right and back before landing.* After jumping, the students twist quickly to the right and back to center.

EQUIPMENT

Mats and raised platforms (e.g., stacked mats, bench, box)

CRITICAL ELEMENTS

Technique

- Start with a small upward jump from the raised platform.
- Land with the feet shoulder-width apart.
- Hold the arms in front of the body and slightly to the side.
- Cushion with the legs on landing.

COMMON ERRORS, CAUSES, AND CORRECTIONS

- The student's landing is jarred (i.e., landing with straight legs). *Cause:* The knees are not bent. *Correction:* Tell the student to land on the balls of the feet and to bend the knees more on landing.
- The student's landing is unstable. *Cause:* The arms are not stretched out. *Correction:* Tell the student to lift the arms.

- The student's jump is uncoordinated. *Cause:* The timing of the arm swing and leg movement is not in sync. *Correction:* The student should practice bending and straightening the legs; as the legs straighten, the arms should move upward. After a few trials, add the jump.

TASK 14: JUMP AND TURN

PURPOSE

Following is the purpose of the task as related to aspects of skilled performance.

Technique: Jumping is a fundamental motor skill used in many gymnastics routines. Landing safely from a jump is a critical safety skill for children. In this task, students learn to jump and turn and then land squarely in the landing position.

DESCRIPTION

Turns are one of the most likely movements in which students might fall. In this task, students progress through quarter, half, and three-quarters turns and then perform 360-degree turns. All students might not be able to perform all the turns. Students should move to the next turn only if they have successfully performed the current turn several times. Students should find eye-level points on the wall they can use as focal points when they turn; this helps maintain balance. It is critical that students prepare for the landing while they are in the air.

EQUIPMENT

Mats or floor area

CRITICAL ELEMENTS

Technique

- Take a small upward jump from the raised platform.
- Perform the turn as directed (e.g., quarter turn). Reach the arms upward and look in the direction you want to land.
- Hold the arms in front of the body and slightly to the side.
- Look forward (not down).
- Land with the feet shoulder-width apart.
- Cushion with legs on landing.

COMMON ERRORS, CAUSES, AND CORRECTIONS

- The student's landing is jarred (i.e., landing with straight legs). *Cause:* The knees not bent. *Correction:* Tell the student to bend the knees more and land on the balls of the feet.
- The student's landing is unstable. *Cause:* The arms are not stretched out. *Correction:* Tell the student to lift the arms.
- The student's landing is unstable. *Cause:* The student is not looking forward. *Correction:* Tell the student to look at something at eye level when landing.
- The student's jump is uncoordinated. *Cause:* The timing of the arm swing and leg movement is not in sync. *Correction:* The student should practice bending and straightening the legs; as the legs straighten, the arms should move upward. After a few trials, add the jump.

TASK 15: ANIMAL WALKS

PURPOSE

Following is the purpose of the task as related to aspects of skilled performance.

Technique: Transferring weight between the feet, between the hands, and between the hands and feet are essential movements for many gymnastic skills. In this task, students learn how to transfer weight.

DESCRIPTION

Introduce students to the animal walks: mouse, crab, seal, monkey, camel, inchworm, and donkey. These are taught as discrete skills and are combined as a game once students learn them. Don't spend too much time on animal walks because students' arms and wrists can get overworked; intersperse them with other activities such as jumping and rolling. Put several mats end to end to allow students to move farther in each walk. Ensure students have space to walk so they do not kick each other. To use the game, the teacher names a walk and students move to that walk. The game can be used to vary the weight bearing demands of the different walks.

EQUIPMENT

Mats

CRITICAL ELEMENTS

Technique

Mouse walk

- Begin on all fours.
- Walk on your hands and feet across the mat and practice scurrying (going faster).

Crab walk (see figure)

- Sit on the ground and place the hands beside the hips.
- Lift the bottom off the mat and walk backward on the feet and hands.
- The fingers should point in the opposite direction of movement.

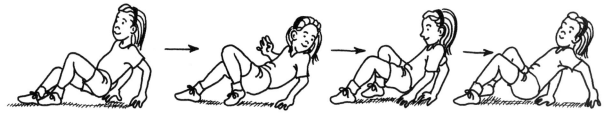

Crab walk

Seal walk (see figure)

- Start in push-up positon but with the toes pointed.
- Walk forward with the arms to drag the legs across the mat. Keep the body straight and tight.

Seal walk

Lame monkey walk (see figure)

- Start in a lunge position (one leg bent and one leg straight) with the arms straight and the hands on the ground about 6-12 inches in front of each foot.
- The student walks forward by kicking the back leg up and lifting the bent leg off the floor, rocking on the hands and landing it closer to the feet and then moving the hands forward together.

Lame monkey walk

Camel walk

- Start with the hands and feet on the ground, the back rounded, and the legs almost straight.
- Walk forward using the hands and feet by raising feet and hands on the same side so they lift off and land together.

Inchworm walk

- Start in a front support or push-up position with the legs, arms, and back straight.
- Walk the hands forward as far as possible and then walk the feet up to the hands while keeping the legs straight. Repeat to move forward.

Donkey kick

- Start in a squat with the hands on the floor.
- Lean forward onto the hands, keep the arms straight, shoulder width apart.
- Kick the feet up and behind the body.
- For a brief moment the feet are in the air and hands and arms support the body,
- Land in a squat.

COMMON ERRORS, CAUSES, AND CORRECTIONS

Mouse walk

- The student moves too fast and too soon. *Cause:* The student is too enthusiastic. *Correction:* Tell the student to start slow and then go faster.

Crab walk

- The student gets sore wrists. *Cause:* The hands are facing the wrong way or there was too much practice. *Correction:* Remind the student that the fingers point in the opposite direction of movement. Have the student choose another walk while the wrists rest.

Seal walk

- The student has difficulty moving across the mat. *Cause:* Weak upper-body strength or loose body. *Correction cue:* Have the student rest between seal walks to recover. Tell the student to keep the body tight by contracting the abs and the buttocks. Perform the seal walk in socks.

Lame monkey walk
- The student's back leg is bent. *Cause:* Lack of awareness. *Correction:* Tell the student to keep the back leg straight like it's in a cast.

Camel walk
- The student is unable to move in the pattern. *Cause:* Lack of awareness. *Correction:* Call the steps slowly and then increase the pace.

Inchworm walk
- The student's legs or arms are bent. *Cause:* Lack of awareness. *Correction:* Remind the student to keep the legs and arms straight.

Donkey kick
- The student's arms bend. *Cause:* Lack of strength. *Correction:* Remind the student to keep the arms straight. The student might need more practice with weight bearing on two hands; the lame monkey walk is a good activity to assess this and for the student to practice.

TASK 16: FROG JUMP

PURPOSE
Following is the purpose of the task as related to aspects of skilled performance.

Technique: The frog jump is an important action for vaulting and for weight bearing. In this task, students learn to perform the frog jump.

DESCRIPTION
The frog jump is characterized by weight transfer from feet to hands and then back to feet.

EQUIPMENT
Mats or floor area

CRITICAL ELEMENTS
Technique
Frog jump from squat position
- Start with the legs a little bent and the hands in front.
- Lean forward on the hands and keep the arms straight.
- Jump the feet between the hands in a tucked position.

Frog jump from straddle position
- Start in the straddle stand.
- Lean forward on the hands and keep the arms straight.
- Jump the feet near the hands.

COMMON ERRORS, CAUSES, AND CORRECTIONS
- The student cannot jump the feet to the hands. *Cause:* The feet are too far away from the hands. *Correction cue:* Tell the student to start closer and then move the feet a little farther away.

TASK 17: FROG JUMP ONTO A RAISED SURFACE

PURPOSE

Following is the purpose of the task as related to aspects of skilled performance.

Technique: The frog jump is an important action for vaulting and for weight bearing. In this task, students learn to perform the frog jump onto a raised surface, which simulates the basic vaulting action.

DESCRIPTION

The frog jump can be challenging for students to learn. It should be taught only after animal walks have been taught. The critical feature to be aware of in the frog jump is that the arms should stay straight. Once the frog jump is performed well on the floor mat, we move it to a raised platform that is 2- to 3-foot (0.6- to 0.9-meter) high.

EQUIPMENT

Mats and mats that are stacked to create a raised platform. Small benches can be used as well.

CRITICAL ELEMENTS

Technique

Frog jump from squat position

- Place the hands on the raised surface.
- Start with legs a little bent, lean forward on flat hands, and keep the arms straight.
- Jump the feet between the hands in a tucked position.

Frog jump from straddle position (see figure)

- Start in the straddle stand.
- Place flat hands on the raised surface, lean forward on the hands, and keep the arms straight.
- Jump the feet near the hands.

COMMON ERRORS, CAUSES, AND CORRECTIONS

- The student's arms collapse. *Cause:* The arms are bent. *Correction:* Tell the student to keep the arms locked straight and to make sure the hands are flat.
- The student cannot make the jump. *Cause:* The distance is too great. *Correction:* Have the student choose a lower height.

TASK 18: STRADDLE OVER A PARTNER

PURPOSE

Following is the purpose of the task as related to aspects of skilled performance.

Technique: The frog jump is an important action for vaulting. In this task, students learn to perform a basic vault over a partner.

DESCRIPTION

Place students into pairs. One student is the vaulter, and the other is the vault. Students vault over their partners at two heights: the partner is crouched on the floor and the partner is kneeling.

EQUIPMENT

Mats

CRITICAL ELEMENTS

Technique (see figure)

Vault

- *Position 1: tucked in a ball.* The knees and lower legs are along the floor and the head is tucked. The hands are on the floor and the arms are straight.
- *Position 2: kneeling.* The hands are on the floor and the arms are straight. The head is tucked.

Vaulter (for either position)

- Stand three steps behind the vault.
- Walk forward and place the hands on the shoulders, *not the back,* of the vault without stopping.
- Straddle over the vault and land in the landing shape taught in task 10.

COMMON ERRORS, CAUSES, AND CORRECTIONS

Vault

- The student's arms collapse. *Cause:* The arms are bent. *Correction:* Tell the student to keep the arms locked straight.

Vaulter

- The student fails to get over the vault. *Cause:* The transition from walk to vault is not smooth. *Correction:* Tell the student to move without stopping. Have the student practice straddled frog jumps.

TASK 19: INTRODUCTION TO THE CARTWHEEL

PURPOSE

Following is the purpose of the task as related to aspects of skilled performance.

Technique: The cartwheel is an important skill in gymnastics routines. It requires a different form of weight transfer than many other skills. This task introduces the cartwheel.

DESCRIPTION

These activities are best taught in a circuit. Be sure that students have enough space to perform. Revisit the lame monkey walk from task 16; although the action is different, the use of the lunge and the leg kicking are similar.

EQUIPMENT

Mats, benches, raised platforms, rope, tape, and foam logs

CRITICAL ELEMENTS

Technique

Cartwheel weight transfer along a bench or floor beam (see figure)

- The bench or beam must be very stable.
- Stand with the feet on either side of the bench at the end of the bench, and face the bench.
- Lean forward and place one hand on each side of the bench top.
- Transfer weight from one side of the bench to the other. To do this, rock from one foot to the other without moving the hands.
- Walk up the bench. Step and rock from side to side but lift the hands one at a time to move them forward as you rock. Continue all the way up the bench.

Cartwheel over an inclined rope (see figure)

- Tape one end of a rope to the wall at a height of 3 feet (0.9 meters). Tape the other end of the rope to the floor mat 4 feet (1.2 meters) from the wall. You can also use a foam log angled against the wall.
- Stand with the back to the wall where the rope touches the mat.
- Place the hands on either side of the rope and kick one leg then the other over the rope.

- *Extension.* Repeat the activity, but start with the hands off the mat and place them on either side of the rope one at a time. Kick the legs over the rope one at a time as soon as the first hand is on the floor.
- As you improve, the legs should be kicked higher over the rope. When you can kick the legs higher, start from a standing position and lunge forward to place the hands on the floor.

Mini cartwheel over a bench or raised platform
- Use a 6-inch (15.2-centimeter) raised platform (mat, box, or bench) that is about 1 foot (0.3 meters) wide.
- Start in a lunge position, lean forward, and place one and then the next hand on the raised platform while kicking the legs up and over the platform to land on the other side.
- Gradually, kick the legs higher as you cartwheel over the platform.

COMMON ERRORS, CAUSES, AND CORRECTIONS

Cartwheel weight transfer along a bench or floor beam
- The student can't transfer weight. *Cause:* The student does not rock from side to side. *Correction:* Tell the student to lean from side to side.

Cartwheel over an inclined rope
- The cartwheel support is not stable. *Cause:* The hands are not flat and the arms are not straight. *Correction:* Tell the student to keep the hands flat and keep the arms straight.
- The student kicks the rope down. *Cause:* The legs are not straight. *Correction:* Tell the student to keep the legs straight.

Mini cartwheel over a bench or raised platform
- The cartwheel support is not stable. *Cause:* The hands are not flat and the arms are not straight. *Correction:* Tell the student to keep the hands flat and keep the arms straight.

TASK 20: CARTWHEEL

PURPOSE

Following is the purpose of the task as related to aspects of skilled performance.

Technique: The cartwheel is an important skill in gymnastics routines. It requires a different form of weight transfer than many other skills. This task introduces advanced progressions to help students perform the cartwheel.

DESCRIPTION

These activities are best taught in a circuit. Be sure that students have enough space to perform. Students should be competent with the activities in task 19 before starting this task. The cartwheel should only be performed on the dominant side.

EQUIPMENT

Mats, tape or chalk, and inclined mat

CRITICAL ELEMENTS

Technique

Cartwheel on curved lines (see figure)

- The teacher makes several curved lines with chalk or ropes. Each is increasingly straighter.
- Start on the most curved line in a lunge position. Face the inside of the curved line.
- Stretch the arms overhead.
- Lean forward and place one hand and then the next hand on the line while kicking the legs overhead.
- As you improve, kick the legs higher and higher.
- As you improve, start with the feet together and step into the lunge.
- From the lunge position the rhythm is hand, hand, foot, foot. From the step position, the rhythm is foot, foot, hand, hand, foot, foot.
- Finish by standing with the arms overhead.

Cartwheel down an inclined mat

- Start in a lunge position at the top of an inclined mat.
- Stretch the arms overhead.
- Lean forward and place one hand and then the next hand on the line while kicking the legs overhead.
- As you improve, kick the legs higher and higher.
- As you improve, start with the feet together and step into the lunge.
- From the lunge position the rhythm is hand, hand, foot, foot. From the step position, the rhythm is foot, foot, hand, hand, foot, foot.
- Finish by standing with the arms overhead.

Cartwheel along a straight line on the floor mat

- Stand with the feet together and the arms overhead.
- Step forward into a lunge, bend the front knee, and place one hand and then the next on the line while kicking the legs overhead.

- As you improve, kick the legs higher and higher.
- Finish by standing with the arms overhead.

COMMON ERRORS, CAUSES, AND CORRECTIONS

- The legs are not moving overhead. *Cause:* Lack of confidence. *Correction:* Go back to task 19 and encourage higher leg lift.
- The cartwheel is not smooth. *Cause:* Incorrect rhythm. *Correction:* Have the student say the rhythm while performing the cartwheel.

TASK 21: STANDING BALANCE

PURPOSE

Following is the purpose of the task as related to aspects of skilled performance.

Technique: Balancing statically on different body parts is essential in gymnastics routines. This task introduces a variety of standing balances that teach students how to maintain a static balance.

DESCRIPTION

The balances are taught as discrete skills and then can be combined as a tag game (students adopt the position when tagged). Mats are not needed for standing balances. Students should be able to hold each balance for at least five seconds.

EQUIPMENT

Floor area

CRITICAL ELEMENTS

Technique

Starting shape

- Stand with the body straight and stretched.
- Look forward.
- Extend the arms overhead by the ears.

Straddle stand

- Stand with the body straight and stretched.
- Move the legs sideways apart and straight (i.e., straddled).
- Look forward.
- Extend the arms overhead by the ears.

Stork stand

- Stand with the body straight and stretched.
- Look forward.
- Place the foot of one leg on the knee of the other.
- Lift the arms to the side for balance.
- Practice using both legs.

Bent-knee stand

- Stand with the body straight and stretched.
- Look forward.
- Bend one leg 90 degrees.
- Point the toes.
- Nonkneeling leg is held straight and behind.

- Lift the arms to the side for balance. Lift them overhead to make it more challenging.
- Practice using both legs.

Two-foot toe stand
- Stand on the toes of both feet with the body straight and stretched.
- Look forward.
- Lift the arms to the side for balance. Lift them overhead to make it more challenging.

One-foot toe stand
- Stand on the toes of one foot with the body straight and stretched.
- Look forward.
- Lift the arms to the side for balance. Lift them overhead to make it more challenging.
- Practice using both legs.

Lunge
- Stand with one foot forward and bend the leg at the knee.
- The back leg is straight and the foot is on the ground.
- Lift the arms overhead.
- Practice using both legs.

Scale
- Stand in the starting shape.
- Extend the arms to a T position.
- Bend at the hip and lift one leg straight backward at the hip level (height will depend on flexibility and strength).
- Both legs should be locked out straight.
- Imagine that there is a log that cannot bend along the toes of the leg in the air to the top of the head.
- Keep the core tight.

COMMON ERRORS, CAUSES, AND CORRECTIONS
- The student is not stable. *Cause:* The support leg is bent. *Correction:* Tell the student to keep the leg locked and straight.
- The student is not stable. *Cause:* The core is not contracted. *Correction:* Tell the student to tighten the core or tighten the belly and buttocks.

TASK 22: SITTING BALANCE

PURPOSE
Following is the purpose of the task as related to aspects of skilled performance.

Technique: Balancing statically on different body parts is essential in gymnastics routines. This task introduces a variety of sitting balances that teach students how to maintain a static balance.

DESCRIPTION
The balances are taught as discrete skills and then can be combined as a tag game (students adopt the position when tagged). Students should be able to hold each balance for at least five seconds.

EQUIPMENT

Mats

CRITICAL ELEMENTS

Technique

Tuck sit

- Sit on the mat with the knees pulled to the chest, the back rounded, and the hands on the knees or the arms out for balance.
- Point the toes.
- To make this a little harder, lift the toes off the ground.

Pike sit

- Sit on the mat with the legs straight and together.
- Stretch the upper body tall.
- Look forward.
- Place the hands beside the hips.
- Point the toes.

Straddle sit

- Sit on the mat with the legs straight and apart.
- Stretch the upper body tall.
- Look forward.
- Place the hands beside the hips or between the legs.
- Point the toes.

Pancake sit

- Sit on the mat with the legs straight and apart.
- Look forward.
- Point the toes.
- Lean the upper body forward as far as possible and point the hands in the direction of the legs. How far you can reach depends on flexibility. (No assistance is needed because this is a self-limiting movement.)

Lying face down

- Lie face down on the mat with the legs together and straight.
- Extend the arms overhead to touch the floor.

Lying face up

- Lie face up on the mat with the legs together and straight.
- Extend the arms overhead to touch the floor.

COMMON ERRORS, CAUSES, AND CORRECTIONS

- The upper body is not straight (when required). *Cause:* Lack of awareness. *Correction:* Tell the student to keep the back straight.

TASK 23: BALANCE ON HANDS AND FEET

PURPOSE

Following is the purpose of the task as related to aspects of skilled performance.

Technique: Balancing statically on different body parts is essential in gymnastics routines. This task introduces a variety of supporting balances using the hands and feet.

DESCRIPTION

These balances are taught as discrete skills and then can be combined as a tag game (students adopt the position when tagged). Students should be able to hold each balance for at least five seconds. Because these activities involve weight bearing on the hands and wrists, intersperse them with other tasks such as jumping and rolling. To help students understand how to hold these positions, emphasize tightening the core, which includes contracting the buttocks and the abdominal muscles.

EQUIPMENT

Mats

CRITICAL ELEMENTS

Technique

Front support

- Assume the push-up position. The arms, back, and legs should be straight.
- The core should be tight.

Rear support

- Assume a reverse push-up position with the body facing the ceiling. The arms, back, and legs should be straight.
- The core should be tight.

Side support

- Assume a push-up position on one hand and face the wall. The arms, back, and legs should be straight.
- Hold the nonsupporting arm above the body for balance.
- The core should be tight.

Shoulders and feet balance

- Lie on the mat with the legs bent and the feet flat on the floor.
- The arms are by the side, palms down, to provide support.
- Raise the body off the floor. Contact with the mat should only occur at the shoulders (*not* the neck or head) and the feet.
- The core should be tight.

Front support with feet raised on a platform

- Lie on the mat with the legs together and straight.
- Extend the arms overhead to touch the floor.

COMMON ERRORS, CAUSES, AND CORRECTIONS

- The student's balance is not stable. *Cause:* The core is not tight. *Correction:* Tell the student to tighten the buttocks and the abdominal muscles.
- The student's balance is not stable. *Cause:* The arms are not straight. *Correction:* Tell the student to keep the arms straight.

TASK 24: BALANCES ON KNEES

PURPOSE

Following is the purpose of the task as related to aspects of skilled performance.

Technique: Balancing statically on different body parts is essential in gymnastics routines. This task introduces a variety of kneeling balances.

DESCRIPTION

The balances are taught as discrete skills and then can be combined as a tag game (students adopt the position when tagged). Students should be able to hold each balance for at least five seconds. Because these activities involve weight bearing on the hand and wrists, intersperse them with other tasks such as jumping and rolling. To help students understand how to hold these positions, emphasize contracting the buttocks and the abdominal muscles.

EQUIPMENT

Mats

CRITICAL ELEMENTS

Technique

Two-knee balance

- Kneel on both legs.
- Keep the upper body upright.
- Lift the arms to the side.

Knee scale

- Kneel with one knee on the mat. Stretch the other leg straight behind and parallel to the floor.
- The hands support the weight of the body under the shoulders. The arms are straight.
- Keep the head up and look forward.
- Practice with both legs.

COMMON ERRORS, CAUSES, AND CORRECTIONS

- The student's balance is not stable. *Cause:* The body is loose and not tight. *Correction:* Tell the student to tighten the buttocks and the abdominal muscles.
- The student's balance is not stable. *Cause:* The arms are not straight. *Correction:* Tell the student to keep the arms straight.

TASK 25: BALANCE ON SHOULDERS

PURPOSE

Following is the purpose of the task as related to aspects of skilled performance.

Technique: Balancing statically on different body parts is essential in gymnastics routines. In this task, students learn to balance on their shoulders. This is an advanced skill.

DESCRIPTION

In this task students emphasize contracting the buttocks and the abdominal muscles to create stability. This is also a key safety feature of this skill. This skill should not be performed if the student cannot contract the buttocks and the abdominal muscles to create stability.

EQUIPMENT

Mats

CRITICAL ELEMENTS

Technique (see figure)

- Lie on the mat and press the arms and hands to the floor.
- Tuck the legs to the chest and then straighten them overhead towards the ceiling.
- Then lift and place the hands on the back.
- The toes should be straight.
- No weight should be placed on the neck or head.
- As students improve, start in a pike position and lift the whole body straight up.

COMMON ERRORS, CAUSES, AND CORRECTIONS

- The student's balance is not stable. *Cause:* The core is not tight. *Correction:* Contract the buttocks and the abdominal muscles.
- The balance is not stable. *Cause:* The arms are not behind the back. *Correction:* Tell the student to place their hands on their back.

TASK 26: HEADSTAND

PURPOSE

Following is the purpose of the task as related to aspects of skilled performance.

Technique: The headstand is an important balance in gymnastics.

DESCRIPTION

The headstand requires a strong triangular base of support between the forehead and the hands. Students should not roll out of headstands, and they should avoid falling with the back toward the floor. To prevent this, the legs should always be angled a little over the hands (never vertical). Students can be taught to spot each other. If they see the legs move too far, they can use their arms or hands to stop the movement. A useful strategy to help students learn where to place their hands and head is to use small carpet squares.

EQUIPMENT

Mats and carpet squares (to show hand and head placement)

CRITICAL ELEMENTS

Technique

Headstand tripod balance (see figures)

- Kneel on the mat and place the hands and head in a triangular formation.
- Lift one leg off the ground and place it on the same-side elbow.
- Repeat this for the other leg.
- There is always a slight backward lean that places most of the weight on the hands.

Headstand tucked balance

- Repeat the previous task, but hold the knees in a tucked position instead of placing them on the elbows.
- There is always a slight backward lean that places most of the weight on the hands.

Headstand

- Once you are proficient in the previous task, repeat the task and straighten each leg to a vertical position.
- There is always a slight lean that places most of the weight on the hands.

COMMON ERRORS, CAUSES, AND CORRECTIONS

- The student complains of too much weight on the head. *Cause:* The hands are not taking enough of the weight. *Correction:* Tell the student to be sure the hands, not the head, are doing the work.
- The student is unbalanced. *Cause:* Triangular formation may be not wide enough. *Correction:* Tell the student to make the triangle a little bigger by moving the hands a little farther apart and back from the head.

TASK 27: HANDSTAND

PURPOSE

Following is the purpose of the task as related to aspects of skilled performance.
   Technique: The handstand is an important balance in gymnastics.

DESCRIPTION

The handstand is the most advanced skill taught in this chapter, and it requires proficiency in many of the previous supports. Students should not roll out of handstands, and they should avoid falling with the back toward the floor. We suggest that the task progressions be part of a circuit. Students might achieve different levels of performance. You should supervise the actual handstand. Students should not support each other.

EQUIPMENT

Mats and a wall

CRITICAL ELEMENTS

Technique

Lame monkey walk

- Revisit the lame money walk from task 15.

Lame monkey without walking

- Start in a lunge position (one leg bent and one leg straight) with the hands on the ground.
- Progressively kick the legs higher and higher while lifting the base leg off the ground. Avoid achieving a balance.
- The arms and swinging (i.e., nonkicking) leg should be locked straight throughout the movement.

Kick to handstand with assist (see figure)

- Step into a lunge position placing the hands on the ground in front of the feet as would occur in the lame monkey walk. The front leg will be bent and the back leg will be straight. Like the lame monkey walk, kick the back leg higher lifting the bent leg off the ground and then join the two legs together in the air.
- The arms and legs should be locked straight.
- The spotter should hold the thighs or lower legs.

Wall walk to handstand

- Start in a front support position with the feet against the wall.
- Walk the hands toward the wall and the feet up the wall.
- Go as high as you wish.

COMMON ERRORS, CAUSES, AND CORRECTIONS

- The student is unbalanced. *Cause:* The arms are not straight. *Correction:* Remind the student to keep the arms straight. Revisit the lame monkey walk.
- The student is unbalanced. *Cause:* The body is loose and not tight. *Correction:* Tell the student to tighten the buttocks and the abdominal muscles.

TASK 28: ROUTINES

PURPOSE

Following is the purpose of the task as related to aspects of skilled performance.

Technique: In this task, students learn to combine several gymnastics movements into a routine.

DESCRIPTION

This application occurs for lessons 1-5 for each block plan as the application activity of the lesson. In lessons 1-5 this application is directed by the teacher asking students to combine in sequence particular content taught that day or on previous lessons. This task is an opportunity for students to combine short sequences of different locomotion activities. This prepares students for the routines they will *practice* in lesson 6 and *present* in lesson 7. Lesson 6 is devoted to designing and practicing the routine, and lesson 7 requires students to present their routines. The complexity and difficulty of the routines are different for each grade. Provide students with instructions for designing a routine. The instructions can be written on cards, provided as pictures that students can use to a create picture boards of the sequence, or placed on a board for the class to see. Following are some sample sequences. Choose the task relative to the grade level you are teaching and your students.

EQUIPMENT

Mats

CRITICAL ELEMENTS

Technique

Lessons 1-5–Daily routine sequences. Depending on the content taught, ask students to sequence the skills taught that day with skills from previous days. The following are some examples:

- Grades K and 1: rock and roll, static balance
- Grades 2 and 3: roll, jump, land, static balance
- Grades 4 and 5: roll, jump, land, static balance, cartwheel
- I want you to start with the seal walk, move to the crab walk, and finish scurrying across the floor in the mouse walk.
- I want you to combine three of the animal walks we learned today.
- Let's perform this routine: forward roll, knee scale, puppy roll, rock to stand.
- Let's perform this routine: cartwheel, scale, forward roll to stand, headstand.

Lesson 6. Have students design a sequence with any combination of skills that is appropriate. Alternately, you can provide the sequence you want students to use. Students will practice the sequence on day 6 and part of day 7.

Lesson 7. Students present their routines. Determine how much time you will allow for students to present their routines. You will need to determine whether students will present their routine to their group, or to the whole class. Teach students who are observers how to behave during a performance (e.g., not to whisper, talk, or move), to applaud at the end, and to appreciate the effort that members of the class put into their performances.

COMMON ERRORS, CAUSES, AND CORRECTIONS

Use these criteria to judge the quality of the movements as students perform the routines.

- All routines start and finish in the with arms overhead.
- The balances are held for three seconds.
- The transitions from one movement to another should flow smoothly without stops and stumbles.
- Students should follow the directions you established.

PART

III

Teaching Sport Skills

Chapter 6

Soccer

Soccer is one of the most popular sports in the world. In addition to being played in schools, in recreational and competitive leagues, and at the professional and Olympic levels, soccer is a lifetime sport. Beginners can learn to play soccer quickly, which makes it an ideal sport to teach in schools, and they can engage in modified games to develop skillfulness, game sense, and enjoyment of the game across their lifespan.

OUR PEDAGOGICAL APPROACH TO SOCCER

The goal of this soccer unit is to teach all students and to have every player touch the ball as much as possible by maximizing time on task. Progression from one task to the next should be done in small steps for the benefit of teachers who are teaching soccer for the first time and for beginner students. There are only a few skills to be taught; what's more important is developing student performance by refining technique and by making each successive task a little more demanding.

A ground game is developmentally appropriate for beginners. The ball should not be in the air in the initial stages of learning. Instead, the focus is on sequential and systematic skill development.

Instruction begins with small-sided games beginning in the 1v1 game and moves to a 4v4 that does not have permanent goalkeepers until the conclusion of level 3 for several reasons:

- Small-sided games create more opportunities to pass, defend, and create more 1v1, 2v1, 2v2, 3v2, 3v3 conditions.
  - More goals are scored.
  - There is more student engagement.
  - The small sided game teaches all the building blocks: ball control, dribbling for possession, penetration and space, shooting, passing, defending, tackling.
  - The 4v4 is the most basic tactical configuration to help students understand the larger game of soccer with a primary focus on individual decision-making and support play.
  - The 4v4 initiates student comprehension of the diamond formation, which is a four-person midfield that is often used in either a 4-4-2 or a 3-4-3 formation of full-sided 11v11 games. It relies on a defensive midfielder, an attacking midfielder, and two wide midfielders. Students have the option of passing the ball forward, sideways, or backward The diamond formation is the simplest way to teach and for students to learn this positioning and strategy.

- Having a student be a permanent goalkeeper provides little advantage to learning the game of soccer. We use a goalkeeper in some of the more advanced games.
- U.S. Youth Soccer recommends the 4v4 approach in the initial stages of learning the game. It is a developmental tool that is used by soccer programs in countries such as Brazil, England, France, Germany, Holland, Italy, and Spain.
- Using the 4v4 game rather than the full game creates more learning opportunities.

- We often use overload situations in which there are more attacking players than defenders. This teaches off-the-ball movement in offense.
- Our tasks accommodate teams of 2, 4, and 8.
- The 4v4 game is an excellent vehicle for enjoyment and activity. The game is particularly helpful for students who do not have a high level of technical development.
- We do not use corner kicks. Instead, the team who didn't kick the ball out of bounds is allowed an unobstructed short pass to a member of their team. Throw-ins are not introduced until level 3 to facilitate passing and control once the ball comes off the ground.
- The restrictions imposed by U.S. Youth Soccer in 2016 preclude children less than 11 years of age from heading a soccer ball. We teach a ground game in 4v4 until students approach level 3 tasks as part of their secondary school physical education curriculum.
- General rules for making tasks easier or more demanding include changing the goal size (wider is easier) and using the overload concept (more players on offense than defense, such as 3v1 or 3v2) for offense.

Modifications to Address Individual Needs of Students

For students with disabilities, appropriate modifications to activities depend on the nature of the disability. When making modifications for individuals with disabilities, be sure to include students in the decision-making process and make the least adaptation necessary for the students to be successful. To modify soccer instruction for students with visual impairments, you can use a brightly colored ball (e.g., bright orange or yellow) or a ball that has a sound source (e.g., a rattle ball) and use brightly colored floor tape, cones, or poly spots to indicate boundaries and goals. In addition, having a paraprofessional or a peer clap behind the goal provides an audio cue to orient a student who is attempting to score. When you are teaching the students about movement around the playing area, allow a student with a visual impairment to become familiar with the area prior to play by running around the area with a peer.

For students with autism spectrum disorder, set up groups that practice in quieter or less chaotic areas of the gymnasium or outdoor space, and present materials using the students' desired communication methods (e.g., picture symbols). You can also add new rules to the game, such as a rule that all students must touch the ball prior to attempting to score, to ensure the inclusion of all students during game play.

Modifications can also be made to include students who use wheelchairs. Rather than striking the soccer ball with the feet, students who use wheelchairs can strike the ball with a hockey stick or with a guard on the front of the wheelchair. All other elements of moving around the soccer playing area should remain similar to the regular game. It is essential that the instruction and the game take place on a flat, hard surface rather than on a field.

For individuals with cerebral palsy, adopt rules from Paralympic soccer. For example, there is a no offside rule, and opposing players must be 7 yards (6.4 meters) from the ball at restart. You can also consider using a half-court playing area and teaching a zone defense so each player defends a small area of the court.

Organization

Place students in groups of 4 to 8. Students stay with their groups for the duration of the unit. The groups should be balanced by gender and in terms of the skillfulness of the students. Each group has a home area where all practices and games occur.

Space

Field organization is important. Where possible, have all fields face the same way with space between each field. This has some limitations because it doesn't prevent the ball from entering another field.

Fields for 4v4 are 35 to 40 yards (32 to 36.6 meters) by 25 yards (22.9 meters). You might place 2 groups of 4, on one field, each on their own half of the field for instructional purposes, and then they can be combined on the whole field for a 4v4 game. You can also reduce the playing area on a field for a specific task. We used fixed field sizes in our lessons to make management of students more efficient.

Equipment Needed

Small (size 4) soccer balls or futsal balls are appropriate for upper-elementary students because they help keep play on the ground. You will also need cones or poly spots to organize fields. Having cones of different colors and sizes is helpful.

CONTENT MAP STRUCTURE

Figure 6.1 is a combined content map that illustrates the flow and connectedness of all the tasks used to develop skillful performance and game sense. It is divided into three levels, and each level has a separate content map that includes the application games used to refine the techniques and tactics for that level. Level 1 (figure 6.2) introduces dribbling and focuses on fundamental and evasion skills in 1v1 modified game play. Passing and shooting are also included at this level, and it concludes with 2v2 application games that combine all three offensive skills. At level 2 (figure 6.3), specific offensive and defensive tactics and skills are taught, and they are used in 4v4 games. At level 3 (figure 6.4), advanced passing and control techniques, offensive and defensive tactics, and initial heading and goalkeeping activities are incorporated into 4v4 games.

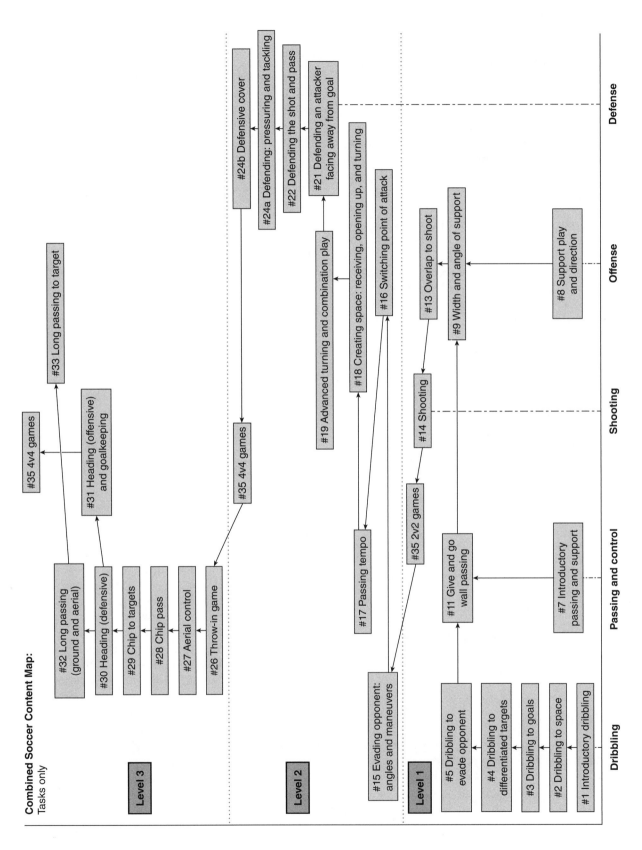

Combined Soccer Content Map:
Tasks only

Level 3
#33 Long passing to target
#31 Heading (offensive) and goalkeeping
#35 4v4 games
#32 Long passing (ground and aerial)
#30 Heading (defensive)
#29 Chip to targets
#28 Chip pass
#27 Aerial control
#26 Throw-in game

Level 2
#24b Defensive cover
#24a Defending: pressuring and tackling
#22 Defending the shot and pass
#21 Defending an attacker facing away from goal
#19 Advanced turning and combination play
#18 Creating space: receiving, opening up, and turning
#16 Switching point of attack
#13 Overlap to shoot
#9 Width and angle of support
#8 Support play and direction
#35 4v4 games
#14 Shooting
#35 2v2 games
#17 Passing tempo
#11 Give and go wall passing
#7 Introductory passing and support
#15 Evading opponent: angles and maneuvers

Level 1
#5 Dribbling to evade opponent
#4 Dribbling to differentiated targets
#3 Dribbling to goals
#2 Dribbling to space
#1 Introductory dribbling

Dribbling   **Passing and control**   **Shooting**   **Offense**   **Defense**

Figure 6.1   Combined content map for soccer.

Level 1 Soccer content map:
Tasks and games

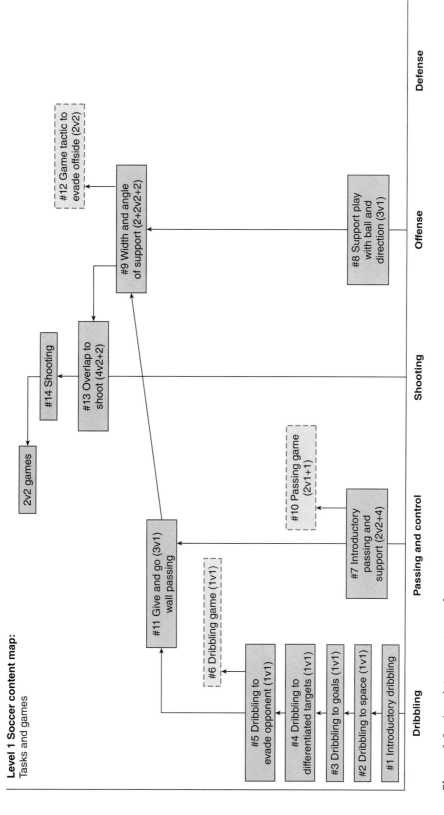

Figure 6.2 Level 1 content map for soccer.

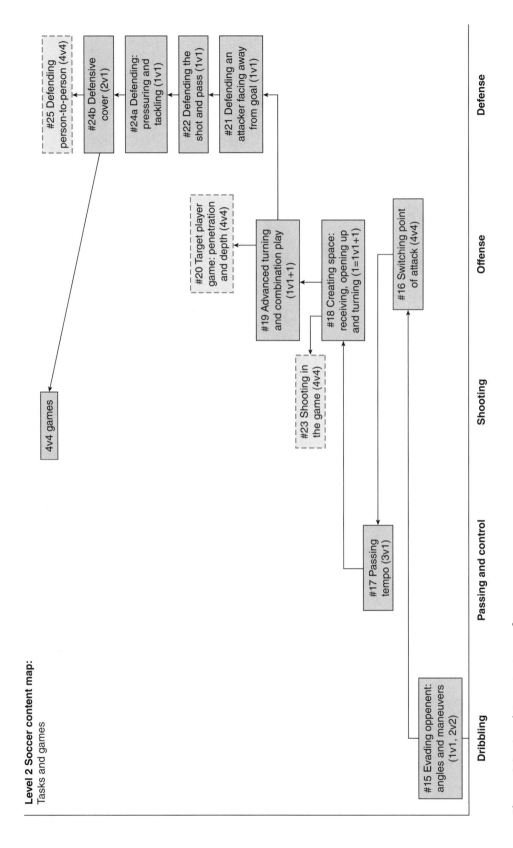

Figure 6.3 Level 2 content map for soccer.

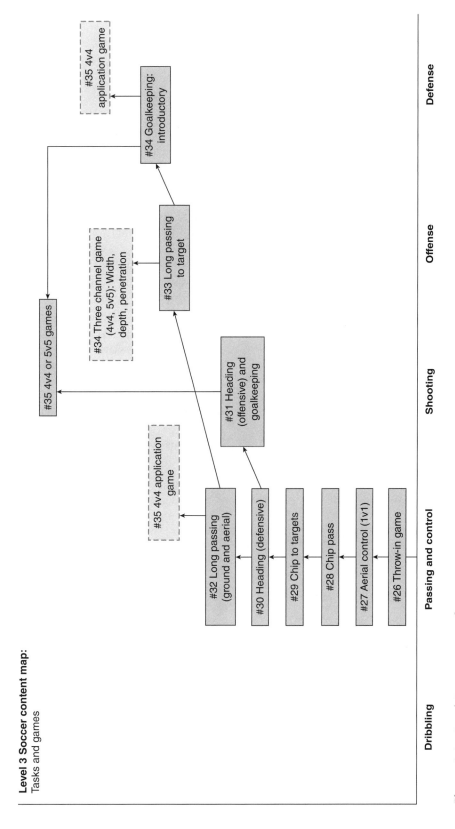

Figure 6.4 Level 3 content map for soccer.

115

STRUCTURE OF THE LESSONS

The following is a sample daily lesson structure for a 50-minute elementary soccer lesson.

Warm-up (6 minutes)

Application task: dribbling to goals (1v1) (5 to 8 minutes)

Informing task: dribbling to differentiated targets (1v1) (10 minutes)

Extension task: dribbling to evade an opponent (1v1) (10 minutes)

Closing application game: dribbling game (1v1) (6 to 10 minutes)

Closure (6 minutes)

Warm-up

We use the same warm-up for elementary and secondary students. The warm-up should be taught to students on the first day of the unit. This might take up most of the lesson.

The warm-up is a circuit. Students move to the next station every 45 seconds to 1 minute. You can use music to time the rotation or set a number of repetitions. Each station can accommodate 4 to 6 students. For larger classes, 2 or 3 sets of stations could be used. The following are the five stations in the circuit (see figure 6.5):

- **Station 1: sideways galloping forward.** Set out 11 to 13 cones about 6 feet (1.8 meters) apart diagonally. Demonstrate how to gallop sideways by moving forward and around each of the cones. When students reach the end of the cones, they jog with high knees (hip level) back to the start. They move along the side of the cones to stay clear of the students performing the gallop.

- **Station 2: sideways galloping facing backward.** This is the same as station 1 except the students are moving backward. Ensure the students do not move too quickly between the cones.

- **Station 3: dribbling in self-space with a soccer ball.** Define a 15-by-15-yard (13.7-by-13.7-meter) area with cones. Each student has a ball. Students dribble with the outside and inside of each foot while imagining that a 1-foot (0.3-meter) string is tied to one foot and to the ball to ensure the ball is kept close.

- **Station 4: dribbling, passing, and trapping.** Place students in groups of four. For each group, have two students stand on one line and the other two students stand 10 yards (9.1 meters) across from them. (Define the area with cones.) One student dribbles toward the two students on the other side. When the dribbler is within 1 yard (0.9 meters), he or she gently passes the ball to one of the two students. The student who receives

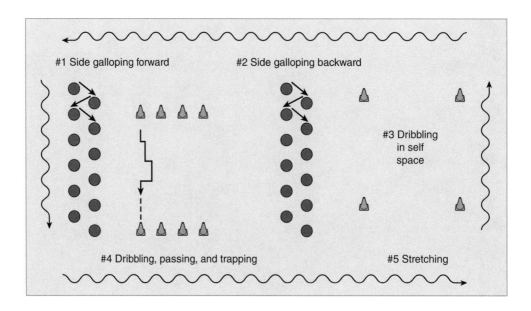

Figure 6.5 Soccer warm-up stations.

the ball should stop it as a trap, dribble back to the original side, and pass the ball to the student standing there who then repeats the dribbling and passing activity. Students continue this pattern until it is time to switch to the next station.

- **Station 5: stretching.** Students complete the following stretches:
  - *Overhead stretch*. Stand upright and stretch the arms straight above the head. The hands are intertwined and the palms point to the ceiling.
  - *Shoulder stretch*. Place the right arm straight across the upper chest. Place the left hand above the right elbow and pull the right arm across the chest. Alternate the arms.
  - *Triceps stretch*. Lift the right hand over the right shoulder and place it between the shoulder blades. Place the left hand on the right elbow and gently pull it toward the midline of the body. Alternate the arms.
  - *Quad stretch*. Support yourself by placing the right hand against a wall or partner at shoulder height. Stand on the right leg. Take hold of the left foot with the left hand and pull the heel toward the buttock. Keep the back straight and the knees together and in line. Alternate the legs.
  - *Hamstring stretch*. Sit on the floor with the left leg straight in front of you and the right leg bent inward. Lean forward and try to touch the toes of the straight leg with both hands. Alternate the legs.
  - *Lower leg stretch*. Place the hands on a wall at shoulder height. Stand with one foot in front of the other. Bend the front knee and lean forward. Keep the back leg straight with the heel on the ground. Alternate the legs.

BLOCK PLANS

The introductory block plan is designed for beginners (see table 6.1). In elementary school, it should not be introduced earlier than second grade. The introductory block plan focuses on helping students to refine their basic dribbling and passing techniques prior to facing more advanced soccer challenges. Although longer units are always preferred, we recognize that there are time limitations at the elementary level; therefore, the elementary unit is five days for the initial grade level in which it is taught.

The secondary block plan follows the elementary block plan and is designed for students in middle school and high school (see table 6.2). It assumes that students were taught basic soccer skills at the elementary level. If this is not the case, follow the introductory block plan. Because middle and high school physical education programs have different requirements, these units should *not* be taught in fewer than 10 days. These units are adjusted for 10-, 15-, and 20-day programs, although we recommend units of 20 or more days.

Table 6.1 Elementary Soccer Block Plan: Five-Day Unit

This is an example of a beginning block plan for elementary students that uses the soccer tasks shown in the level 1 content map. It is based on an initial five-day unit and, as such, it does not encompass all the level 1 tasks on the content map. You can use this as a template for developing an appropriate block plan for beginning students. If you are teaching a longer unit, or if another soccer unit will be taught next year, you can include the remaining level 1 tasks and some level 2 tasks. Your decisions about what tasks to include will depend on your students and their levels of experience.

Lesson 1	Lesson 2	Lesson 3	Lesson 4	Lesson 5

Warm-up
 	
• Teach and rehearse the warm-up
	Warm-up
	
	• Circuit
	  • Sideways galloping facing forward
	  • Sideways galloping facing backward
	  • Dribbling in self-space
	  • Dribbling, passing and trapping
	  • Stretching
		Warm-up
		
		• Same as day 2
			Warm-up
			
			• Same as day 2
				Warm-up
				
				• Same as day 2

Introductory application game None	**Introductory application game** • **(3)** 1v1 dribbling to goals	**Introductory application game** • **(6)** Dribbling game (1v1)	**Introductory application game** • **(10)** Passing game (2v1 + 1)	**Introductory application game** • **(12)** Avoiding being offside (2v2)
Content development • **(1)** Introductory dribbling • **(2)** 1v1 dribbling to space	**Content development** • **(4)** Dribbling to differentiated targets (1v1) • **(5)** 1v1 dribbling to evade an opponent	**Content development** • **(7)** Introductory passing and support (2v2 + 4) • **(8)** Support play with ball and direction (3v1)	**Content development** • **(9)** Width and angle of support (2 + 2v2 + 2) • **(11)** 3v1 give-and-go: wall passing • **(8)** Support play with ball and direction (3v1)	**Content development** • **(13)** Overlap to shoot (4v2 + 2) • **(14)** Shooting
Closing application game • **(3)** 1v1 dribbling to goals	**Closing application game** • **(6)** 1v1 dribbling game	**Closing application game** • **(10)** Passing game (2v1 + 1)	**Closing application game** • **(12)** Avoiding being offside (2v2)	**Closing application game** • **(12)** Avoiding being offside (2v2)

Table 6.2 Secondary Soccer Block Plans: 10-, 15-, and 20-Day Units (With Review of Level 1)

This block plan incorporates 10-, 15-, and 20-day units. The last two days of the 10-day block plan, the last three days of the 15-day block plan, and the last five days of the 20-day block plan are game days and are described at the end of the block plan. The first eight days of the block plan are the same for all units. This block plan reviews level 1 tasks and then addresses the level 2 content map (10- and 15-day units) and the level 3 content map (20-day unit).

Lesson 1 of all block plans	Lesson 2 of all block plans	Lesson 3 of all block plans	Lesson 4 of all block plans	Lesson 5 of all block plans

Warm-up
• Teach and rehearse the warm-up
	Warm-up
	• Circuit
	  • Sideways galloping facing forward
	  • Sideways galloping facing backward
	  • Dribbling in self-space
	  • Dribbling, passing and trapping
	  • Stretching
		Warm-up
		• Same as day 2
			Warm-up
			• Same as day 2
				Warm-up
				• Same as day 2

Introductory application game • **(6)** Dribbling game (1v1)	**Introductory application game** • **(35)** Application games	**Introductory application game** • **(20)** Target player game: penetration and depth (4v4)	**Introductory application game** • **(23)** Shooting in the game (4v4)	**Introductory application game** • **(25)** Defending person to person (4v4)
Content development • **(5)** 1v1 dribbling to evade an opponent • **(15)** Evading an opponent: angles and maneuvers (1v1)	**Content development** • **(18)** Creating space: receiving, opening up, and turning (1 + 1v1 + 1) • **(19)** Advanced turning and combination play (1v1 + 1)	**Content development** • **(21)** Defending an attacker facing away from the goal (1v1) • **(19)** Advanced turning and combination play (1v1 + 1)	**Content development** • **(22)** Defending the shot or pass (1v1)	**Content development** • **(24A)** Defending: pressuring and tackling (1v1) • **(24B)** 2v1 defensive cover
Closing application game • **(35)** Application games	**Closing application game** • **(20)** Target player game: penetration and depth (4v4)	**Closing application game** • **(20)** Target player game: penetration and depth (4v4)	**Closing application game** • **(23)** Shooting in the game (4v4)	**Closing application game** • **(25)** Defending person to person (4v4)

(continued)

Lesson 6 of all block plans	Lesson 7 of all block plans	Lesson 8 of all block plans (last instructional day of 10-day plan)	Lesson 9 of 15- and 20-day block plans (See table 6.3 for lesson 9 for 10-day plan.)	Lesson 10 of 15- and 20-day block plans (See table 6.3 for lesson 10 for 10-day plan.)
Warm-up • Same as day 2	**Warm-up** • Same as day 2	**Warm-up** • Same as day 2	**Warm-up** • Same as day 2	**Warm-up** • Same as day 2
Introductory application game • **(35)** Application games (three passes prior to shot on goal)	**Introductory application game** • **(26)** Throw-in game (3 + 1v3 + 1)	**Introductory application game** • **(26)** Throw-in game (3 + 1v3 + 1)	**Introductory application game** • **(20)** Target player game: penetration and depth (4v4)	**Introductory application game** • **(35)** Application games (final pass must be more than 10 yards [9.1 meters] to target)
Content development • **(16)** 4v4 switching point of attack • **(17)** Passing tempo (3v1)	**Content development** • **(27)** Aerial control (1v1)	**Content development** • **(28)** Chip pass • **(29)** Chip to targets	**Content development** • **(32)** Long passing (ground and aerial) • **(33)** Long passing to target	**Content development** • **(30)** Heading (defensive) • **(29)** Chip to targets
Closing application game • **(35)** Application games (three passes prior to shot on goal)	**Closing application game** • **(26)** Throw-in game (3 + 1v3 + 1)	**Closing application game** • **(20)** Target player game: penetration and depth (4v4)	**Closing application game** • **(35)** Application games (final pass must be more than 10 yards [9.1 meters] to target)	**Closing application game** • **(35)** Application games (final pass must be more than 10 yards [9.1 meters] to target; headed interception scores)

Lesson 11 of 15- and 20-day block plans	Lesson 12 of 15- and 20-day block plans (last instructional day of 15-day plan)	Lesson 13 of 20-day block plan (See table 6.4 for lesson 13 for 15-day plan.)	Lesson 14 of 20-day block plan (See table 6.4 for lesson 14 for 15-day plan.)	Lesson 15 of 20-day block plan (See table 6.4 for lesson 15 for 15-day plan.)
Warm-up • Same as day 2	Warm-up • Same as day 2	Warm-up • Same as day 2	Warm-up • Same as day 2	Warm-up • Same as day 2
Introductory application game • **(34)** Three-channel game: width, depth, and penetration (4v4, 5v5)	**Introductory application game** • **(35)** Application games (final pass or shot must be more than 10 yards [9.1 meters] to target)	**Introductory application game** • **(26)** Throw-in game (3 + 1v3 + 1)	**Introductory application game** • **(23)** Shooting in the game (4v4)	**Introductory application game** • **(25)** Defending person to person (4v4)
Content development • **(16)** 4v4 switching point of attack	**Content development** • **(31)** Goalkeeping: introductory • **(33)** Long passing to target	**Content development** • **(31)** Heading (offensive) and goalkeeping • **(29)** Chip to targets	**Content development** • **(14)** Shooting • **(13)** Overlap to shoot (4v2 + 2)	**Content development** • **(5)** 1v1 dribbling to evade an opponent • **(15)** Evading an opponent: angles and maneuvers 1v1
Closing application game • **(34)** Three-channel game: width, depth, and penetration (4v4, 5v5)	**Closing application game** • **(35)** Application games (final pass or shot must be more than 10 yards [9.1 meters] to target)	**Closing application game** • **(34)** Three-channel game: width, depth, and penetration (4v4, 5v5)	**Closing application game** • **(35)** Application games (shot must follow a backward or sideways pass)	**Closing application game** • **(35)** Application games (players must attempt to evade an opponent with dribbling skill prior to the pass or shot)

Lesson 16 of 20-day block plan	Lesson 17 of 20-day block plan	Lesson 18 of 20-day block plan	Lesson 19 of 20-day block plan	Lesson 20 of 20-day block plan
Warm-up • Same as day 2	**Warm-up** • Same as day 2	**Warm-up** • Same as day 2	**Warm-up** • Same as day 2	**Warm-up** • Same as day 2
Fixed-time 4v4 games against different opponents (nonexclusionary round-robin tournament) Encourage the use of specific skills and tactics. Award an extra point to the score for demonstration of these skills and tactics. We recommend at least two games per lesson.	**Fixed-time 4v4 games against different opponents (nonexclusionary round-robin tournament)** Encourage the use of specific skills and tactics. Award an extra point to the score for demonstration of these skills and tactics. We recommend at least two games per lesson.	**Fixed-time 4v4 games against different opponents (nonexclusionary round-robin tournament)** Encourage the use of specific skills and tactics. Award an extra point to the score for demonstration of these skills and tactics. We recommend at least two games per lesson.	**Fixed-time 4v4 games against different opponents (nonexclusionary round-robin tournament)** Encourage the use of specific skills and tactics. Award an extra point to the score for demonstration of these skills and tactics. We recommend at least two games per lesson.	**Fixed-time 4v4 games against different opponents (nonexclusionary round-robin tournament)** Encourage the use of specific skills and tactics. Award an extra point to the score for demonstration of these skills and tactics. We recommend at least two games per lesson.

Table 6.3 10-Day Block Plan Game Days

Lesson 9 of 10-day block plan	Lesson 10 of 10-day block plan
Warm-up • Same as day 2	**Warm-up** • Same as day 2
Fixed-time single games; fixed-time 4v4 games against different opponents (nonexclusionary round-robin tournament) Encourage the use of specific skills and tactics. Award an extra point to the score for demonstration of these skills and tactics. We recommend at least two games per lesson.	**Fixed-time 4v4 games against different opponents (nonexclusionary round-robin tournament)** Encourage the use of specific skills and tactics. Award an extra point to the score for demonstration of these skills and tactics. We recommend at least two games per lesson.

Table 6.4 15-Day Block Plan Game Days

Lesson 13 of 15-day block plan	Lesson 14 of 15-day block plan	Lesson 15 of 15-day block plan
Warm-up • Same as day 2	**Warm-up** • Same as day 2	**Warm-up** • Same as day 2
Fixed-time 4v4 games against different opponents (nonexclusionary round-robin tournament) Encourage the use of specific skills and tactics. Award an extra point to the score for demonstration of these skills and tactics. We recommend at least two games per lesson.	**Fixed-time 4v4 games against different opponents (nonexclusionary round-robin tournament)** Encourage the use of specific skills and tactics. Award an extra point to the score for demonstration of these skills and tactics. We recommend at least two games per lesson.	**Fixed-time 4v4 games against different opponents (nonexclusionary round-robin tournament)** Encourage the use of specific skills and tactics. Award an extra point to the score for demonstration of these skills and tactics. We recommend at least two games per lesson.

SHAPE AMERICA'S GRADE-LEVEL OUTCOMES
FOR K-12 PHYSICAL EDUCATION

In table 6.5, we identify key grade-level outcomes for soccer for third through seventh grade. These are linked to specific tasks on the content maps that are appropriate for teaching the skill and assessing the outcome.

Table 6.5   Grade-Level Outcomes for Soccer

Outcome	Description	Content map focus and tasks
S1.E1.5c	Combines traveling with manipulative skills for execution to a target (e.g., scoring in soccer, hockey and basketball).	Level 1, task 3
S1. E21.3a	Uses a continuous running approach and intentionally performs a kick along the ground and a kick in the air, demonstrating 4 of the 5 critical elements of a mature pattern for each.	Level 1, task 14
S1.E21.3b	Uses a continuous running approach and kicks a stationary ball for accuracy.	Level 1, task 14
S1.E21.4	Kicks along the ground and in the air, and punts using mature patterns.	Level 1, task 3
S1.E21.5	Demonstrates mature patterns in kicking and punting in small-sided practice task environments.	Level 1, task 3
S1.E26.5	Combines manipulative skills and traveling for execution to a target (e.g., scoring in soccer, hockey and basketball).	Level 2, task 17
S1.M4.7	Passes and receives with feet in combination with locomotor patterns of running and change of direction & speed with competency in invasion games such as soccer or speedball.	Level 1, task 7
S1.M7.6	Performs the following offensive skills without defensive pressure: pivot, give & go, and fakes.	Level 1, task 11
S1.M7.7	Performs the following offensive skills with defensive pressure: pivot, give & go, and fakes.	Level 2, task 18
S1.M9.6	Foot-dribbles or dribbles with an implement with control, changing speed and direction in a variety of practice tasks.	Level 2, task 15
S1.M10.6	Shoots on goal with power in a dynamic environment as appropriate to the activity.	Level 1 task 14
S1.M10.7	Shoots on goal with power and accuracy in small-sided game play.	Level 3, task 35

TASK 1: INTRODUCTORY DRIBBLING

PURPOSE
Following are the purposes of the task as related to aspects of skilled performance.

- Technique: In this task, students learn the appropriate technique for dribbling a soccer ball through space.
- Tactic: Students learn to move to open space.

DESCRIPTION
Two teams of four share one field. Each student has a ball and stands anywhere in the playing area. Ask the students to dribble throughout the playing area and experiment with different surfaces of the foot and various combinations: inside of foot, outside of foot, sole of foot, left foot only, right foot only, toe, heel. Students should keep the ball close to their feet.

- *Extension 1.* Identify north, south, east, and west in the playing square. Ask students to dribble in the direction you call out. Vary the speed at which you call out different directions (e.g., *north* quickly followed by *south*).
- *Extension 2.* Direct students like a traffic officer by using hand signals.
- *Extension 3.* Hold red, yellow, and green poly spots to signify what students should do.
  - Green: Students dribble around the playing area.
  - Yellow: Students slow down and dribble the ball between the insides of the feet.
  - Red: Students stop the ball by placing the foot on top.
- *Extension 4.* When students are dribbling around the playing area, have them switch gears by holding up appropriate fingers. When dribbling at the quickest speed the ball may be pushed out several feet ahead of the dribbler.
  - First gear (one finger): slow dribble
  - Second gear (two fingers): slightly quicker dribble
  - Third gear (three fingers): quick dribble
  - Fourth gear (four fingers): fastest possible dribble
- *Extension 5.* Vary the size of playing area and the number of students in it. Smaller spaces and more students require greater dribbling skills.

EQUIPMENT
One ball per student and red, yellow, and green poly spots

CRITICAL ELEMENTS AND CUES
Technique
- Keep the ball close to feet and the body in a slightly crouched position. *Cue:* Ball close, knees bent.
- When dribbling with the inside of the feet, turn the feet out and nudge the ball forward softly with the arches of the feet. *Cue:* Inside of feet tap ball.
- When dribbling with the outside of the feet, turn the feet in and nudge the ball forward (or to the side) softly with the outsides of the feet. *Cue:* Outside of feet tap ball.
- Dribble at a speed at which you can keep control of the ball. *Cue:* Dribble with care.

Tactics
- Move to open spaces as you dribble. *Cue:* Dribble to the gap.
- Protect the ball from other students by positioning the body between the ball and the player in close proximity. *Cue:* Guard ball with body.

COMMON ERRORS, CAUSES, AND CORRECTIONS
- The student loses control of the ball. *Cause:* The student imparts too much force on the ball or attempts to dribble too fast. *Correction:* Have the student dribble in first or second gear and keep the ball within a stride's length.

- The student focuses only on the ball. *Cause:* The student is looking down at the ball. *Correction:* Return to the traffic officer task; encourage the dribbler to split his or her vision between the ball and the traffic officer to monitor changes of direction.

TASK 2: 1V1 DRIBBLING TO SPACE

PURPOSE
Following is the purpose of the task as related to aspects of skilled performance.

Technique: In this task, students learn to apply dribbling techniques under game conditions.

DESCRIPTION
Position two teams of four students on opposite sides of a field that is 25 by 35 yards (22.9 by 32 meters) (see figure). One team is X's and the other is O's. Place poly spots or cones across the width of the field to indicate 10-, 20-, and 35-yard (9.1-, 18.3-, and 27.4-meter) lines. Each X player attempts to dribble the ball to any location on one of the three lines: line 1 (10 yards) for one point, line 2 (20 yards) for two points, or line 3 (opponent's goal line) for three points. The X player decides which line to advance to and scores the respective number of points by placing a foot on top of the ball on that line. As soon as the X player begins to dribble, the direct opponent (O) can leave the three-point goal line and attempt to put pressure on the dribbler. You can use passive (walking), active (running), or competitive (running and intercepting) defense with players of varying ability levels. If the O player wins the ball (prior to the X player scoring), he or she can dribble the ball to the X player's goal line to earn one point. Dribblers (X) and defenders (O) then alternate roles for the next trial (see figure).

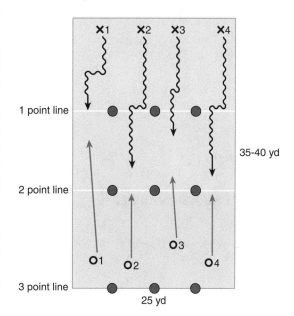

EQUIPMENT
One ball per student and colored poly spots or cones to create lines

CRITICAL ELEMENTS AND CUES

Technique
- Keep the ball close to the feet and hold the body in a slightly crouched position. *Cue:* Ball close, knees bent.
- When dribbling with the inside of the feet, turn the feet out and nudge the ball forward softly with the arches of the feet. *Cue:* Inside of feet tap ball.
- When dribbling with the outside of the feet, turn the feet in and nudge the ball forward (or to the side) softly with the outsides of the feet. *Cue:* Outside of feet tap ball.
- Dribble at a speed at which you can keep control of the ball. *Cue:* Dribble with care.

COMMON ERRORS, CAUSES, AND CORRECTIONS
- The student loses control of the ball. *Cause:* The student imparts too much force on the ball or attempts to dribble too fast. *Correction:* Have the student dribble in first or second gear and keep the ball within a stride's length.

- The student focuses only on the ball. *Cause:* The student is looking down at the ball. *Correction:* With a partner follow-the-leader dribble to follow a partner who is also dribbling a ball (players then alternate leader). The students should use peripheral vision to avoid running into other players who are working in the same space.

TASK 3: 1V1 DRIBBLING TO GOALS

PURPOSE

Following is the purpose of the task as related to aspects of skilled performance.
Technique: In this task, students refine their ball control under game conditions.

DESCRIPTION

The organization of this task is similar to task 2, but each of the three lines has four 2-yard (1.8-meter) goals (marked with cones) that students can attack (see figure). Initially there are no defenders. X students must now dribble the ball through the cone goal on any of the three lines to score the points. Once students have demonstrated their understanding of the tasks, defenders (O's) can move toward the dribblers to create pressure.

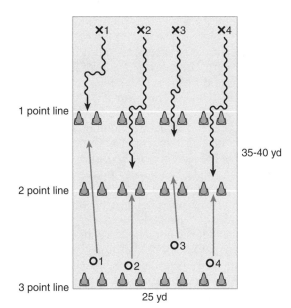

EQUIPMENT

One ball per student and cones or disks

CRITICAL ELEMENTS AND CUES

Technique

- Keep the ball close to the feet and hold the body in a slightly crouched position. *Cue:* Ball close, knees bent.
- When dribbling with the inside of the feet, turn the feet out and nudge the ball forward softly with the arches of the feet. *Cue:* Inside of feet tap ball.
- When dribbling with the outside of the feet, turn the feet in and nudge the ball forward (or to the side) softly with the outsides of the feet. *Cue:* Outside of feet tap ball.
- Dribble at a speed at which you can keep control of the ball. *Cue:* Dribble with care.

COMMON ERRORS, CAUSES, AND CORRECTIONS

- The student loses control of the ball. *Cause:* The student imparts too much force on the ball or attempts to dribble too fast. *Correction:* Have the student dribble in first or second gear and keep the ball within a stride's length.
- The student focuses only on the ball. *Cause:* The student is looking down at the ball. *Correction:* With a partner follow-the-leader dribble to follow a partner who is also dribbling a ball (players then alternate leader). The students should use peripheral vision to avoid running into other players who are working in the same space.

TASK 4: DRIBBLING TO DIFFERENTIATED TARGETS (1V1)

PURPOSE

Following is the purpose of the task as related to aspects of skilled performance.

Technique: In this task, students learn to apply dribbling techniques with tactics under game conditions.

DESCRIPTION

Position two teams of four students on opposite sides of a field that is 25 by 35 yards (22.9 by 32 meters). One team is X's and the other is O's. At the halfway point, position five cones 6 yards (5.5 meters) apart across the width of the field (see figure). Team X students are on offense, and each team X player has a ball. The offensive players attempt to dribble the ball across the opponent's goal line to score two points. If players dribble and touch one of the cones instead, they score one point. The defenders (O) advance toward the ball as soon as the X players begin to dribble. You can use passive, active, or competitive defense with players of varying ability levels. If the O player wins the ball, he or she can dribble it to the X player's goal line to earn one point. Dribblers (X) and defenders (O) then alternate roles for the next trial.

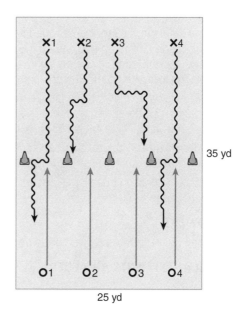

EQUIPMENT

One ball per student and cones or disks

CRITICAL ELEMENTS AND CUES

Technique

- Keep the ball close to the feet and hold the body in a slightly crouched position. *Cue:* Ball close, knees bent.
- When dribbling with the inside of the feet, turn the feet out and nudge the ball forward softly with the arches of the feet. *Cue:* Inside of feet tap ball.
- When dribbling with the outside of the feet, turn the feet in and nudge the ball forward (or to the side) softly with the outsides of the feet. *Cue:* Outside of feet tap ball.
- Dribble at a speed at which you can keep control of the ball. *Cue:* Dribble with care.

COMMON ERRORS, CAUSES, AND CORRECTIONS

- The student loses control of the ball. *Cause:* The student imparts too much force on the ball or attempts to dribble too fast. *Correction:* Have the student dribble in first or second gear and keep the ball within a stride's length.
- The student focuses only on the ball. *Cause:* The student is looking down at the ball. *Correction:* Go back to an earlier task if prompts and cues do not change the performance.

TASK 5: 1V1 DRIBBLING TO EVADE AN OPPONENT

PURPOSE

Following is the purpose of the task as related to aspects of skilled performance.

Technique: In this task, students learn to evade an opponent when dribbling.

DESCRIPTION

Divide teams of four (X's and O's) into pairs. Place two cones 6 yards (5.5 meters) apart as in task 4. Each player has a ball, and teams stand on opposite sides of a line between the cones. The players cannot cross the line between them. One attacker attempts to dribble to either cone (stopping the ball at the cone) before the defender can react and dribble a ball to the same cone. If the attacker touches a cone before the defender reaches it, the attacker scores one point. Players then alternate roles for the next trial.

- *Extension 1.* Only the attacker has a ball. As the attacker gets close to one of the cones, the defender prevents the attacker from reaching the desired cone by placing a foot on it. The attacker then goes to the other cone to try to score.

- *Extension 2.* The attacker can score two points by dribbling across the line to the line behind the defender in addition to scoring one point for touching either cone.

- *Extension 3.* Increase the distance between the two cones to increase the physical challenge.

EQUIPMENT

One ball per student and two cones per pair of students

CRITICAL ELEMENTS AND CUES

Technique

- The keys to success in soccer are deception, ball control, and speed. Use deceptive head, body, and foot movements to throw your opponent off balance. Stand with the feet on either side of the ball and pretend to go right by dropping the right shoulder as you fake to the right side; then, push off the right foot and go to the left with the ball. Exaggerate your movements by initially faking with the head, too. *Cue:* Quick body and head movement one way, dribble in opposite direction.

- Repeat movements by faking to the left and going right in the next trial. *Cue:* Quick body and head movement one way, dribble in opposite direction.

- With the ball in front of both feet, step the right foot around the outside of the ball (so both feet are now on the same side of the ball) and use the outside of the right foot to push the ball right. Repeat with the left foot. *Cue:* Step over, then dribble that way.

COMMON ERRORS, CAUSES, AND CORRECTIONS

- The student's fakes are too complicated. *Cause:* There is too much body or foot movement. *Correction:* A slight feint (one move) that causes the defender to lean away from where the dribbler is going is usually successful.

- The student lacks ball control. *Cause:* The student imparts too much force on the ball or attempts to dribble too fast. *Correction:* Remind the student to keep the ball close to the feet using small steps.

- The student is unable to lose the defender. *Cause:* The student cannot change speed. *Correction:* Have the student move slowly in one direction and then move quickly in the opposite direction after using a body or foot feint.

TASK 6: DRIBBLING GAME (1V1)

PURPOSE

Following is the purpose of the task as related to aspects of skilled performance.

Technique: In this task, students learn to develop dribbling skills in game-like situations.

DESCRIPTION

Position two teams of four students (X's and O's) on opposite ends of the field. At each end there are four 2-yard (1.8-meter) goals. Team X students are on offense, and each team X player has a ball. The goal is to dribble the ball through any of the opponent's goals. Students score one point for a successful goal. The defender attempts to win the ball and score in one of the opposing goals. When a goal is scored or the ball goes out of play, the defender becomes the attacker. Players begin within 5 yards (4.6 meters) of one of their own team's goals (see figure). After five trials, players play a different opponent and create a team win-loss record.

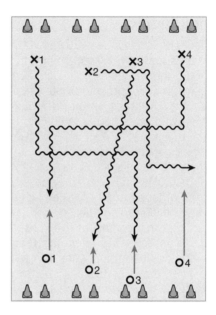

EQUIPMENT

One ball per pair of students and two cones per student

CRITICAL ELEMENTS AND CUES

Technique

- Dribble through any of the four opposing goals to score. *Cue:* Dribble toward one goal and switch to another.

- Draw the defender away from intended point of attack; for example, dribble toward the left side of the defender before accelerating into the space created on the right. *Cue:* Dribble to left of defender, change to right.

- Approach the defender slowly and then accelerate into the space. *Cue:* Dribble slow, then explode.

- Position your body between the defender and the ball. *Cue:* Guard ball with body.

COMMON ERRORS, CAUSES, AND CORRECTIONS

- The student doesn't fake with confidence. *Cause:* The student allows too little time for the fake movement to take effect or watches to see if the defender adapts to the fake. *Correction:* Have the student play defense to see that an opponent will succumb to a calm but well-timed fake.

- The dribbler does not put enough distance between self and defender. *Cause:* The student does not push the ball hard enough in the new direction away from the defender. *Correction:* Remind the student to move quickly in the opposite direction after using a body or foot feint.

TASK 7: INTRODUCTORY PASSING AND SUPPORT (2V2 + 4)

PURPOSE

Following are the purposes of the task as related to aspects of skilled performance.

- Technique: In this task, students learn the push pass in play.
- Tactic: In this task, students learn to maintain ball possession.

DESCRIPTION

Four students divided into pairs (X's and O's) represent opposing teams in a 25-yard (22.9-meter) square. Four remaining support (neutral) players are at the midpoint of each side of the square (see figure). Each team attempts to maintain possession by using the neutral players or each other to create a four-player advantage on offense (6v2). Neutral players have a maximum of three touches to play the ball back into the game. They can move along the sideline but not enter the field of play. Neutral players may pass to each other as well as to the players in the middle. The offense scores a point when it completes five consecutive passes. The defending team assumes possession when the ball is intercepted or the ball goes out of play. After five minutes, the four neutral players rotate positions with the players in the middle.

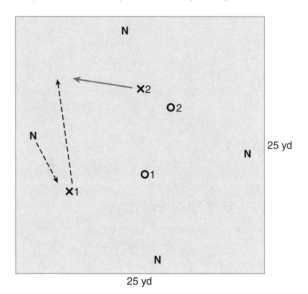

- *Extension 1.* Neutral players cannot pass to each other.
- *Extension 2.* At least one of the five passes must be between two players in the middle.

EQUIPMENT

One ball and four cones per eight students

CRITICAL ELEMENTS AND CUES

Technique

- To complete a push pass with the inside of the foot, keep the eyes on ball when passing, keep the head steady, place the nonkicking foot beside ball, rotate the kicking foot outward and contact the middle of ball (keep the ankle firm), and follow through to the target. *Cue:* Step, strike, follow through.
- Be aware of the defender's position, and use the first touch of the ball to control the ball away from the defender by keeping your body between the defender and the ball. *Cue:* Control ball into space.

Tactic

- Move the ball quickly to avoid being caught in possession. *Cue:* Quick passes.
- When in the middle, stay close enough to help the dribbler but far enough away so that a defender cannot mark both offensive players. *Cue:* Close support but not too close.

COMMON ERRORS, CAUSES, AND CORRECTIONS

- The student's pass is the incorrect speed. *Cause:* The leg swing is too large or small, or the ankle is not rigid. *Correction:* Have the student adjust the length of the back swing of the kicking foot and the rigidity of foot at contact to adjust the speed of the pass.

- The defender closes down the pass and intercepts or deflects the ball out of play. *Cause:* The pass receiver in the middle moves very close to a neutral player or teammate and allows the defender to be close to both the passer and the receiver. *Correction:* Have the receiver move toward the passer initially (2 to 3 yards [1.8 to 2.7 meters]) but then move away quickly (making a V or L cut, similar to basketball). The passer should lead the receiver into space with a pass that facilitates another pass to a neutral player.

TASK 8: SUPPORT PLAY WITH BALL AND DIRECTION (3V1)

PURPOSE

Following is the purpose of the task as related to aspects of skilled performance.

Tactic: Positioning to get open to receive a pass.

DESCRIPTION

Three attackers (X's) attempt to score by advancing and controlling the ball over the goal line (P-Q). The defender (O) attempts to intercept the ball and pass it over the other goal line (R-S). The defender cannot remain on his or her own goal line and must attempt to win possession of the ball (see figure).

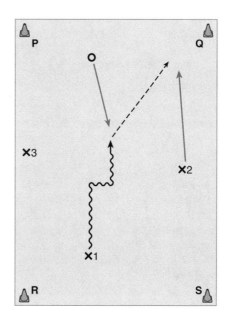

- *Extension 1.* Play the ball in only two touches (one to control and one to pass).
- *Extension 2.* Practice using the other foot to control and pass.
- *Extension 3.* Increase the distance between the passer and the receiver.
- *Extension 4.* Pass and then move with only one touch (first pass).
- *Extension 5.* Play 3v1 but without the direction component. The three offensive players score by completing six passes against the defender. The defender changes after the offense reaches the pass target or the offense makes an error (the pass is intercepted or the ball exits the playing area).

EQUIPMENT

One ball and four cones per four students

CRITICAL ELEMENTS AND CUES

Tactic

- Receivers need to position themselves in space and (if possible) closer to the goal line than the passers and defenders (no offside rules enforced). *Cue:* Find space near goal line.
- Receivers should make runs behind or to the side of the defender in space (where the passer can see them but the defender cannot). *Cue:* Run to space to sides of defender.
- Dribblers should dribble toward the goal line (P-Q), forcing the defender to commit toward the ball. *Cue:* Dribble at defender, then pass.

COMMON ERRORS, CAUSES, AND CORRECTIONS

- The defender tackles the dribbler and wins the ball. *Cause:* The dribbler delays the pass for too long or the receiver is positioned directly behind the defender and cannot be viewed or passed to by the dribbler. *Correction:* Tell the dribbler to pass the ball before the defender is close enough to tackle or to allow the receiver to uncover to collect the pass.

- The defender has time to follow the pass across to the receiver and make a tackle or interception. *Cause:* The dribbler passed the ball too early before drawing the defender toward the ball. *Correction:* Tell the dribbler to delay the pass to a receiver until the defender is committed to the dribbler in possession.

- The student's pass is inaccurate. *Cause:* The passer's shoulders are not square to the target and the kicking foot is not at 90 degrees to the target at the moment of contact. *Correction:* Have the student pass and then run 5 yards (4.6 meters) with a partner.

TASK 9: WIDTH AND ANGLE OF SUPPORT (2 + 2V2 + 2)

PURPOSE

Following is the purpose of the task as related to aspects of skilled performance.

Technique: In this task, students learn to receive with a good first touch and pass with disguise or spontaneity.

DESCRIPTION

Divide students into two teams of four students. Two players from each team start on the field. The other two players on each team take positions as wide players on the touchlines (see figure). The central players are involved in a 2v2 game but can use their wide players to help when they have possession of the ball. The wide players for each team can move up and down the touchlines and can use a maximum of two touches (one touch to control and one to pass) and they cannot score. The objective is for the central players to score by controlling the ball over the opponent's goal line (P-Q or R-S). Students can use individual techniques to evade the opponent, but they must include at least one pass to a supporting wide player before attempting to score during the team's possession. When the ball goes out of play, kick-ins are used from the side of the playing area where the ball exited the field.

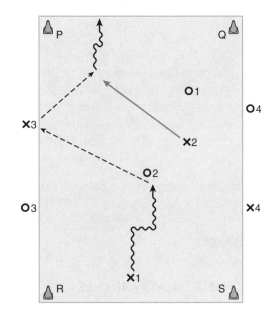

Rotate, central players with wide players every five minutes. As an extension, have wide players use only one touch to play the ball.

EQUIPMENT

One ball and four cones per eight students

CRITICAL ELEMENTS AND CUES

Technique

- Control the ball in space by ensuring that the student uses a "soft" first touch of foot, and moves the ball in the direction of next pass. *Cue:* Control ball into space for pass.
- Disguise the pass by shaping the body to pass in one direction but then passing in another direction. *Cue:* Set body in one direction, turn to pass in another.

- Pretend to kick the ball, but then hold it. This will cause the defender to react and be off balance. *Cue:* Fake pass with foot.
- Pretend to stop the ball, but allow it to run past an attacker into space. *Cue:* Receiver allows ball to roll past and into stride.

COMMON ERRORS, CAUSES, AND CORRECTIONS

- The student passes too soon. *Cause:* The pass is made before the passing angle is created. *Correction:* Have the passer fake and wait for a teammate or support player to position at an angle to the passer to allow space for the pass.
- The student passes too late. *Cause:* The defenders had time to seal off the passing angle and space. *Correction:* Have the student release the pass earlier using a better first touch on the ball to control it and pass quickly or, if possible, use a one-touch pass.

TASK 10: PASSING GAME 2 (2V1 + 1)

PURPOSE

Following is the purpose of the task as related to aspects of skilled performance.

Tactic: In this task, students learn to create space via quick passing and dribbling penetration.

DESCRIPTION

Divide four students into pairs (X's and O's) and position them on opposite sides of a 20-by-30-yard (18.3-by-27.4-meter) playing area. Teams attack 3-yard (2.7-meter) goals at either end of the area (see figure). The game begins with a kickoff. The team in possession (X) attacks with both players passing and dribbling to create a scoring opportunity. The defending team (O) must drop one of their defenders into their own goal, effectively creating a 2v1 advantage for the offense. (Note: The defender positioned in the goal is not a goalkeeper and cannot use the hands to stop the ball.) As soon as the offense loses possession, they must drop one of their players into the goal and the previous defender positioned in the goal joins the teammates on offense, creating a 2v1 overload for the new offensive team. Every time a player on the defending team wins the ball, he or she must play the ball back to the teammate defending the goal prior to mounting a counterattack. Teams score one point for every goal and every time a double pass is successfully completed between two teammates (assuming one of them has run at least 5 yards [4.6 meters] to receive the return pass).

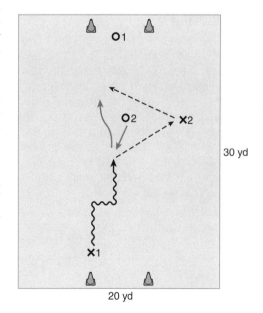

30 yd

20 yd

EQUIPMENT

One ball and four cones per four students

CRITICAL ELEMENTS AND CUES

Tactic

- The support player positions ahead of the ball and creates the option of a first-time return pass by playing the ball behind the defender. *Cue:* Support ahead and to side of dribbler.

- The dribbler draws the defender in, gives the pass, and immediately runs behind the defender for the return pass. *Cue:* Approach the defender, then give and go.
- The support player should create a good angle at which he or she can be seen by a teammate and a passing lane is available. *Cue:* See dribbler at angle through open lane.

COMMON ERRORS, CAUSES, AND CORRECTIONS

- The teammate positions alongside the passer, making the wall pass predictable. *Cause:* The defender can see both offensive players. *Correction:* Tell the support player to move slightly behind the defender's line of vision and make a late run just prior to the pass.
- The defender predicts that the dribbler will pass the ball and positions for it. *Cause:* The dribbler hinted at a pass without attempting to disguise the intention. *Correction:* Tell the dribbler to approach the defender cautiously and position the body to pass to a support player. At last moment, have the attacker dribble past the defender on the opposite side without passing and accelerate quickly past defender; this will prevent the defender from playing the pass every time.

TASK 11: 3V1 GIVE-AND-GO: WALL PASSING

PURPOSE

Following are the purposes of the task as related to aspects of skilled performance.

- Technique: In this task, students learn the wall pass.
- Tactic: In this task, students learn the give and go.
- Communication: Students learn to make eye contact.

DESCRIPTION

Place two pairs of students (X's and O's) in a 20-by-35-yard (18.3-by-32-meter) playing area. Give each pair a ball. Place five 3-yard (2.7-meter) cone gates randomly throughout the playing area. One partner must pass the ball through one of the gates to the teammate. The partner outside the gate must return the ball on the first or second touch. Then, both players travel to a different gate and repeat the process. The goal is for two players to pass the ball through as many gates as possible and receive return passes in one minute. The emphasis is on controlling the ball on the first touch and moving it in the direction of the next passing gate. Use first touch with the inside or outside of the foot to move the ball in the direction of the next gate. Encourage players to move the ball with minimum number of touches (see figure).

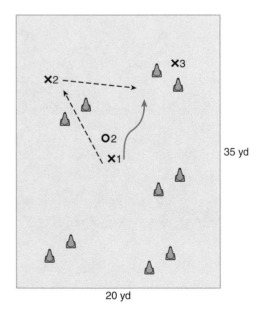

35 yd

20 yd

- *Extension 1.* Three attackers (X's) are joined by one defender (O) to create a 3v1 situation for the offense. The three attackers attempt to create give-and-go situations by dribbling the ball toward the defender and then passing the ball to a teammate and receiving a return pass while evading the defender (see figure). Players score one point for every completed give-and-go and two points when either the initial or return pass is made through one of the gates. The defender must always attack the ball.
- *Extension 2.* Decrease the playing area to ensure a better first touch and quicker feet or increase it to provide more time to pass and move.

EQUIPMENT

Two balls and 10 cones per four students

CRITICAL ELEMENTS AND CUES

Technique

- Dribble toward the defender and pass the ball when you are two paces from the defender. *Cue:* Dribble at defender, then pass.
- Pass with the inside or outside of the foot to the supporting player. (Contact the ball on the side of the foot with the toes pointing down and the ankle firm, and flick the ball with the foot.) *Cue:* Select pass in final dribble approach.

Tactic

- Run quickly into the space behind the defender after releasing the pass. *Cue:* Accelerate into space.
- The wall player aligns with the defensive player 5 yards (4.6 meters) away, which makes it difficult for the defender to react to a wall pass. *Cue:* Align to side of defender.

Communication

- Communication is essential. Make eye contact with the wall player to ensure effective combination play.

COMMON ERRORS, CAUSES, AND CORRECTIONS

- The defender intercepts the give-and-go. *Cause:* If the wall player is very close to the defender (within 2 to 3 yards [1.8 to 2.7 meters]), he or she is likely to intercept the ball. *Correction:* Have the wall players move farther away from the defender (5 yards [4.6 meters] minimum).
- The wall pass is intercepted. *Cause:* The wall player did not release the ball quickly enough. *Correction:* Remind the wall player to try to pass the ball on the first touch.
- The defender tracks the initial passer. *Cause:* The first passer did not disguise her intention or the support player was too far away allowing the defender to react to the passer's ensuing run. *Correction:* The passer should disguise the pass and then accelerate into space after passing the ball. The wall player should move closer to the passer when receiving the ball.

TASK 12: AVOIDING BEING OFFSIDE (2V2)

PURPOSE

Following is the purpose of the task as related to aspects of skilled performance.

Tactic: A 2v2 game using tactics to avoid being offside.

DESCRIPTION

Four students (in two teams) are on opposite sides of a 20-by-30-yard (18.3-by-27.4-meter) playing area. Teams attack 3-yard (2.7-meter) goals at either end of the area (see figure). Team X attacks with both players passing and dribbling to create a scoring opportunity. The defending team (O) must drop one of their defenders into their own goal, effectively creating a 2v1 advantage for the offense. Students can use individual skills to evade the opponent, but they must include at least two passes before attempting to score during their team's possession of the ball. When the ball goes out of play, kick-ins are used from the side of the playing area where the ball exited the field. Players can dribble in from their own goal lines when the ball exits the playing area there.

- *Extension 1.* The defender who is not in the goal must pressure the offense in the attacking half of the playing area, therefore potentially creating space for the offense to attempt a give-and-go play. If the offense scores from the give-and-go, the goal scores two points.

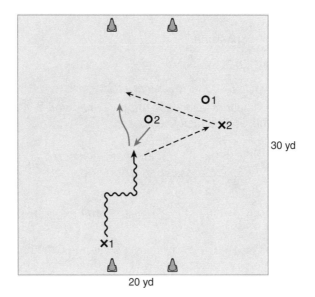

30 yd

20 yd

- *Extension 2.* Introduce the offside rule.
- *Extension 3.* The defense no longer has to drop a defender into the goal, which makes it harder for the offense to score because defenders can pressure both passer and receiver and the offside rule is in play (see figure).

EQUIPMENT

Two balls and 10 cones per four students

CRITICAL ELEMENTS AND CUES

Tactic

- A player is in an offside position if the player is closer to the opponent's goal line than both the ball and the second to last opponent at the moment the ball is passed by the teammate (and the player is involved or interfering in the play).
- A player is not offside if he or she is in his or her own defensive half of the field, level with the second last opponent, level with the last two opponents, or behind the ball.
- There is no offside on a goal kick (place kick), throw-in, or corner kick.
- When a player is judged to be offside, the opposing team is awarded an indirect free kick from the place where the infringement occurred.

COMMON ERRORS, CAUSES, AND CORRECTIONS

- The dribbler or passer delayed passing the ball, which resulted in the player being in an offside position. *Cause:* The receiver moved into the offside position. *Correction:* Tell the passer to release the pass earlier.
- The give-and-go tactic resulted in the player being in an offside position. *Cause:* The initial passer raced past the last defender and anticipated a return pass before the ball was played. *Correction:* Tell the passer to run past the defender as (or even just after) the ball is played. The wall player should pass the ball on first touch to facilitate the process.

TASK 13: OVERLAP TO SHOOT (4V2 + 2)

PURPOSE

Following are the purposes of the task as related to aspects of skilled performance.

- Tactic: Students learn to overlap to create a shooting opportunity.
- Communication: Students learn to talk to teammates.

DESCRIPTION

Divide eight students into two teams (X's and O's) and place them on opposite sides of a 25-by-40-yard (22.9-by-36.6-meter) playing area. The teams defend 8-yard (7.3-meter) goals at either end of the area (see figure). The game begins with a kickoff. The team in possession (X) attacks by passing and dribbling to create a scoring opportunity. The defending team (O) must drop two of their defenders into their own goal, creating a two-player advantage for the offense (4v2). (Note: The defenders positioned in the goal are not goalkeepers and cannot use their hands to stop the ball). As soon as the offense loses possession, they must drop two of their players into the goal. The previous defenders join their teammates on offense, creating a 4v2 overload for the new offensive team. Every time a player on the defending team wins the ball, that player must play it back to one of the two teammates defending the goal prior to mounting a counterattack. Once one of the players defending the goal receives the pass back, that player must immediately pass to one the teammates ahead. Both players who were defending the goal should prepare to make forward runs from behind the ball into a space in front of the teammates on the outside and look to receive a pass and then shoot (see figure). Shots must travel into the goal below the height of the cones (18 inches [45.7 centimeters]).

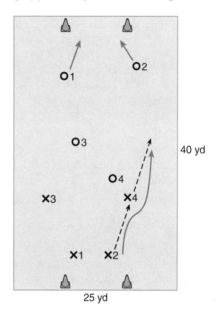

EQUIPMENT

One ball and four cones per eight students

CRITICAL ELEMENTS AND CUES

Tactic

- If you pass to a teammate ahead of you and move into the open space in front of that player on the outside, you have performed an overlapping run. *Cue:* Pass and run on outside of teammate.

Communication

- When making the overlapping run, communicate with the passer about when to release the pass.

COMMON ERRORS, CAUSES, AND CORRECTIONS

- The student cannot assess where the overlapping player will be. *Cause:* The student passes to where the overlapping player was positioned. *Correction:* Tell the student to pass into the space where the overlapping player will run (i.e., on the outside).
- The speed of the pass is too fast or too slow. *Cause:* The student used too much force when passing making it hard to control the ball or causing the ball to go out of play. Too little force means the overlapping student has to slow their run and come back to the ball, which permits defenders to reposition. *Correction:* Tell the student to hit the pass with force that permits the overlapping player to run on to the pass.

TASK 14: SHOOTING

PURPOSE

Following are the purposes of the task as related to aspects of skilled performance.

- Technique: In this task, students learn finishing by striking the ball at goal.
- Tactic: Students learn to place accuracy before power.

DESCRIPTION

Divide eight students into two teams (X's and O's) and place them on opposite sides of a 25-by-40-yard (22.9-by-36.6-meter) playing area. The teams defend 8-yard (7.3-meter) goals at either end of the area. The X1 or X2 player passes the ball into space for X3 and X4 to chase (see figure). The winner (X4) attempts to shoot on the goal defended by O1 and O2 while X3 puts defensive pressure on the shooter (X4). Once a shot is taken or the defender (X3) wins the ball, X3 and X4 run to the far goal and position off the field behind O3 and O4. The process is repeated from the other goal. O1 or O2 passes the ball for O3 and O4 to chase, with the winner shooting on X1 and X2's goal. Next, X1 and X2 attack X3 and X4's new goal, having received a pass from O3 or O4 as the practice rotation continues from the opposite end of the field. Initial passers and receivers for each group should be changed every five trials.

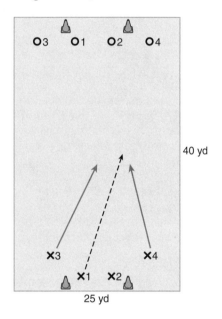

- *Extension 1.* X3 and X4 combine their efforts to score on O1 and O2's goal rather than competing against each other for a shooting opportunity.
- *Extension 2.* After the initial pass from X1, X2 plays as a defender and chases and puts pressure on X3 and X4 from behind.
- *Extension 3.* After the initial pass, X1 overlaps on the outside of either X3 or X4 to create an additional shooting option.
- *Extension 4.* Another defender (O2) is positioned in front of O1's goal and the offense (X3, X4, and X1) must outplay the additional defender and the recovering defender (X2) to create a scoring opportunity and avoid an offside infringement.

EQUIPMENT

One ball per game, poly spots to mark the field and four cones for goals.

CRITICAL ELEMENTS AND CUES

Technique: Shooting

- If you are a few yards from the goal, a push pass (inside of foot pass) or an outside of foot pass may suffice to direct the ball into the goal. *Cue:* Use a push pass.

Technique: Shooting (Drive Technique)

- Keep the eyes focused on ball (the goal does not move but the ball does). *Cue:* Look at ball.
- Step onto the nonkicking foot next to the ball. *Cue:* Step beside ball.
- Bend the knee of the kicking leg during the backswing. *Cue:* Bend leg during backswing.
- Contact the ball with the laces of the kicking foot. The ankle is extended and firm. *Cue:* Contact with laces.
- Hit the ball through the middle. *Cue:* Strike ball center.

- Lean over the ball at contact. *Cue:* Chest over ball.
- The kicking foot follows through to the target. *Cue:* Follow through.

Tactic

- If the ball is off target, it cannot go into the goal no matter how hard you strike it (unless the ball takes a deflection). *Cue:* Accuracy before power.

COMMON ERRORS, CAUSES, AND CORRECTIONS

- The student's shot misses the target. *Cause:* The student does not contact the ball at the midline. *Correction:* Tell the student to put his head down and look at the center of the ball on contact.
- The student's shot lacks power. *Cause:* The foot contacts the ball too high, forcing it into the ground. *Correction:* Tell the student to think of the ball as a clock face and strike it where the hands meet (not at 12 o'clock).
- The student hits the ball above the goal. *Cause:* The student is leaning back on contact or is hitting the ball at six o'clock. *Correction:* Tell the student to think of the ball as a clock face and strike it where the hands meet (not at six o'clock).

TASK 15: EVADING AN OPPONENT: ANGLES AND MANEUVERS (1V1)

PURPOSE

Following are the purposes of the task as related to aspects of skilled performance.

- Technique: The student learns to evade an opponent to create a scoring opportunity.
- Tactic: Students learn to change dribbling speed and protect the ball.

DESCRIPTION

Four defensive players each have a ball and are aligned behind each other at one end of the playing area in the middle of the shooting zone. Four offensive players are arranged similarly opposite them in the other shooting zone (see figure). The first defensive player (O1) passes the ball to the direct opponent (X1) and follows the pass to defend X1. The attacker (X1) attempts to evade O1 by dribbling and attempting to score (in the shooting zone) in either of the two goals. If O1 wins the ball, it can be passed through either of the attackers' goals from anywhere on the field. When a goal is made or the ball goes out of play, X1 and O1 return to their original lines. O2 begins the next round of play by passing to X2. Players complete five trials each against their opponent, and then offensive and defensive roles are switched.

EQUIPMENT

Four balls and eight cones per eight students

CRITICAL ELEMENTS AND CUES

Technique

- When dribbling, move toward the defender and change the angle of the ball's path (on the ground) by using various parts of the feet (insides, outsides, soles). Use any combination. *Cue:* Dribble to left of defender, change to right (and vice versa).

- You should be able to stop the ball and turn with the ball using the inside, outside, and soles of the feet. *Cue:* Stop and turn.
- Roll the ball forward, backward, and sideways with the soles of either foot to evade the defender. *Cue:* Stop and roll.
- Perform a step-over from the outside to the inside and use the same foot to dribble away. *Cue:* Step over, then dribble to outside.
- Perform scissors by stepping over the ball from the inside to the outside using one foot; then, use the outside of the other foot to move the ball in the opposite direction away from the defender. *Cue:* Step over, then dribble opposite way with other foot.

Tactic

- Change the dribbling speed from slow to fast as you approach to evade the defender. *Cue:* Dribble slow, then explode.
- Protect the ball from the defender by using the body to shield the ball. *Cue:* Guard ball with body
- Attacking either goal makes the dribbler's movements unpredictable creating an advantage for the dribbler and a challenge for the defender who does not know which goal the attacker is targeting. *Cue:* Dribble toward one goal and switch to another.

COMMON ERRORS, CAUSES, AND CORRECTIONS

- The defender steals the ball. *Cause:* It is easy to predict the direction the dribbler will move in. *Correction:* Tell the student to disguise the dribbling intention by faking with the head, hips, shoulders, or feet.
- The defender steals the ball. *Cause:* There is no variation in speed. *Correction:* Tell the student to accelerate quickly after the fake or to change directions (and not to wait to see if the defender bought the fake).
- The student loses control of ball while dribbling. *Cause:* The student's feet are not close to the ball. *Correction:* Tell the student to keep the ball within stride length when the defender is close.
- The student loses control of the ball while dribbling. *Cause:* The center of gravity is too high. *Correction:* Tell the student to bend the knees and turn the shoulders in the direction the ball should go.
- The student is unable to change directions. *Cause:* The kicking foot is not in front of the ball. *Correction:* Tell the student to place the kicking foot slightly in front of the ball at the last moment when traveling forward to change directions.

TASK 16: 4V4 SWITCHING POINT OF ATTACK

PURPOSE

Following is the purpose of the task as related to aspects of skilled performance.

Tactic: In this task, students learn to switch the direction of the attack to confuse the defense.

DESCRIPTION

Divide eight students into two teams (X's and O's). Teams attack opposite sides of a 30-by-40-yard (27.4-by-36.6-meter) playing area. Each team attacks two 3-yard (2.7-meter) goals positioned 2 yards (1.8 meters) from the touchline at either end of the playing area (see figure).

EQUIPMENT

One ball and eight cones per eight students

CRITICAL ELEMENTS AND CUES

Tactic

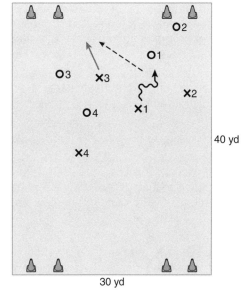

- When dribbling from a deep position, attack one goal and then cut toward the other to wrong-foot the defense. *Cue:* Dribble toward one goal and switch to another.

- When dribbling toward either goal, have support players on each side to spread out the defense to create passing lanes. *Cue:* Supporting players either side of passer.

- Creating passing lanes makes the defense think a pass is likely; the dribbler should use the opportunity for a surprise attack by taking on a defender 1v1 and shooting when close to goal. *Cue:* Dribble and shoot for surprise.

- Switch the direction of the attack when several defenders are occupying space around and closely guarding the goal. *Cue:* Dribbler passes to change point of attack.

- Switch the side of the attack to set up a teammate on the opposite side of the field who is not closely guarded. *Cue:* Cross-field pass to locate player in space.

COMMON ERRORS, CAUSES, AND CORRECTIONS

- The student dribbles instead of passing to a teammate. *Cause:* The defending team has several players close to the dribbler who are restricting the path toward the goal. *Correction:* Tell the student to pass into the space behind the defense that a teammate can run into, which creates a goal-scoring opportunity.

- The dribbler loses possession and the defensive team initiates a fast break. *Cause:* The support players failed to provide any cover behind the dribbler. *Correction:* Tell the closest player to provide support on a diagonal 8 to 10 yards (7.3 to 9.1 meters) behind the dribbler; this provides defensive cover and permits the dribbler to probe the collapsing defense and then play the ball backward on the diagonal to the support player who switches the ball to a teammate who has relocated to the space on the opposite side of the field.

TASK 17: PASSING TEMPO (3V1)

PURPOSE

Following are the purposes of the task as related to aspects of skilled performance.

- Technique: To use quick passing and control via support play.
- Tactic: The offensive players learn to deceive the defender.
- Communication: The receiver and passer communicate to create a fast attack.

DESCRIPTION

Three attackers (X's) control and pass the ball inside the 25-by-35-yard (22.9-by-32-meter) playing area. Three cones are set up in a triangle 5 yards (4.6 meters) apart (see figure). Attackers are permitted only two consecutive touches on the ball prior to passing to a teammate or trying to score by knocking down one of the cones in the triangle. No players may enter the space inside the triangle. The defender (O1) attempts to intercept the ball from the attackers in the playing area, but this can leave the triangle vulnerable to a score.

If the defender wins the ball, he or she switches with one of the attackers. If a cone is knocked down, it is re-erected; the offense continues to see how many points they can score prior to an interception. If the offense misses a cone but maintains possession, the game continues.

- *Extension 1.* Offensive players are allowed a specific number of errors (e.g., interception or ball out of the playing area) before the defender is changed, or they are given a specific amount of time (e.g., two minutes) to see how many cones they can knock over.

- *Extension 2.* Cones knocked down stay down; this makes scoring more difficult for the offense.

- *Extension 3.* Increase the size of the triangle to reduce difficulty for the offense, or reduce the size of the triangle to increase difficulty.

- *Extension 4.* Award two points for knocking a cone over and one point for passing through the triangle to a teammate without knocking a cone over.

- *Extension 5.* Combine groups (6v2) and have the offense attack either set of triangle cones across the full playing area (see figure).

- *Extension 6.* Increase the offensive challenge to five attackers versus three defenders using the entire playing area of 25-by-35-yards (22.9-by-32-meter).

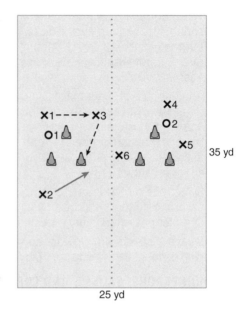

35 yd

25 yd

EQUIPMENT

One ball and three 18-inch (45.7-centimeter) cones per four students

CRITICAL ELEMENTS AND CUES

Technique

- To control the ball with the inside of the foot, move the body in line with the ball, bend the supporting leg slightly and put weight on it, and turn the receiving foot 90 degrees to present a large surface area for the ball to be cushioned in. The foot creates a closed wedge shape with the ground. *Cue:* Position to meet ball, cushion, control.

- To control the ball with the outside of the foot, place the body weight on the nonkicking foot. The ball stays on the kicking-foot side and the body leans in the direction of the approaching ball. The ball is cushioned via backward movement on contact. *Cue:* Position to meet ball, cushion, control.

Tactic

- The attacker fakes with the hips, shoulders, feet, or head before passing the ball. *Cue:* Fake pass with foot, hips, shoulders, or head.

Communication

- All players should prepare for ball at all times.
- The receiver communicates by giving directions (e.g., "out wide") to the passer.
- The passer calls the name of the target followed by *time* or *man-on*.
- With more experience, students can communicate with eye contact, pointing, or nodding.

COMMON ERRORS, CAUSES, AND CORRECTIONS

Technique

- The ball jumps up or over the foot. *Cause:* Controlling foot out in front of the body creates a slope for the ball to roll up. *Correction:* Tell the student to let the ball run under the body by creating a closed angle between the foot and the ground.
- The ball bounces away from the foot, allowing the opponent access to the ball. *Cause:* The foot is too rigid. *Correction:* Tell the student to cushion the ball by moving the foot back during contact.

Tactic

- The pass is intercepted. *Cause:* The intent of the passer is easy for the defender to read. *Correction:* Remind the student to fake with the hips, shoulders, feet, or head before passing the ball.
- The player takes too long to pass. *Cause:* The student is not looking to see where teammates or opponents are before making a pass. *Correction:* Tell the student to take a mental picture of where the opponents, teammates, and goals (cones) are before making the pass.

Communication

- The student is not prepared for the ball. *Cause:* The student is not paying attention to where the ball is located. *Correction:* Tell the student to look at the ball and follow the path of the ball.
- The receiver and passer do not communicate. *Cause:* Students are not used to communicating. *Correction:* Tell the receiver to direct the pass by telling the passer where they are (e.g., I'm wide, I'm forward), and tell the passer to name the person they're passing the ball towards.

TASK 18: CREATING SPACE: RECEIVING, OPENING UP, AND TURNING (1 + 1V1 + 1)

PURPOSE

Following are the purposes of the task as related to aspects of skilled performance.

- Technique: To learn to open up the field by playing sideways-on to the goal to create space and receive the ball under pressure by the defender.
- Tactic: Students learn movements of ball play.
- Communication: The receiver learns to call for the ball.

DESCRIPTION

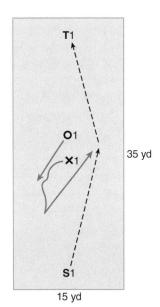

Four players are in a 15-by-35-yard (13.7-by-32-meter) playing area. Two players are servers (T1 and S1) at each end of the area. There is one defender (O1) and one attacker (X1) in the middle of the space (see figure). S1 plays the ball to X1, who scores by passing the ball to T1. If X1 is unable to create space and pass the ball to T1, X1 can pass the ball back to S1 and then receive another pass from S1 when ready. If the ball is successfully played into T1, T1 restarts the task by passing the ball to X1, who is now trying to pass the ball to S1. O1 defends X1 (always positioning behind X1) and attempts to prevent a forward pass by winning the ball or forcing the ball out of the playing area. You can use passive, active, or competitive defense with players of varying ability levels. After five trials, players rotate positions.

EQUIPMENT

One ball per four students

CRITICAL ELEMENTS AND CUES

Technique

- When the ball is close, fake with the head and shoulders to lead the opponent in one direction while turning the other way. *Cue:* Fake with head and shoulders one direction, then turn other way.
- Receive the ball with the outside of the foot reaching across the body (the weight is predominantly on the foot closest to the defender). Then, pivot on the inside foot and rotate 180 degrees, pushing the ball in the new direction with the outside of the kicking foot (reverse hook). *Cue:* Position side-on, pivot 180 degrees hooking ball with outside foot opposite way.

Tactic

- X1 can move at half speed on a 45-degree diagonal run toward the passer and if the defender follows, X1 should change direction and sprint into the space created for S1 to play the ball (see earlier figure in this task). *Cue:* If defender follows run, attacker turns and sprints to space.
- If the defender does not follow the initial movement, X1 should turn immediately and pass the ball by the defender to T1. *Cue:* Defender remains in position, attacker turns, and passes.
- X1 should try to adopt a sideways position when the ball is played toward him or her because it is easier to see the entire field (by quickly turning the head to look) and move into attacking space when standing sideways. A sideways position also enables the offensive player to shield the ball (with the body weight predominantly on the foot closest to the defender) while manipulating the ball with the outside foot. *Cue:* Position side-on to view field, protect ball, and turn.

Communication

- The receiver needs to indicate when the ball should be delivered by saying *ball*, signaling with the hand (pointing), or nodding. The passer also needs to inform the attacker whether he or she is under pressure by calling *man-on* or if the attacker is in space (without immediate defensive pressure) by shouting *turn.*

COMMON ERRORS, CAUSES, AND CORRECTIONS

- The pass is intercepted. *Cause:* The attacker runs straight toward the passer. *Correction:* Tell the student to run away from the defender at a 45-degree angle and not straight to the passer.
- The pass is intercepted. *Cause:* The attacker screens the ball with her back to the defender. *Correction:* Tell the attacker to turn her body sideways to the defender, which permits the ball to be shielded from the defender but also allows the attacker to view the entire field.
- The defender tackles the attacker. *Cause:* The attacker does not disguise the intention to turn. *Correction:* Tell the student to fake with the hips, shoulders, feet, or head before turning in the opposite direction.

TASK 19: ADVANCED TURNING AND COMBINATION PLAY (1V1 + 1)

PURPOSE

Following are the purposes of the task as related to aspects of skilled performance.

- Technique: To learn the Cruyff turn, drag-back, and high wave maneuvers to facilitate turning and passing to a target player.
- Tactic: To learn crossover movement to create space via attacker combination play.

DESCRIPTION

Divide eight students into two groups (X's and O's). Teams attack opposite sides of a 30-by-40-yard (27.4-by-36.6-meter) playing area. The two attackers (X1 and X2) in the center receive a pass from either support player (X3 and X4). They score by passing the ball (along the ground) to O3 or O4. O1 and O2 defend X1 and X2. If O1 or O2 gains possession, these players become the offense and pass the ball back to support players O3 or O4 and then look for a return pass to play the ball to X3 or X4 for a score. X1 and X2 rotate with X3 and X4 every three goals. O1 and O2 follow the same procedure with O3 and O4.

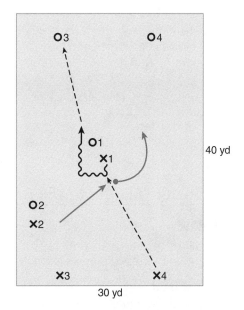

X1 and X2 look for opportunities to turn past defenders using individual skills (Cruyff turn, drag-back, high wave), or they can use combination play (give-and-go, overlap) (see figure). They can also combine for a crossover play (see figure). X1 receives a pass from X4 and screens the ball from the defender O1. X2 makes a crossing run and can either take the ball over or (as in the figure) act as a decoy for X1 to maintain possession of the ball and turn past O2 and finally pass the ball to O3.

EQUIPMENT

One ball per eight students

CRITICAL ELEMENTS AND CUES

Technique

- Cruyff turn: X1 receives the ball with the outside foot (as in task 18) and then fakes to kick the ball to the target player but wraps the foot around the ball and contacts the ball with the inside of the big toe and drags the ball back under the body, turning 180 degrees toward the plant foot and moving back across the defender in the opposite direction. *Cue:* Pull ball back with big toe part of foot.
- Drag-back: X1 receives the ball with the outside foot and then fakes to kick the ball to the target player with the same foot. The nonkicking foot (nearest the defender) is next to the ball and the sole of the outside (kicking) foot is on top of ball, and the player drags the ball back under the body and turns 180 degrees away from the plant foot. The foot will lose contact with ball as the player moves in the opposite direction. *Cue:* Pull ball back with sole of foot.
- High wave: X1 receives the ball with the outside foot, dribbles forward slowly, and waves the foot over the ball as if to perform a drag-back with the sole of foot. Instead, the player brings the foot back behind the ball and pushes the ball forward with the laces while accelerating rapidly in the same direction. *Cue:* Keep wave foot close to top of ball to disguise intent to continue dribble.

Tactic

- Crossover: X1 and X2 are defended person-to-person by O1 and O2 in the center of the field when X1 receives the ball from a support player (X4). X1 and X2 move toward each other, and O1 and O2 follow their opponent (creating space on either side of the defensive players). When X1 and X2 cross each other, X1 can either continue to dribble the ball past the teammate and opponent in the space created by drawing the defenders together or leave the ball for X2 to dribble into the space created on the other side of the defenders. Defenders (O1 and O2) are confused by this arrangement when the attackers cross movements and screen their view of the ball. *Cue:* Attackers cross pathways.

COMMON ERRORS, CAUSES, AND CORRECTIONS

- The defender tackles the attacker as the latter turns. *Cause:* The attacker does not disguise the intention to turn. *Correction:* Tell the student to fake with the hips, shoulders, feet, or head before turning in the opposite direction.

- On the crossover, the defenders react to the position of the ball and read which offensive player will possess the ball. *Cause:* The ball is not screened from defenders' vision until the two attackers cross. *Correction:* Tell the students to delay the execution of which offensive player will possess the ball until the attackers are perfectly aligned on the crossing run and the defenders' view is obscured.

TASK 20: TARGET PLAYER GAME: PENETRATION AND DEPTH (4V4)

PURPOSE

Following is the purpose of the task as related to aspects of skilled performance.

Tactic: In this task, students learn to create penetration and depth using a target.

DESCRIPTION

Divide eight students into two teams (X's and O's). Teams attack opposite sides of a 25-by-40-yard (22.9-by-36.6-meter) playing area. Each team has one offensive player positioned as a target player in the attacking zone (10 yards [9.1 meters] deep across the width of the field; see figure). Defenders and other attackers cannot enter this zone, and the target player cannot score. The objective is for the offensive team to pass the ball into their target player and then receive a lay-off pass to shoot at the goal. There is no offside rule in the game. As an extension, a single defensive player is permitted to position behind (on the goal side of) the target player in the attacking zone. The defender cannot step or move in front of the target player to intercept a pass, and the target player can now attempt to evade the defender and shoot at the goal individually or pass the ball to a supporting player for a shot at the goal.

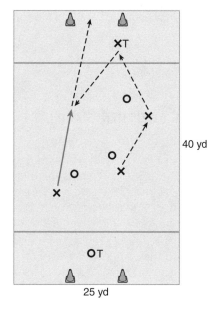

EQUIPMENT

One ball per team and poly spots to mark the field and four cones for goals

CRITICAL ELEMENTS AND CUES

Tactic

- T1 can post up in the attacking zone (like a basketball player). Having received a pass from a teammate, a rapid pass out to a support player (which is particularly effective at a 45-degree angle) can quickly provide a shooting opportunity for the supporting player. *Cue:* Quick pass to support player.
- With a defender present in the attacking zone (in the extension), T1 can execute a diagonal run toward the passer. If the defender follows, T1 should change direction and sprint into the space created by the defender's movement allowing a teammate to play the ball into the space (or T1 could pass the ball backward to a supporting player). *Cue:* If defender follows runner, turn and sprint to space.
- If the defender does not follow the initial movement, T1 can turn immediately and dribble to evade the defender or shoot past the defender at the goal. *Cue:* If defender remains in position, turn and dribble or shoot.

COMMON ERRORS, CAUSES, AND CORRECTIONS

- The target player is isolated from the teammates. *Cause:* The teammates do not move into supporting positions. *Correction:* Tell supporting players to time their runs into open space to receive a return pass from the target player.
- The target player is unable to control the pass and the ball bounces too far away from the feet. *Cause:* The cushioning foot is too rigid. *Correction:* Tell the student to relax the foot (ankle) and give with the ball on contact (like catching an egg).
- The target player does not receive a good pass. *Cause:* Inaccurate pass or passes hit with too much force. *Correction:* Tell students to pass with sympathy to the target player.

TASK 21: DEFENDING AN ATTACKER FACING AWAY FROM THE GOAL (1V1)

PURPOSE

Following is the purpose of the task as related to aspects of skilled performance.

Tactic: In this task, students learn to defend an opponent whose back is to the goal.

DESCRIPTION

Four players are positioned in a 15-by-35-yard (13.7-by-32-meter) playing area. At one end is a pseudo goalkeeper (GK) defending a 5-yard (4.6-meter) goal and at the other end is a server (S1). There is one defender (O1) and one attacker (X1) in the middle of the space (see figure). The attacker (X1) faces the server. The defender (O1) is 5 yards behind the attacker also facing the server. S1 plays the ball to XI who attempts to turn and score in the goal. O1 defends X1 (always positioning behind X1). If O1 wins the ball from X1 (which scores one point), it is returned to S1. You can use passive, active, or competitive offensive play with players of varying ability levels. After five trials, all players rotate positions.

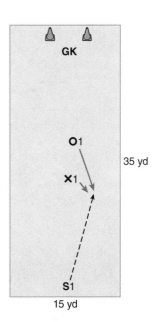

EQUIPMENT

One ball per four students, cones or poly spots and two cones for a goal

CRITICAL ELEMENTS AND CUES

Tactic

As soon as the ball is passed to X1, the defender should move to pressure the ball. Less space means less time for the offensive player. The defender achieves success in the following order of preference:

1. Attempt to intercept the ball if you are sure you can win it. *Cue:* Step in front of attacker.

2. Challenge an opponent if the first touch on the ball is poor. Tackle the ball away (often as the attacker attempts to turn with the ball). *Cue:* Tackle as opponent turns.

3. Stay within touching distance and force the offensive player to protect the ball (facing away from goal) by playing it back to S1 or out of playing area. *Cue:* Force opponent away from goal.

COMMON ERRORS, CAUSES, AND CORRECTIONS

- The attacker shoots past the defender into the goal. *Cause:* The defender is not close enough and puts little pressure on the offensive player. *Correction:* Tell the defender to position "touch tight" (i.e., closing the distance to the attacking player within actual touching distance) to make it difficult to pass or shoot.

- The attacker rolls around the defender. *Cause:* The defender is too close to the attacker and loses sight of the ball. *Correction:* Tell the student to see the ball all the way to the attacker and to position about 1 yard (0.9 meters) away until making the challenge for the ball.

- The defender allows the attacker to turn and shoot for a goal. *Cause:* The attacker disguises the intended direction of the turn. *Correction:* Tell the defender to focus on the ball and avoid watching the attacker's fakes with the hips, shoulders, feet, or head.

TASK 22: DEFENDING THE SHOT OR PASS (1V1)

PURPOSE

Following is the purpose of the task as related to aspects of skilled performance.

Technique: In this task, students learn to prevent a forward pass or shot by an attacker.

DESCRIPTION

Four players are positioned in a 15-by-35-yard (13.7-by-32-meter) playing area. At one end is a server (S1) who positions in the corner. One attacker (X1) positions in the middle at the other end of the playing area. Opposite from X1 (at the same end as S1) is a second attacker (X2). In the middle of the playing area is a defender (O1) who positions on the touchline closest to the server (see figure). S1 passes the ball to X1 who attempts to pass the ball along the ground to X2. X1 cannot pass the ball back to X2 without taking at least one touch to control the ball prior to the pass. O1 defends X1 by running quickly to the center of the playing area (into line between X1 and X2) as soon as S1 passes the ball to immediately cut off the pass by X1 to X2; then O1 moves towards X1. If O1 wins the ball (which scores one point), it is returned to S1. You can use passive, active, or competitive offensive play with players of varying ability levels. After five trials, all players rotate positions.

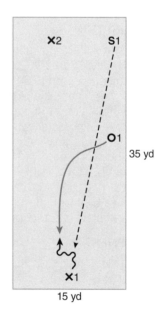

- *Extension 1.* Increase the width and length of the playing area to make the task harder for the defender (O1). More space means more time for the attacker. Reduce the space for the opposite effect.

- *Extension 2.* Convert X2 from an attacker to a goalkeeper who defends a 5-yard (4.6-meter) goal. X1 now attempts to shoot at the goal, and O1 must defend the shot.

EQUIPMENT

One ball per attacking team, poly spots for marking the field and two cones for a goal

CRITICAL ELEMENTS AND CUES

Technique

- Once in line between the passer and the receiver, O1 quickly approaches the attacker and rapidly slows the approach within 2 yards (1.8 meters) of the attacker while maintaining a balanced position. *Cue:* Approach fast, then slow down and balance.
- As the defender approaches the ball, he or she crouches, orients the body slightly sideways, and takes small, choppy steps. *Cue:* Bend knees, angle body sideways, small steps.
- The defender should force the attacker to look down at the ball as he advances towards the attacker encroaching on the attacker's position and prevents a forward pass by winning the ball or forcing the ball out of the playing area. *Cue:* Close down attacker's space.

COMMON ERRORS, CAUSES, AND CORRECTIONS

- The attacker passes past the defender. *Cause:* The defender is not in line or close enough and puts little pressure on the offensive player. *Correction:* Tell the defender to position in line between the passer and the receiver and advance on the offensive player.
- The attacker passes past the defender. *Cause:* The attacker wrong-foots the defender and has a passing lane by disguising the intention of which side of the defender he or she will pass. *Correction:* The defender should focus on the ball and avoid watching the attacker's fakes with the hips, shoulders, feet, or head that are designed to create space.
- The attacker fakes a pass and dribbles past the defender. *Cause:* The defender rushes in to win the ball. *Correction:* Tell the defender to advance quickly but cautiously and to slow down and use small steps in the last 2 to 3 yards (1.8 to 2.7 meters) of the approach.

TASK 23: SHOOTING IN THE GAME (4V4)

PURPOSE

Following are the purposes of the task as related to aspects of skilled performance.

- Technique: In this task, students learn to take opportunities to shoot during games when appropriate.
- Tactic: Students learn to focus on accuracy and not speed in shooting.

DESCRIPTION

Divide eight students into two teams (X's and O's) and position them on opposite sides of a 25-by-25-yard (22.9-by-22.9-meter) playing area. Divide the playing area into three sections with cones or poly spots positioned across the field. Each team defends a 6-yard (5.5-meter) goal at either end of the area (see figure). Each team can have only one player in the offensive section of the field and three players in the defensive section. The middle section of the field is a 5-yard (4.6-meter) neutral zone. Only the player dribbling the ball is permitted in this zone, and that player cannot be directly defended inside this zone. Every time the ball exits the playing area, pass a new ball to one of the three players in the defensive section. Players on both teams combine to shoot at opposite goals. Players score one point for a goal from a team's offensive section or the neutral zone and two points for

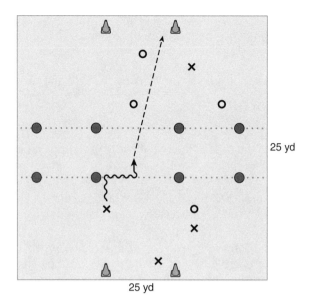

25 yd

25 yd

a goal from the defensive section. Shots must travel into the goal below the height of the cones (18 inches [45.7 centimeters]).

- *Extension 1.* Allow one player per team to enter the neutral zone to receive a pass and then shoot.
- *Extension 2.* Restrict the number of touches a player can take during the possession (one touch to control and one to pass or shoot).
- *Extension 3.* Place cones or poly spots within 1 yard (0.9 meters) of each goal post. Shots that enter the goal in the corners (within 1 yard of the post) count as double.

EQUIPMENT

One ball per student, four 18-inch (45.7-centimeter) cones, and 12 marker disks

CRITICAL ELEMENTS AND CUES

Technique

- Place the nonkicking foot next to the ball. *Cue:* Step beside ball.
- Contact the ball with the laces part of the kicking foot. The ankle is extended and firm. *Cue:* Contact with laces.
- Hit the ball through the middle. *Cue:* Strike ball center.
- Lean over the ball at contact. *Cue:* Chest over ball.
- Extend the kicking foot toward the target after contact. *Cue:* Follow through.

Tactic

- Shots should be on target, so trade speed of shot for accuracy. *Cue:* Accuracy before power.
- Take the first shooting opportunity you get. You may not get another. *Cue:* Shoot on sight.
- When shooting from an angle, try to aim toward the far side of the goal; a rebound may occur and the attacker in the offensive section may arrive to follow up and score. A miss at the near post will always end up out of play. *Cue:* Aim for the far post.
- When playing offense, challenge defenders for rebounds and look for tap-in goals in the offensive section. *Cue:* React fast.

COMMON ERRORS, CAUSES, AND CORRECTIONS

- The player does not shoot at the goal. *Cause:* The player wants a perfect shooting opportunity or lacks confidence in shooting. *Correction:* Tell the player to shoot through defenders or to immediately dribble into the neutral zone where a shot is unchallenged. Encourage players to make very few passes before shooting (provide a limit, such as two passes).

TASK 24A DEFENDING: PRESSURING AND TACKLING (1V1)

PURPOSE

Following is the purpose of the task as related to aspects of skilled performance.

Tactic: In this task, students learn to defend an opponent and win the ball.

DESCRIPTION

Four players are positioned in a 10-by-20-yard (9.1-by-18.3-meter) playing area. The server (S1) is in the corner at one end, and one attacker (X1) is in the adjacent corner. In the corner diagonally opposite the attacker is a defender (O1), who is positioned 3 yards (2.7 meters) in front of a 5-yard (4.6-meter) goal. A goalkeeper (GK) is positioned in the goal (see figure). S1 plays the ball to XI who attempts to dribble the ball into the goal defended by O1 and GK. O1 attempts to prevent X1 from dribbling into the goal by winning the ball. If O1 wins the ball (which scores one point), it is returned to S1. You can use passive, active, or competitive offensive play with players of varying ability levels. After five trials, all players rotate positions.

- *Extension 1.* Increase the width and length of the playing area to make the task harder for the defender.
- *Extension 2.* Give the offensive player the option to pass or shoot the ball into the goal.

EQUIPMENT

One ball per game, two 18-inch (45.7-centimeter) cones and disks

CRITICAL ELEMENTS AND CUES

Tactic

- The defender (O1) quickly approaches the attacker and rapidly slows the approach within 2 to 3 yards (1.8 to 2.7 meters) of the attacker while maintaining a balanced position. *Cue:* Approach fast, then slow down and balance.
- As the defender approaches the ball, he or she crouches, orients the body slightly sideways, and takes small, choppy steps. *Cue:* Bend knees, angle body sideways, small steps.
- When making a block tackle (meeting the dribbler head-on), position the foot sideways (make contact with surface of ball as in a side-foot pass). Keep the tackling foot rigid as it drives through the ball. A block tackle is usually made with the foot farthest from the ball in the defensive stance. *Cue:* Drive foot through ball.
- For a poke tackle (the dribbler is passing to the side), the nonkicking foot is slightly away from the ball and the toe of the kicking foot contacts the ball to knock it away from the opponent (ideally toward the touchline side). A poke tackle is usually made with the foot closest to the ball in the defensive stance. *Cue:* Poke ball with toe.

COMMON ERRORS, CAUSES, AND CORRECTIONS

- The attacker dribbles past the defender on the inside and proceeds directly to the goal or pushes the ball through defender's legs (nutmeg). *Cause:* The defender has not adopted a side-on position. *Correction:* The defender should shepherd the attacker toward the side of the field away from the goal. The defender's inside/front foot is slightly forward of the outside foot (no space available between legs for ball), as she backpedals the legs to keep her body between the attacker and the goal in order to escort the attacker to the side of the field away from the goal.

- The attacker dribbles past the defender. *Cause:* The defender rushes to win the ball. *Correction:* Tell the student to move more cautiously with small steps in last 2 to 3 yards (1.8 to 2.7 meters) of the approach.

- The attacker dribbles past the defender. *Cause:* The attacker wrong-foots the defender. *Correction:* Remind the defender to focus on the ball and avoid reacting to attacker fakes with the hips, shoulders, feet, or head that are designed to create space.

- The defender dives in to win the ball. *Cause:* The defender is impatient and lunges at the ball. *Correction:* Tell the student to wait for the best opportunity to win the ball and to time the tackle when the attacker has the least control of ball.

TASK 24B: 2V1 DEFENSIVE COVER

PURPOSE

Following are the purposes of the task as related to aspects of skilled performance.

- Tactic: In this task, students learn to cover a teammate who is trying to win the ball.
- Communication: Students learn to direct other players.

DESCRIPTION

A second defender (O2) now joins O1 at the side of a 10-by-35-yard (9.1-by-32-meter) playing area (see figure). S1 plays the ball to X1 who attempts to dribble the ball into the goal defended by O1 and O2. O2 will provide defensive cover for O1 if the dribbler evades the player.

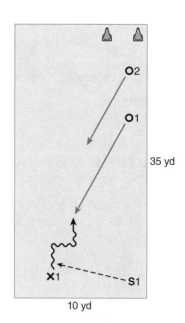

35 yd

10 yd

EQUIPMENT

One ball per game and poly spots to mark the field and two cones for the goal.

CRITICAL ELEMENTS AND CUES

Tactic

- O1 wants to force the attacker to the sideline, and O2 is providing defensive support at an angle that enables O2 to step across to the ball if O1 is evaded by the dribbler on the inside or the outside. The distance between the defenders will depend on the location on the field (if defenders are close to their own goal it will be 2 to 3 yards [1.8 to 2.7 meters], if its midfield: 5 to 6 yards [4.6 to 5.5 meters]). *Cue:* Position to cover inside and outside dribble.

- The speed of the attacker may also influence the distance between the defenders . A very fast attacker may warrant more distance between defenders. *Cue:* Quick attacker requires more space between defenders.

Communication

- The covering defender (O2) provides advice to O1 about where to funnel the attacker and how to position.

COMMON ERRORS, CAUSES, AND CORRECTIONS

- The attacker is able to evade both defenders. *Cause:* Either the covering player is too close and the attacker can evade both defenders with one maneuver, or the covering defender is too far away and the attacker can evade one defender one-on-one and then the second defender one-on-one rather than playing against two defenders. Another possible cause is a poor angle of support. *Correction:* Tell the covering defender to position at a 45-degree angle 4 to 6 yards (3.7 to 5.5 meters) on the goal side of the pressurizing defender.

TASK 25: DEFENDING PERSON TO PERSON (4V4)

PURPOSE

Following is the purpose of the task as related to aspects of skilled performance.

Tactic: Students learn team tactical defense by creating pressure and then covering and recovering.

DESCRIPTION

Divide eight students into two teams (X's and O's). Teams are positioned on opposite sides of 25-by-40-yard (22.9-by-36.6-meter) playing area. Teams defend 5-yard (4.6-meter) goals (with goalkeepers) at either end of the area (see figure). The game begins with a kickoff from the center of the field. When a team is not in possession, they are on defense and must mark (guard) an opponent (person-to-person). Goals scored (along the ground only) are worth one point, and a defender deflecting the ball over his or her goal line (for a corner) scores one point for the offensive player, but the defense retains possession for a goal kick. If a player wins possession from the other team by dispossessing an opponent with the ball via an interception or a tackle, that player scores one point. You can stop the play at any time. If the defensive team has every player within touching distance of his or her immediate opponent (when observed by the teacher at the stoppage) the defensive team scores a point.

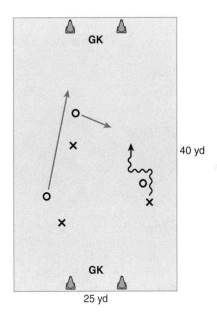

EQUIPMENT

One ball and four cones per eight students

CRITICAL ELEMENTS AND CUES

Tactic

- Defenders should mark offensive players (person-to-person) by positioning themselves between the offensive players and their own goal. The term *goal-side* is used for this tactical concept, and defensive players are usually in a better situation to win the ball from the opponent via tackles or to intercept passes from this position. *Cue:* Stay goal-side.

- The defender closest to the dribbler should be goal-side and a maximum of 2 yards (1.8 meters) from the ball. The first defender pressuring the ball should keep the opponent in front of him or her and deny the ball being passed forward or a shot at the goal. *Cue:* Position to prevent forward pass or shot.

- Defenders should adopt touch-tight positions in relation to attackers to restrict dribbling, passing, and shooting opportunities for the offense. *Cue:* When ball is in close proximity, stay touch tight to opponent.

COMMON ERRORS, CAUSES, AND CORRECTIONS

- The defender does not mark the opponent. *Cause:* The defender watches the ball and loses track of the opponent. *Correction:* Tell the defender to adopt a goal-side position from which the ball and the opponent can be seen.

- The defender does not provide cover when the dribbler evades a teammate. *Cause:* The covering defender remains with the initial opponent rather than positioning to cover the teammate. *Correction:* Tell the covering defender to rotate across and slow the dribbler without committing to the tackle (unless the covering defender is positive that the ball can be won) and to keep both the dribbler and the initial opponent in front of him or her.

- The team is permanently outnumbered when the dribbler evades the first defender. *Cause:* The first defender makes no attempt to recover to a position between the dribbler and the goal (goal-side). *Correction:* Tell the defender to recover as fast as possible on a line toward the closest goalpost to a position that is goal-side of the ball; this permits the defender to mark an opponent, cover teammates, or pressure the ball.

TASK 26: THROW-IN GAME (3 + 1V3 + 1)

PURPOSE

Following is the purpose of the task as related to aspects of skilled performance.

Technique: In this task, students learn to execute a legal throw-in during game situations.

DESCRIPTION

Divide eight students into two teams (X's and O's). Teams attack opposite sides of a 15-by-25-yard (13.7-by-22.9-meter) playing area (see figure). The team with the ball keeps it away from the opponent by throwing the ball (using a throw-in) to a teammate who then controls the ball with the foot, thigh, or chest onto the ground within 1 yard (0.9 meters) of receipt. (If the ball ricochets more than 1 yard away, this is a turnover. The defensive team gains possession, and play is restarted with a throw-in for that team.) The ball is picked up by the player who controlled it, and a throw-in is taken to pass to another teammate; or to their team's target player. Opponents may not stand directly in front of a player taking the throw-in. Students score by throwing the ball to the target player inside a 3-yard (2.7-meter) end zone that runs the width of the field. Target players can move anywhere along their respective goal lines to receive the pass in the air. It must be brought under control with the foot, thigh, or chest entirely within the end zone. No heading is permitted in the game. After the ball reaches a target player, rotate both teams' targets. The field is deliberately narrow to permit multiple throw-ins from the touchlines because the ball will inevitably roll out of play a lot.

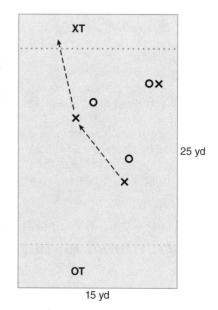

- *Extension 1.* Create a 5v3 (offense to defense) overload game if students have difficulty scoring.

- *Extension 2.* When the offense scores at one target, they immediately change direction and attempt to score at the other target.
- *Extension 3.* Throw-ins that bounce prior to reaching a teammate count as turnovers.
- *Extension 4.* Rather than having a target player, any attacker can run into the end zone to receive a throw-in from a teammate.

EQUIPMENT

One ball per eight students and four cones and multiple cones or poly spots as needed to define the field.

CRITICAL ELEMENTS AND CUES

Technique

A throw-in is awarded to the team not touching the ball last at the point where the ball goes out of play, completely over either touchline (or in this game if it is not controlled by a player within a yard of where he/she first touched the ball). A player taking a throw-in cannot touch the ball a second time until another player has contacted it. A goal cannot be scored directly from a throw-in during a game.

- The thrower must face the field. *Cue:* Face field.
- The thrower keeps part of both feet on the ground on or outside the touchline throughout the throw. *Cue:* Feet on ground.
- The thrower holds the ball with the fingers spread around the back and sides. *Cue:* Two hands.
- The thrower delivers the ball from directly behind and over the head in a continuous movement. *Cue:* Throw overhead.

COMMON ERRORS, CAUSES, AND CORRECTIONS

- The student makes a foul throw. *Cause:* The player's feet are inside the field of play over the touchline. *Correction:* Tell the student to stand behind the touchline.
- The student makes a foul throw. *Cause:* One or both of the player's feet are off the ground when releasing the ball. *Correction:* Tell the student to pretend that both feet are stuck to the ground with glue.
- The student makes a foul throw. *Cause:* The player has not delivered the ball from behind the head. *Correction:* Tell the student to throw the ball in one movement, without pausing, from a position where the ball almost touches the back of the neck.

TASK 27: AERIAL CONTROL (1V1)

PURPOSE

Following is the purpose of the task as related to aspects of skilled performance.
  Technique: In this task, students learn to control a ball that arrives in the air.

DESCRIPTION

Eight students are in pairs in a 25-yard (22.9-meter) square. In each pair, one player is a server or thrower (T1). T1s are positioned in the middle of the area. The other player in each pair is an attacker (X1); X1s are positioned approximately 10 yards (9.1 meters) away from their T1s (see figure). T1 takes a throw-in to X1 with the ball arriving in the air. X1 controls the ball on to the ground using the foot, thigh, or chest within 1 yard (0.9 meters) of where the throw-in was received and then passes the ball along the ground back to T1. After 10 trials, players rotate positions. Throwers can target a specific controlling surface (e.g., thigh) or vary the throws.

- *Extension 1.* Rather than throwing the ball directly to the partner, T1 throws it slightly to the side.

- *Extension 2.* X1 controls the ball and attempts to stop it in either corner of the side of the square with a maximum of three touches.

- *Extension 3.* T1 follows the throw-in as soon as X1 touches it and attempts to prevent X1 from controlling the ball into either corner.

- *Extension 4.* X1 can control to the corners (to score one point) or control and dribble past T1 to the opposite side of the square (to score two points).

- *Extension 5.* T1's throw-in lands midway between T1 and X1 and bounces high before reaching X1 in the air. X1 must select the controlling surface (foot, thigh, chest) and then attempt to dribble past T1 to the opposite side of the square to score.

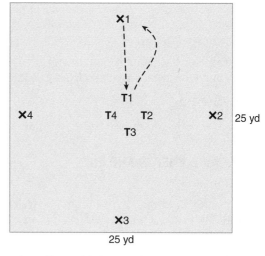

25 yd

25 yd

- *Extension 6.* X1 and T1 change positions so the throw-in is now taken from the side of the square (representing a throw-in during a game). X1 (who is now in the middle of the square) controls the ball thrown in by T1 and passes it back to T1 on the outside. X1 then moves to receive a throw-in from a different server (T2) located on the outside (as do all the other attackers in the middle).

- *Extension 7.* The receiver nominates a specific controlling surface the ball should be thrown to. You can use passive, active, or competitive defensive play with players of varying ability levels.

EQUIPMENT

One ball per pair of players, poly spots to mark the field as needed

CRITICAL ELEMENTS AND CUES

Technique

- Whether you use the foot, thigh, or chest to control the ball, use a cushioning technique and have the arms out for balance. *Cue:* Cushion ball.

- Move in line with the ball and select the controlling surface based on the speed and trajectory of the ball. *Cue:* Select control surface.

- When using the foot, lift it to meet the ball, and with the inside of the foot (or the laces), draw the foot back to the body. *Cue:* Catch ball with foot.

- When using the thigh, lean the trunk forward slightly and bend the knee of the trapping thigh to meet the ball. On contact, the thigh should relax and be withdrawn to cushion the impact, and the ball drops in front of the feet. *Cue:* Thigh gives with ball.

- When using the chest, arch the back as the ball approaches, bring the shoulders in to hollow the chest, and relax on contact so the ball drops to the feet. *Cue:* Relax chest.

COMMON ERRORS, CAUSES, AND CORRECTIONS

- The ball bounces too far away when using the feet. *Cause:* The foot is too rigid. *Correction:* Tell the student to relax the foot and ankle and give with the ball on contact (like catching an egg).

- The ball bounces off the thigh and out of playing distance. *Cause:* The ball hits the knee, the thigh muscle is flexed, or the thigh is moving forward during contact. *Correction:* Tell the student to withdraw the thigh during ball contact.

- The ball bounces too far away when using the chest. *Cause:* The chest muscles are too tight or the student is overarching the back. *Correction:* Tell the student to bend the knees and hollow the chest on contact.

TASK 28: CHIP PASS

PURPOSE

Following are the purposes of the task as related to aspects of skilled performance.

Technique: In this task, students learn to loft the ball over a defender to a target (team-mate or goal) a short distance away.

DESCRIPTION

Eight students are in a 30-yard (27.4-meter) square. One player in each pair is a passer (O); passers are positioned in a 15-yard (13.7-meter) square inside the larger square. The other player in each pair (X) is positioned across from the partner on one sideline just outside a 25-yard (22.9-meter) square (see figure). O1 chip passes the ball from inside the small square to X1 to land outside the second square but inside the third square. X1 controls the ball onto the ground using the foot, thigh, or chest and then chip passes the ball back to O1. This task is completed for a designated period of time (or 10 trials per passer).

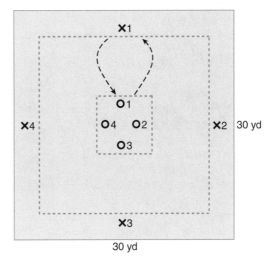

- *Extension 1.* The pair scores one point for each successful chip that goes directly into the partner's square with no bounce.

- *Extension 2.* Add a defender to the middle square for each pair of students. Students chip the ball over the defender and score one point for each pass over the defender. The defender earns a point for each intercepted pass. You should begin with passive defense and then add active, or competitive, defensive play with players of varying ability levels. The defender's position can also be varied; moving the defender closer to the passer increases the task difficulty for the passer.

EQUIPMENT

Four balls per eight students and cones or poly spots to mark squares on the field

CRITICAL ELEMENTS AND CUES

Technique

- Approach the ball straight on (use 1 to 2 steps). *Cue:* Straight approach.
- Keep the nonkicking foot about 6 inches (15.2 centimeters) from the ball. *Cue:* Supporting foot beside ball.
- Keep the head down and focus on the ball. *Cue:* Watch ball.
- Use a short backswing and bend the kicking leg at the knee. *Cue:* Bend kicking knee.
- Move the kicking foot to the ball with a stabbing action aimed at bottom of the ball; there is no follow-through. *Cue:* Stab bottom back of ball with toes.
- Use the lower laces part of the foot (toward the toes) as a wedge to punch the ball into the air and create backspin. *Cue:* Foot punches ball into air.

COMMON ERRORS, CAUSES, AND CORRECTIONS

- The ball stays low and close to the ground. *Cause:* The foot contacted the middle of the ball. *Correction:* Tell the student to strike the bottom of ball close to the ground with the lower laces part of foot near the toes.

- The ball does not follow the intended direction of the pass. *Cause:* The student struck the ball on the side. *Correction:* Tell the student to strike the ball at bottom center (six o'clock) and point the nonkicking foot at the target.

TASK 29: CHIP TO TARGETS

PURPOSE

Following are the purposes of the task as related to aspects of skilled performance.
Technique: In this task, students learn to pass the ball in the air over a short distance.

DESCRIPTION

Divide eight students into two teams (X's and O's). Teams attack opposite sides of a 25-by-50-yard (22.9-by-45.7-meter) playing area (see figure). The team with the ball keeps it away from the opponent by passing and dribbling. When the ball goes out of play over the touchlines, possession changes and the game restarts with a throw-in for the team that did not contact the ball last. Students score by chipping the ball to the target player inside a 5-yard (4.6-meter) end zone that runs the width of the field. The chip must be made from behind the restraining line that is 5 yards in front of each end zone (see dotted line in figure). Only the team's target player is permitted in the end zone, and defenders are not permitted to stand in the space between the dotted line and the end zone. Target players can move anywhere along their respective goal lines to receive a pass in the air; they must bring passes under control with the foot, thigh, or chest completely within the end zone. After the ball is chipped to a target player (to score), the passer and the target player switch positions. No heading is permitted in the game.

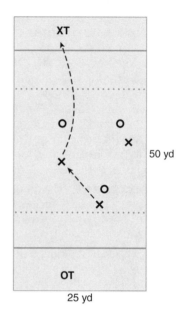

EQUIPMENT

One ball per game, poly spots to mark the field as needed

CRITICAL ELEMENTS AND CUES

Technique

- Move in line with the ball and select the controlling surface based on the speed and trajectory of the ball. *Cue:* Select control surface.
- When using the foot, lift it to meet the ball and with the inside of the foot (or the laces), draw the foot back to the body. *Cue:* Catch ball with foot.
- When using the thigh, lean the trunk forward slightly and bend the knee of the trapping thigh to meet the ball. On contact, the thigh should relax and be withdrawn to cushion the impact, and the ball drops in front of the feet. *Cue:* Thigh gives with ball.
- When using the chest, arch the back as the ball approaches, bring the shoulders in to hollow the chest, and relax on contact so the ball drops to the feet. *Cue:* Relax chest.
- Loft the ball over a defender to a target (teammate or goal) a short distance away.
  - Approach the ball straight on (use 1 to 2 steps). *Cue:* Straight approach.
  - Keep the nonkicking foot about 6 inches (15.2 centimeters) from the ball. *Cue:* Supporting foot beside ball.
  - Keep the head down and focus on the ball. *Cue:* Watch ball.
  - Use a short backswing and bend the kicking leg at the knee. *Cue:* Bend kicking knee.

- Move the kicking foot to the ball with a stabbing action aimed at bottom of the ball; there is no follow-through. *Cue:* Stab bottom back of ball with toes.
- Use the lower laces part of the foot (toward the toes) as a wedge to punch the ball into the air and create backspin. *Cue:* Foot punches ball into air.

COMMON ERRORS, CAUSES, AND CORRECTIONS

- The defender intercepts the chip pass. *Cause:* The passer is too close to the defender. *Correction:* Tell the passer to strike the ball farther back from the defender, which enables the ball to clear the defender at a less acute angle.
- The target player is unable to control the ball, or the ball lands outside the back of the end zone. *Cause:* The passer delivers the chip with low trajectory and too much force. *Correction:* Tell the player to strike the bottom of the ball close to the ground with the lower laces part of the foot (near the toes) to gain greater height and cause the ball to land softly with backspin in the end zone.

TASK 30: HEADING (DEFENSIVE)

PURPOSE

Following are the purposes of the task as related to aspects of skilled performance.

Technique: In this task, students learn to correctly head a soccer ball for passing and clearing.

DESCRIPTION

Divide a group of eight students into pairs. Pairs stand about 5 yards (4.6 meters) apart (see figure). Each student holds the arms out in front of the body and nods the head forward as if heading a ball with the forehead.

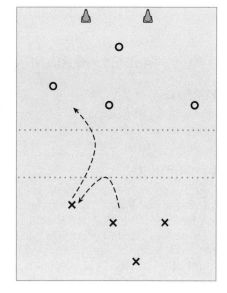

- *Extension 1.* The student holds a ball in front of the forehead and heads it out of the hands to the partner.

- *Extension 2.* The student tosses the ball about 18 inches (38.1 centimeters) above the head. As the ball descends, the student heads the ball to the partner, aiming for the partner's torso (five trials) and then the partner's feet (five trials). Players alternate after each trial.

- *Extension 3.* The student serves the ball (two-handed underarm toss) to the partner. The partner heads the ball at the server's hands, which are offered as a target. The students alternate roles after five trials.

- *Extension 4.* Students play head tennis. Divide students into two teams of four players on a 15-by-12-yard (13.7-by-11-yard) court. A 3-yard (2.7-meter) neutral zone that neither team can enter traverses the middle of the court. One teammate tosses the ball to another teammate who heads it across the neutral zone and into the opposing team's space. If the ball hits the ground before being caught or headed back by an opposing player, the team scores a point.

- Safety: In the United States, players under 11 years of age are precluded by the U.S. Youth Soccer Association from heading the ball during practices or games. For students over 11 years of age, we recommend a gentle introduction to the skill for only a few minutes before the task is changed. Use lightweight, soft-touch, trainer volleyballs for comfort and safety in the initial stages of learning. You can progress to lightweight soccer balls (sizes 3 to 4).

EQUIPMENT

One ball per pair of players and multiple cones or poly spots to designate the neutral zone

CRITICAL ELEMENTS AND CUES

Technique

- Keep the arms out in front of body. *Cue:* Pretend to row a boat.
- Watch the ball approach the forehead (contact area). *Cue:* See design on ball.
- Jerk the elbows back, snap the trunk forward, and tense the neck muscles. *Cue:* Move head like a chicken.
- Nod the head forward through the ball in the direction of the target. *Cue:* Throw eyes at ball.

COMMON ERRORS, CAUSES, AND CORRECTIONS

- The ball hits the player in the face or on top of the head. *Cause:* The player is not looking at the ball or is closing the eyes. *Correction:* Tell the student to watch the ball and strike it with the forehead (hardest and flattest part of the head).
- The header lacks power. *Cause:* The ball is striking the student. *Correction:* Remind the student to strike the ball, snap forward from the trunk to meet the ball, and keep the neck muscles rigid.
- The header lacks accuracy. *Cause:* The target is not located before heading the ball. *Correction:* Tell the student to square the shoulders in the direction of the target.
- The student misses the ball. *Cause:* The ball is not delivered exactly to where the player initially positions. *Correction:* Tell the student to adjust the position of the feet to move the body in line with ball and make the appropriate contact with the forehead.

TASK 31: HEADING (OFFENSIVE) AND GOALKEEPING

PURPOSE

Following are the purposes of the task as related to aspects of skilled performance.

Technique: In this task, students learn how to correctly head a soccer ball for a goal, and students learn to save a shot at different heights.

DESCRIPTION

Divide a group of eight students into pairs. Pairs stand anywhere in general space about 5 yards (4.6 meters) apart inside the 20-by-20-yard (18.3-by-18.3-meter) playing area. One student heads the ball and the partner positions as a goalkeeper. The goalkeeper serves the ball (two-handed underarm toss) in front of the partner. The partner heads the ball at the goalkeeper's hands, which are offered as a target 18 inches (45.7 centimeters) in front of the chest or face. Students alternate roles after five trials (see figure).

- *Extension 1.* The student heads the ball at goalkeeper's waist. Students switch roles after five trials.
- *Extension 2.* The student heads the ball at the goalkeeper's feet so it can be caught on the fly or off the bounce by the goalkeeper. Cones can be added to represent a 2-yard (1.8-meter) goal protected by the goalkeeper.
- *Extension 3.* In a 10-by-10-yard (9.1-by-9.1-meter) playing area with two 6-yard (5.5-meter) goals at either end of the area, X1 and X2 play against O1 and O2. X1 serves (tosses) the ball in front of X2 who attempts to head past students O1 and O2 into the goal being defended. O1 and O2 are both goalkeepers, and they attempt to save the ball. O1 and O2 become attackers when they gain possession of the ball, and they repeat the process. The first team to score five goals wins.

- *Extension 4.* The student serves the ball well in front of the player who is heading it so he or she must move in and jump up to head the ball (simulating the role of an incoming attacker during a game).
- *Extension 5.* Play a modified 4v4 game (see figure) in which students move the ball by throwing, heading, and catching in a 20-by-20-yard (18.3-by-18.3-meter) playing area with four 5-yard (4.6-meter) goals. A goal is scored by heading the ball into either of the opponent's goals (two points) or by heading to a teammate who catches the ball over the opponent's goal line (one point). The goalkeepers can save a header using their hands and then throw to a teammate. The ball must be transferred by sequence of throw-

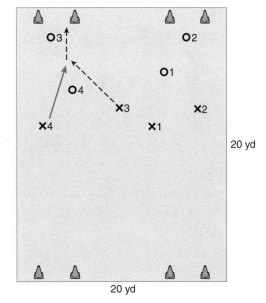

head-catch among teammates. Players may take up to three steps before passing (throwing) the ball for it to be headed. Defenders gain possession of the ball by intercepting an opponent's throw with a header, by recovering a ball that hits the ground, when the ball goes out of bounds, when the passer takes more than three steps, when a goalkeeper saves the ball, or after a goal is scored.

EQUIPMENT

One ball, multiple cones or poly spots to designate the field and eight cones to create four goals

CRITICAL ELEMENTS AND CUES

Technique: Offensive Heading

- Follow the path of ball from the beginning of its flight. *Cue:* Watch ball in flight.
- Take steps toward the ball. Bend the legs slightly as the ball arrives. *Cue:* Move to ball.
- Launch the body into the air by springing off the stronger foot and bringing the arms up and then back. *Cue:* Time jump.
- Watch the ball approach the forehead (contact area). *Cue:* See design on ball.
- Head near the top of the ball to make the ball go down. *Cues:* Head ball at 12 o'clock; punch it at target.

Technique: Goalkeeping

- Bend the knees slightly, lean the body forward, and keep the hands above the waist with the palms facing forward and the fingers upward. *Cue:* Ready position.

Shot-Stopping at Chest Height

- Position hands to form a window with the fingers pointing up and the index fingers and thumbs touching. *Cue:* Diamond-shaped window.
- Extend the arms to the ball, flex the elbows slightly, and catch with the fingers. *Cue:* Sticky fingers and palms.
- Withdraw the arms on contact and bring the ball to the chest. *Cue:* Cushion impact.

Shot-Stopping at Waist Height

- The palms of the hands face outward toward the ball. *Cue:* Palms out, pinkies touch.
- Clasp the ball to the chest as it hits the wrists and forearms. *Cue:* Cup ball into chest.

Shot-Stopping for Ground Shots

- Keep the feet close together (in case you miss the ball with the hands) and bend forward at the waist as the ball arrives. *Cue:* Stoop to collect.
- Extend the arms down with the hands behind the ball and the palms facing outward. Allow the ball to roll up the forearms. *Cue:* Cup ball into chest.

TASK 32: LONG PASSING (GROUND AND AERIAL)

PURPOSE

Following is the purpose of the task as related to aspects of skilled performance.
   Technique: In this task, students learn to pass the ball over longer distances.

DESCRIPTION

Eight players are divided into two groups (all Xs). To show the movement of the ball in the figure, players are Xs. Each group works in a 30-by-20-yard (27.4-by-18.3-meter) area. In each area, two players are the long passers X1 and X3 and the other two X2 and X4 are the supporting players (see figure). X1 plays a short give-and-go with the supporting player (X2) and delivers a long pass (20 to 25 yards [18.3 to 22.9 meters]) to X3. X3'controls the ball and plays a short pass (give-and-go) with the supporting player (X4'). X3' then plays a long return pass to X1', who controls it and plays a give-and-go with X2' as the process is repeated. After 10 long passes, X1 and X3 change positions with X2 and X4.

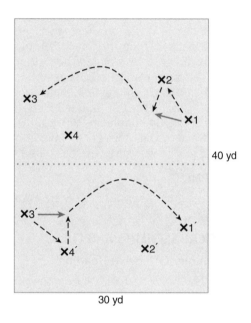

40 yd

30 yd

- *Extension 1.* The support player passes with a one-touch pass.
- *Extension 2.* The long passes are lofted into the air rather than driven along the ground.

EQUIPMENT

Two balls per eight players and multiple cones or poly spots to designate the field

CRITICAL ELEMENTS AND CUES

Technique: Low Drive

- Approach the ball from a slight angle and place the nonkicking foot to the side of the ball and fractionally behind it. *Cue:* Step beside ball.
- Swing the leg back behind the body. *Cue:* Bend leg during backswing.
- Put the head down and lean over the ball with the eyes fixed on it. *Cue:* Look at ball.
- Square the hips and shoulders to the target and hit the ball through the middle. *Cue:* Strike ball center.
- Contact the ball with the laces part of the kicking foot. The ankle is extended and firm. *Cue:* Contact with laces.
- Follow through with the kicking foot low to the passing target. *Cue:* Follow through low.

Technique: Lofted Drive

- Lean back slightly at contact. *Cue:* Lean back.

- The kicking foot contacts the lower half of the ball to make it rise. *Cue:* Strike bottom of ball.
- Swing the kicking leg up and across the body. *Cue:* Follow through high.

COMMON ERRORS, CAUSES, AND CORRECTIONS
- The student contacts the ball with the toes. *Cause:* The nonkicking foot is too far behind the ball or the kicking foot is turned up at contact. *Correction:* Tell the student to place the nonkicking foot closer alongside the ball and to point the toes down at contact.
- The pass is inaccurate. *Cause:* The ball is struck on the left or right side rather than at the center. *Correction:* Tell the student to put the head down and look at the center of the ball on contact.
- The pass is hit higher than required. *Cause:* The player is leaning back on contact, hitting the ball at the bottom part, or turning up the kicking foot. *Correction:* Tell the student to lean forward over the ball, strike the center of the ball, or point the toes toward the ground, respectively.

TASK 33: LONG PASSING TO TARGET

PURPOSE
Following is the purpose of the task as related to aspects of skilled performance.
   Tactic: In this task, students learn to deliver the ball over distance in game situations.

DESCRIPTION
Divide eight students into two teams (X's and O's). Teams attack opposite sides of a 25-by-40-yard (22.9-by-36.6-meter) playing area. The team with the ball keeps it away from the opponent by passing and dribbling. When the ball goes out of play over the touchlines, possession changes and the game restarts with a throw-in for the team that did not contact the ball last. Students score by long passing the ball to their goalkeeper's hands inside a 5-yard (4.6-meter) end zone that runs the width of the field. Initially, goalkeepers represent an offensive passing target for their respective team. The long pass may be made from anywhere on the field. Only the team's goalkeeper is permitted in the end zone. Goalkeepers can move anywhere along their respective goal lines to receive a pass. After the ball is passed (to score) to a goalkeeper, the passer and goalkeeper switch positions (see figure).

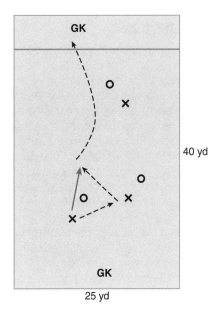

- *Extension 1.* Pass the ball to the goalkeeper in the air. Only a pass caught without bouncing will score.
- *Extension 2.* Remove the end zone, add goals and change the role of the team goalkeepers. Rather than play as a target in the opposing end zone for their team to pass towards the goalkeepers now play for their own team and defend their own team goal as they would in a conventional soccer game. A goal scored from a long pass in build up or a long shot counts double.

EQUIPMENT
One ball, multiple cones or poly spots to designate the end zones and 4 cones to create two goals

CRITICAL ELEMENTS AND CUES

Tactic

- Pass the ball long to the goalkeeper as soon as an opening exists. *Cue:* First opportunity, pass to target.
- Play short passes using give-and-go's, crossovers, and overlaps to create openings for long passes. *Cue:* Create space for long passes.

COMMON ERRORS, CAUSES, AND CORRECTIONS

- The defender intercepts the long pass. *Cause:* The passer is too close to the defender. *Correction:* Tell the passer to strike the ball farther from the defender, which will enable the ball to clear the defender at a less acute angle.
- The goalkeeper is unable to save the ball, or the ball lands outside the back of the end zone. *Cause:* The passer delivers an inaccurate long pass, or the pass has too much force. *Correction:* Tell the passer to strike the bottom middle of the ball close to the ground.

TASK 34: THREE-CHANNEL GAME: WIDTH, DEPTH, AND PENETRATION (4V4 OR 5V5)

PURPOSE

Following is the purpose of the task as related to aspects of skilled performance.
    Tactic: In this task, students learn to develop width, depth, and penetration.

DESCRIPTION

Divide 8 to 10 students into two teams (X's and O's). Teams attack opposite sides of a 25-by-40-yard (22.9-by-36.6-meter) playing area. Each team has a goalkeeper. If playing 4v4, teams nominate one player as a "rush" goalkeeper who leaves the goal and plays on the field to support their team when they are on offense (in possession of the ball). If playing 5v5 the goalkeeper remains in goal during offensive and defensive situations. The team with the ball keeps it away from their opponents by passing and dribbling and scores in the opponent's goal. The field is divided into three 8-yard (7.3-meter) channels that run the length of the pitch. Three players on each team operate in their own 1v1 zones (see figure). One player from each team (PO or PX) is the playmaker (could be the goalkeeper in 4v4). When the playmaker's team is on offense, this player is the only one allowed to move from zone to zone. The game is played for 4 to 5 two-minute periods. Players rotate from zone to zone, to the goalkeeper position, and/or the playmaker role every two minutes.

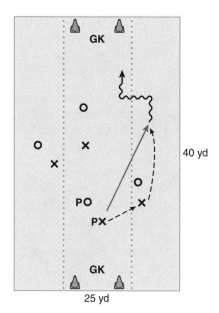

EQUIPMENT

One ball, multiple cones or poly spots to designate the field channels/zones and 4 cones to create two goals

CRITICAL ELEMENTS AND CUES

Tactic

- The playmaker should try to create a 2v1 situation by supporting a teammate in one of the zones. *Cue:* Playing zones permit numerical overload.

- Offensive players have the opportunity to take on an opponent 1v1 because covering defenders cannot leave their respective zones. *Cue:* Playing zones encourage 1v1 situations.

- Players will spread out across the width of the field and not be congested around the ball because of the specific zones that they must function in during the game. Space is available for dribbling against an opponent or passing to a teammate. *Cue:* Playing zones facilitate width and dribbling at opponent.

- Use a longer diagonal pass hit into space behind a defender for an offensive player to chase from the middle channel to either side channel or from one side channel to the opposite one. *Cue:* Hit diagonal passes over distance.

COMMON ERRORS, CAUSES, AND CORRECTIONS

- The dribbler loses the ball to the defender. *Cause:* The playmaker passed the ball to the teammate but did not support the teammate in that channel. *Correction:* Tell the playmaker to try to provide offensive penetration (past teammate) or depth (behind teammate) to receive a return pass in the channel to help the teammate evade the defender by creating a 2v1 offensive passing advantage.

- The offense lacks creativity when in possession. *Cause:* Students do not utilize offensive tactics to evade defenders with a numerical player advantage in the channel. *Correction:* Tell players to employ give-and-go, crossover, or overlap tactics to evade the defender and create scoring opportunities.

TASK 35: APPLICATION GAMES

PURPOSE

Following are the purposes of the task as related to aspects of skilled performance.

- Technique: In this task, students apply learned skills in game-like situations.

- Tactic: Students apply learned tactical elements in game-like situations.

- Communication: Students apply communication requirements in game-like situations.

DESCRIPTION

- **1v1 games.** These are soccer's most basic equation. Students are introduced to the basics of playing small-sided games in level 1. Technique and the ability to judge space and read intentions are crucial at this initial stage. There is a focus on the customs and traditions of playing the game; such as giving the ball back after a player deflects the ball out of play. There is also a focus is on dribbling and evasion skills. The 1v1 game requires a passive, moving on to active and then competitive defense. The players will likely experience some game stress because they either evade an opponent or are unsuccessful in the attempt.

- **2v2 games.** In these games, players learn that teamwork begins with two students. By working with teammates, they learn to share responsibilities and are dependent on each other on offense. They are constantly involved with the ball or in assisting the player with it. Players learn when to attack an opponent and when to keep possession. Different skills can be applied to these games to work on offensive maneuvers to get open. Students can score in a variety of ways: (a) attacking an end line, (b) maintaining possession for a number of passes, (c) passing to a target, or (d) scoring in a goal.

- **Moving from 2v2 to 4v4 games.** Games with staggered numbers that create overload situations (more offensive than defensive players or vice versa) can help students move from 2v2 to 4v4 games (e.g., 2v2 + 4, 2v1 + 1, 3v1, 2 + 2v2 + 2, 4v2 + 2, 4v3 + 1). Players learn that larger numbers on offense can be advantageous. Conditions and rules can also be modified to facilitate this numerical overload (e.g., a restricted number of touches of the ball results in a quick passing tempo, which creates scoring openings). Players recognize the value of having three players on offense (in a 3v1 application task). A triangle guarantees there is an open space somewhere in the game and enables players to potentially send the ball to the most open offensive player. Defensive principles are also emphasized in games with defensive player overload during level 2, including pressurizing an opponent, tackling, defending the pass or shot, and defensive cover.

- **4v4 games.** The 4v4 modified game is the initial manifestation of the adult game. Four offensive principles (support, penetration, width, and depth) and four defensive principles (engagement, depth, contraction, and expansion) provide a learning context for the eight tactical principles of the adult game. A ground game is initially emphasized in this unit to simplify play. An aerial game is added at level 3 once players have mastered skills and tactics on the ground. Various game conditions are employed in specific application games to facilitate player development around these principles. For example, the following four conditions may be employed in application games to develop the offensive principles mentioned previously:

  1. *Support.* Three consecutive passes must be made prior to a goal attempt.
  2. *Penetration.* Players must attempt to evade an opponent with a dribbling skill prior to passing, or the shot or final pass must be over 10 yards (9.1 meters) before reaching the target.
  3. *Width.* The ball must be switched from a 5-yard (4.6-meter) channel running along the flank of the field to the equivalent channel on the opposite side prior to a goal attempt.
  4. *Depth.* A shot at the goal cannot be attempted unless the previous pass was backward.

  The 4v4 (or 5v5 if you include goalkeepers toward the end of level 3) is the concluding game of the advanced level in our approach.

EQUIPMENT
One ball per game

CRITICAL ELEMENTS AND CUES
Apply all the previous skills and tactical cues.

COMMON ERRORS, CAUSES, AND CORRECTIONS
Look for all previously discussed errors and provide corrections.

Chapter 7

Flag Football

American football is a popular sport in U.S. culture, and its popularity is beginning to spread across the world. It is important for students to understand this sport so they can become participants and informed spectators. Flag football is an alternative to the more violent tackle football. Boys and girls can participate in flag football through youth leagues, and the sport has been used in physical education curricula for years to teach fundamentals of football. One criticism of how flag football is taught in schools is that large teams are often used in game play; this results in a few students dominating play and most students not being actively engaged, which results in low moderate to vigorous physical activity (MVPA). Our approach to flag football aims to increase learning through active participation and MVPA by using small-sided games (5v5 is the largest game). Although this chapter uses flags instead of tackling, this material could also be used in a touch football unit (with minor modifications to a couple of tasks) if flags are not available.

OUR PEDAGOGICAL APPROACH TO FLAG FOOTBALL

Flag football uses many of the basic techniques of American football. Instruction in the elementary and secondary units focuses on developing skillful performance and game sense through tasks and instructional sequences that teach flag football skills and quickly using these skills in modified games.

The basic offensive techniques are ball carrying, centering, passing, catching, and route running. The shape of a football makes throwing and catching it a challenge to beginning learners; therefore, early learning experiences focus on the running game and introduce the techniques of passing and catching. Once the techniques of passing and catching are developed, the passing game is incorporated. The basic defensive techniques are flag pulling (as part of the running game), person-to-person defensive movement, and zone defense principles (when the passing game is introduced).

Levels 1 and 2 focus on the running and passing games, respectively, and the two are combined in level 3. Overload games (e.g., 3v1, 3v2) are used to emphasize particular offensive or defensive elements such as ball carrying, pass reception, pass routes, and defensive principles. Overload games increase student engagement and allow for greater student success as they apply the learned techniques.

We use the PAC progression when adding defensive pressure: *passive* defense stands still or walks and does not interfere with the play, *active* defense runs but does not interfere, and *competitive* defense interrupts the play.

Modifications to Address Individual Needs of Students

For students with disabilities, appropriate modifications to activities depend on the nature of the disability. To modify flag football instruction for students with visual impairments, you can (a) place stripes of brightly colored floor tape on the football to create high contrast, (b) use brightly colored floor tape or caution tape to mark off boundaries, (c) use physical guidance to demonstrate plays and show positioning prior to the game, and (d) use tactile modeling (i.e., demonstration by touch rather than sight) to demonstrate the proper form for various skills (e.g., throwing, catching). Some positions in football require more modifications to include individuals with visual impairments (e.g., quarterback), but others might not require any (e.g., center).

For students with autism spectrum disorder, teach each role or activity in isolation prior to its use in a game-like environment. Because children with autism spectrum disorder tend to be more successful in quieter, less chaotic environments, you may want to have students play on smaller teams before introducing full-sided games. You can also modify game rules, such as making a rule that each student must score a touchdown before a team wins.

To accommodate individuals who use wheelchairs, flag football needs to be played on a hard surface (e.g., gymnasium, outdoor basketball court). Other than this, students who use wheelchairs should be able to fully participate in games of flag football with traditional rules. Rather than placing flags around the waist, attach them to the vertical supports of the wheelchair behind the student's back.

For individuals with cerebral palsy, a larger football may make catching easier, but this can also make it more difficult for students to throw the ball. Determine whether to use the larger ball based on the student's position (e.g., quarterback, receiver). Because students with cerebral palsy can have limited mobility, include a rule that the defense must give the offense a 3-yard (2.7-meter) cushion when attempting to make a reception. After the reception, defenders can pull the receiver's flag.

Organization

A full-sided game of flag football varies in size from 5 (U.S. Flag Football Association) to 8 (International Federation of American Football) players per team. While it is not uncommon for flag football to be played with teams of more than five in a school setting, we limit the size of the teams to no more than five. We feel that this allows the basic character of football, which involves running and receiving the ball, to be met. When the running game is the focus, we advocate the use of teams of no more than three. When pass routes are introduced, the team size moves up to a maximum of five.

Space

We recommend that you teach flag football outdoors. A full-sized football field is preferred, but if one is not available you can use a large, open space that can accommodate multiple fields. The number of fields needed in a physical education class depends on class size and field space available. Multiples of 10 determine the number of fields needed for game-play if all students are engaged at the same time; if your space cannot accommodate this, set it up so the maximum number of games can be played. While a full field is needed for game play, most of the tasks in this unit do not require a full field. If you have your class divided into sport education teams or groups, you need a field for every two teams with each team doing their tasks on an opposite end of the field. Because kicking is not a part of our game, goal posts are not needed.

Equipment Needed

While footballs come in a variety of size classifications it is important to have a variety of football sizes available for students so they can practice passing and receiving techniques using footballs that are appropriately scaled to their hands. If a football is too large for a student's hand it will have a negative impact on that student's performance. Footballs are also made from a variety of materials such as leather, synthetics, and rubber, and there are also soft and grip balls; have a variety of these on hand to meet the needs of students. There should be one ball for every two students to accommodate tasks involving pairs. Flags and belts are also needed. The type of flag and belts used are a choice of the teacher but one flag and belt set is needed for each student.

CONTENT MAP STRUCTURE

Figure 7.1 is a combined content map that illustrates the flow and connectedness of all the tasks used to develop flag football techniques and tactics. It is divided into three levels, and each level has a separate content map that includes the application games used to refine the techniques and tactics for that level. Although passing and receiving are introduced in level 1 (figure 7.2), the primary focus is on the running game, and it ends with an application game that focuses on the run. In level 2 (figure 7.3), snapping, pass routes, and defense are added, and the end game is a 3v3 passing game. In level 3 (figure 7.4), more pass routes are included and further refinement of defensive tactics and passing and receiving are stressed. This level ends with a 5v5 game that uses all the offensive components.

In the content maps, we have numbered the tasks. These numbers are used to cross reference tasks' descriptions in the body of the chapter with the content maps. The task numbers should not be interpreted as the order in which they should be taught. It is important that tasks are taught and progressed from simpler to more complex forms, which is shown in the upward progress of the task sequence on the content map. This is particularly necessary before tasks are combined. For instance in flag football whether you teach defensive flag pulling first or running with the ball, the progressions of both need to be taught before they are combined in task 4.

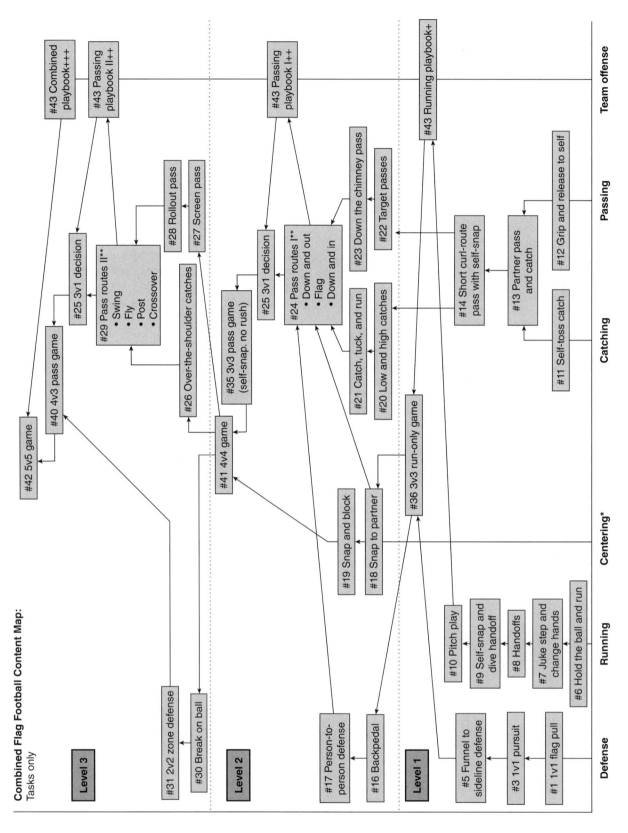

Figure 7.1 Combined content map for flag football.

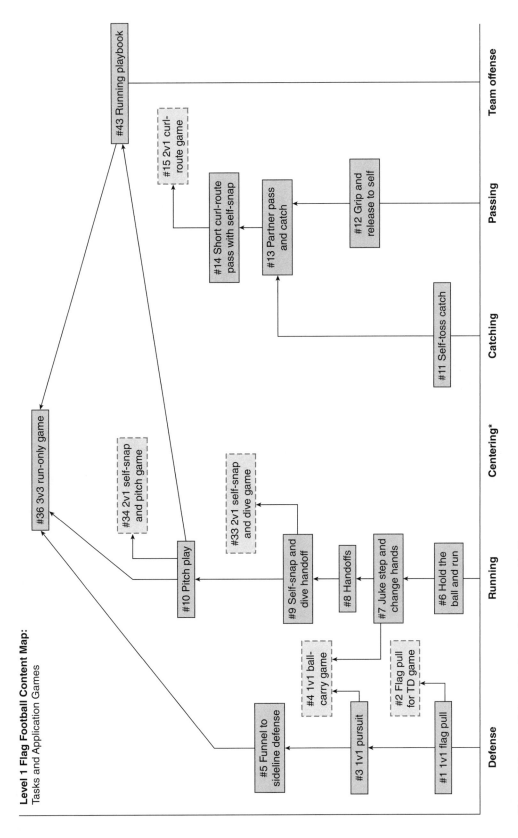

Level 1 Flag Football Content Map:
Tasks and Application Games

Figure 7.2 Level 1 content map for flag football.

171

172

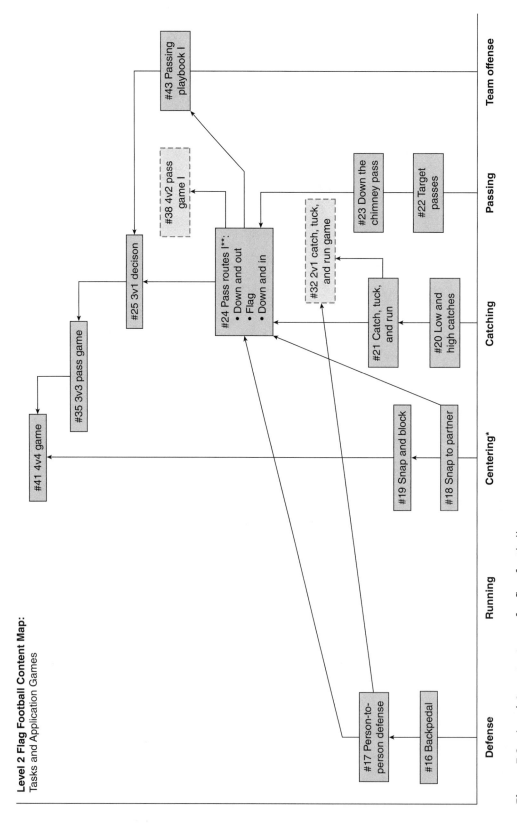

Figure 7.3 Level 2 content map for flag football.

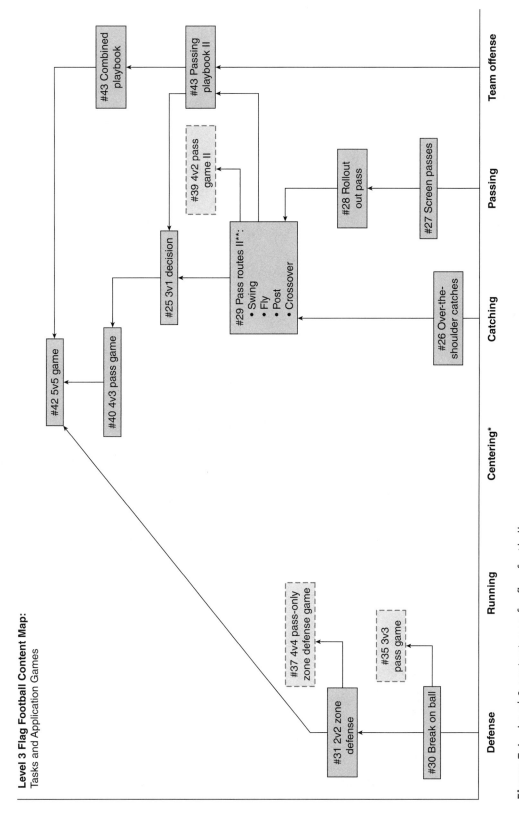

Level 3 Flag Football Content Map:
Tasks and Application Games

Figure 7.4 Level 3 content map for flag football.

173

STRUCTURE OF THE LESSONS

The following is a sample daily lesson structure for a 50-minute secondary flag football lesson.

Warm-up (5 to 6 minutes)

Application game: 2v1 self-snap and dive game (5 minutes)

Informing task: short curl route with self-snap (5 minutes)

Extension task: short curl route with self-snap (from other side) (3 minutes)

Extension task: passive defense added to the 2v1 self-snap and dive game (3 minutes)

Extension task: active defense added to the 2v1 self-snap and dive game (3 minutes)

Informing task: pitch play (to right side) (6 minutes)

Extension task: defender moves to active defense against the pitch play (3 minutes)

Extension task: defender moves toward running back during the pitch play (3 minutes)

Extension task: defender choice during the pitch play (3 minutes)

Application game: 2v1 pass game (5 minutes)

Closure (1 to 2 minutes)

Warm-up

Elementary School

The warm-up should be taught to students on the first or second day of the unit. If a skill used in the warm-up has not been taught, it should not be included in the warm-up circuit until the day after you teach it. The warm-up includes four components: passing, catching, flag pulling, and handing off. In the first lesson, passing, catching, and flag pulling are introduced; on the second day, you can include those three techniques in the warm-up. Handoffs are introduced in the third lesson, so you can include this in the warm-up on the fourth day.

For passing and catching, partners stand approximately 10 feet (3 meters) apart and pass the ball back and forth. For flag pulling, students are divided into two groups that attempt to pull each other's flags. Once all the flags of one team have been pulled, the flags are returned and play begins again. For handing off, students stand two steps behind their partners, who each have a ball. The student with the ball executes a self-snap and hands off the ball to the partner, who is moving forward. After the handoff, the partners change positions. The warm-up time should allow for multiple trials. Once students have learned the warm-up, it should not last more than 5 to 6 minutes.

How you organize your students for the warm-up will depend on the decisions you make about the organization of the class. If you use a circuit, divide the class into three groups and include the appropriate equipment at each of the stations (see figure 7.5). The passing and catching station and the handoff station require footballs for each pair of students, and the flag-pulling station requires flags and flag belts for each student. Students should begin each day in the same area and rotate through the stations. If you decide to have the whole class do the warm-up tasks together, you need to have footballs for every pair of students and flags and flag belts for each student. You can determine the order in which the tasks are done.

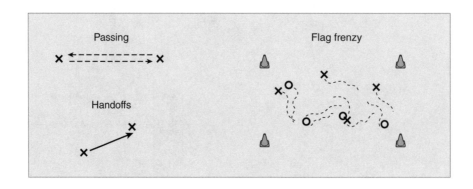

Figure 7.5 Sample elementary school warm-up circuit for flag football.

Secondary School

This warm-up can begin right when students enter the gym or after roll call and introductory messages. The secondary warm-up involves passing and catching, snapping, flag pulling, and defensive movement. For passing and catching, partners pass the ball back and forth. As they gain expertise, they can pass to a moving target. To do this, the partners stand next to each other. One partner jogs forward while the other partner passes the ball to the jogger. After the pass, the partners switch roles. For snapping, partners snap the ball back and forth to each other. For flag pulling, students are divided into two groups that attempt to pull each other's flags. For defensive movement, set up a 10-yard (9.1-meter) square and have students line up on one side and face out. Students then move around the square using backpedaling, forward running, and sideways shuffling.

The warm-up can be done with stations or in teams. If you use stations, divide the class into four groups (or combine teams into four larger groups) and have each group spend about 90 seconds at each station before rotating to the next one (see figure 7.6). The warm-up continues until students have completed each station. If the warm-up is done within teams, you will need enough footballs for each pair of students and flags and belts for each student within each team.

When warming up within teams, each team will stay in their team area and will do each warm-up task there. Teams spend 60 to 90 seconds on each warm-up task.

BLOCK PLAN

The introductory block plan is designed for beginners. In elementary school, it should not be introduced earlier than fourth grade. This allows students to refine their basic throwing and catching techniques in other activities prior to facing the challenges of throwing and catching a football. Although longer units are always preferred, we recognize that there are time limitations at the elementary level; therefore, the elementary unit is five days for the initial grade level in which it is taught.

The secondary block plan follows the elementary block plan and is designed for students in middle school and high school. It assumes that students were taught the basic flag football skills at the elementary level. If this is not the case, follow the introductory block plan. Because middle and high school physical education programs have different requirements, these units should *not* be taught in fewer than 10 days. These units are adjusted for 10-, 15-, and 20-day programs, although we recommend units of 20 or more days.

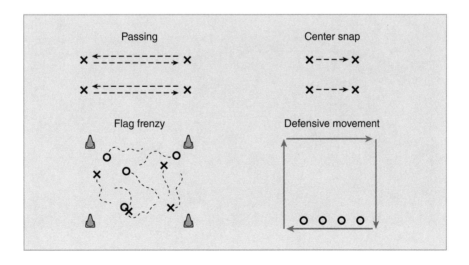

Figure 7.6 Sample secondary school warm-up circuit for flag football.

Table 7.1 Elementary Flag Football Block Plan: Five-Day Unit

This is an example of a beginning block plan for elementary students that uses the flag football tasks shown in the level 1 content map. It is based on an initial five-day unit and, as such, it does not encompass all of the level 1 tasks on the content map. You can use this as a template for developing an appropriate block plan for beginning students. If you are teaching a longer unit, you can include the remaining level 1 and some level 2 tasks.

Lesson 1	Lesson 2	Lesson 3	Lesson 4	Lesson 5

Warm-up
• Nonspecific warm-up
	Warm-up
	• Circuit
	  • Passing
	  • Catching
	  • Flag pulling
		Warm-up
		• Circuit
		  • Passing
		  • Catching
		  • Flag pulling
		  • Handing off
			Warm-up
			• Same as day 3
				Warm-up
				• Same as day 3

Introductory application game None	**Introductory application game** • **(2)** Flag pull for touchdown game	**Introductory application game** • **(4)** 1v1 ball-carry game	**Introductory application game** • **(33)** 2v1 self-snap and dive game	**Introductory application game** • **(15)** 2v1 curl-route game
Content development • **(11)** Self-toss catch • **(12)** Grip and release to self • **(13)** Partner pass and catch • **(1)** 1v1 flag pull	**Content development** • **(6)** Hold the ball and run • **(7)** Juke step and change hands	**Content development** • **(8)** Handoffs • **(9)** Self-snap and dive handoff	**Content development** • Review previous tasks as determined by teacher • **(14)** Short curl route pass with self-snap	**Content development** • Review previous tasks as determined by teacher • **(10)** Pitch play
Closing application game • **(2)** Flag pull for touchdown game	**Closing application game** • **(4)** 1v1 ball-carry game	**Closing application game** • **(33)** 2v1 self-snap and dive game	**Closing application game** • **(15)** 2v1 curl-route game	**Closing application game** • **(34)** 2v1 self-snap and pitch game

Table 7.2 Secondary Flag Football Block Plans: 10-, 15-, and 20-Day Units

This block plan incorporates 10-, 15-, and 20-day units. The last two days of the 10-day block plan, the last three days of the 15-day block plan, and the last five days of the 20-day block plan are game days, which are described at the end of the block plan. The first eight days of the block plan are the same for all units.

Lesson 1 of all block plans	Lesson 2 of all block plans	Lesson 3 of all block plans	Lesson 4 of all block plans	Lesson 5 of all block plans
Warm-up • Nonspecific warm-up (e.g., movements for agility and stretching)	**Warm-up** • Teach the warm-up	**Warm-up** • Teach the warm-up	**Warm-up** • Passing • Catching • Snapping • Flag pulling • Handing off	**Warm up** • Same as day 4
Introductory application game None	**Introductory application game** • **(2)** Flag pull for touchdown game	**Introductory application game** • **(4)** 1v1 ball-carry game	**Introductory application game** • **(33)** 2v1 self-snap and dive game	**Introductory application game** • **(15)** 2v1 curl-route game
Content development • **(11)** Self-toss catch • **(12)** Grip and release to self • **(13)** Partner pass and catch • **(1)** 1v1 flag pull	**Content development** • **(6)** Hold the ball and run • **(7)** Juke step and change hands • **(8)** Handoffs	**Content development** • **(9)** Self-snap and dive handoff • **(5)** Funnel to sideline defense • **(18)** Snap to partner	**Content development** • **(14)** Short curl-route pass with self-snap • **(10)** Pitch play (to right)	**Content development** • **(10)** Pitch play (to left) • **(34)** 2v1 self-snap and pitch game
Closing application game • **(2)** Flag pull for touchdown game	**Closing application game** • **(4)** 1v1 ball-carry game	**Closing application game** • **(33)** 2v1 self-snap and dive game	**Closing application game** • **(15)** 2v1 curl-route game	**Closing application game** • **(36)** 3v3 run-only game
Lesson 6 of all block plans	**Lesson 7 of all block plans**	**Lesson 8 of all block plans (last instructional day of 10-day plan)**	**Lesson 9 of 15- and 20-day block plans (See table 7.3 for lesson 9 for 10-day plan.)**	**Lesson 10 of 15- and 20-day block plans (See table 7.3 for lesson 10 for 10-day plan.)**
Warm-up • Same as day 4	**Warm-up** • Same as day 4	**Warm-up** • Same as day 4	**Warm-up** • Same as day 4	**Warm-up** • Same as day 4
Introductory application game • **(36)** 3v3 run-only game	**Introductory application game** • **(32)** 2v1 catch, tuck, and run game	**Introductory application game** • **(32)** 2v1 catch, tuck, and run game	**Introductory application game** • **(38)** 4v2 pass game I	**Introductory application game** **(38)** 4v2 pass game I
Content development • **(16)** Backpedal • **(17)** Person-to-person defense • **(20)** Low and high catches • **(21)** Catch, tuck, and run	**Content development** • **(19)** Snap and block • **(22)** Target passes • **(23)** Down the chimney pass	**Content development** • **(24)** Pass routes I	**Content development** • **(24)** Pass routes I	**Content development** • Review all pass routes • **(25)** 3v1 decision
Closing application game • **(32)** 2v1 catch, tuck, and run game	**Closing application game** • **(32)** 2v1 catch, tuck, and run game	**Closing application game** • **(38)** 4v2 pass game I	**Closing application game** • **(38)** 4v2 pass game I	**Closing application game** • **(35)** 3v3 pass game

(continued)

Lesson 11 of 15- and 20-day block plans	Lesson 12 of 15- and 20-day block plans (last instructional day of 15-day plan)	Lesson 13 of 20-day block plan (See table 7.4 for lesson 13 for 15-day plan.)	Lesson 14 of 20-day block plan (See table 7.4 for lesson 14 for 15-day plan.)	Lesson 15 of 20-day block plan (See table 7.4 for lesson 15 for 15-day plan.)
Warm-up • Same as day 4	**Warm-up** • Same as day 4	**Warm-up** • Same as day 4	**Warm-up** • Same as day 4	**Warm-up** • Same as day 4
Introductory application game • **(35)** 3v3 pass game	**Introductory application game** • **(41)** 4v4 game	**Introductory application game** • **(35)** 3v3 pass game	**Introductory application game** • **(39)** 4v2 pass game II	**Introductory application game** • **(37)** 4v4 pass-only zone defense game
Content development • **(26)** Over-the-shoulder catches • **(27)** Screen passes	**Content development** • **(28)** Rollout pass • **(29)** Pass routes II (fly, crossover)	**Content development** • **(29)** Pass routes II (swing, post) • **(30)** Break on ball	**Content development** • **(25)** 3v1 decision • **(31)** 2v2 zone defense • Passing Playbook design and practice	**Content development** • Review techniques as needed • **(40)** 4v3 pass game • Passing Playbook design and practice
Closing application game • **(41)** 4v4 game	**Closing application game** • **(35)** 3v3 pass game	**Closing application game** • **(39)** 4v2 pass game II	**Closing application game** • **(37)** 4v4 pass-only zone defense game	**Closing application game** • **(42)** 5v5 game

Lesson 16 of 20-day block plan	Lesson 17 of 20-day block plan	Lesson 18 of 20-day block plan	Lesson 19 of 20-day block plan	Lesson 20 of 20-day block plan
Warm-up • Same as day 4	**Warm-up** • Same as day 4	**Warm-up** • Same as day 4	**Warm-up** • Same as day 4	**Warm-up** • Same as day 4
Fixed-time 5v5 games against different opponents (nonexclusionary round-robin tournament) Encourage the use of specific skills. Award an extra point to the score for demonstration of these skills. We recommend at least two games per lesson.	**Fixed-time 5v5 games against different opponents (nonexclusionary round-robin tournament)** Encourage the use of specific skills. Award an extra point to the score for demonstration of these skills. We recommend at least two games per lesson.	**Fixed-time 5v5 games against different opponents (nonexclusionary round-robin tournament)** Encourage the use of specific skills. Award an extra point to the score for demonstration of these skills. We recommend at least two games per lesson.	**Fixed-time 5v5 games against different opponents (nonexclusionary round-robin tournament)** Encourage the use of specific skills. Award an extra point to the score for demonstration of these skills. We recommend at least two games per lesson.	**Fixed-time 5v5 games against different opponents (nonexclusionary round-robin tournament)** Encourage the use of specific skills. Award an extra point to the score for demonstration of these skills. We recommend at least two games per lesson.

Table 7.3 10-Day Block Plan Game Days

Lesson 9 of 10-day block plan	Lesson 10 of 10-day block plan
Warm-up • Same as day 4	**Warm-up** • Same as day 4
Fixed-time 4v4 games (include running and passing) against different opponents (nonexclusionary round-robin tournament) Encourage the use of specific skills. Award an extra point to the score for demonstration of these skills. We recommend at least two games per lesson.	**Fixed-time 4v4 games (include running and passing) against different opponents (nonexclusionary round-robin tournament)** Encourage the use of specific skills. Award an extra point to the score for demonstration of these skills. We recommend at least two games per lesson.

Table 7.4 15-Day Block Plan Game Days

Lesson 13 of 15-day block plan	Lesson 14 of 15-day block plan	Lesson 15 of 15-day block plan
Warm-up • Same as day 4	**Warm-up** • Same as day 4	**Warm-up** • Same as day 4
Fixed-time 4v4 games (include running and passing) against different opponents (nonexclusionary round-robin tournament) Encourage the use of specific skills. Award an extra point to the score for demonstration of these skills. We recommend at least two games per lesson.	**Fixed-time 4v4 games (include running and passing) against different opponents (nonexclusionary round-robin tournament)** Encourage the use of specific skills. Award an extra point to the score for demonstration of these skills. We recommend at least two games per lesson.	**Fixed-time 4v4 games (include running and passing) against different opponents (nonexclusionary round-robin tournament)** Encourage the use of specific skills. Award an extra point to the score for demonstration of these skills. We recommend at least two games per lesson.

SHAPE AMERICA'S GRADE-LEVEL OUTCOMES FOR K-12 PHYSICAL EDUCATION

In table 7.5, we identify key outcomes for flag football for 4th through 8th grade. These are linked to specific tasks on the content maps that are appropriate for teaching the skill and assessing the outcome.

Table 7.5 Grade-Level Outcomes for Flag Football

Outcome	Description	Content map focus and tasks
S1.E14.4a	Throws overhand using a mature pattern in nondynamic environments (closed skills).	Level 1, task 13
S1.E14.4b	Throws overhand to a partner or at a target with accuracy at a reasonable distance.	Level 1, task 13
S1.E15.4	Throws to a moving partner with reasonable accuracy in a nondynamic environment (closed skills).	Level 1, task 14
S1.E15.5a	Throws with accuracy, both partners moving.	Level 3, task 30
S1.E15.5b	Throws with reasonable accuracy in dynamic, small-sided practice tasks.	Level 2, task 3
S1.E16.4	Catches a thrown ball above the head, at chest or waist level, and below the waist using a mature pattern in a nondynamic environment (closed skills).	Level 2, task 20
S1.E16.5c	Catches with reasonable accuracy in dynamic, small-sided practice tasks.	Level 2, task 37
S1.E26.4	Combines traveling with the manipulative skills of dribbling, throwing, catching and striking in teacher- and/or student-designed small-sided practice-task environments.	Level 2, task 24 Level 3, task 29
S2.M1.6	Creates open space by using locomotor movements (e.g., walking, running, jumping & landing) in combination with movement (e.g., varying pathways; change of speed, direction or pace).	Level 2, tasks 24, 40 Level 3, tasks 29, 39
S2.M1.7	Reduces open space by using locomotor movements (e.g., walking, running, jumping & landing, changing size and shape of body) in combination with movement concepts (e.g., reducing the angle in the space, reducing distance between player and goal).	Level 2, task 17

(continued)

Grade-Level Outcomes for Flag Football *(continued)*

Outcome	Description	Content map focus and tasks
S2.M1.8	Opens and closes space during small-sided game play by combining locomotor movements with movement concepts.	Level 3, tasks 30-31
S2.M2.7	Executes at least 2 of the following offensive tactics to create open space: uses a variety of passes, pivots and fakes; give & go.	Level 2, task 41 Level 3, task 42
S2.M3.6	Creates open space by using the width and length of the field/court on offense.	Levels 2 and 3, task 43
S2.M4.7	Reduces open space on defense by staying close to the opponent as he/she nears the goal.	Level 2, task 17 Level 3, task 30
S2.M4.8	Reduces open space on defense by staying on the goal side of the offensive player and reducing the distance to him/her (third-party perspective).	Level 2, tasks 17, 35, 41 Level 3, tasks 30, 40, 42
S2.M5.7	Reduces open space by not allowing the catch (denial) or anticipating the speed of the object and person for the purpose of interception or deflection.	Level 2, task 17 Level 3, task 30
S2.M5.8	Reduces open space by not allowing the catch (denial) and anticipating the speed of the object and person for the purpose of interception or deflection.	Level 2, tasks 17, 35, 41 Level 3, tasks 30, 40, 42

TASK 1: 1V1 FLAG PULL

PURPOSE

Following are the purposes of the task as related to aspects of skilled performance.

- Technique: In this task, students learn how to properly pull a flag.
- Fair play: Students hand back the flag after pulling it and holding it in the air.
- Communication: Students hold the flag up after pulling it to indicate that it has been pulled.

DESCRIPTION

Have students pair up and stand about 5 yards (4.6 meters) apart. One student is the offensive runner and the other is the defensive puller. The students walk toward each other and the defensive student pulls the flag of the offensive student as the latter walks past. The defensive student raises the flag into the air and then hands it back to the offensive student. Students switch roles and repeat the task. Students perform the task for a designated time. If students need motivation, award one point for each successful pull.

- *Extension 1.* Have the offensive student use the nondominant hand to pull the flag.
- *Extension 2.* Have the two students jog toward each other.

EQUIPMENT

Flag belts and flags for each student

CRITICAL ELEMENTS AND CUES

Technique

- Look at the flag you intend to pull. *Cue:* Eyes on flag.
- Reach out with the arm without bending too much at the waist. *Cue:* Reach, don't lean.
- Pull the flag down and raise it overhead. *Cue:* Pull and raise.

Fair Play

- Hand the flag back to the offensive student after raising it.

Communication

- Raise the flag to indicate that the offensive student is down.

COMMON ERRORS, CAUSES, AND CORRECTIONS

- The students misses the flag when reaching for it. *Cause:* The student is not looking at the flag. *Correction:* Have the offensive student stand still while the defender approaches and pulls the flag.
- The student does not raise the flag after pulling it. *Cause:* The student forgets that it needs to be raised. *Correction:* Remind the defensive student to stop and raise the flag high so the play will stop and to indicate where the next play will begin.

TASK 2: FLAG PULL FOR TOUCHDOWN GAME

PURPOSE

Following are the purposes of the task as related to aspects of skilled performance.

- Technique: In this task, students apply the flag-pulling technique in a game setting.
- Tactic: Offensive students attempt to run past the defenders.
- Fair play: Students hand back the flag after pulling it and holding it in the air.
- Communication: Students hold the flag up in the air after pulling it.

DESCRIPTION

Divide students into two teams (offense and defense) of no more than six students. The offense stands between two cones 30 yards (27.4 meters) in front of an end zone that is designated by two cones. The defense stands about 15 yards (13.7 meters) in front of the offense. On the teacher's signal, the offensive students attempt to jog toward the goal line to score a touchdown while the defenders attempt to pull their flags. Offensive students are encouraged not to try to juke the defenders but rather to jog past them. Once the students either get the flag pulled or cross the goal line and score a touchdown, the pulled flags are returned. The offensive students then reverse the direction and repeat the task. If students need motivation, award one point for each flag pulled and one point for each touchdown. As an extension, have students run as they attempt to score.

EQUIPMENT

Flag belts and flags for each student and 4 cones per six students

CRITICAL ELEMENTS AND CUES

Technique

- Look at the flag you intend to pull. *Cue:* Eyes on flag.
- Reach out with the arm without bending too much at the waist. *Cue:* Reach, don't lean.
- Pull the flag down and raise it overhead. *Cue:* Pull and raise.

Tactic

- Move straight toward the goal line and do not to juke to evade the defenders.

Fair Play

- Hand the flag back to the offensive student after raising it.
- Move only straight forward on offense.

Communication

- Raise the flag to indicate that the offensive student is down.

COMMON ERRORS, CAUSES, AND CORRECTIONS

- Two or more defenders attempt to pull the same offensive student's flag. *Cause:* Defenders are not working together. *Correction:* Have each defender line up across from an offensive student and attempt to pull only that student's flag.

TASK 3: 1V1 PURSUIT

PURPOSE

Following are the purposes of the task as related to aspects of skilled performance.

- Technique: In this task, students learn to pull the flag of a student who is moving away from them.
- Fair play: Students hand back the flag after pulling it and holding it in the air.
- Communication: Students hold the flag up after pulling it.

DESCRIPTION

Pair students and designate one student in each pair as the offense and the other as the defense. The offensive student stands at a line indicated by a cone and the defensive student starts at a cone 3 to 4 yards (2.7 to 3.7 meters) behind the offensive student. On your signal, the offensive student slowly walks away from the defender while the defender quickly walks toward the offensive student in an attempt to pull the flag. Once the flag is pulled and raised, the flag is returned and the students reverse roles.

- *Extension 1.* Have the defender pull the flag with the nondominant hand.
- *Extension 2.* Have students move from a walk to a jog and then to a controlled run.

EQUIPMENT

Flag belts and flags for each student and two cones

CRITICAL ELEMENTS AND CUES

Technique

- Look at the flag you intend to pull. *Cue:* Eyes on flag.
- When you are approaching the offensive student from the rear, keep the flag-pulling side of your body behind the flag. *Cue:* Arm to hip.
- Lean forward slightly with the upper body when reaching for the flag. *Cue:* Reach and lean.
- Pull the flag down and raise it overhead. *Cue:* Pull and raise.

Fair Play

- Hand the flag back to the offensive student after the student stops moving.

Communication

- Hold the flag overhead to indicate that it has been pulled.

COMMON ERRORS, CAUSES, AND CORRECTIONS

- The defender's legs contact the offensive student's legs. *Cause:* The defender is approaching the middle of the offensive student's back. *Correction:* Have the students slow down, and stress the need for the defender to approach to the side of the offensive student.
- The defender loses balance when reaching for the flag. *Cause:* The defender reaches for the flag before he or she is in range to pull it. *Correction:* Have the students slow down so the defenders can get a feel for how close they need to be to pull the flag.

TASK 4: 1V1 BALL-CARRY GAME

PURPOSE

Following are the purposes of the task as related to aspects of skilled performance.

- Technique: In this task, students learn to pull the flag of a student who is carrying the ball.
- Agility: The offensive student uses a juke step to avoid the defender. The defender must react quickly to the movement.
- Fair play: Students hand back the flag after play stops.
- Communication: Students hold the flag up after pulling it.

DESCRIPTION

This task is set up like task 2 except the offensive student carries a football. The offensive student begins at a line marked by two cones set 40 yards (36.6 meters) from the goal line also marked by two cones, and the defender is 15 yards (13.7 meters) in front of the offensive student. On your signal, the offensive student jogs toward the goal line and is allowed to use a juke step to avoid the defender. The defender can pursue the offensive student to the goal line. After the attempt, the students turn and repeat the task toward the other goal. After four trials, the students reverse roles. If students need motivation, award one point for each flag that is pulled and one point for each touchdown. As an extension, have students move from a jog to a controlled run and then to a sprint.

EQUIPMENT

One football per pair of students, flag belts and flags for each student, and four cones

CRITICAL ELEMENTS AND CUES

Technique

- Look at the flag you intend to pull. *Cue:* Eyes on flag.
- When you are approaching the offensive student from the rear, keep the flag-pulling side of your body behind the flag. *Cue:* Arm to hip.
- Lean forward slightly with the upper body when reaching for the flag. *Cue:* Reach and lean.
- Pull the flag down and raise it overhead. *Cue:* Pull and raise.

Fair Play

- Hand the flag back to the offensive student after the student stops moving.

Communication

- Hold the flag overhead to indicate that it has been pulled.

COMMON ERRORS, CAUSES, AND CORRECTIONS

- The defender's legs contact the offensive student's legs. *Cause:* The defender is approaching the middle of the offensive student's back. *Correction:* Have the students slow down, and stress the need for the defender to approach to the side of the offensive student.
- The defender loses balance when reaching for the flag. *Cause:* The defender reaches for the flag before he or she is in range to pull it. *Correction:* Have the students slow down so the defenders can get a feel for how close they need to be to pull the flag.

TASK 5: FUNNEL TO SIDELINE DEFENSE

PURPOSE

Following are the purposes of the task as related to aspects of skilled performance.

- Technique: In this task, students learn to position themselves on defense so a ball carrier moves toward the sideline.
- Tactic: Students use the sideline to limit the number of options the ball carrier has when running.

DESCRIPTION

Create a sideline using a chalk line or cones. Approximately 5 yards (4.6 meters) from the sideline, set up stations of two cones that are 20 yards (18.3 meters) apart (see figure). Place students in pairs, and have 2 to 3 pairs work at each station. One pair stands back-to-back between the two cones facing the cones. The other pairs stand to the side and wait in two lines: ball carriers and defenders.

One student holds a ball and the other student is the defender. On your signal, the two students run in opposite directions and circle the cones they are facing. Then the two students run toward each other at a controlled speed. The defender tries to funnel the ball carrier toward the sideline (the ball carrier allows this) and keep the ball carrier from moving toward the middle of the field. Once the ball carrier makes it past the opposite cone, the two students return to the side, switch roles, and take their places in the appropriate lines. The next pair in line then steps into the middle of the two cones and repeats the task. As an extension, have the ball carrier try to avoid the defender's intent, and have the defender try to pull the ball carrier's flag. Once the flag is pulled or the ball carrier gets past the defender, the task ends and the two students return to the waiting line. If students need motivation, award one point to the defender for funneling the ball carrier and pulling the flag and one point to the ball carrier for successfully avoiding the defender.

EQUIPMENT

One football, flag belts, and flags for each student; two cones per station and cones or chalk to indicate the sideline

CRITICAL ELEMENTS AND CUES

Technique

- Approach the ball carrier on at the inside shoulder to funnel the player toward the sideline. *Cue:* Inside shoulder.
- When approaching the ball carrier, slow down slightly until the ball carrier moves toward the sideline. *Cue:* Approach under control.

Tactic

- Use the sideline as an extra defender by funneling the ball carrier toward the sideline. This makes it easier to pull the flag by limiting the space the ball carrier has to move in.

COMMON ERRORS, CAUSES, AND CORRECTIONS

- The ball carrier moves toward the center of the field. *Cause:* The defender is moving toward the center of the ball carrier's body or the outside shoulder, or the defender approaches the ball carrier too fast. *Correction:* Tell the defender to slow down to judge the approach that should be made.

TASK 6: HOLD THE BALL AND RUN

PURPOSE

Following is the purpose of the task as related to aspects of skilled performance.
  Technique: In this task, students learn how to hold a football while running.

DESCRIPTION

Students stand on a line marked by two cones and hold a football in the dominant hand. On your signal, students run to a line marked by two cones 20 yards (18.3 meters) away. Repeat this several times. As an extension, have students hold the ball in the nondominant hand.

EQUIPMENT

One football per student and four cones

CRITICAL ELEMENTS AND CUES

Technique

- To hold a football we use the acronym REEF that stands for Rib cage, Elbow, Eagle Claw and Forearm. *Cue:* REEF (see figure)
    - Tuck the ball into the rib cage. *Cue:* Rib cage
    - Tuck the elbow in. *Cue:* Elbow
    - Spread the fingers over the point of the ball. *Cue:* Eagle claw
    - Cover the ball with the forearm. *Cue:* Forearm

COMMON ERRORS, CAUSES, AND CORRECTIONS

The ball moves away from the body as the student runs. *Cause:* The student is not holding the ball firmly against the body. *Correction:* Have the student slow down and concentrate on holding the ball in tight.

TASK 7: JUKE STEP AND CHANGE HANDS

PURPOSE

Following are the purposes of the task as related to aspects of skilled performance.

- Technique: In this task, students learn to quickly change directions when running with the ball (to avoid the defense) and to change the hand holding the ball.
- Tactic: Students protect the ball from the defender and make it harder for the defender to pull the flag.
- Agility: Students take quick side steps.

DESCRIPTION

Pair students and give one student in each pair a ball and have them stand at the cone. The other student (defender) stands at a cone set 5 yards (4.6 meters) in front of the offensive student. The offensive student jogs toward the defender, who is standing still, and executes a juke step while switching the ball to the other hand (away from the defender). The student continues to run to a line 5 yards away. Once there, the student turns and, on the teacher's signal, repeats the task. After a set number of trials, the two students switch roles.

- *Extension 1.* Have the offensive student do the juke step with the nondominant foot.
- *Extension 2.* Have the defender walk toward the offensive student instead of standing still.

EQUIPMENT

One football and two cones per pair of students

CRITICAL ELEMENTS AND CUES

Technique

- Move the ball to the side away from the defender when executing the juke step. *Cue:* SOAP (switch outside arm position).

Tactic

- Use this move when you are trying to avoid a defender.

Agility

- Place the plant foot (the foot on the side you are running to) to the side and push off it as you step in the other direction. *Cue:* Plant and cut.

COMMON ERRORS, CAUSES, AND CORRECTIONS

The student does not change the ball position when executing the juke. *Cause:* The student is going too fast and forgets. *Correction:* Tell the student to slow down.

TASK 8: HANDOFFS

PURPOSE

Following is the purpose of the task as related to aspects of skilled performance.

Technique: In this task, students learn how to receive a handoff for a dive play.

DESCRIPTION

Place students in groups of three. Two students stand in a line, and the third student stands 5 yards (4.6 meters) away and faces them. The student at the front of the two-student line is the ball carrier, and the third student is the receiver. The ball carrier slowly approaches toward the left of the receiver and hands off the ball to the right (see figure). The receiver stands with arms ready to receive the handoff (see figure). When the ball carrier reaches the receiver, he or she places the ball into the opening created by the receiver. When the receiver feels the ball in the opening, the student closes the arms around the ball and moves toward the opposite student and hands the ball off to that student. Students practice handing off and receiving handoffs for a set number of trials. *Note:* Ideally this should be done in groups of three, but use the smallest group size possible depending on the number of footballs available. If students need motivation, have students see how many successful handoffs their group can do in a row.

- *Extension 1.* Have the students handoff to the opposite side.
- *Extension 2.* Move students back a few yards and have both students move toward each other to complete the handoff.

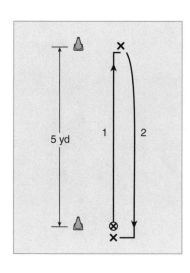

EQUIPMENT

One football and two cones per three students

CRITICAL ELEMENTS AND CUES

Technique

- Use two hands to place the ball into the receiver's arms. *Cue:* Two hands.
- When you receive the ball, the elbow closest to the handoff is up with the forearm across the chest. The other arm is about 1 foot (0.3 meters) below and parallel. *Cue:* Shark's mouth.
- When the ball is placed into this pocket, close a hand around each end of the football and hold it there as you move forward. *Cue:* Shut the shark's mouth.

COMMON ERRORS, CAUSES, AND CORRECTIONS

- The ball carrier cannot easily place the ball in the receiver's arms. *Cause:* The inside elbow is down. *Correction:* Remind the receiver to keep the inside elbow up.
- The ball is dropped during the handoff. *Cause:* The receiver is reaching out to receive the ball. *Correction:* Make sure the receiver stands with the arms in the proper position.
- The ball is dropped during the handoff. *Cause:* The receiver does not close the hands around the ball. *Correction:* Have the ball carrier slow down to allow the receiver time to close the hands around the ball.

TASK 9: SELF-SNAP AND DIVE HANDOFF

PURPOSE

Following are the purposes of the task as related to aspects of skilled performance.

- Technique: In this task, students learn to make a quarterback handoff to a running back and to receive that handoff on a dive play.
- Tactic: Students use this play to run straight at a defense, especially if only a few yards are needed for a first down or the defense's attention is on the receivers.
- Agility: Students use quick sideways steps to avoid the defense.
- Communication: The quarterback signals the beginning of the play with a verbal cue (e.g., *hut, hike*).

DESCRIPTION

Place students into pairs. One student in each pair is the quarterback (QB) and the other is the running back (RB). The RB lines up 2 to 3 yards (1.8 to 2.7 meters) behind the QB, who has the ball. The QB calls *hike* and turns to the left to hand the ball off to the RB, who is moving forward to receive the handoff. Once the RB receives the handoff, the RB runs forward 15 yards (13.7 meters) as if running for a touchdown (see figure). The two then exchange roles. This drill can be performed a number of times down the field (if this method is used, set up markers every 15 yards). Once students are comfortable receiving the ball from the right side, repeat the task from the left side. As an extension, add a single passive defender who stands 5 yards (4.6 meters) in front of the QB; this forces the RB to cut around the defender.

15 yd

2-3 yd

EQUIPMENT

One football and cones set up every 15 yards (length of field will determine number of cones needed) per pair of students

CRITICAL ELEMENTS AND CUES

Technique: Handing Off

- Hold the back half of the ball with two hands. *Cue:* Two hands.
- At the snap, take a short step to the side with the foot that is on the side the RB is approaching, and then step across with the opposite foot. *Cue:* Pivot and step across.
- Place the ball between the RB's arms. *Cue:* Place the ball.

Technique: Receiving the Handoff

- Keep the elbow closest to the handoff up and the forearm across the chest. The other arm is about 1 foot (0.3 meters) below and parallel. *Cue:* Shark's mouth.

- When the ball is placed into this pocket, close a hand around each end of the football and hold it there as you move forward. *Cue:* Shut the shark's mouth.

Tactic
- Use this play if only a few yards are needed for a first down or a touchdown (if running for a short touchdown is allowed).
- Use this play when the defenders are expecting a pass and the defense's focus is on the receivers.

Agility
- Use a juke step to evade the defender.

Communication
- Decide on a verbal cue to signal the start of the play (e.g., *hike*).

COMMON ERRORS, CAUSES, AND CORRECTIONS
- The handoff is not successful. *Cause:* The RB has the inside elbow down instead of up, which blocks the opening. *Correction:* Have the RB approach the QB with the inside elbow up and the outside hand in position.
- The RB reaches for the ball with both hands. *Cause:* The RB is anxious to get the ball and is not comfortable with the ball being placed against the body. *Correction:* Have the RB stand with the arms in position; then, have the QB repeatedly place the ball into the opening with the RB holding it tight each time.

TASK 10: PITCH PLAY

PURPOSE
Following are the purposes of the task as related to aspects of skilled performance.
- Technique: In this task, students learn how to execute a pitch play.
- Tactic: Offensive students use the pitch play to spread out the defenders by running the ball wide of the line of scrimmage (LOS). The QB reacts to the defensive pressure when deciding whether to toss the ball to the RB or keep it.
- Communication: The QB signals the beginning of the play with a verbal cue (e.g., *hike*).

DESCRIPTION
This play is done in a 2v1 formation: the QB and RB against a single defender. The QB and RB line up in a stacked position and the defender is wide left (the defender's left) just beyond the LOS. Cones are placed to indicate the LOS, where the QB starts, where the RB starts, where the RB must run, and where the QB must run (see figure). After calling *hike,* the QB and the RB run to the right toward their respective cones. The defender is passive and walks toward the QB, who then underhand tosses the ball to the RB. The RB cuts up field after passing the cone. After the play, students switch positions: defender to QB, QB to RB, and RB to defender if there are more than 3 students in a group have the extra students stand in a line 5 yards behind the defender. After the RB runs, the RB will get into the line and the student at the front of the line steps into the defender's role and then rotate through the 3 positions.
- *Extension 1.* The defender is active and jogs toward the QB.
- *Extension 2.* Have the defender move toward the RB, which causes the QB to fake a toss, keep the ball, and cut up field.
- *Extension 3.* Have the defender move toward either the QB or the RB, which forces the QB to make a decision. If the QB is covered, the pitch is made to the RB and if the RB is covered, the QB fakes a toss, keeps the ball and runs up field with the ball.
- *Extension 4.* Perform the task toward the left side of the field.

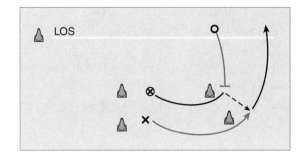

EQUIPMENT

One football and six cones per group of students

CRITICAL ELEMENTS AND CUES

Technique

- Hold the ball in both hands and place the fingers wide on the ball. *Cue:* Wide fingers.
- Use an underhand toss and keep the arms straight. *Cue:* Arms straight.
- Aim the ball at the RB's chest. *Cue:* Aim for the chest.

Tactic

- The QB must read the defender. If the defender is moving toward the QB, the QB must pitch the ball to the defender. If the defender is moving toward the RB, the QB should fake a pitch and then keep the ball. *Cue:* Read the defense.

Communication

- The QB signals the start of play by calling *hike.*

Rule

- The pitch has to go behind or to the side. If it goes forward, it is a forward pass behind the LOS, which is illegal in our version of flag football.

COMMON ERRORS, CAUSES, AND CORRECTIONS

- The pitch is too high. *Cause:* The ball is released too late. *Correction:* Have the student practice the pitch while both students are standing still.
- The QB makes an incorrect decision about whether to pitch. *Cause:* The QB is looking at the RB and not the defender. *Correction:* Have the defender hold up a number of fingers that the QB must recall after the play.

TASK 11: SELF-TOSS CATCH

PURPOSE

Following is the purpose of the task as related to aspects of skilled performance.
Technique: In this task, students learn how to toss and catch a football.

DESCRIPTION

Each student has a football and stands in self-space. Each student holds the football with one hand, tosses the ball up with a spin, and catches it as it comes back down. Students repeat this for the designated time. If students need motivation, have them see how many catches they can make in a row. As an extension, have the students toss the ball higher.

EQUIPMENT

One football per student

CRITICAL ELEMENTS AND CUES

Technique: Toss

- Hold the ball on one end with one hand. *Cue:* One hand on end.
- Place the thumb on top of the ball and spread the fingers across the bottom of the ball. *Cue:* Wide hand.
- Start with the ball below the waist. As you toss the ball up, turn the tossing hand toward the thumb. This causes the ball to spin. *Cue:* Make it spin.

Technique: Catch

- Spread the fingers of both hands out wide. *Cue:* Big hands.
- Point the thumbs and index fingers of both hands toward each other with the palms facing away from the body, creating an open diamond shape. *Cue:* Diamond hands.
- Watch the ball all the way into the chest. *Cue:* Eyes on ball.
- After catching the ball, pull the ball into the chest. *Cue:* Ball to chest.

COMMON ERRORS, CAUSES, AND CORRECTIONS

- The student's palms are facing the body. *Cause:* The little fingers are pointing toward each other. *Correction:* Have the student toss the ball higher and look through the diamond formed by the hands.

TASK 12: GRIP AND RELEASE TO SELF

PURPOSE

Following are the purposes of the task as related to aspects of skilled performance.
   Technique: In this task, students learn how to grip and release a football when passing.

DESCRIPTION

Each student has a football and stands in self-space. Each student grips the football, executes a soft self-throws up into the air, and catches the ball as it comes down.

EQUIPMENT

One football per student

CRITICAL ELEMENTS AND CUES

Technique: Grip (see figure)

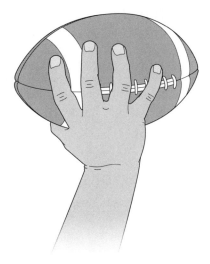

- Place the throwing hand on the back half of the football by forming a *C* with the index finger and thumb. *Cue:* Make a *C*.
- Spread the four fingers apart. *Cue:* Spread fingers.
- Place 2 to 3 fingers on the laces. *Cue:* Laces.
- Rest the ball on the top pads of the palm (not the entire palm). There should be a slight gap between the ball and the palm. *Cue:* Keep the window open.

Technique: Throw (see figure)

- Stretch the throwing arm back by making an *L* with the elbow. *Cue:* Make an *L*.
- Put the throwing elbow at shoulder level. *Cue:* Elbow up.
- Take a short or medium step with the opposite foot. *Cue:* Step.

Technique: Follow Through

- On the release, turn the palm out so the ball rolls off the index finger. *Cue:* Palm out.
- After the ball is released, the passing hand should continue to move to the opposite hip. *Cue:* Opposite hip.

COMMON ERRORS, CAUSES, AND CORRECTIONS

- The student grasps the ball in the middle rather than on the back half. *Cause:* The student is used to holding a ball in the middle. *Correction:* Have the student hold the ball in the nonthrowing hand with the point of the ball down and then place the throwing hand on the back half of the ball.
- The student's middle knuckle is on the laces. *Cause:* The thumb is not on the bottom side of the ball. *Correction:* Place the student's hand on the ball to help the student get the feel of it.
- The ball tumbles out of the hand when thrown and there is no spiral. *Cause:* The hand is not releasing to the outside; rather, the football is being released like a baseball. *Correction:* Have the student throw toward you and stress the outward movement of the hand.

TASK 13: PARTNER PASS AND CATCH

PURPOSE

Following are the purposes of the task as related to aspects of skilled performance.

- Technique: In this task, students work on passing and catching a football.
- Communication: Students hold their hands up to indicate that they are ready for the pass.

DESCRIPTION

Place students in pairs, and have each student stand across from each other at cones set about 10 yards (9.1 meters) from each other. One student passes the football to the other student, who catches it. Students repeat the task for the designated time. If students need motivation, have the students count how many successful passes and catches they can make within a set time or in a row. As an extension, have students stand at a cone 15 yards (13.7 meters) and then at a cone 20 yards (18.3 meters) apart.

EQUIPMENT

One football and four cones per pair of students

CRITICAL ELEMENTS AND CUES

Technique: Pass—Use Grip, Throw, and Follow Through Techniques From Task 12

Grip

- Place the throwing hand on the back half of the football by forming a *C* with the index finger and thumb. *Cue:* Make a *C*.
- Spread the four fingers apart. *Cue:* Spread fingers.
- Place 2 to 3 fingers on the laces. *Cue:* Laces.
- Rest the ball on the top pads of the palm (not the entire palm). There should be a slight gap between the ball and the palm. *Cue:* Keep the window open.

Throw

- Stretch the throwing arm back by making an *L* with the elbow. *Cue:* Make an *L*.
- Put the throwing elbow at shoulder level. *Cue:* Elbow up.
- Take a short or medium step with the opposite foot. *Cue:* Step.

Follow Through

- On the release, turn the palm out so the ball rolls off the index finger. *Cue:* Palm out.
- After the ball is released, the passing hand should continue to move to the opposite hip. *Cue:* Opposite hip.

Technique: Catch

- Spread the fingers of both hands out wide. *Cue:* Big hands.
- Point the thumbs and index fingers of both hands toward each other with the palms facing away from the body, creating an open diamond shape. *Cue:* Diamond hands.
- After catching the ball, pull the ball into the chest. *Cue:* Ball to chest.
- Watch the ball all the way into the chest. *Cue:* Eyes on ball.

Communication

- The receiver holds the hands up in the diamond shape to indicate he or she is ready to receive a pass.

COMMON ERRORS, CAUSES, AND CORRECTIONS

- The student grasps the ball in the middle rather than on the back half. *Cause:* The student is used to holding a ball in the middle. *Correction:* Have the student hold the ball in the nonthrowing hand with the point of the ball down and then place the throwing hand on the back half of the ball.
- The student's middle knuckle is on the laces. *Cause:* The thumb is not on the bottom side of the ball. *Correction:* Place the student's hand on the ball to help the student get the feel of it.
- The ball tumbles out of the hand when thrown and there is no spiral. *Cause:* The hand is not releasing to the outside; rather, the football is being released like a baseball. *Correction:* Have the student throw toward you and stress the outward movement of the hand.
- The ball goes over the receiver's head or to the receiver's feet. *Cause:* The student releases the ball too early or too late. *Correction:* Have the receiver move in closer to the passer.

TASK 14: SHORT CURL-ROUTE PASS WITH SELF-SNAP

PURPOSE

Following are the purposes of the task as related to aspects of skilled performance.

- Technique: In this task, students learn to throw a pass to a receiver who is running a curl route.
- Tactic: Students complete a short pass for a short gain against a defender who is playing off the receiver.
- Agility: The receiver makes a quick stopping step with the outside foot (the foot away from the QB) and moves quickly back toward the QB.
- Communication: The QB signals the beginning of the play with a verbal cue (e.g., *hike*).

DESCRIPTION

Divide students into groups of three. In each group, one student stands along the LOS at a cone approximately 5 yards (4.6 meters) to the side of the QB, another student serves as the QB and stands at a cone 3 to 4 yards (2.7 to 3.7 meters) behind the LOS with the football, and the third student stands at a cone 5 yards (4..6 meters) behind the QB with a football and is ready to rotate in after the pass. The QB calls *hike,* executes a self-snap, and takes a couple of steps backward while the receiver runs out 5 yards (marked with a cone) and executes a curl route to the inside (the receiver's left). As the receiver is completing the curl, the QB passes the ball to the receiver. After catching the ball, the receiver tucks the ball and runs down the field for 10 yards (9.1 meters). The student standing out with the ball then moves into the QB position, the QB moves out to the receiver position, and the receiver jogs back with the ball and stands behind the QB ready to rotate in after the next pass. If students need motivation, have them see how many completed passes their group can make.

- *Extension 1.* The receiver moves to the left side and does the curl from that side, turning toward the inside (right).
- *Extension 2.* Have the student standing out play the role of a passive defender who starts 5 yards back and walks backward while the receiver is moving forward.
- *Extension 3.* Move the defender to active defense.

EQUIPMENT

Two footballs and 3 cones per three students

CRITICAL ELEMENTS AND CUES

Technique: Self-Snap

- Hold the ball in front of the body at waist height with both hands with the point of the ball toward the LOS. *Cue:* Ball out front.
- On the *hike* signal, bring the ball back to the throwing position while adjusting the hand to the passing grip on the ball. *Cue:* Adjust and back.
- While bringing the ball back, turn slightly to the ball side, step back with the foot on the throwing hand side, and take two side steps back to the throwing position. *Cue:* Turn and slide.

Technique: Curl Route

- Run straight down the field for 5 yards. *Cue:* Run for five.
- Plant the outside foot (the foot closest to the sideline) and turn quickly back toward the LOS. *Cue:* Plant, turn, and move.
- Take a couple of steps toward the QB with the hands in position to catch the pass. *Cue:* Hands up.
- Tuck the ball into the body after catching it and turn to run down the field. *Cue:* Tuck and run.

Tactic

- Use this route when a defender is playing off the receiver or when a short gain is needed.

Agility

- When planting the outside foot, the change of direction back toward the QB must be made quickly.

Communication

- The QB signals the start of the play by calling a designated signal (e.g., *hike*).

COMMON ERRORS, CAUSES, AND CORRECTIONS

- The receiver turns and waits for the pass instead of moving back toward the QB. *Cause:* The receiver does not step firmly with the outside foot when turning in order to move toward the QB. *Correction:* Place a second cone 3 yards (2.7 meters) at an angle to the cut cone and have the receiver run toward it after making the cut.

TASK 15: 2V1 CURL-ROUTE GAME

PURPOSE

Following are the purposes of the task as related to aspects of skilled performance.

- Technique: In this task, students learn to apply the pass and curl route to a game-like setting.
- Tactic: Students pass to the open receiver.

DESCRIPTION

Divide students into groups of three and a LOS is established using two cones. One student is the receiver and one is the QB and they huddle to decide which side to set up on. The third student is the defender and sets up 5 yards (4.6 meters) off the LOS on the same side as the receiver. On the teacher's signal the play begins with a self-snap, the receiver runs approximately 5 yards and executes a curl. The defender moves backward while the receiver runs straight. When the cut is made, the defender moves forward but not close enough to interfere with the pass. If the pass is completed, the receiver tucks the ball and runs toward a designated goal line while the defender tries to pull the flag. The offense gets three tries to score a touchdown before students switch positions.

- *Extension 1.* Add a second receiver and defender on the opposite side and have the QB decide who to pass to.
- *Extension 2.* Have the defenders play on the LOS and try to disrupt the pass.

EQUIPMENT

Flag belts and flags for each student, one football and two cones per group of three

CRITICAL ELEMENTS AND CUES

Technique: Curl route

- Plant the outside foot (the foot closest to the sideline) and turn quickly back toward the LOS. *Cue:* Plant, turn, and move.

Tactic

- The QB must time the pass so the defender cannot interfere with it.

Rules

- The offense has three tries to score a touchdown.
- If the offense scores, they get six points.
- If the offense doesn't score, they get three points.
- The defender is not allowed to contact the receiver.

COMMON ERRORS, CAUSES, AND CORRECTIONS

- The defender is too aggressive and either intercepts or contacts the receiver before he or she can catch the ball. *Cause:* The defender is too eager to disrupt the play and doesn't move back as the receiver moves forward. *Correction:* Ask the defender to stand 10 yards (9.1 meters) off the LOS and not move until the pass is thrown.

TASK 16: BACKPEDAL

PURPOSE

Following are the purposes of the task as related to aspects of skilled performance.

- Technique: In this task, students learn how to move backward when playing defense.
- Tactic: Backpedaling is used by defensive backs when covering receivers.
- Agility: Students must use quick, low steps.

DESCRIPTION

Have students stand on a line marked with a cone and face forward. When you give the *hike* command, students backpedal to a cone set 5 yards (4.6 meters) away. Students return to the line and repeat the exercise.

- *Extension 1.* When the students get to the 5-yard marker, they turn and run to a cone that is 15 yards from the starting line while still looking at you.
- *Extension 2.* When the students get to the 5-yard marker, they break and run back to the starting line.
- *Extension 3.* As the students backpedal to the 5-yard marker, point forward to indicate that students should break and run down the field, or raise your hand to indicate that students should run back toward the starting line.

EQUIPMENT

Three cones

CRITICAL ELEMENTS AND CUES

Technique: Backpedal

- Stand with the knees bent, the feet shoulder-width apart and slightly staggered, and the weight on the balls of the feet. *Cue:* Athletic stance.
- Push off the front foot and keep the balls of feet close to the ground as you move backward. *Cue:* Low to the ground.
- Stay in an athletic stance and move the arms. *Cue:* Stay low.

Technique: Backpedal break

- Open the back foot and the hips 90 degrees and push off of back foot. *Cue:* T stop.
- Remain in an athletic stance. *Cue:* Stay low.

Tactic

- When covering a receiver, the defender moves in this position while the receiver runs the route.

Agility

- For the defender to move and react quickly, the feet must remain low to the ground and the weight must be on the balls of the feet.
- When the receiver adjusts the route, the defender must make a quick break to react to the movement.

COMMON ERRORS, CAUSES, AND CORRECTIONS

- The defender slips when making the break. *Cause:* The defender plants the back foot too far behind the body. *Correction:* Tell the student to keep the feet low to the ground and take short steps.
- The defender takes additional steps when making the break. *Cause:* The body raises up and the weight goes back. *Correction:* Tell the student to slow down the backpedal and remain in the athletic stance throughout the break.

TASK 17: PERSON-TO-PERSON DEFENSE

PURPOSE

Following are the purposes of the task as related to aspects of skilled performance.

- Technique: In this task, students practice backpedaling against an offensive receiver.
- Agility: Defenders must react quickly to the break of the receiver who is running the route.

DESCRIPTION

This is the same as task 16 except now you add a receiver, a QB, and an alternate (four students total). The receiver sets up at a cone along the LOS, the defender is at a cone 5 yards (4.6 meters) in front of the receiver, the QB is at a cone behind the LOS with a football, and the alternate is to the rear of the QB with a football. On your signal, the receiver runs to the 5-yard indicator and then executes a route and receives a pass from the QB while the defender moves and breaks in reaction to the receiver. We recommend that the receiver run at a pace the defender can easily move against. The defender is also active, meaning he or she can move and break with the receiver but does not try to interrupt the catch. The routes the receiver can use in this task are the fly (run straight down the field), the curl (move back toward the QB), or the down and in or out (break at a 90-degree angle toward the middle or sideline). You can determine the order in which students run these routes. After the pass, the QB moves to the receiver position, the defender moves to receiver, the receiver brings the ball back and moves to alternate, and the alternate moves to QB. As an extension, move both the receiver and the defender to competitive defense.

EQUIPMENT

Two footballs and 3 cones per group of four students

CRITICAL ELEMENTS AND CUES

Technique

- Stand with the knees bent, the feet shoulder-width apart and slightly staggered, and the weight on the balls of the feet. *Cue:* Athletic stance.
- Push off the front foot and keep the balls of feet close to the ground as you move backward. *Cue:* Low to the ground.
- Stay in an athletic stance and move the arms. *Cue:* Stay low.
- Keep your eyes on the receiver's belt. *Cue:* Eyes on belt.
- When the receiver makes the break, look for the ball. *Cue:* Look for the ball.
- The defender must always keep the receiver in front of them and not allow a receiver to get behind them. *Cue:* Don't get beat.

Agility

- As the receiver makes the break, the defender must quickly mirror the receiver's move. *Cue:* React fast.

COMMON ERRORS, CAUSES, AND CORRECTIONS

- The defender slips when making the break. *Cause:* The defender plants the back foot too far behind the body. *Correction:* Tell the student to keep the feet low to the ground and take short steps.
- The defender takes additional steps when making the break. *Cause:* The body raises up and the weight goes back. *Correction:* Tell the student to slow down the backpedal and remain in the athletic stance throughout the break.

TASK 18: SNAP TO PARTNER

PURPOSE

Following are the purposes of the task as related to aspects of skilled performance.

- Technique: In this task, students learn the center snap.
- Tactic: The center must remain onside when snapping the ball.
- Communication: The QB signals the snap by calling *hike*.

DESCRIPTION

Pair students and have them stand 3 to 4 yards (2.7 to 3.7 meters) apart with a football. The student with the ball snaps it to the partner, who is the QB. Once the snap is made, the QB snaps the ball back to the partner. Students continue the exercise for a designated time. If students need motivation, have them see how many successful snaps they can make in a row.

EQUIPMENT

One football per pair of students

CRITICAL ELEMENTS AND CUES

Technique (see figure)

- Stand on the side of the ball as the hand you will snap with (right side if right handed). *Cue:* Stand on the dominant side.
- Stand facing the ball with both feet to the side and behind the ball. *Cue:* Feet behind ball.
- Knees should be bent with the feet shoulder-width apart and pointed straight ahead. *Cue:* Get low.
- Place the snapping hand on the ball as if making a pass. *Cue:* Thumb up.
- On the snap, keep the arm straight. *Cue:* Straight arm.

Tactic

- The ball marks the LOS, so the center's feet must be behind the ball or they are offside.

Communication

- Snap the ball on the QB's signal.

COMMON ERRORS, CAUSES, AND CORRECTIONS

- The student picks up the ball and tosses it back to the QB. *Cause:* The arm is not straight during the snap. *Correction:* Have the partner move in closer, and have the student softly snap the ball while concentrating on keeping the arm straight.
- As the ball goes back to the QB, it turns end over end. *Cause:* The center's hand isn't on the ball as if gripping the ball to pass it (thumb is down). *Correction:* Have the center grip the ball properly while standing and then turn the hand while placing the ball down to snap it.

TASK 19: SNAP AND BLOCK

PURPOSE
Following are the purposes of the task as related to aspects of skilled performance.

- Technique: In this task, students learn how to block a defender after snapping the ball.
- Tactic: Students block the defender away from the play.

DESCRIPTION
Divide students into groups of four. One student is the QB, one is the running back (RB), one is the center, and one is the defender. A cone is used to mark the LOS where the ball will be placed. The defender lines up 1 yard (0.9 meters) in front of the ball and center, and the center, QB, and RB line up in their positions. On the snap, the offense executes a dive-right play and the center blocks against the passive defender. After the play, students rotate and the RB becomes the center, the center becomes the defender, the defender becomes the QB, and the QB becomes the RB.

- *Extension 1.* Have the RB do a dive-left play.
- *Extension 2.* Change the action to active and then competitive, in which the defender tries to pull the RB's flag.

EQUIPMENT
One football and 1 cone per four students

CRITICAL ELEMENTS AND CUES

Technique (see figure)

- Stand with the knees slightly bent, the feet shoulder-width apart, and the chest up. *Cue:* Athletic stance.
- Cross the arms in front of the body. *Cue:* Arms crossed.
- Face the defender. *Cue:* Face the defender.
- As the RB runs towards the LOS, the center needs to move the feet in a sideways motion and keep in slight contact with the defender while keeping the body between the defender and the RB. *Cue:* Be a shield.

Tactic

- When the play is to the right, the center who is blocking is to the right of the defender and when the play is to the left, the center who is blocking is to the left of the defender.

COMMON ERRORS, CAUSES, AND CORRECTIONS

- The defender gets around the blocker. *Cause:* The blocker doesn't remain in contact with the defender or isn't moving the feet while blocking. *Correction:* Have the blocker and the defender work one-on-one at a slower pace and focus on staying in contact.

TASK 20: LOW AND HIGH CATCHES

PURPOSE

Following are the purposes of the task as related to aspects of skilled performance.

Technique: In this task, students learn how to catch passes that are above the waist and below the waist.

DESCRIPTION

Students and their partners stand across from each other at cones set 5 to 8 yards (4.6 to 7.3 meters) apart and pass a football back and forth. The passes should be completed and caught above the waist. After a set number of successful catches, students throw passes and catch them below the waist. If students need motivation, have them see if they can catch a set number of passes in a row.

- *Extension 1.* Have students stand 10 to 12 yards (9.1 to 11 meters) apart.
- *Extension 2.* Have the students make the passes high or low so the receiver must adjust to the pass.

EQUIPMENT

One football and two cones per pair of students

CRITICAL ELEMENTS AND CUES

Technique: High Pass Catching

- Spread the fingers of both hands out wide. *Cue:* Big hands.
- Point the thumbs and index fingers of both hands toward each other with the palms facing away from the body, creating an open diamond shape. *Cue:* Diamond hands.
- Watch the ball all the way into the hands. *Cue:* Eyes on ball.
- After catching the ball, pull the ball into the chest. *Cue:* Ball to chest.

Technique: Low Pass Catching

- Spread the fingers of both hands out wide. *Cue:* Big hands.
- Hold the hands so the little fingers are pointed toward each other. *Cue:* Pinkies in.
- Watch the ball all the way into the hands. *Cue:* Eyes on ball.
- After catching the ball, pull the ball up to the chest. *Cue:* Ball to chest.

COMMON ERRORS, CAUSES, AND CORRECTIONS

- The student does not adjust the hands properly for passes to the abdominal area. *Cause:* This is the transition point for the low and high pass hand positions. *Correction:* Have students use underhand tosses to the midsection so the receiver can practice adjusting the hand position.

TASK 21: CATCH, TUCK, AND RUN

PURPOSE

Following are the purposes of the task as related to aspects of skilled performance.

- Technique: In this task, students learn to transition from catching a pass to running with the ball after the catch.
- Tactic: After catching a pass, the receiver must run and move toward the goal line.

DESCRIPTION

Students are in pairs, and each pair has a football. Set up two cones that are 5 yards (4.6 meters) apart and set up another pair of cones the same way 15 yards (13.7 meters) down the field (see figure a). One student is standing with a football at the first cone and passes

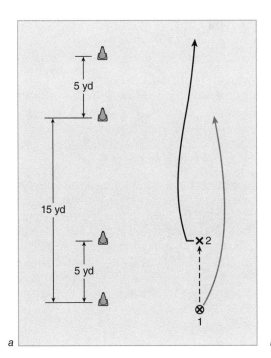

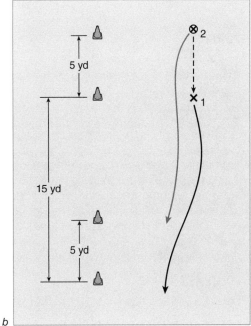

the ball to the other student who is standing at the second cone 5 yards (4.6 meters) apart. The student who catches the ball then tucks, turns, and runs to the farthest cone (the fourth cone). The student who passes the ball runs after the receiver but stops at the third cone that is 15 yards (13.7 meters) away (see figure *b*). Then, students reverse roles and repeat the pass and run back toward the initial set of cones. Students continue the exercise for a designated time. If students need motivation, have them see how many times they can successfully complete the down-and-back task within the designated time.

EQUIPMENT

One football and four cones per pair of students

CRITICAL ELEMENTS AND CUES

Technique

- After catching the ball, the receiver moves the ball down to the dominant side hip and grasps the ball using the REEF technique. *Cue:* Tuck the ball in.
- While tucking the ball in, the receiver turns the shoulders and hips toward the goal line and begins running for a touchdown. *Cue:* Tuck and run.

Tactic

- After catching the pass, think of yourself as a runner and move toward the goal line to attempt to score a touchdown.

COMMON ERRORS, CAUSES, AND CORRECTIONS

- The student drops the ball while attempting to tuck and run. *Cause:* The receiver is in a hurry to run and takes the eyes off the ball before tucking and turning. *Correction:* Tell the receiver to slow down and perform the task in three steps: catch, tuck, and run. As the student gets the hang of it, increase the speed.
- The student drops the ball while attempting to tuck and run. *Cause:* The receiver's hand strength and/or control are not developed enough to control the catch. *Correction:* Have the partner shorten or soften the throw to the receiver. One type of throw that could be used is an underhand spin toss.

TASK 22: TARGET PASSES

PURPOSE

Following is the purpose of the task as related to aspects of skilled performance.

Tactic: In this task, students learn how to control a pass so it can be thrown away from the defender.

DESCRIPTION

Students are in pairs and stand across from each other at cones that are 5 yards (4.6 meters) apart. The receiver holds the hands in a position, and the passer attempts to pass the ball such that the receiver does not have to move the hands very much to make the catch. Once the pass is made, the two students reverse roles and continue the exercise for a designated time. The hand positions should include the following: above the right shoulder, above the left shoulder, to the right of the hips, and to the left of the hips. If students need motivation, have passers count how many times they can pass to the target without making the receiver move the hands more than 1 foot (0.3 meters). As an extension, have the students move farther apart.

EQUIPMENT

One football and two cones per pair of students

CRITICAL ELEMENTS AND CUES

Tactic

- Learn to control your passes so you can pass away from the defender and give the receiver a great opportunity to catch the pass.

COMMON ERRORS, CAUSES, AND CORRECTIONS

- The receiver has to move the hands too much. *Cause:* The pass is too soft and the passer is trying to guide the pass. *Correction:* Have the passer step toward the receiver and pass with more velocity (but be sure it is not too fast for the receiver to catch).

TASK 23: DOWN THE CHIMNEY PASS

PURPOSE

Following are the purposes of the task as related to aspects of skilled performance.

- Technique: In this task, students learn how to loft the ball over the shoulder of the receiver (who is running away from the LOS) and how to catch a ball over the shoulder.
- Tactic: Students pass the ball deep down the field against a defender who is playing close.
- Communication: The receiver begins running down the field when a signal is called by the QB.

DESCRIPTION

Divide students into groups of three. One student is the receiver, one is the QB (with a ball), and the other is an alternate (with a ball). The receiver is at a cone that marks the LOS and is to the right side of the QB. The QB sets up at a cone off the LOS behind where a center would be set and the alternate stands at a cone set up 5 yards (4.6 meters) behind the QB's cone. On a signal from the QB, the receiver runs straight down the field, and the QB tries to pass the ball over the receiver's inside (left) shoulder. When the receiver returns to the LOS, the students rotate: receiver to alternate, alternate to QB, and QB to receiver. If students need motivation, have them count the number of successful passes they can make over the inside shoulder. As an extension, move the cone to the left side and repeat the task; this means the pass must be over the right (inside) shoulder.

EQUIPMENT

Two footballs and three cones per three students

CRITICAL ELEMENTS AND CUES

Technique

- When throwing, release the ball high so it arches over the shoulder of the receiver. *Cue:* High release.
- When throwing, keep the arms out, the fingers spread, and the little fingers pointed toward each other. *Cue:* Make a basket.

Tactic

- If a defender is playing close and the receiver has more speed, the receiver can run past the defender for a long pass to increase the opportunity for a touchdown.

Communication

- The QB uses a snap command (e.g., *hike*) to signal the receiver to start running.

COMMON ERRORS, CAUSES, AND CORRECTIONS

- The pass is off the mark and is not completed. *Cause:* The pass is too long or too short and the timing with the receiver is unsuccessful. *Correction:* Have the receiver move slower and have the QB pass the ball before the receiver gets too far down the field.

TASK 24: PASS ROUTES I
(DOWN AND OUT, DOWN AND IN, FLAG)

PURPOSE

Following are the purposes of the task as related to aspects of skilled performance.

- Technique: In this task, students learn how to run the down-and-in, down-and-out, and flag pass routes.
- Tactic: Students get open against a defender to catch a pass.
- Agility: Students must use quick jab steps to get open.
- Fair play: The receiver hands the ball to the defender after catching it.
- Communication: The QB signals to begin the play.

DESCRIPTION

Use the following task progressions when you teach each of these pass routes. Place students in groups of five. One is the center, one is the QB, one is the receiver, one is the defender, and one is the alternate. Set up one cone to indicate where the center will stand to snap the ball from (LOS cone), one cone to indicate where the QB will pass from (QB cone), one cone to indicate where the receiver will stand along the LOS to begin the route (receiver cone), one cone to indicate where the receiver runs to and makes the cut (cut cone), and a final cone 5 yards (4.6 meters) in the direction the receiver moves after making the cut (route cone) (see figure). Move the cut and route cones appropriately for the route being run. To begin the task, the QB and the receiver stand at their cones, and the defender stands one step behind the cut cone. On the QB's signal, the ball is snapped by the center, and the receiver runs toward the defender and the cut cone to make the cut and then runs toward the route cone. After the receiver makes the cut, the QB throws the pass and the receiver catches it. The defender is passive and does not move. After the receiver catches the pass, he or she hands the ball to the defender, and students rotate positions. The QB moves to center, the center moves to receiver, the receiver moves to defender, the defender takes the ball back and becomes the alternate, and the alternate becomes the new QB.

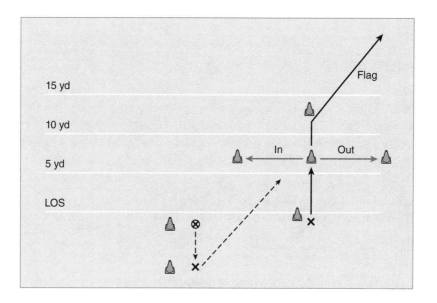

- *Extension 1.* The defender moves to active defense and trails the receiver after the cut is made.
- *Extension 2.* The defender is active and tries to disrupt the route and pass.
- *Extension 3.* Move students along the LOS to the other side of the center and run the route with extensions 1 and 2.

EQUIPMENT

Two footballs and seven cones per five students

CRITICAL ELEMENTS AND CUES

Technique: Down-and-in Route

- The receiver runs straight for 5 to 8 yards (4.6 to 7.3 meters). *Cue:* Down.
- When making the cut for the in move, the receiver plants the outside foot, steps with the inside foot, and makes a 90-degree angle turn toward the inside of the field. *Cue:* In.
- After the cut is made, the receiver raises the hands in preparation for catching the pass. *Cue:* Hands up.

Technique: Down-and-out Route

- The receiver runs straight for 5 to 8 yards (4.6 to 7.3 meters). *Cue:* Down.
- When making the cut for the out move, the receiver plants the inside foot, steps with the outside foot, and makes a 90-degree angle turn toward the outside of the field. *Cue:* Out.
- After the cut is made, the receiver raises the hands in preparation for catching the pass. *Cue:* Hands up.

Technique: Flag Route

- The receiver runs straight for 10 to 12 yards (9.1 to 11 meters).
- The receiver cuts toward the outside corner of the goal line at an approximately 45-degree angle. *Cue:* Forty-five-degree out.
- Once the cut is made, the receiver looks back over the inside shoulder at the QB and locates the thrown ball to make the catch. *Cue:* See the ball.

COMMON ERRORS, CAUSES, AND CORRECTIONS

Errors will vary according to the route being run, but most will be one of the following:

- *Error:* The cut is made too soon or too late. *Cause:* The receiver does cut at the cut cone. *Correction:* Have the alternate stand at the cut cone and have the receiver cut when they get to the alternate.

- *Error:* The receiver is not ready to catch the pass after the cut is made. *Cause:* The receiver is not looking at the QB after the cut. *Correction:* Add the cue "Cut and look".

- *Error:* The pass is not thrown accurately or in a timely manner. *Cause:* Pass is either thrown at the receiver instead of leading the receiver or the pass is thrown too long after the cut is made. *Correction:* Shorten the route to make the pass easier to complete, or allow more practice time with each route.

TASK 25: 3V1 DECISION

PURPOSE

Following are the purposes of the task as related to aspects of skilled performance.

- Tactic: In this task, students learn to pass to the open (undefended) student.
- Communication: The QB calls *hike* to begin the play.

DESCRIPTION

Divide students into groups of four. Three students are on offense and one is a defender with two cones marking the LOS. The offensive students (QB and two receivers) huddle and decide the two routes that the receivers will run (choose from down-and-in, down-and-out, or flag routes). The two receivers then line up a step apart on one end of the LOS (one is on the inside and the other is on the outside). The defender stands 5 yards (4.6 meters) in front of them (see figure). The QB self-snaps the ball, and the receivers run their assigned routes. The defender decides which receiver to defend, which leaves the other receiver open. The QB passes the ball to the undefended receiver. After the catch, the receiver turns and runs up the field, and the defender then comes and tries to pull the flag. After 3 to 4 passes are completed, the QB becomes the inside receiver, the inside receiver becomes the outside receiver, the outside receiver becomes the defender, and the defender becomes the QB. Students stay in their positons for several passes before rotating so the QB gets multiple opportunities to make the correct passing decision. If students need motivation, award one point when the QB passes to the undefended receiver and see how many points can be scored on the QB's allotted passes. As an extension, add an RB as a receiver out of the backfield and a second defender.

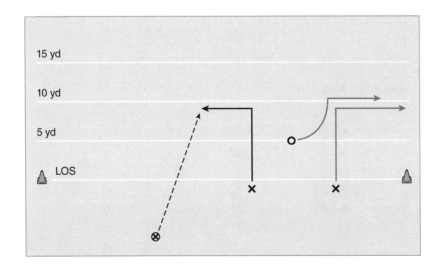

EQUIPMENT

One football and two cones per four students and flag belts and flags for each student

CRITICAL ELEMENTS AND CUES

Tactic

- The QB looks at the defense to see which receiver is being covered.
- The QB passes to the open (undefended) receiver.

Communication

- The QB calls *hike* to begin the play.

COMMON ERRORS, CAUSES, AND CORRECTIONS

- The QB passes to the defended receiver. *Cause:* The QB does not look at the defender. *Correction:* Have the defender wear a pinnie.
- The QB passes to the defended receiver. *Cause:* The QB wants to pass to a particular student regardless of whether that student is defended. *Correction:* Switch the receiver to another group or rearrange the rotation so the friend is the defender instead of a receiver.

TASK 26: OVER-THE-SHOULDER CATCHES

PURPOSE

Following are the purposes of the task as related to aspects of skilled performance.

- Technique: In this task, students learn to catch a pass thrown over the shoulder on a fly route.
- Tactic: Students catch a long pass on a fly route, which is used to beat the defender by getting behind the defender down the field.

DESCRIPTION

Divide students into groups of three. One student is the QB (with a ball), one is the receiver, and one is an alternate (with a ball). The receiver stand 3 to 4 yards (2.7 to 3.7 yards) in front of the QB. On the QB's signal, the receiver jogs forward, the QB makes a high pass over the shoulder of the receiver, and the receiver catches it. After the toss, students rotate positions. The QB moves to receiver, the receiver returns with the ball and becomes the alternate, and the alternate moves to QB. Students continue the exercise for a designated time. If students need motivation, award one point for each successful catch.

- *Extension 1.* The QB throws the pass over the other shoulder (outside).
- *Extension 2.* The receiver runs faster and the QB makes the pass farther out.

EQUIPMENT

Two footballs per three students

CRITICAL ELEMENTS AND CUES

Technique

- Turn the head and see the ball in the air. *Cue:* Eyes on ball.
- Extend the arms out and up. *Cue:* Arms up and out.
- Keep the palms up and the little fingers together. *Cue:* Hands together.
- Allow the hands to give a little as the ball contacts them. *Cue:* Soft hands.
- After the catch, pull the ball into the chest. *Cue:* Ball to chest.

Tactic

- If the defender is playing close or the receiver is faster than the defender, a route that requires an over-the-shoulder catch is preferred.

COMMON ERRORS, CAUSES, AND CORRECTIONS

- The receiver drops the ball. *Cause:* The receiver's eyes do not stay on the ball all the way into the hands. *Correction:* Tell the receiver to imagine the hands in a picture frame; the receiver needs to see both the ball and the hands in the frame.
- The receiver drops the ball. *Cause:* The hands do not give a little on the catch. *Correction:* Have the receiver stand still and catch a tossed ball that comes over the body; the receiver should concentrate absorbing the ball with the hands.

TASK 27: SCREEN PASSES

PURPOSE

Following are the purposes of the task as related to aspects of skilled performance.

- Technique: In this task, students learn to make short, soft passes to moving targets.
- Tactic: Students use this pass when a short gain is needed and the defenders are looking for a running play.
- Agility: The center must quickly move down the LOS after the snap.

DESCRIPTION

Divide students into groups of five. One student is a QB (with a ball), one is a center, one is an RB, one is a defender, and one is an alternate (with a ball). The RB lines up behind the QB (see figure). On the snap, the center turns and runs down the LOS to get into position between the defender and the RB to block. The defender plays passive defense and stands in position. The RB runs to the right side in a curve around a cone set 3 to 4 yards (2.8 to 3.7 meters) to side and behind the LOS. The QB passes the ball to the RB who then catches, tucks, and runs with the ball, keeping the center between him or her and the defender. After the play, students change positions: QB to center, center to RB, RB to defense, and defender to alternate.

- *Extension 1.* Move the cone to the left of the RB and run the route that direction.
- *Extension 2.* Move passive defender to active and then to competitive defense where they attempt to pull the RB's flag.

EQUIPMENT

Flag belts and flags for each student and two footballs and one cone per four students

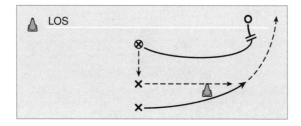

CRITICAL ELEMENTS AND CUES

Technique

- After the snap, the center quickly moves down the LOS and positions between the defender and the RB. *Cue:* Block a defender.
- The RB runs straight out to the side 3 to 4 steps and stays 3 to 4 yards (2.8 to 3.7 meters) behind the LOS as the pass is made. *Cue:* Stay wide.
- After receiving the pass, the RB turns upfield, keeping the center between the defender and the RB. *Cue:* Run behind the center.

Tactic

- If you need only a few yards for a first down or touchdown, then the defenders are expecting a run. This gets the ball into the RB's hands and allows more space to maneuver.

Agility

- The center must immediately move down the LOS so he or she has time to locate a defender and position between the defender and the RB.

COMMON ERRORS, CAUSES, AND CORRECTIONS

- The RB is too close to the QB when the pass is made. *Cause:* The RB runs at an angle straight toward the LOS. *Correction:* Place a cone out to the side that the RB must run around before heading upfield.
- The RB's flag is pulled right as he passes the LOS. *Cause:* The center doesn't position between the defender and the RB. *Correction:* Have the center run one step past the defender he or she is blocking and then turn to face the defender.
- The pass is made before the RB is wide enough or when the RB is too close to the LOS. *Cause:* The QB is in a hurry to pass the ball or passes the ball too late. *Correction:* Tell the QB not to pass the ball until the RB circles the cone out to the side.

TASK 28: ROLLOUT PASS

PURPOSE

Following are the purposes of the task as related to aspects of skilled performance.

- Technique: In this task, students learn how to roll out and pass while moving.
- Tactic: If the receivers are covered, then the QB running with the ball is an option.
- Agility: Students must make a quick first step.

DESCRIPTION

Divide students into groups of four. One student is a center, one is a QB, one is a receiver, and one is a defender. The QB lines up behind the center, the receiver is in position to the right, and the defender is lined up 5 yards in front of the receiver. After the center snaps the ball, the receiver runs a down-and-out route while the QB rolls out to the right and runs in an arc around a cone that is set up 2 to 3 yards (1.8 to 2.7 meters) back and to the right of the QB. The defender moves towards the QB and the QB completes the pass to the receiver (see figure). When the play is completed, the receiver moves to center, the center to QB, and the QB to defender and the defender to receiver. If students need motivation, award one point when the QB successfully throws to the down-and-out route, and then change routes.

- *Extension 1.* Have the receiver line up on the left side and have the QB roll out to the left.
- *Extension 2.* Have defender drop back to cover the receiver causing the QB to tuck the ball and run.
- *Extension 3.* Have defender choose whether to rush the QB or cover the receiver making the QB have to make the proper decision as to passing or running.

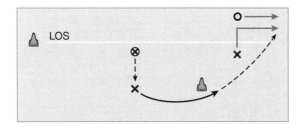

EQUIPMENT

Flag belts and flags per student and one football and two cones per four students

CRITICAL ELEMENTS AND CUES

Technique

- After the snap, turn and take a quick step back with the foot that is on the side you are rolling to. *Cue:* Drop step.
- Take three steps in an arc (around the cone) and look for the receiver. *Cue:* Three steps and look.
- When releasing the ball for the pass, be sure your shoulders are square to the receiver. *Cue:* Square shoulders to target.
- Continue running as you pass the ball. *Cue:* Run and throw.

Tactic

- The QB must look at the defenders. If the receivers are covered and there is not an open pass, the QB can tuck the ball and run.

Agility

- The QB's first steps must be quick to enable the QB to get to the outside while the routes are being run.

COMMON ERRORS, CAUSES, AND CORRECTIONS

- The pass is off the mark. *Cause:* The shoulders are not squared to the receiver. *Correction:* Have the QB and the receiver slow down so the shoulders can be squared on release.
- The QB does not run in an arc when rolling out. *Cause:* The QB turns and runs straight down the LOS. *Correction:* Place the cone back down for the student to run around.

TASK 29: PASS ROUTES II
(SWING, FLY, POST, AND CROSSOVER)

PURPOSE

Following are the purposes of the task as related to aspects of skilled performance.

- Technique: In this task, students learn how to run the swing, fly, post, and crossover pass routes.
- Tactic: Students get open against a defender to catch a pass.
- Agility: Students must use quick jab steps to get open.
- Fair play: The receiver hands the ball to the defender after catching.
- Communication: A verbal QB signal begins the play.

DESCRIPTION

Use the following task progressions when you teach these pass routes. Place students in groups of five. One is the center, one is the QB, one is the receiver, one is the defender, and one is the alternate. Set up one cone to indicate where the ball will be snapped from (LOS cone), one cone to indicate where the QB will pass from (QB cone), one cone to indicate where the receiver will stand to begin the route (receiver cone), one cone to indicate where the receiver runs to and makes the cut (cut cone), and a final cone 5 yards (4.6 meters) in the direction the receiver moves after making the cut (route cone). To begin the task, the QB and receiver stand at their cones, and the defender stands one step behind the cut cone. On the QB's signal, the ball is snapped, and the receiver runs toward the defender and the cut cone and cuts and then runs toward the route cone. After the receiver makes the cut, the QB throws the pass and the receiver catches it. The defender is passive and does not move. After the receiver catches the pass, he or she hands the ball to the defender, and students rotate positions. The QB moves to center, the center moves to receiver, the receiver moves to defender, the defender takes the ball back and becomes the alternate, and the alternate becomes the new QB.

- *Extension 1.* The defender moves to active defense and trails the receiver after the cut is made.
- *Extension 2.* The defender is active and tries to disrupt the route and pass.
- *Extension 3.* Move students along the LOS to the other side of the center and run the route with extensions 1 and 2.

EQUIPMENT

Two footballs and five cones per five students

CRITICAL ELEMENTS AND CUES

Technique: Swing Route (see figure)

- The RB runs in an arc towards the LOS. *Cue:* Run in an arc.
- The QB looks to the side opposite the RB before looking back to the RB. *Cue:* Look the defender off.
- The QB throws a soft-arcing pass to the RB. *Cue:* Soft toss.

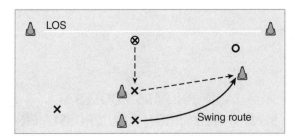

Technique: Fly Route (see figure)

- The receiver runs straight down the field to get behind the defender. *Cue:* Run fast.
- Catch – same cues as over the shoulder catch:
  - Turn the head and see the ball in the air. *Cue:* Eyes on ball.
  - Extend the arms out and up. *Cue:* Arms up and out.
  - Keep the palms up and the little fingers together. *Cue:* Hands together.
  - Allow the hands to give a little as the ball contacts them. *Cue:* Soft hands.
  - After the catch, pull the ball into the chest. *Cue:* Ball to chest.

Technique: Post Route (see figure)

- The receiver runs straight for 10 to 12 yards (9.1 to 11 meters). *Cue:* Run straight.
- The receiver cuts toward the middle of the field at an approximately 45-degree angle. *Cue:* Forty-five degree in.
- Once the cut is made, the receiver should look back over the inside shoulder at the QB and locate the thrown ball to make the catch. *Cue:* See the ball.

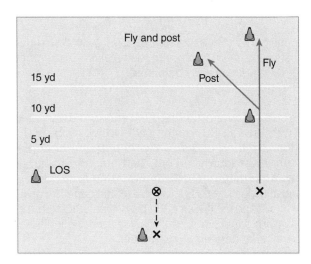

Technique: Crossover Route (see figure)

- Two receivers begin on opposite ends of the LOS. At the snap, the receivers run the same route, which takes them toward each other in the middle of the field (e.g., they both run the down-and-in route or post route). The intent is that the defenders will interfere with each other and open up at least one receiver. *Cue:* Pass right shoulder to right shoulder.
- After the two receivers pass each other, the QB passes to the open receiver. *Cue:* Pass to the open receiver.

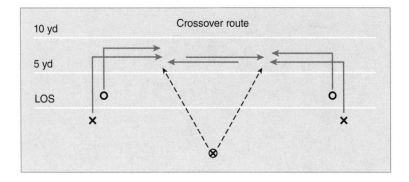

COMMON ERRORS, CAUSES, AND CORRECTIONS

Errors will vary according to the route being run, but most will be one of the following:

- *Error:* The cut is made too soon or too late. *Cause:* The receiver does cut at the cut cone. *Correction:* Have the alternate stand at the cut cone and have the receiver cut when they get to the alternate.
- *Error:* The receiver is not ready to catch the pass after the cut is made. *Cause:* The receiver is not looking at the QB after the cut. *Correction:* Add the cue "Cut and look".

- *Error:* The pass is not thrown accurately or in a timely manner. *Cause:* Pass is either thrown at the receiver instead of leading the receiver or the pass is thrown too long after the cut is made. *Correction:* Shorten the route to make the pass easier to complete, or allow more practice time with each route.

TASK 30: BREAK ON BALL

PURPOSE
Following is the purpose of the task as related to aspects of skilled performance.

Tactic: In this task, students learn to move to the receiver to attempt to pull the receiver's flag and stop the play when the pass is completed.

DESCRIPTION
Place students into groups of five; two groups (offense and defense) are used in this task. The offense sets up with the QB, RB, center, and two receivers, and the defense sets up with one rusher and four defensive backs. At the snap, one receiver runs a long route (flag), the other runs a shorter route (down and out), and the RB runs out and does a curl. Any combination of routes is permitted. The defenders play active defense, moving with the offensive students and allowing the pass to be made and caught. The QB passes to the RB, who catches the ball and stands still. Once the pass is caught, all the defenders run to the RB as if to pull the flag (with passive defense, the flag is not pulled) (see figure). No rotation is necessary because all defenders break on the ball.

- *Extension 1.* The RB turns up field and jogs toward the goal line (this is active defense, but the flag is still not pulled).
- *Extension 2.* The receiver and the defenders are competitive (the defense tries to pull the flag) and the pass can be made to any receiver.

EQUIPMENT
One football per 10 students and flag belts and flags for each student

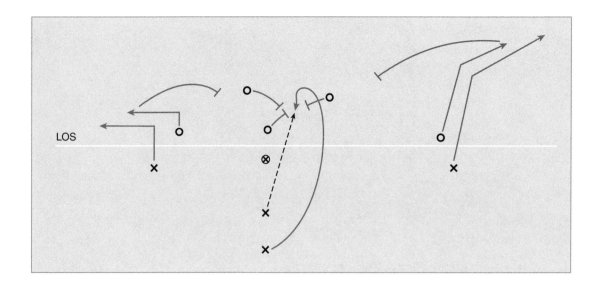

CRITICAL ELEMENTS AND CUES
Tactic
- All defenders need to pursue the receiver once the pass has been caught. This is how big gains and touchdowns are avoided, and it is every defender's responsibility.

COMMON ERRORS, CAUSES, AND CORRECTIONS

- Some defenders do not run to the receiver after the catch. *Cause:* The defenders are concentrating on the receivers they are covering and do not see the ball being passed. *Correction:* Have defenders call out *pass* when the ball is in the air, which alerts everyone that a pass has been thrown.

TASK 31: 2V2 ZONE DEFENSE

PURPOSE

Following are the purposes of the task as related to aspects of skilled performance.

- Technique: In this task, students practice defending a receiver in their zone.
- Tactic: Students cover an area of the field instead of a particular student.
- Communication: Students identify a receiver in the zone or one moving out of the zone.

DESCRIPTION

The zone defense is common in flag football, but sometimes it is difficult to teach if students do not develop communication skills. If your students do not have time to develop these communication skills, we do not recommend that you use zone defenses when playing games. What follows is a basic task to teach zone defensive principles in a 5v5 setting. This five-student defensive scheme is based on having one defender across from the center who rushes the QB or stops the run while the other four defenders act as defensive backs in their zone positions. While in a full 5v5 game play situation there would be four defensive backs, this basic task focuses on the defensive responsibilities of two opposite defensive backs and can be adapted to any type of zone defense or situation you want to teach.

Use cones to mark the field into four zones. Zones 1 and 2 are side by side and extend out 10 yards (9.1 meters) from the LOS and meet in line with the center. Zones 3 and 4 begin 10 yards out from the LOS and are stacked on zones 1 and 2. One student is the QB, one is the receiver, and two are defensive backs. The QB sets up in positon behind the LOS, and the receiver lines up in position on one side of the LOS. The defenders stand 2 yards (1.8 meters) off the LOS across from the receiver; one defender is in zone 1 and the other is in zone 2 (see figure *a*). On the self-snap, the receiver runs a down-and-in route and crosses from zone 2 into zone 1. The defender backs up and covers the receiver until the receiver enters zone 1, at which point the defender drops off and calls *out,* and the second defender begins to cover the receiver and calls *mine.* The QB doesn't pass the ball until the receiver enters zone 1. After the pass, the QB moves to the receiver (but on the opposite end of the LOS as the previous snap), and the receiver moves to the QB while the two defenders remain in their zones. After six passes the offense and defense switch places. If more than four students are in the group, extra students can line up behind the QB and rotate after each attempt. The defenders must remain on defense until the sides switch.

- *Extension 1.* Have the receiver run a fly route and move the second defender to zone 3 (just above zone 2). Have defenders switch positions after three passes (see figure *b*).
- *Extension 2.* Use the same structure to add routes and defenders as you see fit.

EQUIPMENT

One football per four students and ten markers to indicate the four zones

CRITICAL ELEMENTS AND CUES

Technique

Use person-to-person defensive principles when covering the receiver in your zone:

- Stand with the knees bent, the feet shoulder-width apart and slightly staggered, and the weight on the balls of the feet. *Cue:* Athletic stance.
- Push off the front foot and keep the balls of feet close to the ground as you move backward. *Cue:* Low to the ground.

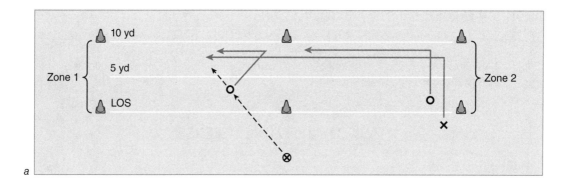

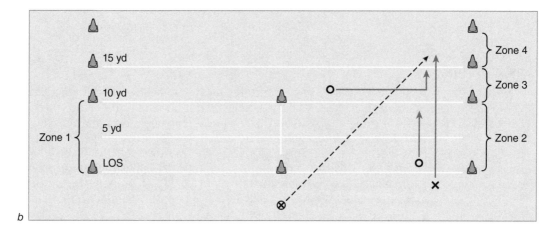

- Stay in an athletic stance and move the arms. *Cue:* Stay low.
- Keep your eyes on the receiver's belt. *Cue:* Eyes on belt.
- When the receiver makes the break, look for the ball. *Cue:* Look for the ball.
- The defender must always keep the receiver in front of them and not allow a receiver to get behind them. *Cue:* Don't get beat.

Tactic
- Recognize when receivers are in your zone and cover those receivers. Zone defense means you are responsible for your area.
- If a receiver enters your zone, you must cover that receiver until the play is over, the ball crosses the LOS on a running play, or the receiver leaves your zone.
- Understand your zone and the areas you have to cover depending on the down and the distance in front of you or behind you.
- Anticipate where the receivers are going by reading the QB's eyes and shoulders. *Cue:* Read the quarterback.

Communication
- Say *mine* when the receiver enters your zone.
- Let your teammate know when a receiver is leaving your zone and entering another zone by saying *out*.

COMMON ERRORS, CAUSES, AND CORRECTIONS
- Students fail to communicate with each other. *Cause:* Students are focused on their receivers and forget to communicate. *Correction:* Award one point each time the defender communicates correctly.

- Students follow their receivers into the next zone rather than dropping off and remaining in their zones. *Cause:* Students are focused on their receivers and forget about the zone boundaries. *Correction:* Add more cones to mark the zone boundaries so the defenders can see them better, or slow the receivers down to allow defenders to see the zones and the positions of the receivers within the zones.

TASK 32: 2V1 CATCH, TUCK, AND RUN GAME

PURPOSE

Following are the purposes of the task as related to aspects of skilled performance.

- Technique: In this task, students apply the tuck and run in a game situation.
- Tactic: Students catch the ball and run with it to avoid getting the flag pulled.
- Agility: Students must use quick juke steps to avoid the flag puller.
- Fair play: Students hand the flag back to the receiver after pulling it.
- Communication: A signal is given by the QB to indicate the beginning of the play.

DESCRIPTION

Place students into groups of three. One is the defender, one is the QB, and one is the receiver. The receiver stands 5 yards (4.6 meters) in front and to the side of the QB, and the defender stands 5 yards behind the receiver. The QB calls *hike* to signal the beginning of play and then passes the ball to the receiver who is standing still. The receiver catches and tucks the ball and then turns and runs toward a goal line indicated by two cones. Once the catch is made, the defender approaches the receiver in an attempt to pull the flag. Students rotate positions and repeat the task: QB moves to receiver, receiver moves to defender, and defender moves to QB. If students need motivation, award one point if the receiver scores a touchdown before the flag is pulled, and award one point if the defender successfully pulls the flag of the receiver before the touchdown is scored. Students maintain their total points earned.

EQUIPMENT

One football and two cones per three students and flag belts and flags for each student

CRITICAL ELEMENTS AND CUES

Technique:

- After catching the ball and bringing it into the chest, the receiver needs to take the ball to one side. *Cue:* Tuck.
- Grip the ball with one hand using REEF. *Cue:* REEF.
  - Tuck the ball into the rib cage. *Cue:* Rib cage.
  - Tuck the elbow in. *Cue:* Elbow.
  - Spread the fingers over the point of the ball. *Cue:* Eagle claw.
  - Cover the ball with the forearm. *Cue:* Forearm.
- Turn towards the goal line and run. *Cue:* Run.

Rules

- The defender cannot move toward the receiver until the pass has been caught.
- The receiver must turn and run straight toward the goal line and can only use a juke step to avoid the defender.
- Spin moves to avoid defenders are not allowed.
- If a flag is pulled, the defender raises the flag above the head to signal the end of the play and then hands the flag back to the receiver.
- If a flag falls off and is not pulled, the play ends and no one earns a point.

COMMON ERRORS, CAUSES, AND CORRECTIONS

- The defender moves to disrupt the pass or pulls the flag as the catch is being made. *Cause:* The defender is anxious to stop the play. *Correction:* Do not allow the defender to move until the receiver turns and takes a step toward the goal line.

TASK 33: 2V1 SELF-SNAP AND DIVE GAME

PURPOSE

Following are the purposes of the task as related to aspects of skilled performance.

- Technique: In this task, students apply the dive play in a game situation.
- Tactic: The QB and RB huddle to decide which side to run the play on.
- Agility: The RB uses juke steps and quick movements to avoid the defender.
- Fair play: The RB does not spin to avoid getting the flag pulled.
- Communication: The QB calls *hike* to indicate the start of the play.

DESCRIPTION

The object of this game is to score a touchdown using only the dive play. Set up the playing area with two cones that are 5 yards (4.6 meters) apart to indicate the line of scrimmage (LOS) and the area through which the RB must run and two cones set 5 yards (4.6 meters) apart and 10 to 15 yards (9.1 to 13.7 meters) away from the LOS indicating the goal line. The game begins with the ball on the LOS, which is 10 to 15 yards (9.1 to 13.7 meters) from the goal line. Students are in groups of three: a QB, an RB, and a defender. The offense huddles, and the QB calls either the dive-right or the dive-left play. The defender stands 5 yards in front of the QB just across the LOS. When the QB calls *hike,* the play begins. The defender allows the ball to be handed off and then tries to pull the RB's flag as he or she runs between the cones toward the goal line. Students rotate through each position: QB to RB, defender to QB, and RB to defender. If students need motivation, award one point if the RB makes it to the goal line without having the flag pulled, and award one point if the defender successfully pulls the RB's flag.

EQUIPMENT

One football and four cones per three students and flag belts and flags for each student

CRITICAL ELEMENTS AND CUES

Rules

- The offense gets one try to score a touchdown.
- The defender cannot cross the LOS until the ball is handed off.
- After each play, the students rotate positions.
- The QB has 15 seconds to call the play.
- Spin moves to avoid the defender are not allowed.
- Play begins when the QB calls *hike.*

COMMON ERRORS, CAUSES, AND CORRECTIONS

- The defender moves across the LOS when the QB calls *hike. Cause:* The defender is anxious to get to the flag. *Correction:* Have the defender count to three out loud before moving across the LOS.
- The runner does a spin move to avoid the flag puller. *Cause:* The student is athletic and wants to avoid getting the flag pulled. *Correction:* Award the runner two points if he or she scores without doing a spin move.

TASK 34: 2V1 SELF-SNAP AND PITCH GAME

PURPOSE

Following are the purposes of the task as related to aspects of skilled performance.

- Technique: In this task, students apply the pitch play in a game situation.
- Tactic: The QB and RB huddle to decide which side to run the play on.
- Agility: The RB uses juke steps and quick movements to avoid the defender.
- Fair play: The RB does not spin to avoid getting the flag pulled.
- Communication: The QB calls *hike* to indicate the start of the play.

DESCRIPTION

The object of this game is to score a touchdown using only the pitch play. Set up the playing area with two cones to indicate the LOS. The game begins with the ball on the LOS, which is 10 to 15 yards (9.1 to 13.7 meters) from the goal line which is also marked with two cones. Students are in groups of four: a QB and RB on offense and two defenders, one on each end of the LOS (since this is a 2v1 game, the defender opposite the direction of the pitch play is not involved in the play). The offense huddles and the QB calls the pitch-right or pitch-left play. The defenders stands toward the end of the LOS, and the play begins when the QB calls *hike*. The defenders read the play, and the defender to whose side the play is being run moves toward the QB or RB approaching that side. The QB reads the defender and decides whether to pitch or keep the ball. After the play, the defense and offense switch roles. If students need motivation, award one point if the RB makes it to the goal line without having the flag pulled, and award one point if the defender successfully pulls the RB's flag.

EQUIPMENT

One football and four cones per four students and flag belts and flags for each student

CRITICAL ELEMENTS AND CUES

Rules

- The offense gets one try to score a touchdown.
- The RB cannot spin to avoid the defender.
- After each play, the students rotate positions.
- The ball must move sideways or backward when pitched.

COMMON ERRORS, CAUSES, AND CORRECTIONS

- The defender moves across the LOS when the QB calls *hike*. *Cause:* The defender is anxious to get to the flag. *Correction:* Have the defender count to three out loud before moving across the LOS.
- The RB is too close to the QB when the pitch is executed. *Cause:* The RB runs toward the QB and doesn't keep proper spacing. *Correction:* Place a cone at both sides that the RB must run around.

TASK 35: 3V3 PASS GAME

PURPOSE

Following are the purposes of the task as related to aspects of skilled performance.

- Technique: In this task, students apply passing, catching, defense, and route running to a game situation.
- Tactic: Students use of set plays to get open for a reception.
- Agility: Students make quick cuts to get open.

- Fair play: Defensive students return pulled flags to offensive students.
- Communication: Students hold up the pulled flag to indicate a down. A signal is called by the QB to begin the play. Students use a huddle to call the play.

DESCRIPTION

Two teams of three are set against each other on a field marked with six cones. Two cones indicate the 40 yard line, two cones mark the goal line, and one cone is set half way between the LOS and goal line to mark each side line. The offense consists of a QB and two receivers. The defense has three defensive backs; two play person-to-person defense and the other is a rover. The offense huddles to call the play, and the play begins when the QB calls a signal followed by a self-snap. Play begins at the 40-yard line (marked by two cones), and the offense has four plays to cross the goal line (marked by two cones) to score a touchdown. The receivers run their set routes and the two defenders cover them. The rover double-teams one of the receivers. After a score, or if the defense stops the offense or intercepts the ball, the ball goes to the defense and they begin on the 40-yard line and attempt to score.

EQUIPMENT

One football per six students, six cones, flag belts, flags, and pinnies for each student

CRITICAL ELEMENTS AND CUES

Technique

- Apply the critical elements of all previous techniques.

Tactic

- Use play cards to call plays in the huddle.

Agility

- Make quick cuts when running routes.

Fair Play

- Hand flags to receivers.
- Penalties will be assessed for rule infractions.

Communication

- Immediately raise a pulled flag to indicate the new LOS.
- In the huddle, only the QB calls the plays or routes.
- QB signals the start of play with a verbal command (e.g., ready, set, *hike*).

Rules

- All previous game rules apply to this game.
- Five-yard (4.6-meter) penalties will be assessed for rule infractions.
- Do not rush the QB.
- The offense has four plays to score a touchdown.
- The offensive series always begins on the 40-yard line.

COMMON ERRORS, CAUSES, AND CORRECTIONS

- Students will make common errors that were previously discussed.
- The student pulls the flag but does not raise it up. *Cause:* In the excitement of the game, the student forgets to do this. *Correction:* The first time this happens you can remind the student, but for each successive failure to raise the flag, assess a 5-yard penalty.

TASK 36: 3V3 RUN-ONLY GAME

PURPOSE

Following are the purposes of the task as related to aspects of skilled performance.

- Technique: In this task, students apply the techniques of running plays in a game situation.
- Tactic: Students use dive plays for short yardage situations and pitches for attacking the edge of the defense.
- Agility: Students use jab steps to avoid flag defenders.
- Fair play: Students hand flags to play carriers after they are pulled. Students abide by the rules.
- Communication: The QB use a verbal snap command. Raise flags after they are pulled.

DESCRIPTION

Two teams of three are set against each other on a field marked with six cones. Two cones indicate the 40 yard line, two cones mark the goal line and one cone is set half way between the LOS and goal line to mark each side line. The offense consists of a QB, an RB, and a center. The role of the center will depend on whether you taught the snap. If you taught the snap, the center will snap the ball and then move to block a defender. If you did not teach the snap, the center will start on the LOS in the center position and then move to block a defender. The offense huddles and calls one of the four running plays. The defense lines up 5 yards (4.6 meters) in front of the LOS; there is one defender on each end of the LOS 5 to 7 yards (4.6 to 6.4 meters) out from the center and one in front of the center. On the snap, defenders can move forward after a count of three. Play begins at the 40 yard (36.6 meters) line from the end zone, and the offense has four plays to score. Students rotate offensive positions on every series of downs so everyone has an opportunity to play in each position.

EQUIPMENT

One ball and six cones per six students, flag belts, flags, and pinnies for each student

CRITICAL ELEMENTS AND CUES

Technique

- Apply all previous running play techniques.

Rules

- Use only running plays.
- The offense has four downs to score.
- If the offense scores or is stopped, the defense gains control of the ball.
- On a change of possession, the ball always starts on the 40-yard line.
- The ball carrier cannot use spins or hand shielding.
- The defense raises the pulled flag to mark a new LOS.
- The offense has 20 seconds to huddle and start the play.

COMMON ERRORS, CAUSES, AND CORRECTIONS

- The ball carrier spins or hand shields to avoid the defender. *Cause:* The student instinctively tries to avoid getting the flag pulled. *Correction:* Stop the play. The new LOS is placed where the infraction occurred.

TASK 37: 4V4 PASS-ONLY ZONE DEFENSE GAME

PURPOSE

Following are the purposes of the task as related to aspects of skilled performance.

- Technique: Students will apply the learned critical elements and cues from the previous techniques of passing (tasks 12, 13, 23), receiving (tasks 13, 14, 24), and zone defensive movement (task 31).
- Tactic: Students apply the zone defense to defend pass routes.
- Agility: Students use quick cuts to get open and to break on the ball.
- Fair Play: Defensive students return pulled flags to offensive students.
- Communication: Students hold up the pulled flag to indicate a down. A *hike* signal is called by the QB to begin play. Defenders communicate with each other as receivers move through zones.

DESCRIPTION

Two teams of four are set against each other on a field marked with six cones. Two cones indicate the 40 yard line, two cones mark the goal line, and one cone is set half way between the LOS and goal line to mark each side line. The offense consists of a center, a QB, and two receivers, and the defense consists of four defensive backs. Set the original LOS approximately 40 yards (36.6 meters) from the goal line. The two receivers set up 5 yards (4.6 meters) out from the center on opposite sides, and the defensive backs set up in the four defensive zones. The offense huddles, and the QB assigns the routes to be run by the receivers. On the snap, the receivers run their routes while being actively defended (receivers are defended when they are in the defender's zone, but defenders allow the catch to be made before the flag can be pulled). The offense has four snaps to get a touchdown. After a touchdown is scored or four snaps are made, the students rotate in pairs. The center and QB change places with the receivers, and the two front defenders switch places with the two deep defenders. If students need motivation, award three points if the offense scores within four snaps, and award three points if the defense stops the offense from scoring. As an extension, have defenders switch to competitive defense.

EQUIPMENT

One ball and six cones per eight students, flag belts, flags, and pinnies for each student

CRITICAL ELEMENTS AND CUES

Rules

- The offense can use any route.
- Each new team possession starts on the 40-yard line.
- Only passes can advance the ball.
- Do not rush the QB.
- Do not contact the receiver.
- Do not pull the flag until the pass is received.
- The offense has 20 seconds to call and execute the play.
- The ball is placed on the new LOS where the flag was pulled.

COMMON ERRORS, CAUSES, AND CORRECTIONS

- Students fail to communicate with each other. *Cause:* Students are focused on their receivers and forget to communicate. *Correction:* Award one point each time the defender communicates correctly.
- Students follow their receivers into the next zone rather than dropping off and remaining in their zones. *Cause:* Students are focused on their receivers and forget about the

zone boundaries. *Correction:* Add more cones to mark the zone boundaries so the defenders can see them better, or slow the receivers down to allow defenders to see the zones and the positions of the receivers within the zones.

TASK 38: 4V2 PASS GAME I

PURPOSE

Following are the purposes of the task as related to aspects of skilled performance.

- Technique: In this task, students apply the down and in, down and out, curl, and flag passing routes to a game-like setting.
- Tactic: Students use routes to get open against the defense.
- Agility: Students make quick cuts to get open.
- Fair play: Defensive students return pulled flags to offensive students.
- Communication: Students hold up the pulled flag to indicate a down. A *hike* signal is called by the QB to begin play.

DESCRIPTION

Divide students into groups of six and place them on a field marked with six cones. Two cones indicate the 40 yard line, two cones mark the goal line, and one cone is set half way between the LOS and goal line to mark each side line. Four students play offense (QB, center, and two receivers) and two students play defense. Set the original LOS approximately 40 yards (36.6 meters) from the goal line. The two receivers set up 5 yards (4.6 meters) out, one to each side of the center. The defenders set up 5 yards opposite each of the receivers. The offense huddles, and the QB assigns the routes to be run by the receivers. On the snap, the receivers run their routes while being actively defended (defenders move with the receivers but allow the catch to be made before the flag can be pulled). The offense has four snaps to get a touchdown. After a touchdown is scored or four snaps are made, the students rotate in pairs. The center and QB change places with the receivers, the receivers become defenders, and the defenders move to center and QB. If students need motivation, award three points if the offense scores within four snaps, and award three points if the defense stops the offense from scoring. Students tally their own points. As an extension, have defenders switch to competitive defense.

EQUIPMENT

One ball and six cones per six students, flag belts and flags for each student

CRITICAL ELEMENTS AND CUES

Rules

- Use only the down and out, down and in, curl, and flag routes.
- Each new team possession starts on the 40-yard line.
- Only passes can advance the ball.
- Do not rush the QB.
- Do not contact the receiver.
- Do not pull the flag until the pass is received.
- The offense has 20 seconds to call and execute the play.
- The ball is placed on the new LOS where the flag was pulled.

COMMON ERRORS, CAUSES, AND CORRECTIONS

- Students do not run the routes correctly. *Cause:* Students get excited and forget how to run the routes. *Correction:* Take more time in the huddle and make sure the receivers know how to run the routes. If the problem persists, go back and practice the routes individually.

TASK 39: 4V2 PASS GAME II

PURPOSE

Following are the purposes of the task as related to aspects of skilled performance.

- Technique: In this task, students apply the swing, fly, post, and crossover passing routes to a game-like setting.
- Tactic: Students use routes to get open against the defense.
- Agility: Students make quick cuts to get open.
- Fair play: Defensive students return pulled flags to offensive students.
- Communication: Students hold up the pulled flag to indicate a down. A *hike* signal is called by the QB to begin play.

DESCRIPTION

Divide students into groups of six and place them on a field marked with six cones. Two cones indicate the 40 yard line, two cones mark the goal line, and one cone is set half way between the LOS and goal line to mark each side line. Four students play offense (QB, center, and two receivers) and two students play defense. Set the original LOS approximately 40 yards (36.6 meters) from the goal line. The two receivers set up 5 yards (4.6 meters) out, one to each side of the center. The defenders set up 5 yards opposite each of the receivers. The offense huddles, and the QB assigns the routes to be run by the receivers. On the snap, the receivers run their routes while being actively defended (defenders move with the receivers but allow the catch to be made before the flag can be pulled). The offense has four snaps to get a touchdown. After a touchdown is scored or four snaps are made, the students rotate in pairs. The center and QB change places with the receivers, the receivers become defenders, and the defenders move to center and QB. If students need motivation, award three points if the offense scores within four snaps, and award three points if the defense stops the offense from scoring. Students tally their own points. As an extension, have defenders switch to competitive defense.

EQUIPMENT

One ball and six cones per six students, flag belts and flags for each student

CRITICAL ELEMENTS AND CUES

Rules

- Use only the swing, fly, post, and crossover routes.
- Each new team possession starts on the 40-yard line.
- Only passes can advance the ball.
- Do not rush the QB.
- Do not contact the receiver.
- Do not pull the flag until the pass is received.
- The offense has 20 seconds to call and execute the play.
- The ball is placed on the new LOS where the flag was pulled.

COMMON ERRORS, CAUSES, AND CORRECTIONS

- Students do not run the routes correctly. *Cause:* Students get excited and forget how to run the routes. *Correction:* Take more time in the huddle and make sure the receivers know how to run the routes. If the problem persists, go back and practice the routes individually.

TASK 40: 4V3 PASS GAME

PURPOSE

Following are the purposes of the task as related to aspects of skilled performance.

- Technique: In this task, students apply passing, catching, defense, and route running to a game situation.
- Tactic: Students use set plays to get open for a reception.
- Agility: Students make quick cuts to get open.
- Fair play: Defensive students return pulled flags to offensive students.
- Communication: Students hold up the pulled flag to indicate a down. A signal is called by the quarterback to begin the play. Students use huddles to call the play.

DESCRIPTION

Seven students are set up in an overload situation with four students on offense and three students on defense. The game is played on a field marked with six cones. Two cones indicate the 40 yard line, two cones mark the goal line, and one cone is set half way between the LOS and goal line to mark each side line. The offense consists of a QB, a center, and two receivers. The defense has three defensive backs; two play person-to-person defense and the other is a rover. The offense huddles to call the play, and the play begins with a center snap. Play begins at a 40-yard line, and the offense has four plays to score a touchdown. The receivers run their set routes and the two defenders cover them. The rover double-teams one of the receivers. After a score, or if the defense stops the offense or intercepts the ball, the ball goes to the defense and they begin on the 40-yard line and attempt to score.

EQUIPMENT

One ball and six cones per eight students, flag belts, flags, and pinnies for each student

CRITICAL ELEMENTS AND CUES

Technique

- Apply the critical elements of all previous techniques.

Tactic

- Use play cards to call plays in the huddle.

Agility

- Make quick cuts when running routes.

Fair Play

- Hand flags to receivers.
- Penalties will be assessed for rule infractions.

Communication

- Immediately raise a pulled flag to indicate the new LOS.
- In the huddle, only the QB calls the plays or routes.
- A signal is called by the QB to begin the play (e.g., ready, set, *hike*).

Rules

- All previous game rules apply to this game.

COMMON ERRORS, CAUSES, AND CORRECTIONS

- Students will make common errors that were previously discussed.
- The student pulls the flag but does not raise it up. *Cause:* In the excitement of the game, the student forgets to do this. *Correction:* The first time this happens you can remind the student, but for each successive failure to raise the flag, assess a 5-yard penalty.

TASK 41: 4V4 GAME

PURPOSE

Following are the purposes of the task as related to aspects of skilled performance.

- Technique: In this task, students apply passing, catching, defense, ball carrying, and route running to a game situation.
- Tactic: Students use set pass and receiving plays to advance the ball.
- Agility: Students make quick cuts to get open.
- Fair play: Defensive students return pulled flags to offensive students. Students abide by the rules.
- Communication: Students hold up the pulled flag to indicate a down. A signal is called by the QB to begin the play. Students use a huddle to call the play.

DESCRIPTION

Two teams of four are set against each other. The offense consists of a QB, a center, and either two receivers or an RB and a receiver. The defense has three defensive backs (two play person-to-person defense and the other is a rover) and one rusher. Use a full 80-yard (73.2-meter) field marked by 14 cones (2 cones each to mark the 2 end lines, 2 goal lines, the 2 five yard lines and the 40 yard line). Play begins at the 5-yard line in front of the offensive own goal line. The offense huddles to call the play, and the play begins with a center snap. The RB is an eligible receiver and can catch the ball coming out of the backfield or can line up as a second receiver. The rover double-teams one of the receivers or rushes the ball carrier. The rusher rushes the QB after the designated count and is blocked by the center. The offense has four plays to get across the midline for a new set of downs. If the defense stops the offense or intercepts the ball, the ball goes over to the defense and they begin play at that point. After a score, the defense moves to offense and begins play on the 5-yard line heading in the other direction toward their goal line. If students need motivation, award points if the QB uses good judgment in completing a touchdown or a pass to the receiver using a designated route.

EQUIPMENT

One football and 14 cones per eight students and flag belts, flags, and pinnies for each student

CRITICAL ELEMENTS AND CUES

Technique

- Apply the critical elements of all previous techniques.

Tactic

- Use play cards to call plays in the huddle.

Agility

- Make quick cuts when running routes.

Fair Play

- Hand flags to receivers.
- Penalties will be assessed for rule infractions.

Communication

- Immediately raise a pulled flag to indicate the new LOS.
- In the huddle, only the QB calls the plays or routes.
- A signal is called by the QB to begin the play (e.g., ready, set, *hike*).

Rules

- All previous game rules apply to this game.
- The defender must count out loud to eight before rushing the QB.

- If the offense gets across the midfield line within four plays, they get a new set of four downs.
- On fourth down, the offense can call a punt, which means the ball is given to the defense and they begin on their own 5-yard line.
- If the defense stops the offense in four plays or intercepts the ball, they gain possession of it at that spot.
- A ball passed to the end zone must be caught within the end zone to count as a touchdown.
- When the LOS is within 5 yards of the goal line, only a pass play can be used to score.

COMMON ERRORS, CAUSES, AND CORRECTIONS

- Students will make common errors that were previously discussed.

TASK 42: 5V5 GAME

PURPOSE

Following are the purposes of the task as related to aspects of skilled performance.

- Technique: In this task, students apply all techniques in a game situation.
- Tactics: Students use set plays to advance the ball.
- Agility: Students make quick cuts to get open.
- Fair play: Defensive students return pulled flags to offensive students. Students abide by the rules.
- Communication: Students hold up the pulled flag to indicate a down. A signal is called by the QB to begin the play. Students use a huddle to call the play.

DESCRIPTION

Two teams of five are set against each other. The offense consists of a QB, an RB, a center, and two receivers. The five defenders can play either person-to-person defense or zone defense. Use a full 80-yard (73.2-meter) field marked by 14 cones (2 cones each to mark the 2 end lines, 2 goal lines, the 2 five yard lines and the 40 yard line). Play begins at the 5-yard line in front of the offensive goal line. The offense huddles to call the play, and the play begins with a center snap. The RB is an eligible receiver and can catch the ball coming out of the backfield. The rusher rushes the QB after the designated count and is blocked by the center. The offense has four plays to get across the midline (40 yards [36.6 meters]) for a new set of downs. After a score, the defense becomes the offense and begins play on the 5-yard line in front of their goal. If the defense stops the offense or intercepts the ball, the ball goes over to the defense and they then become the offense and begins play at that point. Use a marker to indicate the new LOS. Have students rotate through each of the offensive positions every series so everyone has an opportunity to play each position.

EQUIPMENT

One football and 14 cones per eight students and flag belts, flags, and pinnies for each student

CRITICAL ELEMENTS AND CUES

Technique

- Apply the critical elements of all previous techniques.

Tactics

- Use play cards to call plays in the huddle.

Agility

- Make quick cuts when running routes.

Fair Play

- Hand flags to receivers.
- Penalties will be assessed for rule infractions.

Communication

- Immediately raise a pulled flag to indicate the new LOS.
- In the huddle, only the QB calls the plays or routes.
- A signal is called by the QB to begin the play (e.g., ready, set, *hike*).

Rules

- All previous game rules apply to this game.

COMMON ERRORS, CAUSES, AND CORRECTIONS

- Students will make common errors that were previously discussed.

TASK 43: PLAYBOOKS

PURPOSE

Football is a strategic game in which students perform specific roles so the team will be successful. Football is also a game of deception in which students try to get open to advance the ball. The use of set plays helps define the students' roles and how they will get open.

You can set up the playbooks as outlined in this chapter, or the students can create their own plays. The play must use only the offensive tactics taught within the class. We recommend that you make play cards the QB can use to call plays in the huddle.

RUNNING PLAYBOOK (LEVEL 1)

There are four basic running plays taught at this level: dive right, dive left, pitch right, and pitch left. Make diagrams of each running play that show the movements of the RB and QB. The QB uses these diagrams when calling the plays. Use this playbook for the 3v3 run-only game that concludes level 1 (task 36).

PASSING PLAYBOOK I (LEVEL 2)

This playbook includes the four pass routes learned in level 1 (curl) and level 2 (down and out, down and in, and flag). Diagram each route on a single page for student reference as they learn the routes. You can then design plays that combine these four routes. In the huddle, the QB uses the diagrams when calling these pass plays. Use this playbook for the 3v3 pass game (task 35). For the 4v4 game that concludes level 2 (task 41), use the running and passing I playbooks to call plays.

PASSING PLAYBOOK II (LEVEL 3)

This playbook contains the four pass routes learned in level 2: swing, fly, post, and crossover. Diagram each route on a single page for student reference as they learn the routes. You can then design plays that combine these four routes. In the huddle, the QB uses the diagrams when calling these pass plays. Use this playbook for the 4v4 game in level 3 (task 41).

COMBINED PLAYBOOK (LEVEL 3)

When you are ready to play the concluding 5v5 game, combine the techniques from the running and passing playbooks (minus individual route diagrams) into one playbook. Diagram plays using all running and passing plays. The QB uses the diagrams to call the plays in the huddle. When designing plays, combine short routes (curl, down and in, down and out), longer routes (fly, flag, and post), or crossover routes for each play.

Chapter 8

Basketball

Basketball is the second most popular sport in the world, and it is played in more than 200 countries. In the United States, the home of basketball, it is a staple of many physical education programs in elementary, middle, and high schools. It is also becoming more popular in the physical education curricula in other countries. Research conducted in the United States shows that basketball is among the top four activities (after camping, swimming, and biking) that nonparticipants in physical activity aged 6 to 12 years would like to learn (Physical Activity Council, 2016). Although basketball is common in the U.S. school curriculum, research shows that it is one of the least-liked sports among U.S. students aged 5 to 17 years (Bailey, Hillman, Arent, & Petipas, 2013; Rikard & Baneville, 2006). What is the reason for this seeming contradiction? We propose that students dislike basketball in physical education because it is often taught in ways that do not help them develop skillfulness and game sense. Failure to develop these aspects hinders children from pursuing basketball and enjoying the game. We have designed this chapter to ensure that skillfulness and game sense are progressively taught and that the organization and use of pedagogies ensure that students have frequent opportunities to learn in every lesson.

OUR PEDAGOGICAL APPROACH TO BASKETBALL

Basketball is a small-sided court invasion game. Instruction in the elementary and secondary units focuses on developing skillful performance and game sense through tasks and instructional sequences that teach basketball skills and quickly using these skills in modified games.

Developing skillful performance involves the basic offensive techniques of shooting, passing, and dribbling. Because dribbling is challenging, we focus on passing and shooting performance with beginners and introduce dribbling in tasks and during the warm-up. Once students develop dribbling skills, these are incorporated into the tasks and game play as part of the triple-threat (pass, dribble, or shoot) decision-making process.

We begin with person-to-person defensive principles. We do not add zone defense until late in the learning sequence, because effective zones are founded on person-to-person principles.

We use modified games that emphasize passing in level 1, 3v3 half-court games in level 2, and 4v4 full-court games in level 3. We use overload games (e.g., 2v1, 3v2) to develop game sense because they can be used to emphasize specific elements such as dribbling and shooting in game-like conditions. Overload games increase student engagement and allow for greater student success as they apply the learned techniques. We use the PAC progression when adding defensive pressure. See chapter 7 for a detailed description of the PAC progression.

Modifications to Address Individual Needs of Students

For students with disabilities, appropriate modifications depend on the nature of the disability. To modify basketball instruction for students with visual impairments, you can (a) use brightly colored basketballs (e.g., bright orange or yellow), (b) use brightly colored floor tape to mark off boundaries, or (c) use tactile modeling when demonstrating the proper form for various basketball skills.

For students with autism spectrum disorder, set up groups that practice in quieter or less chaotic areas of the gymnasium. You can also present materials using the students' desired communication methods (e.g., using picture symbols).

For students who use wheelchairs, adopt rules from wheelchair basketball. Rather than holding students to the same dribbling technicalities, introduce and enforce wheelchair basketball dribbling rules (e.g., students are not allowed to take more than two consecutive pushes without bouncing a ball).

For individuals with cerebral palsy, you may need to limit the speed at which students move between locations. To accommodate this, consider decreasing the playing area (e.g., playing half-court) and teaching zone defense so each student defends only a small area within the court.

Organization

A full-sided basketball game is 5v5. We question the appropriateness of 5v5 in a physical education setting relative to teaching beginners. The development of game sense in basketball is based on three general game tactics: on-the-ball play, off-the-ball play, and opposite-the-ball play. When these are taught to beginners in a 5v5 setting, the fifth student (and to a lesser extent the fourth student) congests the midcourt and limits students' abilities to apply the techniques and tactics being learned. As such, we advocate the use of a 3v3 team structure with beginners to develop the skillful play and game sense needed for basketball. We don't recommended adding the fourth student until students can somewhat successfully apply the elements of skillful play and game sense they have learned. We do not recommend that you use a 5v5 game in a typical physical education setting.

Space

We recommend that you have one basketball court and at least 4 to 6 baskets. At the elementary level, when equipment might be limited, we suggest detachable baskets with suction cups or targets that are attached to the wall (students strike the targets with the ball). If fixed baskets are available, they should be adjustable down to 6 or 8 feet (1.8 to 2.4 meters) for elementary and middle school students. Adjustable goals are also preferred at the high school level, but this is not mandatory. The court space should be large enough to be divided into home areas for groups of 4 to 8 students, and you should have enough goals to accommodate each group of students. If you use an outdoor space, a wall is helpful for some tasks.

Equipment Needed

Having a variety of basketballs sizes (e.g., 4, 5, 6) is important at the elementary level regardless of skill level. Balls must be scaled to the students' hands. At the middle and high school levels, basketball sizes 6 (intermediate) and 7 (official) need to be available. You should have enough balls for each student.

CONTENT MAP STRUCTURE

Figure 8.1 is a combined content map that illustrates the flow and connectedness of all the tasks used to develop skillful play and game sense in basketball. It is divided into three levels, and each level has a separate content map that includes the application games used to refine the elements of skillful play and game sense at that level. Although dribbling is introduced in level 1 (figure 8.2), the primary focus is on passing and shooting, and it ends with an application game that combines those two techniques. At level 2 (figure 8.3), dribbling, defense, and individual offensive tactics are added, and the end game is a 3v3 game. At level 3 (figure 8.4), offensive and defensive tactics are stressed; this level ends in a 4v4 game.

In the content maps, we have numbered the tasks. These numbers are used to cross reference tasks descriptions in the body of the chapter with the content maps. The task numbers should not be interpreted as the order in which they should be taught. It is important that tasks are taught and progressed from simpler to more complex forms which is shown in the upward progress of the task sequence on the content map. This is particularly necessary before tasks are combined. For instance in basketball whether you teach shooting first or dribbling, the progressions of both need to be taught before they are combined in task 19.

STRUCTURE OF THE LESSONS

The following is a sample daily lesson structure for a 50-minute elementary basketball lesson.

Warm-up (5 to 6 minutes)

Application game: end line passing game (5 to 6 minutes)

Informing task: 2v1 passing (5 minutes)

Extension task: 2v1 passing from the other side (4 minutes)

Extension task: PAC defense applied to the 2v1 passing task (5 minutes)

Informing task: individual dribbling (5 minutes)

Extension task: nondominant side dribbling (4 minutes)

Application game: mat basketball with shooting game (10 minutes)

Closure (3 to 5 minutes)

Warm-up

Elementary School

The warm-up should be taught to students on the first or second day of the unit. If a technique used in the warm-up has not been taught, it should not be included in the warm-up circuit until the day after you teach it. Passing, dribbling, and shooting are the initial techniques used in the warm-up. In the first lesson, passing and wall shots are introduced; therefore, you can include passing and shooting practice in the warm-up for lesson 2. Lesson 2 introduces individual dribbling, so you can include that technique in the warm-up for lesson 3. Each day you can add new techniques, such as step back shots for wall shots (see the five-day block plan), or you can stick with the same warm-up.

For the passing task, pairs of students stand 8 to 10 feet (2.4 to 3 meters) apart and pass the ball back and forth using the techniques that have been taught. For the shooting task, students begin with wall shots and move to step-back shots with a partner after a couple of days. For the dribbling task, students dribble in a stationary position using the dominant and nondominant hands. After a couple days, students can add movement to the dribbling if their skills have progressed appropriately. The warm-up time should allow for multiple trials. Once students have learned the warm-up, it should not last more than 5 to 6 minutes.

How you organize your students for the warm-up will depend on the decisions you make about the organization of the class. If you use a circuit, divide the class into three groups and include the appropriate equipment at each of the three stations (see figure 8.5). The passing and shooting stations require basketballs for each pair of students, and the dribbling station

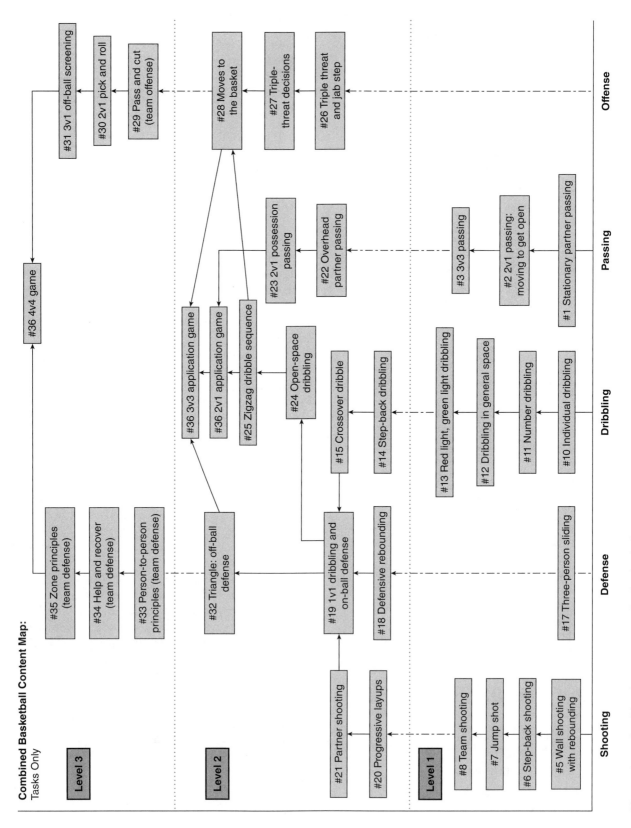

Figure 8.1 Combined content map for basketball.

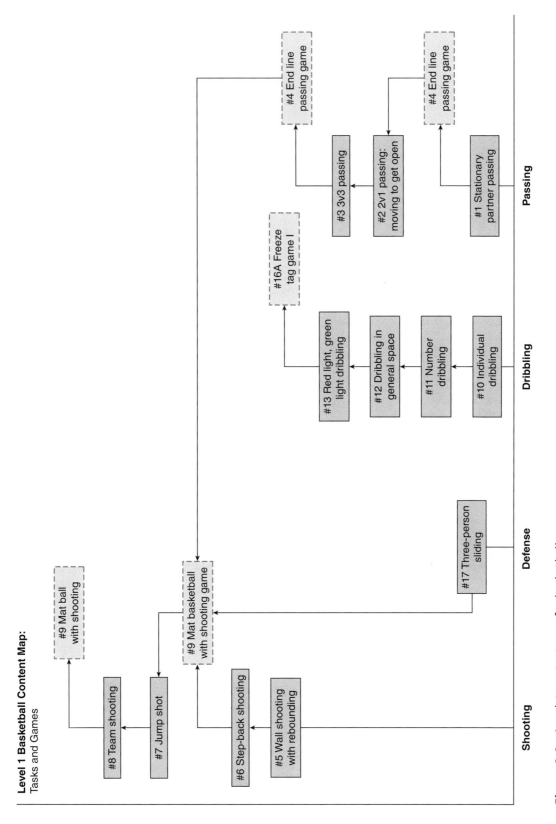

Figure 8.2 Level 1 content map for basketball.

231

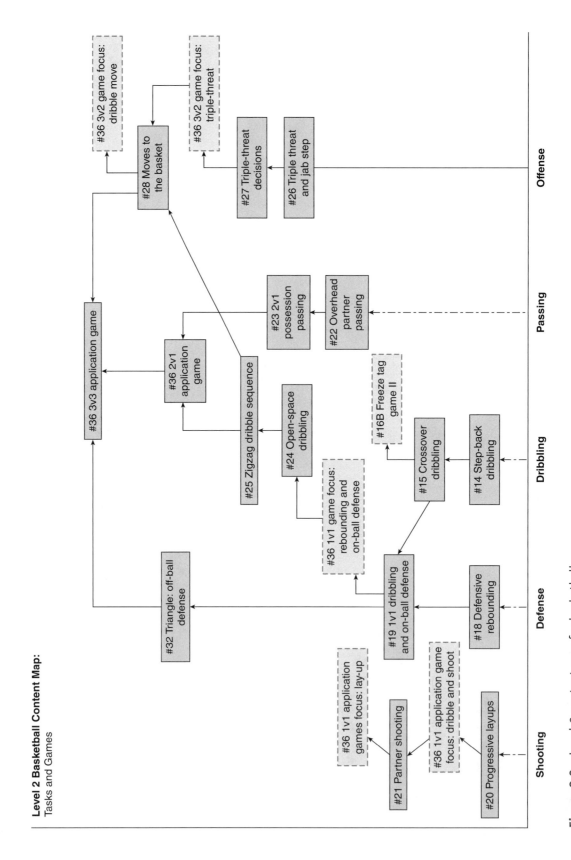

Figure 8.3 Level 2 content map for basketball.

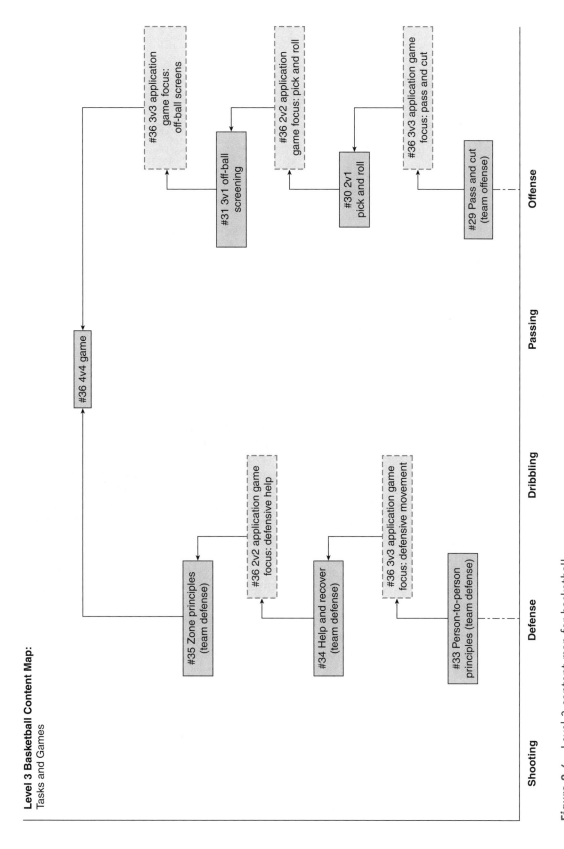

Level 3 Basketball Content Map:
Tasks and Games

Figure 8.4 Level 3 content map for basketball.

233

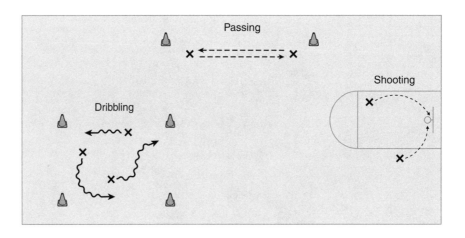

Figure 8.5   Sample elementary school warm-up circuit for basketball.

requires a ball for each student. Students should begin each day in the same area and rotate through the stations. The tasks can be done in any order. Provide instructions for what students should do once they have completed all the stations. If you decide to have the whole class do the warm-up activities together, you need to have enough baskets to accommodate the entire class with no more than 8 students at a basket. You can add stick-on baskets to the walls if needed. We recommend that the warm-up not last more than 5-6 minutes once it has been learned.

Secondary School

Teach the warm-up in lessons 2 through 4; once students know the warm-up, it should take 4 to 5 minutes. Students work in pairs. In the first task, students alternate between open-space and close-control dribbling in the court space. Each pair has a ball, and one student assumes the role of offense and the other assumes the role of defense. The defensive student moves along with the offensive student and provides active defense as the offensive student dribbles under control. Students switch roles after each trial. In the next task, students practice left- and right-handed layups; one student shoots and the other student rebounds. After rebounding, the rebounder moves to the shooting line and the shooter moves to the rebounding line. After a determined number of right-handed layups, have students attempt left-handed layups. In the last task, students practice open shooting and attempt shots they would take in a game situation. If a student makes a shot, the partner returns the ball and the student continues shooting until a shot is missed or a set number of shots have been attempted; then, the partner becomes the shooter.

This warm-up can be done with stations or in teams. If you use stations, divide the class into three groups and have each group spend about 90 seconds at each station. The lay-ups should be done at one end basket, the open shooting at the opposite end basket with the open- and closed-space dribbling occurring in the middle of the court (see figure 8.6). If the warm-up is done in teams, have groups of 6 to 8 students complete each part of the warm-up in the home area. This requires one basket for each group. Provide students with instructions for what they should do once they finish the warm-up (e.g., put balls away, ball rake, sit down in an assigned space, line up, repeat tasks).

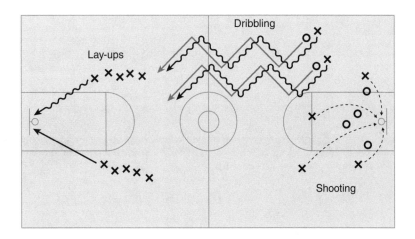

Figure 8.6   Sample secondary school warm-up circuit for basketball stations.

BLOCK PLAN
. . . .

The introductory block plan is designed for begin-ners. In elementary school, this should not be introduced earlier than fourth grade. This allows students to refine their basic ball-handling tech-niques in other activities prior to facing the chal-lenges of manipulating a basketball. Although longer units are always preferred, we recognize that there are time limitations at the elementary level; therefore, the elementary unit is five days for the initial grade in which it is taught.

The secondary block plan follows the elemen-tary block plan and is designed for students in middle school and high school. It assumes that students were taught the basic basketball tech-niques at the elementary level. If this is not the case, follow the introductory block plan. Because middle and high school physical education pro-grams have different requirements, these units should *not* be taught in fewer than 10 days. These units are adjusted for 10-, 15-, and 20-day programs, although we recommend units of 20 or more days.

Table 8.1 Elementary Basketball Block Plan: Five-Day Unit

This is an example of a beginning block plan for elementary students that uses the basketball tasks shown in the level 1 content map. It is based on an initial five-day unit and, as such, it does not encompass all the level 1 tasks on the content map. You can use this as a template for developing an appropriate block plan for beginning students. If you are teaching a longer unit, or if another basketball unit will be taught next year, you can include the remaining level 1 tasks and some level 2 tasks. Your decisions about what tasks to include will depend on your students and their levels of experience.

Lesson 1	Lesson 2	Lesson 3	Lesson 4	Lesson 5

Warm-up
• Nonspecific warm-up
	Warm-up
	• Circuit
	  • Passing: chest passes and bounce passes
	  • Shooting: wall shots
		Warm-up
		• Circuit
		  • Passing: chest passes and bounce passes
		  • Shooting: wall shots
		  • Individual dribbling: on dominant side and on non-dominant side
			Warm-up
			• Circuit
			  • Passing: chest passes and bounce passes
			  • Shooting: step-back shots
			  • Individual dribbling: on dominant side and on non-dominant side
				Warm-up
				• Same as day 4

Introductory application game None	**Introductory application game** • **(4)** End line passing game	**Introductory application game** • **(4)** End line passing game	**Introductory application game** • **(4)** End line passing game	**Introductory application game** • **(9)** Mat basketball with shooting game
Content development • **(1)** Stationary partner passing • **(17)** Three-person sliding • **(5)** Wall shooting with rebounding	**Content development** • **(2)** 2v1 passing: moving to get open • **(10)** Individual dribbling	**Content development** • **(3)** 3v3 passing • **(6)** Step-back shooting • **(11)** Number dribbling	**Content development** • **(3)** 3v3 passing • **(11)** Number dribbling • **(12)** Dribbling in general space	**Content development** • **(13)** Red light, green light dribbling
Closing application game • **(4)** End line game	**Closing application game** • **(4)** End line game	**Closing application game** • **(4)** End line game	**Closing application game** • **(9)** Mat basketball with shooting game	**Closing application game** • **(16A)** Freeze tag game I • **(9)** Mat basketball with shooting game

Table 8.2 Secondary Basketball Block Plans: 10-, 15-, and 20-Day Units

This block plan incorporates 10-, 15-, and 20-day units. The last two days of the 10-day block plan, the last three days of the 15-day block plan, and the last five days of the 20-day block plan are game days, which are described at the end of the block plan. The first eight days of the block plan are the same for all units. This block plan reviews level 1 tasks and then addresses the level 2 content map (10- and 15-day units) and the level 3 content map (20-day unit).

Lesson 1 of all block plans	Lesson 2 of all block plans	Lesson 3 of all block plans	Lesson 4 of all block plans	Lesson 5 of all block plans
Warm-up • Nonspecific warm-up (e.g., movements for agility and stretching)	**Warm-up** • Teach the warm-up	**Warm-up** • Teach the warm-up	**Warm-up** • Dribbling • Shooting • Layups	**Warm-up** • Same as day 4
Introductory application game • 3v3 game to assess level of previously learned skills	**Introductory application game** • **(36)** 1v1 application game	**Introductory application game** • **(36)** 1v1 application game	**Introductory application game** • **(36)** 2v1 application game	**Introductory application game** • **(16B)** Freeze tag game II
Content development • **(6)** Step-back shooting • **(12)** Dribbling in general space	**Content development** • **(7)** Jump shot • **(20)** Progressive layups • **(21)** Partner shooting	**Content development** • **(1)** Stationary partner passing • **(22)** Overhead partner passing • **(23)** 2v1 possession passing	**Content development** • **(14)** Step-back dribbling • **(15)** Crossover dribbling	**Content development** • **(26)** Triple threat and jab step
Closing application game • **(36)** 1v1 application game	**Closing application game** • **(36)** 1v1 application game	**Closing application game** • **(36)** 2v1 application game	**Closing application game** • **(16B)** Freeze tag game II	**Closing application game** • **(36)** 2v2 application game

Lesson 6 of all block plans	Lesson 7 of all block plans	Lesson 8 of all block plans (last instructional day of 10-day block plan)	Lesson 9 of 15- and 20-day block plans (See table 8.3 for lesson 9 for 10-day plan.)	Lesson 10 of 15- and 20-day block plans (See table 8.3 for lesson 10 for 10-day plan.)
Warm-up • Same as day 4	**Warm-up** • Same as day 4	**Warm-up** • Same as day 4	**Warm-up** • Same as day 4	**Warm-up** • Same as day 4
Introductory application game • **(36)** 2v2 application game	**Introductory application game** • **(36)** 1v1 application game	**Introductory application game** • **(36)** 3v2 application game	**Introductory application game** • **(36)** 3v2 application game	**Introductory application game** • **(36)** 3v3 application game
Content development • **(18)** Defensive rebounding • **(19)** 1v1 dribbling and on-ball defense	**Content development** • **(26)** Triple threat and jab step • **(27)** Triple-threat decisions	**Content development** • **(28)** Moves to the basket	**Content development** • **(29)** Pass and cut (team offense)	**Content development** • **(30)** 2v1 pick and roll • **(36)** 2v2 application game • **(31)** 3v1 off-ball screening
Closing application game • **(36)** 1v1 application game	**Closing application game** • **(36)** 3v2 application game	**Closing application game** • **(36)** 3v2 application game	**Closing application game** • **(36)** 3v3 application game	**Closing application game** • **(36)** 3v3 application game

(continued)

Lesson 11 of 15- and 20-day block plans	Lesson 12 of 15- and 20-day block plans (last instructional day of 15-day plan)	Lesson 13 of 20-day block plan (See table 8.4 for lesson 13 for 15-day plan.)	Lesson 14 of 20-day block plan (See table 8.4 for lesson 14 for 15-day plan.)	Lesson 15 of 20-day block plan (See table 8.4 for lesson 15 for 15-day plan.)
Warm-up • Same as day 4	**Warm-up** • Same as day 4	**Warm-up** • Same as day 4	**Warm-up** • Same as day 4	**Warm-up** • Same as day 4
Introductory application game • **(36)** 3v2 application game	**Introductory application game** • **(36)** 3v3 application game	**Introductory application game** • **(36)** 3v3 application game	**Introductory application game** • **(36)** 2v2 application game	**Introductory application game** • **(36)** 4v4 application game
Content development • **(32)** Triangle: off-ball defense	**Content development** • **(33)** Person-to-person principles (team defense)	**Content development** • **(34)** Help and recover (team defense)	**Content development** • **(35)** Zone principles (team defense)	**Content development** • Review previous defensive tasks
Closing application game • **(36)** 3v3 application game	**Closing application game** • **(36)** 3v3 application game	**Closing application game** • **(36)** 2v2 application game	**Closing application game** • **(36)** 4v4 application game	**Closing application game** • **(36)** 4v4 application game
Lesson 16 of 20-day block plan	**Lesson 17 of 20-day block plan**	**Lesson 18 of 20-day block plan**	**Lesson 19 of 20-day block plan**	**Lesson 20 of 20-day block plan**
Warm-up • Same as day 4	**Warm-up** • Same as day 4	**Warm-up** • Same as day 4	**Warm-up** • Same as day 4	**Warm-up** • Same as day 4
Fixed-time 4v4 games against different opponents (nonexclusionary round-robin tournament) Encourage the use of specific skills. Award an extra point to the score for demonstration of these skills. We recommend at least two games per lesson.	**Fixed-time 4v4 games against different opponents (nonexclusionary round-robin tournament)** Encourage the use of specific skills. Award an extra point to the score for demonstration of these skills. We recommend at least two games per lesson.	**Fixed-time 4v4 games against different opponents (nonexclusionary round-robin tournament)** Encourage the use of specific skills. Award an extra point to the score for demonstration of these skills. We recommend at least two games per lesson.	**Fixed-time 4v4 games against different opponents (nonexclusionary round-robin tournament)** Encourage the use of specific skills. Award an extra point to the score for demonstration of these skills. We recommend at least two games per lesson.	**Fixed-time 4v4 games against different opponents (nonexclusionary round-robin tournament)** Encourage the use of specific skills. Award an extra point to the score for demonstration of these skills. We recommend at least two games per lesson.

Table 8.3   10-Day Block Plan Game Days

Lesson 9 of 10-day block plan	Lesson 10 of 10-day block plan
Warm-up • Same as day 4	**Warm-up** • Same as day 4
Fixed-time 4v4 games against different opponents (nonexclusionary round-robin tournament) Encourage the use of specific skills. Award an extra point to the score for demonstration of these skills. We recommend at least two games per lesson.	**Fixed-time 4v4 games against different opponents (nonexclusionary round-robin tournament)** Encourage the use of specific skills. Award an extra point to the score for demonstration of these skills. We recommend at least two games per lesson.

Table 8.4 15-Day Block Plan Game Days

Lesson 13 of 15-day block plan	Lesson 14 of 15-day block plan	Lesson 15 of 15-day block plan
Warm-up • Same as day 4	**Warm-up** • Same as day 4	**Warm-up** • Same as day 4
Fixed-time 4v4 games against different opponents (nonexclusionary round-robin tournament) Encourage the use of specific skills. Award an extra point to the score for demonstration of these skills. We recommend at least two games per lesson.	**Fixed-time 4v4 games against different opponents (nonexclusionary round-robin tournament)** Encourage the use of specific skills. Award an extra point to the score for demonstration of these skills. We recommend at least two games per lesson.	**Fixed-time 4v4 games against different opponents (nonexclusionary round-robin tournament)** Encourage the use of specific skills. Award an extra point to the score for demonstration of these skills. We recommend at least two games per lesson.

SHAPE AMERICA'S GRADE-LEVEL OUTCOMES FOR K-12 PHYSICAL EDUCATION

In table 8.5, we identify key grade-level outcomes for basketball for 2nd through 8th grade. These are linked to specific tasks on the content maps that are appropriate for teaching the skill and assessing the outcome.

Table 8.5 Grade-Level Outcomes for Basketball

Outcome	Description	Content map focus and tasks
S1.E17.2a	Dribbles in self-space with preferred hand demonstrating a mature pattern.	Level 1, task 10
S1.E17.2b	Dribbles using the preferred hand while walking in general space.	Level 1, tasks 11, 12
S1.E17.3	Dribbles and travels in general space at slow to moderate jogging speed, with control of ball and body.	Level 1, task 12
S1.E17.4a	Dribbles in self-space with both the preferred and the non-preferred hands using a mature pattern.	Level 1, task 10
S1.E17.4b	Dribbles in general space with control of ball and body while increasing and decreasing speed.	Level 1, task 13
S1.E17.5	Combines hand dribbling with other skills during 1v1 practice tasks.	Level 2, tasks 19, 36
S1.M4.6	Passes and receives with hands in combination with loco-motor patterns of running and change of direction & speed with competency in invasion games such as basketball, flag football, speedball or team handball.	Level 1, tasks 2-3
S1.M5.6	Throws, while stationary, a leading pass to a moving receiver.	Level 1, task 2 Level 2, task 21
S1.M5.7	Throws, while moving, a leading pass to a moving receiver.	Level 1, task 3
S1.M5.8	Throws a lead pass to a moving partner off a dribble or a pass.	Level 2, tasks 23, 36
S1.M6.6	Performs pivots, fakes and jab steps designed to create open space during practice tasks.	Level 2, tasks 26-27
S1.M6.7	Executes at least one of the following designed to create open space during small-sided game play: pivots, fakes, jab steps.	Level 2, task 36
S1.M6.8	Executes at least two of the following to create open space during modified game play: pivots, fakes, jab steps, screens.	Levels 2 and 3, task 36

(continued)

Outcome	Description	Content map focus and tasks
S1.M7.8	Executes the following offensive skills during small-sided game play: pivot, give & go, and fakes.	Level 2, task 36
S1.M8.6	Dribbles with dominant hand using a change of speed and direction in a variety of practice tasks.	Level 2, tasks 14-15, 24-25
S1.M8.7	Dribbles with dominant and nondominant hands using a change of speed and direction in a variety of practice tasks.	Level 2, tasks 14-15, 24-25
S1.M8.8	Dribbles with dominant and nondominant hands using a change of speed and direction in small-sided game play.	Level 2, task 36
S1.M10.6	Shoots on goal with power in a dynamic environment as appropriate to the activity.	Level 1, task 8 Level 2, task 21
S1.M10.7	Shoots on goal with power and accuracy in small-sided game play.	Level 2, task 36
S1.M11.6	Maintains defensive-ready position, with weight on balls of feet, arms extended and eyes on midsection of the offensive player.	Level 1, task 17
S1.M11.7	Slides in all directions while on defense without crossing feet.	Level 1, task 17
S1.M11.8	Drop-steps in the direction of the pass during player-to-player defense.	Level 2, task 32

TASK 1: STATIONARY PARTNER PASSING

PURPOSE

Following are the purposes of the task as related to aspects of skilled performance.

- Technique: In this task, students learn the basic techniques of passing and catching a basketball without a defender.
- Fair play: Students pass the ball where the partner can receive it.
- Communication: Students hold their hands out to indicate they are ready to receive the pass.

DESCRIPTION

Divide students into pairs and have them stand 10 to 15 feet (3 to 4.6 meters) apart. On your signal, the students continuously pass a ball back and forth using the assigned pass (chest and bounce) and catch techniques. If students need motivation, have pairs count how many successful passes they can make in a row or within a designated time. As an extension, have students move back one step until they are 20 feet (6.1 meters) apart.

EQUIPMENT

One ball per pair of students

CRITICAL ELEMENTS AND CUES

Technique: Chest Pass

- Place both hands on the side of the ball and spread the fingers and thumbs. *Cue:* Fingers spread.
- Start with the ball close to chest. *Cue:* Ball to chest.
- Look at the receiver's chest. *Cue:* Eyes on target.
- Step toward the receiver with one leg. *Cue:* Step to receiver.
- Move the ball away from the chest by extending the elbows. *Cue:* Push.
- As the arms extend, pronate the arms and end in a thumb-down position. *Cue:* Thumbs down.

Technique: Bounce Pass

- Place both hands on the side of the ball and spread the fingers and thumbs. *Cue:* Fingers spread.
- Start with the ball close to chest. *Cue:* Ball to chest.
- Step toward the receiver with one leg. *Cue:* Step to receiver.
- Move the ball away from the chest by extending the elbows. *Cue:* Push.
- Push the ball toward the floor so it bounces two-thirds of the distance to your partner. *Cue:* Down and close.
- The target is between the receiver's knees and waist. *Cue:* Keep it low.
- Actively push the thumbs through the pass (thumbs back to thumbs down) to create backspin. *Cue:* Slam the door.

Technique: Receive a Pass

- Look at the ball as it comes into the hands. *Cue:* Eyes on ball.
- Step toward the ball as it comes toward you. *Cue:* Step to ball.
- As the ball contacts the hands, pull the ball into the body as you catch it. *Cue:* Absorb the ball.
- End with the ball close to the body and the elbows flexed. *Cue:* Bring it in.

Fair Play

- Pass the ball directly to the receiver.
- The pass must have enough force to reach the receiver, but it should not be so hard that the receiver cannot catch it.

Communication

- When you are ready to receive a pass, create a target with both hands by placing the hands in the target area and spreading the fingers and palms. *Cue:* Big target.

COMMON ERRORS, CAUSES, AND CORRECTIONS

Catching

- The receiver does not step toward the ball. *Cause:* The receiver doesn't understand that a defender can intercept a passed ball. *Correction:* Place a student slightly behind and to the side of the receiver who tries to disrupt the catch.
- The receiver doesn't follow the ball into the hands. *Cause:* The receiver keeps the eyes on the passer. *Correction:* Remind the student to keep the eyes on the ball.
- On the catch, the ball is away from the body. *Cause:* The receiver does not absorb the ball into the body. *Correction:* Ask the student to exaggerate the flexing of the elbows such that the elbows are almost out to the side.

Chest Pass

- The ball does not make it to the receiver. *Cause:* The passer does not step toward the receiver. *Correction:* Place a poly spot in front of the passer and have the student step over it when making the pass.
- The ball does not make it to the receiver. *Cause:* The arms do not extend quickly. *Correction:* Remind the student to "slam the gate."
- The thumbs do not point down after release. *Cause:* The wrists are not pronated. *Correction:* Remind the student that the thumbs should end up pointing toward the wall. (This is an exaggeration, but it will help the student understand the need to pronate.)
- The pass does not arrive at the receiver's chest. *Cause:* The passer is not looking at the receiver's chest. *Correction:* Have the receiver create a number with one hand and then have the passer tell what the number was after the pass is made.
- The pass does not arrive at the receiver's chest. *Cause:* The passer doesn't have the strength to get the pass to the chest. *Correction:* Have partners move closer together.

Bounce Pass

- The ball has topspin as it hits the floor. *Cause:* The thumbs moved over the top of the ball. *Correction:* Stress the pronation of the wrists by reminding the student to keep the thumbs down.
- The ball does not make it to the receiver. *Cause:* The passer does not step toward the receiver. *Correction:* Place a poly spot in front of the passer and have the student step over it when making the pass.
- The ball does not make it to the receiver. *Cause:* The arms do not extend quickly. *Correction:* Remind the student to "slam the gate."
- The student catches the ball on the downward arc. *Cause:* The ball is bounced less than two-thirds of the way to the receiver. *Correction:* Place a marker two-thirds of the way to the receiver and have the passer aim for that spot.

TASK 2: 2V1 PASSING: MOVING TO GET OPEN

PURPOSE

Following are the purposes of the task as related to aspects of skilled performance.

- Technique: In this task, students learn to use a V-cut to create open space for a pass.
- Tactic: The receiver moves the defender to create an open passing lane.
- Agility: The receiver moves away from the intended direction of the pass, and then makes a quick cut back toward the intended pass.
- Communication: Students hold their outside hand out to indicate they are ready to receive the pass.

DESCRIPTION

Divide students into groups of three. Two students are on offense and one is on defense. One offensive student has the ball, faces the basket, stands at the top of the key, and stays here throughout the task. The other offensive student stands on a wing and is guarded by the defender (see figure). The student on the wing moves toward the basket and draws the defender back. When the student reaches the poly spot that is set 5-8 feet towards the basket, he or she executes a jab step and quickly darts back out to the wing while holding the outside hand out to the side away from the defender; this indicates that the student is ready to receive a pass. After receiving the pass, the student must stop within two steps or is considered traveling. The defender plays active defense, meaning the defender moves with the wing person and allows the wing to receive the ball once the V-cut is made. The student passes to the receiver on the side opposite where the defender is positioned using a chest pass. Students rotate positions after two successful passes or four attempts: passer to defender, defender to receiver, and receiver to passer. If there is a group of 4 or 5, have the extra students line up behind the passer. When a student rotates into the passing position, the receiver moves to the waiting line. If students need motivation, award a point to the offense for two successful consecutive passes.

- *Extension 1.* Have the defender use competitive defense, in which the defender tries to disrupt the pass.
- *Extension 2.* Have the passer use the bounce pass against an active defender and then a competitive defender.
- *Extension 3.* Have the wing student move in different directions using the V-cut to get open.

EQUIPMENT

One basketball and one poly spot per three students

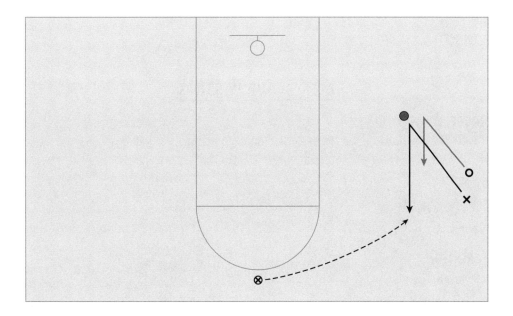

CRITICAL ELEMENTS AND CUES

Technique

- The passer passes the ball to the side of the receiver away from the defender. *Cue:* Lead the receiver.
- The receiver moves a few steps away from the passer to draw the defender away from the anticipated pass. *Cue:* Move the defender.

Tactic

- The receiver creates an open passing lane so a pass can be made.

Agility

- The receiver quickly stops and cuts back out to receive the pass by speeding up. *Cue:* Quick cut.

Communication

- As the receiver moves back out after the cut, both hands are out on the side away from the defender as a target. *Cue:* Give a target.

COMMON ERRORS, CAUSES, AND CORRECTIONS

- The receiver does not get open to receive the pass. *Cause:* The offensive student does not execute the V-cut quickly enough to lose the defender. *Correction:* Have the student practice making a good jab step to initiate the V-cut by adding a second cone to cut toward.
- The pass is intercepted by the defender. *Cause:* The ball is passed toward the defender side of the receiver. *Correction:* In a partner pass situation, have the defender stand by the inside shoulder of the receiver, and have the passer pass to the side of the receiver away from the defender.
- The pass is too far in front of the receiver. *Cause:* The passer is passing the ball too soon. *Correction:* In a partner pass situation, have the students practice the V-cut and pass without a defender.

- The pass is too far in front of the receiver. *Cause:* The receiver does not present a good target. *Correction:* Remind the receiver to give a target.

TASK 3: 3V3 PASSING

PURPOSE

Following are the purposes of the task as related to aspects of skilled performance.

- Technique: In this task, students learn to pass against pressure.
- Agility: Students move to get open.
- Fair play: When playing passive or active defense, students do not pressure too much.
- Communication: Receivers indicate that they are ready to receive a pass by putting an arm up.

DESCRIPTION

Divide groups of six students into two teams of three. One team has the ball and is on offense, and the other team is on defense. The offensive student with the ball begins at the top of the key, and the other two teammates are each on a wing (free-throw line extended). The defenders begin by playing passive defense and staying 1 yard (0.9 meters) away from the offensive students and allowing the passes to be made. The offensive students use the V-cut and quick movements to get open and indicate when they are open by raising the arm that is away from the defender. When the pass is caught, the receiver becomes the new passer and must stand still while the other two offensive students execute V-cuts to get open. These movements continue until five successful passes have been made; then, the offensive and defensive students switch positions.

- *Extension 1.* Defenders move to active defense, in which they play on the offensive student but still allow passes to be made.
- *Extension 2.* Defenders play competitive defense, in which they try to deny and disrupt the passes. If students need motivation, award the defense one point for each pass that is not made.

EQUIPMENT

One ball per six students

CRITICAL ELEMENTS AND CUES

Technique

- On offense, extend the arms and ball-side leg as if you are going to pass in one direction; then, cross the ball-side leg across the body and pull the ball in close before passing in the opposite direction. This can help you get an open pass. *Cue:* Pass fake.
- On defense, watch both the passer and the offensive student who is being guarded. *Cue:* Watch.
- Stay between the student you are defending and the basket. *Cue:* Basket side.

Agility

- Use V-cuts to get open. *Cue:* Cut to get open.

Fair play

- Use PAC defense.

Communication

- Raise the arm on the side away from the defender if you are open for a pass. *Cue:* Call for the ball.

COMMON ERRORS, CAUSES, AND CORRECTIONS

- Students without the ball are not able to get open. *Cause:* Students are not cutting sharply enough. *Correction:* Go back to the 2v1 passing task.
- The ball is knocked out of the passer's hands when attempting a pass fake. *Cause:* The passer does not bring the ball back in close to the body while moving to pass in the opposite direction. *Correction:* Have the student attempt the pass fake without being guarded and stress bringing the ball back in before passing.
- During the pass fake, the student travels (both feet move). *Cause:* When the student makes the pass fake, one foot steps toward the fake and the other foot does not remain as the pivot foot but instead step towards the pass when the ball is brought back and across the body. *Correction:* Have the student execute the pass fake without a defender, and stress that the stepping foot, not the pivot foot, crosses in front of the body and steps toward the receiver.

TASK 4: END LINE PASSING GAME

PURPOSE

Following are the purposes of the task as related to aspects of skilled performance.
- Technique: In this task, students apply passing skills, defensive movement, and moving to get open in a game-like setting.
- Agility: Students make quick cuts and movements to get open and use shuffle steps on defense.
- Fair play: Students report their own violations, and disputes are resolved using rock, paper, scissors. The ball is not taken away from the person in possession of it.
- Communication: Students raise a hand when they are open for a pass.

DESCRIPTION

Divide students into two teams of 5 to 6 players. Play the game on half of the court from sideline to sideline. Each team has a student that is designated as the goalie; this student stands behind opposite sideline (the goal line). The other team members stand within the playing area. The object is for a team to pass the ball as they move toward their team's end zone and to pass the ball to the goalie within their end zone. This is a passing-only game; dribbling and running with the ball are not allowed. The defenders try to intercept the pass, but the ball cannot be taken out of another student's hands. If the ball is intercepted, the intercepting team then moves the ball toward its goal by passing. A team scores a goal when the ball is passed successfully across the goal line and caught by the goalie. Defenders are not allowed in the goal area. When a goal is scored, the student who passed the ball to the goalie becomes the new goalie, and the goalie plays on the court. Play continues for a designated time.

EQUIPMENT

One ball per 10 to 12 students

CRITICAL ELEMENTS AND CUES

Technique
- Students apply the passing critical elements and cues learned in tasks 2 and 3.
- Teachers need to stress the need for the defenders to stay on one person. *Cue:* Person-to-person.
- Teachers need to stress the need for students to move when they do not have the ball. *Cue:* Move to get open.
- Teachers need to stress the importance of short passes. *Cue:* Keep passes short.

Agility

- Move the feet quickly whether you are on defense (shuffling) or on offense (moving to get open).

Fair Play

- Do not take or slap at the ball when it is in an offensive player's hands.
- Do not take any steps when you have the ball. This is called *traveling,* and it results in a loss of the ball.
- At the start of play, allow one short free pass before playing defense.
- When defending the student with the ball, stand 3 feet (0.9 meters) away.
- When you are on defense, do not make body contact with offensive team members.
- If a dispute arises, resolve it by playing rock, paper, scissors.

Communication

- Raise your hand to indicate that you are open.

COMMON ERRORS, CAUSES, AND CORRECTIONS

- The defender makes contact with the passer or tries to take the ball away. *Cause:* The defender is not 3 feet (0.9 meters) away. *Correction:* Have the student stretch out an arm and take one step back.
- Students are not open to receive a pass. *Cause:* Students are not moving in different directions (away from and toward the passer). *Correction:* Tell students to move away from the ball and then back to the ball.
- Passes are regularly intercepted. *Cause:* The receiver is too far away from the passer. *Correction:* Remind students to make short passes and to move to the ball.

TASK 5: WALL SHOOTING WITH REBOUNDING

PURPOSE

Following are the purposes of the task as related to aspects of skilled performance.

- Technique: In this task, students learn the set shot and basic rebounding.

DESCRIPTION

Each student stands a couple feet away from a wall with a basketball. Students practice shooting against the wall to targets that are approximately 7 feet (2.1 meters) high. As an extension, have students jump to rebound the ball after the shot.

EQUIPMENT

One ball per student

CRITICAL ELEMENTS AND CUES

Technique: Shot (see figure)

- Spread the fingers on the ball. Make an L position with the wrist and elbow. Balance the hand lightly on the side of the ball. *Cue:* Waiter tray position.
- Maintain a *balanced* position. Keep the *elbow* bent and pointed toward the basket. *Eyes* look at the basket. *Follow* through with the hand in the cookie jar. *Cue:* BEEF.
- Set the shot so both feet stay on the floor. *Cue:* Feet stuck.

Technique: Rebound

- Push off the floor and extend the legs. *Cue:* Jump high.
- Extend the arms straight up. *Cue:* Reach high.
- Place the hands on opposite sides of the ball. *Cue:* Grab the ball.
- Pull the ball down to chest level with the elbows out. *Cue:* Rip it down.

COMMON ERRORS, CAUSES, AND CORRECTIONS

- The student shoots with both hands. *Cause:* The shooting elbow is not below the ball. *Correction:* Have the student practice the shot without the wall. Stress the BEEF position and the ball dropping straight down in front of the student after release.

- The ball is not going straight. *Cause:* The elbow is not pointed at the target. *Correction:* Have the student practice the shot without the wall. Stress the BEEF position and the ball dropping straight down in front of the student after release.

- The movements of the student's legs and arms are not coordinated. *Cause:* The knees are not bent before the shot. *Correction:* Have the student practice the shot without the wall, and remind the student to bend the knees and to begin the shot by extending the shooting arm.

- The student does not catch the ball at the height of the jump. *Cause:* The timing of the jump is off. *Correction:* Remind the student to catch the ball high.

- The student does not bring the ball down to chest level. *Cause:* The elbows are not flexed after the hands are placed on the ball. *Correction:* Remind the student to "rip it down."

TASK 6: STEP-BACK SHOOTING

PURPOSE

Following are the purposes of the task as related to aspects of skilled performance.

- Technique: In this task, students learn to get the ball into the basket when shooting a set shot.

- Fair play: Students do not shoot when another student is shooting.

DESCRIPTION

Set up rows of poly spots 3, 5, 7, and 9 feet (0.9, 1.5, 2.1, and 2.7 meters) in front of the basket as shown in the figure. Students are in pairs, and one student from each pair stands on each spot in the first arc and shoots at the basket using a set shot. After the student makes three shots from the first spot, the student moves back to the poly spot on the next

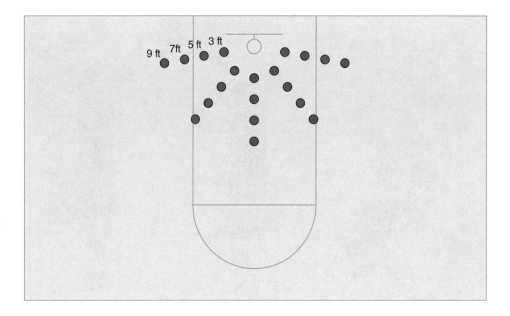

9 ft 7ft 5 ft 3 ft

arc. The task is repeated on each arc. The partner who is not shooting rebounds the ball and passes it back to the shooter. Students shoot for two minutes and then switch roles with their partners. If students need motivation, award one point for each made basket.

EQUIPMENT

One ball and 4 poly spots per pair of students

CRITICAL ELEMENTS AND CUES

Technique

- Keep the eyes on the middle eyelet of the back of the rim. *Cue:* Eyes on back of rim.
- Spread the fingers on the ball. Make an L position with the wrist and elbow. Balance the hand lightly on the side of the ball. *Cue:* Waiter tray position.
- Maintain a *balanced* position. Keep the *elbow* bent and pointed toward the basket. *Eyes* look at the basket. *Follow* through with the hand in the cookie jar. *Cue:* BEEF.
- Set the shot so both feet stay on the floor. *Cue:* Feet stuck.

Fair Play

- Do not shoot when someone else is shooting. *Cue:* Wait your turn.

COMMON ERRORS, CAUSES, AND CORRECTIONS

- The student does not get the ball over the front of the rim. *Cause:* The student is not extending the knees or is not extending with enough force to help get the ball up. *Correction:* Have the student add the jump to the shot. Remind the student to bend and extend the knees.

TASK 7: JUMP SHOT

PURPOSE

Following are the purposes of the task as related to aspects of skilled performance.

- Technique: In this task, students learn to get the ball into the basket when shooting a jump shot.
- Fair play: Students do not shoot when another student is shooting.

DESCRIPTION

Set up rows of poly spots as in task 7 but 5, 7, 9, and 11 feet (1.5, 2.1, 2.7, and 3.4 meters) in front of the basket. Students are in pairs, and one student from each pair stands on each spot in the first arc and shoots at the basket using a jump shot. After the student makes three shots from the first spot, the student moves back to the poly spot on the next arc. The task is repeated on each arc. The partner who is not shooting rebounds the ball and passes it back to the shooter. Students shoot for two minutes and then switch roles with their partners. If students need motivation, award one point for each made basket.

EQUIPMENT

One ball and 4 poly spots per pair of students

CRITICAL ELEMENTS AND CUES

Technique

- Keep the eyes on the middle eyelet of the back of the rim. *Cue:* Eyes on back of rim.
- Spread the fingers on the ball. Make an L position with the wrist and elbow. Balance the hand lightly on the side of the ball. *Cue:* Waiter tray position.
- Maintain a *balanced* position. Keep the *elbow* bent and pointed toward the basket. *Eyes* look at the basket. *Follow* through with the hand in the cookie jar. *Cue:* BEEF.
- Bend your knees and push off the ground with both feet. *Cue:* Bend and push.
- Shoot at the highest point of the jump. *Cue:* Shoot at the highest point.

Fair Play

- Do not shoot when another student is shooting so your ball does not interfere with the other student's shot.

COMMON ERRORS, CAUSES, AND CORRECTIONS

- The student does not get the ball over the front of the rim. *Cause:* The student is not extending the knees or is not extending with enough force to help get the ball up. *Correction:* Remind the student to bend and quickly extend the knees when jumping.

TASK 8: TEAM SHOOTING

PURPOSE

Following are the purposes of the task as related to aspects of skilled performance.

- Technique: In this task, students make jump and set shots in a competitive environment.
- Agility: Students move quickly to retrieve shots and get back to attempt additional shots.
- Fair play: Students only call out made shots.
- Communication: The number of made shots is called out loudly.

DESCRIPTION

Using one basket for each team of students, set up one arc of poly spots approximately 7 feet (2.1 meters) in front of the basket and another arc at the free throw line to create a shooting zone (see figure) at each team's basket. In their teams each student has a basketball within the shooting zone and, on your signal, all the students attempt to make a shot at their team's basket. After each shot, the shooter retrieves the ball and returns to the shooting zone to attempt another shot. When a student makes a shot, the team loudly calls out the number of made shots thus far. When the time is up, the team with the most made shots wins. If there are not enough balls for each person, have the students work in pairs in which one student shoots and the other rebounds. Students switch positions after the time is up. If students need motivation, allow them to attempt shots from outside the free-throw line arc; if made, these count as two shots.

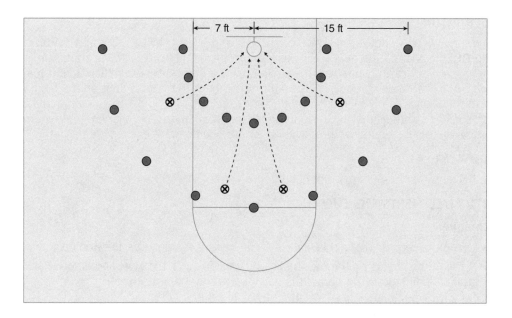

EQUIPMENT

One ball per student and a minimum of 10 poly spots for each basket

CRITICAL ELEMENTS AND CUES

Technique

- Keep the eyes on the middle eyelet of the back of the rim. *Cue:* Eyes on back of rim.
- Spread the fingers on the ball. Make an L position with the wrist and elbow. Balance the hand lightly on the side of the ball. *Cue:* Waiter tray position.
- Maintain a *balanced* position. Keep the *elbow* bent and pointed toward the basket. *Eyes* look at the basket. *Follow* through with the hand in the cookie jar. *Cue:* BEEF.
- Bend your knees and push off the ground with both feet. *Cue:* Bend and push.
- Shoot at the highest point of the jump. *Cue:* Shoot at the highest point.

Agility

- After each shot, move quickly to recover the ball and get back to the shooting zone for the next attempt.

Fair Play

- Only call out the number of the shot if you make it. Work with your teammates to accumulate shots.

Communication

- Loudly call out each made shot.

COMMON ERRORS, CAUSES, AND CORRECTIONS

- The students are not making many shots or are in too big of a hurry. *Cause:* The time limit causes the students to hurry their shots too much. *Correction:* Set a number of shots to be made and see which team can make the required number of shots first.

TASK 9: MAT BASKETBALL WITH SHOOTING GAME

PURPOSE

Following are the purposes of the task as related to aspects of skilled performance.

- Technique: In this task, students apply passing, defense movement, and shooting skills.
- Tactic: Students move to open space to get open.
- Agility: Students move their feet quickly on both offense and defense.
- Fair play: Students report their own violations, and disputes are resolved using rock, paper, scissors.
- Communication: Students raise a hand when they are open.

DESCRIPTION

This game is played the same as the end line passing game (task 4) except the goalie is on a mat under the basket and must remain there to receive a pass, and a shot is incorporated into the game. Two goals are needed per game; these can be permanent side baskets, baskets attached by suction cups to the walls, or targets attached to the walls. Once a pass is successfully made to the goalie, the student who made the pass gets a free shot at the basket from the spot from which he or she made the pass. Defenders should not interfere with the shot. After the shot (whether made or missed), the other team gets the ball and begins play with a free pass.

EQUIPMENT

One basketball per 10 to 12 students

CRITICAL ELEMENTS AND CUES

Technique

- Apply all critical elements and cues from passing task 1, defensive task 17, and shooting task 7.

Tactic

- Be sure to use V-cuts and move to open space.

Agility

- Be sure to keep the feet moving on both offense and defense.

Fair Play

- Do not take or slap at the ball when it is in an offensive player's hands.
- Do not take any steps when you have the ball. This is called *traveling,* and it results in a loss of the ball.
- At the start of play, allow one free pass before playing defense.
- Allow the shooter to attempt the shot without any physical or vocal distractions.
- Shake hands with the other team after the game is over.

Communication

- If an open passing lane is available, raise your hand or call for the ball to inform the passer.

COMMON ERRORS, CAUSES, AND CORRECTIONS

- The shot attempt is too far away from the basket. *Cause:* The pass to the goalie was too long. *Correction:* Tell the student to make shorter passes.
- The pass cannot be made to the goalie. *Cause:* A defender is standing in front of the goalie instead of guarding a student. *Correction:* Remind the defender to stay on his or her student.

TASK 10: INDIVIDUAL DRIBBLING

PURPOSE

Following is the purpose of the task as related to aspects of skilled performance.

Technique: In this task, students learn the proper technique for dribbling a basketball while stationary.

DESCRIPTION

Students spread out in general space within the home area. Each student has a basketball. Students stand still and dribble using the dominant hand. When students demonstrate a basic level of control, have them switch the ball to the nondominant hand. If students need motivation, have them count how many dribbles they can make in 30 seconds.

EQUIPMENT

One ball per student

CRITICAL ELEMENTS AND CUES

Technique

- Stand with the knees slightly bent. *Cue:* Knees bent.
- Stagger the feet so the toes of one foot are even with the heel of the other foot and the feet are shoulder-width apart. *Cue:* Feet shoulder-width apart.
- Spread the fingers. Only the finger pads contact the ball. *Cue:* Spider fingers.
- Keep the head up and look forward (not at the ball). *Cue:* Eyes up.
- The ball should be at or below waist level after the bounce. *Cue:* Ball low.
- Extend the elbow and flex the wrist downward as the ball contacts the finger pads. *Cue:* Push.
- Hold the nondribbling arm away from the body with the elbow slightly bent to protect the dribble. *Cue:* Protect.

COMMON ERRORS, CAUSES, AND CORRECTIONS

- The student is looking at the ball. *Cause:* The student lacks confidence in controlling the ball. *Correction:* Allow the student to look at the ball for one dribble; then have the student raise the head and eyes up on the next dribble. Gradually increase the number of dribbles done with the head and eyes up.
- The student is slapping at the ball. *Cause:* The student is contacting the ball with the palm of the hand instead of the finger pads. *Correction:* Remind the student to use spider fingers, and emphasize the flexion of the wrist.
- The student's arm is moving at the shoulder. *Cause:* The shoulder is exerting most of the force for the dribble. *Correction:* Have the student dribble while kneeling on both knees.
- The student's body is too upright. *Cause:* The legs are stiff. *Correction:* Remind the student to keep the knees bent.

TASK 11: NUMBER DRIBBLING

PURPOSE

Following is the purpose of the task as related to aspects of skilled performance.

- Technique: In this task, students learn to dribble a basketball while moving without looking at it.
- Fair play: The teammate holds the hand up so the dribbler can see the fingers.
- Communication: Students can effectively communicate during play because they are not looking at the ball.

DESCRIPTION

Place students into groups of three. Two students (A and C) line up facing the other partner (B) who is about 20 to 30 feet (6.1 to 9.1 meters) away. Student A has a basketball and walks while dribbling toward student B. While student A dribbles, student B holds up a number of fingers with one hand and student A calls out the number. After the correct number is called out, student B shows another number to student A. This continues until student A reaches student B. Then, student B takes the ball and walks while dribbling toward student C. Student C holds up fingers and B calls out the numbers. Students repeat the task until all three students have dribbled a set number of times.

- *Extension 1.* Have students dribble using their nondominant hand.
- *Extension 2.* Have dribblers increase their speed once they demonstrate control.

EQUIPMENT

One ball per three students

CRITICAL ELEMENTS AND CUES

Technique

- Keep the head up while dribbling so you can see the number of fingers being held up. *Cue:* Eyes up.
- Move at a speed at which you can control the dribble. *Cue:* Controlled speed.

Fair Play

- Do not stop holding up your fingers until your teammate correctly calls out the number.

Communication

- Hold up a number of fingers (0 through 5) using one hand.

COMMON ERRORS, CAUSES, AND CORRECTIONS

- The student looks down while dribbling. *Cause:* The student lacks confidence in knowing where the ball will bounce. *Correction:* Allow the student to look down for one dribble and then look back up.
- The student loses control of the ball while dribbling. *Cause:* The student is moving too fast. *Correction:* Tell the dribbler to slow down to a speed at which he or she can control the ball.

TASK 12: DRIBBLING IN GENERAL SPACE

PURPOSE

Following are the purposes of the task as related to aspects of skilled performance.

- Technique: In this task, students learn to control a dribble while moving in traffic by stopping, changing directions, and changing hands while dribbling.
- Agility: Students quickly stop and change directions.
- Fair play: Students purposefully avoid contact with other dribblers.

DESCRIPTION

Combine two groups of 6 to 8 students in one playing area to provide more space. Each student has a basketball and begins to dribble while moving slowly in different directions within the space. On your signal, students stop, switch hands, and begin moving again. If a student needs to turn in the opposite direction while moving to avoid contact with another dribbler, the student should reverse directions and change hands. As an extension, have students move faster as they demonstrate control; on your signal, have them reverse directions and change hands without stopping.

EQUIPMENT

One ball per student

CRITICAL ELEMENTS AND CUES

Technique

- Push the ball out slightly ahead of your body as you move. The faster you move the farther in front of the body the ball should be. *Cue:* Push the ball.
- Keep your eyes up to be aware of other dribblers. *Cue:* Eyes up.
- When dribbling in reverse, step forward with and push off the foot opposite the dribbling hand; as you do this, change dribbling hands. *Cue:* Step, push, and switch.

Agility

- While moving through open space, quickly stop and change directions to avoid contacting other dribblers.

Fair Play

- Avoid contacting other dribblers while moving through open space.

COMMON ERRORS, CAUSES, AND CORRECTIONS

- The student loses control of the ball. *Cause:* The student is moving too fast. *Correction:* Have the student slow down to maintain control and then slowly increase the speed.
- The student is dribbling into other dribblers. *Cause:* The student is not looking up or is not scanning the court while dribbling. *Correction:* Eyes up.

TASK 13: RED LIGHT, GREEN LIGHT DRIBBLING

PURPOSE

Following is the purpose of the task as related to aspects of skilled performance.

Technique: In this task, students learn to execute a controlled stop while dribbling with either hand.

DESCRIPTION

Students are in the home area, and each student has a basketball. On your signal, students move counterclockwise and dribble with the right hand within the area at a speed at which they can control the dribble. When you say "red light," students stop moving and continue dribbling while standing still. When you say "green light," the students begin to move forward again. When students demonstrate good control, have them switch hands and move clockwise while dribbling (continue the red and green light cues).

- *Extension 1.* As their confidence increases, the students can increase their speed.
- *Extension 2.* When you say "reverse," students turn and move in the opposite direction while maintaining the dribble.

EQUIPMENT

One ball per student

CRITICAL ELEMENTS AND CUES

Technique

- Keep the ball to the side while dribbling. *Cue:* Ball on the outside.
- Bend the knees slightly when you stop. *Cue:* Knees bent.
- The foot opposite the dribbling hand is forward when you are dribbling in place. *Cue:* Opposite foot forward.
- To turn around, step forward with the foot opposite the dribbling hand, push off that foot, and turn. *Cue:* Step, push, and turn.

- As the body turns, switch hands and begin dribbling with the opposite hand (the ball should always be dribbled with the side opposite the center of the circle). *Cue:* Switch hands.

COMMON ERRORS, CAUSES, AND CORRECTIONS

- The student continues to move forward while trying to stop. *Cause:* The student is not bending knees when slowing down. *Correction:* Remind the student to keep the knees bent.
- The student continues to move forward while trying to stop. *Cause:* The student is going too fast. *Correction:* Have the student return to the last controllable speed. The student should accelerate only when control is demonstrated.
- The student loses control of the dribble while switching directions. *Cause:* The student is not pushing hard off the opposite foot on the turn. *Correction:* Have the student practice stepping and pushing off with the opposite foot without using a ball. Once the student understands that action, the student can dribble while walking and practice the step, push, and turn. The student can increase the speed when control is demonstrated.

TASK 14: STEP-BACK DRIBBLING

PURPOSE

Following are the purposes of the task as related to aspects of skilled performance.

- Technique: In this task, students learn to perform a retreat dribble, which is used to avoid defensive pressure by creating open space between the dribbler and the defender. This can lead to a crossover dribble and go, a shot, or a pass.
- Agility: Students stop quickly and move in the opposite direction while facing forward.

DESCRIPTION

Scatter 7 to 10 domes within each team's home area marked by 4 cones. Each student has a basketball and dribbles from dome to dome within the zone (see figure). When a student reaches a dome, he or she performs a retreat dribble and then a crossover dribble; then the student proceeds to another dome. Students continue this for approximately one minute. If students need motivation, award one point for each controlled retreat and crossover dribble the student executes in one minute.

EQUIPMENT

One ball per student, 4 cones, and 7 to 10 domes per group

CRITICAL ELEMENTS AND CUES

Technique

- Keep the head up. *Cue:* Eyes up.
- Change to the retreat dribble with the ball at knee level. *Cue:* Ball low.
- Protect the ball with the body and the nondribbling hand. *Cue:* Protect.

Agility

- Use short, quick retreat steps, *Cue:* Quick feet.

COMMON ERRORS, CAUSES, AND CORRECTIONS

- The ball is too far in front of body. *Cause:* The dribbling arm is extended too far. *Correction:* Remind the student to keep the elbow bent and the ball close.
- The student doesn't retreat quickly. *Cause:* The student's steps are too big. *Correction:* Tell the student to make small, quick steps.

TASK 15: CROSSOVER DRIBBLING

PURPOSE

Following is the purpose of the task as related to aspects of skilled performance.

Technique: In this task, students learn to change hands while dribbling using a crossover dribble.

DESCRIPTION

Scatter 7 to 10 domes within each team's home area marked by 4 cones. Each student has a basketball and dribbles from dome to dome within the zone (see figure). When the student reaches a dome, he or she performs a crossover dribble and then proceeds to another dome. Students continue this for approximately one minute. If students need motivation, award one point for each controlled crossover dribble the student completes in one minute. As an extension, remove the domes and add two defenders that walk around the area. When a defender approaches a dribbler, the dribbler retreats and executes a crossover dribble before continuing.

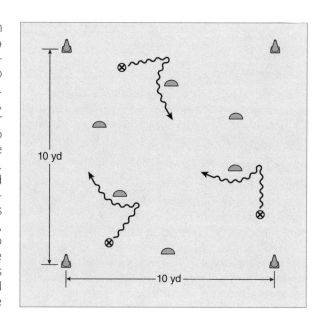

EQUIPMENT

One ball per student, 4 cones, and 7 to 10 domes per group

CRITICAL ELEMENTS AND CUES

Technique

- Push the ball from right to left (or vice versa) while keeping the ball in front of the body. *Cue:* Push across body.
- Push with the foot on the same side as the dribbling hand and step to the side. *Cue:* Push and step.
- Keep the ball low. *Cue:* Ball low.

COMMON ERRORS, CAUSES, AND CORRECTIONS

- The student loses control of the ball as the cross is made. *Cause:* The student is going too fast. *Correction:* Have the student slow down to a speed at which the dribble can be controlled.

- The ball is too high when crossing. *Cause:* The hand rises above the waist and the knees are not bent. *Correction:* Remind the student to stay low.
- The student reaches for ball with the opposite hand (rather than letting it come to the hand). *Cause:* The student does not push the ball hard enough on the dribble. *Correction:* Remind the student to push hard.
- The student bounces the ball off the ball-side foot. *Cause:* The ball-side foot doesn't step to the side when the hand begins the crossover dribble. *Correction:* Have the student practice the crossover dribble by starting from a stationary position and taking a sideway step with the ball-side foot before executing the crossover dribble.

TASK 16A: FREEZE TAG GAME I

PURPOSE

Following are the purposes of the task as related to aspects of skilled performance.

- Technique: In this task, students dribble with both hands with control.
- Tactic: Students move away from opponents.
- Agility: Students quickly change directions while maintaining possession of the ball.
- Fair play: Students should not tag too hard or try to knock the ball away from the dribbler.

DESCRIPTION

Set up four cones in a 20-by-20-foot (6.1-by-6.1-meter) home area. Five students have balls, and the sixth student does not and is the tagger. On your signal, the students with the balls begin dribbling and try to avoid being tagged. The tagger walks to try to tag the dribblers. If a dribbler is tagged, that dribbler stands still and holds the ball until touched by another dribbler and freed; then the student can begin dribbling again. If a dribbler loses control of the ball, that dribbler retrieves the ball and then stands still and holds the ball until freed. Continue the game for 1 to 2 minutes. Students rotate through the tagger position, and the game begins again.

- *Extension 1.* Have the students dribble with the nondominant hand.
- Extension 2. Have the tagger jog instead of walking. Increase area as needed.

EQUIPMENT

Five basketballs and four cones per six students

CRITICAL ELEMENTS AND CUES

Technique

- Apply all dribbling critical elements and cues from dribbling tasks 10,11,12,13,14 and 15.
- The tagger is only allowed to walk (or jog in the task extension). *Cue:* Walk.

Tactic

- Dribblers move away from the tagger.

Agility

- Dribblers need to change directions quickly when being pursued by the tagger.

Fair Play

- The tagger lightly touches the dribbler on the shoulder or back.
- The tagger does not touch the ball as it is being dribbled.

COMMON ERRORS, CAUSES, AND CORRECTIONS

- The tagger runs after the dribblers. *Cause:* The tagger gets too excited and forgets to walk. *Correction:* Remind the student to walk. If that is not effective, impose a rule that frees all tagged dribblers if the tagger runs.
- The dribblers lose control when the tagger is allowed to jog. *Cause:* The dribblers get too excited and lose control. *Correction:* Have the tagger go back to walking until the dribblers gain more confidence and control in their dribbling.

TASK 16B: FREEZE TAG GAME II

PURPOSE

Following are the purposes of the task as related to aspects of skilled performance.

- Technique: In this task, students change hands while dribbling and maintain control.
- Tactic: Students keep the body between the tagger and the ball.
- Agility: Students take quick reverse steps to avoid other dribblers or the tagger.
- Fair play: Students do not contact the dribbler while trying to make the dribbler lose control.

DESCRIPTION

The game is set up like task 16A. The tagger moves at a jog and freezes the dribbler by causing the dribbler to lose control of the dribble. The tagger can do this by knocking the ball away or by causing the dribbler to make an error. If a dribbler makes a dribbling error or loses control of the ball, the dribbler retrieves and then stands in the playing area until freed. Frozen dribblers are freed when touched by another dribbler. Continue the game for 1 to 2 minutes. Students rotate through the tagger position, and the game begins again. As an extension, enlarge the playing area and allow the tagger to run.

EQUIPMENT

Five basketballs and four cones per six students

CRITICAL ELEMENTS AND CUES

Technique

- Apply all dribbling critical elements and cue from dribbling tasks 10,11,12,13,14 and 15.
- When you are approached by the tagger, dribble with the hand that is away from the tagger. *Cue:* Protect the ball.
- The tagger must get in front of or behind the dribbler to knock the ball out. This can be done by using a feint step to get around (step in one direction and then quickly move in the other direction). *Cue:* Get around.

Tactic

- Dribblers move away from the tagger.
- The tagger uses the feint step to cause the dribbler to react in one direction, which allows the tagger to move in the other direction.

Agility

- Dribblers need to change directions quickly when being pursued by the tagger.
- Execute the feint step quickly.

Fair Play

- The tagger is not allowed to contact the body of the dribbler.

COMMON ERRORS, CAUSES, AND CORRECTIONS

- The tagger reaches across the dribbler when attempting to knock the ball out. *Cause:* The tagger does not feint with the feet quickly enough to get around the dribbler's body. *Correction:* Remind the tagger to get around.
- The dribblers allow the tagger to get too close. *Cause:* The dribblers don't move away from the tagger soon enough. *Correction:* Remind the dribblers to keep moving away.

TASK 17: THREE-PERSON SLIDING

PURPOSE

Following are the purposes of the task as related to aspects of skilled performance.

- Technique: In this task, students learn a good defensive position and learn how to slide in that defensive position.
- Agility: Students move the feet in a sliding motion without crossing them and stop and change directions quickly.

DESCRIPTION

Set two cones 10 feet (3 meters) apart for each group of three students. One student (A) stands in the middle of the two cones. Another student (B) stands 8 to 10 feet (2.4 to 3 meters) in front of and facing student A. The third student (C) stands 8 to 10 feet behind student B and faces the same direction. All students assume a defensive position. Student A slides toward one of the side cones. Students B and C mirror student A's movement. Student A moves to the cone on one side and then changes directions and slides toward the other cone. Students B and C continue to mirror student A's movements. After 30 seconds, students stop and rotate positions: student B moves to A's position, A moves to C's position, and C moves to B's position. This continues until all three students have lead the task. After students demonstrate the ability to maintain a good defensive position while sliding, the leader can add forward and backward movements.

EQUIPMENT

Two cones per three students

CRITICAL ELEMENTS AND CUES

Technique

- Bend both knees and stand with the feet shoulder-width apart. *Cue:* Knees bent.
- Keep the upper body up with a slight bend at the waist. *Cue:* Chest up.
- Put both arms up with the hands out to the side at or slightly below shoulder height. *Cue:* Arms up.
- Lead with the foot that is on the side of the body you are moving. Close the other foot to the lead foot without crossing the feet. *Cue:* Slide.
- Keep the weight on the balls of both feet. *Cue:* Balls of your feet.

Agility

- Move the feet quickly without crossing when sliding and when stopping and changing directions.

COMMON ERRORS, CAUSES, AND CORRECTIONS

- The student's feet cross. *Cause:* The student is taking a closing step that is too big or is turning the hips in the direction they are moving. *Correction:* Have the student move more slowly and concentrate on the movement of the feet and maintaining the weight on the balls of the feet.
- The student stands too tall. *Cause:* The legs get tired or the hips turn in the direction of movement. *Correction:* Have the student hold the defensive stance in a static position, or slow the movement down to stress positioning.

TASK 18: DEFENSIVE REBOUNDING

PURPOSE

Following is the purpose of the task as related to aspects of skilled performance.

Technique: In this task, students learn how to box out to get a rebound. This is done primarily for defensive purposes.

DESCRIPTION

Pairs of students stand 5 feet (1.5 meters) from a wall. One student is on defense and the other is on offense. The offensive student tosses a ball up to the wall, and the defender pivots to block out the offensive student, who is passive and does not move, while the defensive student jumps to catch the ball high. After securing the ball, the defensive student dribbles the ball out from under the basket (wall spot) and switches positions with the offensive student.

- *Extension 1.* Have three pairs of students stand 5 feet in front of a basket for rebounding with the offensive students being passive. Have the middle offensive student toss the ball towards the basket's rim or back board while the defenders pivot and rebound the ball.
- *Extension 2.* Have students use active movements where the offensive student moves towards the ball but does not rebound.
- *Extension 3.* Have students use competitive movements where both defensive and offensive students attempt to rebound the ball.

EQUIPMENT

One ball per pair of students

CRITICAL ELEMENTS AND CUES

Technique

- Reverse pivot on the front foot. *Cue:* Reverse pivot.
- Move backward so your back is on the opponent's chest. *Cue:* Feel the student.
- Spread the feet to create a wide base, and keep the hands up. *Cue:* Box out.
- Go for the ball at your highest point and catch it with two hands. *Cue:* Reach high.
- Protect the ball in front of the forehead with the elbows out. *Cue:* Protect the ball.

COMMON ERRORS, CAUSES, AND CORRECTIONS

- The offensive student moves around the defender to get the ball. *Cause:* The defender does not make contact with the offensive student. *Correction:* After the pivot step, tell the defender to keep the back toward the offensive student.

TASK 19: 1V1 DRIBBLING AND ON-BALL DEFENSE

PURPOSE

Following are the purposes of the task as related to aspects of skilled performance.

- Technique: In this task, students learn defensive position and movement when playing the ball and to protect the ball while dribbling against defensive pressure.
- Tactic: While on defense, students stay between the dribbler and the basket.
- Agility: While on defense, students move the feet quickly and change directions when the dribbler moves.
- Fair play: Students allow a passive defender to stay between the ball and the basket by not dribbling too fast.

DESCRIPTION

Students attempt to dribble from the midcourt line to the end line within their team's zone. Students are paired up, and one student is the dribbler and the other is the defender. The dribbler dribbles slowly down the zone toward the basket while the defender moves in passive defense and attempts to stay in front of the dribbler. The defender cannot contact the dribbler. The dribbler takes a shot within 5 to 8 feet (1.5 to 2.4 meters) of the basket. After the shot, students switch positions and begin again from the midcourt line.

- *Extension 1.* Defenders use active defense.
- *Extension 2.* Defenders move to competitive defense and the dribblers move faster, resulting in a competitive 1v1 situation. If students need motivation during competitive defense, award one point when a student successfully dribbles the ball and makes a basket and one point if a defender causes a turnover or the dribbler cannot make the shot.

EQUIPMENT

One ball per pair of students

CRITICAL ELEMENTS AND CUES

Technique: Dribbling

- Push the ball out slightly ahead of your body as you move. The faster you move the farther in front of the body the ball should be. *Cue:* Push the ball.
- Keep your eyes up to be aware of other dribblers. *Cue:* Eyes up.
- Push the ball from right to left (or vice versa) while keeping the ball in front of the body. *Cue:* Push across body.
- Push with the foot on the same side as the dribbling hand and step to the side. *Cue:* Push and step.
- Keep the ball low. *Cue:* Ball low.

Technique: Defending

- Maintain a balanced and athletic position with the feet spread, the knees bent, and the weight on balls of the feet. *Cue:* Athletic position.
- Keep the eyes on midsection of the dribbler. *Cue:* Eyes on belly button.

Tactic

- On defense, maintain your position between the dribbler and the basket. *Cue:* Back to basket.

Agility

- On defense, your feet move as the dribbler moves. *Cue:* Quick feet.

Fair Play

- During the initial task and the first extension, the defender allows the offensive student to dribble while staying in the back-to-the-basket position.

COMMON ERRORS, CAUSES, AND CORRECTIONS

- The defender is slow in reacting to the movement of the dribbler. *Cause:* The weight is on the heels rather than the balls of the feet. *Correction:* Remind students to use a good defensive stance.
- When the dribbler changes directions, the defender cannot react quickly enough. *Cause:* The feet cross when the student changes direction. *Correction:* Have the dribbler slow down and allow the defender to execute the drop step when changing directions.
- The defender reacts to a feint by the dribbler. *Cause:* The defender is looking at their feet or at the ball. *Correction:* Remind the student to keep the eyes on the offensive student's belly button.

TASK 20: PROGRESSIVE LAYUPS

PURPOSE

Following is the purpose of the task as related to aspects of skilled performance.
Technique: In this task, students learn to execute the layup shot in basketball.

DESCRIPTION

These tasks teach beginning students the proper form for executing a layup. Each progression is explained using the right-hand layup. Left-handed layups would be the opposite. It is important that students practice layups from both sides. Experienced students may not need all the tasks in this progression for the dominant side, but they might need them for the nondominant side. Divide students into groups based on the number of baskets available.

Progression 1: Walking with the ball. Have students start approximately 3 walking steps at an angle to the basket. The student then takes 3 walking steps beginning with the left foot towards the basket while carrying the ball. On the third step, the student will extend the ball up while lifting the right knee without taking a shot.

Progression 2: Bounce one-two layup. Students stand at an angle to the right side of the basket 3 steps from the basket with the feet together and then step forward on the left foot while pushing the ball down with both hands. As the ball rebounds, students take a small forward jump off that foot and catch the ball while it is in the air. On landing (on the right foot), students take a step onto the left foot and shoot the ball using one or both hands, aiming for the corner of the box on the backboard.

Progression 3: Walking dribble with a shot. For the progression, divide the students into 2 groups with one group as the shooters and one group as the rebounders. The offensive students begin approximately 10 feet at an angle to the basket on the right side, and the rebounding students stand similarly on the left side. The offensive students each have a ball and the first offensive student in line dribbles while walking toward the basket and executes a layup. As the first offensive student approaches the basket the first rebounding student moves towards the basket to get the ball after the layup attempt. The students then switch positions with the rebounder taking the ball and getting in the shooting line and the offensive student getting in the back of the rebounding line. As an extension, students can increase the distance and the speed of dribble

Progression 4: Layups with a Trailing Defender. At the group's basket and starting 30 feet (9.1 meters) out at a 45-degree angle to the basket, a student dribbles toward the basket with the outside hand and executes a layup (see figure). A defender moves alongside the shooter. The defender does not attempt to disrupt the shot. As an extension, the defender begins 8 feet (2.4 meters) behind the dribbler and attempts to catch the dribbler and disrupt the layup.

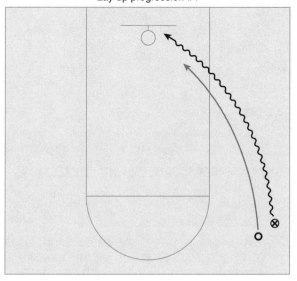
Lay-up progression #4

EQUIPMENT

One ball per student

CRITICAL ELEMENTS AND CUES

Technique

- Keep the eyes on the corner of the white box on the backboard. *Cue:* See the box.
- Jump off the inside foot and raise the outside knee and arm. *Cue:* Inside foot, outside knee.
- Raise the inside arm to shoulder height to help shield the shot. *Cue:* Protect the ball.
- Shoot with the palm facing the basket. *Cue:* Palm out.

COMMON ERRORS, CAUSES, AND CORRECTIONS

- The student cannot control the ball. *Cause:* The student is going too fast. *Correction:* Have the student slow down.
- When shooting from the nondominant side, the student uses the dominant hand. *Cause:* The student is not comfortable with the nondominant hand. *Correction:* Go back to an earlier step and move forward as the student becomes more comfortable.
- The student jumps off the preferred leg on both sides. *Cause:* The student is not comfortable jumping off the nonpreferred leg. *Correction:* Go back to the earlier steps and move forward as the student becomes more comfortable.
- The student's takeoff is either too close to or too far away from the basket. *Cause:* The timing of the approach and the jump is off. *Correction:* Place a marker to the side where the student should take off.

TASK 21: PARTNER SHOOTING

PURPOSE

Following are the purposes of the task as related to aspects of skilled performance.

- Technique: In this task, students learn to identify appropriate areas of the court from which to shoot the ball.
- Agility: Students will utilize directional movement while relocating between shots.
- Fair play: Students make appropriate passes to partners during jump shots and layups.
- Communication: Students make a nonverbal call for the ball by reaching out with their hands when in position and indicating that they are ready to catch the ball and shoot.

DESCRIPTION

Place 3 pairs of students at each basket. In their pairs, students shoot independently at the basket. Students should attempt appropriate shots that will be used in future game play with an equal emphasis on game-like speed and shooting techniques. When student A makes a shot, student B rebounds the ball and makes an appropriate pass to a relocated student A, who attempts another shot. This continues until student A misses a shot, at which point student B rebounds the ball and makes a pass as student A moves to the basket for a layup. Student A retrieves the ball after the layup and makes an appropriate pass to student B for a midrange shot. If the shot is successful, student B relocates and shoots off another pass from student A. If not, student B makes a layup and students switch positions. This continues for a designated time.

EQUIPMENT

One basketball per pair of students

CRITICAL ELEMENTS AND CUES

Technique: Layups

- Keep the eyes on the corner of the white box on the backboard. *Cue:* See the box.

- Jump off the inside foot and raise the outside knee and arm. *Cue:* Inside foot, outside knee.
- Raise the inside arm to shoulder height to help shield the shot. *Cue:* Protect the ball.
- Shoot with the palm facing the basket. *Cue:* Palm out.

Technique: Jump Shots

- Keep the eyes on the middle eyelet of the back of the rim. *Cue:* Eyes on back of rim.
- Spread the fingers on the ball. Make an L position with the wrist and elbow. Balance the hand lightly on the side of the ball. *Cue:* Waiter tray position.
- Maintain a *balanced* position. Keep the *elbow* bent and pointed toward the basket. *Eyes* look at the basket. *Follow* through with the hand in the cookie jar. *Cue:* BEEF.
- Bend your knees and push off the ground with both feet. *Cue:* Bend and push.
- Shoot at the highest point of the jump. *Cue:* Shoot at the highest point.

Agility

- Move in different directions after attempting each shot.

Fair Play

- Make appropriate passes that enable the shooter to catch and quickly shoot.

Communication

- When you are the shooter, call for the ball as you move into position to take the next shot, by placing your hands where you want the pass to be made.

COMMON ERRORS, CAUSES, AND CORRECTIONS

Jump Shots:

- The student does not get the ball over the front of the rim. *Cause:* The student is not extending the knees or is not extending with enough force to help get the ball up. *Correction:* Remind the student to bend and quickly extend the knees.

Layups:

- The student cannot control the ball. *Cause:* The student is going too fast. *Correction:* Have the student slow down.
- When shooting from the nondominant side, the student uses the dominant hand. *Cause:* The student is not comfortable with the nondominant hand. *Correction:* Go back to an earlier step and move forward as the student becomes more comfortable.
- The student jumps off the preferred leg on both sides. *Cause:* The student is not comfortable jumping off the nonpreferred leg. *Correction:* Go back to the earlier steps and move forward as the student becomes more comfortable.
- The student's takeoff is either too close to or too far away from the basket. *Cause:* The timing of the approach and the jump is off. *Correction:* Place a marker to the side where the student should take off.

TASK 22: OVERHEAD PARTNER PASSING

PURPOSE

Following are the purposes of the task as related to aspects of skilled performance.

- Technique: In this task, students learn the basic techniques of the overhead pass.
- Fair play: Students pass the ball so it can be caught.
- Communication: Students reach out with the hands to indicate readiness to receive a pass.

DESCRIPTION

Have students pair up and stand 10 feet (3 meters) apart. On your signal, the students continuously pass a ball back and forth using the overhead pass technique. As an extension, have pairs move back one step until they are 15 feet (4.6 meters) apart.

EQUIPMENT

One ball per pair of students

CRITICAL ELEMENTS AND CUES

Technique

- Hold the ball with both hands above the head. *Cue:* Ball high.
- The arms are straight. *Cue:* Arms straight.
- The hands are on the sides of the ball with the thumbs pointed toward each other. *Cue:* Thumbs pointed in.
- Push the thumbs through the ball by snapping the wrists and ending in a forward position pointed towards the receiver. *Cue:* Snap the wrists.
- Step forward with one foot to add more power. *Cue:* Step.
- Pass toward the receiver's head. *Cue:* Aim for the head.

Fair Play

- Pass the ball where the receiver can catch it.

Communication

- Place the hands out to indicate you are ready to receive a pass.

COMMON ERRORS, CAUSES, AND CORRECTIONS

- The student catches the pass below the head area. *Cause:* The release point is too low. *Correction:* Have the student move closer to the receiver. The student can move back out when better control is demonstrated.
- The ball is dropping before reaching the receiver. *Cause:* The student did not use enough force on the pass. *Correction:* Have the passer step toward the receiver and snap the wrists when passing.

TASK 23: 2V1 POSSESSION PASSING

PURPOSE

Following are the purposes of the task as related to aspects of skilled performance.

- Technique: In this task, students learn to maintain critical elements of passing while keeping possession in open space.
- Agility: Students move quickly to get open and receive the pass.
- Fair play: Defenders do not make contact with the offense.
- Communication: Students make verbal and nonverbal calls for the ball.

DESCRIPTION

Using four cones set up a 10-by-10-foot (3-by-3-meter) playing area (no basket is needed) for each group of three students. Two students are on offense with the ball, and the other student is on defense (see figure). The objective is for the offense to maintain possession using the passes and fakes learned while maintaining legal positioning (e.g., keeping a pivot foot). The two offensive students can move only if they do not have the ball, and the defender must always move to mark (defend) the ball, eliminating a zone defense. Students continue this for a designated time; then students rotate. One offensive student changes places with

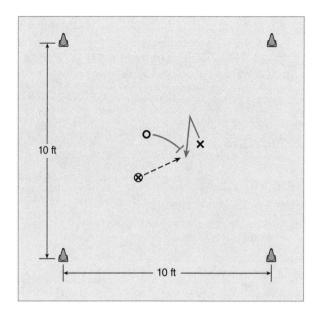

the defender. If there are 4 or 5 in the group, pair the students up and have them rotate in pairs, and alternate between the two when they are playing defense. The teacher needs to discuss points such as making appropriate, timely passes with students as need arises.

EQUIPMENT

One basketball and 4 cones per three students

CRITICAL ELEMENTS AND CUES

Technique

- Continue to be mindful of the critical elements of all previous passing tasks.

Agility

- Use V-cuts and feints to get open.

Fair Play

- Avoid making contact with the offensive students.
- Defend only the student with the ball.

Communication

- Use hand signals or verbal calls for the ball when you are open.

COMMON ERRORS, CAUSES, AND CORRECTIONS

- The student compromises form to make accurate or necessary passes. *Cause:* The defender is guarding too tightly. *Correction:* Have the defender stand an arm's length away from the ball.
- The pass is being knocked down. *Cause:* The passer telegraphs the pass by continually looking at the receiver before passing the ball. *Correction:* Have the passer use a pass fake.
- The student cannot make the pass to the receiver. *Cause:* The student has limited understanding of floor spacing. *Correction:* Have the receiver move more aggressively to the sides away from the defender.
- The defender is moving with the receiver. *Cause:* The defensive student is not marking the ball. *Correction:* Have the defender stay an arm's length away from the passer.

TASK 24: OPEN-SPACE DRIBBLING

PURPOSE

Following are the purposes of the task as related to aspects of skilled performance.

- Technique: In this task, students learn to dribble in open space at a fast speed.
- Fair play: Students practice spatial awareness and share space on the court.

DESCRIPTION

Place students in groups of three. Two students are stacked (standing one behind the other) on one side of the court and one student is on the other side. The student at the front of the stacked pair has a ball. On your signal, the student with the ball dribbles to the other side at the fastest speed that allows him or her to maintain possession of the ball. Once at the other side, the student hands the ball to the next person, who moves back across the court. This continues for a designated time. As an extension, have the dribbler use the nondominant hand. *Note:* We do not recommend that this task be done as a relay.

EQUIPMENT

One basketball per three students

CRITICAL ELEMENTS AND CUES

Technique

- Push the ball out several feet and run after it. *Cue:* Push and run.
- Push the dribble forward at waist level. *Cue:* Waist level.
- Dribble the ball to the side away from the defender. *Cue:* Ball on the side.

Fair Play

- While dribbling in open space, be aware of others and avoid contact.

COMMON ERRORS, CAUSES, AND CORRECTIONS

- The ball is bouncing off the student's leg. *Cause:* The ball is either not pushed far enough ahead, or the ball is being dribbled at the middle of the body and not to the side. *Correction:* Either stress that the student should push and run, or have the dribbler slow down and dribble along a line with the body on one side of the line and the ball on the other.

TASK 25: ZIGZAG DRIBBLE SEQUENCE

PURPOSE

Following are the purposes of the task as related to aspects of skilled performance.

- Technique: In this task, students apply the elements of dribbling while moving and adding the quick crossover.
- Agility: Students must advance the ball in a zigzag pattern, forcing them to use both hands in the dribble.
- Fair play: Students provide appropriate defensive pressure without touching the ball.

DESCRIPTION

Have students pair up and place half the pairs on the right baseline corner on each end of the court. One student will be the dribbler while the partner is an active defender. One pair of students begins at each right baseline corner and moves left (one dribbling and one defending) to the free-throw elbow. The students then cross over and dribble right to the half-court line, cross over left to the free-throw elbow at the other end, and cross over right to finish the full-court-length zigzag pattern. Each trial requires three changes in direction.

Extra pairs line up behind the initial dribbling pair at both right baseline corners. Once the first crossover occurs, the next pair in both lines can begin. Once every pair is at the other end, the first pair switches roles and dribbles back using the same zigzag pattern but now from the left baseline corner where they had stopped. This means the first dribbling direction will be to the right. *Note:* We do not recommend that this task be done as a relay.

EQUIPMENT

One ball per pair of students

CRITICAL ELEMENTS AND CUES

Technique: Open Space Dribbling

- Push the ball out several feet and run after it. *Cue:* Push and run.
- Push the dribble forward at waist level. *Cue:* Waist level.
- Dribble the ball to the side away from the defender. *Cue:* Ball on the side.

Technique: Cross Over Dribbling

- Keep your eyes up to be aware of other dribblers. *Cue:* Eyes up.
- Push the ball from right to left (or vice versa) while keeping the ball in front of the body. *Cue:* Push across body.
- Push with the foot on the same side as the dribbling hand and step to the side. *Cue:* Push and step.
- Keep the ball low. *Cue:* Ball low.
- Stress defensive stance and movement critical elements and cues from tasks 17 and 19.

Agility

- When changing directions, make the cuts quickly.

Fair Play

- During the zigzag movements, the defenders move appropriately without touching the dribbler or the ball.

COMMON ERRORS, CAUSES, AND CORRECTIONS

- The student is dribbling in a straight line rather than in the zigzag pattern. *Cause:* The student is going too fast. *Correction:* Add cones where the crossover dribble should occur.

TASK 26: TRIPLE THREAT AND JAB STEP

PURPOSE

Following are the purposes of the task as related to aspects of skilled performance.

- Technique: In this task, students learn to execute a jab step from the triple-threat position to start the dribble.
- Fair play: Students react to the jab step by allowing the offensive players to dribble around them.

DESCRIPTION

Divide students into groups of three in their home areas. One attacker is at the top of the key with the ball, and the other attacker stands on the free-throw lane box with an active defender. The attacker with the ball passes to the other attacker who is moving out toward the wing. That student catches the ball on the wing and assumes a triple-threat position. The attacker then executes a jab step toward the weak side, and the active defender reacts to the jab step by allowing the dribbler to dribble to the dominant side for a layup.

- *Extension 1.* Have students use the nondominant side to dribble off the jab step to the dominate side.

- *Extension 2.* Have the dribbler pull up for a jump shot after the crossover dribble.
- *Extension 3.* Have the defenders move from active to competitive defense.

EQUIPMENT

One ball per three students

CRITICAL ELEMENTS AND CUES

Technique: Triple Threat

- Bend the knees. *Cue:* Bend knees.
- Keep the feet even and shoulder-width apart. *Cue:* Shoulder-width apart.
- Hold the ball close to the belly with both hands. *Cue:* Ball close.
- Hold your head up and look at the defender. *Cue:* Look at the defender.

Technique: Jab Step

- Establish a pivot foot by moving only one foot. *Cue:* Pivot foot.
- Take a short step with the nonpivot foot at a 45-degree angle. *Cue:* Jab step.
- Look at the reaction of the defender. *Cue:* Read the defender.
- Pull the stepping foot back and across the body and step forward with the nonpivot foot to begin the dribble. *Cue:* Step across.

Fair Play

- Move with the fake and trail the dribbler as he or she moves toward the basket.

COMMON ERRORS, CAUSES, AND CORRECTIONS

- The student travels. *Cause:* The pivot foot steps forward as the dribble begins instead of the jab foot crossing over. *Correction:* Have the student practice the jab step and step across without moving and without a defender.

TASK 27: TRIPLE-THREAT DECISIONS

PURPOSE

Following are the purposes of the task as related to aspects of skilled performance.

- Technique: In this task, students assume a triple-threat position off a pass and decide whether to pass, shoot, or dribble.
- Fair play: Defenders execute the correct action so the attackers can make the correct decision.

DESCRIPTION

Divide students into groups of three in their home areas. One attacker is at the top of the key with the ball, and the other attacker stands on the free-throw lane box with an active defender. The attacker at the baseline quickly moves out to the wing to receive a pass. On receiving the pass, that student assumes a triple-threat position and then reads the defender to decide what to do. Initially the defender will stay back, so the choice is for the attacker to shoot. To rotate positions, the passer becomes the defender, the defender becomes the new receiver, and the receiver becomes the new passer. If there are 4 or 5 in the group, the extra students line up behind the passer and rotate into the position; in this case, the receiver moves to the back of the waiting line after the shot.

- *Extension 1.* Have the defender move up to the attacker after the catch. In this scenario, the attacker would execute a jab step and then dribble for a layup or a shot with the defender trailing.
- *Extension 2.* Have the defender move up with the receiver. After catching the ball, the receiver passes it back to the passer because the receiver is closely guarded.
- *Extension 3.* Have the defender move randomly, switching from one coverage to another.

EQUIPMENT

One ball per three students

CRITICAL ELEMENTS AND CUES

Technique: Triple Threat

- Bend the knees. *Cue:* Bend knees.
- Keep the feet even and shoulder-width apart. *Cue:* Shoulder-width apart.
- Hold the ball close to the belly with both hands. *Cue:* Ball close.
- Hold your head up and look at the defender. *Cue:* Look at the defender.

Technique: Jab Step

- Establish a pivot foot by moving only one foot. *Cue:* Pivot foot.
- Take a short step with the nonpivot foot at a 45-degree angle. *Cue:* Jab step.
- Look at the reaction of the defender. *Cue:* Read the defender.

Fair Play

- Stay back after the pass is received, and then make the appropriate defensive movement based on the extension being used.

COMMON ERRORS, CAUSES, AND CORRECTIONS

- The receiver makes the wrong decision. *Cause:* The receiver is not reading the defender and recognizing the defender's position. *Correction:* Slow the task down and remind the student to look at the defender and review the decisions through situational replays.

TASK 28: MOVES TO THE BASKET

PURPOSE

Following are the purposes of the task as related to aspects of skilled performance.

- Technique: In this task, students learn the pump fake and how to make offensive moves off the dribble.
- Agility: Students use the jab step to move the defender out of position.
- Fair play: Defenders allow offensive students to make the moves and shots.

DESCRIPTION

Place students in groups of three. One offensive student is at the top of the key with the ball, and the other offensive student is on the wing (free-throw line extended) and guarded by the defensive student. The student with the ball passes to the wing student, who then makes a pump fake and dribble drives around the defender for a shot. The task is repeated, and the receiver executes one of the following dribble moves: jab step single dribble to layup or jumper, jab step dribble and cross to layup, jab step to jumper, pump fake, or dribble cross. The defense is passive. Use the same rotation as in task 27. As an extension, have the defense move to active and then competitive.

EQUIPMENT

One ball per three students

CRITICAL ELEMENTS AND CUES

Technique

- For the pump fake, quickly move the ball up a little bit by raising the shoulders and head. *Cue:* Head fake.

Agility

- Execute the jab step in a short, quick motion.

Fair Play

- React to the pump fake by jumping up slightly, which allows the offensive student to drive toward the basket.

COMMON ERRORS, CAUSES, AND CORRECTIONS

- The defender plays too aggressively at the beginning. *Cause:* The defender forgets to be passive or active. *Correction:* Remind the defender to play off the offensive student a couple of steps and to allow the move and shot.

TASK 29: PASS AND CUT (TEAM OFFENSE)

PURPOSE

Following are the purposes of the task as related to aspects of skilled performance.

- Technique: In this task, students learn to pass and move in an offensive set.
- Agility: Students make quick cuts after passes have been made.
- Fair play: Students play passive or active defense, which allows the passes and cuts to be made.
- Communication: Students reach out with the hands to indicate that a pass should be made.

DESCRIPTION

This is often called a *cut-through offense.* A group students of six students is ideal for this task, but you can use larger groups. Begin in a 3v0 format (see figure *a*) with three offensive students around the perimeter with one student at the top of the key (position 1) and the other two on opposite wings (positions 2 and 3). The first pass should be made from the top of the key to a wing student. After the first pass, the passer will cut to the basket and moves out towards the wing position opposite the pass. When the passer leaves his position to make the cut the wing student opposite the pass moves to the point position to replace the initial passer (see figure *a*). The wing with the ball then passes back to the point and the point person passes to the opposite wing (formerly the initial passer) and then cuts towards the basket to be replaced by the wing opposite the pass who has moved up to the point position (see figure *b*). Run this through until everyone has been the point person a designated number of times, and then have the other group of three step in to run the cut-through offense.

- *Extension 1.* Add this to create another cut. When a pass is made back to the top of the key from a wing, the wing student should cut to the basket and then circle back into the original position. This offensive strategy promotes continuous motion and maintaining spacing.
- *Extension 2.* Add three active defenders to the 3v0 formation that move along with the cutters but do not interfere with the passes or cuts making it a 3v3 situation.
- *Extension 3.* Add a pass to a cutter if one is open (between the defender and the basket). The defenders remain active.

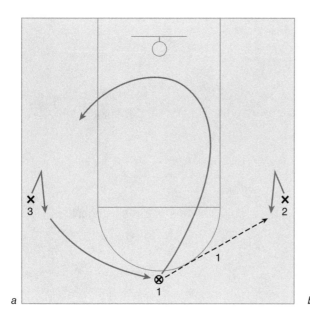

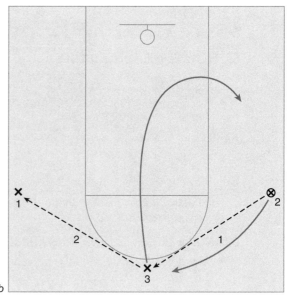

- *Extension 4.* Have defenders play competitive defense. If a basket is made, the pass is intercepted, or a turnover occurs, the ball goes to the defenders who become the new offensive players. The defense checks the ball by tossing the ball to the offensive point person to indicate the beginning of play.

EQUIPMENT
One ball per group of six students

CRITICAL ELEMENTS AND CUES

Technique
- Look at the ball when cutting to the basket. *Cue:* Look for the ball.

Agility
- When defenders are present, wings must do V-cuts to get open for a pass. *Cue:* V-cuts.

Fair Play
- During the first three extensions, defenders allow cuts, passes, and shot to be made.

Communication
- If you are open, call for the ball by holding your hands out. *Cue:* Call for the ball.

COMMON ERRORS, CAUSES, AND CORRECTIONS
- While being defended, the cutter gets hit with a pass. *Cause:* The cutter is not looking for the pass. *Correction:* Go back to playing without a defender. Have the passer hold up a number of fingers, and have the cutter call out the number.

TASK 30: 2V1 PICK AND ROLL

PURPOSE
Following are the purposes of the task as related to aspects of skilled performance.
- Technique: In this task, students attempt to get open for a return pass after setting a pick to create a scoring opportunity.
- Agility: Students execute a reverse pivot.

- Fair play: Students play passive or active defense, which allows offensive students to make the passes and picks.
- Communication: Students reach out with the hands to indicate readiness for a pass.

DESCRIPTION

Within the home areas, divide students into groups of three (two offensive attackers and one student on defense). One attacker stands at the top of the key (point) with the ball, and the other attacker stands in a wing position and is guarded loosely by the passive defender. The point attacker with the ball passes the ball to the wing attacker and runs over to set a pick or screen on the defender. The wing person then dribbles over the top of the pick or screen and looks back at the student setting the screen. After the dribbler has dribbled over the pick or screen, the student setting the pick or screen does a reverse pivot and rolls to the basket to look for a return pass. The defender is passive and stands still. After the pass back is made, the student with the ball executes a layup. Use the same rotation as in task 27.

- *Extension 1.* Have the defender play active defense. The defender moves around the pick and follows the student rolling to the basket for the shot without interfering with either the pass or the shot.
- *Extension 2.* The defender plays competitive defense and tries to interfere with the pass and the shot.

EQUIPMENT

One ball per three students

CRITICAL ELEMENTS AND CUES

Technique

- Set up on the shoulder of the defender. *Cue:* Shoulder.
- Stand in one of two positions: arms straight and hands crossed (male) or arms crossed at the chest (female). *Cue:* Set the pick.
- As the dribbler dribbles off the pick, the dribbler's shoulder should pass close to the shoulder of the student setting the pick. *Cue:* Shoulder to shoulder.
- When rolling, keep the body between the basket and the defender. *Cue:* Block the defender.

Agility

- After the dribbler has executed two dribbles over the top of the screen, the screener does a reverse pivot using the basket-side foot as the pivot foot. *Cue:* Roll.
- After the roll, the screener executes a slide step toward the basket. *Cue:* Slide toward the basket.

Communication

- Put the outside arm up for the pass. *Cue:* Call for the pass.

Fair Play

- During the initial task and the first extension, defenders move with the offense but allow passes to be made.

COMMON ERRORS, CAUSES, AND CORRECTIONS

- The pivot doesn't keep defender to the rear away from the basket. *Cause:* The pivot is too late. *Correction:* Tell the student to pivot as soon as the dribbler passes the shoulder.
- The pivot doesn't keep defender to the rear away from the basket. *Cause:* The pick is set too far away from the defender. *Correction:* Have the picker lightly touch the shoulder of the defender when setting the pick.

TASK 31: 3V1 OFF-BALL SCREENING

PURPOSE

Following are the purposes of the task as related to aspects of skilled performance.

- Technique: In this task, students learn to set a screen on a student away from the ball so that student can move to get open to receive a pass and take a shot.
- Agility: Students cut quickly off the screen.
- Fair play: Students play passive or active defense, which allows offensive students to make the passes and picks.
- Communication: Students reach out with the hands to indicate readiness for a pass.

DESCRIPTION

Divide students into groups of four (three attackers and one student on defense). One attacker is in each wing position and the other is in the middle at the top of the key with a basketball (see figure). The passive defender is on one of the wing students. The attacker with the ball passes to the wing away from the defender and then moves toward the defender (on the wing opposite the pass) and sets a screen on the defender. The wing attacker moves over the top of the screen, cuts across the lane, and receives a pass for either a layup or a shot. The defender remains behind the screen playing passive defense. The rotation for this task is as follows: the cutter moves to the wing that made the pass, the wing that passed the ball moves to the top of the key, the passer becomes the defender, and the defender becomes the cutter. If there are 5 or 6 in the group, have the extra students line up behind the passer. When a student rotates into the passer position, the wing passer moves to the waiting line.

- *Extension 1.* Have the defenders play active defense while the screen is being set by moving around the screen and following the cutter.
- *Extension 2.* Have the defender play competitive defense and actively attempt to disrupt play.

EQUIPMENT

One ball per four students

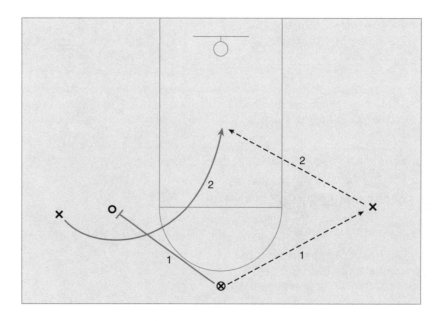

CRITICAL ELEMENTS AND CUES

Technique

- Set the screen away from the ball. *Cue:* Off-ball screen.
- Set up on the shoulder of the defender. *Cue:* Shoulder.
- Stand in one of two positions: arms straight and hands crossed (male) or arms crossed at the chest (female). *Cue:* Set the pick.
- After setting the pick the student needs to remain stationary. *Cue:* Don't move.

Agility

- When cutting off the screen, the offensive student must move quickly.

Fair Play

- During the initial task and the first extension, defenders allow offensive students to move and make passes.

Communication

- When moving off the screen, raise your arm to indicate you are open.

COMMON ERRORS, CAUSES, AND CORRECTIONS

- The defender moves around the screen. *Cause:* The screen is set too far away from the defender. *Correction:* Practice setting the screen against the defender.
- The cutter moves during the screen. *Cause:* The cutter moves before the screen is set, which causes the defender to move. *Correction:* Remind the cutter not to move until the screen is set.
- The student setting the screen moves during the screen. *Cause:* The screen is set too far away from the defender. *Correction:* Have the screener lightly touch the shoulder of the defender when setting the screen.

TASK 32: TRIANGLE: OFF-BALL DEFENSE

PURPOSE

Following are the purposes of the task as related to aspects of skilled performance.

- Technique: In this task, students learn how to move in a defensive position when the student they are defending does not have the ball.
- Tactic: Students protect the basket.

DESCRIPTION

Divide students into groups of six and have the students pair up within the home area. Pairs spread out on the three-point arc in front of the team basket; one pair is on each wing and one is at the top of the key. One student is playing defense and the other is playing offense. The ball starts in the middle with the middle person's defender standing one step in front of the middle person in-line with the basket. The defenders for the two wing students are also one step off the offensive student they are guarding, but they are also one step towards the ball because their offensive student is one pass away from the ball (see figure *a*). The ball is slowly passed around the perimeter by the offensive students, who remain stationary. The defenders adjust their defensive positions based on the position of the ball by taking one step off and one step towards the ball from the offensive student they are guarding for every pass they are away from the ball (see figure *b*). In figure *b,* the numbers by the defenders indicate how many steps the defender is off their offensive student based on the number of passes they are away. In this example a defender is never more than two steps off the offensive student because they are never more than two passes away. As an extension, have the students make faster passes once the defenders display competence in changing positions.

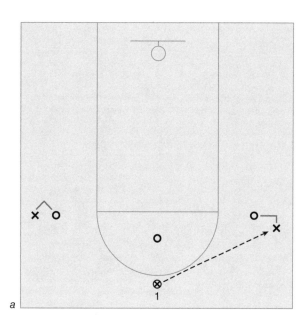 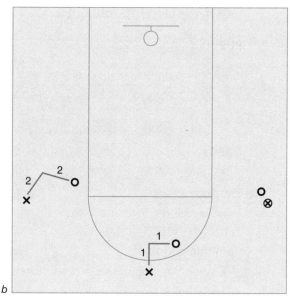

EQUIPMENT

One ball per six students

CRITICAL ELEMENTS AND CUES

Technique

- When defending off the ball, focus your eyes at a point in space that is midway between the ball and the student you are defending. This keeps both in your peripheral vision. *Cue:* Student-ball-you-man.
- If your offensive student is away from the ball, drop back and over one step for every pass they are away from the ball. *Cue:* Keep your triangle.

Tactic

- If your offensive student has the ball, assume a normal defensive position on a line between the offensive student and the basket.
- If your offensive student is one pass away from the ball, assume a position that is one step farther away from the offensive student and one step toward the ball. This forms a triangle between you, the offensive student, and the ball. *Cue:* One step off and one step toward the ball.
- If your offensive student is two passes away from the ball, assume a position that is two steps farther away from the offensive student and two steps toward the ball. This forms a larger triangle between you, the offensive student, and the ball. *Cue:* Two steps off and two steps toward the ball.

COMMON ERRORS, CAUSES, AND CORRECTIONS

- The student does not react to the movement of the ball or the offensive student. *Cause:* The defender looks at the student with the ball or the student he or she is defending. *Correction:* Place a cone where the student should look when off the ball.
- The defender turns the back toward their offensive student while adjusting his or her position. *Cause:* The defender is not watching the ball and the student. *Correction:* Place a cone where the student should look when in the triangle position.

TASK 33: PERSON-TO-PERSON PRINCIPLES (TEAM DEFENSE)

PURPOSE

Following are the purposes of the task as related to aspects of skilled performance.

- Technique: In this task, students move accordingly depending on their position from the ball (e.g., one pass away, two passes away).
- Agility: Students will execute directional movement while relocating on and off the ball.
- Fair play: Students make passes at an appropriate pace to allow the defenders time to adjust their positions accordingly.
- Communication: Defenders make verbal calls to indicate their position relative to the position of the ball.

DESCRIPTION

Divide students into groups of 8 or 10 in a 4v4 or 5v5 setup. The offensive students spread out around the arc with one defender on each offensive student. The offensive students pass the ball around the arc with a 2- to 3-second delay between passes so they can observe all the defenders moving into different defensive positions based on the new location of the ball (one step off and one step towards the ball for every pass the defender is away from the ball). The defenders call out their position in relation to the ball by calling out, "Ball" if they are defending the ball and "One" if they are one pass away from the ball and "Two" if two passes away and "Three" if three passes away. After a set time, have students switch roles from offense to defense.

- *Extension 1.* Students increase the speed of the passes once the defenders demonstrate an understanding of the movement principles.
- *Extension 2.* On your signal, the offensive students become live and can move toward the basket by dribbling or passing to attempt get off a shot.

EQUIPMENT

One basketball and one hoop (half-court setup) per 8 to 10 students

CRITICAL ELEMENTS AND CUES

Technique

- Defenders need to differentiate between on-the-ball and 1-, 2-, and 3-pass responsibilities for each defensive student. For each pass the defender is away from the ball, the defender is one step off the offensive student and one step toward the ball. *Cue: Adjust to the ball*

Agility

- Adjust your position by making the proper defensive movement after the ball is passed (or moved) from the original position.

Fair Play

- Allow defensive students to have a realistic look.
- Participate at the correct speed.

Communication

- Call your new position (e.g., ball, one, two) to identify your position and role in the team defense.

COMMON ERRORS, CAUSES, AND CORRECTIONS

- Students are in the wrong position. *Cause:* The students have limited experience and knowledge. *Correction:* With beginning students, take an approach in which you explain, demonstrate, and perform the tasks. The expectations apply to playing person-to-person defense in any formation (not just 5v5).

- When the offensive person moves, the defender does not react. *Cause:* The defender is looking at the offensive student who has the ball. *Correction:* Remind the defender to look at an area halfway between the two offensive students to keep both the ball and the offensive student he is guarding in the peripheral vision. You can also have passers away from the ball hold up fingers and see if the defenders can call out the number.

TASK 34: HELP AND RECOVER (TEAM DEFENSE)

PURPOSE

Following are the purposes of the task as related to aspects of skilled performance.

- Technique: In this task, students abide by the ball-you-student principle, in which the defender is positioned to see both the ball and the student being defended.
- Agility: Student A moves closer to and farther away from the ball using the proper footwork depending on the position of the opposing student B.
- Fair play: Students participate in appropriate drills that apply the help and recover concept. Students focus on this defensive concept.

DESCRIPTION

Divide students into groups of three (two offensive students and one defensive student). Offensive student A has the ball at the right wing extended and is not guarded. Offensive student B is positioned at the free-throw line and is guarded by the defender, who is in a one pass off defensive position. Student A dribbles to the right baseline and as they dribble the defender drops off student B and moves to become the helping defender and cuts off the dribbler at the right baseline; student B stays stationary. Once student A is cutoff at the baseline by the defender or the ball is passed back out to student B, student A exits the drill and the defender moves out to defend student B who now has the ball. The drill finishes with a 1v1 possession between student B and the defender (see figure). Student B allows time for the defender to get back out in a defensive position before attempting to attack the basket. In this task, the defender helps at the baseline and then recovers to the original offensive student. Stress to defenders that they need to maintain the appropriate defensive ball adjustment position. In doing so, the defender should be able to see everything and when the ball is farther away from your offensive student, the defender can provide more support to the on-the-ball defender. For the rotation, student A becomes the defender, the defender becomes student B, and student B becomes student A. If there are 4 to 5 students in the group, the extra students line up behind student B's position and the defender moves to the waiting line. As an extension, once the defender demonstrates an understanding of the task, student B can immediately attack the basket after the pass back.

EQUIPMENT

One basketball and one hoop (half-court setup) per three students

CRITICAL ELEMENTS AND CUES

Technique

- When defending off the ball, focus your eyes at a point in space that is midway between the ball and the student you are defending. This keeps both in your peripheral vision. *Cue:* Student-ball-you-man.

Agility

- The defensive student and her or his movements should be the main focus. A quick step towards the dribbler is needed.

Fair Play

- Clarify to the students the speed at which the task is being executed. Time must be allowed for the defender to move appropriately so that a good simulation of help and recover for all persons can be achieved.

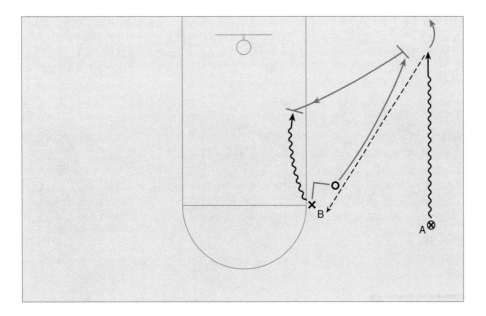

COMMON ERRORS, CAUSES, AND CORRECTIONS

- The defensive student is late to help defend at the baseline. *Cause:* The student got a late start or was too far from the ball at the original position. *Correction:* Have the student move to a middle position.

TASK 35: ZONE PRINCIPLES (TEAM DEFENSE)

PURPOSE

Following are the purposes of the task as related to aspects of skilled performance.

- Technique: In this task, students learn to take an athletic position and move accordingly depending on their position from the ball (e.g., one pass away, two passes away) in a zone defense.
- Agility: Students make quick, directional movements when relocating to on- and off-the-ball positions.
- Fair play: Students make passes at speeds that defenders can effectively react to.
- Communication: Students verbally call out "ball" when a defender is on the ball, and they use nonverbal pointing to indicate the positions defensive students are moving to.

DESCRIPTION

Divide students into groups of seven (four offensive students and three defensive students). In this 4v3 situation, we use a 2-1 defensive formation. The four offensive students are in an arc on the 3-point line while two defensive students begin with one on each of the free throw line elbows and the third defender is in the middle of the lane in front of the basket. The one-student offensive advantage requires the defense to mark spaces rather than people while maintaining the general defensive principles of pressuring the ball, employing the ball-you-man position, and shifting roles based on offensive developments. Offensive students pass the ball around the arc with a 2- to 3-second delay between passes so they can observe all three defenders moving into different defensive positions based on the new location of the ball. The ball is always marked by the nearest defender, and the other two defenders adjust to the position of the ball and defend their space. The ball begins with one of the two middle offensive students. The defender closest to the ball steps out and guards the ball while the other top defender moves slightly into the lane and the bottom defender moves towards the free throw lane line on the side of the ball (figure *a*). If the ball is passed to the baseline student the bottom defender steps out to guard the ball while the top defender on the side of the ball moves back into the free throw lane and the top defender opposite the ball moves deeper into the lane (figure *b*). As the ball moves around the arc these defensive positions adjust according to the position of the ball with the bottom defender always on the side that the ball is on.

- *Extension 1.* Students increase the speed of the passing once defenders demonstrate an understanding of the proper defensive movement.
- *Extension 2.* After making a number of passes, the offensive students attempt to attack the basket with the ball and the defenders react accordingly.
- *Extension 3.* Move the defenders to a 2-2. In this extension the added defender is added to the position next to the single defender and each defender is located on opposite sides of the lane towards the basket. As the ball moves around the arc, the defenders adjust to the position of the ball an indicated in figures *c* and *d*.

EQUIPMENT

One basketball and one hoop (half-court setup) per seven students

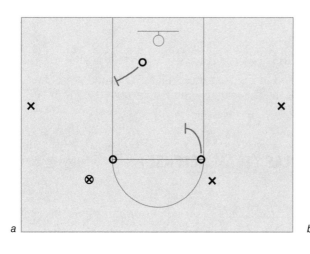

a

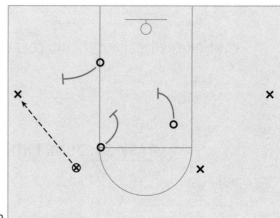

b

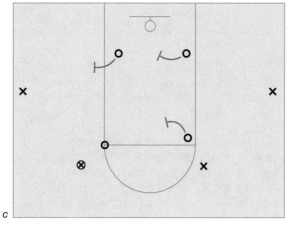

c

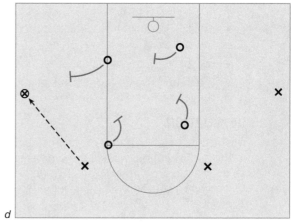

d

CRITICAL ELEMENTS AND CUES

Technique

- Make sure students can differentiate between zone responsibilities for each defensive student in formations such as a 2-1 and 2-2.

Agility

- Quickly adjust your position after the ball is passed (or moved) from the original position.

Fair Play

- Allow defensive students time to adjust appropriately to the ball movement.
- Participate at the correct speed.

Communication

- Call your new position (*ball*) to identify your position and role in the team defense.
- Point to identify offensive students who are moving into any observed holes in the zone.

COMMON ERRORS, CAUSES, AND CORRECTIONS

- Students are in the wrong position. *Cause:* The students have limited experience and knowledge. *Correction:* With beginning students, take an approach in which you explain, demonstrate, and perform the tasks. The expectations apply to playing person-to-person defense in any formation.

TASK 36: APPLICATION GAMES

PURPOSE

Following are the purposes of the task as related to aspects of skilled performance.

- Technique: In this task, students apply learned skills in game-like situations.
- Tactic: Students apply learned tactical elements in game-like situations.
- Agility: Students apply agility requirements in game-like situations.
- Fair play: Students call their own fouls and violations.
- Communication: Students apply communication requirements in game-like situations.

DESCRIPTION

- **1v1 games.** Introduce students to basic norms of playing small-sided games. The beginning games of this level emphasize different types of defense (active, passive, competitive), checking the ball to the on-the-ball defender, and options for scoring in a 1v1 formation. There is a focus on the customs and traditions of playing the game, such as taking the ball back after a defensive rebound and providing the appropriate level of defense. At this level, shooting, dribbling, and rebounding provide focus points for the 1v1 game, and the defender provides PAC defense and rebounding. There is also a focus on shooting the ball in a modified game situation from a stationary position or off 1 or 2 dribbles.
- **2v1 games.** Each possession begins with checking the ball, and the defender is required to mark the ball. When the ball is checked, one offensive student makes a pass to the other offensive student on the left or right wing. After the first pass, the defender can mark space rather than the ball, and the offensive students are advised to space out so the defender is at a disadvantage. After the first pass, the emphasis is on offensive students attempting appropriate shots when open; this is set up by quick passes and shifting the defender across space. Given the one-student advantage in a 2v1 game, offensive students can use dribbling, spacing, and passing to get good shots off. Because passing is the focus, emphasize multiple passes to get a good shot.

- **2v2 games.** Start this formation in a passive or active defense situation. The defender checks the ball to the offensive student they are guarding, and that offensive student makes the first pass to the other offensive student who is on either the right or left wing and makes a cut to get open from their defender. After the first pass, students get open by changing speed and direction. Defensive pressure should not be so much that students cannot make a move to get a shot off if able to. Different skills can be applied to these games such as defensive principles and offensive moves to get open.
- **3v2 games.** The individual offense is the focus here. Emphasize getting the ball to the most open offensive student and attacking the basket using individual offensive moves. The defensive principles of guarding the ball are also emphasized.
- **3v3 games.** Because team offense, individual defense, and team defense are the foci, the emphasis is different during game play. Here the use of offensive tactics such as pick and roll, off-ball screens or other offensive tactics as well as defensive movements can be stressed.
- **4v4 games.** This is the concluding game of the advanced level. We do not include the fifth student because this student clogs up the court and limits the ability of students to apply the skills learned in a physical education setting. We believe the fifth student should be used only in competitive athletic teams.

EQUIPMENT

One ball per game

CRITICAL ELEMENTS AND CUES

Apply all the previous skills and cues.

Rules

- Check the ball at each possession at the top of the key.
- Once the ball is checked, allow a free first pass to the right or left wing extended.
- Alternate possessions at made baskets.
- Offensive students make calls when fouled.
- Head coaches settle all disputes.
- The default level of defense is active. Give opponents a good look and play to win fairly.

COMMON ERRORS, CAUSES, AND CORRECTIONS

- Look for all previously discussed errors and provide corrections.

Chapter 9

Volleyball

Volleyball has grown in popularity around the world since it was invented in 1895. The advent of beach (sand) volleyball has contributed to a recent growth in popularity. Volleyball has been a part of most physical education curricula for many years, and it is played in a variety of recreational settings. Volleyball is not a complicated game. There is an element of fear, however, that has to be overcome when using the hit (spike) and block. Although teaching strategies for volleyball vary, the typical method involves practicing techniques individually and with a partner and then applying those techniques in a 6v6 (or larger) game setting. We believe the techniques need to be taught and applied in small game settings that provide students with multiple opportunities to practice them and gain the confidence needed to enjoy a full-sized volleyball game.

OUR PEDAGOGICAL APPROACH TO VOLLEYBALL

Volleyball is a net game. Instruction in the elementary and secondary units focuses on developing skillful performance and game sense through tasks and instructional sequences that teach volleyball techniques and quickly using these skills in modified games.

The basic volleyball techniques are passing, setting, hitting, blocking, and serving. We recognize that each of these can be challenging for beginning students; therefore, we first focus on passing and setting (individually and with a partner) and using these skills in games. After students learn these basic offensive techniques, they are applied to the triad tactic and we introduce serving, basic blocking, and tipping the ball over the net. After students learn these techniques, we add playing the ball off the net, hitting the ball, and coordinating blocks with teammates.

The level 1 tasks can be performed with balloons, beach balls, foam balls, or trainer volleyballs. You might want to incorporate the level 1 tasks in each year of an elementary program but change the type of ball used (start with balloons and then progress to beach balls and then to foam balls or trainer volleyballs).

Students should only use regulation volleyballs at the secondary level when they demonstrate the ability to execute basic forearm passes, sets, and serves using trainer volleyballs. This way, students will have less fear about executing these techniques.

We use modified 2v2 games that emphasize passing and setting in level 1. We add the triad along with serving, tipping, and blocking in 3v3 and 4v4 games in level 2. In level 3, we move to 6v6 games that include hitting and double blocks. Before you add the serve to the games, begin with self-toss or over-the-net toss games.

Modifications to Address Individual Needs of Students

For students with disabilities, appropriate modifications depend on the nature of the disability. To modify volleyball instruction for students with visual impairments, you can use a trainer ball or beach ball instead of a regulation volleyball, and you can use brightly colored floor tape to mark off boundaries. You can also use the whole-part-whole method, in which you show the student the entire skill from the beginning to end, then you break it down into pieces for instruction, and then you teach the entire skill. In addition, you can modify the rules to better suit individuals with visual impairments, such as allowing students to touch the net to help with orientation or allowing the student to serve the ball out of the support hand rather than throwing it in the air prior to the serve.

For students with autism spectrum disorder, modify activities by allowing students to practice bumps, sets, and hiking motions against a wall where there are minimal distractions. You can also communicate using students' desired methods (e.g., picture symbols). Consider modifying game rules by allowing students to catch and throw the ball over the net when playing initial games or putting students in smaller teams in which each student must touch the ball prior to hitting it over the net.

For students who use wheelchairs, few modifications should be needed. You might want to adopt a one-bounce rule to ensure students can get to the ball in time. This rule might also be beneficial for other students who have limited movement, such as those with cerebral palsy.

In sports that include flying implements (e.g., volleyballs), it is possible for students to get hit in the head. Ensure that there are no serious issues with this. For example, a child with a retinal detachment might lose residual vision if struck in the head with a flying volleyball. Refer to the student's IEP for information on this matter.

Organization

The full-sided game of volleyball is six players per team. We question the appropriateness of 6v6 in a physical education setting relative to learning techniques and tactics. Volleyball is based on two general game tactics: offensive attack and transitioning to the attack. In a 6v6 setting, the team size doesn't provide beginners with ample opportunities to practice the techniques and tactics; often, the more skilled students dominate play. We advocate the use of 2v2, 3v3, and eventually 4v4 team structures to apply and practice the various techniques and tactics of volleyball. The use of the full-sided 6v6 game is not recommended until all the students demonstrate the ability to apply learned techniques and tactics competently.

Space

In smaller games, a full-sized volleyball court is not mandatory. You can divide a volleyball court in half so two games can be played next to each other on the full court. If volleyball courts are not available, set up nets across a gymnasium and designate mini courts with cones. Many initial learning tasks can be done without courts or nets.

Equipment Needed

At the elementary level, we recommended that you use balloons, beach balls, foam balls, and trainer volleyballs. We discourage the use of regulation volleyballs due to the fear and control issues that arise when students are first learning volleyball techniques. At the secondary level, students can use trainer and regulation volleyballs, but you might need foam balls or beach balls for early learners. Although nets are preferred, they are not mandatory for early learning tasks. In place of nets, use ropes draped between chairs or standards that can be adjusted for height as appropriate.

CONTENT MAP STRUCTURE

Figure 9.1 is a combined content map that illustrates the flow and connectedness of all the tasks used to develop volleyball techniques and tactics. It is divided into three levels, and each level has a separate content map that includes the application games used to refine the techniques and tactics in that level. The primary focus of level 1 (figure 9.2) is passing and setting, and it ends with an application game that combines those techniques. At level 2 (figure 9.3), the triad tactic is added, the serve is introduced, the concept of the attack is introduced with the tip, and a defensive block is added; this level concludes with a 4v4 game. At level 3 (figure 9.4), the spike, coordinated blocking, and extended forearm passing (off-center passes and digging the ball out of the net) are introduced, and the level ends with a full-sided 6v6 game.

In the content maps, we have numbered the tasks. These numbers are used to cross reference tasks descriptions in the body of the chapter with the content maps. The task numbers should not be interpreted as the order in which they should be taught. It is important that tasks are taught and progressed from simpler to more complex

forms which is shown in the upward progress of the task sequence on the content map. This is particularly necessary before tasks are combined. For instance in volleyball whether you teach the forearm pass first or the set, the progressions of both need to be taught before they are combined in task 11.

STRUCTURE OF THE LESSONS

The following is a sample daily lesson structure for a 50-minute secondary volleyball lesson.

Warm-up (5 to 6 minutes)

Application game: 2v2 captain's toss game (8 minutes)

Informing task: triad toss, pass, set, and catch (5 minutes)

Extension task: triad toss, pass, set and catch with extension (5 minutes)

Informing task: 1v3 toss over the net to a triad with a jump catch (7 minutes)

Informing task: wall serves (underhand) (4 minutes)

Extension task: wall serves (overhand) (5 minutes)

Application game: 3v3 captain's toss game (catch allowed) (7 minutes)

Closure (3 minutes)

Warm-up

Our elementary and secondary school warm-ups for volleyball are presented here.

Elementary School

The warm-up should be taught to students on the second and third days of the unit. If a technique used in the warm-up has not been taught, it should not be included in the warm-up circuit until the day after you teach it. Passing, movement, and setting are the initial techniques used in the warm-up. Passing is introduced in lesson 1, so the lesson 2 warm-up includes partner passing. Movement with passing is introduced in lesson 2, so lateral sliding and shuffling are added to the warm-up for lesson 3. Setting is introduced in lesson 3, so this is added to the warm-up for lesson 4. Each day you can add new techniques (see level 1 block plan), or you can stick with the same warm-up.

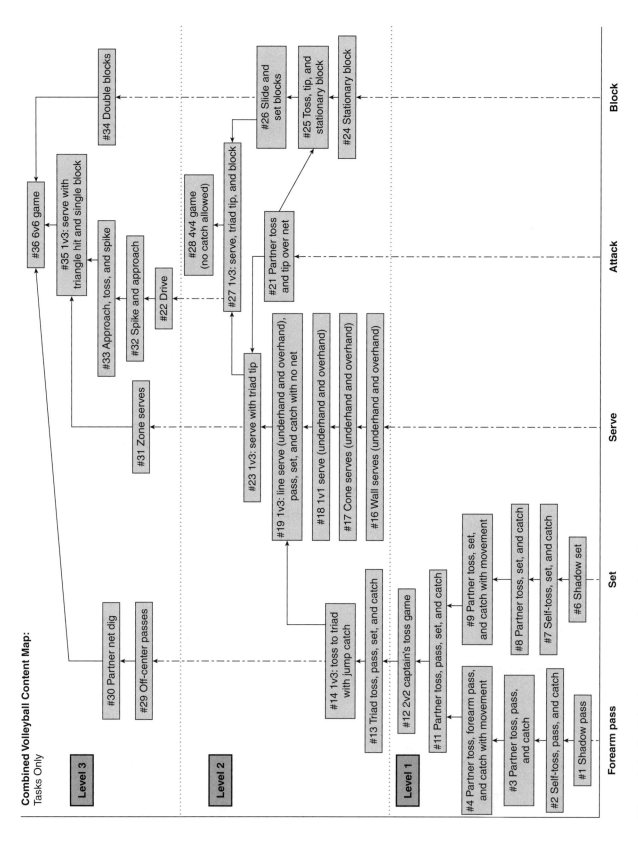

Combined Volleyball Content Map:
Tasks Only

Figure 9.1 Combined content map for volleyball.

286

Level 1 Volleyball Content Map:
Application Games

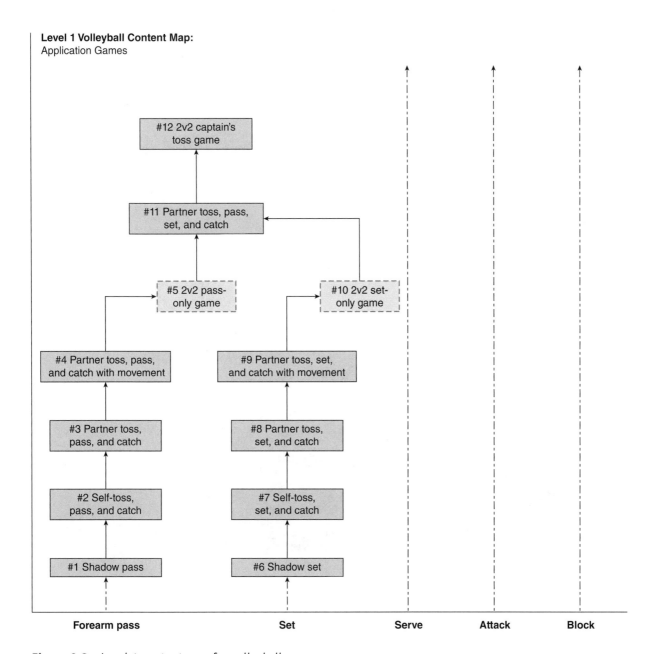

Figure 9.2 Level 1 content map for volleyball.

Level 2 Volleyball Content Map:
Application Games

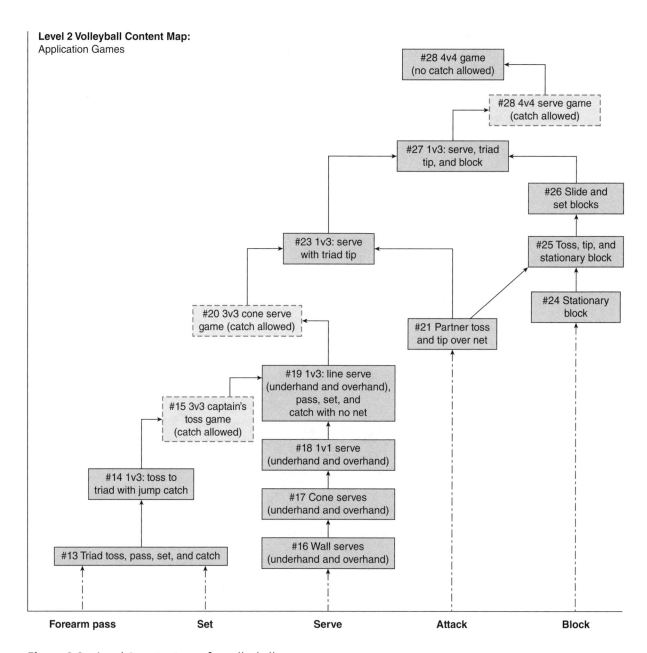

Figure 9.3 Level 2 content map for volleyball.

Level 3 Volleyball Content Map:
Application Games

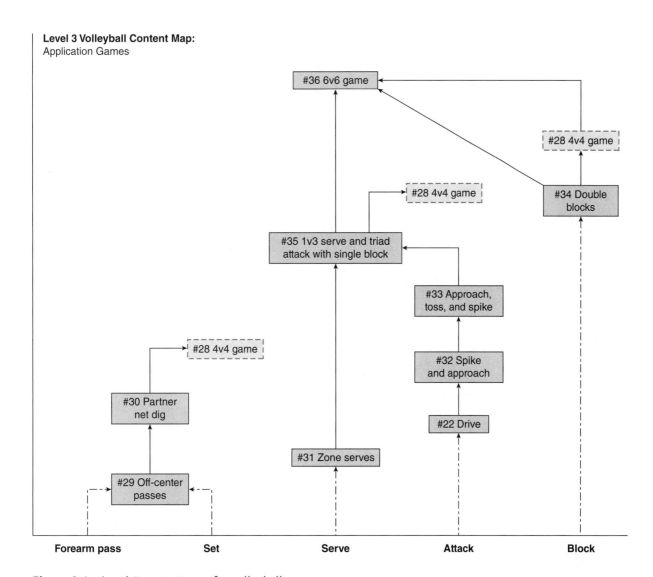

Figure 9.4 Level 3 content map for volleyball.

For the passing task, pairs of students stand 8 to 10 feet (2.4 to 3 meters) apart. One student tosses the ball and the partner passes it back. After five tosses, the students switch roles and repeat the task. You can challenge students to do continuous passes back and forth if their passing control warrants this. For the movement task, set up a 10-foot square with cones. Students do slide steps along the back and front edges of the square and shuffle steps forward and backward on the sides of the square. Students focus on not crossing the feet when going sideways and using a step-close-step action when moving forward or backward. For the setting task, pairs of students stand 8 to 10 feet apart and execute chest passes (as in basketball) back and forth. Hands start on the sides of the ball with the thumbs and fingers pointing back at the student. On release of the ball, the thumbs point toward the floor and fingers point at the partner. Emphasize this wrist action, which mimics the toss and catch hand action of the overhead set. In later grades, you can change this task to a partner toss with a set back to the tosser. The warm-up should provide enough time for multiple trials to be attempted, but it should not last more than 4 to 5 minutes once students have learned all the techniques.

How you organize your students for the warm-up will depend on the decisions you make about the organization of the class. If you use a circuit, divide the class into three groups and include the appropriate equipment at each of the three stations (see figure 9.5). The passing and setting stations require balls for each pair of students, and the movement station requires cones to mark the 10-foot square. Students should begin each day in the same area and rotate through the stations. The tasks can be done in any order. Provide instructions for what students should do once they have completed all the stations. If you decide to have the whole class do the warm-up activities together, you need to have enough balls to accommodate the entire class (one for every two students) and enough 10-foot squares to accommodate 5 to 6 students each.

Secondary School

Introduce the secondary warm-up over the first few days of the unit as techniques are taught. The forearm pass is reviewed (including movement) in lesson 1, so in lesson 2 the warm-up begins with defensive sliding and the forearm passing "t" drill. Setting is reviewed in lesson 2, so it is added to the warm-up for lesson 3. Although spiking is not introduced until later in the unit, a spiking-related task is included in the lesson 3 warm-up. This mimics the arm, hand, and follow-through motions of the spike and is a good arm and upper-body warm-up. Students do not know the relevance of this task to the spiking technique they will learn later. For a unit that lasts more than 10 days, there is an extension for the spiking task. Once learned, the warm-up should be completed in the first 5 to 6 minutes of the lesson.

For the defensive sliding task, use the 3-meter, side, and service lines on a volleyball court. Students assume a defensive stance and then move around the lines using a slide and shuffle step and intermittently assuming the forearm pass position. The objective is to quickly move sideways, forward, and backward without crossing the feet

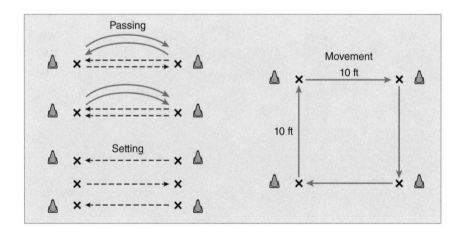

Figure 9.5 Sample elementary school warm-up circuit for volleyball.

while integrating a forearm passing position. For the forearm passing task, use the "t" drill. Students work in pairs. One student tosses the ball to the partner, and the partner forearm passes it back to the tosser. Then the student tosses the ball to the right, and the passer must move one slide step to the right to pass the ball back and then return to the starting position. The third toss is to the left for a return pass. The fourth toss forces the passer to move back one step to execute the pass, and the fifth toss forces the passer to move forward one step to complete the pass. The movement of the passer mimics the shape of the lowercase letter *t*. After each set of "t" movements, the students switch roles. For the setting task, students follow the same instructions but use the set instead of the pass to return the ball. These three tasks are foundational techniques that need to be practiced, and they remain the same through the unit regardless of the unit's length. For the spiking task, emphasize the wrist snap and follow-through motion of the spike. Pairs of students stand 8 to 10 feet (2.4 to 3 meters) apart. One student makes a soccer-style, two-hand overhead throw toward the ground with a high bounce to the partner. The thrower should see the elbows in front of the body prior to the throw, extend the arms quickly, and snap the wrists and the ball to the ground on release. If the unit extends past 10 days, change the task. In this extension, the student hits the ball out of the hand to the ground and it bounces up to a partner (or this can be done against a wall using a self-catch). Again, the focus is on a high elbow, quick extension, and snapping the wrist so the ball bounces as high as possible. The throwing hand should follow through to hip on the throwing side.

This warm-up can be done with stations or in teams. If you use stations, divide the class into four groups and have students spend about 90 seconds at each station (see figure 9.6). If the warm-up is done in teams, have groups of 6 to 8 students complete each part of the warm-up in the home area. This requires that each home area have a 20-foot (6.1-meter) square for the sliding task. Provide students with instructions for what they should do once they finish the warm-up tasks (e.g., put balls away, ball rake, sit down in an assigned space, line up, or repeat the tasks).

BLOCK PLAN

The introductory block plan (see table 9.1) is designed for beginners. In elementary school, this should be not be introduced earlier than third grade. In third and fourth grades, students should start with balloons and move to beach balls. In fifth grade, students might advance to the use of trainer volleyballs, but we do not advocate the use of regulation volleyballs at the elementary level. Although some passing and setting tasks can be done with balloons, all of the tasks on the elementary block plan can be accomplished with beach balls, foam balls, or trainer volleyballs. When you change the type of ball used, repeat the early tasks to address the challenge presented by the new ball. Although students in each grade do similar tasks, this allows them to refine their

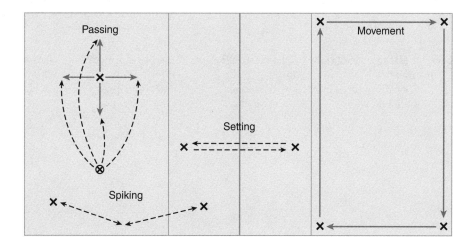

Figure 9.6 Sample secondary warm-up circuit for volleyball.

basic passing and setting techniques prior to the challenges of manipulating a regulation volleyball. Although longer units are always preferred, we recognize that there are time limitations at the elementary level; therefore, the elementary unit is five days for the initial grade in which it is taught.

The secondary block plan (see table 9.2) follows the elementary block plan and is designed for students in middle school and high school. It assumes that students were taught the basic volleyball skills at the elementary level. If this is not the case, follow the introductory block plan and use the appropriate type of ball. In most secondary programs, we recommend that students begin with trainer volleyballs and move to regulation volleyballs when they demonstrate control. Because middle and high school physical education programs have different requirements, these units should *not* be taught in fewer than 10 days. These units are adjusted for 10-, 15-, and 20-day programs, although we recommend units of 20 or more days.

Table 9.1   Elementary Volleyball Block Plan: Five-Day Unit

This is an example of a beginning block plan for elementary students that uses all the volleyball tasks shown in the level 1 content map. You can use this as a template for developing an appropriate block plan for beginning students. If you are teaching a longer unit, or if another volleyball unit will be taught next year, repeat these tasks using different types of balls (e.g., move from balloons to beach balls in third grade, move from beach balls to foam balls in fourth grade, and move from foam balls to trainer balls in fifth grade). The type of ball used is a critical decision that will affect student success. Your decisions about what balls to use depend on your students and their levels of experience.

Lesson 1	Lesson 2	Lesson 3	Lesson 4	Lesson 5

Warm-up
• Nonspecific warm-up
	Warm-up
	• Passing
		Warm-up
		• Circuit
		  • Passing
		  • Lateral sliding and shuffling
			Warm-up
			• Circuit
			  • Partner passing
			  • Lateral sliding and shuffling
			  • Setting
				Warm-up
				• Same as day 4

Introductory application game None	**Introductory application game** • **(3)** Partner toss, pass, and catch	**Introductory application game** • **(5)** 2v2 pass-only game	**Introductory application game** • **(8)** Partner toss, set, and catch	**Introductory application game** • **(10)** 2v2 set-only game
Content development • **(1)** Shadow pass • **(2)** Self-toss, pass, and catch	**Content development** • **(4)** Partner toss, forearm pass, catch with movement	**Content development** • **(6)** Shadow set • **(7)** Self-toss, set, and catch	**Content development** • **(9)** Partner toss, set, and catch with movement	**Content development** • **(11)** Partner toss, pass, set, and catch
Closing application game • **(3)** Partner toss, pass, and catch	**Closing application game** • **(5)** 2v2 pass-only game	**Closing application game** • **(8)** Partner toss, set, and catch	**Closing application game** • **(10)** 2v2 set-only game	**Closing application game** • **(12)** 2v2 captain's toss game

Table 9.2 Secondary Volleyball Block Plans: 10-, 15-, and 20-Day Units

This block plan incorporates 10-, 15-, and 20-day units. The last two days of the 10-day block plan, the last three days of the 15-day block plan, and the last five days of the 20-day block plan are game days and are described at the end of the block plan. The first eight days of the block plan are the same for all units. This block plan includes level 1 tasks and then addresses the level 2 content map (10- and 15-day units) and the level 3 content map (20-day unit). Use the level 1 tasks as a review or for initial instruction. Begin the tasks with a trainer ball, and switch to a regulation ball when students demonstrate control.

Lesson 1 of all block plans	Lesson 2 of all block plans	Lesson 3 of all block plans	Lesson 4 of all block plans	Lesson 5 of all block plans

Warm-up
• Nonspecific warm-up
	Warm-up
	• Tasks
	  • Defensive sliding
	  • Forearm passing "t" drill
		Warm-up
		• Tasks
		  • Defensive sliding
		  • Forearm passing "t" drill
		  • Setting
		  • Spiking
			Warm-up
			• Same as day 3
				Warm-up
				• Same as day 3

Introductory application game None	**Introductory application game** • **(5)** 2v2 pass-only game	**Introductory application game** • **(10)** 2v2 set-only game	**Introductory application game** • **(12)** 2v2 captain's toss game	**Introductory application game** • **(15)** 3v3 captain's toss game (catch allowed)
Content development • **(1)** Shadow pass • **(2)** Self-toss, pass, and catch • **(3)** Partner toss, pass, and catch	**Content development** • **(4)** Partner toss, forearm pass, and catch with movement • **(6)** Shadow set • **(7)** Self-toss, set, and catch • **(8)** Partner toss, set, and catch	**Content development** • **(9)** Partner toss, set, and catch with movement • **(11)** Partner toss, pass, set, and catch	**Content development** • **(13)** Triad toss, pass, set, and catch • **(14)** 1v3 toss over the net to a triad with a jump catch • **(16)** Wall serves (underhand and overhand)	**Content development** • **(17)** Cone serves (underhand and overhand) • **(18)** 1v1 serve (underhand and overhand) • **(21)** Partner toss and tip over the net
Closing application game • **(5)** 2v2 pass-only game	**Closing application game** • **(10)** 2v2 set-only game	**Closing application game** • **(12)** 2v2 captain's toss game	**Closing application game** • **(15)** 3v3 captain's toss game (catch allowed)	**Closing application game** • **(20)** 3v3 cone serve game (catch allowed)

(continued)

Lesson 6 of all block plans	Lesson 7 of all block plans	Lesson 8 of all block plans (last instructional day of 10-day block plan)	Lesson 9 of 15- and 20-day block plans (See table 9.3 for lesson 9 for 10-day plan.)	Lesson 10 of 15- and 20-day block plans (See table 9.3 for lesson 10 for 10-day plan.)
Warm-up • Same as day 3	**Warm-up** • Same as day 3	**Warm-up** • Same as day 3	**Warm-up** • Same as day 3	**Warm-up** • Same as day 3
Introductory application game • **(20)** 3v3 cone serve game (catch allowed)	**Introductory application game** • **(20)** 3v3 cone serve game (catch allowed)	**Introductory application game** • **(28)** 4v4 game	**Introductory application game** • **(28)** 4v4 game	**Introductory application game** • **(28)** 4v4 game
Content development • **(19)** 1v3 line serve (underhand and overhand), pass, set, and catch with no net • **(24)** Stationary block • **(25)** Toss, tip, and stationary block	**Content development** • **(23)** 1v3 serve with triad tip • **(26)** Slide and set blocks	**Content development** • **(27)** 1v3 serve, triad tip, and block • Review tasks as needed	**Content development** • **(31)** Zone serves • **(22)** Drive • Review tasks as needed	**Content development** • **(32)** Spike and approach • **(33)** Approach, toss, and spike • Review tasks as needed
Closing application game • **(20)** 3v3 cone serve game (catch allowed)	**Closing application game** • **(28)** 4v4 game	**Closing application game** • **(28)** 4v4 game • **(36)** 6v6 game (for 10-day unit)	**Closing application game** • **(28)** 4v4 game	**Closing application game** • **(28)** 4v4 game

Lesson 11 of 15- and 20-day block plans	Lesson 12 of 15- and 20-day block plans (last instructional day of 15-day plan)	Lesson 13 of 20-day block plan (See table 9.4 for lesson 13 for 15-day plan.)	Lesson 14 of 20-day block plan (See table 9.4 for lesson 14 for 15-day plan.)	Lesson 15 of 20-day block plan (See table 9.4 for lesson 15 for 15-day plan.)

Warm-up
• Tasks
  • Defensive sliding
  • Forearm passing "t" drill
  • Setting
  • Spiking extension
	Warm-up
	• Same as day 11
		Warm-up
		• Same as day 11
			Warm-up
			• Same as day 11
				Warm-up
				• Same as day 11

Introductory application game • **(28)** 4v4 game	**Introductory application game** • **(28)** 4v4 game	**Introductory application game** • **(28)** 4v4 game	**Introductory application game** • **(28)** 4v4 game	**Introductory application game** • **(36)** 6v6 game
Content development • **(29)** Off-center passes • **(30)** Partner net dig	**Content development** • Review tasks as needed	**Content development** • **(27)** 1v3 serve, triad tip, and block • **(34)** Double blocks	**Content development** • Review tasks as needed	**Content development** • Review tasks as needed
Closing application game • **(28)** 4v4 game	**Closing application game** • **(28)** 4v4 game	**Closing application game** • **(28)** 4v4 game	**Closing application game** • **(28)** 4v4 game	**Closing application game** • **(36)** 6v6 game

Lesson 16 of 20-day block plan	Lesson 17 of 20-day block plan	Lesson 18 of 20-day block plan	Lesson 19 of 20-day block plan	Lesson 20 of 20-day block plan
Warm-up • Same as day 11	**Warm-up** • Same as day 11	**Warm-up** • Same as day 11	**Warm-up** • Same as day 11	**Warm-up** • Same as day 11
Fixed-time 6v6 games against different opponents (nonexclusionary round-robin tournament) Encourage the use of specific skills. Award an extra point to the score for demonstration of these skills. We recommend at least two games per lesson.	**Fixed-time 6v6 games against different opponents (nonexclusionary round-robin tournament)** Encourage the use of specific skills. Award an extra point to the score for demonstration of these skills. We recommend at least two games per lesson.	**Fixed-time 6v6 games against different opponents (nonexclusionary round-robin tournament)** Encourage the use of specific skills. Award an extra point to the score for demonstration of these skills. We recommend at least two games per lesson.	**Fixed-time 6v6 games against different opponents (nonexclusionary round-robin tournament)** Encourage the use of specific skills. Award an extra point to the score for demonstration of these skills. We recommend at least two games per lesson.	**Fixed-time 6v6 games against different opponents (nonexclusionary round-robin tournament)** Encourage the use of specific skills. Award an extra point to the score for demonstration of these skills. We recommend at least two games per lesson.

Table 9.3   10-Day Block Plan Game Days

Lesson 9 of 10-day block plan	Lesson 10 of 10-day block plan
Warm-up • Same as day 3	**Warm-up** • Same as day 3
Fixed-time 4v4 games against different opponents (nonexclusionary round-robin tournament) Encourage the use of specific skills. Award an extra point to the score for demonstration of these skills. We recommend at least two games per lesson.	**Fixed-time 4v4 games against different opponents (nonexclusionary round-robin tournament)** Encourage the use of specific skills. Award an extra point to the score for demonstration of these skills. We recommend at least two games per lesson.

Table 9.4   15-Day Block Plan Game Days

Lesson 13 of 15-day block plan	Lesson 14 of 15-day block plan	Lesson 15 of 15-day block plan
Warm-up • Same as day 11	**Warm-up** • Same as day 11	**Warm-up** • Same as day 11
Fixed-time 4v4 or 6v6 games against different opponents (nonexclusionary round-robin tournament) Encourage the use of specific skills. Award an extra point to the score for demonstration of these skills. We recommend at least two games per lesson.	**Fixed-time 4v4 or 6v6 games against different opponents (nonexclusionary round-robin tournament)** Encourage the use of specific skills. Award an extra point to the score for demonstration of these skills. We recommend at least two games per lesson.	**Fixed-time 4v4 or 6v6 games against different opponents (nonexclusionary round-robin tournament)** Encourage the use of specific skills. Award an extra point to the score for demonstration of these skills. We recommend at least two games per lesson.

SHAPE AMERICA'S GRADE LEVEL OUTCOMES
FOR K-12 PHYSICAL EDUCATION

In table 9.5, we identify key grade-level outcomes for volleyball for 2nd through 8th grade. These are linked to specific tasks on the content maps that are appropriate for teaching the skill and assessing the outcome.

Table 9.5 Grade-Level Outcomes for Volleyball

Outcome	Description	Content map focus and tasks
S1.E22.2	Volleys an object upward with consecutive hits.	Level 1, task 7
S1.E22.3	Volleys an object with an underhand or sidearm striking pattern, sending it forward over a net, to the wall or over a line to a partner, while demonstrating 4 of the 5 critical elements of a mature pattern.	Level 1, task 3
S1.E22.4	Volleys underhand using a mature pattern, in a dynamic environment (e.g., 2 square, 4 square, handball).	Level 1, task 10
S1.E23.4	Volleys a ball with a 2-hand overhead pattern, sending it upward, demonstrating 4 of the 5 critical elements of a mature pattern.	Level 1, task 7
S1.E23.5	Volleys a ball using a 2-hand overhead pattern sending it upward to a target.	Level 1, tasks 8-9
S1.M13.6	Strikes with a mature overhand pattern in a nondynamic environment for net/wall games such as volleyball, handball, badminton or tennis.	Level 2, task 16
S1.M13.7	Strikes with a mature overhand pattern in a dynamic environment for net/wall games such as volleyball, handball, badminton or tennis.	Level 2, task 27
S1.M13.8	Strikes with a mature overhand pattern in a modified game for net/wall games such as volleyball, handball, badminton or tennis.	Level 2, task 29
S1.M15.6	Transfers weight with correct timing for the striking pattern.	Level 2, task 17
S1.M17.6	Two-hand-volleys with control in a variety of practice tasks.	Level 1, tasks 8-9, 11 Level 2, tasks 13-14
S1.M17.7	Two-hand-volleys with control in a dynamic environment.	Level 1, task 9
S1.M17.8	Two-hand-volleys with control in a small-sided game.	Level 1, tasks 10, 12 Level 2, task 29 Level 3, task 38

TASK 1: SHADOW PASS

PURPOSE

Following is the purpose of the task as related to aspects of skilled performance.

Technique: In this task, students learn the critical elements of the forearm pass.

DESCRIPTION

Students are in a scattered formation. After your instruction, students perform the forearm passing action (without a ball) in self space. Move around and provide feedback to students based on the critical elements displayed.

EQUIPMENT

None

CRITICAL ELEMENTS AND CUES

Technique: Grip

- Join the hands together in one of these two positions:
  - Wrapped fist position: Make a fist with your dominant hand and wrap it in the palm of your other hand with the thumbs side by side (figure *a-b*). *Cue:* Wrapped fist.

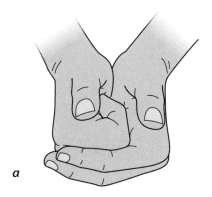 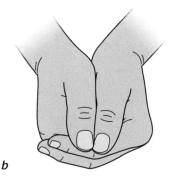

a   *b*

  - Cupped palms position: Bring your hands together as if you were going to take a sip of water from them, and lay your thumbs side by side across the top (figure *c-d*). *Cue:* Cupped palms.

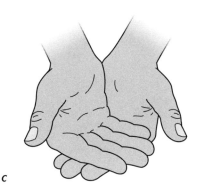 

c   *d*

Technique: Forearm Pass

- Touch the forearms together between the wrists and the elbows at the thickest portion of the forearm. *Cue:* Forearms.
- Press the wrists and hands down to hyperextend the arms. *Cue:* Make a platform.
- Lock the elbows to keep the arms locked. *Cue:* Straight arms.
- Bend the knees before the ball gets to you. *Cue:* Bend knees.
- Move your shoulders toward your target on impact. *Cue:* Lift your shoulders.

COMMON ERRORS, CAUSES, AND CORRECTIONS

- Students will interlock fingers. *Cause:* This is a more natural feel for them when putting hands together to strike something. *Correction:* Have students show the teacher their hands after assuming the grip.
- Students will have their thumbs crossed when assuming their grip. *Cause:* This is a more natural feel for them when putting their hands together. *Correction:* After assuming their grips, have students tap their thumbs together and if they can't, have them tap their thumbs and then stop with the thumbs next to each other.

TASK 2: SELF-TOSS, PASS, AND CATCH

PURPOSE

Following is the purpose of the task as related to aspects of skilled performance.
   Technique: In this task, students apply the critical elements of the forearm pass using a ball.

DESCRIPTION

Each student has a ball in self-space. On your signal, students toss the ball into the air in front of the body, forearm pass the ball straight up, and catch it as it comes down. Students repeat this until you tell them to stop. Start with an appropriate ball (e.g., balloon, beach ball, trainer), but as students demonstrate control extend the task to include other types of balls. If students need motivation, have them see how many passes they can make in a row. As an extension, challenge students to do multiple passes before catching the ball.

EQUIPMENT

One ball per student

CRITICAL ELEMENTS AND CUES

Technique

- See critical elements and cues for task 1.
- Allow the ball to come to the arms; do not swing the arms at the ball. *Cue:* Arms still.

COMMON ERRORS, CAUSES, AND CORRECTIONS

- The ball goes over the student's head. *Cause:* The student swings the arms at the ball. *Correction:* Have the student practice keeping the ball at head height on the pass, and remind the student to lift the shoulders on contact.
- The ball rebounds at an angle to the side. *Cause:* The ball contacts the hands or wrists. *Correction:* Have the student use a balloon to practice the contact point.

TASK 3: PARTNER TOSS, PASS, AND CATCH

PURPOSE

Following are the purposes of the task as related to aspects of skilled performance.

- Tactic: In this task, students practice passing to a partner.
- Fair play: Students toss the ball in a manner that allows the partner to pass it.
- Communication: Students say *mine* to indicate possession as the ball comes.

DESCRIPTION

Students pair up, and each pair has a ball. One student gently tosses the ball to the other student; this student calls out *mine* and then forearm passes the ball back to the tosser. The tosser catches the ball and repeats the action. After a set number of times, students switch roles.

- *Extension 1.* When control is evident, have the student toss the ball short (so if missed it would hit the passer's feet). This requires the passer to step forward one step to forearm pass the ball.
- *Extension 2.* Have partners pass back and forth a set number of times before the catch.

EQUIPMENT

One ball per pair of students

CRITICAL ELEMENTS AND CUES

Technique

- See tasks 1 and 2.

Tactic

- Contact the ball lower in the arc to direct the flight to the target. *Cue:* Low contact.

Communication

- Call out *mine* to indicate that you will contact the ball. *Cue:* Call for it.

COMMON ERRORS, CAUSES, AND CORRECTIONS

- The ball angles to the side after contact. *Cause:* The student's arms are not even. *Correction:* Remind the student to make a platform with the arms.
- The ball angles to the side after contact. *Cause:* The toss is to the side. *Correction:* Move the tosser closer to the passer.
- The ball does not go directly to the tosser. *Cause:* The passer's shoulders are not pointed toward the tosser. *Correction:* Make sure the passer faces the tosser before the toss.
- The passer doesn't get under the ball. *Cause:* The student's knees aren't bent. *Correction:* Remind the student to bend the knees.
- The toss is inaccurate. *Cause:* The tosser is too far away or the ball is tossed too high or too low. *Correction:* Have the tosser move closer to the passer.
- The passer forgets to call *mine*. *Cause:* The student is excited and is concentrating on the contact. *Correction:* Have the tosser remind the passer each time the passer fails to call *mine*.

TASK 4: PARTNER TOSS, FOREARM PASS, AND CATCH WITH MOVEMENT

PURPOSE

Following are the purposes of the task as related to aspects of skilled performance.

- Technique: In this task, students move to get under the ball to execute a forearm pass.
- Fair play: Students toss the ball in a manner that allows the partner to pass it.
- Communication: Students say *mine* to indicate possession as the ball comes.

DESCRIPTION

Students pair up, and each pair has a ball. One student gently tosses the ball to the side of the partner, which forces the partner to slide step to the side to execute the forearm pass (see figure). The passer calls out *mine* and forearm passes the ball back to the tosser. The tosser catches the ball and repeats the action. After a set number of times, students switch roles. If students need motivation, have them see how many passes they can make in a row.

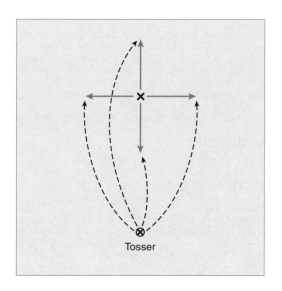

Tosser

- *Extension 1.* When control is evident, increase the number of steps the passer takes before the pass (not more than three).
- *Extension 2.* Have students use short or long tosses that require the passer to step forward (short) or backward (long).

EQUIPMENT

One ball per pair of students

CRITICAL ELEMENTS AND CUES

Technique

- See tasks 1 and 2.
- Use a slide step to move in each direction. *Cue:* Slide step.

COMMON ERRORS, CAUSES, AND CORRECTIONS

- See tasks 1 and 2.
- The student is slow in getting under the ball. *Cause:* The student stands up when moving. *Correction:* Have the student practice by sliding a couple of steps with the knees bent and without a ball.
- The student turns the shoulders away from the passer while moving. *Cause:* The student crosses the feet when sliding, which forces the shoulders to turn. *Correction:* Have the student practice making a couple of correct sliding steps with the knees bent and without a ball.

TASK 5: 2V2 PASS-ONLY GAME

PURPOSE

Following are the purposes of the task as related to aspects of skilled performance.

- Technique: In this task, students begin to incorporate the forearm pass in a modified game situation.
- Fair play: Students begin to apply rules to the game of volleyball.

DESCRIPTION

Divide students into groups of four; groups will play 2v2. Students play on a modified court. This modified court can either be a regulation court divided into half using the 3 meter line as the end line or in a 10-by-20-foot (3.05-by-6.1-meter) playing area. The teams stand on each side of a net that is 4 to 6 feet (1.2 to 1.8 meters) high. One player self-tosses the ball and makes a forearm pass to the teammate. Then the team attempts to pass the ball over the net to the other team. The other team returns the ball after a minimum of two passes. Students can use only forearm passes. Award teams one point each time they make 2 or 3 forearm passes before returning the ball across the net. Students can earn multiple points on a single rally. After each rally, the next rally is started by the opposing team. Team members alternate the beginning self-tosses. Students play the game for a designated time.

EQUIPMENT

One ball (beach, trainer, or regulation) per four students

CRITICAL CUES AND ELEMENTS

Technique

- See tasks 1 and 2.

Fair Play

- Follow the rules and self-officiate the game.

Rules

- Play begins with a self-toss and a pass to your teammate.
- Only three touches are allowed before the ball must go back over.
- Do not touch the ball twice in a row.
- Pass the ball toward the partner on the initial forearm pass.
- One point is earned every time 2 or 3 passes are made before the ball is passed over the net.

COMMON ERRORS, CAUSES, AND CORRECTIONS

- Students consistently struggle to control their passes. *Cause:* Students are not applying the learned critical elements properly. *Correction:* Go back and have the students practice the partner toss, pass, and catch with movement (task 4), and have them increase the number of passes before the catch to three.

TASK 6: SHADOW SET

PURPOSE

Following is the purpose of the task as related to aspects of skilled performance.
  Technique: In this task, students learn the critical elements of the set.

DESCRIPTION

Students are in a scattered formation. After your instruction, students perform the setting action (without a ball) in self-space. Move around and provide feedback to students based on the critical elements displayed.

EQUIPMENT

None

CRITICAL ELEMENTS AND CUES

Technique

- Stand with your knees bent. *Cue:* Knees bent.
- Hold your hands above your head and look at the ball through the opening between your hands. *Cue:* Look through the hole.
- Contact the ball with the finger pads of both hands simultaneously. Keep the ball off the palms. *Cue:* Spider fingers.
- Snap the ball out of your finger pads while extending the arms and legs. *Cue:* Snap and get tall.

COMMON ERRORS, CAUSE, AND CORRECTIONS

- Hands are too far apart when above the head. *Cause:* They will raise their hands straight up above their shoulders since this is a more common action when raising their hands. *Correction:* Tell students to touch their thumb and index finger tips together when they raise their hands to create a hole. While this is not the proper technique, it will get across to the student the need to bring the hands closer together.

TASK 7: SELF-TOSS, SET, AND CATCH

PURPOSE

Following is the purpose of the task as related to aspects of skilled performance.
  Technique: In this task, students begin executing the set using critical elements.

DESCRIPTION

Each student is in self-space with a ball. On your signal, students toss the ball into the air above the head, set the ball straight up, and catch it as it comes down. Students repeat this until you tell them to stop. Start with an appropriate ball (e.g., balloon, beach ball, trainer), but as students demonstrate control extend the task to include other balls. As an extension, challenge students to do multiple sets before catching the ball. If students need motivation, have them see how many sets they can make in a row.

EQUIPMENT

One ball per student

CRITICAL ELEMENTS AND CUES

- See task 6.

COMMON ERRORS, CAUSES, AND CORRECTIONS

- The student uses only one hand to set the ball. *Cause:* The toss is too high and doesn't go straight up. *Correction:* Remind the student to toss the ball no higher than the arm's reach.
- The student contacts the ball too hard and can't control it. *Cause:* The ball contacts the palm and the student slaps at it. *Correction:* Have the student lie down with the arms up and form a hole with the hands. A partner drops a ball down to the hands, and the setter snaps the ball back up to be caught.

TASK 8: PARTNER TOSS, SET, AND CATCH

PURPOSE

Following are the purposes of the task as related to aspects of skilled performance.

- Technique: In this task, students learn to set the ball in a determined direction.
- Fair play: Students toss the ball in a manner that allows the partner to set it.
- Communication: Students say *mine* to indicate possession as the ball comes.

DESCRIPTION

Students pair up and stand 6 to 8 feet (1.8 to 2.4 meters) apart. Each pair has an appropriate ball. One student gently tosses the ball to the partner, and the partner sets it back to the tosser. The tosser catches the ball and then repeats the task. Do this a designated number of times and then switch roles. As an extension, increase the number of sets before the catch when control is evident.

EQUIPMENT

One ball per pair of students

CRITICAL ELEMENTS AND CUES

Technique

- Square your shoulders to the tosser. *Cue:* Face the ball.
- Extend the arms slightly in the direction that the ball will travel. *Cue:* Ball out front.

Fair Play

- Toss the ball gently to the setter.

Communication

- As the ball comes to the setter, the setter calls out *mine* to indicate that she will set the ball.

COMMON ERRORS, CAUSES, AND CORRECTIONS

- The ball goes straight toward the tosser and there is no arc. *Cause:* The setter extends the arms out towards the tosser instead of more up and slightly in the direction of the tosser. *Correction:* Tell the student to contact the ball above the forehead.
- The setter doesn't get under the ball. *Cause:* The student does not bend the knees. *Correction:* Remind the student to bend the knees.
- The toss is inaccurate. *Cause:* The tosser isn't facing the setter. *Correction:* Remind the tosser to face the setter.

TASK 9: PARTNER TOSS, SET, AND CATCH WITH MOVEMENT

PURPOSE

Following are the purposes of the task as related to aspects of skilled performance.

- Technique: In this task, students get into position to set the ball in a determined direction.
- Fair play: Students toss the ball in a manner that allows the partner to set it.
- Communication: Students say *mine* to indicate possession as the ball comes.

DESCRIPTION

Students pair up, and each pair has an appropriate ball. One student gently tosses the ball to the side of the partner, which forces the partner to step to the side to execute the set back to the tosser. The tosser catches the ball and then repeats the task. Do this a designated number of times and then switch roles.

- *Extension 1.* When control is evident, increase the number of steps before the set (not more than three).
- *Extension 2.* Increase the number of sets before the catch. If students need motivation, have them see how many sets they can make in a row.

EQUIPMENT

One ball per pair of students

CRITICAL ELEMENTS AND CUES

Technique

- See task 6.
- Keep the knees bent as you step sideways. *Cue:* Knees bent.
- Use a shuffle step to get under the ball. *Cue:* Shuffle step.
- Keep the shoulders square to the tosser. *Cue:* Face the target.

COMMON ERRORS, CAUSES, AND CORRECTIONS

- The student turns away from the tosser during the set. *Cause:* The student crosses the legs or doesn't do a shuffle step. *Correction:* Have the student practice the shuffle step without a ball.
- The student's shoulders turn away from the direction of the set. *Cause:* The setter reaches for the ball and doesn't move the feet. *Correction:* Have the setter practice shuffling without the ball.
- The setter doesn't get under the ball. *Cause:* The setter isn't bending the knees. *Correction:* Remind the student to bend the knees.
- The setter doesn't get under the ball. *Cause:* The setter is slow to react to the toss. *Correction:* Use a lighter ball.
- The toss is inaccurate. *Cause:* The tosser is too far away or tosses too hard or too soft. *Correction:* Have tosser stand closer or toss across a net or rope set at the correct height.

TASK 10: 2V2 SET-ONLY GAME

PURPOSE

Following are the purposes of the task as related to aspects of skilled performance.

- Technique: In this task, students begin to incorporate the set in a modified game situation.
- Fair play: Students begin to apply rules to the game of volleyball.

DESCRIPTION

Divide students into groups of four; groups will play 2v2. Students play on a modified court. This modified court can either be a regulation court divided into half using the 3 meter line as the end line or in a 10-by-20-foot (3.05-by-6.1-meter) playing area. The teams stand on each side of a net that is 4 to 6 feet (1.2 to 1.8 meters) high. One player self-tosses the ball and sets it to the teammate who sets the ball over the net. The other team returns the ball. Students continue the rally using only the set. A team cannot make more than three sets before passing the ball over the net. Award teams one point each time they get the ball over the net legally with two or three sets. There are no points awarded for forcing an error, or if only a set is used to get the ball over the net.

EQUIPMENT

One ball per four students

CRITICAL ELEMENTS AND CUES

Technique

- See tasks 6 and 7.

Fair Play

- Follow the rules and self-officiate the game.

Rules

- Play begins with a self-toss.
- No more than three sets are allowed before returning the ball.
- One point is earned each time the ball is set over with three or fewer sets.

COMMON ERRORS, CAUSES, AND CORRECTIONS

- See tasks 6 and 7.
- The self-toss is not successful. *Cause:* It is difficult to control the toss and get right into the set sequence. *Correction:* Have the student toss the ball to the partner to begin the set sequence.

TASK 11: PARTNER TOSS, PASS, SET, AND CATCH

PURPOSE

Following are the purposes of the task as related to aspects of skilled performance.

- Technique: In this task, students apply the forearm pass and set in sequence.
- Tactic: Students sequence the forearm pass and set to initiate an offensive try.
- Communication: Passers and setters communicate that they will control the ball by calling out *mine*.

DESCRIPTION

Students pair up, and each pair has an appropriate ball (balloon, beach ball, trainer, or regulation volleyball). Student A gently tosses the ball to student B. Student B calls out *mine* and then passes the ball back to student A. Student A calls *mine* and sets the ball back to student B, who calls *mine* and catches the ball. Student B then becomes the tosser, and the students repeat the task a set number of times. As an extension, have the student toss the ball such that the passer has to move one step to the right or left, forward, or backward.

EQUIPMENT

One ball per pair of students

CRITICAL ELEMENTS AND CUES

Technique

- See tasks 1, 2, 6, and 7.

Tactic

- The first touch on the volleyball after it comes over the net should be a forearm pass toward a setter.

Communication

- The passer and the setter both call out *mine* before contacting the ball.

COMMON ERRORS, CAUSES, AND CORRECTIONS

- See tasks 1, 2, 6, and 7.
- The student doesn't call out *mine* before contacting the ball. *Cause:* The student forgets to call it. *Correction:* Award one point each time a group calls the ball when doing the task.

TASK 12: 2V2 CAPTAIN'S TOSS GAME

PURPOSE

Following are the purposes of the task as related to aspects of skilled performance.

- Technique: In this task, students apply the forearm pass and set combination in a game setting.
- Tactic: Having students properly sequence the forearm pass and set is key to the offensive part of the game.
- Fair play: Students follow game rules. The initial toss is made in a friendly manner.
- Communication: Students use verbal cues to denote possession of the ball.

DESCRIPTION

Divide students into groups of four; groups will play 2v2. Students play on a modified court. This modified court can either be a regulation court divided into half using the 3 meter line as the end line or in a 10-by-20-foot (3.05-by-6.1-meter) playing area. The teams stand on each side of a net that is 4 to 6 feet (1.2 to 1.8 meters) high. The team with the ball tosses it over the net to the other team. The other team returns the ball with a pass and set combination. Each side is allowed three touches to get the ball back over the net. The sequence of touches should be pass, set, and set over, but a pass and set over is allowed. Play continues until one team cannot get the ball back over the net. Points are awarded in two ways based on hitting sequences resulting in forced errors. Award one point if the two touches that are used to get the ball over the net are the same type (set-set or pass-pass), and it is not returned. Award two points if the team uses a forearm pass-set combination to get the ball over and it is not returned. No point is awarded if the ball is set or passed over with one touch, and it is not returned.

EQUIPMENT

One ball per four students

CRITICAL ELEMENTS AND CUES

Technique

- See tasks 1, 2, 6, and 7.
- All passes and sets should be high. *Cue:* Keep it high.

Tactic

- The triad three-touch sequence begins with the forearm pass-set combination.

Fair Play

- Follow the rules and self-officiate the game.
- Toss the ball in a friendly manner and directly toward an opponent so he or she can initiate the forearm pass.

Communication

- Call *mine* before receiving a pass or set.

Rules

- Play begins with one team tossing the ball over the net.
- Only three touches are allowed.
- Play continues until one team does not successfully return the ball.
- One point is earned by the attacking team if the return is not successful. Two points are awarded if the forearm pass-set combination was used to force the error.
- The team that earns the points is the tosser for the next point.

COMMON ERRORS, CAUSES, AND CORRECTIONS

- Students lack control of the pass and the set. *Cause:* The ball is coming too fast. *Correction:* Have students play the game with a slower ball (trainer or beach ball).
- Students lack control of the pass and the set. *Cause:* The forearm pass or set technique is off. *Correction:* Go back to pass-only and set-only games.
- Two students go after the ball. *Cause:* Students do not call *mine*. *Correction:* Have the students go back to task 3 and practice the call.

TASK 13: TRIAD TOSS, PASS, SET, AND CATCH

PURPOSE

Following are the purposes of the task as related to aspects of skilled performance.

- Technique: In this task, students make accurate passes and sets to appropriate targets.
- Tactic: Students use the triad hit (forearm pass, set, and attack), which is the basic team strategy used in volleyball.
- Fair play: Students make friendly tosses to initiate the task.
- Communication: Students say *mine* to indicate possession.

DESCRIPTION

Divide students into groups of three, and give each triad an appropriate ball (balloon, beach ball, trainer, or regulation volleyball). The triad members are designated as the tosser, the passer, and the setter, and they form a 10-foot (3-meter) equilateral triangle. The tosser and the setter have their backs to the net, and the passer faces the net (see figure). The tosser gently tosses the ball to the passer. The passer calls out *mine* and then passes the ball to the setter. The setter calls *mine* and then sets the ball over to the tosser, who catches it. Students repeat this a set number of times, and then students rotate positions. This continues until students have fulfilled each role. As an extension, have the student toss the ball such that the passer has to move one step to the right or left, forward, or backward.

EQUIPMENT

One ball per three students

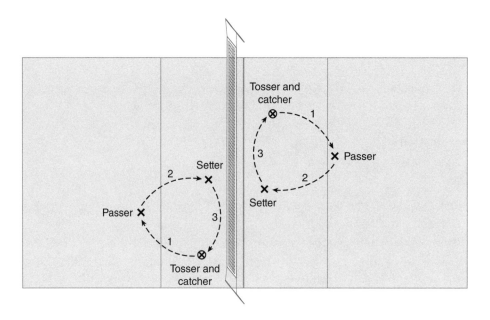

CRITICAL ELEMENTS AND CUES

Technique

- See tasks 1, 2, 6, and 7.
- When passing, contact the ball a bit lower in the arc to direct the flight to the setter. *Cue:* Contact the ball lower.
- When setting, square the shoulders to the target. *Cue:* Face the target.
- When setting, move to a position along the net facing the passer. *Cue:* Face the passer.
- When setting, guide the ball by turning the shoulders slightly toward the target. *Cue:* Guide the ball.

Tactic

- The use of the triad lays the foundation for the offense in volleyball. The first touch on the ball should be the forearm pass, which stops the ball and redirects it to the setter. The setter sets the ball along the net so it can be hit by an attacker. Since the attack has not yet been taught, in this task the tosser who catches the set substitutes for the attacker.

Fair Play

- Toss the ball in a friendly manner that allows the passer to attempt the initial forearm pass.

Communication

- When passing or setting, communicate to the other students that you will get the ball by calling out *mine*.

COMMON ERRORS, CAUSES, AND CORRECTIONS

- The toss is inaccurate. *Cause:* The ball is tossed to low or too high. *Correction:* Have the tosser practice without the triangle.
- The set goes over the net or is too far away from the net. *Cause:* The student does not turn the shoulders slightly to guide the ball to the catcher. *Correction:* Toss to the setter so he or she can practice guiding the ball.

TASK 14: 1V3 TOSS OVER THE NET TO A TRIAD WITH A JUMP CATCH

PURPOSE

Following are the purposes of the task as related to aspects of skilled performance.

- Technique: In this task, students apply the forearm pass technique to begin the triad when receiving a ball coming over a net.
- Fair play: Students make friendly tosses to initiate the task.

DESCRIPTION

Divide students into groups of four, and place two groups on one court. Each group has a tosser on one side of the court and a passer, a setter, and a catcher on the other side (see figure). If you want to place a second group on the same court to do this task set it up so the tosser is on the opposite side that the first group's tosser is on. The tosser in each group tosses the ball across the net to the passer, who is standing outside the 3-meter line. The passer passes the ball to the setter, who is standing forward toward the sideline. The setter sets the ball toward the catcher, who jumps and catches the ball. After a set number of tosses, the students rotate positions as follows: the tosser goes to the passer's position, the passer moves up to the setter's position, the setter moves to the catcher's position, and the catcher takes the ball back to the 3-meter line and becomes the tosser. Students continue the activity for a set number of rotations.

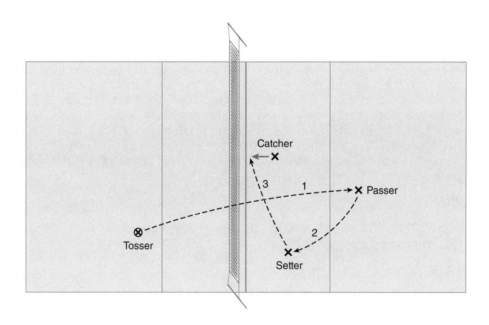

EQUIPMENT

One ball per four students

CRITICAL ELEMENTS AND CUES

Technique

- See task 13.

Fair Play

- Toss the ball in a friendly manner that allows the passer to attempt the initial forearm pass.

COMMON ERRORS, CAUSES, AND CORRECTIONS

- The student cannot control the pass. *Cause:* The passer is not moving to get behind and under the ball. *Correction:* Use a lighter, slower ball or have the passer practice receiving a ball without passing to the setter.
- The student cannot control the pass. *Cause:* The ball contacts the arms too high or too low. *Correction:* Stress lifting the shoulders rather than moving the arms.
- The toss is inaccurate. *Cause:* The tosser is too far away from the net. *Correction:* Have the tosser stand as close to the net as is needed to get the toss over.

TASK 15: 3V3 CAPTAIN'S TOSS GAME (CATCH ALLOWED)

PURPOSE

Following are the purposes of the task as related to aspects of skilled performance.

- Technique: In this task, students use the forearm pass and set to maintain possession of the ball.
- Tactic: Students use the triad touch sequence, which is used to form the attack.
- Fair play: Students begin the game with a friendly toss. Students follow game rules.
- Communication: Students call out *mine* to indicate possession of the ball.

DESCRIPTION

Divide students into groups of three, and place one group on each side of the net. The team with the ball tosses it over the net. The other team starts its return with a pass-set-set combination. Each side is allowed three touches to get the ball back over the net. If a student does not feel comfortable in contacting the ball, the student is allowed to catch the ball. After catching the ball, the student would do a self-toss and contact the ball using the appropriate touch (pass or set). The sequence of touches should be pass, set, and set over, but a pass and set over is allowed. This continues until one side is unable to get the ball back over the net. Award one point if the team uses two touches (forearm pass, set) and two points if the team uses three touches (forearm pass, set, set) to get the ball over and it is not returned.

EQUIPMENT

One ball per six students

CRITICAL ELEMENTS AND CUES

Technique

- The critical elements of previously learned techniques of forearm pass, set and triad need to be applied.
- Remind students that all passes and sets should be high. *Cue:* Keep it high.

Tactic

- The triad three-touch sequence begins with the forearm pass-set combination.

Fair Play

- Follow the rules and self-officiate the game.
- Toss the ball in a friendly manner and directly toward an opponent so he or she can initiate the forearm pass.

Communication

- Call *mine* before receiving a pass or set.

Rules

- Play begins with one team tossing the ball over the net.
- Only three touches are allowed.
- Play continues until one team does not successfully return the ball.
- One point is earned by the attacking team if two touches (pass and set) are used to return the ball and the other team is not successful in returning the ball. Two points are awarded if three touches are used (forearm pass-set -set combination) to force the error.
- The team that earns the point(s) is the tosser for the next point.
- If a student doesn't feel confident making a forearm pass or set, he or she can catch the ball and put it back in play using the appropriate technique off a self-toss.

COMMON ERRORS, CAUSES, AND CORRECTIONS

- Students lack control of the pass and the set. *Cause:* The ball is coming too fast. *Correction:* Have students play the game with a slower ball (trainer or beach ball).
- Students lack control of the pass and the set. *Cause:* The forearm pass or set technique is off. *Correction:* Go back to pass-only and set-only games.
- Two students go after the ball. *Cause:* Students do not call *mine. Correction:* Have the students go back to task 3 and practice the call.

TASK 16: WALL SERVES (UNDERHAND AND OVERHAND)

PURPOSE

Following is the purpose of the task as related to aspects of skilled performance.

Technique: In this task, students learn the critical elements of the underhand and overhand serves.

DESCRIPTION

Each student has a ball (balloon, beach ball, trainer, or regulation volleyball) and stands approximately 10 feet (3 meters) in front of a wall. Students serve the ball to the wall, retrieve the ball, and repeat the task. As an extension, have students move to the overhand serve.

EQUIPMENT

One ball per student

CRITICAL ELEMENTS AND CUES

Technique: Underhand Serve

- Step forward with the nondominant foot (the foot opposite the serving hand). *Cue:* Step with opposite foot.
- Transfer the weight from the back foot to the front foot. *Cue:* Rock forward.
- Hold the ball in the palm of the nondominant hand with the arm extended at waist level on the side of the hitting arm. *Cue:* Arm extended at waist.
- Keep the dominant arm straight; it acts as a pendulum and swings back and forward. *Cue:* Tick tock.
- Keep the fingers of the striking hand open and pointed back. *Cue:* Hand open.
- Transfer weight from the back foot to the front foot to help generate momentum and get the ball over the net. *Cue:* Rock step.
- Drop the ball from the extended arm as the dominant arm swings through. *Cue:* Drop and hit.

- Contact the ball with the heel of the hand. *Cue:* Heel of the hand.
- The contact point is in front of the body. *Cue:* Out front.
- After striking the ball, the arm follows through in a straight line toward the net. *Cue:* Follow through.

Technique: Overhand Serve

- Place the feet in a staggered position with the nondominant foot slightly forward. *Cue:* Opposite foot forward.
- Align the feet, hips, and shoulders with the wall. *Cue:* Feet, hips, shoulders forward.
- Rest the ball in the tossing hand at shoulder height in front of the striking shoulder. The arm is extended. *Cue:* Hold the ball out.
- The body weight is on the back foot. *Cue:* Weight back.
- Toss the ball up and slightly forward with no rotation just above the outstretched arm. *Cue:* Toss up and forward.
- Cock the striking arm back with the elbow high (like drawing a bow and arrow). *Cue:* Arm back, elbow up.
- As the elbow is driven forward, the weight goes forward. *Cue:* Rock step.
- Make contact with the heel of the hand and with the arm fully extended. *Cue:* Open hand.
- Stop the arm action on contact (like giving a high five). *Cue:* High five.

COMMON ERRORS, CAUSES, AND CORRECTIONS

Underhand Serve

- The student tosses the ball up at release instead dropping it. *Cause:* The student raises the arm holding the ball as the hitting arm comes forward. *Correction:* Have the student drop the ball without the hitting arm moving forward.
- The student strikes the ball with a closed fist. *Cause:* The student thinks a fist is needed to hit the ball over. *Correction:* Stress the cues "hand open" and "heel of the hand."
- The ball goes straight up when contacted. *Cause:* The student tosses the ball prior to contact. *Correction:* Remind the student to drop the ball without contacting it.
- The ball goes straight up when contacted. *Cause:* The student strikes the ball directly on the bottom. *Correction:* Tell the student to extend the arm and hold the ball so the contact point is behind the ball.
- The student steps with the foot that is on the same side as the striking arm. *Cause:* The student has opposition issues. *Correction:* Have the student stand with the opposite foot slightly forward and stress starting with the weight on the back foot.

Overhand Serve

- The student makes an erratic toss. *Cause:* The student does not hold the arm in a consistent location. *Correction:* Have the student stand and practice pushing the ball up so it lands on a target (poly spot, hoop, piece of paper) in front of the body and the striking shoulder.
- The student makes an erratic toss. *Cause:* The student drops the arm below the waist prior to the toss. *Correction:* Have the student hold the ball at shoulder height and drop it minimally (not below waist) prior to the toss.
- The student makes an erratic toss. *Cause:* The student is using only the arm to toss and not the legs. *Correction:* Prior to the toss, tell the student to bend knees to help push the ball into the air.
- The student doesn't transfer weight to the front foot. *Cause:* The student does not step forward as the ball is tossed. *Correction:* Have the student do a shadow serve (motion without striking the ball), stress that the toss should be pushed up and forward, and emphasize the weight shift.

- The student's arm follows through after contact. *Cause:* The arm is not moving forward quickly enough. *Correction:* Stress the cue "high five."
- The student contacts the ball early or late. *Cause:* The toss is too high, too low, too far forward, or behind the head. *Correction:* Have the student stand and practice pushing the ball up and slightly forward so it lands on a target (poly spot, hoop, piece of paper).
- The student steps with the foot that is on the same side as the striking arm. *Cause:* The student has opposition issues. *Correction:* Have the student stand with the opposite foot slightly forward and stress starting with the weight on the back foot.

TASK 17: CONE SERVES (UNDERHAND AND OVERHAND)

PURPOSE

Following is the purpose of the task as related to aspects of skilled performance.

Technique: In this task, students create enough force to get the ball over the net from the service line.

DESCRIPTION

Students are in pairs. Place cones on the sideline of the court on both sides of the net: one at the end of the 3-meter line, one halfway between the 3-meter line and the service line, and one on the service line. Starting at the first cone (3-meter line), have 3 to 4 students serve the ball over the net to their partners (see figure). After five successful serves, have students move back to the middle cone and serve; then, after five more successful serves, have them move back to the service line. If a student has trouble getting the ball over the net from a new position, have the student move back up to the previous successful line. The students on the opposite side of the net retrieve the balls and serve them back by following the same progression.

EQUIPMENT

One ball per pair of students and 12 cones per court

CRITICAL ELEMENTS AND CUES

Technique

- See task 16.

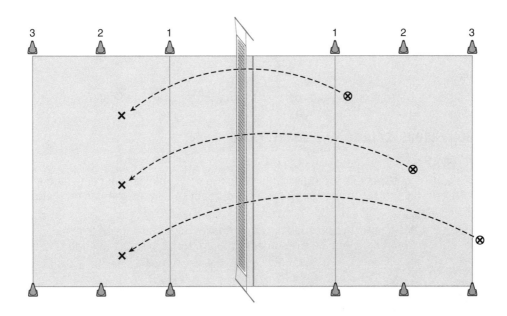

COMMON ERRORS, CAUSES, AND CORRECTIONS

- The ball does not go over the net on the underhand serve. *Cause:* The student does not generate enough force to get ball over the net. *Correction:* Have the student move closer to the net, and emphasize the use of the rock step.
- The ball goes too high or too low on the underhand serve. *Cause:* The student uses inconsistent contact points. *Correction:* Have the student practice dropping the ball and doing a shadow serve until the drop is consistent.
- The ball does not go over the net on the overhand serve. *Cause:* The student uses inconsistent contact points. *Correction:* Have the student practice tossing the ball up and forward so it drops in front of the feet on the contact side.

TASK 18: 1V1 SERVE (UNDERHAND AND OVERHAND)

PURPOSE
Following are the purposes of the task as related to aspects of skilled performance.

- Technique: In this task, students learn to serve directionally.
- Fair play: Students work cooperatively with partners to catch the serve.

DESCRIPTION
Students are in pairs with no more than four pairs per court. Place cones on the sideline of the court on both sides of the net: one at the end of the 3-meter line, one halfway between the 3-meter line and the service line, and one on the service line. Starting at the first cone (3-meter line), students serve the ball over to the net to their partners. The receiver attempts to catch the ball by taking less than one step and then returns to the 3-meter line and serves the ball back to the partner, who also tries to catch it by taking less than one step. When partners catch three serves each, they move to the middle cone and repeat the process. Students remain at each set of cones until three catches are completed. If partners are successful at serving and catching from the serving line, they can then move to other areas of the court (not directly in front of the partner). When students are no longer standing in front of their partners when receiving the serve, the teacher needs to stress the importance of safety by watching out for the serves of other pairs.

EQUIPMENT
One ball per pair of students and 12 cones per court

CRITICAL ELEMENTS AND CUES
Technique
- See task 16.

Fair Play
- Serve the ball directly to your partner to work on accuracy and control rather than how hard the ball can be served.

COMMON ERRORS, CAUSES, AND CORRECTIONS
Underhand Serve
- The ball is not going in the intended direction. *Cause:* The student contacts the ball at the wrong point. *Correction:* Remind the student to contact the ball on the lower half and in the middle.
- The ball is not going in the intended direction. *Cause:* The student follows through across the body. *Correction:* Remind the student to follow through to the intended target.

Overhand Serve

- The ball is not going in the intended direction. *Cause:* The student contacts the ball inconsistently. *Correction:* Have the student practice tossing the ball up and forward so it drops in front of the feet on the contact side.
- The ball is not going in the intended direction. *Cause:* The student's feet, hips, and shoulders do not face the intended target during the toss or on contact with the ball. *Correction:* Have the student practice tossing the ball up and forward, stepping, and catching the ball high and in front of the body.

TASK 19: 1V3 LINE SERVE (UNDERHAND AND OVERHAND), PASS, SET, AND CATCH WITH NO NET

PURPOSE

Following are the purposes of the task as related to aspects of skilled performance.

- Technique: In this task, students practice serving, passing, and setting in a game-like situation.
- Fair Play: Students serve when the passer is ready.
- Communication: Passers indicate they are taking the ball.

DESCRIPTION

Divide students into groups of four, and place two groups on one court. Each group has a server on one side of the court and a passer, setter, and target (catcher) on the other side. The other group is set up so the server is on the opposite side of the court as the other server (see figure). The servers from both groups should serve from opposite end lines (the server can move up if needed). The server serves the ball across to the passer who is standing outside the 3-meter line. This student passes the ball to the setter, who is standing in the middle of the court inside the 3-meter line. The setter sets the ball toward the target (who is standing an arm's length away from the net), who catches the ball. After a set number of serves, the students rotate positions as follows: the server goes to the passer's position, the passer moves to the setter's position, the setter moves to the target's position, and the target takes the ball back to the serve line on that side of the court and becomes the server. This continues for a set number of rotations. As an extension, add the net if the serves warrant it.

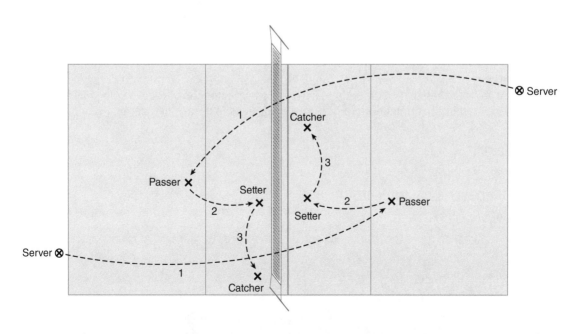

EQUIPMENT

One ball per four students

CRITICAL ELEMENTS AND CUES

Technique

- Apply technique critical elements and cues from previous forearm pass, set, and serve tasks.

Fair Play

- Prior to serving, make sure the passer is ready so he or she doesn't get hit with the ball and so the task can be completed as described.

Communication

- Calls *mine* to indicate that you are going to pass the ball.
- When setting, call *here* to indicate where you are located so the passer can pass the ball there.

COMMON ERRORS, CAUSES, AND CORRECTIONS

- See tasks 2, 3, 4, 7, 8, 9, and 16.
- The students do not rotate correctly. *Cause:* Students don't remember the progression. *Correction:* Have students practice the rotation without the serve.

TASK 20: 3V3 CONE SERVE GAME (CATCH ALLOWED)

PURPOSE

Following are the purposes of the task as related to aspects of skilled performance.

- Technique: In this task, students apply the volleyball skills learned in a modified game situation that allows for multiple touches by all students.
- Fair play: Students self-officiate and make passable serves.
- Communication: Students indicate they are going to make a play on the ball.

DESCRIPTION

Divide students into teams of three. Place one team on each side of the net in a triangle formation (two students on the back and one at the front along the net). Cones are set up along the sideline with one at the end of the 3-meter line, one halfway between the 3-meter line and the service line, and one on the service line. Play begins with a serve from any cone along the side of the court. Students should use the pass-set-set sequence when returning the ball. If the team catches the ball, they can play the ball off a self-toss (this counts as a touch). When the serving team loses the point, the ball goes over to the other team. When a team gains the serve, the students rotate in a clockwise direction. Regular volleyball rules apply concerning open underhand hits, boundary lines, net interference, and number of touches. No spikes are allowed.

EQUIPMENT

One ball per six students and 12 cones per court

CRITICAL ELEMENTS AND CUES

Technique

- Apply technique critical elements and cues from previous forearm pass, set and serve tasks.

Fair Play

- Your team will self-officiate. If an infraction occurs, stop play.
- Serve a ball that is playable and can be passed rather than for a point.

Communication

- Call *mine* to indicate you are taking the ball, and call *here* for a set to indicate where you are located.

Rules

- No open underhand touches allowed.
- A ball on the boundary line is in.
- No more than three touches on a side.
- The ball can be played off a single bounce or a catch, but touches remain the same.
- No touching the net during game play.
- Return the ball by rolling it under the net.

COMMON ERRORS, CAUSES, AND CORRECTIONS

If you observe repeated technical errors during play, have students go back and repeat those learning tasks in the next lesson.

TASK 21: PARTNER TOSS AND TIP OVER THE NET

PURPOSE

Following are the purposes of the task as related to aspects of skilled performance.

- Technique: In this task, students learn the tip, which is the first step in learning to attack.
- Fair play: Students make tosses that are tippable.

DESCRIPTION

Divide students into groups of three. One student is on one side of the net (retriever) and the other two (tosser and attacker) are on the other side and an arm's length from the net. The attacker (tipper) faces the net. The tosser tosses the ball toward the attacker slightly above the height of the net. The attacker jumps up and tips the ball over the net. The student on the other side of the net catches or retrieves the ball and hands the ball under the net to the tosser. This continues for a set number of trials, and then students rotate positions: the tosser moves to attacker, attacker to catcher, and catcher to tosser. As an extension, have students tip with one hand.

EQUIPMENT

One ball per three students

CRITICAL ELEMENTS AND CUES

Technique

- Stand 2 to 3 feet (0.6 to 0.9 meters) from the net when tipping the ball over. *Cue:* Close to the net.
- Face the net when tipping the ball. *Cue:* Face the net.
- Use both hands when tipping the ball. *Cue:* Two hands.
- The fingers are spread and strong. *Cue:* Strong fingers.
- The ball rebounds off the finger pads. *Cue:* Tap the ball.

Fair Play

- Toss the ball directly in front of the attacker with no spin a couple of feet above the net so the attacker has the best opportunity to tip the ball over the net.

COMMON ERRORS, CAUSES, AND CORRECTIONS

- The attacker moves into the net. *Cause:* The attacker starts too close to or too far from the net and steps and jumps forward. *Correction:* Move the attacker to within an arm's length of the net, and have the tosser move closer to the attacker and toss the ball an arm's length from the net.

- The attacker gets in front of the ball or the ball is behind the attacker's head or body. *Cause:* The attacker starts too close to the net. *Correction:* Put a poly spot on the ground for the starting position.
- The attacker gets in front of the ball or the ball is behind the attacker's head or body. *Cause:* The toss is inaccurate or the ball is tossed too far away from the net. *Correction:* Have the tosser move closer to the attacker, and remind the student to toss the ball just above the height of the net.

TASK 22: DRIVE

PURPOSE

Following are the purposes of the task as related to aspects of skilled performance.

- Technique: In this task, students learn contact points and arm swing for attacking.
- Fair play: Students makes tosses that are attackable and hand the ball underneath the net to return it to the tosser.

DESCRIPTION

Place students in groups of three at the net. One student is on one side of the net (retriever) and the other two (tosser and attacker) are on the other side of the net. The tosser stands inside the 3-meter line, and the attacker stands just beyond the 3-meter line (see figure). The tosser has the ball and makes a high, rainbow-like toss that is approximately 10 feet (3 meters) in the air (basketball rim height) and toward the attacker. The attacker lines up behind and underneath the ball and, without jumping, attacks the ball. The student on the other side of the net catches or retrieves the ball and hands it under the net to the tosser. This continues for a set number of trials, and then students rotate positions: the tosser moves to attacker, attacker to retriever, and retriever to tosser. As an extension, have the attacker jump to contact the ball. It is recommended that a variety of net heights be available for students to choose from. The net height should be one that the attacking student can reasonably be able to get the ball over. The differing net heights can be achieved one of two ways, either have varying net heights at each court or angle the net on the court starting with one side set at the women's height (7 ft. 4" – 2.24 m) and then angled down to a lower height that is reasonable for your lowest student. Once the net heights have been set, allow students to choose the net height they are most comfortable with.

EQUIPMENT

One ball per three students and nets of different heights

CRITICAL ELEMENTS AND CUES

Technique

- Stand with the feet, hips, and shoulders square to the net and in a slightly staggered stance. *Cue:* Square to the net.
- The nonattacking arm points to the incoming ball to help you keep the ball in front of the body and the shoulders level. *Cue:* Point.
- The contact point is in front of the body. Reach as high as possible. *Cue:* Reach.
- Make contact with an open hand and the fingers spread and firm. *Cue:* Contact.
- On contact, snap the wrist forward over the top of the ball to give it forward rotation. *Cue:* Snap.
- Follow through to the hip of the attacking arm. *Cue:* Hand in the pocket.

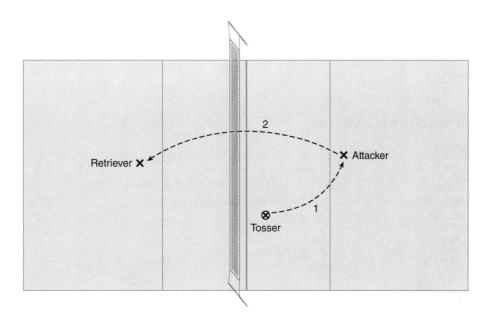

Fair Play

- Toss the ball with no rotation and high enough that the attacker can contact it. Rotation on the ball can cause it to drop and makes it is harder to contact.
- Hand the ball under the net. A rolling ball could be stepped on and a thrown ball could hit the net or not be caught.

COMMON ERRORS, CAUSES, AND CORRECTIONS

- The attacker is not square to the net. *Cause:* The student's body is turned. *Correction:* Have the student face the net prior to the toss.
- The ball goes over the net really high or goes out of bounds. *Cause:* The student contacts the ball behind the head. *Correction:* Tell the student to point at the ball with the opposite hand to keep the ball in front of the body.
- The ball goes over the net really high or goes out of bounds. *Cause:* The student does not snap the wrist on contact. *Correction:* Have the student stand with the ball, and hit it out of the student's hand by snapping his or her wrist so the ball goes to the floor.
- The ball doesn't clear the net. *Cause:* The contact point is too low. *Correction:* Have the tosser stand closer to the attacker and toss the ball straight up and in front of the attacker. Prior to contact with the ball, the student should be able to see the elbow.

TASK 23: 1V3 SERVE WITH TRIAD TIP

PURPOSE

Following is the purpose of the task as related to aspects of skilled performance.

Technique: In this task, students learn to sequence the pass, set, and tip combination off a serve.

DESCRIPTION

Place students in groups of four. The tosser is on one side of the net and the passer, setter, and attacker are on the other side. Use a net that is at the appropriate height. The tosser tosses the ball to the passer. The passer forearm passes the ball to the setter, who is standing an arm's length from the net. The setter sets the ball up for the attacker to tip the ball over the net.

- *Extension 1.* Instead of tossing the ball across the net, have the tosser serve to the passer.
- *Extension 2.* Have the attacker change to the left and right front positions.

EQUIPMENT

One ball per four students and nets of different heights

CRITICAL ELEMENTS AND CUES

Technique

- See tasks 1, 6, and 16.
- Pass the ball above setter's outstretched arms and within one step of the setter's beginning location. *Cue:* Hit your target.
- Set the ball high and an arm's length away from the net. *Cue:* High and off.

Fair Play

- The toss or the serve in the extension should go directly to the passer to start the task and not to score a point.

COMMON ERRORS, CAUSES, AND CORRECTIONS

- The ball is passed too low or too high. *Cause:* The angle of the platform is too high or too low. *Correction:* Have the student push the thumbs toward the floor so the platform is even.
- The ball is passed too high. *Cause:* The student is swinging on contact. *Correction:* Remind the student not to swing the arms.
- The ball is passed too low. *Cause:* The student's hand position is incorrect. *Correction:* Make sure the student's hands are away from the body and almost parallel to the floor.
- The toss or the serve in the extension does not get to the passer. *Cause:* The tosser or server is too far away from the net. *Correction:* Have the tosser or server move closer to the net (use a cone for placement).
- When serving in the extension the serve does not get to the passer. *Cause:* The server cannot direct the ball to the passer. *Correction:* If the serve cannot be successful, the student can toss the ball over the net to the passer.

TASK 24: STATIONARY BLOCK

PURPOSE

Following is the purpose of the task as related to aspects of skilled performance.
Technique: In this task, students learn to perform a block.

DESCRIPTION

Students stand at the net and face it. On your signal, the students stand and simulate a blocking position without jumping.

- *Extension 1.* Add a jump to the block.
- *Extension 2.* Have students face a partner across the net. On your signal, the partners jump and attempt to touch each other's fingers over the net.

EQUIPMENT

Net

CRITICAL ELEMENTS AND CUES

Technique: Ready position

- Stand with the knees bent and the feet shoulder-width apart. The hands are open and the fingers are spread and strong. *Cue:* Ready position.
- Extend the fingers and point the thumbs to the ceiling (hands make a butterfly shape). *Cue:* Butterfly.
- Hold the hands slightly in front of the body and just above shoulder level. *Cue:* Hands slightly up and out.

Technique: Block

- Push off hard against the floor using both feet. *Cue:* Jump up and high.
- Extend the arms straight up with the hands above the net. *Cue:* Extend.
- Roll the shoulders forward to move the hands at a slight angle over the net. *Cue:* Shoulder press.
- The thumbs should be close enough that a ball can't get through. *Cue:* Thumbs up.
- The hands should be close enough to the net that a ball cannot fit between them and the net. *Cue:* Seal the net.
- Land in the ready position. *Cue:* Ready.

COMMON ERRORS, CAUSES, AND CORRECTIONS

- The student does not reach above the net. *Cause:* The student cannot jump high enough. *Correction:* Have the student soft block by "breaking" the wrists so the palms are facing the ceiling. This way, the ball is deflected up and into the court and is playable.
- The student jumps off one foot. *Cause:* The weight is not distributed evenly between the feet. *Correction:* Have the student stand in the ready position prior to jumping or take time between blocks.
- The student hits the net while jumping. *Cause:* The hands drop below the shoulders to assist with the jump and contact the net on the way up. *Correction:* Remind the student to keep the hands above the shoulders at all times.
- The student hits the top of the net. *Cause:* The student extends the hands over the net by chopping down with their arms. *Correction:* Have the student stand still and roll the shoulders forward to demonstrate the shoulder press.
- The ball falls between the blocker's hands and the net. *Cause:* The student's hands are too far away from the net. *Correction:* Have the student move closer to the net, lower the net, or have the student stand on a box to practice pressing over the net.

TASK 25: TOSS, TIP, AND STATIONARY BLOCK

PURPOSE

Following are the purposes of the task as related to aspects of skilled performance.

- Technique: In this task, students learn to time the jump for the block.
- Tactic: This is a team's first line of defense as a ball comes over the net.

DESCRIPTION

Divide students into groups of three. One student is the blocker, one is the tosser, and one is the attacker (see figure). The tosser tosses the ball up to the attacker, who jumps and tips the ball over the net. The blocker reacts to the jump of the attacker and jumps to block the tip. After a set number of tries, students rotate roles: the blocker moves to the tosser, tosser to attacker, and attacker to blocker.

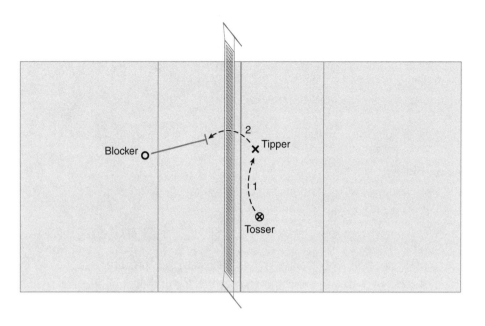

EQUIPMENT

One ball per three students

CRITICAL ELEMENTS AND CUES

Technique

- See task 24.
- The blocker jumps just *after* the attacker jumps. *Cue:* Time your jump.
- The blocker's hands should meet the ball on the offensive side of the net. *Cue:* Hands up and over.

Tactic

- Tell students that the blockers are the first students who can stop the ball from coming over the net or deflect the ball to slow it down so it is easier for the defense to make a play on it.

COMMON ERRORS, CAUSES, AND CORRECTIONS

- The blocker is coming down as the ball is tipped. *Cause:* The timing of the jump is off. *Correction:* Have the blocker practice reacting to the jump of the hitter without a ball.
- The ball goes through the blocker's hands. *Cause:* The fingers are loose and are not spread with the thumbs pointing at each other. *Correction:* Emphasize the cues "butterfly" or "thumbs up."
- See task 21.

TASK 26: SLIDE AND SET BLOCKS

PURPOSE
Following are the purposes of the task as related to aspects of skilled performance.

- Technique: In this task, students learn blocking footwork so they will be able to line up with the attacker in a game.
- Tactic: The ability of the student to move into a block is a team's first line of defense.
- Agility: Students slide step to the left and right.

DESCRIPTION
Divide students into groups of six. Three students are on each side of the net facing each other. On your signal, students make slide steps in a designated direction. You dictate the number of steps (2 or 3) and the direction. After the designated number of slides, the student jumps up as if blocking. On landing, the student slides in the opposite direction the same number of steps and executes another block. This continues for a set number of trials or a designated time.

EQUIPMENT
Net

CRITICAL ELEMENTS AND CUES

Technique: Slide step
- Make the first step (lead step) laterally in the direction of movement. Do not cross the feet. Push hard off the back foot (trail foot) to travel quickly and as low as possible. *Cue:* Step and push.
- On the final step, stop the momentum with the lead foot. *Cue:* Brake.
- Close the trail foot to shoulder width (jumping position) and then jump. *Cue:* Close and jump.

Technique: Arms
- The blocker's hands should meet the ball on the offensive side of the net. *Cue:* Hands up and over.

Tactic
- See task 25.

Agility
- Keep the entire body square to the net while moving. *Cue:* Square to net.
- Maintain the ready position throughout the movement.
- When moving stays on the balls of the feet and push off. *Cue:* Push.
- Limit the vertical lift as the student slides. *Cue:* Low and fast.

COMMON ERRORS, CAUSES, AND CORRECTIONS
- The student makes contact with the net. *Cause:* The student turns the shoulders when moving laterally or the lead foot steps toward the net instead of laterally. *Correction:* Put tape on the floor for the student to step on and to provide a visual reference for shoulder position.
- The student contacts the net. *Cause:* The student's hands drop below the shoulders. *Correction:* Remind the student that the hands must stay above the shoulders. Have the student hold a ball with both hands in front of the body and above the shoulders (blocking position) while practicing sliding.
- The student loses balance when planting both feet. *Cause:* The student is going too fast or feet are together. *Correction:* Tell the student to slow the slide steps down to help maintain balance and to end with the feet shoulder-width apart.

TASK 27: 1V3 SERVE, TRIAD TIP, AND BLOCK

PURPOSE

Following are the purposes of the task as related to aspects of skilled performance.

- Technique: In this task, students learn to sequence the pass-set-tip combination with a block off a serve.
- Tactic: This is a team's first line of defense as a ball comes over the net.
- Agility: Students slide step to the left and right.
- Fair play: Students serve a passable ball.

DESCRIPTION

Place students in groups of four. There is a server on one side of the net and a passer, setter, and tipper on the other side. Use a net that is at the appropriate height. The server serves the ball to the passer, who is standing behind the 3-meter line. After serving the ball, the server moves to the net to become a blocker. The passer forearm passes the ball up to the setter, who is at the net near the center of the court. The setter sets the ball up for the attacker to approach and tip the ball over as the blocker jumps to block the tip. As an extension, have the attacker tip from the left and right sides of the court.

EQUIPMENT

One ball per four students and nets of different heights

CRITICAL ELEMENTS AND CUES

Technique: Serve

- See task 16.

Technique: Tip

- See task 21.

Technique: Setting the block

- Keep your eyes on the attacker and not on the ball. *Cue:* Look at the attacker.
- Line up your nose with the attacker's swinging shoulder. *Cue:* Nose to shoulder.
- Jump just after the attacker jumps. *Cue:* Wait and jump.

Tactic

- See task 25.

Agility

- See task 26.

Fair Play

- Serve the ball so the passer can pass the ball to the setter to initiate the task rather than to score a point. Work on gaining control of your serve.

COMMON ERRORS, CAUSES, AND CORRECTIONS

- See tasks 16, 21, and 26.

TASK 28: 4V4 GAMES

PURPOSE

Following are the purposes of the task as related to aspects of skilled performance.

- Technique: In this task, students apply learned techniques in a modified game.
- Tactic: Students apply learned tactics in a modified game.
- Agility: Students apply agility demands in a modified game.
- Fair play: Students apply fair play practices in a modified game.
- Communication: Students apply learned communication strategies in a modified game.

DESCRIPTION

Divide students into teams of four; students will play 4v4. Place students in a square formation with two students at the back and two at the front along the net. Play begins with a serve from any area within the court that the server chooses. Students should use the pass-set-set or the pass-set-tip (or spike) sequence when returning the ball. If the ball hits the floor, the attacking team earns a point. When the serving team loses the point, the ball goes over to the other team. When a team gains the serve, the students rotate in a clockwise direction. Regular volleyball rules apply concerning open underhand hits, boundary lines, net interference, and number of touches. Teams should not be larger than four students; have extra students rotate into the game when students rotate after each point.

Level 2 4v4 Game Variations

- If a catch is allowed, a student can catch the ball and then self-toss to pass or set the ball.
- If a bounce is allowed, a student can play the ball off a bounce using an appropriate technique.

Level 3 4v4 Game Variations

- If a catch is not allowed, the games can be shaped to emphasize the techniques learned. Shaping is a *Play Practice* (Launder and Piltz 2013) teaching strategy where game variables can be manipulated to emphasize the application of desired techniques during game play. For example, after the net dig is taught in task 30, award an extra point to a team that executes a net dig during a rally. Examples of techniques that can be shaped are net digs, double blocks, consistent use of the triad or any other technique the teacher wants to emphasize.

EQUIPMENT

One ball per eight students

CRITICAL ELEMENTS AND CUES

Apply all previous skills and cues.

Rules

- No open underhand hits allowed.
- A ball on the boundary line is in.
- No more than three touches on a side.
- No touching the net during game play.
- Return the ball to the server by rolling it under the net.

COMMON ERRORS, CAUSES, AND CORRECTIONS

Look for all previously discussed errors and provide corrections.

TASK 29: OFF-CENTER PASSES

PURPOSE

Following are the purposes of the task as related to aspects of skilled performance.

- Technique: In this task, students learn to pass a ball when they cannot properly place their bodies.
- Fair play: Students make gentle tosses.

DESCRIPTION

Pairs of students are in a scattered formation, and each pair has a ball. Partners stand about 10 feet (3 meters) apart facing each other. The tosser has the ball, and the passer assumes a ready position. The tosser gently throws the ball slightly to the side of the passer, who tries to forearm pass the ball back to the tosser without moving the body to get in line with the ball. The tosser catches the passed ball and repeats the task. After a set number of tosses to one side, the tosser repeats the action to the passer's other side. After a set number of passes, students switch roles. As an extension, have students increase the speed of the toss.

EQUIPMENT

One ball per pair of students

CRITICAL ELEMENTS AND CUES

Technique (see figure)

- Lower the inside shoulder (the shoulder away from the toss). *Cue:* Drop inside shoulder.
- The arms (platform) face the target. *Cue:* Platform to target.
- Keep the body behind the ball (not in line with the ball). *Cue:* Body behind ball.
- Stay as balanced as possible. *Cue:* Balanced.

Fair Play

- Toss gently so the passer can react to the flight of the ball and get the platform into position.

COMMON ERRORS, CAUSES, AND CORRECTIONS

- The student swings the arms instead of maintaining a platform. *Cause:* The student does not drop the outside shoulder. *Correction:* Have the student practice the outside shoulder drop without the ball.

TASK 30: PARTNER NET DIG

PURPOSE

Following are the purposes of the task as related to aspects of skilled performance.

- Technique: In this task, students use the forearm pass to contact the ball after it has been hit into the net.
- Tactic: Students must use the dig to keep the rally alive after an initial contact sends the ball into the net.
- Fair play: Students throw the ball such that the dig can be attempted.

DESCRIPTION

Pairs of students face the net, and each pair has a ball. The passer stands about 5 feet (1.5 meters) from the net, and the tosser stands about 10 feet (3 meters) from the net and to the side of the passer (see figure). The passer assumes a ready position. The tosser throws the ball into the net slightly to the side of the passer. The passer tries to dig the ball out of the net using a forearm pass back to the tosser. The tosser catches the passed ball and repeats the throw. After a set number of throws to one side, the tosser repeats the action to the passer's other side. After a set number of passes, students switch roles. As an extension, have students throw the ball into the net at varied heights.

EQUIPMENT

One ball per pair of students

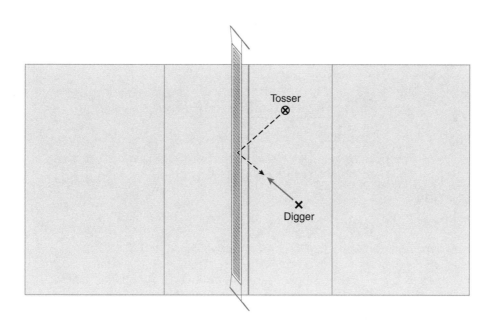

CRITICAL ELEMENTS AND CUES

Technique

- Get into a crouched position. *Cue:* Get low.
- Spread the legs wide and bend them to get under the ball (see figure). *Cue:* Legs spread, knees bent.
- Face the sideline. *Cue:* Face the sideline.
- Use the forearm pass with an upward and backward striking motion. *Cue:* Arms up and back.

COMMON ERRORS, CAUSES, AND CORRECTIONS

- The student is too far away from or too close to the net. *Cause:* The student's timing of their approach steps to the net is off. *Correction:* Have the student move closer to or farther from the net.
- The student can't get the body under the ball. *Cause:* The student is not bending the knees enough. *Correction:* Have the student start with the knees bent and then move to the ball.

TASK 31: ZONE SERVES

PURPOSE

Following is the purpose of the task as related to aspects of skilled performance.
   Technique: In this task, students learn how to place a serve.

DESCRIPTION

Divide the court into six zones using cones or poly spots: three across the back court and three in the forecourt. Number the zones as follows: (1) right back, (2) right front, (3) center front, (4) left front, (5) left back, (6) center back (see figure). Students work in pairs; one student stands on each side of the net. The server attempts to serve the ball into zone 1. After five successful serves, the student serves to zone 2. This continues until the student serves to all six zones. The student on the other side of the net retrieves the balls and serves them back, attempting to hit the zones on the opposite side.

- *Extension 1.* Call out a zone number. Students attempt to serve into that zone. If successful, the student earns one point.
- *Extension 2.* Have the receiver return the serve using a forearm pass.

EQUIPMENT

One volleyball per pair of students and 8 half-cones or poly spots to mark zones

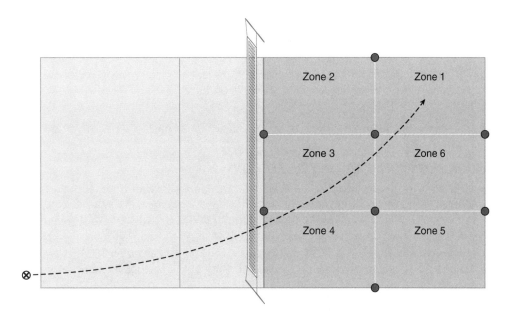

CRITICAL ELEMENTS AND CUES

Technique

- See task 16.
- Feet, hips, and shoulders must face the target. *Cue:* Square to target.

COMMON ERRORS, CAUSES, AND CORRECTIONS

- See task 16.

TASK 32: SPIKE AND APPROACH

PURPOSE

Following is the purpose of the task as related to aspects of skilled performance.

Technique: In this task, students learn the step sequence and arm action for the spike.

DESCRIPTION

Four students stand on both sides of the net at the 3-meter line facing the net at a slight angle to the left as if spiking with the right hand. On a signal from the teacher, students take a four-step approach starting with the right foot as described in the technique. After the last step (fourth step) the students jump straight up and swing the striking hand as if contacting the ball. Repeat as needed.

EQUIPMENT

Net

CRITICAL ELEMENTS AND CUES

Technique

- Complete the following four-step sequence (right handed):
  - First step: Starting with the right foot, take a short and slow step toward the ball.
  - Second step: After taking the first step, make a longer, faster, and directional step with the left foot.

- Third step: The right foot steps towards the net to stop momentum (brake step)
- Fourth step: The left foot step then closes onto the right foot quickly (step-close). *Cue:* Four steps.
- The third and fourth step are parallel with the net to stop forward momentum and transfer it into the vertical jump. *Cue:* Brake and up.
- Use both arms to help propel the jump. *Cue:* Swing up.
- As the student leaves the ground, the hitting arm goes back and up with elbow above ear and hand above head. *Cue:* Arm back, elbow up.

COMMON ERRORS, CAUSES, AND CORRECTIONS

- The attacker jumps into the net. *Cause:* The student's forward momentum isn't converted to the vertical jump because steps 3 and 4 are not parallel to the net. *Correction:* Have the student eliminate the first step (right) and stand with the weight on the left foot. From this position, have the student take steps 3 (right) and 4 (left) to ensure they are parallel with the net.
- The attacker jumps into the net. *Cause:* The student takes steps 3 and 4 slowly, which causes the weight to transfer toward the net. *Correction:* Have the student eliminate the first step (right) and stand with weight on the left foot. From this position, have the student take steps 3 (right) and 4 (left) to ensure they are done quickly and are parallel to the net.

TASK 33: APPROACH, TOSS, AND SPIKE

PURPOSE

Following are the purposes of the task as related to aspects of skilled performance.

- Technique: In this task, students learn the timing needed to spike a ball over a modified net.
- Communication: Attackers communicate their locations to setters.

DESCRIPTION

Students work in pairs with a height-modified net. One student tosses the ball up about 4 to 6 feet (1.2 to 1.8 meters) above the net. The spiker begins the approach after the toss and then spikes the ball over the net. The tosser retrieves the ball. After a designated number of tosses, the partners switch roles. As an extension, adjust the net height to accommodate spikers' abilities.

EQUIPMENT

One volleyball per pair of students and nets at different heights

CRITICAL ELEMENTS AND CUES

Technique

- See task 32.
- The attacker begins the approach after the ball is tossed. *Cue:* Wait.
- Fully extend the arm on contact. *Cue:* Reach.
- Contact the ball with the heel of the hand. *Cue:* Heel of the hand.
- Contact the top center and top half of the ball. *Cue:* Top of ball.
- Snap the wrist and finish with the fingers over the top of the ball. *Cue:* Snap wrist.
- After contact, follow through to the hip on the side of the attacking arm. *Cue:* Hand in the pocket.

Communication

- Prior to the toss, call your location so the setter is aware that you are ready to attack. Use the following cues:
  - From the left front position: *outside*
  - From the center front position: *middle*
  - From the right front position: *back*

COMMON ERRORS, CAUSES, AND CORRECTIONS

- The student cannot get good contact on the ball. *Cause:* The coordination of the arm action with the jump is out of sequence. *Correction:* Have the student go back to a shadow spike without the ball. Then, add a ball and have the student catch it instead of hitting it.
- The ball flies up on contact. *Cause:* The student contacts the underside of the ball. *Correction:* Toss the ball higher and have the student reach as high as possible to contact it.
- The ball flies up on contact. *Cause:* The student contacts the ball behind the head. *Correction:* Have the student shorten the first and second steps of the approach. Remind student to wait until after the ball is tossed to start the approach.
- The student's arm contacts the net. *Cause:* The student is too close to the net. *Correction:* Have the partner toss the ball farther from the net. Ensure that the final two steps are parallel to the net.
- The attacker is not communicating with the setter. *Cause:* The student forgets the name of the location or forgets to call it. *Correction:* Have the tosser hold the ball until the attacker calls out the position.

TASK 34: DOUBLE BLOCKS

PURPOSE

Following are the purposes of the task as related to aspects of skilled performance.

- Technique: In this task, students learn how to set a double block.
- Tactic: The block is the team's first line of defense and a double block makes a more effective block.
- Agility: Students slide step to the left and right.
- Communication: Outside blockers communicate with inside blockers.

DESCRIPTION

Divide students into groups of five. Use a half-court setup with an offensive student triad on one side of the net and two defenders (blockers) on the other side. One blocker is near the sideline and the other is near the center front (see figure). One blocker tosses the ball over the net to begin the triad action ending in a jump and catch instead of a hit (pass, set, jump catch sequence). As the ball is in the air from the setter, the outside blocker sets the block and then calls the middle blocker (by saying *here*) to set a double block. After the catch, students rotate as follows: the outside blocker rotates to middle blocker, middle blocker to setter, setter to passer, passer to attacker and attacker to outside blocker.

- *Extension 1.* Replace the jump and catch with an attack.
- *Extension 2.* Add another blocker (left side, middle, and right side) and move to full-court formation.
- *Extension 3.* Add attackers to the left and right sides of the court so the middle blocker must watch where the setter sets the ball and then react.

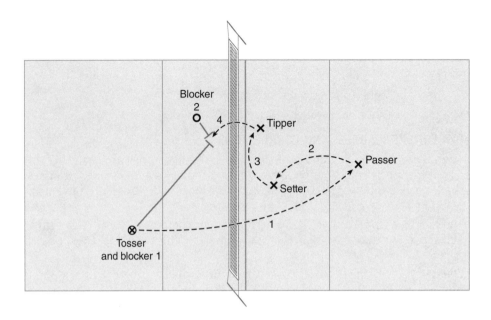

EQUIPMENT

One ball per five students

CRITICAL ELEMENTS AND CUES

Technique

- Apply the blocking critical elements and cues from task 26.
- The inside blocker slides and finds the outside blocker. *Cue:* Find them.
- The inside blocker places the brake foot next to the outside blocker's trail foot. *Cue:* Close the block.
- When blockers are together (foot to foot and shoulder to shoulder), the outside blocker says *up* so they jump together. *Cue:* Up.
- The outside blocker turns the outside hand in so it faces the middle of the court. *Cue:* Outside hand in.

Tactic

- Apply the tactics as described in task 25.

Agility

- See agility requirements as presented in task 26.

Communication

- The outside blocker calls the middle blocker for the double block by saying *here.*
- When blockers are together, the outside blocker says *up* so the blockers jump at the same time to form a wall of hands.

COMMON ERRORS, CAUSES, AND CORRECTIONS

- The blockers are too far apart. *Cause:* The middle blocker does not close the gap between the feet, shoulders, or hands, or the outside blocker doesn't call out *here.* *Correction:* Slow the blockers down so they can practice setting the block, communicating, and closing the block.
- One blocker jumps before or after the other. *Cause:* The outside blocker does not communicate to coordinate the jump. *Correction:* Remind the outside blocker to call *up* so the inside blocker jumps on cue.

- The blockers miss the ball. *Cause:* The outside blocker incorrectly sets the block. *Correction:* Instead of attacking the ball, have the attacker catch it so the blocker can see the alignment. You can also have offensive students catch and toss the ball instead of playing it live so the blockers have time to read, react, and move into position.

TASK 35: 1V3 SERVE AND TRIAD ATTACK WITH SINGLE BLOCK

PURPOSE

Following are the purposes of the task as related to aspects of skilled performance.

- Technique: In this task, students learn to sequence the pass, set, and spike combination with a block.
- Communication: All students on the court communicate their intentions to play the ball.

DESCRIPTION

Place students in groups of four. Use a net that is at the appropriate height. There is one passer, one setter, and one attacker on one side of the net and a server (who is also a blocker) on the other side. The server serves the ball over the net to the passer, who forearm passes the ball up to the setter at the net. The setter sets the ball up for the attacker to approach and hit the ball. After the serve, the server moves to the net to become the blocker and jumps to block the shot.

- *Extension 1.* Have the spiker attack from all three positions: left front, middle front, and right front.
- *Extension 2.* Add a second blocker.

EQUIPMENT

One ball per four students and nets of different heights

CRITICAL ELEMENTS AND CUES

Technique

- See tasks 1, 6, 16, 26, and 33.

Communication

- All students must communicate so collisions don't occur. The passer calls *mine,* setter calls *here,* and the attacker calls *outside, middle,* or *back.*

COMMON ERRORS, CAUSES, AND CORRECTIONS

- See tasks 1, 6, 16, 26, and 33.

TASK 36: 6V6 GAME

PURPOSE

Following are the purposes of the task as related to aspects of skilled performance.

- Technique: In this task, students apply learned techniques in a modified game.
- Tactic: Students apply learned tactics in a modified game.
- Agility: Students apply agility demands in a modified game.
- Fair play: Students apply fair play practices in a modified game.
- Communication: Students apply learned communication strategies in a modified game.

DESCRIPTION

Divide students into teams of six; students will play 6v6. On each team, three students are in the back and three are in front along the net. Play begins with a serve from the service line. If a student is not comfortable serving from there, the student can serve from anywhere on the court. Students should use the pass-set-set or pass-set-tip (or spike) sequence when returning the ball. If the ball hits the floor, the attacking team earns a point. When the serving team loses the point, the ball goes over to the other team. When a team gains the serve, the students rotate in a clockwise direction. Regular volleyball rules apply concerning open underhand hits, boundary lines, net interference, and number of touches. Teams should not be larger than six students; have extra students rotate into the game when students rotate after each point.

EQUIPMENT

One ball per 12 students

CRITICAL ELEMENTS AND CUES

Apply all previous skills and cues.

Rules

- No open underhand hits allowed.
- A ball on the boundary line is in.
- No more than three touches on a side.
- No touching the net during game play.
- Return the ball to the server by rolling it under the net.

COMMON ERRORS, CAUSES, AND CORRECTIONS

Look for all previously discussed errors and provide corrections.

Chapter 10

Badminton

Badminton is played around the world and is often included in school physical education curricula. It is very popular in Europe, China, Korea, Malaysia, and Indonesia, and its popularity has grown around the world, and especially in the United States, since it was added as a medal sport in the Olympics. One of the attractions of badminton is that it can be played in coed settings. Although the basic nature of badminton is to simply hit a shuttle over a net, doing so effectively takes practice. Badminton is often taught using a variety of strokes to get the shuttle over the net. We believe that to effectively develop badminton abilities, students must learn not only basic strokes but also how to control the direction of the shot and how to combine shots to create scoring opportunities. We suggest that students be placed into predesigned situations in which these techniques and tactics can be developed and then practice the techniques in controlled game-like settings. This chapter shows you how to accomplish this.

OUR PEDAGOGICAL APPROACH TO BADMINTON

Badminton is a fast-paced racket and net sport. This unit focuses on developing skillful performance and game sense through tasks. Initially, we address handling the racket and placement of the shuttle, and then we move to a modified game. Our focus is on developing technique and refining performance. Each successive task and tactic builds on the previous ones and is a little more demanding. Our goal is to enable students to maintain a rally, which is the primary strategy we use to introduce and have students practice techniques and tactics. We base the techniques and game sense on the game of singles. Doubles should not be used until techniques can be effectively demonstrated in singles play.

Games are central to our pedagogy. The key games that we use for teaching are forehand and forehand, backhand and backhand, forehand and backhand, and long and short games. As students learn to play these games, you will learn to better identify errors. There are three ways you can respond to these errors: (1) provide feedback to correct errors and keep the task the same, (2) modify the task to make it easier, or (3) return to an earlier progression and then come back to the game. For example, if you observe that, despite your prompts, students are not hitting the shuttle at the highest point for a high clear shot, we suggest that you have students stop at the contact point and see if they hit the shuttle at the highest point. Similarly, if you observe that students are not quickly moving under the shuttle, revisit the shadow badminton task and then return to the game you were playing.

We use targets to develop and refine specific shots (e.g., down-in-line shots or cross-court shots). Court spaces are often manipulated (e.g., using diagonally opposite squares) and game rules are shaped (e.g., earning a point only when hitting a smash) to emphasize particular techniques or tactics. Most task progressions go from a static context (e.g., hitting the shuttle directly tossed or served while standing still) to a dynamic context (e.g., hitting the shuttle indirectly tossed or served from various distances or directions).

Modifications to Address Individual Needs of Students

For students with disabilities, appropriate modifications to activities depend on the nature of the disability. To modify badminton instruction for students with visual impairments, you can (a) use a larger, slower shuttle; (b) use a racket with a short shaft and a larger head; and (c) use brightly colored tape to highlight boundaries and the top of the net.

For students with autism spectrum disorder, place the students in areas of the gymnasium that are quieter and less distracting. Children with autism spectrum disorder may benefit from having targets on the floor that they try to hit when practicing their swings. You can also place colored tape on the handle of the racket to indicate where students should grip it.

For students who use wheelchairs, adopt rules from wheelchair badminton. For example, rather than returning the shuttle with one touch, students can return the shuttle with two touches.

For individuals with cerebral palsy, a common concern in badminton is lateral mobility. To accommodate the students, (a) allow them to play with larger and slower shuttles, (b) adopt a two-touch or three-touch return rule, or (c) use half of the width of the court during game play to limit movement.

Organization

Divide students into groups of four and assign each group to a badminton court. Students can practice most of the techniques with a partner on a half-width court. Some tasks assign students to various roles (e.g., tossers or servers, hitters, retrievers). The use of these roles result in an increase in student engagement and allow for the tasks to help students learn the skills and develop game sense in game-like conditions.

Space

Badminton requires a hard, flat surface that is clear of obstacles. It can be played outside, but the wind limits shot control. The U.S. Badminton Association recommends court dimensions of 44 by 20 feet (13.4 by 6.1 meters). The front service line should be marked 6.5 feet (2 meters) away from the net. The court can be modified to 30 by 15 feet (9.1 by 4.6 meters) with the service line 4 feet (1.2 meters) from the net. The use of smaller courts allows novice students to demonstrate more control, positions them closer to the net, and helps them focus on using proper techniques. Begin with smaller badminton courts to allow for more control over technique, and then move to full-court badminton. The court can be marked with floor tape or poly spots. For students in lower grades, you can eliminate boundaries.

Nets are not necessary in introductory lessons, but their use is encouraged. If badminton nets are not available, poly spots or cones can be used to mark the net area, string can be strung between two tall cones or chairs, and mini nets, lowered volleyball nets, or higher tennis nets can be used. Nets can be lowered 4 inches (10 centimeters) from the official height of 5 feet 1 inch (1.53 meters), but they should not be higher than the official height.

The following are important safety considerations relative to the organization of space:

- Have students spread out so they are not struck by rackets or shuttles.

- Construct activities in a way that minimizes the chances of students being hit by other students' shuttles.

- Ensure that students have sufficient space to swing their rackets.

- Place left-handed students in appropriate positions to avoid racket collisions with right-handed students.

- Ensure that shuttles are regularly cleared from the court to prevent students from stepping on them. Court activity should cease when students are clearing shuttles.

Equipment Needed

Modified equipment helps you provide developmentally appropriate learning experiences and increases student success. Students in lower grades can use shortened rackets, shortened racket grips, or bigger racket heads. Upper-grade students should use regulation rackets.

Students can use feathered or synthetic shuttlecocks. Synthetic shuttlecocks are used in most school settings because feathers break easily and need to be replaced several times during a unit. Larger and slower shuttles should be used in elementary schools and for beginners in secondary settings. These give students more time to move under the shuttle and execute a shot with control. In secondary settings, use regulation badminton shuttles. We recommend having one shuttle for each student. Although one shuttle per pair of students will suffice for most tasks, having 3 to 4 shuttles per court increases opportunities to execute shot tries.

CONTENT MAP STRUCTURE

Figure 10.1 is a combined content map that illustrates the flow and connectedness of all of the tasks used to develop badminton techniques and tactics. It is divided into three levels, and each level has a separate content map that includes the application games used to refine the techniques and tactics in that level. The primary focus of level 1 (figure 10.2) is developing the foundational techniques of the underhand clear, the overhead clear, and the serve so students can participate in a simplified singles games. In level 2 (figure 10.3), we emphasize controlling the direction of the overhead and underhand clear and introduce the drop shot and backhand serves; this level also concludes with a singles game. In level 3 (figure 10.4), the smash is introduced, and students learn to combine shots for better scoring opportunities. Doubles strategies and doubles games are also introduced at this level and conclude in doubles games.

In the content maps, we have numbered the tasks. These numbers are used to cross reference tasks descriptions in the body of the chapter with the content maps. The task numbers should not be interpreted as the order in which they should be taught. It is important that tasks are taught and progressed from simpler to more complex forms which is shown in the upward progress of the task sequence on the content map. This is particularly necessary before tasks are combined. For instance in badminton whether you teach the underhand clear first or the overhead clear, the progressions of both need to be taught before they are combined in task 20.

338

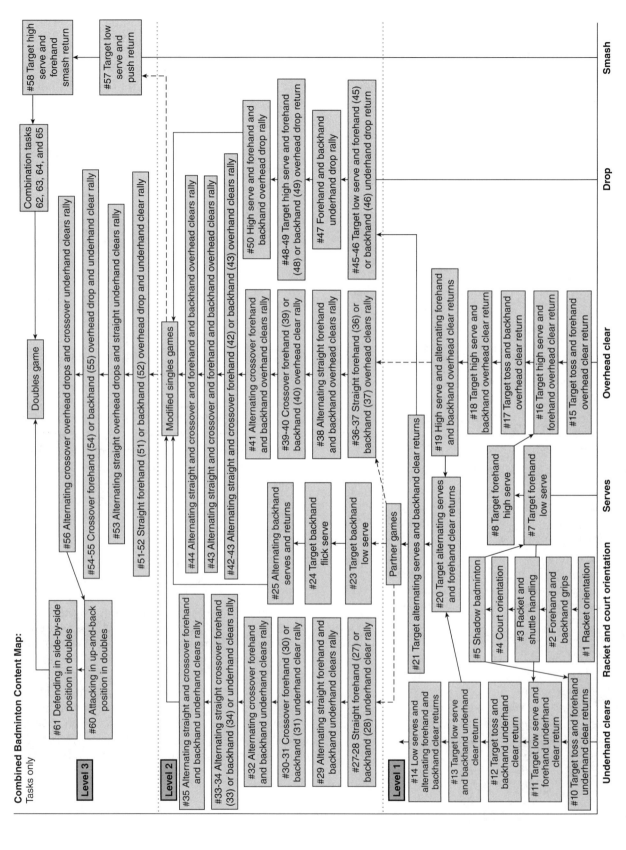

Figure 10.1 Combined content map for badminton.

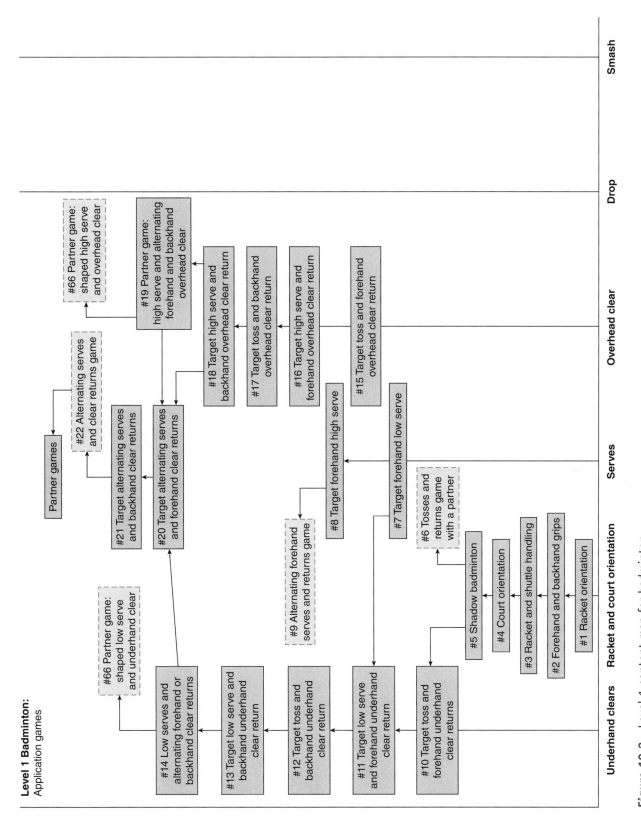

Level 1 Badminton:
Application games

Figure 10.2 Level 1 content map for badminton.

339

Level 2 Badminton:
Application games

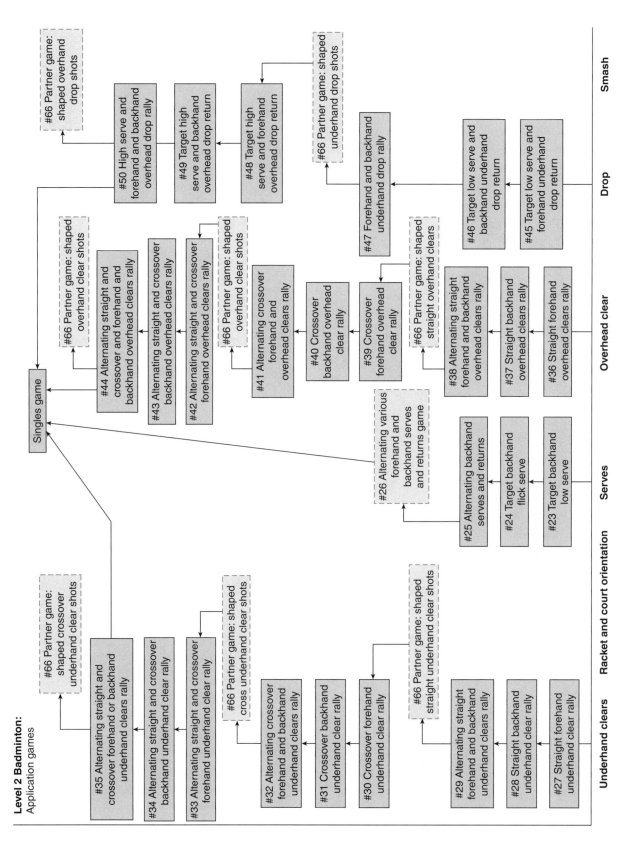

Figure 10.3 Level 2 content map for badminton.

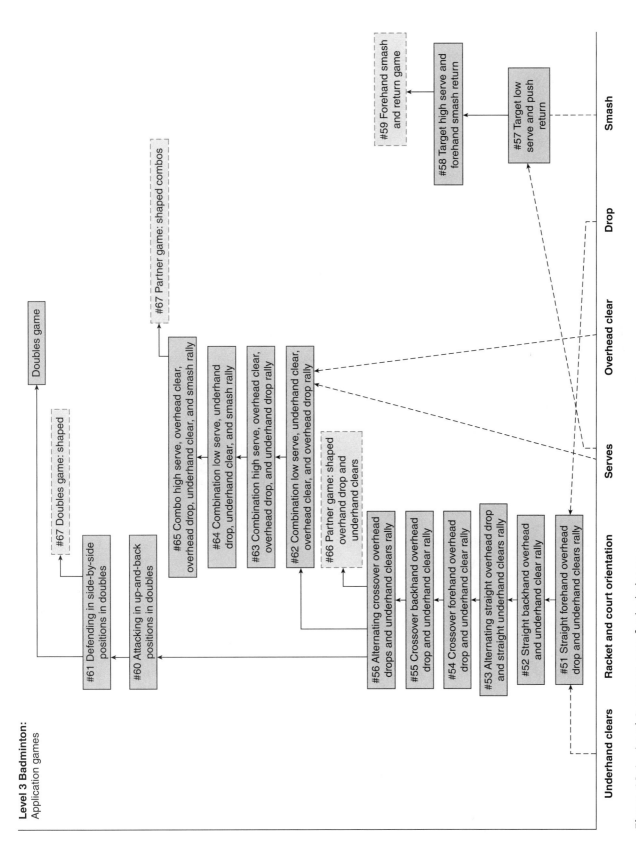

Figure 10.4 Level 3 content map for badminton.

STRUCTURE OF THE LESSONS

The following is a sample daily lesson structure for a 50-minute secondary badminton lesson.

Warm-up (5 to 6 minutes)

Application game: Shaped partner game (straight underhand clear shots) (5 minutes)

Informing task: target backhand low serve (7 minutes)

Extension task: add targets to target backhand low serve task (6 minutes)

Informing task: target backhand flick serve (7 minutes)

Extension task: add targets to target backhand flick serve task (6 minutes)

Informing task: alternating backhand serves and returns (5 minutes)

Application game: alternating various forehand and backhand serves and returns game (6 minutes)

Closure (2 minutes)

Warm-up

Our elementary and secondary school warm-ups for badminton are presented here.

Elementary School

The elementary warm-up focuses on students controlling the shuttle as it comes off the racket strings. On the first day of the unit, teach students three shuttle handling drills: (1) carrying the shuttle, (2) bouncing the shuttle, and (3) bouncing the shuttle while walking. Students will perform these drills on days 2 through 5. These can be done as whole-class drills or as a circuit. If done as a circuit, divide the class into three groups and have the groups rotate through the drills. The warm-up should last about 5 minutes, which is approximately 90 seconds for each drill.

Secondary School

These warm-ups change throughout the unit and apply techniques after they are taught. These warm-ups provide students with more opportunities to refine the basic badminton techniques. The warm-up for day 2 is a review of the shuttle-handling drills reviewed or learned in lesson 1. For days 3 and 4, the warm-up uses the forehand and backhand underhand clear shots in a rally

as a review of the techniques taught in lesson 2. On days 5 through 9, the warm-up is a forehand and backhand overhead clear rally that refines the overhead clears taught in lesson 4. On day 10, the warm-up focuses on the underhand drop rally from lesson 9, and in lesson 11, the warm-up is the overhead drop with the underhand clear rally. Students should do each warm-up with their group at their assigned home area (net) for 5 to 6 minutes.

BLOCK PLAN

The introductory block plan (see table 10.1) is designed for beginners at the elementary or secondary level. In elementary school, this should not be introduced earlier than fourth grade. (Before fourth grade, students should work on developing striking skills starting with their hands or short-handled implements and working toward long-handled implements.) The lack of badminton courts or nets should not be a limitation at this level. You can effectively teach using the modified courts and nets mentioned earlier. Although longer units are always preferred, we recognize that there are time limitations at the elementary level; therefore, the elementary unit is five days for the initial grade in which it is taught. If the unit is being taught across two grades, modify the block plan by teaching some tasks in fourth grade and the remaining tasks in fifth grade. It might be appropriate to use some of the level 2 tasks for the fifth-grade students depending on their technique development. Limit games to singles so students have ample opportunities to apply learned techniques.

The secondary block plan (see table 10.2) follows the elementary block plan and is designed for students in middle and high school. It assumes that students were taught the level 1 techniques at the elementary level. If this is not the case, follow the introductory block plan. Because middle and high school physical education programs have different requirements, these units should *not* be taught in fewer than 10 days. These units are adjusted for 10-, 15-, and 20-day programs, although we recommend units of 20 or more days. In a 10-day unit, limit games to singles so each student has an opportunity to apply learned techniques in the game. For units of 15 or 20 days, use a mixture of singles and doubles games based on student progress.

Table 10.1   Elementary Badminton Block Plan: Five-Day Unit

This is an example of a beginning block plan for elementary students that uses the badminton tasks shown in the level 1 content map. It is based on an initial five-day unit, and it encompasses some of the level 1 tasks on the content map. You can use this as a template for developing an appropriate block plan for beginning students. If you are teaching a longer unit, or if another badminton unit will be taught next year, you can include the remaining level 1 tasks and some level 2 tasks. Your decisions about what tasks to include will depend on your students and their levels of experience.

Lesson 1	Lesson 2	Lesson 3	Lesson 4	Lesson 5
Warm-up • Nonspecific warm-up	**Warm-up** • Shuttle-handling activities	**Warm-up** • Same as day 3	**Warm-up** • Same as day 3	**Warm-up** • Same as day 3
Introductory application game • Pre-assessment: partner rally (10 feet [3 meters] away)	**Introductory application game** • **(6)** Tosses and returns game with a partner	**Introductory application game** • **(9)** Alternating forehand serves and returns game	**Introductory application game** • **(66)** Shaped partner games	**Introductory application game** • **(19)** High serve and alternating forehand and backhand overhead clear returns
Content development • **(1)** Racquet orientation • **(2)** Forehand and backhand grips • **(3)** Racket and shuttle handling • **(5)** Shadow badminton	**Content development** • **(4)** Court orientation • **(7)** Target forehand low serve • **(8)** Target forehand high serve	**Content development** • **(10)** Target toss and forehand underhand clear returns • **(11)** Target low serve and forehand underhand clear return • **(12)** Target toss and backhand underhand clear return • **(13)** Target low serve and backhand underhand clear return	**Content development** • **(14)** Low serve and alternating forehand and backhand underhand clear returns • **(15)** Target toss and forehand overhead clear return • **(16)** Target high serve and forehand overhead clear return	**Content development** • **(17)** Target toss and backhand overhead clear return • **(18)** Target high serve and backhand overhead clear return
Closing application game • **(6)** Tosses and returns game with a partner	**Closing application game** • **(9)** Alternating forehand serves and returns game	**Closing application game** • **(66)** Shaped partner game	**Closing application game** • **(19)** High serve and alternating forehand and backhand overhead clear returns	**Closing application game** • **(19)** High serve and alternating forehand and backhand overhead clear returns

Table 10.2 Secondary Badminton Block Plans: 10-, 15-, and 20-Day Units

This block plan incorporates 10-, 15-, and 20-day units. The last two days of the 10-day block plan, the last three days of the 15-day block plan, and the last five days of the 20-day block plan are game days and are described at the end of the block plan. The first eight days of the block plan are the same for all units. If students are new to badminton or if a review of level 1 tasks is needed, refer to table 10.1 for appropriate task progressions.

Lesson 1 of all block plans	Lesson 2 of all block plans	Lesson 3 of all block plans	Lesson 4 of all block plans	Lesson 5 of all block plans
Warm-up • None	**Warm-up** • Shuttle-handling activities	**Warm-up** • Forehand and backhand underhand clear rally	**Warm-up** • Same as day 3	**Warm-up** • Forehand and backhand overhead clear rally
Introductory application game • Pre-assessment: Modified singles game to assess skill level	**Introductory application game** • **(22)** Alternating serves and clear returns game	**Introductory application game** • **(66)** Shaped partner games	**Introductory application game** • **(26)** Alternating various forehand and backhand serves and returns game	**Introductory application game** • **(66)** Shaped partner games
Content development • Review of forehand and backhand clears and high and low serves (as needed) • **(20)** Target alternating serves and forehand clear returns • **(21)** Target alternating serves and backhand clear returns	**Content development** • **(27)** Straight forehand underhand clear rally • **(28)** Straight backhand underhand clear rally • **(29)** Alternating straight forehand and backhand underhand clears rally	**Content development** • **(23)** Target backhand low serve • **(24)** Target backhand flick serve • **(25)** Alternating backhand serves and returns	**Content development** • **(30)** Crossover forehand underhand clear rally • **(31)** Crossover backhand underhand clear rally • **(32)** Alternating crossover forehand and backhand underhand clear rally	**Content development** • **(33)** Alternating straight and crossover forehand underhand clears rally • **(34)** Alternating straight and crossover backhand underhand clears rally • **(35)** Alternating straight and crossover forehand and backhand underhand clears rally
Closing application game • **(22)** Alternating serves and clear returns game	**Closing application game** • **(66)** Shaped partner games	**Closing application game** • **(26)** Alternating various forehand and backhand serves and returns game	**Closing application game** • **(66)** Shaped partner games	**Closing application game** • **(66)** Shaped partner games

Lesson 6 of all block plans	Lesson 7 of all block plans	Lesson 8 of all block plans (last instructional day of 10-day block plan)	Lesson 9 of 15- and 20-day block plans (See table 10.3 for lesson 9 for 10-day plan.)	Lesson 10 of 15- and 20-day block plans (See table 10.3 for lesson 10 for 10-day plan.)
Warm-up • Same as day 5	**Warm-up** • Same as day 5	**Warm-up** • Same as day 5	**Warm-up** • Same as day 5	**Warm-up** • Forehand and backhand under-hand drop rally
Introductory application game • **(66)** Shaped partner games	**Introductory application game** • **(66)** Shaped partner games	**Introductory application game** • **(66)** Shaped partner games	**Introductory application game** • **(66)** Shaped partner games	**Introductory application game** • **(66)** Shaped partner games
Content development • **(36)** Straight forehand overhead clear rally • **(37)** Straight back-hand overhead clear rally • **(38)** Alternating straight forehand and backhand overhead clears rally	**Content development** • **(39)** Crossover forehand overhead clear rally • **(40)** Crossover backhand over-head clear rally • **(41)** Alternating crossover forehand and backhand overhead clears rally	**Content development** • **(42)** Alternat-ing straight and crossover forehand overhead clears rally • **(43)** Alternating straight and cross-over backhand overhead clears rally • **(44)** Alternating straight and cross-over forehand and backhand over-head clears rally	**Content development** • **(45)** Target low serve and forehand underhand drop return • **(46)** Target low serve and back-hand underhand drop return • **(47)** Forehand and backhand under-hand drop rally	**Content development** **(48)** Target high serve and forehand over-head drop return **(49)** Target high serve and backhand over-head drop return **(50)** High serve and forehand and back-hand overhead drop rally
Closing application game • **(66)** Shaped partner games	**Closing application game** • **(66)** Shaped partner games	**Closing application game** • **(66)** Shaped partner games	**Closing application game** • **(66)** Shaped partner games	**Closing application game** • **(66)** Shaped partner games

(continued)

Lesson 11 of 15- and 20-day block plans	Lesson 12 of 15- and 20-day block plans (last instructional day of 15-day plan)	Lesson 13 of 20-day block plan (See table 10.4 for lesson 13 for 15-day plan.)	Lesson 14 of 20-day block plan (See table 10.4 for lesson 14 for 15-day plan.)	Lesson 15 of 20-day block plan (See table 10.4 for lesson 15 for 15-day plan.)
Warm-up • Overhead drop with underhand clear rally	**Warm-up** • Same as day 11	**Warm-up** • Same as day 11	**Warm-up** • Same as day 11	**Warm-up** • Same as day 11
Introductory application game • **(66)** Shaped partner games	**Introductory application game** • **(66)** Shaped partner games	**Introductory application game** • **(66)** Shaped partner games	**Introductory application game** • **(59)** Forehand smash and return game	**Introductory application game** • **(67)** Shaped doubles game
Content development • **(51)** Straight forehand overhead drop and underhand clear rally • **(52)** Straight backhand overhead drop and underhand clear rally • **(53)** Alternating straight overhead drops and straight underhand clears rally	**Content development** • **(54)** Crossover forehand overhead drop and underhand clear rally • **(55)** Crossover backhand overhead drop and underhand clear rally • **(56)** Alternating crossover overhead drops and crossover underhand clears rally	**Content development** • **(62)** Combination low serve, underhand clear, overhead clear, and overhead drop rally • **(57)** Target low serve and push return • **(58)** Target high serve and forehand smash return	**Content development** • **(63)** Combination high serve, overhead clear, overhead drop, and underhand drop rally • **(64)** Combination low serve, underhand drop, underhand clear, and smash rally • **(60)** Attacking in the up-and-back position in doubles	**Content development** • **(65)** Combination high serve, overhead clear, overhead drop, underhand clear, and smash rally • (61) Defending in side-by-side position in doubles
Closing application game • **(66)** Shaped partner games	**Closing application game** • **(66)** Shaped partner games	**Closing application game** • **(59)** Forehand smash and return game	**Closing application game** • **(67)** Shaped doubles game	**Closing application game** • **(67)** Shaped doubles game

Lesson 16 of 20-day block plan	Lesson 17 of 20-day block plan	Lesson 18 of 20-day block plan	Lesson 19 of 20-day block plan	Lesson 20 of 20-day block plan
Warm-up • Forehand and backhand overhead rally, forehand and backhand underhand rally, or overhead drop and underhand clear rally	**Warm-up** • Same as day 16	**Warm-up** • Same as day 16	**Warm-up** • Same as day 16	**Warm-up** • Same as day 16
Fixed-time full singles against different opponents (nonexclusionary round-robin tournament) Encourage the use of regular game rules. We recommend at least two games per lesson.	**Fixed-time full singles against different opponents (nonexclusionary round-robin tournament)** Encourage the use of regular game rules. We recommend at least two games per lesson.	**Fixed-time full doubles against different opponents (nonexclusionary round-robin tournament)** Encourage the use of regular game rules. We recommend at least two games per lesson.	**Fixed-time full doubles against different opponents (nonexclusionary round-robin tournament)** Encourage the use of regular game rules. We recommend at least two games per lesson.	**Fixed-time full doubles against different opponents (nonexclusionary round-robin tournament)** Encourage the use of regular game rules. We recommend at least two games per lesson.

Table 10.3 10-Day Block Plan Game Days

Lesson 9 of 10-day block plan	Lesson 10 of 10-day block plan
Warm-up • Same as day 3	**Warm-up** • Same as day 3
Fixed-time modified singles against different opponents (nonexclusionary round-robin tournament) Encourage the use of specific skills. Award an extra point to the score for demonstration of these skills. We recommend at least two games per lesson.	**Fixed-time modified singles against different opponents (nonexclusionary round-robin tournament)** Encourage the use of specific skills. Award an extra point to the score for demonstration of these skills. We recommend at least two games per lesson.

Table 10.4 15-Day Block Plan Game Days

Lesson 13 of 15-day block plan	Lesson 14 of 15-day block plan	Lesson 15 of 15-day block plan
Warm-up Same as day 3	**Warm-up** Same as day 3	**Warm-up** Same as day 3
Fixed-time modified singles and doubles against different opponents (nonexclusionary round-robin tournament) Encourage the use of specific skills. Award an extra point to the score for demonstration of these skills. We recommend at least two games per lesson.	**Fixed-time modified singles and doubles against different opponents (nonexclusionary round-robin tournament)** Encourage the use of specific skills. Award an extra point to the score for demonstration of these skills. We recommend at least two games per lesson.	**Fixed-time modified singles and doubles against different opponents (nonexclusionary round-robin tournament)** Encourage the use of specific skills. Award an extra point to the score for demonstration of these skills. We recommend at least two games per lesson.

SHAPE AMERICA'S GRADE LEVEL OUTCOMES FOR K-12 PHYSICAL EDUCATION

In table 10.5, we identify key grade-level outcomes for badminton for 4th grade through 8th grade. These are linked to specific tasks on the content maps that are appropriate for teaching the skill and assessing the outcome.

Table 10.5 Grade-Level Outcomes for Badminton

Outcome	Description	Content map focus and tasks
S1.E24.4a	Strikes an object with a short-handled implement while demonstrating a mature pattern.	Level 1, task 22
S1.E24.5	Strikes an object consecutively, with a partner, using a short-handled implement, over a net or against a wall, in either a competitive or cooperative environment.	Level 1, tasks 22, 66
S1.E25.4	Strikes an object with a long-handled implement (e.g., hockey stick, golf club, bat, tennis racket, badminton racket), while demonstrating 3 of the 5 critical elements of a mature pattern for the implement (grip, stance, body orientation, swing plane and follow through).	Level 1, task 10
S1.M13.6	Strikes with a mature overhand pattern in a nondynamic environment for net/wall games such as volleyball, handball, badminton or tennis.	Level 1, tasks 15-16
S1.M13.7	Strikes with a mature overhand pattern in a dynamic environment for net/wall games such as volleyball, handball, badminton or tennis.	Level 1, task 20
S1.M13.8	Strikes with a mature overhand pattern in a modified game for net/wall games such as volleyball, handball, badminton or tennis.	Level 1, task 22
S1.M14.7	Demonstrates the mature form of forehand and backhand strokes with a long-handled implement in net games such as badminton or tennis.	Level 1, task 19
S1.M14.8	Demonstrates the mature form of forehand and backhand strokes with a short- or long-handled implement with power and accuracy in net games such as pickleball, tennis, badminton or paddle ball.	Level 1, tasks 20-21
S1.M15.6	Transfers weight with correct timing for the striking pattern.	Level 1, task 8
S1.M15.7	Transfers weight with correct timing using low to high striking pattern with a short-handled implement on the forehand side.	Level 1, task 15
S1.M15.8	Transfers weight with correct timing using low to high striking pattern with a long-handled implement on the forehand and backhand sides.	Level 1, tasks 20-21

TASK 1: RACKET ORIENTATION

PURPOSE

Following are the purposes of the task as related to aspects of skilled performance.

- Technique: In this task, students learn the names and parts of the badminton racket.
- Fair play: Students demonstrate teamwork in determining a correct answer on a team.

DESCRIPTION

Have students stand in a half circle around you. Introduce students to the following parts of the badminton racket (see figure):

- **Handle.** The handle is the part of the racket you grip.
- **Shaft.** The shaft connects the handle to the head. It can also include the throat, but not all rackets have throats.
- **Head.** The head encircles the stringed area.
- **Stringed area.** The stringed area is the part used to hit the shuttle. The stringed area is also called the *face* of the racket.
- **Frame.** The frame is the head, throat, shaft, and handle collectively.

Then, point to the parts of the racket and ask each team to name the part. If students need motivation, you can award a point for each part the team correctly names.

EQUIPMENT

One racket

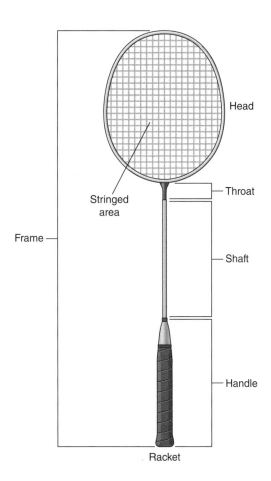

Racket

TASK 2: FOREHAND AND BACKHAND GRIPS

PURPOSE

Following is the purpose of the task as related to aspects of skilled performance.

Technique: In this task, students learn the forehand and backhand grips in badminton.

DESCRIPTION

To demonstrate the Eastern forehand grip to right-handers, hold the racket in the left hand by the middle of the shaft and place the open right hand on the face of the racket, which should be perpendicular to the ground. Next, slide the open right hand down the shaft to "shake the hand" of the racket handle. Reverse the process for left-handed students. To demonstrate the backhand grip, change only the thumb: straighten it on the top instead of wrapping it around the handle. Each student should perform 10 forehand and backhand grips with the racket before moving on to the next task.

EQUIPMENT

One racket per student

CRITICAL ELEMENTS AND CUES

Technique: Eastern Forehand Grip (see figure)

- Position the wrist slightly to the right of the center of the handle if you are right-handed and to the left if you are left-handed. *Cue:* Right (or left) of center.

- Wrap the fingers around the handle so the home knuckle of the index finger is on the right panel of the handle. *Cue:* Knuckle on panel.

Technique: Backhand Grip (see figure)

- The thumb is straight up and down on the top instead of wrapped around the handle. *Cue:* Thumb up.

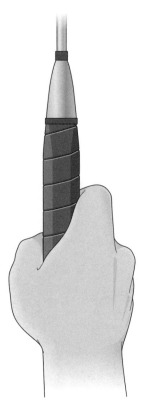

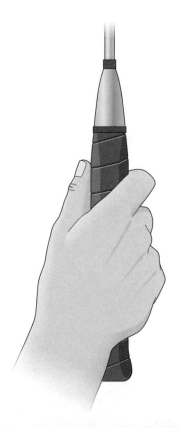

COMMON ERRORS, CAUSES, AND CORRECTIONS

- The student has the wrist turned too far to the side of the handle. *Cause:* The student is not able to use proper force when switching the grip. *Correction:* Have the student check the thumb and index finger positions around the handle.
- The student opens the pointing finger so it is along the handle. *Cause:* The student is not yet comfortable with the grip. *Correction:* Be very attentive to grip, and remind the student of the proper grip. This is an error that occurs very frequently until students are comfortable with the correct Eastern grip.
- The student holds the racket too tightly. *Cause:* The student is not relaxed. *Correction:* Ask the student to relax the grip by pretending to hold a little bird.

TASK 3: RACKET AND SHUTTLE HANDLING

PURPOSE

Following is the purpose of the task as related to aspects of skilled performance.

Technique: In this task, students learn basic racket- and shuttle-handling skills and become comfortable holding and manipulating the racket and the shuttle.

DESCRIPTION

Use the forehand grip to progressively teach basic racket- and shuttle-handling skills using the following three tasks:

- **Carry the shuttle.** Students hold the racket with the palm and the face of the racket pointing toward the sky, place the shuttle on the face of the racket, and carry the shuttle along the boundary of the court or across the court. If students need motivation, see how many students can keep control of the shuttle while moving for 30 seconds. As an extension, have students speed up.
- **Bounce the shuttle.** Students hold the racket with the palm and the face of the racket pointing toward the sky and continuously bounce the shuttle five times. The shuttle should not go higher than eye level. If students need motivation, see how many consecutive hits students can make.
  - *Extension 1.* Increase the number of consecutive hits to 10, 15, and 20.
  - *Extension 2.* Encourage practice at different levels: eye level, above the head, and really high.
- **Bounce the shuttle while walking.** Students hold the racket with the palm and the face of the racket pointing toward the sky and bounce the shuttle above the head while walking in self-space. If students need motivation, see how many consecutive hits students can make.
  - *Extension 1.* Have students alternate between the palm facing the sky and the palm facing the floor.
  - *Extension 2.* Encourage practice at different levels: eye level, above the head, and really high.

EQUIPMENT

One racket and one shuttle per student

CRITICAL ELEMENTS AND CUES

Technique

- To carry the shuttle, keep the face of the racket horizontal and the shuttle in the middle of the face. *Cue:* Palm up.
- When bouncing the shuttle, keep your eyes on it. *Cue:* Eyes on shuttle.
- Hit the shuttle to eye level, then above the head, and then really high. *Cues:* Eye high; above head; really high.

COMMON ERRORS, CAUSES, AND CORRECTIONS

- The student gets too close to another student. *Cause:* The student walks too fast. *Correction:* Be sure students are spaced far enough apart.
- The shuttle falls off the racket while the student is carrying it. *Cause:* The student does not hold the racket horizontal or hits the shuttle in the middle of the racket face. *Correction:* Remind the student to keep the palm up and keep the shuttle on the middle of the racket without hitting it.
- The student does not look to where he or she is moving. *Cause:* The student's eyes are continuously glued to the shuttle. *Correction:* Remind the student to briefly look up every 2 to 3 steps.
- The student bounces the shuttle too high or too low. *Cause:* The student uses too much or too little force. *Correction:* Stress that the shuttle should rebound at head level.
- The student misses the shuttle. *Cause:* The student does not look at the shuttle. *Correction:* Have the student stand to the side and practice the alternating hits without moving while keeping the eyes on the shuttle.
- The student does not have enough time to change the racket position. *Cause:* The student does not hit the shuttle high enough. *Correction:* Stress that the shuttle go slightly above the head.

TASK 4: COURT ORIENTATION

PURPOSE

Following are the purposes of the task as related to aspects of skilled performance.

- Tactic: In this task, students learn the location and purpose of the home line, sidelines, center line, and net.
- Fair play: Students correctly tally earned points on a team.

DESCRIPTION

Introduce students to the following parts of the badminton court (see figure), and have them stand on each line or court part as you identify it (on the home line, they should be facing the net):

- **Sidelines for singles.** These are the inside lines or edges of each side of the court. Shuttles that land outside the sidelines are considered out-of-bounds. Shuttles that land on the sidelines are considered inbounds.
- **Sidelines for doubles.** These are the outer lines or edges of each side of the court.
- **Center line.** This line creates the left and right service courts. Serves occur diagonally from one side of the court to the other and must land in the service court.
- **Net.** The net is 5 feet 1 inch high at each side and is a little lower in the center.
- **Right and left service courts.** When serving, students must place the shuttle in the opponent's service court on the opposite diagonal side from the serve.
- **Back boundary line.** This is the end line at each end of the court. Serves occur behind this line. A shuttle that lands beyond this line is out-of-bounds. If it lands on the line, it is inbounds.
- **Short service line.** This is the line at the front of the service boxes that the shuttle must land past and within the appropriate service court to be fair.
- **Long service line for doubles.** This line is used when a serve is made in a doubles game only. This served shuttle must land in front of the line in the appropriate service court to be fair. Once the service is legally made, the line is no longer impacts the play and the back boundary line indicates the legal court that play must occur in.

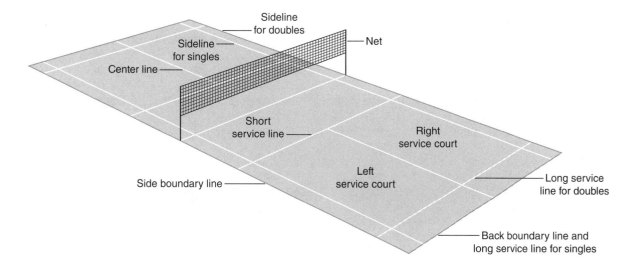

Once you have explained each area, use the following game as a warm-up activity. Place teams of four students on each side of a court (use as many courts as you have teams). Students cannot touch the net. When you call out the name of a court location, the students run to that location within their assigned side of the court. Then ask the significance of that location (e.g., Why is the boundary line important?). If students need motivation, award a point for each correct location students move to and for each correct answer.

EQUIPMENT

Courts

CRITICAL ELEMENTS AND CUES

Tactic

- Stand at each location as it is being explained.
- When students stand on the baseline instruct them to "face the net".

Fair Play

- Make sure students are accurately accumulating their points.

COMMON ERRORS, CAUSES, AND CORRECTIONS

- Students may be moving to the wrong line or court area; *Cause:* Will happen mostly in the first trials practiced since students are not yet acquainted with the various court lines; *Correction:* Add several repetitions to sprint to a line or area which students still confuse with another.

TASK 5: SHADOW BADMINTON

PURPOSE

Following are the purposes of the task as related to aspects of skilled performance.

- Technique: In this task, students learn the proper ready position and footwork to move into position to receive the shuttle.
- Tactic: Students learn to cover a playing area by quickly moving back to the middle of the court after each shot.
- Agility: Students quickly move the feet into position.

DESCRIPTION

Divide groups of four students into pairs. One pair is on the court (one student on each side) and one pair watches from the side. Begin the game by determining which student is the lead and which is the shadow (one student mirrors what the other student does). Indicate on each side of the court eight areas using either poly spots or simply explain the eight positions. The eight areas marked are as follows: one at each corner of the half court (4), one at the end of the center line, one at the middle of the net and one on each singles side line (2) halfway between the net and back boundary line. The lead student starts at the center of the half court in the proper ready position (see figure), moves at a half pace to one of the positions (1 through 8), and pretends to hit a shot. The shadow must mirror the movement of the lead by moving to the same location and performing the same actions. The lead returns to the midpoint and stands in the proper ready position between each movement. The other pair of students rotates in after eight trials (one for each number on the court). If pairs do this multiple times, the two partners can switch roles between lead and mirror.

- *Extension 1.* The lead student moves at the normal pace.
- *Extension 2.* To make the game more challenging and encourage lots of fast footwork, have students play an opposite shadow game in which the shadow moves opposite the lead.

EQUIPMENT

One racket per student

CRITICAL ELEMENTS AND CUES

Technique

- Assume the ready position: Stand with your upper body in an up-and-back position with the feet shoulder-width apart and with the knees slightly bent. Put both arms up, and hold the racket head up slightly toward the backhand side. Keep the weight on the balls of the feet. *Cue:* Ready position.
- For the proper footwork for the forehand side, pivot and reach with the dominant arm and leg, and shuffle using a step-close-step action. *Cues:* Pivot; step-close-step.
- For the backhand side, cross over with the dominant side leg and then reach with the dominant arm and use a step-close-step action. *Cue:* Cross, step-close-step.

Tactic

- Return to the middle of the court after each mock shot so you are in position to react to the next one. *Cue:* Push back.

Agility

- Watch your partner and then move fast to get into position. *Cue:* Fast feet.

COMMON ERRORS, CAUSES, AND CORRECTIONS

- The student does not shadow the lead student. *Cause:* The student does not watch the lead. *Correction:* Have lead student hold up a number of fingers and have the shadow student call out the number while moving.
- The student does not return to the midpoint between trials. *Cause:* The student is in a hurry to get to the next spot. *Correction:* Have the lead student move to a spot and return to the midpoint on your command.

- For the forehand side, the student reaches with the nondominant leg. *Cause:* The student uses cross-steps. *Correction:* Have the student reach for the shuttle with the dominant arm and leg.
- For the backhand side, the student reaches with the nondominant leg. *Cause:* The student fails to cross over with the dominant leg. *Correction:* Have the student cross over with the dominant leg and then use cross-steps.

TASK 6: TOSSES AND RETURNS GAME WITH A PARTNER

PURPOSE

Following are the purposes of the task as related to aspects of skilled performance.

- Technique: In this task, students learn the proper ready position and footwork to move into position to receive and return the shuttle.
- Tactic: Students learn to cover a playing area when returning shuttles by quickly moving back to the middle of the court after each shot.
- Agility: Students quickly move the feet into the correct position.

DESCRIPTION

Divide groups of four students into pairs. One pair is on the court (one student on each side) and one pair watches from the side. Begin the game by determining which student is the tosser and which is the hitter. The tosser stands close to the net and tosses a shuttle to one of the eight numbered areas explained in the previous task. The hitter hits the shuttle over the net and then returns to the middle of the court and assumes the ready position. The tosser then tosses a shuttle to one of the other areas. The other pair of students rotates in after 15 trials. When pairs rotate in, the two students change roles. If a student is having trouble tossing the shuttle over the net, allow the tosser to stand on the same side of the court as the hitter and toss from there. If students need motivation, award one point when a student hits a shuttle over the net or each time you see the proper ready position and footwork before the hit.

- *Extension 1.* To challenge the hitter, the tosser can increase the speed of the throw.

EQUIPMENT

Four rackets and up to 15 shuttles per four students

CRITICAL ELEMENTS AND CUES

Technique

- Assume the ready positon. *Cue:* Ready position.
- For the forehand side, pivot and reach with the dominant arm and leg and shuffle using a step-close-step action. *Cues:* Pivot; step-close-step.
- Only for the backhand side use the dominant side cross step followed by a step-close-step. *Cue:* Cross; step-close-step.

Tactic

- Begin at a half pace and then move to a full pace.
- Good footwork allows you to get to the shuttle with enough time to perform a good swing on a good contact point. *Cue:* Get to the shuttle.

Agility

- Watch your opponent and then move fast to get into position. *Cue:* Watch and move fast.

COMMON ERRORS, CAUSES, AND CORRECTIONS

- The student does not return to the midpoint between shots. *Cause:* The student is not ready to move after making a shot. *Correction:* Emphasize returning to the midpoint after each shot.

- The student fails to contact the shuttle or hit it over the net. *Cause:* The student does not look at the shuttle, has the wrong grip, lacks eye coordination or power, or contacts the shuttle with the racket facing down. *Correction:* Grip issue - check the student's grip; contact point issue - make sure the racket face is slightly up at contact; and looking and coordination issues - allow the student to practice racket-handling drills to stress eyes on the shuttle and eye-hand coordination.
- The student contacts the shuttle too early or too late. *Cause:* The student fails to hold the racket head up after each shot. *Correction:* Have the student hold the racket head up after every shot.
- For the forehand side, the student reaches with the nondominant arm and leg. *Cause:* The student uses cross-steps. *Correction:* Have the student reach for the shuttle with the dominant arm and leg.
- For the backhand side, the student reaches with the nondominant leg. *Cause:* The student fails to cross over with the dominant leg. *Correction:* Have the student cross over with the dominant leg and then use cross-steps.

TASK 7: TARGET FOREHAND LOW SERVE

PURPOSE

Following are the purposes of the task as related to aspects of skilled performance.
- Technique: In this task, students learn the forehand low serve.
- Tactic: Students learn to serve the shuttle to target areas.

DESCRIPTION

Although the low serve is used more often in doubles than singles games, we begin with the low serve because it provides more control for students. In this task, focus on the technique of the forehand low serve and the placement of the shuttle. Groups of four students stand on a court (one in each service box). If available, have at least 5 shuttles available for each server. Two students on one side of the court serve their shuttles diagonally across the net into the opposite service box. The goal is to land the shot in that box. The student standing in that box collects the shuttles; once all shuttles have been served, that student serves them back. If students need motivation, award one point each time the shuttle lands in the target area or each time you see students use the correct technique. As an extension, place three hula hoops as targets along the short serve line for the servers to serve into.

EQUIPMENT

One racket per student and five or more shuttles and three hula hoops per pair of students

CRITICAL ELEMENTS AND CUES

Technique: Stance
- Stand 2 to 3 feet (0.6 to 0.9 meters) behind the front service line close to the center line with the upper body in an up-and-back stance and the feet staggered (nonracket side forward and racket side back). *Cue:* Up-and-back stance.
- Use the forehand grip. *Cue:* Forehand grip.
- Start with the weight on the rear foot (racket foot). *Cue:* Weight on the rear foot.
- Hold the racket in the backswing position. *Cue:* Racket arm back.
- Cock the wrist backward. *Cue:* Cock your wrist.

Technique: Action
- Hold the shuttle at the base between the thumb and the index finger with the cork facing downward, and drop it to the front and to the racket side of the body before swinging. *Cue:* Drop it in front.

- Contact the shuttle below the waist (at knee level). *Cue:* Hit below the waist.
- The wrist should remain cocked. *Cue:* Firm wrist.
- Watch the shuttle contact the racket. *Cue:* Eyes on the shuttle.
- Shift the weight back to the front on execution. *Cue:* Back to front.
- Push or guide the shuttle rather than hitting it. *Cues:* Guide the shuttle; gently push.
- Follow through by extending your arm in the direction of the serve (see figure). *Cue:* Follow through.
- Aim for the white top of the net to keep the shot low and close to the net. *Cues:* Low and close to the net; aim for the white top.

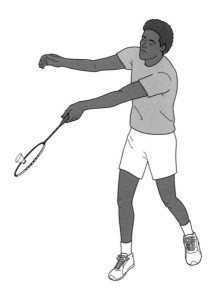

Tactic
- Land the shot in the front corners of the diagonal service box. *Cue:* Diagonal front corners.

COMMON ERRORS, CAUSES, AND CORRECTIONS
- The student tosses the shuttle rather than dropping it. *Cause:* The student does not understand the preparation phase of the serving movement. *Correction:* Have the student practice dropping the shuttle onto the target.
- The student misses the shuttle contact. *Cause:* The student does not watch the shuttle as it contacts the racket. *Correction:* Ask the student to watch the shuttle at contact.
- The student contacts the shuttle too far in front of the body or above the waist. *Cause:* The student is not in the correct position or fails to wait the shuttle until is dropped to the thigh level. *Correction:* Ask the student to use the correct preparation position for the serve or wait until the shuttle drops to the thigh level.
- On the serve the shuttle travels in a high trajectory. *Cause:* The student uses too much wrist action. *Correction:* Ask the student to use limited wrist action by keeping the wrist firm.
- On the serve the shuttle travels in a high trajectory. *Cause:* The shuttle is contacted too far above the knee. *Correction:* Have the student hit the shuttle into the net a few times so that the contact point is low.
- The student hits the shuttle rather than guiding it. *Cause:* The student uses too much force and wrist action on contact. *Correction:* Have the student shorten the backswing and follow through with limited wrist action.

TASK 8: TARGET FOREHAND HIGH SERVE

PURPOSE
Following are the purposes of the task as related to aspects of skilled performance.
- Technique: In this task, students learn the forehand high serve.
- Tactic: Students learn to serve the shuttle to target areas.

DESCRIPTION
This is a high and deep serve; it is not flat like the low serve. In this task, focus on the technique of the forehand high serve and the placement of the shuttle. Groups of four students stand on a court (one in each service box). Two students on one side of the court have at least five shuttles (if available) that they serve diagonally across the net into the opposite

service box. The goal is to land the shot in that box. The student standing in that box collects the shuttles; once all shuttles have been served, that student serves them back. If students need motivation, award one point each time the shuttle lands in the target area or each time you see students use the correct technique. As an extension, place three hula hoops as targets along the back boundary line within the service box.

EQUIPMENT

One racket per student and five shuttles and three hula hoops per pair of students

CRITICAL ELEMENTS AND CUES

Technique: Stance

- Stand 2 to 3 feet (0.6 to 0.9 meters) behind the front service line close to the center line with the upper body in an up-and-back stance. *Cue:* Up-and-back stance.
- Point your nonracket shoulder toward the net. *Cue:* Sideways.
- Use the forehand grip. *Cue:* Forehand grip.
- Put your weight on your back foot in preparation. *Cue:* Weight on your back foot.

Technique: Action (see figure)

- Cock the wrist backward. *Cue:* Cock your wrist.
- Hold the shuttle at the base between the thumb and the index finger with the cork facing downward, and drop it to the front and to the racket side of the body before swinging. *Cue:* Drop it in front.
- Transfer your weight from your back foot to your front foot. *Cue:* Shift your weight from back to front.
- Contact the shuttle below the waist (around knee level). *Cue:* Knee level.
- At contact, use a strong wrist action and forearm rotation. *Cue:* Strong wrist and rotate.
- Exaggerate the follow-through by allowing your racket head to swing over your nonracket shoulder. *Cue:* Full follow-through.

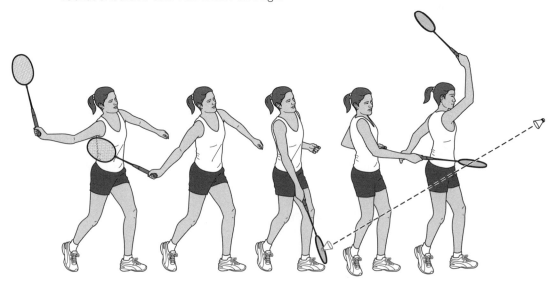

Tactic

- Aim for the rear corners of the service box. *Cue:* Rear corners.
- Keep the shot high and deep. *Cue:* High and deep.

COMMON ERRORS, CAUSES, AND CORRECTIONS

- The student lacks hitting power. *Cause:* The student does not transfer weight from the back foot to the front foot and is not using forearm rotation or wrist action.

Correction: Have the student practice the weight-shifting movement, forearm rotation, and wrist action without the shuttle.

- The student fails to contact the shuttle. *Cause:* The student does not watch the shuttle make contact with the racket. *Correction:* Remind the student to watch the shuttle at contact.

- The student contacts the shuttle too far forward or above the knee. *Cause:* The student has the incorrect grip or preparation position, or the student tosses the shuttle rather than dropping it. *Correction:* Ask the student to double-check the grip, stance, and drop motion on the serve.

- The shuttle does not land in the target area. *Cause:* The student does not follow through after hitting the shot. *Correction:* Make sure the student finishes the swing over the nonracket shoulder.

- The flight path is too low. *Cause:* The racket face is closed at contact. *Correction:* Ask the student to slightly open the racket face at contact.

TASK 9: ALTERNATING FOREHAND SERVES AND RETURNS GAME

PURPOSE

Following are the purposes of the task as related to aspects of skilled performance.

- Technique: In this task, students alternately use the forehand low and high serves.
- Tactic: Students learn how to serve to challenge a receiver and to return alternating serves.
- Agility: Students quickly move the feet into position.

DESCRIPTION

Alternately using low and high serves makes it difficult for the receiver to return or attack the serve. Groups of four students stand on a court (one in each service box). The two students on one side are servers and each has at least five shuttles, if available. Each server hits a low or high serve to their partner from the service court to the appropriate diagonal service court. Encourage students to use serves alternating randomly between low and high serves. The receiving partner returns each serve with any shot. You don't need to explain the skills for returning at this time. Students should switch roles after 5 trials. If students need motivation, award one point to the server when the receiver misses the return shot and one point to the receiver when the server misses the serve or the receiver returns the serve to the opponent's court.

EQUIPMENT

One racket per student and five shuttles per pair

CRITICAL ELEMENTS AND CUES

Technique

- See tasks 7 and 8.

Tactic

- Stand in the service box (about 2 to 3 feet [0.6 to 0.9 meters] behind the front service line near the center line) with your nonracket shoulder pointing toward the net, and decide which serve to perform. *Cue:* Side-hitting stance.
- Land the shot in the opposite and diagonal court. *Cue:* Opposite and diagonal.

Agility

- React to the serve and quickly move into position to return the serve.

COMMON ERRORS, CAUSES, AND CORRECTIONS

- Look for the common errors and their causes and corrections from tasks 7 and 8.

TASK 10: TARGET TOSS AND FOREHAND UNDERHAND CLEAR RETURNS

PURPOSE

Following are the purposes of the task as related to aspects of skilled performance.

- Technique: In this task, students learn the forehand underhand clear and the placement of the shuttle.
- Tactic: When students are in the frontcourt area, they move the shuttle to the opponent's backcourt.
- Agility: Students quickly move the feet into position.

DESCRIPTION

Have four students at a court and divide them into two groups of two. Place one pair of students on each side of the court and designate one student in each pair as the tosser. Set up four hoops deep in each service box as targets (see figure). The student who is not the tosser holds a racket and stands in middle of a service box with their dominant side towards the other service court, and the tosser stands without a racket on the forehand side of the student with the racket in the other service box about 5 feet (1.5 meters) from net with five shuttles (if available). The other pair of students stands in the service boxes on the opposite side of the court in the same setup. The tossers toss a shuttle to their partners, who perform the forehand underhand clear. The students' goals are to use good technique and to place the shuttle in a target. After the shuttles have all been tossed and returned, the partners switch roles and repeat the task. If students need motivation, award one point each time a shuttle lands in a target.

- *Extension 1.* To make the task more challenging, specify which hoop the shuttle should land in.
- *Extension 2.* Ask the student with the racket to stand in the middle of the center line (home position), move and hit the shuttle, and then return to the home position.

EQUIPMENT

Four rackets, ten shuttles (if available), and eight hoops per four students

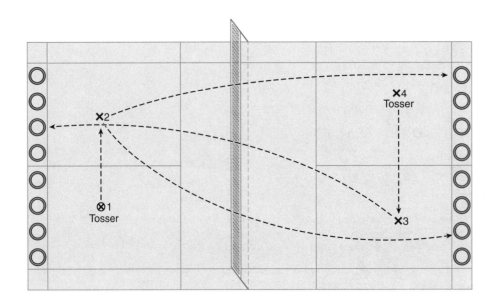

CRITICAL ELEMENTS AND CUES

Technique

- Begin with forehand grip. *Cue:* Forehand grip.
- Extend and lift your racket up with the palm pointed upward when performing the shot. *Cue:* Palm up and swing upward.
- The point of impact should be out in front of the body with the racket leg leading in a lunge position. *Cue:* Lunge.
- Swing the racket upward as the shuttle drops in the hitting area. *Cue:* Wait until the shuttle drops.
- Unlock your wrist as you contact the shuttle, producing a whip action. *Cue:* Whip action.
- Follow through with the racket in the direction of the shuttle's trajectory. *Cue:* Follow through.

Tactic

- The underhand clear is typically played from the frontcourt to an opponent's backcourt. Whether to play it high and deep or flat and crosscourt will depend on the situation at that time and your opponent's positioning on the court.

Agility

- Push with both legs and quickly move back to your home position. *Cue:* Back to home.

COMMON ERRORS, CAUSES, AND CORRECTIONS

- The student has weak wrist action. *Cause:* The student fails to cock the wrist backward before hitting. *Correction:* Have the student practice a whip action with a towel.
- The contact is too low or too high. *Cause:* The student does not wait when dropping the shuttle or makes late contact. *Correction:* Have the student practice contacting the shuttle at the knee level.
- The student is not following through. *Cause:* The student stops swinging after contacting the shuttle. *Correction:* Have the student check the position of the racket arm after each shot.
- The flight path is too low. *Cause:* The student overuses the whip action or has a closed racket face at contact. *Correction:* Check the student's whip action or the racket face at contact.
- The student fails to return to the home position after each shot. *Cause:* The student stays at the hitting position after making a shot. *Correction:* Have the student practice moving back to the home position after hitting the shuttle.

TASK 11: TARGET LOW SERVE AND FOREHAND UNDERHAND CLEAR RETURN

PURPOSE

Following are the purposes of the task as related to aspects of skilled performance.

- Technique: In this task, students learn to perform the forehand underhand clear when returning the shuttle from a low serve.
- Tactic: Students learn where to place the shuttle when returning the low serve.
- Agility: Students quickly move the feet into position.

DESCRIPTION

Have four students at a court and divide them into two groups of two. Place one pair of students on each side of the court and designate one student in each pair as student A and the other as student B. Set up four hoops deep in each service box as targets. Both A students stand in the middle of a diagonal service court on opposite sides of the net and the B students stand in the service court directly opposite their partner. Student B has five shuttles and makes a low serve from the service court to the forehand side of student A straight across from them. Student A then returns the low serve with a forehand underhand clear towards the back of the opposite service court. The students' goals are to use good technique for the forehand underhand clear and place the shuttle towards a target. After five tries, paired students change roles. If students need motivation, award one point each time the shuttle lands in the target.

- *Extension 1.* To make the task more challenging, specify which hoop the shuttle should land in.
- *Extension 2.* Ask student A to stand in the middle of the center of the service court, move and hit the served shuttle, and then return to the home position at the center of the center line (home base).

EQUIPMENT

Four rackets, ten shuttles, and four hoops per four students.

CRITICAL ELEMENTS AND CUES

Technique

- Apply critical elements and cues from tasks 7 and 10.

Agility

- Apply agility points indicated in task 10.

Tactic

- When returning a low serve to the forehand side, use a forehand underhand clear shot that moves the opposing student to the back of the court to give you time to return to your home position.

COMMON ERRORS, CAUSES, AND CORRECTIONS

Look for errors, and their causes and corrections indicated in tasks 7 and 10.

TASK 12: TARGET TOSS AND BACKHAND UNDERHAND CLEAR RETURN

PURPOSE

Following are the purposes of the task as related to aspects of skilled performance.

- Technique: In this task, students learn the backhand underhand clear and placement of the shuttle.
- Agility: Students quickly move the feet into position.

DESCRIPTION

Have four students at a court and divide them into two groups of two. Place one pair of students on each side of the court and designate one student in each pair as student A and the other as student B. Set up four hoops deep in each service box as targets (see figure in task 10). Student A holds a racket and stands in middle of a service box with their nondominant side towards the other service court, and student B stands without a racket on the backhand side of student A in the other service box about 5 feet (1.5 meters) from net with five shuttles (if available). The other pair of students stands in the service boxes on the opposite side of the court in the same setup. Both B students toss a shuttle to their student A, who performs the backhand underhand clear. The students' goals are to use good technique and to place the shuttle in a target. After the shuttles have all been tossed and returned, the partners switch roles and repeat the task. If students need motivation, award one point each time a shuttle lands in a target.

- *Extension 1.* To make the task more challenging, specify which hoop the shuttle should land in.
- *Extension 2.* Ask student A to stand in the middle of the center line (home position), move and hit the shuttle, and then return to the home position.

EQUIPMENT

Four rackets, ten shuttles, and eight hoops per four students

CRITICAL ELEMENTS AND CUES

Technique (see figure)

- Begin with the backhand grip. *Cue:* Backhand grip.
- Extend and lift your racket up with the palm down when performing the shot. *Cues:* Palm down; swing low to high.
- The point of impact should be out in front of the body with the racket leg leading in a lunge position. *Cue:* Lunge.
- Swing the racket upward as the shuttle drops in the hitting area. *Cue:* Wait until the shuttle drops.
- Unlock your wrist as you contact the shuttle, producing a whip action. *Cue:* Whip action.
- Follow through with the racket in the direction of the shuttle's trajectory. *Cue:* Follow through.

Agility

- Push with both legs and quickly move back to your home position. *Cue:* Back to home.

COMMON ERRORS, CAUSES, AND CORRECTIONS

- The student has weak wrist action. *Cause:* The student fails to cock the wrist backward before hitting. *Correction:* Have the student practice a whip action with a towel.
- The contact is too low or too high. *Cause:* The student does not wait when dropping the shuttle or makes late contact. *Correction:* Have the student practice contacting the shuttle at the knee level.
- The student is not following through. *Cause:* The student stops swinging after contacting the shuttle. *Correction:* Have the student check the position of the racket arm after each shot.
- The flight path is too low. *Cause:* The student overuses the whip action or has a closed racket face at contact. *Correction:* Check the student's whip action or the racket face at contact.

- The students fails to return to the home position after each shot. *Cause:* The student stays at the hitting position after making a shot. *Correction:* Have the student practice moving back to the home position after hitting the shuttle.

TASK 13: TARGET LOW SERVE AND BACKHAND UNDERHAND CLEAR RETURN

PURPOSE
Following are the purposes of the task as related to aspects of skilled performance.
- Technique: In this task, students learn to perform the backhand underhand clear when returning the shuttle.
- Tactic: Students learn where to place the shuttle when returning the low serve.
- Agility: Students quickly move the feet into position.

DESCRIPTION
Have four students at each court and divide into two pairs with the pair of students across from each other on each side of the half court with a racket. Set up four hoops deep in each service box as targets. Designate one student in each group as student A and the other as student B. Both A students stand in the middle of a diagonal service court on opposite sides of the net and the B students stand in the service court directly opposite their partner. Student B has five shuttles and makes a low serve from the service court to the backhand side of student A who is straight across from them. Student A then returns the low serve with a backhand underhand clear towards the back of the opposite service court. The students' goals are to use good technique for the backhand underhand clear and place the shuttle towards a target. After five tries, paired students change roles. If students need motivation, award one point each time the shuttle lands in the target.
- *Extension 1.* To make the task more challenging specify which hoop the shuttle should land in.
- *Extension 2.* Ask student A to stand in the middle of the center of the service court, move and hit the served shuttle, and then return to the home position at the center of the center line (home base).

EQUIPMENT
Four rackets, ten shuttles, and four hoops per four students

CRITICAL ELEMENTS AND CUES
Technique
- Apply critical elements and cues from tasks 7 and 12.

Agility
- Apply agility points from task 12.

Tactic
- When returning a low serve to the backhand side, use a backhand underhand clear that moves the opposing student to the back of the court to give you time to return to your home position.

COMMON ERRORS, CAUSES, AND CORRECTIONS
- Look for common errors, causes and corrections from tasks 7 and 12.

TASK 14: LOW SERVE AND ALTERNATING FOREHAND AND BACKHAND UNDERHAND CLEAR RETURNS

PURPOSE

Following are the purposes of the task as related to aspects of skilled performance.

- Technique: In this task, students learn to perform the forehand and backhand underhand clears when returning the shuttle.
- Tactic: Students learn where to place the shuttle when returning the low serve.
- Agility: Students quickly move the feet into position.

DESCRIPTION

At each court, divide groups of four into two pairs; partners set up in diagonal courts with one partner the server and the other partner the returner. Both servers serve and alternate between hitting low serves to their partner's forehand and backhand sides. The partner returns each serve with the appropriate forehand or backhand underhand clear. Partners should switch roles after 10 trials. If students need motivation, award one point to the server when the receiver misses the return shot and one point to the receiver when the server misses the serve. As an extension, ask the receiving partner to stand in the middle of center court (home position), move to hit the shuttle, and then return to the home position.

EQUIPMENT

Four rackets and several shuttles per four students

CRITICAL ELEMENTS AND CUES

- Apply critical elements and cues from tasks 7, 10, and 12.

COMMON ERRORS, CAUSES, AND CORRECTIONS

- Look for common errors and their causes and corrections from tasks 7, 10, and 12.

TASK 15: TARGET TOSS AND FOREHAND OVERHEAD CLEAR RETURN

PURPOSE

Following are the purposes of the task as related to aspects of skilled performance.

- Technique: In this task, students learn the forehand overhead clear and placement of the shuttle.
- Tactic: Students return the shuttle to the back corners of the service court.
- Agility: Students quickly move the feet into position.

DESCRIPTION

Have four students at a court and divide them into two groups of two. Place one pair of students on each side of the court and designate one student in each pair as student A and the other as student B. Set up four hoops deep in each service box as targets (see figure in task 10). Student A holds a racket and stands in middle of a service box with their dominant side toward the other service court, and student B stands without a racket on the forehand side of student A in the other service box about 5 feet (1.5 meters) from net with five shuttles (if available). The other pair of students stands in the service boxes on the opposite side of the court in the same setup. Both B students toss a shuttle to their student A, who performs the forehand overhead clear. The students' goals are to use good technique and to place the shuttle in a target. After the shuttles have all been tossed and returned, the partners switch roles and repeat the task. If students need motivation, award one point each time a shuttle lands in a target.

- *Extension 1.* To make the task more challenging, specify which hoop the shuttle should land in.
- *Extension 2.* Ask student A to stand in the middle of the center line (home position), move and hit the shuttle, and then return to the home position.

EQUIPMENT

Four rackets, ten shuttles, and eight hoops per four students

CRITICAL ELEMENTS AND CUES

Technique (see figure)

- Begin with forehand grip. *Cue:* Forehand grip.
- Assume a sideways hitting stance. *Cue:* Sideways.
- Hold the racket head up. *Cue:* Both arms up.
- Hold the racket arm in a back-scratch position and cock the wrist. *Cues:* Back scratch; cock your wrist.
- Quickly position yourself under the shuttle with balance. *Cue:* Get under the shuttle.
- Swing the racket forward and contact the shuttle as high as possible (like scraping the ceiling). *Cues:* Contact at the highest point; scrape the ceiling.
- Unlock your wrist as you contact the shuttle, producing a whip action. *Cue:* Whip action.
- Follow through with the racket down in the direction of the shuttle's trajectory. *Cue:* Follow through.

Tactic

- The overhead clear is typically played from the frontcourt to an opponent's backcourt. Whether to play it high and deep or flat and crosscourt depends on the situation at that time and the opponent's positioning on the court.
- Move the server backward by aiming for the back service line corners. *Cue:* Back corners.

Agility

- Push with both legs and move back to your home position. *Cue:* Back to home.

COMMON ERRORS, CAUSES, AND CORRECTIONS

- The student lacks hitting power. *Cause:* The student fails to make a full backswing motion in preparation. *Correction:* Ask the student to make a back-scratch motion with the racket before hitting the shuttle.
- The student lacks hitting power. *Cause:* The student fails to use a wrist action at contact. *Correction:* Have the student practice a whip action at contact.
- The student has weak wrist action. *Cause:* The student fails to cock the wrist backward before hitting. *Correction:* Have the student practice a whip action with a towel.
- The contact is too low. *Cause:* The student fails to contact the shuttle at the highest point. *Correction:* Have the student practice contacting the shuttle at the highest point.
- The student is not following through. *Cause:* The student stops swinging after contacting the shuttle. *Correction:* Ask the student to look at the position of the racket arm after each shot.
- The flight path moves from high to low. *Cause:* The student makes contact late or with a closed racket face. *Correction:* Check the student's racket face and location at contact.
- The student fails to return to the home position after each shot. *Cause:* The student stays at the hitting position after making a shot. *Correction:* Have the student practice moving back to the home position after hitting the shuttle.

TASK 16: TARGET HIGH SERVE AND FOREHAND OVERHEAD CLEAR RETURN

PURPOSE

Following are the purposes of the task as related to aspects of skilled performance.

- Technique: In this task, students learn to perform the forehand overhead clear when returning the shuttle.
- Tactic: Students learn where to place the shuttle with the forehand overhead clear.
- Agility: Students quickly move the feet into position.

DESCRIPTION

The forehand overhead stroke is probably the most powerful aspect of a student's game. Have four students at a court and divide them into two groups of two. Place one pair of students on each side of the court and designate one student in each pair as student A and the other as student B. Set up four hoops deep in each service box as targets. Both A students stand in the middle of a diagonal service court on opposite sides of the net and the B students stand in the service court directly opposite their partner. Student B has five shuttles and makes a high serve from the service court to the forehand side of student A straight across from them. Student A then returns the high serve with a forehand overhead clear towards the back of the opposite service court. The students' goals are to use good technique for the forehand overhead clear and place the shuttle towards a target. After five tries, paired students change roles. If students need motivation, award one point each time the shuttle lands in the target.

- *Extension 1.* If the servers struggle with the correct serve, ask students to use a toss to set up the play.
- *Extension 2.* To modify the complexity of the task, you can change the target sizes or locations.
- *Extension 3.* Ask the receiver to stand in the middle of the center box (home position), move and hit the shuttle, and then return to the home position.

EQUIPMENT

Four rackets, ten shuttles, and eight hoops per four students

CRITICAL ELEMENTS AND CUES

Technique

- Apply critical elements and cues from tasks 8 and 15.

Tactic

- When receiving a high serve to the racket side, use a forehand overhead clear to move the server to the back of the court to give you time to return to your home position.

Agility

- Apply agility factors from task 15.

COMMON ERRORS, CAUSES, AND CORRECTIONS

- Look for common errors, and their causes and corrections from tasks 8 and 15.

TASK 17: TARGET TOSS AND BACKHAND OVERHEAD CLEAR RETURN

PURPOSE

Following are the purposes of the task as related to aspects of skilled performance.

- Technique: In this task, students learn the backhand overhead clear and placement of the shuttle.
- Tactic: Students hit the shuttle to the back of the court and move the server back.
- Agility: Students quickly move the feet into position.

DESCRIPTION

Have four students at a court and divide them into two groups of two. Place one pair of students on each side of the court and designate one student in each pair as student A and the other as student B. Set up four hoops deep in each service box as targets (see figure in task 10). Student A holds a racket and stands in middle of a service box with their nondominant side towards the other service court, and student B stands without a racket on the backhand side of student A in the other service box about 5 feet (1.5 meters) from net with five shuttles (if available). The other pair of students stands in the service boxes on the opposite side of the court in the same setup. Both B students toss a shuttle to their student A, who performs the backhand overhead clear. The students' goals are to use good technique and to place the shuttle in a target. After the shuttles have all been tossed and returned, the partners switch roles and repeat the task. If students need motivation, award one point each time a shuttle lands in a target.

- *Extension 1.* To make the task more challenging, specify which hoop the shuttle should land in.
- *Extension 2.* Ask student A to stand in the middle of the center line (home position), move and hit the shuttle, and then return to the home position.

EQUIPMENT

Four rackets, ten shuttles, and eight hoops per four students

CRITICAL ELEMENTS AND CUES

Technique (see figure)

- Begin with the backhand grip. *Cue:* Backhand grip.
- Assume a sideways backhand hitting stance. *Cue:* Sideways.

- Hold the racket arm parallel to the floor with a cocked wrist. *Cues:* Parallel to the floor; cock your wrist.
- Point the racket head downward. *Cue:* Racket downward.
- Quickly position yourself under the shuttle with balance. *Cue:* Get under the shuttle.
- Swing the racket facing up and outward. *Cue:* Swing up and outward.
- Contact the shuttle at the highest point. *Cues:* Contact at the highest point; scrape the ceiling.
- Unlock your wrist as you contact the shuttle, producing a whip action. *Cue:* Whip action.
- Follow through with the racket down in the direction of the shuttle's trajectory. *Cue:* Follow through.

Tactic
- Apply tactic factors from task 15.

Agility
- Apply agility factors from task 15.

COMMON ERRORS, CAUSES, AND CORRECTIONS
- The student lacks hitting power. *Cause:* The student fails to make a full backswing motion in preparation. *Correction:* Ask the student to make a back-scratch motion with a racket before hitting the shuttle.
- The student lacks hitting power. *Cause:* The student fails to use a wrist action at contact. *Correction:* Have the student practice a whip action with a towel.
- The contact is too low. *Cause:* The student fails to contact the shuttle at the highest point.
- *Correction:* Have the student practice contacting the shuttle at the highest point.
- The student is not following through. *Cause:* The student stops swinging after contacting the shuttle. *Correction:* Ask the student to look at the position of the racket arm after each shot.
- The flight path moves from high to low. *Cause:* The student makes contact late or with a closed racket face. *Correction:* Check the student's racket face and location at contact.
- The students fails to return to the home position after each shot. *Cause:* The student stays at the hitting position after making a shot. *Correction:* Have the student practice moving back to the home position after hitting the shuttle.

TASK 18: TARGET HIGH SERVE AND BACKHAND OVERHEAD CLEAR RETURN

PURPOSE

Following are the purposes of the task as related to aspects of skilled performance.

- Technique: In this task, students learn to perform the backhand overhead clear when returning the shuttle. Students also learn placement of the shuttle.
- Tactic: Students learn where to place the shuttle with the backhand overhead clear.
- Agility: Students quickly move the feet into position.

DESCRIPTION

The backhand overhead stroke is used to return the opponent's shots from the backhand side. Have four students at each court and divide into two pairs with the pair of students across from each other on each side of the half court with a racket. Set up four hoops deep in each service box as targets. Designate one student in each group as student A and the other as student B. Both A students stand in the middle of a diagonal service court on opposite sides of the net and the B students stand in the service court directly opposite their partner. Student B has five shuttles and makes a high, friendly, underhand serve from the service court to the backhand side of student A who is straight across from them. Student A then returns the high serve with a backhand overhead clear towards the back of the opposite service court. The students' goals are to use good technique for the backhand overhead clear and place the shuttle towards a target. After five tries, paired students change roles. If students need motivation, award one point each time the shuttle lands in the target.

- *Extension 1.* If the servers struggle with the correct serve, ask students to use a toss to set up the play.
- *Extension 2.* To make the task more challenging specify which hoop the shuttle should land in.
- *Extension 3.* Ask student A to stand in the middle of the center of the service court, move and hit the served shuttle, and then return to the home position at the center of the center line (home base).

EQUIPMENT

Four rackets, ten shuttles, and eight hoops per four students

CRITICAL ELEMENTS AND CUES

Technique

- Apply critical elements and cues from task 17.

Tactic

- When receiving a high serve to the backhand side, use a backhand overhead clear to move the server to the back of the court to give you time to return to your home position.

Agility

- Apply agility points from task 17.

COMMON ERRORS, CAUSES, AND CORRECTIONS

- Look for common errors and their causes and corrections from tasks 8 and 17.

TASK 19: HIGH SERVE AND ALTERNATING FOREHAND AND BACKHAND OVERHEAD CLEAR RETURNS

PURPOSE

Following are the purposes of the task as related to aspects of skilled performance.

- Technique: In this task, students learn to alternately use forehand and backhand overhead clears to return the shuttle.
- Tactic: Students learn where to place the shuttle using forehand or backhand overhead clears in the opposite court so they are not returnable.
- Agility: Students quickly move the feet into position.

DESCRIPTION

At each court, divide groups of four into two pairs; partners set up in diagonal courts with one partner the server and the other partner the returner. Both servers serve and alternate between hitting high serves to their partner's forehand and backhand sides. The partner returns each serve with the appropriate forehand or backhand overhead clear. Partners should switch roles after 10 trials. If students need motivation, award one point to the server when the receiver misses the return shot and one point to the receiver when the server misses the serve. As an extension, ask the receiving partner to stand in the middle of center court (home position), move to hit the shuttle, and then return to the home position.

EQUIPMENT

Four rackets and several shuttles per four students

CRITICAL ELEMENTS AND CUES

Technique

- Apply critical elements and cues from tasks 8, 15, and 17.

Tactic

- Apply tactic factors from tasks 8, 15, and 17.

Agility

- Apply agility factors from tasks 15 and 17.

COMMON ERRORS, CAUSES, AND CORRECTIONS

- Look for common errors, and their causes and corrections from tasks 8, 15, and 17.

TASK 20: TARGET ALTERNATING SERVES AND FOREHAND CLEAR RETURNS

PURPOSE

Following are the purposes of the task as related to aspects of skilled performance.

- Technique: In this task, students learn to alternately use forehand underhand and overhead clears to return low and high shuttles.
- Tactic: Students learn where to place the shuttle using forehand overhead or underhand clears in the opposite court so they are not returnable.
- Agility: Students quickly move the feet into position.

DESCRIPTION

On each court, divide groups of four students into two pairs; partners set up on opposite sides of the court in diagonal service courts with one as the server and one as the returner. The two servers hit either a friendly low, short or a high, deep underhand serve to the partner's forehand side. The partner returns each serve with the appropriate forehand underhand or overhead clear. Encourage students to alternate between low and high serves and forehand underhand or overhead clear returns. Students switch roles after 10 trials. If students need motivation, award one point to the server when the receiver misses the return shot and one point to the receiver when the server misses the serve. As an extension, ask the receiving partner to stand in the middle of center court (home position), move to hit the shuttle, and then return to the home position.

EQUIPMENT

Four rackets and several shuttles per four students

CRITICAL ELEMENTS AND CUES

Technique

- Apply critical elements and cues from tasks 7, 8, 10, and 15.

Tactic

- Apply tactic factors from tasks 7, 8, 10, and 15.

Agility

- Apply agility factors from tasks 10 and 15.

COMMON ERRORS, CAUSES, AND CORRECTIONS

- Look for common errors and their causes and corrections from tasks 7, 8, 10, and 15.

TASK 21: TARGET ALTERNATING SERVES AND BACKHAND CLEAR RETURNS

PURPOSE

Following are the purposes of the task as related to aspects of skilled performance.

- Technique: In this task, students learn to alternately use backhand underhand and overhead clears to return low and high shuttles.
- Tactic: Students learn where to place the shuttle using backhand overhead or underhand clears in the opposite court so they are not returnable.
- Agility: Students quickly move the feet into position.

DESCRIPTION

On each court, divide groups of four students into two pairs; partners set up on opposite sides of the court in diagonal service courts with one as the server and one as the returner. The two servers hit either a friendly low, short or a high, deep underhand serve to the partner's backhand side. The partner returns each serve with the appropriate backhand underhand or overhead clear. Encourage students to alternate between low and high serves and backhand underhand or overhead clear returns. Students switch roles after 10 trials. If students need motivation, award one point to the server when the receiver misses the return shot and one point to the receiver when the server misses the serve. As an extension, ask the receiving partner to stand in the middle of center court (home position), move to hit the shuttle, and then return to the home position.

EQUIPMENT

Four rackets and several shuttles per four students

CRITICAL ELEMENTS AND CUES

Technique

- Apply critical elements and cues from tasks 7, 8, 12, and 17.

Tactic

- Apply tactic factors from tasks 7, 8, and 17.

Agility

- Apply agility factors from tasks 12 and 17.

COMMON ERRORS, CAUSES, AND CORRECTIONS

- Look for common errors and their causes and corrections from tasks 7, 8, 12, and 17.

TASK 22: ALTERNATING SERVES AND CLEAR RETURNS GAME

PURPOSE

Following are the purposes of the task as related to aspects of skilled performance.

- Technique: In this task, students learn to alternately use low and high serves to the opponents' forehand and backhand sides and to alternately use forehand and backhand and overhead and underhand clear returns.
- Tactic: In this task, students place the shuttle using clear shots in the opposite court that are not returnable.
- Agility: Students quickly move the feet into position.

DESCRIPTION

At each net, divide groups of four students into two pairs; partners set up in diagonal courts with one student the server and the other student the returner. Set two hoops as targets at the back of each service court and one cone on each singles sideline 14 feet (4.3 meters) from the net to mark the back third of both halves of the court. One pair's server serves five serves alternately hitting friendly low and short serves or high and deep underhand serves to the partner's forehand or backhand side. The partner returns each serve with the appropriate forehand or backhand underhand clear or the appropriate forehand or backhand overhead clear to the target zone in an attempt to place the shuttle in a target hoop. After the first pair's server completes its five serves, the other pair's server serves from their service courts. After both pairs' first servers have served, the partners change roles. Three points are earned if the shuttle lands within a target and one point is earned if the shuttle lands in the back third of a service court. Total points are kept to determine the pair that wins. Encourage students to alternate serving and returning the shots by changing the right or left side of the service boxes after each round of services.

- *Extension 1.* Have the server send the alternating serves as quickly as possible.
- *Extension 2.* Ask the receiver to stand in the middle of center court (home position), move to hit the shuttle, and then return to the home position.

EQUIPMENT

Four rackets, four cones, and several shuttles per four students

CRITICAL ELEMENTS AND CUES

Technique

- Apply critical elements and cues from tasks 7, 8, 10, 12, 15, and 17.

Tactic

- Apply tactic factors from tasks 7, 8, 10, 15, and 17.

Agility

- Apply agility factors from tasks 10, 12, 15, and 17.

COMMON ERRORS, CAUSES, AND CORRECTIONS

- Look for common errors and their causes and corrections from tasks 7, 8, 10, 12, 15, and 17.

TASK 23: TARGET BACKHAND LOW SERVE

PURPOSE

Following are the purposes of the task as related to aspects of skilled performance.

- Technique: In this task, students learn the backhand low serve and placement of the shuttle.
- Tactic: Students learn to move the receiver forward in the service box.

DESCRIPTION

In this task, focus on the technique of the backhand low serve and placement of the shuttle. Groups of four students stand on a court (one in each service court). Two students on one side of the court have five shuttles and serve their shuttles diagonally across the net into the opposite service court using a backhand low serve. The servers should stand close to the T formed by the short service line and center line. The goal is to land the shot in the opposite diagonal service court. The student standing in that service court collects the shuttles; once all shuttles have been served, the students change roles and that student who has collected the shuttles serves them back from by the T of the service court they are standing in. If students need motivation, award one point each time the shuttle lands in the target area or each time you see students use the correct technique. As an extension, challenge students to use hula hoops placed at the front of the service court as targets.

EQUIPMENT

Four rackets, ten shuttles, and eight hula hoops per four students

CRITICAL ELEMENTS AND CUES

Technique (see figure)

Short Backhand Grip

- Place your thumb against the back bevel on the handle for greater leverage and power. *Cue:* Backhand grip.
- Shorten the grip by placing it nearer to the shaft to increase control. *Cue:* Shorten grip.

Stance

- Stand near the T short service with an up-and-back stance with the weight on the back foot. *Cue:* Weight on the back foot.
- Relax the shoulders, square them towards the opponent. *Cue:* Face the opponent.
- Turn the racket counterclockwise so that the V shape moves towards the body. *Cue:* V in.
- Hold racket with the arm up and across the chest. *Cue:* Elbow up and out.
- Slightly cock the wrist backward. *Cue:* Slightly cock your wrist.
- Hold the shuttle at waist level. *Cue:* Waist.

Action

- Transfer your weight from the back to the front. *Cue:* Transfer weight.
- Contact the shuttle below the waist at thigh level. *Cue:* Below waist.
- Use little or no wrist action. *Cue:* Limit your wrist action.
- Push or guide the shuttle rather than hitting it. *Cue:* Push or guide.
- Finish with the racket upward. *Cue:* Racket up.
- Aim for the white top of the net to keep the shot low and close to net. *Cue:* Low and close.

Tactic

- If the receiver is towards the middle or back of the service court, move the receiver forward by hitting the backhand low serve in the opposite and diagonal front corners of the service box. *Cue:* Front corners.

COMMON ERRORS, CAUSES, AND CORRECTIONS

- The student contacts the shuttle too far forward or above the waist. *Cause:* The student tosses the shuttle rather than dropping it. *Correction:* Have the student practice dropping and hitting the shuttle.
- The student misses the shuttle contact. *Cause:* The student does not watch the shuttle as it contacts the racket. *Correction:* Ask the student to watch the shuttle at contact.
- The trajectory of the shot is too high. *Cause:* The student uses too much wrist action. *Correction:* Have the student limit the wrist action at contact.
- The student makes inconsistent shuttle placements. *Cause:* The follow-through is inconsistent and is either too full or is stopped at contact. *Correction:* Have the student practice a shortened follow-through after the hit.

TASK 24: TARGET BACKHAND FLICK SERVE

PURPOSE

Following are the purposes of the task as related to aspects of skilled performance.

- Technique: In this task, students learn a backhand flick serve and placement of the shuttle.
- Tactic: Students learn to serve the shuttle toward the back of the service court.

DESCRIPTION

In this task, focus on good technique of the backhand flick serve and placement of the shuttle. Groups of four students stand on a court (one in each service court). Two students on one side of the court with five shuttles act as servers while their partners set up in the middle of the diagonal service court as receivers. As the server begins to serve, the receiver moves towards the short serve line and the server then uses the backhand flick serve to hit the shuttles diagonally across the net into the opposite service court. The goal is to land the shot toward the back of the opposite diagonal service court. The student standing in that service court collects the shuttles; once all shuttles have been served, the students change roles and that student who has collected the shuttles serves them back from by the T of the service court they are standing in. If students need motivation, award one point each time the shuttle lands in the target area or each time you see students use the correct technique. As an extension, challenge students to use hula hoops placed at the back of the service court as targets.

EQUIPMENT

Four rackets, ten shuttles, and eight hula hoops per four students

CRITICAL ELEMENTS AND CUES

Technique (see figure)

- Apply short backhand critical elements and cues from task 23.
- Apply stance critical elements and cues from task 23.

Action

- Transfer your weight from the back to the front. *Cue:* Transfer weight.
- Contact the shuttle below the waist at thigh level. *Cue:* Below waist.
- Use a lot of wrist action. *Cue:* Whip your wrist.
- Finish with the racket high. *Cue:* Racket up high.
- Aim to get the shuttle just higher than the opponent can reach. *Cue:* Over and high.

Tactic

- If the receiver is either standing close to the short serve line or is moving towards the net as the serve is beginning then use the backhand flick serve to move the receiver back by serving the shuttle to the opposite diagonal back service box. *Cue:* Back service box.

COMMON ERRORS, CAUSES, AND CORRECTIONS

- The student contacts the shuttle too far forward or above the waist. *Cause:* The student tosses the shuttle rather than dropping it. *Correction:* Have the student practice dropping and hitting the shuttle.
- The student misses the shuttle contact. *Cause:* The student does not watch the shuttle as it contacts the racket. *Correction:* Ask the student to watch the shuttle at contact.

- The shot has a low trajectory. *Cause:* The student uses limited wrist action. *Correction:* Have the student use a quick and full wrist action at contact.
- The student makes inconsistent shuttle placements. *Cause:* The follow-through is inconsistent and the wrist is not quickly and fully released at contact. *Correction:* Have the student practice a shortened follow-through with proper wrist action after the hit.

TASK 25: ALTERNATING BACKHAND SERVES AND RETURNS

PURPOSE

Following are the purposes of the task as related to aspects of skilled performance.
- Technique: In this task, students alternately use the backhand low and flick serves.
- Tactic: Students learn to use backhand low and flick serves that challenge the receiver, and they learn placement of the shuttle.
- Agility: Students quickly move the feet to get into position.

DESCRIPTION

Groups of four students stand on a court (one in each service court). Two students on one side of the court with five shuttles act as servers while their partners set up in the diagonal service court as receivers. The servers hit the backhand low serve or flick serve to the partner from the service court. Encourage the receivers to set up both in the front and middle of the service court so the servers have to alternate between backhand low and flick serves. Alternately using backhand low and flick serves makes it difficult for the receiver to return or attack the serve. The receiver returns each serve with any shot. Students switch roles after 5 trials. If students need motivation, award one point when the receiver misses the return shot, the server misses the serve, or the receiver returns the serve to the opponent's court inbounds.

EQUIPMENT

Four rackets and ten shuttles per four students

CRITICAL ELEMENTS AND CUES

Technique
- Apply critical elements and cues from tasks 23 and 24.

Tactic
- Apply tactic factors from tasks 23 and 24.

COMMON ERRORS, CAUSES, AND CORRECTIONS
- Look for common errors and their causes and corrections from tasks 23 and 24.

TASK 26: ALTERNATING VARIOUS FOREHAND AND BACKHAND SERVES AND RETURNS GAME

PURPOSE

Following are the purposes of the task as related to aspects of skilled performance.
- Technique: In this task, students use various forehand and backhand serving skills.
- Tactic: Students learn to use various forehand and backhand serves that challenge the receiver, and they learn placement of the shuttle.
- Agility: Students quickly move into position.

DESCRIPTION

Groups of four students stand on a court (one in each service court). Two students on one side of the court with five shuttles act as servers while their partners set up in the diagonal service court as receivers. The servers hit alternating forehand and backhand serves to the partner. Encourage the receivers to set up in various areas of the service court so that the servers use various forehand low and high serves and backhand low and flick serves. Alternately using various forehand and backhand low, high, and flick serves makes it difficult for the receiver to return or attack the serve. The receiver returns each serve with any shot. Students switch roles after 5 trials. If students need motivation, award one point when the receiver misses the return shot and when the server misses the serve or the receiver returns the serve to the opponent's court inbounds.

EQUIPMENT

Four rackets and ten shuttles per four students

CRITICAL ELEMENTS AND CUES

Technique

- Apply critical elements and cues from tasks 7, 8, 23, and 24.

Tactic

- Apply tactic factors from tasks 7, 8, 23, and 24.

COMMON ERRORS, CAUSES, AND CORRECTIONS

- Look for common errors and their causes and corrections from tasks 7, 8, 23, and 24.

TASK 27: STRAIGHT FOREHAND UNDERHAND CLEAR RALLY

PURPOSE

Following are the purposes of the task as related to aspects of skilled performance.

- Technique: In this task, students apply the straight forehand underhand clear during a rally.
- Tactic: Students learn to place the shuttle in a straight direction using the straight forehand underhand clear during a rally.
- Agility: Students quickly move their feet to get into position.

DESCRIPTION

Divide groups of four into two pairs; partners set up across from each other on each half court (see figure) with one partner the server and the other the receiver. The rally starts with a forehand low serve directly (not diagonally) across the net to the opposite service court; the receiver returns the serve straight across the net using forehand underhand clears. Part-ners continuously hit the shuttle back and forth using straight forehand underhand clears. After five serves, have partners change the serving and receiving roles. Each student should show the proper technique for the forehand low serve, forehand underhand clears and the placement of the shuttle (back corner of the single sideline). If students need motivation, award one point when the partner misses the shot or hits the shuttle out-of-bounds. As an extension, ask students to return to the middle of the court (home position) after every shot.

EQUIPMENT

Four rackets and two shuttles per four students

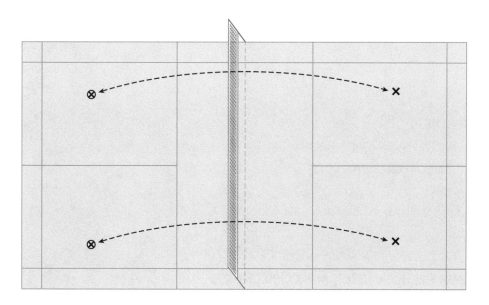

CRITICAL ELEMENTS AND CUES

Technique

- Apply critical elements and cues from tasks 7, 10, and 12.

Tactic

- Apply tactic factors from tasks 7, 10, and 12.
- If an opponent is positioned diagonally from the returner, then the return shot should be straight toward the back corner of the court so that the opponent has to move to return the shot.

Agility

- Apply agility factors from task 10.

COMMON ERRORS, CAUSES, AND CORRECTIONS

- Look for common errors and their causes and corrections from tasks 7, 10, and 12.

TASK 28: STRAIGHT BACKHAND UNDERHAND CLEAR RALLY

PURPOSE

Following are the purposes of the task as related to aspects of skilled performance.

- Technique: In this task, students apply the straight backhand underhand clear during a rally.
- Tactic: Students learn to place the shuttle in a straight direction using the straight backhand underhand clear during a rally.
- Agility: Students quickly move their feet to get into position.

DESCRIPTION

Divide groups of four into two pairs; partners set up across from each other on each half court (see figure in task 27) with one partner the server and the other the receiver. The rally starts with a forehand low serve directly (not diagonally) across the net to the opposite service court. The receiver returns the serve straight across the net using backhand underhand clears. Partners continuously hit the shuttle back and forth using straight backhand underhand clears. After five serves, have partners change the serving and receiving roles. Each student should show the proper technique for the forehand low serve, backhand underhand clears and the placement of the shuttle (back corner of the single sideline). If students need motivation, award one point when the partner misses the shot or hits the shuttle out-of-bounds. As an extension, ask students to return to the middle of the court (home position) after every shot.

EQUIPMENT
Four rackets and two shuttles per four students

CRITICAL ELEMENTS AND CUES

Technique
- Apply critical elements and cues from tasks 12 and 23.

Tactic
- Apply tactic factors from tasks 7, 12, and 27.

COMMON ERRORS, CAUSES, AND CORRECTIONS
- Look for common errors and their causes and corrections from tasks 12 and 23.

TASK 29: ALTERNATING STRAIGHT FOREHAND AND BACKHAND UNDERHAND CLEARS RALLY

PURPOSE
Following are the purposes of the task as related to aspects of skilled performance.
- Technique: In this task, students use alternating straight forehand and backhand underhand clears during a rally.
- Tactic: Students learn where to place the shuttle using the straight forehand and backhand underhand clears during a rally.
- Agility: Students quickly move into position.

DESCRIPTION
Divide groups of four into two pairs; partners set up across from each other on each half court (see figure in task 27) with one partner the server and the other the receiver. The rally starts with a forehand low serve directly (not diagonally) across the net to the opposite service court. The receiver returns the serve straight across the net using the appropriate forehand or backhand underhand clear, and students continuously hit the shuttle by alternating between straight forehand and backhand underhand clears. After 5 trials, have students switch roles between server and receiver. Each student should show the proper technique for the short serve, forehand and backhand underhand clears, and the placement of the shuttle (back corners of the straight single sideline). If students need motivation, award one point when the partner misses the shot or hits the shuttle out-of-bounds. As an extension, ask students to return to the middle of the court (home position) after every shot.

EQUIPMENT
Four rackets and two shuttles per four students

CRITICAL ELEMENTS AND CUES

Technique
- Apply critical errors and cues from tasks 7, 10, and 12.

Tactic
- Apply tactic factors from tasks 7, 10, 12, and 27.

Agility

- Apply agility factors from task 10.

COMMON ERRORS, CAUSES, AND CORRECTIONS

- Look for common errors and their causes and corrections from tasks 7, 10, and 12.

TASK 30: CROSSOVER FOREHAND UNDERHAND CLEAR RALLY

PURPOSE

Following are the purposes of the task as related to aspects of skilled performance.

- Technique: In this task, students use the crossover forehand underhand clear during a rally.
- Tactic: Students learn where to place the shuttle using the crossover forehand underhand clear during a rally.
- Agility: Students quickly move into position.

DESCRIPTION

Divide groups of four into two pairs; partners set up diagonally across from each other on each side of the court (see figure) with one partner the server and the other the receiver. The rally starts with a forehand low serve diagonally across the net to the appropriate service court. The receiver returns the serve diagonally across the net using forehand underhand clears. Partners continuously hit the shuttle back and forth using crossover forehand underhand clears. After five serves, have partners change the serving and receiving roles. Each student should show the proper technique for the forehand low serve, forehand underhand clears, and the placement of the shuttle (back corner of the single sideline). If students need motivation, award one point when the partner misses the shot or hits the shuttle out-of-bounds. As an extension, ask students to return to the middle of the court (home position) after every shot.

EQUIPMENT

Four rackets and two shuttles per four students

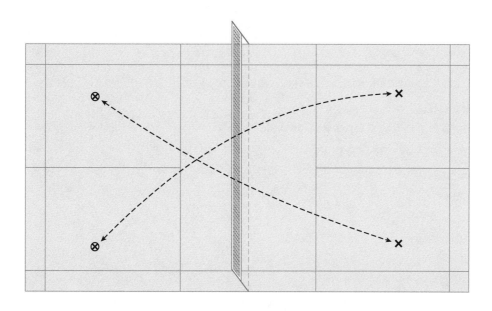

CRITICAL ELEMENTS AND CUES

Technique

- Apply critical elements and cues from tasks 7 and 10.

Tactic

- Apply tactic factors from tasks 7 and 10.
- If an opponent is positioned directly across from the returner, then the return shot should be toward the opposite side of the court so that the opponent has to move to return the shot.

Agility

- Apply agility factors from task 10.

COMMON ERRORS, CAUSES, AND CORRECTIONS

- Look for common errors and their causes and corrections from tasks 7 and 10.

TASK 31: CROSSOVER BACKHAND UNDERHAND CLEAR RALLY

PURPOSE

Following are the purposes of the task as related to aspects of skilled performance.

- Technique: In this task, students use the crossover backhand underhand clear during a rally.
- Tactic: Students learn where to place the shuttle using the crossover backhand underhand clear during a rally.
- Agility: Students quickly move into position.

DESCRIPTION

Divide groups of four into two pairs; partners set up diagonally across from each other on each side of the court (see figure in task 30) with one partner as the server and the other the receiver. The rally starts with a forehand low serve diagonally across the net to the appropriate service court. The receiver returns the serve diagonally across the net using backhand underhand clears. Partners continuously hit the shuttle back and forth using crossover backhand underhand clears. After five serves, have partners change the serving and receiving roles. Each student should show the proper technique for the forehand low serve, backhand underhand clears, and the placement of the shuttle (back corner of the single sideline). If students need motivation, award one point when the partner misses the shot or hits the shuttle out-of-bounds. As an extension, ask students to return to the middle of the court (home position) after every shot.

EQUIPMENT

Four rackets and two shuttles per four students

CRITICAL ELEMENTS AND CUES

Technique

- Apply critical elements and cues from tasks 7 and 12.

Tactic

- Apply tactic factors from tasks 30.

Agility

- Apply agility factors from task 30.

COMMON ERRORS, CAUSES, AND CORRECTIONS

- Look for common errors and their causes and corrections from tasks 7 and 12.

TASK 32: ALTERNATING CROSSOVER FOREHAND AND BACKHAND UNDERHAND CLEARS RALLY

PURPOSE

Following are the purposes of the task as related to aspects of skilled performance.

- Technique: In this task, students use alternating crossover forehand and backhand underhand clears during a rally.
- Tactic: Students learn where to place the shuttle using the crossover forehand and backhand underhand clears during a rally.
- Agility: Students quickly move into position.

DESCRIPTION

Divide groups of four into two pairs; partners set up diagonally across from each other on each side of the court (see figure in task 30) with one partner as the server and the other the receiver. The rally starts with a forehand low serve diagonally across the net to the appropriate service court. The receiver returns the serve diagonally across the net using the appropriate (either forehand or backhand) underhand clear. Partners continuously hit the shuttle back and forth alternating between crossover forehand and backhand underhand clears until the shuttle is not returned using an appropriate underhand clear. After five serves, have partners change the serving and receiving roles. Each student should show the proper technique for the forehand low serve and forehand and backhand underhand clear. If students need motivation, award one point for every successful underhand clear return. As an extension, ask students to return to the middle of the court (home position) after every shot

EQUIPMENT

Four rackets and two shuttles per four students

CRITICAL ELEMENTS AND CUES

Technique

- Apply critical elements and cues from tasks 7, 10, and 12.

Tactic

- Apply tactical factors from tasks 30 and 31.

Agility

- Apply agility factors from tasks 30 and 31.

COMMON ERRORS, CAUSES, AND CORRECTIONS

- Look for common errors and their causes and corrections from tasks 30 and 31.

TASK 33: ALTERNATING STRAIGHT AND CROSSOVER FOREHAND UNDERHAND CLEARS RALLY

PURPOSE

Following are the purposes of the task as related to aspects of skilled performance.

- Technique: In this task, students use alternating straight and crossover forehand underhand clears during a rally.
- Tactic: Students learn where to place the shuttle using the straight and crossover forehand underhand clears during a rally.
- Agility: Students quickly move into position.

DESCRIPTION

Place one member of each group of four in each of the service courts and number them 1 through 4 with students 1 and 2 on one side of the net and 3 and 4 on the other side. The task begins with a forehand low serve by student 1 diagonally across the net to student 3 who returns the serve using a straight forehand underhand clear across the net to student 2. Student 2 returns the shot using a forehand underhand clear crosscourt to student 4 who returns the crosscourt shot to student 1 using a straight forehand underhand clear (see figure). This sequence of forehand underhand clears continues until a shot is missed. After each rally or after a set number of serves, students rotate in a clockwise manner with student 1 going to student 2's position, student 2 to student 3, student 3 to student 4, and student 4 moving to student 1's position as the server. If students need motivation, award one point for every successful forehand underhand clear sequence of four hits. As an extension, ask students to return to the middle of the court (home position) after every shot.

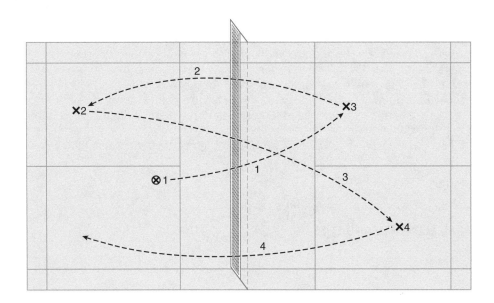

EQUIPMENT

Four rackets and one shuttle per four students

CRITICAL ELEMENTS AND CUES

Technique

- Apply critical elements and cues from tasks 7 and 10.

Tactic

- Apply tactic factors from tasks 7, 10, 27, and 30.

Agility

- Apply agility factors from task 10.

COMMON ERRORS, CAUSES, AND CORRECTIONS

- Look for common errors and their causes and corrections from tasks 7 and 10.

TASK 34: ALTERNATING STRAIGHT AND CROSSOVER BACKHAND UNDERHAND CLEARS RALLY

PURPOSE

Following are the purposes of the task as related to aspects of skilled performance.

- Technique: In this task, students use alternating straight and crossover backhand underhand clears during a rally.
- Tactic: Students learn where to place the shuttle using the straight and crossover backhand underhand clears during a rally.
- Agility: Students quickly move into position.

DESCRIPTION

Place one member of each group of four in each of the service courts and number them 1 through 4 with numbers 1 and 2 on one side of the net and 3 and 4 on the other side. The task begins with a forehand low serve by student 1 diagonally across the net to student 3 who returns the serve using a backhand underhand clear across the net to student 2. Student 2 returns the shot using a backhand underhand clear crosscourt to student 4 who returns the crosscourt shot to student 1 using a straight backhand underhand clear (see figure in task 33). This sequence of backhand underhand clears continues until a shot is missed. After each rally or after a set number of serves, students rotate in a clockwise manner with student 1 going to student 2's position, student 2 to student 3, student 3 to student 4, and student 4 moving to student 1's position as the server. If students need motivation, award one point for every successful backhand underhand clear sequence of four hits. As an extension, ask students to return to the middle of the court (home position) after every shot.

EQUIPMENT

Four rackets and one shuttle per four students

CRITICAL ELEMENTS AND CUES

Technique

- Apply critical elements and cues from tasks 7 and 12.

Tactic

- Apply tactic factors from tasks 7, 10, 28, and 31.

COMMON ERRORS, CAUSES, AND CORRECTIONS

- Look for common errors and their causes and corrections from tasks 7 and 12.

TASK 35: ALTERNATING STRAIGHT AND CROSSOVER FOREHAND AND BACKHAND UNDERHAND CLEARS RALLY

PURPOSE

Following are the purposes of the task as related to aspects of skilled performance.

- Technique: In this task, students use alternating straight and crossover forehand and backhand underhand clears during a rally.
- Tactic: Students learn where to place the shuttle using the straight and crossover forehand and backhand underhand clears during a rally.
- Agility: Students quickly move into position.

DESCRIPTION

Place one member of each group of four in each of the service courts and number them 1 through 4 with numbers 1 and 2 on one side of the net and 3 and 4 on the other side. The task begins with a forehand low serve by student 1 diagonally across the net to student 3 who returns the serve using an appropriate (forehand or backhand) underhand clear across the net to student 2. Student 2 returns the shot using an appropriate underhand clear crosscourt to student 4 who returns the crosscourt shot to student 1 using an appropriate underhand clear (see figure in task 33). This sequence of underhand clears continues until a shot is missed. After each rally or after a set number of serves, students rotate in a clockwise manner with student 1 going to student 2's position, student 2 to student 3, student 3 to student 4, and student 4 moving to student 1's position as the server. If students need motivation, award one point for every successful underhand clear sequence of four hits. As an extension, ask students to return to the middle of the court (home position) after every shot.

EQUIPMENT

Four rackets and one shuttle per four students

CRITICAL ELEMENTS AND CUES

Technique

- Apply critical elements and cues from tasks 7, 10, and 12.

Tactic

- Apply tactic factors from tasks 7, 10, 29, and 32.

Agility

- Apply agility factors from tasks 10, 12, 29, and 32.

COMMON ERRORS, CAUSES, AND CORRECTIONS

- Look for common errors and their causes and corrections from tasks 7, 10, 12, 29, and 32.

TASK 36: STRAIGHT FOREHAND OVERHEAD CLEAR RALLY

PURPOSE

Following are the purposes of the task as related to aspects of skilled performance.

- Technique: In this task, students use the straight forehand overhead clear during a rally.
- Tactic: Students learn where to place the shuttle using the straight forehand overhead clear during a rally.
- Agility: Students quickly move into position.

DESCRIPTION

Divide groups of four into two pairs; partners set up across from each other on each half court (see figure in task 27) with one partner the server and the other the receiver. The rally starts with a forehand high serve directly (not diagonally) across the net to the opposite service court; the receiver returns the serve straight across the net using forehand overhead clears. Partners continuously hit the shuttle back and forth using straight forehand overhead clears. After five serves, have partners change the serving and receiving roles. Each student should show the proper technique for the forehand high serve, forehand overhead clears and the placement of the shuttle (back corner of the single sideline). If students need motivation, award one point when the partner misses the shot or hits the shuttle out-of-bounds. As an extension, ask students to return to the middle of the court (home position) after every shot.

EQUIPMENT

Four rackets and two shuttles per four students

CRITICAL ELEMENTS AND CUES

Technique

- Apply critical elements and cues from tasks 8 and 15.

Tactic

- Apply tactic factors from task 15.
- If an opponent is positioned diagonally from the returner, then the return shot should be straight towards the back corner of the court so that the opponent has to move to return the shot.

Agility

- Apply agility factors from tasks 8 and 15.

COMMON ERRORS, CAUSES, AND CORRECTIONS

- Look for common errors and their causes and corrections from tasks 8 and 15.

TASK 37: STRAIGHT BACKHAND OVERHEAD CLEAR RALLY

PURPOSE

Following are the purposes of the task as related to aspects of skilled performance.

- Technique: In this task, students use the straight backhand overhead clear during a rally.
- Tactic: Students learn where to place the shuttle using the straight backhand overhead clear during a rally.
- Agility: Students quickly move into position.

DESCRIPTION

Divide groups of four into two pairs; partners set up across from each other on each half court (see figure in task 27) with one partner the server and the other the receiver. The rally starts with a forehand high serve directly (not diagonally) across the net to the opposite service court; the receiver returns the serve straight across the net using backhand overhead clears. Partners continuously hit the shuttle back and forth using straight backhand overhead clears. After five serves, have partners change the serving and receiving roles. Each student should show the proper technique for the forehand high serve, backhand overhead clears and the placement of the shuttle (back corner of the single sideline). If students need motivation, award one point when the partner misses the shot or hits the shuttle out-of-bounds. As an extension, ask students to return to the middle of the court (home position) after every shot.

EQUIPMENT

Four rackets and two shuttles per four students

CRITICAL ELEMENTS AND CUES

Technique

- Apply critical elements and cues from tasks 8 and 17.

Tactic

- Apply tactic factors from tasks 8 and 17.

Agility

- Apply agility factors from task 17.

COMMON ERRORS, CAUSES, AND CORRECTIONS

- Look for common errors and their causes and corrections from tasks 8 and 17.

TASK 38: ALTERNATING STRAIGHT FOREHAND AND BACKHAND OVERHEAD CLEARS RALLY

PURPOSE

Following are the purposes of the task as related to aspects of skilled performance.

- Technique: In this task, students use the alternating straight forehand and backhand overhead clears during a rally.
- Tactic: Students learn where to place the shuttle using the straight forehand and backhand overhead clears during a rally.
- Agility: Students quickly move into position.

DESCRIPTION

Divide groups of four into two pairs; partners set up across from each other on each half court (see figure in task 27) with one partner the server and the other the receiver. The rally starts with a forehand high serve directly (not diagonally) across the net to the opposite service court; the receiver returns the serve straight across the net using the appropriate forehand or backhand overhead clear and students continuously hit the shuttle by alternating between straight forehand and backhand overhead clears. After 5 trials, have students switch roles between server and receiver. Each student should show the proper technique for the short serve, forehand and backhand overhead clears and the placement of the shuttle (back corners of the straight single sideline). If students need motivation, award one point when the partner misses the shot or hits the shuttle out-of-bounds. As an extension, ask students to return to the middle of the court (home position) after every shot.

EQUIPMENT

Four rackets and two shuttles per four students

CRITICAL ELEMENTS AND CUES

Technique

- Apply critical elements and cues from tasks 8, 15, and 17.

Tactic

- Apply tactic factors from tasks 8, 15, 17, 36, and 37.

Agility

- Apply agility from tasks 15 and 17.

COMMON ERRORS, CAUSES, AND CORRECTIONS

- Look for common errors and their causes and corrections from tasks 8, 15, and 17.

TASK 39: CROSSOVER FOREHAND OVERHEAD CLEAR RALLY

PURPOSE

Following are the purposes of the task as related to aspects of skilled performance.

- Technique: In this task, students use the crossover forehand overhead clear during a rally.
- Tactic: Students learn where to place the shuttle using the crossover forehand overhead clear during a rally.
- Agility: Students quickly move into position.

DESCRIPTION

Divide groups of four into two pairs; partners set up diagonally across from each other on each side of the court (see figure in task 30) with one partner the server and the other the receiver. The rally starts with a forehand high serve diagonally across the net to the appropriate service court, the receiver returns the serve diagonally across the net using forehand overhead clears. Partners continuously hit the shuttle back and forth using crossover forehand overhead clears. After five serves, have partners change the serving and receiving roles. Each student should show the proper technique for the forehand high serve, forehand overhead clears and the placement of the shuttle (back corner of the single sideline). If students need motivation, award one point when the partner misses the shot or hits the shuttle out-of-bounds. As an extension, ask students to return to the middle of the court (home position) after every shot.

EQUIPMENT

Four rackets and two shuttles per four students

CRITICAL ELEMENTS AND CUES

Technique

- Apply critical elements and cues from tasks 8 and 15.

Tactic

- Apply tactic factors from task 15.
- If an opponent is positioned directly across from the returner, then the return shot should be towards the opposite side of the court so that the opponent has to move to return the shot.

Agility

- Apply agility factors from task 15.

COMMON ERRORS, CAUSES, AND CORRECTIONS

- Look for common errors and their causes and corrections from tasks 8 and 15.

TASK 40: CROSSOVER BACKHAND OVERHEAD CLEAR RALLY

PURPOSE

Following are the purposes of the task as related to aspects of skilled performance.

- Technique: In this task, students use the crossover backhand overhead clear during a rally.
- Tactic: Students learn where to place the shuttle using the crossover backhand overhead clear during a rally.
- Agility: Students quickly move into position.

DESCRIPTION

Divide groups of four into two pairs; partners set up diagonally across from each other on each side of the court (see figure in task 30) with one partner the server and the other the receiver. The rally starts with a forehand high serve diagonally across the net to the appropriate service court; the receiver returns the serve diagonally across the net using backhand overhead clears. Partners continuously hit the shuttle back and forth using crossover backhand overhead clears. After five serves, have partners change the serving and receiving roles. Each student should show the proper technique for the forehand high serve, backhand overhead clears and the placement of the shuttle (back corner of the single sideline). If students need motivation, award one point when the partner misses the shot or hits the shuttle out-of-bounds. As an extension, ask students to return to the middle of the court (home position) after every shot.

EQUIPMENT

Four rackets and two shuttles per four students

CRITICAL ELEMENTS AND CUES

Technique

- Apply critical elements and cues from tasks 17 and 24.

Tactic

- Apply tactic factors from tasks 8 and 17.
- If an opponent is positioned directly across from the returner, then the return shot should be towards the opposite side of the court so that the opponent has to move to return the shot.

Agility

- Apply agility from task 17.

COMMON ERRORS, CAUSES, AND CORRECTIONS

- Look for common errors and their causes and corrections from tasks 17 and 24.

TASK 41: ALTERNATING CROSSOVER FOREHAND AND BACKHAND OVERHEAD CLEARS RALLY

PURPOSE

Following are the purposes of the task as related to aspects of skilled performance.

- Technique: In this task, students use alternating crossover forehand and backhand overhead clears during a rally.
- Tactic: Students learn where to place the shuttle using the crossover forehand and backhand overhead clears during a rally.
- Agility: Students quickly move into position.

DESCRIPTION

Divide groups of four into two pairs; partners set up diagonally across from each other on each side of the court (see figure in task 30) with one partner the server and the other the receiver. The rally starts with a forehand high serve diagonally across the net to the appropriate service court; the receiver returns the serve diagonally across the net using the appropriate (either forehand or backhand) overhead clear. Partners continuously hit the shuttle back and forth alternating between crossover forehand and backhand overhead clears until the shuttle is not returned using an appropriate overhead clear. After five serves, have partners change the serving and receiving roles. Each student should show the proper technique for the forehand high serve and the forehand and backhand overhead clear. If students need motivation, award one point for every successful underhand clear return. As an extension, ask students to return to the middle of the court (home position) after every shot.

EQUIPMENT

Four rackets and two shuttles per four students

CRITICAL ELEMENTS AND CUES

Technique

- Apply critical elements and cues from tasks 8, 15, and 17.

Tactic

- Apply tactic factors from tasks 8, 39, and 40.

Agility

- Apply agility factors from tasks 15 and 17.

COMMON ERRORS, CAUSES, AND CORRECTIONS

- Look for common errors and their causes and corrections from tasks 8, 15, and 17.

TASK 42: ALTERNATING STRAIGHT AND CROSSOVER FOREHAND OVERHEAD CLEARS RALLY

PURPOSE

Following are the purposes of the task as related to aspects of skilled performance.

- Technique: In this task, students use alternating straight and crossover forehand overhead clears during a rally.
- Tactic: Students learn where to place the shuttle using the straight and crossover forehand overhead clears during a rally.
- Agility: Students quickly move into position.

DESCRIPTION

Place one member of each group of four in each of the service courts and number them 1 through 4 with numbers 1 and 2 on one side of the net and 3 and 4 on the other side. The task begins with a forehand high serve by student 1 diagonally across the net to student 3 who returns the serve using a forehand overhead clear across the net to student 2. Student 2 returns the shot using a forehand overhead clear crosscourt to student 4 who returns the crosscourt shot to student 1 using a straight forehand overhead clear (see figure in task 33). This sequence of forehand overhead clears continues until a shot is missed. After each rally or after a set number of serves, students rotate in a clockwise manner with student 1 going to student 2's position, student 2 to student 3, student 3 to student 4, and student 4 moving to student 1's position as the server. If students need motivation, award one point for every successful forehand overhead clear sequence of four hits. As an extension, ask students to return to the middle of the court (home position) after every shot.

EQUIPMENT

Four rackets and one shuttle per four students

CRITICAL ELEMENTS AND CUES

Technique

- Apply critical elements and cues for tasks 8 and 15.

Tactic

- Control and alternate the direction of the forehand overhead clears to move your opponent and set up a scoring opportunity.

Agility

- Apply agility factors from task 15.

COMMON ERRORS, CAUSES, AND CORRECTIONS

- Look for common errors and their causes and corrections from tasks 8 and 15.

TASK 43: ALTERNATING STRAIGHT AND CROSSOVER BACKHAND OVERHEAD CLEARS RALLY

PURPOSE

Following are the purposes of the task as related to aspects of skilled performance.

- Technique: In this task, students use alternating straight and crossover backhand overhead clears during a rally.
- Tactic: Students learn where to place the shuttle using the straight and crossover backhand overhead clears during a rally.
- Agility: Students quickly move into position.

DESCRIPTION

Place one member of each group of four in each of the service courts and number them 1 through 4 with numbers 1 and 2 on one side of the net and 3 and 4 on the other side. The task begins with a forehand high serve by student 1 diagonally across the net to student 3 who returns the serve using a backhand overhead clear across the net to student 2. Student 2 returns the shot using a backhand overhead clear crosscourt to student 4 who returns the crosscourt shot to student 1 using a straight backhand overhead clear (see figure in task 33). This sequence of backhand overhead clears continues until a shot is missed. After each rally or after a set number of serves, students rotate in a clockwise manner with student 1 going to student 2's position, student 2 to student 3, student 3 to student 4, and student 4 moving to student 1's position as the server. If students need motivation, award one point for every successful backhand overhead clear sequence of four hits. As an extension, ask students to return to the middle of the court (home position) after every shot.

EQUIPMENT

Four rackets and one shuttle per four students

CRITICAL ELEMENTS AND CUES

Technique

- Apply critical elements and cues from tasks 8 and 17.

Tactic

- Control and alternate the direction of the backhand overhead clears to move your opponent and set up a scoring opportunity.

Agility

- Apply agility factors from task 17.

COMMON ERRORS, CAUSES, AND CORRECTIONS

- Look for common errors and their causes and corrections from tasks 8 and 17.

TASK 44: ALTERNATING STRAIGHT AND CROSSOVER AND FOREHAND AND BACKHAND OVERHEAD CLEARS RALLY

PURPOSE

Following are the purposes of the task as related to aspects of skilled performance.

- Technique: In this task, students use alternating straight and crossover forehand and backhand overhead clears during a rally.
- Tactic: Students learn where to place the shuttle using the straight and crossover forehand and backhand overhead clears during a rally.
- Agility: Students quickly move into position.

DESCRIPTION

Place one member of each group of four in each of the service courts and number them 1 through 4 with numbers 1 and 2 on one side of the net and 3 and 4 on the other side. The task begins with a forehand high serve by student 1 diagonally across the net to student 3 who returns the serve using an appropriate (forehand or backhand) overhead clear across the net to student 2. Student 2 returns the shot using an appropriate overhead clear crosscourt to student 4 who returns the crosscourt shot to student 1 using an appropriate overhead clear (see figure in task 33). This sequence of overhead clears continues until a shot is missed. After each rally or after a set number of serves, students rotate in a clockwise manner with student 1 going to student 2's position, student 2 to student 3, student 3 to student 4, and student 4 moving to student 1's position as the server. If students need motivation, award one point for every successful overhead clear sequence of four hits. As an extension, ask students to return to the middle of the court (home position) after every shot.

EQUIPMENT

Four rackets and one shuttle per four students

CRITICAL ELEMENTS AND CUES

Technique

- Apply critical elements and cues from tasks 8, 15, and 17.

Tactic

- Combine straight and crossover overhead clears to move the opponent and open up a scoring opportunity.

Agility

- Apply agility factors from tasks 15 and 17.

COMMON ERRORS, CAUSES, AND CORRECTIONS

- Look for common errors and their causes and corrections for tasks 8, 15, and 17.

TASK 45: TARGET LOW SERVE AND FOREHAND UNDERHAND DROP RETURN

PURPOSE

Following are the purposes of the task as related to aspects of skilled performance.

- Technique: In this task, students learn to perform the forehand underhand drop when returning the shuttle.
- Tactic: Students learn where to place the shuttle using the forehand underhand drop.
- Agility: Students quickly move the feet into position.

DESCRIPTION

Groups of four students stand on a court (one in each service box) with two students as servers on one side of the net and two students as receivers on the opposite side. If available, have at least 5 shuttles available for each server. The two servers serve their shuttles diagonally across the net into the appropriate service box using a low serve to their receiver's forehand side. The receiver returns the shuttle using a forehand underhand drop into the opposite forecourt area. Place two hoops on the floor between the short serve line for both service courts and net to serve as targets for the drop shot (four total). The goal is to land the shot in the opposite forecourt area with the targets as an objective. Once all the shuttles have been served and returned, the student serving collects the shuttles and students switch roles. If students need motivation, award one point each time the shuttle lands in a target.

- *Extension 1.* To make the task more challenging, specify which hoop the shuttle should land in.
- *Extension 2.* Ask student receiving the serve to stand in the middle of the center box (home position), move and hit the shuttle, and return to the home position.

EQUIPMENT

Four rackets, four hoops, and ten shuttles per four students

CRITICAL ELEMENTS AND CUES

Technique (see figure)

- Begin with the forehand grip. *Cue:* Forehand grip.
- Quickly get behind the shuttle. *Cue:* Get behind the shuttle.
- To fool your opponent, disguise the drop shot by preparing your racket and body as if you were going to play a forehand underhand clear. *Cue:* Disguise.
- Contact the shuttle out in front of the body with the racket leg leading in a lunge position. *Cue:* Lunge.
- Swing the racket upward in a controlled manner as the shuttle drops in the hitting area. *Cue:* Wait until the shuttle drops.
- Guide or block the shuttle gently. *Cue:* Guide or block.
- Gently follow through with the racket in the direction of the shuttle's trajectory. *Cue:* Gentle follow-through.

Tactic

- If your opponent is in the back court area or on the opposite side of the court, use the drop shot to force your opponent to move to the net for the return.

Agility

- Push with both legs and move back to your home position. *Cue:* Back to home.

COMMON ERRORS, CAUSES, AND CORRECTIONS

- The contact point is too low. *Cause:* The student contacted the shuttle too late. *Correction:* Have the student practice contacting the shuttle before dropping it.
- The shuttle lands in the middle or backcourt. *Cause:* The student does not use a full follow-through motion. *Correction:* Have the student practice gentle follow-throughs.
- The flight path is too low or too high. *Cause:* The racket face is open or closed at contact. *Correction:* Check the student's racket face at contact.
- The student doesn't return to the home position after each shot. *Cause:* The student stays at the hitting position. *Correction:* Have the student practice hitting the shuttle and moving from the home position.

TASK 46: TARGET LOW SERVE AND BACKHAND UNDERHAND DROP RETURN

PURPOSE

Following are the purposes of the task as related to aspects of skilled performance.

- Technique: In this task, students learn to perform the backhand underhand drop when returning the shuttle.
- Tactic: Students learn where to place the shuttle using the backhand underhand drop.
- Agility: Students quickly move the feet into position.

DESCRIPTION

Groups of four students stand on a court (one in each service box) with two students as servers on one side of the net and two students as receivers on the opposite side. If available, have at least 5 shuttles available for each server. The two servers serve their shuttles diagonally across the net into the appropriate service box using a low serve to their receiver's backhand side. The receiver returns the shuttle using a backhand underhand drop into the opposite forecourt area. Place two hoops on the floor between the short serve line for both service courts and net to serve as targets for the drop shot (four total). The goal is to land the shot in the opposite forecourt area with the targets as an objective. Once all the shuttles have been served and returned, the student serving collects the shuttles and students switch roles. If students need motivation, award one point each time the shuttle lands in a target.

- *Extension 1.* To make the task more challenging, specify which hoop the shuttle should land in.
- *Extension 2.* Ask student receiving the serve to stand in the middle of the center box (home position), move and hit the shuttle, and return to the home position.

EQUIPMENT

Four rackets, four hoops, and ten shuttles per four students

CRITICAL ELEMENTS AND CUES

Technique

- Begin with backhand grip. *Cue:* Backhand grip.
- Quickly get behind the shuttle. *Cue:* Get behind the shuttle.
- To fool your opponent, disguise the drop shot by preparing your racket and body as if you were going to play a backhand underhand clear. *Cue:* Disguise.
- Contact the shuttle out in front of the body with the racket leg leading in a lunge position. *Cue:* Lunge.
- Swing the racket upward in a controlled manner as the shuttle drops in the hitting area. *Cue:* Wait until the shuttle drops.
- Guide or block the shuttle gently. *Cue:* Guide or block.
- Gently follow through with the racket in the direction of the shuttle's trajectory. *Cue:* Gentle follow-through.

Tactic

- Use a drop shot to force your opponent to move to the net for the return.

Agility

- Push with both legs and move back to your home position. *Cue:* Back to home.

COMMON ERRORS, CAUSES, AND CORRECTIONS

- Look for the common errors and their causes and corrections for task 45.

TASK 47: FOREHAND AND BACKHAND UNDERHAND DROP RALLY

PURPOSE

Following are the purposes of the task as related to aspects of skilled performance.

- Technique: In this task, students use the forehand and backhand underhand drop shots in a rally.
- Agility: Students quickly move the feet into position.

DESCRIPTION

In this task, the four students on the court are divided into two teams of two with one team on each side of the net. The serving team serves the shuttle using a low serve diagonally across the net into the appropriate service court. The receiving student is standing in the middle of the service court and returns the serve using an appropriate (forehand or backhand) underhand drop shot, and the serving team then tries to return the shuttle also using an appropriate underhand drop shot. The only shots allowed in this rally are forehand and backhand underhand drop shots. After each drop shot, the hitter must return to their home base position. The rally ends when one team either does not get the shuttle over the net and in bounds successfully or a returner uses a shot other than an underhand drop shot to return the shuttle. For motivation, award the team that forces an error with a drop shot a point. Once the rally is completed, the other student on the serving team serves from the other service court to begin another underhand drop rally. After both team members have served, the other team then gets the serve. The task continues until either a set score is obtained or a set amount of time has been completed. The goal of this task is to perform a good underhand drop technique and place the shuttle in the near forecourt area.

EQUIPMENT

Four rackets and one shuttle per four students

CRITICAL ELEMENTS AND CUES

Technique

- Apply critical elements and cues from tasks 7, 23, 45, and 46.

Agility

- Apply agility factors from tasks 45 and 46.

COMMON ERRORS, CAUSES, AND CORRECTIONS

- Look for common errors and their causes and corrections from tasks 7, 23, 45, and 46.

TASK 48: TARGET HIGH SERVE AND FOREHAND OVERHEAD DROP RETURN

PURPOSE

Following are the purposes of the task as related to aspects of skilled performance.

- Technique: In this task, students learn to perform the forehand overhead drop when returning the shuttle.
- Tactic: Students learn where to place the shuttle using the forehand overhead drop.
- Agility: Students quickly move the feet into position.

DESCRIPTION

Groups of four students stand on a court (one in each service box) with two students as servers on one side of the net and two students as receivers on the opposite side. If available, have at least 5 shuttles available for each server. The two servers serve their shuttles diagonally across the net into the appropriate service box using a high serve to their receiver's forehand side. The receiver returns the shuttle using a forehand overhead drop into the opposite forecourt area. Place two hoops on the floor between the short serve line for both service courts and net to serve as targets for the drop shot (four total). The goal is to land the shot in the opposite forecourt area with the targets as an objective. Once all the shuttles have been served and returned, the student serving collects the shuttles and students switch roles. If students need motivation, award one point each time the shuttle lands in a target.

- *Extension 1.* To make the task more challenging, specify which hoop the shuttle should land in.
- *Extension 2.* Ask student receiving the serve to stand in the middle of the center box (home position), move and hit the shuttle, and return to the home position.
- *Extension 3.* Ask student receiving the serve to change the speed of the shot (slow drop to fast drop).

EQUIPMENT

Four rackets, four hoops, and ten shuttles per four students

CRITICAL ELEMENTS AND CUES

Technique: Forehand Overhead Drop (see figure)

- Begin with the forehand grip. *Cue:* Forehand grip.
- Turn your body sideways. *Cue:* Sideways.
- Disguise the shot by making the racket setup and backswing look like how you would play a forehand overhead clear. *Cue:* Disguise.
- Shift your weight from back to front. *Cue:* Shift your weight.
- Contact the shuttle as high as possible by straightening your elbow. *Cue:* Straighten elbow.
- Slice or tap the shuttle by using little wrist action to reduce the racket head speed. *Cue:* Tap.
- The point of impact should be above the racket shoulder for the slow shot and farther out in front of the body for the fast shot. *Cue:* Above and out front.
- Gently follow through with the racket in the direction of the shuttle's trajectory. *Cue:* Gentle follow-through.

Tactic

- For the slow drop shot, if the opponent is either in the back court or on the opposite side of the court aim for the forecourt as close to the net as possible. *Cue:* Close to the net.
- If the opponent is on one side then use the fast drop shot and aim for the middle court toward the opposite side. *Cue:* Middle sides.

Agility

- Push with both legs and move back to your base position. *Cue:* Back to base.

COMMON ERRORS, CAUSES, AND CORRECTIONS

- The shuttle hits the net. *Cause:* The student contacts the shuttle too late, which results in the racket head contacting the shuttle too low. *Correction:* Have the student practice contacting the shuttle as high as possible.
- The shuttle lands in the middle of the court. *Cause:* The student hits the shuttle too hard. *Correction:* Ask the student to practice tapping the shuttle with a gentle follow-through, aiming for the forecourt area.
- The flight path is too low or too high each time. *Cause:* The student has inconsistent contact points or the racket face is open or closed at contact. *Correction:* Check the student's contact points and racket face at contact.
- The student doesn't return to the home position after each shot. *Cause:* The student stays at the hitting position. *Correction:* Have students practice hitting the shuttle and moving from the home position.

TASK 49: TARGET HIGH SERVE AND BACKHAND OVERHEAD DROP RETURN

PURPOSE

Following are the purposes of the task as related to aspects of skilled performance.

- Technique: In this task, students learn to perform a backhand overhead drop when returning the shuttle.
- Tactic: Students learn where to place the shuttle using the backhand overhead drop.
- Agility: Students quickly move the feet into position.

DESCRIPTION

Groups of four students stand on a court (one in each service box) with two students as servers on one side of the net and two students as receivers on the opposite side. If available, have at least 5 shuttles available for each server. The two servers serve their shuttles diagonally across the net into the appropriate service box using a high serve to their receiver's backhand side. The receiver returns the shuttle using a backhand overhead drop into the opposite forecourt area. Place two hoops on the floor between the short serve line for both service courts and net to serve as targets for the drop shot (four total). The goal is to land the shot in the opposite forecourt area with the targets as an objective. Once all the shuttles have been served and returned, the student serving collects the shuttles and students switch roles. If students need motivation, award one point each time the shuttle lands in a target.

- *Extension 1.* To make the task more challenging, specify which hoop the shuttle should land in.
- *Extension 2.* Ask student receiving the serve to stand in the middle of the center box (home position), move and hit the shuttle, and return to the home position.
- *Extension 3.* Ask student receiving the serve to change the speed of the shot (slow drop to fast drop).

EQUIPMENT

Four rackets, four hoops, and ten shuttles per four students

CRITICAL ELEMENTS AND CUES

Technique: Backhand Overhead Drop (see figure)

- Begin with the backhand grip. *Cue:* Backhand grip.
- Turn your body sideways. *Cue:* Sideways.
- Step with the racket side foot towards the back corner of the court turning your back to the net. *Cue:* Step to the corner.
- Disguise the shot by making the racket setup and backswing look like how you would play a backhand overhead clear. *Cue:* Disguise.
- The point of impact should be in front of your body and as high as possible. *Cue:* Contact in front and high.
- Angle your racket face to the direction of your shot. *Cue:* Racket face to target.
- At contact, snap the wrist. *Cue:* Snap the wrist.
- Guide the shuttle by hitting it gently and smoothly. *Cue:* Gently and smoothly.
- Gently follow through with the racket in the direction of the shuttle's trajectory. *Cue:* Gentle follow-through.

Tactic

- Apply tactic factors from task 48.

Agility

- Apply agility factors from task 48.

COMMON ERRORS, CAUSES, AND CORRECTIONS

- The shuttle hits the net. *Cause:* The student contacts the shuttle too far out in front of the shoulder. *Correction:* Have the student practice contacting the shuttle at the highest point above the shoulder by pretending to scrape the ceiling with the racket.

- The shuttle goes too high. *Cause:* The student does not move back quick enough to get fully behind the shuttle. *Correction:* Have the student practice shuffling back towards the back corner.
- The student doesn't return to the home position after each shot. *Cause:* The student stays at the hitting position. *Correction:* Have the student practice hitting the shuttle and moving from the home position.

TASK 50: HIGH SERVE AND FOREHAND AND BACKHAND OVERHEAD DROP RALLY

PURPOSE
Following are the purposes of the task as related to aspects of skilled performance.
- Technique: In this task, students learn to perform the forehand and backhand overhead drops when returning the shuttle.
- Tactic: Students learn which overhead drop to use to return the shuttle.
- Agility: Students quickly move the feet into position.

DESCRIPTION
Divide groups of four into two pairs; partners set up across from each other on half the court with one as the server and the other as the receiver. The servers serve the shuttle using a high serve straight across the net into the opposite service court. The receiving student is standing in the middle of the service court and returns the serve using an appropriate (forehand or backhand) overhead drop shot and the server then tries to return the shuttle also using an appropriate overhead drop shot. The only shots allowed in this rally are forehand and backhand overhead drop shots. After each drop shot, the hitter must return to their home base position. The rally ends when one team either does not get the shuttle over the net and in bounds successfully or a returner uses a shot other than an overhead drop to return the shuttle. For motivation, award a point to the partner that forces an error with a drop shot. Once the rally is completed, the partners switch roles and the new server serves from the side of the court they are on to begin another overhead drop rally. The task continues until either a set score is obtained or a set amount of time has been completed. The goal of this task is to perform a good overhead drop technique and place the shuttle in the near forecourt area.

EQUIPMENT
Four rackets and several shuttles per four students

CRITICAL ELEMENTS AND CUES
Technique
- Apply critical elements and cues for tasks 8, 48, and 49.

Tactic
- Apply tactic factors for tasks 8, 48, and 49.

Agility
- Apply agility factors for tasks 48 and 49.

COMMON ERRORS, CAUSES, AND CORRECTIONS
- Look for common errors and their causes and corrections for tasks 8, 48, and 49.

TASK 51: STRAIGHT FOREHAND OVERHEAD DROP AND UNDERHAND CLEAR RALLY

PURPOSE

Following are the purposes of the task as related to aspects of skilled performance.

- Technique: In this task, students use the straight forehand overhead drop and the forehand underhand clear during a rally.
- Tactic: Students learn that an underhand clear is an effective shot for returning a drop shot.
- Agility: Students quickly move into position.
- Fair play: All shots are friendly.

DESCRIPTION

Divide groups of four into two pairs; partners set up in the service courts directly across the net from each other with one partner the server and the other partner the receiver. Each server starts a rally with a straight forehand high serve directly across the net to the receiver. The receiver returns the serve with a forehand overhead drop. The server then returns the drop shot using an underhand clear shot. For this rally, the partner who receives the serve always returns the shuttle using a forehand overhead drop and the partner who served always returns the shuttle using an underhand clear. Each student should show the proper technique for the forehand underhand clear, the forehand overhead drop, and the placement of the shuttle (backcourt close to the single end line for the forehand underhand clear and forecourt close to the net for the forehand overhead drop). After each rally, students switch shots. If students need motivation, award one point when the partner misses the designated shot or hits the shuttle out-of-bounds. As an extension, ask students to return to the middle of the court (home position) after every shot.

EQUIPMENT

Four rackets and two shuttles per four students

CRITICAL ELEMENTS AND CUES

Technique

- Apply critical elements and cues for tasks 10 and 48.

Tactic

- Attempt a drop shot when the receiver is in the backcourt. When returning a drop shot, the underhand clear gives you time to return to your home base and be prepared for the return shot.

Agility

- Apply agility factors for tasks 10 and 48.

Fair Play

- All shots are friendly; the goal is a continuous rally.

COMMON ERRORS, CAUSES, AND CORRECTIONS

- Look for common errors and their causes and corrections for tasks 10 and 48.

TASK 52: STRAIGHT BACKHAND OVERHEAD DROP AND UNDERHAND CLEAR RALLY

PURPOSE

Following are the purposes of the task as related to aspects of skilled performance.

- Technique: In this task, students use the straight backhand overhead drop and the backhand underhand clear during a rally.
- Tactic: Students learn that an underhand clear is an effective shot for returning a drop shot.
- Agility: Students quickly move into position.
- Fair play: Students make friendly shots.

DESCRIPTION

Divide groups of four into two pairs; partners set up in the service courts directly across the net from each other with one partner the server and the other partner the receiver. Each server starts a rally with a straight forehand high serve directly across the net to the receiver. The receiver returns the serve with a backhand overhead drop. The server then returns the drop shot using an underhand clear shot. For this rally, the partner who receives the serve always returns the shuttle using a backhand overhead drop and the partner who served always returns the shuttle using an underhand clear. Each student should show the proper technique for the backhand underhand clear, the backhand overhead drop, and the placement of the shuttle (backcourt close to the single end line for the backhand underhand clear and forecourt close to the net for the backhand overhead drop). After each rally, students switch shots. If students need motivation, award one point when the partner misses the designated shot or hits the shuttle out-of-bounds. As an extension, ask students to return to the middle of the court (home position) after every shot.

EQUIPMENT

Four rackets and two shuttles per four students

CRITICAL ELEMENTS AND CUES

Technique

- Apply critical elements and cues for tasks 8, 12, and 49.

Tactic

- Apply tactic factors for task 51.

Agility

- Apply agility factors for tasks 12 and 49.

Fair Play

- Apply fair play factor for task 51.

COMMON ERRORS, CAUSES, AND CORRECTIONS

- Look for common errors and their causes and corrections for tasks 12 and 49.

TASK 53: ALTERNATING STRAIGHT OVERHEAD DROPS AND STRAIGHT UNDERHAND CLEARS RALLY

PURPOSE

Following are the purposes of the task as related to aspects of skilled performance.

- Technique: In this task, students use alternating straight forehand and backhand overhead drops and straight forehand and backhand underhand clears during a rally.
- Tactic: Students learn where to place the shuttle using the straight forehand and backhand overhead drops and straight forehand and backhand underhand clears during a rally.
- Agility: Students quickly move into position.
- Fair play: Students make friendly shots.

DESCRIPTION

Divide groups of four into two pairs; partners set up in the service courts directly across the net from each other with one partner the server and the other partner the receiver. Each server starts a rally with a straight forehand high serve directly across the net to the receiver. The receiver returns the serve with an appropriate overhead drop (forehand or backhand). The server then returns the drop shot using an appropriate clear shot (forehand or backhand). For this rally, the partner who receives the serve always returns the shuttle using an overhead drop and the partner who served always returns the shuttle using an underhand clear. Each student should show the proper technique for the underhand clears, the overhead drops, and the placement of the shuttle (backcourt close to the single end line for the underhand clears and forecourt close to the net for the overhead drops). After each rally, students switch shots. If students need motivation, award one point when the partner misses the designated shot or hits the shuttle out-of-bounds. As an extension, ask students to return to the middle of the court (home position) after every shot.

EQUIPMENT

Four rackets and two shuttles per four students

CRITICAL ELEMENTS AND CUES

Technique

- Apply critical elements and cues for tasks 8, 10, 12, 48, and 49.

Tactic

- Apply tactic factors for tasks 8, 10, 48, and 49.

Agility

- Apply agility factors for tasks 10, 12, 48, and 49.

Fair Play

- Apply fair play factor from task 51.

COMMON ERRORS, CAUSES, AND CORRECTIONS

- Look for common errors and their causes and corrections for tasks 10, 12, 48, and 49.

TASK 54: CROSSOVER FOREHAND OVERHEAD DROP AND UNDERHAND CLEAR RALLY

PURPOSE

Following are the purposes of the task as related to aspects of skilled performance.

- Technique: In this task, students use the crossover forehand overhead drop and the forehand underhand clear during a rally.
- Tactic: Students learn where to place the shuttle using the crossover forehand overhead drop and forehand underhand clear during a rally.
- Agility: Students quickly move into position.
- Fair play: Students make friendly shots.

DESCRIPTION

Divide groups of four into two pairs; the partners for each pair set up across from each other diagonally on the court with one side designated as the serving side and the other side designated as the receiving side. The rally begins with the two servers serving a crossover forehand high serve. The receiving students on one side of the net hit their shuttles using the crossover forehand overhead drop to their partners, who hit the shuttles back using the crossover forehand underhand clear. The student that serves always returns the shuttle using a crossover forehand underhand clear while the receiver always returns the shuttle using a crossover forehand overhead drop. After each rally, students switch roles. Each student should show the proper technique for the forehand underhand clear, the forehand overhead drop, and the placement of the shuttle (backcourt close to the single end line for the forehand underhand clear and forecourt close to the net for the forehand overhead drop). If students need motivation, award one point when the partner misses the shot or hits the shuttle out-of-bounds. As an extension, ask students to return to the middle of the court (home position) after every shot.

EQUIPMENT

Four rackets and two shuttles per four students

CRITICAL ELEMENTS AND CUES

Technique

- Apply critical elements and cues for tasks 8, 10, and 48.

Tactic

- Apply tactic factors for tasks 8, 10, and 48.

Agility

- Apply agility factors for tasks 10 and 48.

Fair Play

- Apply fair play factor from task 51.

COMMON ERRORS, CAUSES, AND CORRECTIONS

- Look for common errors and their causes and corrections for tasks 8, 10, and 48.

TASK 55: CROSSOVER BACKHAND OVERHEAD DROP AND UNDERHAND CLEAR RALLY

PURPOSE

Following are the purposes of the task as related to aspects of skilled performance.

- Technique: In this task, students use the crossover backhand overhead drop and the backhand underhand clear during a rally.
- Tactic: Students learn where to place the shuttle using each crossover backhand overhead drop and crossover backhand underhand clear during a rally.
- Agility: Students quickly move into position.
- Fair play: Students make friendly shots.

DESCRIPTION

Divide groups of four into two pairs; the partners for each pair set up across from each other diagonally on the court with one side designated as the serving side and the other side designated as the receiving side. The rally begins with the two servers serving a crossover forehand high serve. The receiving students on one side of the net hit their shuttles using the crossover backhand overhead drop to their partners, who hit the shuttles back using the crossover backhand underhand clear. The student that served always returns the shuttle using a crossover backhand underhand clear while the receiver always returns the shuttle using a crossover backhand overhead drop. After each rally, students switch roles. Each student should show the proper technique for the backhand underhand clear, the backhand overhead drop, and the placement of the shuttle (backcourt close to the single end line for the backhand underhand clear and forecourt close to the net for the backhand overhead drop). If students need motivation, award one point when the partner misses the shot or hits the shuttle out-of-bounds. As an extension, ask students to return to the middle of the court (home position) after every shot.

EQUIPMENT

Four rackets and two shuttles per four students

CRITICAL ELEMENTS AND CUES

Technique

- Apply critical elements and cues for tasks 8, 12, and 49.

Tactic

- Apply tactic factors for tasks 8 and 49.

Agility

- Apply agility factors for tasks 12 and 49.

Fair Play

- Apply fair play factor from task 51.

COMMON ERRORS, CAUSES, AND CORRECTIONS

- Look for common errors and their causes and corrections for tasks 18, 12 and 49.

TASK 56: ALTERNATING CROSSOVER OVERHEAD DROPS AND CROSSOVER UNDERHAND CLEARS RALLY

PURPOSE

Following are the purposes of the task as related to aspects of skilled performance.

- Technique: In this task, students use alternating crossover forehand and backhand overhead drops and crossover forehand and backhand underhand clears during a rally.
- Tactic: Students learn where to place the shuttle using the crossover forehand and backhand overhead drops and crossover forehand and backhand underhand clears during a rally.
- Agility: Students quickly move into position.
- Fair play: Students make friendly shots.

DESCRIPTION

Divide groups of four into two pairs; the partners for each pair set up across from each other diagonally on the court with one side designated as the serving side and the other side designated as the receiving side. The rally begins with the two servers serving a crossover forehand high serve. The receiving students on one side of the net hit their shuttles using the appropriate crossover overhead (forehand or backhand) drop to their partners, who hit the shuttles back using the appropriate crossover underhand clear (forehand or backhand). The student that served always returns the shuttle using a crossover underhand clear while the receiver always returns the shuttle using a crossover overhead drop. After each rally, students switch roles. Each student should show the proper technique for the underhand clears, the overhead drops, and the placement of the shuttle (backcourt close to the single end line for the underhand clear and forecourt close to the net for the overhead drop). If students need motivation, award one point when the partner misses the shot or hits the shuttle out-of-bounds. As an extension, ask students to return to the middle of the court (home position) after every shot.

EQUIPMENT

Four rackets and two shuttles per four students

CRITICAL ELEMENTS AND CUES

Technique

- Apply critical elements and cues for tasks 8, 10, 12, 48, and 49.

Tactic

- Apply tactic factors for tasks 8, 10, 12, 48, and 49.

Agility

- Apply agility factors for tasks 10, 12, 48, and 49.

Fair Play

- Apply fair play factor for task 51.

COMMON ERRORS, CAUSES, AND CORRECTIONS

- Look for common errors and their causes and corrections for tasks 8, 10, 12, 48, and 49.

TASK 57: TARGET LOW SERVE AND PUSH RETURN

PURPOSE

Following are the purposes of the task as related to aspects of skilled performance.

- Technique: In this task, students learn to perform the push shot when returning the oncoming low serve.
- Tactic: Students learn how to use the forehand and backhand push shots in a game play.
- Agility: Students quickly move into position.

DESCRIPTION

Divide groups of four into two pairs; partners set up across from each other on the court with one partner as the server, who has five shuttles, and the other partner as the receiver. The two servers make either a forehand or backhand low serve to their receiver. The receiver performs a forehand or backhand push shot to return the serve. The receiver's goal is to hit the shuttle into the backcourt area. Student switch roles after the five shuttles have been served. As an extension, set up four hoops as targets in the backcourt and ask students to hit a specific target. If students need motivation, award one point when the student successfully hits the target.

EQUIPMENT

Four rackets, four hoops, and ten shuttles per four students

CRITICAL ELEMENTS AND CUES

Technique: Push Return (see figure)

- For forehand push shot, use a forehand grip. *Cue:* Forehand grip.
- For backhand push shot, use a backhand grip. *Cue:* Backhand grip.
- Shorten your grip. *Cue:* Shorten grip.
- Push the shuttle in front of the body. *Cue:* Push in front of you.
- Use a wrist snap at contact. *Cue:* Wrist snap.
- Keep the shuttle as low as possible. *Cue:* Hit as low as possible.
- Move your racket leg in a lunge position at contact. *Cue:* Lunge.
- Gently follow through with the racket in the direction of the shuttle's trajectory. *Cue:* Gentle follow-through.

Tactic

- Aim for the opposite backcourt. *Cue:* Backcourt.

Agility

- Push with both legs and move back to your base position. *Cue:* Back to base.

COMMON ERRORS, CAUSES, AND CORRECTIONS

- The student has a weak swing. *Cause:* The student doesn't use a wrist snap at contact or has weak wrist action. *Correction:* Ask the student to practice a quick wrist action at contact.
- The student misses the shuttle. *Cause:* The student is not in the ready position before hitting the shuttle or is not looking at the shuttle. *Correction:* Remind the student to be ready for hitting in an up-and-back stance with the eyes on the shuttle at contact.
- Look for low serve common errors and their causes and corrections for tasks 7 and 23.

TASK 58: TARGET HIGH SERVE AND FOREHAND SMASH RETURN

PURPOSE

Following are the purposes of the task as related to aspects of skilled performance.

- Technique: In this task, students learn to perform the forehand smash when returning the shuttle.
- Tactic: Students learn where to place the shuttle when using the forehand smash.
- Agility: Students quickly move into position.
- Fair play: Students begin the task with a friendly serve.

DESCRIPTION

Divide groups of four into two pairs; partners set up across from each other on the court with one as the server and the other as the receiver. Set up two hoops along both sidelines with one at the short serve line and the other halfway between the short serve line and the doubles long serve line. The servers stand next to the center line with five shuttle each and makes a forehand high serve to the partner who is straight across from them. The receiver is in the middle of the service court and returns the serve with a forehand overhead smash towards the target areas. Students switch roles after five trials. As an extension, change the size and location of the targets. If students need motivation, award one point each time the shuttle lands in a target area.

EQUIPMENT

Four rackets, four hoops, and several shuttles per four students

CRITICAL ELEMENTS AND CUES

Technique

- Assume the ready position. *Cue:* Ready.
- Use a forehand grip. *Cue:* Forehand grip.
- Stand in a sideways hitting stance. *Cue:* Sideways.
- Hold the racket arm up with a cocked wrist. *Cue:* Racket up and cocked.
- Use a strong throwing action as if you are going to throw your racket high and forward through the air (but don't let go of the racket!). *Cue:* Racket up and out.
- Contact the shuttle as high as possible with the racket face down. *Cue:* Contact high with face slightly down.
- Keep your balance. *Cue:* Balance.
- Reach with your racket leg in a lunge position. *Cue:* Lunge.

- Unlock your wrist as you contact the shuttle, producing a powerful swing. *Cue:* Unlock your wrist.
- Follow through with the racket down in the direction of the shuttle's trajectory. *Cue:* Follow-through.
- Aim for a spot on the court low and away from your opponent. *Cue:* Low and away.

Tactic

- The smash is a main point-getting shot that gives your opponent very little time to prepare for or return the shot. Beginners should use the smash when in the front half of the court and you feel the opponent is not in a good position to return the smash.

Agility

- Push with both legs and move back to your base position. *Cue:* Back to base.

Fair Play

- Make the initial high serve friendly so the partner can attempt the smash.

COMMON ERRORS, CAUSES, AND CORRECTIONS

- The student has a weak swing. *Cause:* The student uses a weak wrist action or there is no backswing. *Correction:* Have the student practice using a wrist snap and back-scratch position before hitting.
- The flight path is too straight. *Cause:* The student contacts the shuttle low or fails to make the racket face down at contact. *Correction:* Ask the student to check the contact and make sure the racket face is down at contact.
- The student doesn't return to the base position after each shot. *Cause:* The student stays in the hitting position. *Correction:* Have the student practice hitting the shuttle and moving from the base position.

TASK 59: FOREHAND SMASH AND RETURN GAME

PURPOSE

Following are the purposes of the task as related to aspects of skilled performance.

- Technique: In this task, students use the forehand smash and return shots during a game.
- Tactic: Students use the forehand smash to try and score.
- Agility: Students quickly move into position.
- Fair play: Students begin the task with a friendly serve.

DESCRIPTION

Divide groups of four into two pairs; partners set up across from each other on half the court with one as the server and the other as the receiver. The servers serve the shuttle using a high serve straight across the net into the opposite service court. The receiving student is standing in the middle of the service court and returns the serve using a smash, and the server team then tries to return the shuttle also using an appropriate underhand clear or drop. The only shots allowed in this rally are the smash by the receiver and underhand clears or drops by the server. After each shot, the hitters must return to their home base position. The rally ends when one partner either does not get the shuttle over the net and in bounds successfully or a returner uses a shot other than the prescribed shot to return the shuttle. For motivation award the partner that forces an error with a smash. Once the rally is completed, the partners switch roles and the partner serves from the side of the net they are on. The task continues until either a set score is obtained or a set amount of time has been completed. The goal of this task is to perform a good smash technique and place the shuttle in an area that the return cannot be made from.

EQUIPMENT

Four rackets and two shuttles per four students

CRITICAL ELEMENTS AND CUES

Technique

- Apply critical elements and cues from task 58.

Tactic

- Apply tactic factors from task 58.

Agility

- Apply agility factors from task 58.

Fair Play

- Apply fair play factor from task 58.

COMMON ERRORS, CAUSES, AND CORRECTIONS

- Pairs cannot keep their shots on their half of the court. *Cause:* The students cannot control the direction of their shots. *Correction:* While the structure of the task is meant to keep all four students active, allow one pair to play using the entire court while the other playing pair is off to the side. Rotate pairs in after both partners have served one time.
- Look for common errors and their causes and corrections for task 58.

TASK 60: ATTACKING IN THE UP-AND-BACK POSITION IN DOUBLES

PURPOSE

Following are the purposes of the task as related to aspects of skilled performance.

- Technique: In this task, students apply attacking shots in doubles from an up-and-back position.
- Tactic: Students learn the up-and-back attacking position used in doubles.
- Agility: Student quickly move into position.
- Fair play: Students start the task with a friendly serve.

DESCRIPTION

Divide students into groups of three and place one group on each court. Two students stand on one side of the net in an up-and-back position (see court side A in the figure) while the single student stands on the opposite side of the court. The up student in the up-and-back position serves the shuttle using a low and short serve. The single student returns the serve using any clear or drop shot. Depending on where the return shot goes, one of the two up-and-back students returns the shuttle using an attacking shot. If the shot is coming to the forecourt area, then the up partner returns the shot and if the return is coming to the back court area, then the back partner returns the shot using any clear or drop shot. This is not a rally, so the three students need to play and stop after three hits (i.e., serve-return-attack). After three trials, students rotate with the back position going to up position, the up position to the serve position, and the serve position going to the back position. If you have a fourth person, have that person stand as an alternate and then rotate into the back position and have the serve position move to the alternate position. The goal of the task is to have the two students attack the initial server from an up-and-back position in doubles. As an extension, allow the students to continuously hit the shuttle without stopping. If students need motivation, award one point when the up-and-back positions correctly return the shuttle.

EQUIPMENT

Three rackets and one shuttle per three students

CRITICAL ELEMENTS AND CUES

Technique

- Apply critical elements and cues from tasks 57 and 58.

Tactic

- The up-and-back position is one formation to cover the court in doubles by covering either the front portion of the court or the back half of the court.
- If you are the up (front) attacker, position yourself in the front middle court and cover the frontcourt area. *Cues:* Front middle; cover the front area.
- If you are the back attacker, position yourself in the back middle court and cover the backcourt area. *Cues:* Back middle; cover the back area.

Agility

- Quickly move into the up-and-back position after the serve. *Cue:* Up-and-back position.

Fair Play

- Students begin the task with a friendly serve.

COMMON ERRORS, CAUSES, AND CORRECTIONS

- Students try to return a shot that they should not attempt (i.e., up student moves back to hit a deep shot or the back student moves up to hit a short shot). *Cause:* Students focus on the shuttle and lose their orientation to where they are on the court. *Correction:* Have students call *mine* when they are moving to the shuttle.
- Look for common errors and their causes and corrections from tasks 57 and 58.

TASK 61: DEFENDING IN THE SIDE-BY-SIDE
POSITION IN DOUBLES

PURPOSE

Following are the purposes of the task as related to aspects of skilled performance.

- Technique: In this task, students apply attacking shots in doubles from a side-by-side position.
- Tactic: Students learn the side-by-side attacking position used in doubles.
- Agility: Students quickly move into position.
- Fair play: Students start the task with a friendly serve.

DESCRIPTION

Divide students into groups of three and place one group on each court. Two students stand on one side of the net in a side-by-side position while the single student stands on the opposite side of the court (see court side B in the figure in task 60). The student in the right side of the side-by-side position serves the shuttle using a high serve. The single student returns the serve using any clear or drop shot. Depending on where the return shot goes, one of the two side-by-side students returns the shuttle using an attacking shot. If the shot is coming to the right side of the court, then the partner on the right side returns the shot and if the return is coming to the left side of the court, then the left side partner returns the shot. This is not a rally so the three students need to play and stop after three hits (i.e., serve-return-attack). After three trials, students rotate with the left side position going to right side position, the right side position to the serve position and the serve position going to the left side position. If you have a fourth person, have that person stand as an alternate and then rotate into the left side position and have the serve position move to the alternate position. The goal of the task is to have the two students attack the initial server from a side by side position in doubles. As an extension, allow the students to continuously hit the shuttle without stopping. If students need motivation, award one point when the side-by-side positions correctly return the shuttle.

EQUIPMENT

Three rackets and two shuttles per three students

CRITICAL ELEMENTS AND CUES

Technique

- Apply critical elements and cues from tasks 57 and 58.

Tactic

- The side-by-side position in doubles is used to cover the court. Play both forward and back on your side of the court.
- If the shot comes to the middle of the court, if in position, the defender on the left side takes the shot using the forehand.
- If you are the right-side defender, position yourself in the middle of the right court and cover the right side of the court. *Cues:* Right middle; cover the right court.
- If you are the left-side defender, position yourself in the middle of the left court and cover the left side of the court. *Cues:* Left middle; cover the left court.

Agility

- Quickly move yourself into the side-by-side defending position when your partner hits the clear shot. *Cue:* Side-by-side.

COMMON ERRORS, CAUSES, AND CORRECTIONS

- A shot toward the middle of the court is not returned. *Cause:* The students are uncertain about who should return the shuttle when it comes to the middle. *Correction:* Remind students that the student whose forehand side the shuttle is moving toward is responsible for returning the shuttle.

TASK 62: COMBINATION LOW SERVE, UNDERHAND CLEAR, OVERHEAD CLEAR, AND OVERHEAD DROP RALLY

PURPOSE

Following are the purposes of the task as related to aspects of skilled performance.

- Technique: In this task, student use a combination of shots resulting from a low serve.
- Tactic: Students learn where to place the shuttle to move an opponent when combining shots.
- Agility: Students quickly move into position.
- Fair play: Students make friendly shots.

DESCRIPTION

Place one pair of students on each court with one as the server and the other as the receiver. The server starts the task with a forehand or backhand short serve. The receiver, who stands in the diagonal service court, returns the serve with a forehand or backhand underhand clear, aiming for the server's backcourt. The server then returns that shot with a forehand or backhand overhead clear, aiming for the receiver's backcourt. The receiver then finishes the rally with a forehand or backhand overhead drop. Students switch roles after a set number of combination plays. If students need motivation, award one point when both students successfully perform the designated combination shots.

EQUIPMENT

Two rackets and one shuttle per pair of students

CRITICAL ELEMENTS AND CUES

Technique

- Apply critical elements and cues from tasks 7 or 23, 10 or 12, 15 or 17, and 48 or 49.

Tactic

- Use different shots to affect the shot selection of the opponent and this can lead to a scoring opportunity.
- Applying the low serve brings the receiver up resulting in the return being an underhand clear. If the underhand clear is deep, that drives the initial server to the backcourt to use an overhead clear as a return. With the initial server in the backcourt, this sets up the opportunity for a drop shot being made in an attempt to score.

Agility

- Use quick movements to cover the court.

Fair Play

- Work cooperatively and use friendly shots.

COMMON ERRORS, CAUSES, AND CORRECTIONS

- The sequence of shots is not successful. *Cause:* The shots are not executed properly. *Correction:* See corrections for shots not performed properly (forehand and backhand low serves, tasks 7 and 23; forehand and backhand underhand clears, tasks 10 and 12; forehand and backhand overhead clears, tasks 15 and 17; forehand and backhand overhead drops, tasks 48 and 49).

TASK 63: COMBINATION HIGH SERVE, OVERHEAD CLEAR, OVERHEAD DROP, AND UNDERHAND DROP RALLY

PURPOSE

Following are the purposes of the task as related to aspects of skilled performance.

- Technique: In this task, students use combination shots off a high serve during a rally.
- Tactic: Students learn where to place the shuttle to move an opponent when combining shots.
- Agility: Students quickly move into position.
- Fair play: Students make friendly shots.

DESCRIPTION

Place one pair of students on each court with one as the server and the other as the receiver. The server starts the task with a forehand high or backhand flick serve. The receiver, who stands in the diagonal service court, returns the serve with a forehand or backhand overhead clear, aiming for the initial server's backcourt. The initial server then returns that shot with a forehand or backhand overhead drop, aiming for the initial receiver's forecourt. The receiver then finishes the rally with a forehand or backhand underhand drop. Students switch roles after a set number of combination plays. If students need motivation, award one point when both students successfully perform the designated combination shots.

EQUIPMENT

Two rackets and one shuttle per pair of students

CRITICAL ELEMENTS AND CUES

Technique

- Apply the critical elements and cues from tasks 8 or 25, 15 or 17, 45 or 46, and 48 or 49.

Tactic

- Use different shots to affect the shot selection of the opponent, and this can lead to a scoring opportunity.
- Applying the high serve forces the receiver back resulting in the only return being an overhead clear. If the overhead clear is not too deep, the initial server can use an overhead drop to force the receiver to the net. But if the receiver who rushed the net gets there in time, an underhand drop is an effective return shot for a scoring opportunity.

Agility

- Make quick movements to cover the court.

Fair Play

- Work cooperatively and use friendly shots.

COMMON ERRORS, CAUSES, AND CORRECTIONS

- The sequence of shots is not successful. *Cause:* The shots are not executed properly. *Correction:* See corrections for shots not performed properly (forehand high serve, task 8 and backhand flick serve, task 25; forehand and backhand overhead clears, tasks 15 and 17; forehand and backhand underhand drops, tasks 45 and 46; forehand and backhand overhead drops, tasks 48 and 49).

TASK 64: COMBINATION LOW SERVE, UNDERHAND DROP, UNDERHAND CLEAR, AND SMASH RALLY

PURPOSE

Following are the purposes of the task as related to aspects of skilled performance.

- Technique: In this task, students use combination shots off a low serve during a rally.
- Tactic: Students learn where to place the shuttle to move an opponent when combining shots.
- Agility: Students quickly move into position.
- Fair play: Students make friendly shots.

DESCRIPTION

Place one pair of students on each court with one as the server and the other as the receiver. The server starts the task with a forehand or backhand low serve. The receiver, who stands in the diagonal service court, returns the serve with a forehand or backhand underhand drop, aiming for the server's front court. The server then returns that shot with a forehand or backhand underhand clear, aiming for the receiver's backcourt. The receiver then finishes the rally with a forehand smash, aiming for the mid-backcourt. Students switch roles after a set number of combination plays. If students need motivation, award one point when both students successfully perform the designated combination shots.

EQUIPMENT

Two rackets and one shuttle per pair of students

CRITICAL ELEMENTS AND CUES

Technique

- Apply critical elements and cues from tasks 7 or 23, 45 or 46, 10 or 12 and 58.

Tactic

- Using a combination of shots can set up a smash shot to score a point.
- Applying the low serve forces the receiver up which can result in an underhand drop as the return. A possible return is an underhand clear, which could then set up a smash attempt as a scoring opportunity.

Agility

- Make quick movements to cover the court.

Fair Play

- Work cooperatively and use friendly shots.

COMMON ERRORS, CAUSES, AND CORRECTIONS

- The sequence of shots is not successful. *Cause:* The shots are not executed properly. *Correction:* See corrections for shots not performed properly (forehand and backhand low serves, tasks 7 and 23; forehand and backhand underhand clears, tasks 10 and 12; forehand and backhand underhand drops, tasks 45 and 46; forehand smash, task 58).

TASK 65: COMBINATION HIGH SERVE, OVERHEAD CLEAR, OVERHEAD DROP, UNDERHAND CLEAR, AND SMASH RALLY

PURPOSE
Following are the purposes of the task as related to aspects of skilled performance.

- Technique: In this task, students use combination shots off a high serve during a rally.
- Tactic: Students learn where to place the shuttle to move an opponent when combining shots.
- Agility: Students quickly move into position.
- Fair play: Students make friendly shots.

DESCRIPTION
Place one pair of students on each court with one as the server and the other as the receiver. The server starts the task with a forehand high serve. The receiver, who is standing in the diagonal service court, returns the serve with a forehand or backhand overhead clear, aiming for the opponent's backcourt. The server then performs a forehand or backhand overhead drop, and the receiver performs a forehand or backhand underhand clear, aiming for the opponent's backcourt. The server then finishes the rally with a forehand smash that is not returnable. Students switch roles after a set number of combination plays. If students need motivation, award one point when both students successfully perform the designated combination shots.

EQUIPMENT
Two rackets and one shuttle per pair of students

CRITICAL ELEMENTS AND CUES

Technique
- Apply critical elements and cues from tasks 8, 10 or 12, 15 or 17, 48 or 49, and 58.

Tactic
- Using a combination of shots off a high serve can set up a smash shot to score a point.
- Applying a high serve forces the receiver to return the serve with an overhead clear. With the receiver in the backcourt, the server can do an underhand drop shot to pull the receiver up to the net. At the net the receiver can use an underhand clear and if that shot does not go to the back court, the server can use a smash to score a point.

Agility
- Make quick movements to cover the court.

Fair Play
- Work cooperatively and use friendly shots.

COMMON ERRORS, CAUSES, AND CORRECTIONS
- The sequence of shots is not successful. *Cause:* The shots are not executed properly. *Correction:* See corrections for shots not performed properly (forehand and backhand underhand clears, tasks 10 and 12; forehand high serve, task 8; forehand and backhand overhead clears, tasks 15 and 17; forehand and backhand overhead drops, tasks 48 and 49; forehand smash, task 58).

TASK 66: SHAPED PARTNER GAMES

PURPOSE

Following are the purposes of the task as related to aspects of skilled performance.

- Technique: In this task, students apply learned techniques in a game-like situation.
- Tactic: Students apply learned tactics to improve game strategies for doubles and singles.
- Agility: Student move quickly into position.
- Fair play: Students self-officiate games in a fair manner and settle disputes cooperatively.
- Communication: The server calls out the game score before serving the next point.

DESCRIPTION

Students play singles with a partner. During the games, students are expected to perform the learned techniques of the shots and strategies learned in the lesson. The games are shaped by awarding bonus points if the techniques learned in the lesson are applied in the game. For example, if the straight backhand and forehand overhead clears were taught in the lesson, two points are awarded if a straight overhead clear is used. If a shot other than a straight overhead clear is used to win the point, only one point is awarded. This encourages students to apply the techniques and strategies learned in that lesson in the game situation. Another shaping strategy is to award a point only if the desired technique (e.g., the straight overhead clear) is used to score the point. Either strategy is appropriate; it is your decision.

Score games with a 10- or 15-rally point system where every time a student wins a rally they gain a point and the serve. If the intent is to play multiple games, do not require the winner of the game to win by two points.

EQUIPMENT

Two rackets and one shuttle per pair of students

CRITICAL ELEMENTS AND CUES

Technique

- Apply all previous critical elements and cues for techniques learned.

Tactic

- Apply previous tactics learned.

Agility

- Make quick movements to cover the court.

Fair Play

- Work cooperatively and use friendly shots.

Communication

- The server needs to call out the game score by stating the server's score then the receiver's score by saying, i.e. "5 serving 3."

COMMON ERRORS, CAUSES, AND CORRECTIONS

Look for all previously discussed errors and provide corrections.

TASK 67: SHAPED DOUBLES GAME

PURPOSE

Following are the purposes of the task as related to aspects of skilled performance.

- Technique: In this task, students apply learned techniques in a game-like situation.
- Tactic: Students apply techniques to improve game strategies for doubles.
- Agility: Students quickly move into position.
- Fair play: Students self-officiate games in a fair manner and settle disputes cooperatively.
- Communication: The server calls out the game score before serving the next point.

DESCRIPTION

Students play with a partner against another pair of students. During the games, students are expected to perform the learned techniques of the shots and the doubles strategies learned in the lesson. The games are shaped by awarding bonus points if the strategies learned in the lesson are applied in the game. For example, if the attacking up-and-back position was taught in the lesson, then a point can only be earned if that strategy is used. This encourages students to apply the strategy learned in that lesson in a game situation. Score games with a 10- or 15-rally point system where every time a student wins a rally they gain a point and the serve. If the intent is to play multiple games, do not require the winner of the game to win by two points.

EQUIPMENT

Four rackets and one shuttle per four students

CRITICAL ELEMENTS AND CUES

Technique

- Apply all previous critical elements and cues for techniques learned.

Tactic

- Apply previous tactics learned.

Agility

- Make quick movements to cover the court.

Fair Play

- Work cooperatively and use friendly shots.

Communication

- The server needs to call out the game score by stating the server's score then the receiver's score by saying, i.e. "5 serving 3."

COMMON ERRORS, CAUSES, AND CORRECTIONS

- Look for all previously discussed technique common errors and their causes and corrections.
- Look for common errors and their causes and corrections from tasks 60 and 61.

Chapter 11

Tennis

Tennis is a lifetime sport that can be played by the young and old alike. Many teachers do not include tennis in their curriculum because they lack tennis courts and equipment. In this chapter, we address ways that tennis can be taught very successfully with and without tennis courts and nets.

Learning tennis begins with the grip. You must revisit this skill to ensure that students are using it consistently. Our goal is for beginners to quickly engage in modified games that develop skillfulness, games sense, and enjoyment of the game.

OUR PEDAGOGICAL APPROACH TO TENNIS

In this chapter, we begin with short-court tennis and move to full-court tennis. In short-court tennis, students are closer to the net, which provides more control. We use the rally as a primary teaching strategy. In this unit, we focus on developing skillful performance and game sense through the use of instructional sequences that progressively teach each tennis technique and tactic.

Games are central to our pedagogy. The key that games we use for teaching are forehand and forehand, backhand and backhand, forehand and backhand, and progressive friend-rival games. As students learn to play these games, you will learn to better identify errors. There are three ways you can respond to these errors: (1) provide feedback to correct errors while keeping the task the same, (2) modify the task to address the students' needs, or (3) return to an earlier progression and then come back to the game. For example, if you observe that, despite your prompts, the students are not starting in the ready position, we suggest that after the game you have students practice the ready position to forehand position (task 10). If you observe that students are not moving quickly to the ball, you should revisit the fast feet game (task 4) and then return to the game you were playing.

An important pedagogoical consideration is the role of the feeder for some tasks that can influence the success of lessons. For all tasks that require a feeder, the feeder should stand inside the service box and the receiver should stand on the service line (at the beginning level), a line that marks three-quarters of the court length, or the baseline (full court) (at the intermediate level). A good toss is one for which the ball is placed a little past the service line.

Modification to Address Individual Needs of Students

For students with disabilities, appropriate modifications to activities depend on the nature of the disability. To modify tennis instruction for students with visual impairments, you can (a) use slower foam balls, (b) use a racket that has a shorter shaft, and (c) use brightly colored tape to highlight boundaries and the top of the net.

For students with autism spectrum disorder, use playing areas that are quieter and less distracting. You can also use colored tape on the handle of the racket to indicate where the student should grip it. Children with autism spectrum disorder may also benefit from having targets on the wall that they can try to hit when practicing their swings.

For students who use wheelchairs, use larger, slower foam balls that allow students more time to get to the needed location on the court. This modification may also be appropriate for individuals with cerebral palsy who have limited lateral mobility. Each of these modifications should be discussed with students prior to implementation to ensure that students are being fully and appropriately accommodated.

Organization

Divide students into groups of four, and assign each group to a home court. Though there are four on a court, students typically play 1v1 on a half court.

Space

Tennis requires a hard, flat surface that is clear of obstacles. The United States Tennis Association (USTA) recommends that courts be 60 by 21 feet (18.3 by 6.4 meters). Courts can be marked with floor tape, poly spots, cones, or chalk (outdoors). On a regulation tennis court, the short court is the length of the service box. The intermediate court, or three-quarters court, is 9 feet (2.7 meters) beyond the service box line. Available space may determine the size of your courts. We use short courts for many of the beginning activities and the three-quarters court for intermediate activities.

The following are important safety considerations relative to the organization of space:

- Have students spread out so they are not struck by rackets or balls.
- Construct activities in a way that minimizes the chances of students being hit by balls from other games.
- Ensure that students have sufficient space to practice their swings.
- Place left-handed students in appropriate positions (e.g., on the left side of the court) to avoid racket collisions with right-handed students.

- Ensure that balls are regularly cleared from the court to prevent students from stepping on them.

Equipment Needed

Nets are not necessary. Poly spots or cones can be used to mark the net area, or you can use string or plastic barrier tape strung between two tall cones or chairs in place of a net. You can also use mini nets or lowered badminton or volleyball nets. Nets should not be higher than 3 feet (0.9 meters).

The USTA recommends that students ages 8 and under use 21- to 23-inch (53.3- to 58.4-centimeter) rackets and that 9- and 10-year-olds use 23- to 25-inch (58.4- to 63.5-centimeter) rackets. After 11 years of age, 27-inch (68.5-centimeter) rackets can be used. If this is not possible, paddles are appropriate.

Foam balls or low-compression balls should be used rather than tennis balls for most of the tasks in the first two levels of the content map. Low-compression balls bounce lower and slower, which gives students more time to execute shots with control. Use regular tennis balls as students profiency increases during level 2 of the content map. Although one ball per pair of students will suffice for most tasks, having 3 to 4 balls per court increases opportunities to respond by decreasing the need to recover balls that are played out-of-bounds.

CONTENT MAP STRUCTURE

Figure 11.1 is a combined content map that illustrates the flow and connectedness of all of the tasks used to develop skillful performance and game sense in tennis. It is divided into three levels, and each level has a separate content map that includes the application games used to refine the techniques and tactics in that level. The primary focus of level 1 (figure 11.2) is to introduce students to the court and to teach the fundamentals of grips, footwork, and stance so they can produce a sustained rally. In levels 2 and 3 (figures 11.3 and 11.4), we use rallies as a core teaching strategy to teach the techniques and tactics of basic tennis.

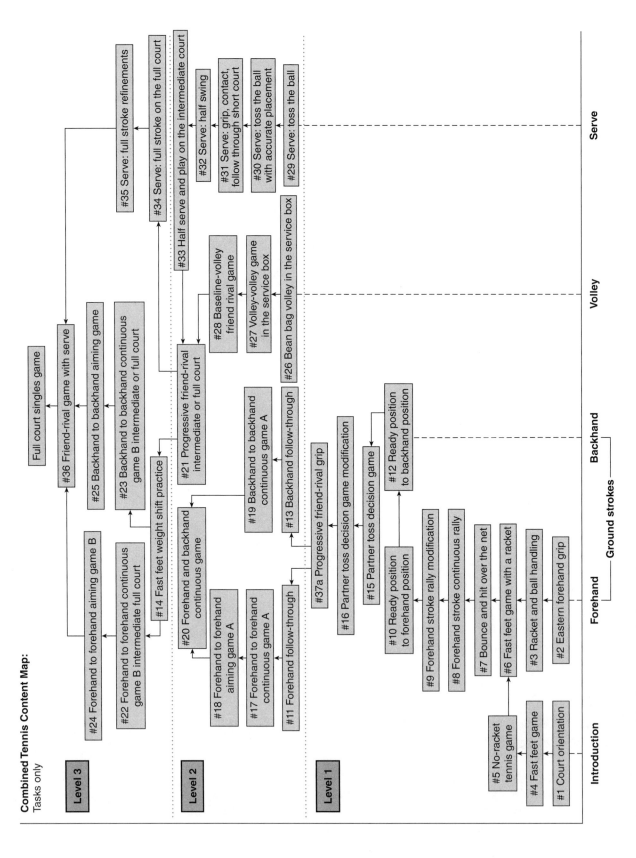

Figure 11.1 Combined content map for tennis.

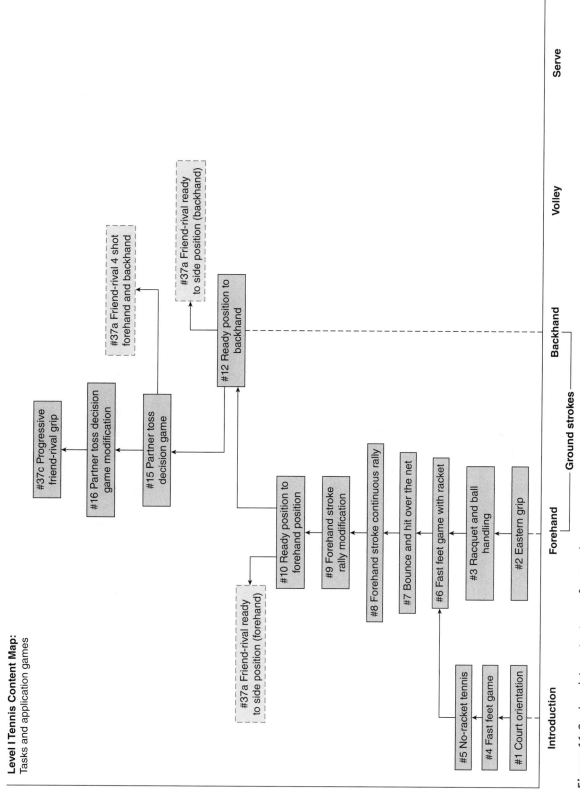

Figure 11.2 Level 1 content map for tennis.

423

Level 2 Tennis Content Map:
Tasks and games

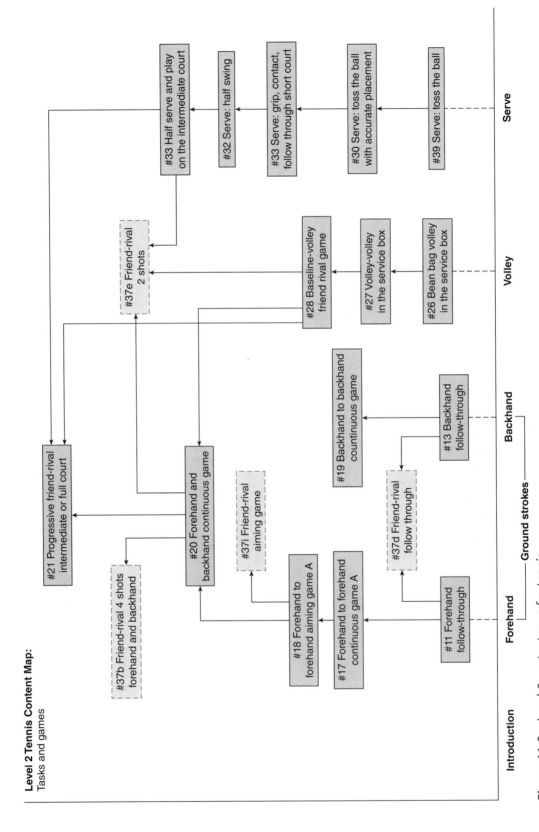

Figure 11.3 Level 2 content map for tennis.

Level 3 Tennis Content Map:
Tasks and games

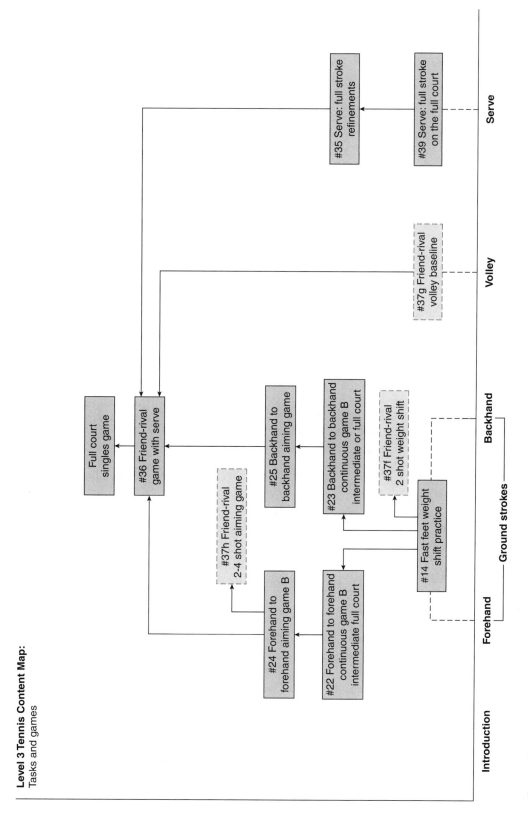

Figure 11.4 Level 3 content map for tennis.

STRUCTURE OF THE LESSONS

The following is a sample daily lesson structure for a 50-minute secondary tennis lesson.

Warm-up (6 minutes)

Informing task: Eastern forehand grip (4 minutes)

Informing task: fast feet game (5 minutes)

Extension task: fast feet game with a racket (8 to 10 minutes)

Extension task: bounce and hit over the net (8 to 10 minutes)

Application game: forehand stroke rally (10 minutes)

Closure (5 minutes)

Warm-up

We recommend using the same introductory warm-up for elementary students and secondary school students. After the first five days of secondary instruction, change the warm-up to include more advanced skills.

Elementary School

The warm-up should be taught to students on the first day of the unit, and it will likely take up at least half of the lesson. The warm-up introduces tennis-specific tasks that underlie the fundamentals of tennis: (a) racket and ball handling, (b) ball tossing, and (c) the ready position. The warm-up also includes jump rope and stretching activities that are designed to warm up the body for the active movement in the lesson. Once learned, the warm-up should last 5 to 7 minutes. You may decide to spend more time on the warm-up early in the unit so students can master the basic skills.

The warm-up is set up as a five-station circuit. The students begin at one station and rotate to a new station every 45 to 75 seconds. We typically use music to time the rotation. You can also set a number of repetitions to be done before rotating. To teach the warm-up, teach the tasks to be performed at each station to the class as a whole. Demonstrate the rotation, and then give the students time to rehearse it. Each station can accommodate 4 to 8 students. For larger classes, you can use 2 or 3 sets of stations.

Include the appropriate equipment at each station. The racket- and ball-handling station requires a racket and a ball for each student. The ball tossing station requires a ball for each pair

of students. The ready position station requires a racket, a ball, and a hoop for each pair of students. The jump rope station requires jump ropes for each student. The stretching station does not require equipment, but you can use task cards as prompts for the activities.

Racket- and Ball-Handling Station

At this station, students perform the following tasks:

- **Racket bounce.** Students hold the racket using the Eastern forehand grip (tell students to shake hands with the racket) with the palm facing up. Have students continuously bounce the tennis ball no higher than eye level. To develop more control, encourage students to practice at different levels: eye level, above the head, and really high.

- **Tennis ball dribble.** Students hold the racket using the Eastern forehand grip with the palm facing the ground. Students continuously dribble the tennis ball using the racket (similar to basketball dribbling). Students can dribble at different heights, but they should start slightly below hip height.

- **Dribble along the baseline and sidelines.** Students continuously dribble the tennis ball along the sidelines and baselines of the court.

Ball Tossing Station

One student slowly tosses a tennis ball to the left or right of the partner. The partner runs to catch the ball and then returns the ball to the partner in the same manner.

Ready Position Station

Two students stand 30 feet (9.1 meters) apart with a hoop placed halfway between them. One student bounces the ball on the ground and then softly hits the ball so it bounces inside the hoop. The partner catches the ball with the hand and the racket and then returns the ball in the same manner.

Jump Rope Station

Students practice jumping rope. We assume that students know how to jump rope; if they don't, you will need to teach this activity.

Stretching Station

At this station, students perform the following stretches:

- **Overhead stretch.** Students stand upright and stretch the arms straight above the head with the hands clasped and the palms pointing to the ceiling. Students continue the stretch by moving the clasped hands to the right and to the left above the head.

- **Shoulder stretch.** Students place the right arm straight across the upper chest and place the left arm above the right elbow and pull the right arm across the chest. Students then switch arms.

- **Triceps stretch.** Students lift the right hand over the right shoulder and place it between the shoulder blades. Students place the left hand on the right elbow and gently pull toward the midline of the body. Students then switch arms.

- **Quad stretch.** Students support themselves by placing the right hand at shoulder height against a wall. Students stand on the right leg and take hold of the left foot with the left hand and pull the heel toward the buttock. Students keep the back straight and the knees together and in line. Students then switch legs.

- **Hamstring stretch.** Students sit on the floor with the left leg straight in front of the body and the right leg bent. Students lean forward and try to touch the toes of the straight leg with both hands. Students then switch legs.

- **Lower leg stretch.** Students place the hands at shoulder height on a wall. Students stand with both feet forward and one foot in front of the other. The front knee is bent. Students lean forward. The back leg is straight with the heel on the ground. Students then switch legs.

Secondary School

For the the first 5 lessons of the secondary lessons the warm up is the same same as the elementary warm up because there are essential tasks to learn. Beginning with lesson 6, students perform the stretches from the elementary warm-up in their home court areas. Then students will perform 10 repetitions of specific shots they have been taught in previous lesson (these are indicated on the block plan).

BLOCK PLAN

The introductory block plan (see table 11.1) is designed for beginners at the elementary or secondary level. In elementary school, this should not be introduced earlier than third grade. Although longer units are always preferred, we recognize that there are time limitations at the elementary level; therefore, the elementary unit is five days for the initial grade in which it taught.

The secondary block plan (see table 11.2) follows the elementary block plan and is designed for students in middle and high school. It assumes that students were taught the level 1 skills at the elementary level. If this is not the case, follow the introductory block plan. Because middle and high school physical education programs have different requirements, these units should *not* be taught in fewer than 10 days. These units are adjusted for 10-, 15-, and 20-day programs, although we recommend units of 20 or more days.

Table 11.1 Elementary Tennis Block Plan: Five-Day Unit

This is an example of beginning block plan for elementary students that uses the tennis tasks shown in the level 1 content map. It is based on an initial five-day unit, and it encompasses all the level 1 tasks on the content map. You can use this as a template for developing an appropriate block plan for beginning students. If you are teaching a longer unit, you can include some level 2 tasks. Your decisions about what tasks to include will depend on your students and their levels of experience.

Lesson 1	Lesson 2	Lesson 3	Lesson 4	Lesson 5

Warm-up
• Teach the warm-up
	Warm-up
	• Circuit
	  • Racket and ball handling
	  • Ball tossing
	  • Ready position
	  • Jump rope
	  • Stretching
		Warm-up
		• Same as lesson 2
			Warm-up
			• Same as lesson 2
				Warm-up
				• Same as lesson 2

Introductory application game • **(1)** Court orientation	**Introductory application game** • **(5)** No-racket tennis game	**Introductory application game** • **(8)** Forehand stroke continuous rally	**Introductory application game** • **(8)** Forehand stroke continuous rally	**Introductory application game** • **(8)** Forehand stroke continuous rally
Content development • **(2)** Eastern forehand grip • **(3)** Racket and ball handling • **(4)** Fast feet game	**Content development** • **(6)** Fast feet game with a racket • **(7)** Bounce and hit over the net	**Content development** • **(9)** Forehand stroke rally modification • **(10)** Ready position to forehand position • **(12)** Ready position to backhand position • **(37A)** Friend-rival application game	**Content development** • **(15)** Partner toss decision game • **(37A)** Friend-rival application game	**Content development** • **(37B)** Friend-rival application game • **(16)** Partner toss decision game modification • **(37C)** Friend-rival application game
Closing application game • **(5)** No-racket tennis game	**Closing application game** • **(8)** Forehand stroke continuous rally	**Closing application game** • **(37A)** Friend-rival application game	**Closing application game** • **(37B)** Friend-rival application game	**Closing application game** • **(37C)** Friend-rival application game

Table 11.2 Secondary Tennis Block Plans: 10-, 15-, and 20-Day Units

This block plan incorporates 10-, 15-, and 20-day units. The last two days of the 10-day block plan, the last three days of the 15-day block plan, and the last five days of the 20-day block plan are game days and are described at the end of the block plan. The first eight days of the block plan are the same for all units.

Lesson 1 of all block plans	Lesson 2 of all block plans	Lesson 3 of all block plans	Lesson 4 of all block plans	Lesson 5 of all block plans

Warm-up
• Teach the warm-up
	Warm-up
	• Circuit
	  • Racket and ball handling
	  • Ball tossing
	  • Ready position
	  • Jump rope
	  • Stretching
		Warm-up
		• Same as lesson 2
			Warm-up
			• Same as lesson 2
				Warm-up
				• Same as lesson 2

Introductory application game • **(4)** Fast feet game • **(5)** No-racket tennis game	**Introductory application game** • **(6)** Fast feet game with a racket • **(37C)** Friend-rival application game	**Introductory application game** • **(22)** Forehand to forehand continuous game B • **(37A)** Friend-rival application game	**Introductory application game** • **(20)** Forehand to backhand continuous game	**Introductory application game** • **(37D)** Friend-rival application game
Content development • **(2)** Eastern forehand grip • **(7)** Bounce and hit over the net • **(10)** Ready position to forehand position	**Content development** • **(6)** Fast feet game with a racket • **(37C)** Friend-rival application game • **(10)** Ready position to forehand position • **(12)** Ready position to backhand position • **(15)** Partner toss decision game • **(16)** Partner toss decision game modification	**Content development** • **(17)** Forehand to forehand continuous game A • **(15)** Partner toss decision game • **(10)** Ready position to forehand position • **(12)** Ready position to backhand position • **(16)** Partner toss decision game modification	**Content development** • **(12)** Ready position to backhand position • **(16)** Partner toss decision game modification • **(17)** Forehand to forehand continuous game A • **(19)** Backhand to backhand continuous game A	**Content development** • **(37B)** Friend-rival application game • **(17)** Forehand to forehand continuous game A • **(18)** Forehand to forehand aiming game A • **(19)** Backhand to backhand continuous game A • **(20)** Forehand to backhand continuous game
Closing application game • **(37C)** Friend-rival application game • **(8)** Forehand stroke continuous rally	**Closing application game** • **(17)** Forehand to forehand continuous game A	**Closing application game** • **(17)** Forehand to forehand continuous game A • **(20)** Forehand to backhand continuous game	**Closing application game** • **(37B)** Friend-rival application game • **(21)** Progressive friend-rival rally	**Closing application game** • **(21)** Progressive friend-rival rally

(continued)

Lesson 6 of all block plans	Lesson 7 of all block plans	Lesson 8 of all block plans (last instructional day of 10-day block plan)	Lesson 9 of 15- and 20-day block plans (See table 11.3 for lesson 9 for 10-day plan.)	Lesson 10 of 15- and 20-day block plans (See table 11.3 for lesson 10 for 10-day plan.)
Warm-up • Stretching • Forehand shots • Backhand shots	**Warm-up** • Stretching • Forehand shots • Backhand shots • Serve practice: accurate tossing with nondominant hand	**Warm-up** • Stretching • Forehand shots • Backhand shots • Serve: contact shots	**Warm-up** • Same as day 8	**Warm-up** • Circuit • Forehand shots • Backhand shots • Forehand volley shots • Backhand volley shots
Introductory application game • **(37F)** Friend-rival application game	**Introductory application game** • **(37H)** Friend-rival application game	**Introductory application game** • **(37I)** Friend-rival application game • **(26)** Beanbag volley in the service box	**Introductory application game** • **(37B)** Friend-rival application game	**Introductory application game** • **(20)** Forehand to backhand continuous game
Content development • **(18)** Forehand to forehand aiming game A • **(25)** Backhand to backhand aiming game • **(29)** Serve: toss the ball	**Content development** • **(18)** Forehand to forehand aiming game A • **(25)** Backhand to backhand aiming game • **(26)** Beanbag volley in the service box • **(33)** Half serve and play on the intermediate court	**Content development** • **(20)** Forehand to backhand continuous game • **(30)** Serve: toss the ball with accurate placement • **(33)** Half serve and play on the intermediate court • **(27)** Volley game in the service box	**Content development** • **(20)** Forehand to backhand continuous game • **(30)** Serve: toss the ball with accurate placement • **(33)** Half serve and play on the intermediate court • **(27)** Volley game in the service box	**Content development** • **(20)** Forehand to backhand continuous game • **(30)** Serve: toss the ball with accurate placement • **(33)** Half serve and play on the intermediate court • **(27)** Volley game in the service box
Closing application game • **(37H)** Friend-rival application game	**Closing application game** • **(37B)** Friend-rival application game	**Closing application game** • **(37B)** Friend-rival application game	**Closing application game** • **(37B)** Friend-rival application game	**Closing application game** • **(37G)** Friend-rival application game • **(21)** Progressive friend-rival rally

Lesson 11 of 15- and 20-day block plans	Lesson 12 of 15- and 20-day block plans (last instructional day of 15-day plan)	Lesson 13 of 20-day block plan (See table 11.4 for lesson 13 for 15-day plan.)	Lesson 14 of 20-day block plan (See table 11.4 for lesson 14 for 15-day plan.)	Lesson 15 of 20-day block plan (See table 1.4 for lesson 15 for 15-day plan.)
Warm-up • Stretching • Forehand shots • Backhand shots • Forehand volley shots • Backhand volley shots	**Warm-up** • Same as day 11	**Warm-up** • Stretching • Forehand shots • Backhand shots • Forehand volley shots • Backhand volley shots • Serves to each side (five)	**Warm-up** • Same as day 13	**Warm-up** • Same as day 13
Introductory application game • **(20)** Forehand to backhand continuous game	**Introductory application game** • **(20)** Forehand to backhand continuous game	**Introductory application game** • **(37G)** Friend-rival application game	**Introductory application game** • **(33)** Half serve and play on the intermediate court	**Introductory application game** • **(34)** Serve: full stroke
Content development • **(17)** Forehand to forehand continuous game A • **(19)** Backhand to backhand continuous game A • **(30)** Serve: toss the ball with accurate placement • **(31)** Serve: grip, contact, and follow through short court • **(27)** Volley game	**Content development** • **(17)** Forehand to forehand continuous game A • **(19)** Backhand to backhand continuous game A • **(33)** Half serve and play on the intermediate court • **(27)** Volley game in the service box	**Content development** • **(17)** Forehand to forehand continuous game A • **(19)** Backhand to backhand continuous game A • **(33)** Half serve and play on the intermediate court • **(27)** Volley game in the service box	**Content development** • **(17)** Forehand to forehand continuous game A • **(19)** Backhand to backhand continuous game A • **(35)** Serve: full-stroke refinements • **(27)** Volley game in the service box	**Content development** • **(17)** Forehand to forehand continuous game A • **(19)** Backhand to backhand continuous game A • **(35)** Serve: full-stroke refinements • **(27)** Volley game in the service box
Closing application game: • **(34)** Serve: full stroke	**Closing application game:** • **(34)** Serve: full stroke	**Closing application game:** • **(34)** Serve: full stroke	**Closing application game:** • **(34)** Serve: full stroke	**Closing application game:** • **(34)** Serve: full stroke

(continued)

Lesson 16 of 20-day block plan	**Lesson 17 of 20-day block plan**	**Lesson 18 of 20-day block plan**	**Lesson 19 of 20-day block plan**	**Lesson 20 of 20-day block plan**
Warm-up Same as day 13	**Warm-up** Same as day 13	**Warm-up** Same as day 13	**Warm-up** Same as day 13	**Warm-up** Same as day 13
Singles progressive friend-rival game with serve (first to score 11 points; non-exclusionary round-robin tournament) Award one extra point for correct grip, correct contact, follow through, and weight shift. Award two extra points for accurate placement, volley shot, and ace serve.	**Singles progressive friend-rival game with serve (first to score 11 points; non-exclusionary round-robin tournament)** Award one extra point for correct grip, correct contact, follow through, and weight shift. Award two extra points for accurate placement, volley shot, and ace serve.	**Singles progressive friend-rival game with serve (first to score 11 points; non-exclusionary round-robin tournament)** Award one extra point for correct grip, correct contact, follow through, and weight shift. Award two extra points for accurate placement, volley shot, and ace serve.	**Singles progressive friend-rival game with serve (first to score 11 points; non-exclusionary round-robin tournament)** Award one extra point for correct grip, correct contact, follow through, and weight shift. Award two extra points for accurate placement, volley shot, and ace serve.	**Singles progressive friend-rival game with serve (first to score 11 points; non-exclusionary round-robin tournament)** Award one extra point for correct grip, correct contact, follow through, and weight shift. Award two extra points for accurate placement, volley shot, and ace serve.

Table 11.3   10-Day Block Plan Game Days

Lesson 9 of 10-day block plan	**Lesson 10 of 10-day block plan**
Warm-up • Same as day 8	**Warm-up** • Same as day 8
Singles progressive friend-rival game with serve (first to score 11 points; nonexclusionary round-robin tournament) Award one extra point for correct grip, correct contact, follow through, and weight shift. Award two extra points for accurate placement, volley shot, and ace serve.	**Singles progressive friend-rival game with serve (first to score 11 points; nonexclusionary round-robin tournament)** Award one extra point for correct grip, correct contact, follow through, and weight shift. Award two extra points for accurate placement, volley shot, and ace serve.

Table 11.4   15-Day Block Plan Game Days

Lesson 13 of 15-day block plan	**Lesson 14 of 15-day block plan**	**Lesson 15 of 15-day block plan**
Warm-up • Same as day 11	**Warm-up** • Same as day 11	**Warm-up** • Same as day 11
Singles progressive friend-rival game with serve (first to score 11 points; nonexclusionary round-robin tournament) Award one extra point for correct grip, correct contact, follow through, and weight shift. Award two extra points for accurate placement, volley shot, and ace serve.	**Singles progressive friend-rival game with serve (first to score 11 points; nonexclusionary round-robin tournament)** Award one extra point for correct grip, correct contact, follow through, and weight shift. Award two extra points for accurate placement, volley shot, and ace serve.	**Singles progressive friend-rival game with serve (first to score 11 points; nonexclusionary round-robin tournament)** Award one extra point for correct grip, correct contact, follow through, and weight shift. Award two extra points for accurate placement, volley shot, and ace serve.

SHAPE AMERICA'S GRADE LEVEL OUTCOMES FOR K-12 PHYSICAL EDUCATION

In table 11.5, we identify key grade-level outcomes for tennis for 3rd through 8th grade. These are linked to specific tasks on the content maps that are appropriate for teaching the skill and assessing the outcome. Some outcomes refer to short-handled implements; we include them here because you might use short-handled rackets in elementary school tennis.

Table 11.5 Grade-Level Outcomes for Tennis

Outcome	Description	Content map focus and tasks
S1.E24.3a	Strikes an object with a short-handled implement, sending it forward over a low net or to a wall.	Level 1, task 6
S1.E24.3b	Strikes an object with a short-handled implement while demonstrating 3 of the 5 critical elements of a mature pattern.	Level 1, tasks 9-11
S1.E24.4a	Strikes an object with a short-handled implement while demonstrating a mature pattern.	Level 1, tasks 16-17
S1.E24.4b	Strikes an object with a short-handled implement, alternating hits with a partner over a low net or against a wall.	Level 1, tasks 16-17
S1.E24.5	Strikes an object consecutively, with a partner, using a short-handled implement, over a net or against a wall, in either a competitive or cooperative game environment.	Level 1, tasks 7, 26
S1.M13.6	Strikes with a mature overhand pattern in a nondynamic environment for net/wall games such as volleyball, handball, badminton or tennis.	Level 2, task 8
S1.M13.7	Strikes with a mature overhand pattern in a dynamic environment for net/wall games such as volleyball, handball, badminton or tennis.	Level 2, tasks 8-9, 21
S1.M13.8	Strikes with a mature overhand pattern in a modified game for net/wall games such as volleyball, handball, badminton or tennis.	Level 2, tasks 9, 21
S1.M14.6	Demonstrates the mature form of the forehand and backhand strokes with a short-handled implement in net games such as paddle ball, pickleball or short-handled racket tennis.	Level 2, tasks 17-20
S1.M14.7	Demonstrates the mature form of forehand and backhand strokes with a long-handled implement in net games such as badminton or tennis.	Level 2, tasks 17-21
S1.M14.8	Demonstrates the mature form of forehand and backhand strokes with a short- or long-handled implement with power and accuracy in net games such as pickleball, tennis, badminton or paddle ball.	Level 2, tasks 17-21
S1.M15.6	Transfers weight with correct timing for the striking pattern.	Level 1, tasks 4, 6
S1.M15.7	Transfers weight with correct timing using low to high striking pattern with a short-handled implement on the forehand side.	Level 1, tasks 6, 11
S1.M15.8	Transfers weight with correct timing using low to high striking pattern with a long-handled implement on the forehand and backhand sides.	Level 2, task 8
S1.M16.6	Forehand-volleys with a mature form and control using a short-handled implement.	Level 2, task 27
S1.M16.7	Forehand- and backhand-volleys with a mature form and control using a short-handled implement.	Level 2, tasks 27-28

(continued)

Outcome	Description	Content map focus and tasks
S1.M16.8	Forehand- and backhand-volleys with a mature form and control using a short-handled implement during modified game play.	Level 2, task 27
S1.M17.6	Two-hand-volleys with control in a variety of practice tasks.	Level 2, tasks 25-26
S1.M17.7	Two-hand-volleys with control in a dynamic environment.	Level 2, task 27
S1.M17.8	Two-hand-volleys with control in a small-sided game.	Level 2, tasks 26-27
S1.H1.L1	Demonstrates competency and/or refines activity-specific movement skills in two or more lifetime activities (outdoor pursuits, individual-performance activities, aquatics, net/wall games or target games).	Level 2, tasks 20, 35 Level 3, tasks 20, 35
S1.H1.L2	Refines activity-specific movement skills in one or more lifetime activities (outdoor pursuits, individual-performance activities, aquatics, net/wall games or target games).	Level 2, tasks 23-24, 34 Level 3, tasks 23-24, 34

TASK 1: COURT ORIENTATION

PURPOSE

Following is the purpose of the task as related to aspects of skilled performance.

Technique: In this task, students learn the locations and purposes of the baseline, sidelines, center line, and net.

DESCRIPTION

Have students line up on the baseline facing the net. Introduce students to the following parts of the modified tennis court for their lessons:

- **Baseline.** The baseline is the end line at each end of the tennis court (line 1 in figure 11.5). Serving occurs behind the baseline. Much of the game occurs along the baseline. A ball that lands beyond the baseline is out-of-bounds. If it lands on the baseline, the ball is considered inbounds.
- **Sidelines.** This is the outer edge of each side of the tennis court (line 2). Balls that bounce outside of the sidelines are considered out-of-bounds. Balls that bounce on the sidelines are considered inbounds.
- **Center service line.** This line divides the court in half and creates two service boxes (line 3). Serves occur diagonally from one side of the court to the other, and a ball must bounce in the service box, which is the rectangular box formed by the sideline, centerline, and baseline.
- **Net.** The net divides the two playing areas of the court (line 4). Remind students not to touch the net. You can also describe alternatives that you are using in place of a net, such as cones or string between chairs. Remind students not to cross the court by going under the net.

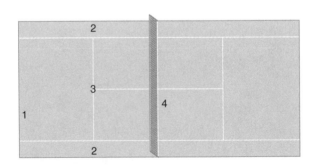

Use the following game as an introductory activity. Place one team on each side of a court (use as many courts as you have teams). Students cannot touch the net or step over or around it. When you call out a court location, students run to that location within their assigned court. Then, ask the significance of that location (e.g., Why is the baseline important?).

EQUIPMENT

Courts

CRITICAL ELEMENTS AND CUES

Technique

- Stand at each location as the teacher explains. *Cue:* Listen.
- Face the net when standing on the baseline. *Cue:* Face the net.

COMMON ERRORS, CAUSES, AND CORRECTIONS

- Students move to the wrong line. *Cause:* Students are not yet acquainted with the various court lines. *Correction:* Repeat the activity and focus on the areas students have trouble with.

TASK 2: EASTERN FOREHAND GRIP

PURPOSE

Following is the purpose of the task as related to aspects of skilled performance.

Technique: In this task, students learn the Eastern forehand grip. This is the basic grip in tennis.

DESCRIPTION

Have students line up on the baseline facing the net. Each student has a racket at their feet. Describe the three parts of the tennis racket you will use in this task: the head (also called strings and face), the shaft, and the handle (see figure).

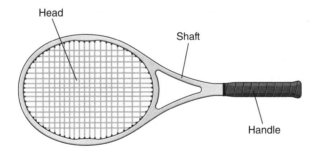
Head / Shaft / Handle

To demonstrate the Eastern forehand grip, hold the racket in the nondominant hand by the middle of the shaft and place the open dominant hand on the face of the racket, which should be perpendicular to the ground. Next, slide the open dominant hand down the shaft to "shake the hand" of the racket handle.

EQUIPMENT

One racket per student

CRITICAL ELEMENTS AND CUES

Technique

- Position the wrist slightly to the right of the center of the handle if you are right-handed (to the left if you are left-handed). *Cue:* Right (or left) of center.

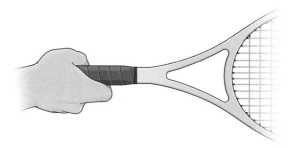

- Wrap the fingers around the handle so the home knuckle of the index finger is on the right panel of the handle (see figure). *Cue:* Knuckle on panel.

COMMON ERRORS, CAUSES, AND CORRECTIONS

- The student's wrist is turned too far toward the upper side of the handle. *Cause:* The grip is incorrect. *Correction:* Draw an imaginary diagonal line on the palm to help the student visualize the placement of the hand on the racket. Have the student perform at least 30 strikes using the proper grip without attending to any other critical elements such as distance, target, or height.
- The student opens the index finger so it is along the handle. *Cause:* The student uses the finger for additional support on contact with the ball. *Correction:* Draw an imaginary diagonal line on the palm to help the student visualize the placement of the hand on the racket. Have the student perform at least 30 strikes using the proper grip without attending to any other critical elements such as distance, target, or height.

TASK 3: RACKET AND BALL HANDLING

PURPOSE

Following is the purpose of the task as related to aspects of skilled performance.

Technique: In this task, students learn basic racket- and ball-handling skills and become comfortable holding and manipulating the racket and the ball.

DESCRIPTION

Use the following tasks to teach basic racket- and ball-handling skills:

1. **Racket bounce.** Students hold the racket using the Eastern forehand grip (tell students to shake hands with the racket) with the palm pointing toward the sky. Have students continuously bounce the tennis ball no higher than eye level. To develop more control, encourage students to practice at different levels: eye level, above the head, and really high.
2. **Tennis ball dribble.** Students hold the racket using the Eastern forehand grip with the palm facing down. Students continuously dribble the tennis ball using the racket (similar to basketball dribbling). Students can dribble at different heights, but they should start slightly below hip height.
3. **Dribble along the baseline and sidelines.** Students continuously dribble the tennis ball along the sidelines and baselines of the court.

EQUIPMENT

One ball and one racket per student

CRITICAL ELEMENTS AND CUES

Technique: Dribble

- Focus on your hand position. Your stiff wrist is an extension of the racket. *Cue:* Keep wrist stiff.

- Choke up on the racket for more control if needed. *Cue:* Move your hands down the racket.
- Dribble the ball softly with a short and brisk hand movement. *Cue:* Keep it soft.
- Dribble waist high, and then vary the height. *Cue:* No higher than the waist.
- Perform lots of repetitions. *Cue:* Keep working, don't stop.

Technique: Racket Bounce

- Do not chase the ball if it gets away from you (so you don't run into other students). *Cue:* Wait till the ball moves past player before retrieving it or call me.
- Stand away from other students. *Cue:* Stay in self space away from others.
- Hit the ball eye high. *Cue:* Only as high as the eye.
- Bump the ball softly. *Cue:* Hit softly.
- Use a stiff wrist. *Cue:* Keep the wrist stiff.
- Perform lots of repetitions. *Cue:* Keep working, don't stop.

COMMON ERRORS, CAUSES, AND CORRECTIONS

Dribble

- The student struggles to start the dribble with a tennis ball. *Cause:* The task requires arm strength and racket-ball coordination. *Correction:* Revert to an upward dribble (ball dribbled upward on the racket), or use low-compression balls that are easier to dribble and return slower from the ground.
- The student struggles to control the ball. *Cause:* The student lacks mastery over racket-ball control and the weight of racket. *Correction:* Have the student kneel or sit to make the task easier, or instruct the student to assume more control over the racket by holding it closer to the shaft (the student can gradually go back to holding the handle).
- The student's wrist is turned too far toward the upper side of the handle. *Cause:* The grip is incorrect. *Correction:* Draw an imaginary diagonal line on the palm to help the student visualize the placement of the hand on the racket. Have the student perform at least 30 strikes using the proper grip without attending to any other critical elements such as distance, target, or height.

Bounce

- The student opens the index finger so it is along the handle. *Cause:* The student uses the finger for additional support on contact with the ball. *Correction:* Draw an imaginary diagonal line on the palm to help the student visualize the placement of the hand on the racket. Have the student perform at least 30 strikes using the proper grip without attending to any other critical elements such as distance, target, or height.
- The student moves around too much while trying to accumulate bounces. *Cause:* The student has little control over the racket and applies low power on the bounce. *Correction:* Have the student start with a foam ball and then move to the low-compression ball and keep a radius of 1 to 2 steps.
- The student struggles to control the ball. *Cause:* The student lacks ball-racket control. *Correction:* Have the student use a low bounce (eye height or below).

TASK 4: FAST FEET GAME

PURPOSE

Following are the purposes of the task as related to aspects of skilled performance.

- Technique: In this task, students learn the correct footwork to move into position to receive the ball.
- Agility: Students practice fast footwork for optimal movement on the court.
- Fair play: Students challenge their peers for practice purposes.

DESCRIPTION

Divide students into pairs and position one student on each side of a court. On each side of the court, place six equally spaced circles in two rows (see figure). Each circle is numbered 1 through 6 and is about the size of a regular hula hoop, approximately 39 inches (100 centimeters).

One student tosses and is called the feeder, and the other student is the receiver. The feeder begins in the middle about 4 feet (1.2 meters) back from the net. The feeder underhand tosses the ball upward so it flies about 1 to 2 feet (0.3 to 0.6 meters) over the height of the net and lands in one of the circles. The receiver starts in the center of the baseline and moves toward the circle as if to catch the ball but stays behind the circle. The receiver lets the ball bounce and says *bounce* when it hits the ground. Then the receiver should be in position to catch the ball. Students then switch roles.

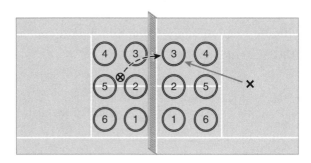

EQUIPMENT

One ball per pair of students hoops or chalk to draw circles

CRITICAL ELEMENTS AND CUES

Technique

- Use longer steps when you are farther from the ball and smaller steps as you get closer to the ball for optimal positioning. *Cue:* Long steps for distance or short steps if you are close
- Toss the ball to the closest center circle, then to the far center circle, and then to the outside circles. *Cue:* Be precise.
- Be sure to say *bounce* when the ball bounces so you can judge whether you are in the correct position. *Cue:* Don't forget to say *bounce*.

Agility

- Move fast to get into position. *Cue:* Move fast.

Fair Play

- Gradually challenge your partner with the tosses (begin with close tosses and gradually proceed to more distant tosses that the partner can reach). *Cue:* Challenge your partner.

COMMON ERRORS, CAUSES, AND CORRECTIONS

- Students do not take the quickest route to the spot. *Cause:* The student lacks agility and is not proactive in moving toward the spot. *Correction:* Have the student quickly call out the direction the ball is tossed in (e.g., right, left) and practice short sprints forward or diagonally to focus their attention on where the ball will bounce.
- The student moves too slowly. *Cause:* The student has slow identification and response times. *Correction:* Have the feeder indicate which circle he or she will toss to moments before the toss. Then, proceed to a task in which the receiver calls the direction in which the ball is tossed.

TASK 5: NO-RACKET TENNIS GAME

PURPOSE

Following are the purposes of the task as related to aspects of skilled performance.

- Technique: In this task, students learn the correct footwork on a short court, and they learn to return to the center after a pass over the net.
- Tactic: Students learn to aim their throw to an open area on the opponent's court and to move their opponent around. Students also learn how to score the game.
- Agility: Students practice fast footwork for optimal movement on the court.

DESCRIPTION

Divide students into pairs and position one student on each side of the court. Students are on the service line, and one student has a ball. Students play a tennis game using only their hands. Each player must catch the ball after no more than one bounce and throw it to the other side of the court. When throwing to the other side, the student must aim for an open space on the opponent's court. When receiving the ball, the student must move toward it to catch it. Elementary students and other beginners can play on one service box; more advanced students can play on two service boxes.

EQUIPMENT

One ball per pair of students

CRITICAL ELEMENTS AND CUES

Technique

- Use large steps when you are far from the ball and small steps when you are close to the ball for optimal positioning.
- Slide back to the center point after passing the ball to the other side.

Agility

- Move fast to get into position.

Tactic

- Alternate sides when making tosses.
- Aim the ball to areas within the court that are far from the opponent.

COMMON ERRORS, CAUSES, AND CORRECTIONS

- Students do not take the quickest route to the spot to receive the ball. *Cause:* The student lacks agility and is not proactive in moving toward the spot. *Correction:* Have the student quickly call out the direction the ball is tossed in (e.g., right, left) and practice short sprints forward or diagonally.
- The student moves too slowly. *Cause:* The student has slow identification and response times. *Correction:* Have the feeder indicate the area he or she will toss to moments before the toss. Then, proceed to a task in which the receiver calls the direction in which the ball is tossed.
- The student throws the ball to the center or at the opponent. *Cause:* The student focuses on the partner as the target rather than looking for open spots. *Correction:* Award the student two points (instead of one) when the ball is untouched by the opponent and one point if the throw hits one of the far corners of the opponent's court, even if the play was not won.

TASK 6: FAST FEET GAME WITH A RACKET

PURPOSE

Following are the purposes of the task as related to aspects of skilled performance.

- Technique: In this task, students learn the correct footwork to get to the ball, and they learn to position themselves to better strike the ball.
- Agility: Students practice fast footwork for optimal positioning to strike a ball.

DESCRIPTION

This is an extension of the fast feet game (task 4). Divide students into pairs and position one student on each side of the court. The receiver stands at the center of the baseline, and the feeder stands at the center halfway between the baseline and the net. (If the feeder has difficulties aiming and reaching the proper circles, he or she can take 2 to 3 more steps into the court.)

The feeder begins by tossing the ball to the middle circles. As the receiver gets better, the feeder can toss the ball to the outer circles. We recommend that the feeder toss five balls in a row to the same circle before changing circles. Once all the circles have been used, the feeder can randomly toss the ball to any circle.

The receiver has a racket and gently hits the ball back to the feeder, who then retrieves the ball. The receiver needs to be in position before calling *bounce* when the ball bounces. Students switch roles after every 15 tosses.

EQUIPMENT

One ball and one racket per pair of students

CRITICAL ELEMENTS AND CUES

Technique

- Use the Eastern forehand grip. *Cue:* Use Eastern grip. Toss to the closest center circle, then to the far center circle, then to the outside circles closest to the net, and then to outside circles closest to the baseline.

Agility

- Move fast to get into position.
- Say *bounce* when the ball bounces so you can judge whether you are in position.
- Move fast to get into position. Use large steps when you are far from the ball and small steps when you are close to the ball.

COMMON ERRORS, CAUSES, AND CORRECTIONS

- The student moves too slowly. *Cause:* The student has slow identification and response times. *Correction:* Have the feeder indicate the circle he or she will toss to moments before the toss.
- The student's wrist is turned too far toward the upper side of the handle. *Cause:* The grip is incorrect. *Correction:* Draw an imaginary diagonal line on the palm to help the student visualize the placement of the hand on the racket. Have the student perform at least 30 strikes using the proper grip without attending to any other critical elements such as distance, target, or height.
- The student opens the index finger so it is along the handle. *Cause:* The student uses the finger for additional support on contact with the ball. *Correction:* Draw an imaginary diagonal line on the palm to help the student visualize the placement of the hand on the racket. Have the student perform at least 30 strikes using the proper grip without attending to any other critical elements such as distance, target, or height.

TASK 7: BOUNCE AND HIT OVER THE NET

PURPOSE

Following is the purpose of the task as related to aspects of skilled performance.

Technique: In this task, students learn to hit the ball with a straight racket face.

DESCRIPTION

Divide students into pairs and position one student on each side of the court. Each student has a racket and one student has a ball. They will switch roles in this task so both will serve in each role. Students stand on their baselines (see figure).

First, the server softly self-tosses the ball up (with the nonhitting hand), lets it bounce, and hits it over the net with a straight racket face (i.e., strings facing the net). The receiver attempts to catch the ball with the hand, the racket, or both. The receiver then performs the same task. Then, the first student softly tosses the ball up, lets it bounce, and hits it over the net with a straight racket face. The receiver lets the ball bounce on the ground and attempts to return it over the net. After two hits, the server catches the ball with the hand and racket.

To make the task easier, you can keep the nets low or remove them. You can also modify the difficulty level by adjusting the students' distance from the net (closer is easier, farther is more challenging).

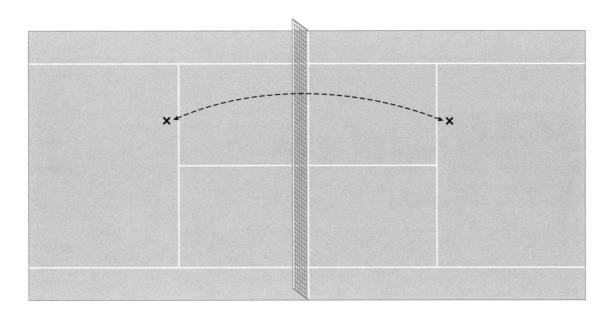

EQUIPMENT

One ball and two rackets per pair of students

CRITICAL ELEMENTS AND CUES

Technique

- Hold the racket in the dominant hand with the handle pointed away from the ground. The strings and palm should face the net. *Cue:* Strings and palm should face the net.
- Hit the ball at waist level. *Cue:* Hit at the waist.
- Use the Eastern forehand grip. *Cue:* Use Eastern grip.

COMMON ERRORS, CAUSES, AND CORRECTIONS

- The student does not hold the racket correctly. *Cause:* The student lacks mastery of racket handling. *Correction:* Repeat the racket- and ball-handling activities, and remind the student of the proper grip.

- The student contacts the ball too low or above the waist. *Cause:* The student makes an inaccurate self-toss or assumes an inaccurate position to the ball. *Correction:* Return to the self-toss from a stationary position, repeat the fast feet activities, or have the student identify and call out the contact level of the ball (e.g., low, high) and say *yes* after each strike.

- The student's wrist is turned too far toward the upper side of the handle. *Cause:* The grip is incorrect. *Correction:* Draw an imaginary diagonal line on the palm to help the student visualize the placement of the hand on the racket. Have the student perform at least 30 strikes using the proper grip without attending to any other critical elements such as distance, target, or height.

- The student opens the index finger so it is along the handle. *Cause:* The student uses the finger for additional support on contact with the ball. *Correction:* Draw an imaginary diagonal line on the palm to help the student visualize the placement of the hand on the racket. Have the student perform at least 30 strikes using the proper grip without attending to any other critical elements such as distance, target, or height.

TASK 8: FOREHAND STROKE CONTINUOUS RALLY

PURPOSE

Following is the purpose of the task as related to aspects of skilled performance.

Technique: In this task, students learn to consistently rally over the net and develop rally competence. The rally is the basic teaching strategy for tennis.

DESCRIPTION

Students are in pairs, and one student is on each side of the court on the baseline. Students start at the back-left corner (for right-handed students) to increase the probability of only forehand shots. Left-handed students start at the back-right corner.

One student with the ball begins the rally with an underhand serve. The server drops the ball with the nonhitting hand, lets it bounce, and strikes it over the net with the racket. The partner returns the ball over the net after it bounces. If the partner misses the ball, or if it bounces more than once, the partner should retrieve the ball and restart. This is the basic rally. Students should see how many times they can pass the ball over the net. Begin by setting a goal of two times, and then increase this (e.g., to 5, 10, 15, 20 times). When errors occur, the students restart the game. As students gain more competence, encourage them to say *bounce* when they are in position. Adjust students' distance from the net to modify the level of difficulty (closer is easier, farther away is more challenging).

EQUIPMENT

One ball and two rackets per pair of students

CRITICAL ELEMENTS AND CUES

Technique

- The strings (or racket face) should face the net once you are in position to hit. *Cue:* Strings face the net.
- The balls should bounce halfway between your partner and the net. *Cue:* Gentle hits.
- Use the Eastern forehand grip. *Cue:* Eastern grip.
- Call *bounce* when you are in position before the ball bounces. *Cue:* Call bounce.

COMMON ERRORS, CAUSES, AND CORRECTIONS

- The student does not hold the racket correctly. *Cause:* The student lacks mastery of racket handling. *Correction:* Repeat the racket- and ball-handling activities, and remind the student of the proper grip.
- The student's wrist is turned too far toward the upper side of the handle. *Cause:* The grip is incorrect. *Correction:* Draw an imaginary diagonal line on the palm to help the student visualize the placement of the hand on the racket. Have the student perform at least 30 strikes using the proper grip without attending to any other critical elements such as distance, target, or height.
- The student opens the index finger so it is along the handle. *Cause:* The student uses the finger for additional support on contact with the ball. *Correction:* Draw an imaginary diagonal line on the palm to help the student visualize the placement of the hand on the racket. Have the student perform at least 30 strikes using the proper grip without attending to any other critical elements such as distance, target, or height.
- The student makes hard or long hits that make the return difficult. *Cause:* The student lacks power regulation. *Correction:* Have the student practice hitting a self-toss ball with a forehand shot inbounds to various distances from the starting point.

TASK 9: FOREHAND STROKE RALLY MODIFICATION

PURPOSE

Following are the purposes of the task as related to aspects of skilled performance.

- Technique: In this task, students learn the positioning of their bodies relative to the incoming ball so they can perform a forehand stroke.
- Agility: Students use speed and appropriate strides to reach the moving ball.

DESCRIPTION

Students are in pairs, and one student is on each side of the court on the baseline. Students start at the back-left corner (for right-handed students) to increase the probability of only forehand shots. Left-handed students start at the back-right corner.

One student with the ball begins the rally with an underhand serve. The server drops the ball with the nonhitting hand, lets it bounce, and strikes it over the net with the racket. The partner returns the ball over the net after it bounces. If the partner misses the ball, or if it bounces more than once, the partner should retrieve the ball and restart. This is the basic rally. Students should see how many times they can pass the ball over the net. Begin by setting a goal of two times, and then increase this (e.g., to 5, 10, 15, 20 times). When errors occur, the students restart the game. As students gain more competence, encourage them to say *bounce* when they are in position. Adjust students' distance from the net to modify the level of difficulty (closer is easier, farther away is more challenging).

Students stand with the left shoulder pointing toward the target area. (Reverse this for left-handed students.) We call this *showing the shoulder*. The body weight should be placed primarily on the front foot.

EQUIPMENT

One ball and two rackets per pair of students

CRITICAL ELEMENTS AND CUES

Technique

- Point the nonracket shoulder toward the net, and set the feet with the toes parallel to the target and the racket foot slightly behind the other foot. *Cue:* Nonracket shoulder point toward the net
- Hold the racket perpendicular to the court with the strings facing the net.

- Make gentle hits. *Cue:* Gentle hits.
- Use the Eastern forehand grip. *Cue:* Use Eastern grip.
- The path of the racket should move from low to high, especially when you are playing on a full court. *Cue:* Low to high.
- Make contact with the ball in front of the lead foot. *Cue:* Contact in front of foot.
- Keep the racket strings pointed where you want the ball to go (straight, left, right) on contact. *Cue:* Racket face to target.
- After contacting the ball, promptly return to a squared position with the shoulders and the body facing the net. *Cue:* Square up.

Agility

- Make long steps when you are far from the ball and short strides as you reach the ball.

COMMON ERRORS, CAUSES, AND CORRECTIONS

- The student places the weight on the back foot instead of the front foot. *Cause:* The student has slow footwork. *Correction:* Practice the fast feet task and have the student turn the shoulder to the net on the ball's first bounce on the court. Have the student take two steps forward into the court immediately after the strike.
- The student does not hold the racket correctly. *Cause:* The student lacks mastery of racket handling. *Correction:* Repeat the racket- and ball-handling activities, and remind the student of the proper grip.
- The student's grip is incorrect. The student's wrist is turned too far toward the upper side of the handle. *Cause:* The grip is incorrect. *Correction:* Draw an imaginary diagonal line on the palm to help the student visualize the placement of the hand on the racket. Have the student perform at least 30 strikes using the proper grip without attending to any other critical elements such as distance, target, or height.
- The student opens the index finger so it is along the handle. *Cause:* The student uses the finger for additional support on contact with the ball. *Correction:* Draw an imaginary diagonal line on the palm to help the student visualize the placement of the hand on the racket. Have the student perform at least 30 strikes using the proper grip without attending to any other critical elements such as distance, target, or height.
- The student turns the shoulder too much and is in a closed position to the net. *Cause:* The student steps into the ball incorrectly. *Correction:* Instruct the student to step with the front foot diagonally rather than crossing the foot laterally over the other.
- After contact with the ball, the student keeps the shoulder pointed toward the target rather than returning to a squared position to the net. *Cause:* The student does not shift the weight forward. *Correction:* Have the student step forward with the back leg so the waist rotates back to a squared position.

TASK 10: READY POSITION TO FOREHAND POSITION

PURPOSE

Following is the purpose of the task as related to aspects of skilled performance.

Technique: In this task, students learn the positioning of their bodies relative to the incoming ball so they can perform a forehand stroke from a ready position.

DESCRIPTION

Each student is located on each side of the court. One student with racket and one with a ball. The receiver stands on the baseline (center), feeder at the center, half way between the baseline and the net. In this task we introduce the ready position to give the students the ability to use both arms and use their energy more efficiently. We teach them how to move from the ready position to a position to execute a forehand stroke and in later pro-

gressions a backhand stroke. We introduce the ready position first. The ready position is considered the "decision position". From this position you can decide to go to a forehand or a backhand or approach to volley based on the ball that is hit to you from an opponent. As such, it is the foundation for playing tennis. The ready position is similar to the defensive stance in basketball. The feet are a little wider than the shoulders, the knees are bent, and the weight is slightly forward on the balls of the feet (see figure). Both hands are on the racket, and the striking hand is on the bottom of the handle. The other hand is closer to the neck of the racket. The racket is held at the midline between the right and left sides of the body. The racket head is tilted slightly forward and away (about 45 degrees to the net).

Students are in pairs with one student is on each side of the court. Students first practice the movement from the ready position to the forehand position without a ball to ensure fluency. Students point the shoulder toward the target and step toward the target with the front foot.

The feeder stands about halfway between the baseline and the net and uses an underhand toss so the ball hits the ground halfway down the other side of the court. The receiver stands on the baseline on the other side of the net in the ready position with the racket. As the ball is tossed, the receiver moves to the proper position with the shoulder to the net and returns the ball over the net. The feeder catches the ball. Students should repeat this 10 times before changing roles.

EQUIPMENT

One ball and one racket per pair of students

CRITICAL ELEMENTS AND CUES

Technique

- Assume the ready position: The feet are a little wider than the shoulders, your knees are bent, and your weight is slightly forward on the balls of your feet. The arms are bent, and the hands are on the racket. *Cue:* Ready position.

- Turn to the forehand position. *Cue:* Forehand position.

- On contact, the nonracket shoulder should point toward the net and the feet should be in a staggered position with the racket foot slightly behind the other foot (for right-handers). *Cue:* Non-racket shoulder point toward the net.

- Step forward diagonally with opposite foot with the shoulder to the net. *Cue:* Step to the net.

- Make gentle hits. *Cue:* Gentle hits.

- Use the Eastern forehand grip. *Cue:* Use Eastern grip.
- Call out *open* when you see the ball move over the net to prompt you to ensure you have a straight racket (strings facing the net). *Cue:* Open.

COMMON ERRORS, CAUSES, AND CORRECTIONS

- The student's wrist is turned too far toward the upper side of the handle. *Cause:* The grip is incorrect. *Correction:* Draw an imaginary diagonal line on the palm to help the student visualize the placement of the hand on the racket. Have the student perform at least 30 strikes using the proper grip without attending to any other critical elements such as distance, target, or height
- The student opens the index finger so it is along the handle. *Cause:* The student uses the finger for additional support on contact with the ball. *Correction:* Draw an imaginary diagonal line on the palm to help the student visualize the placement of the hand on the racket. Have the student perform at least 30 strikes using the proper grip without attending to any other critical elements such as distance, target, or height.
- The student moves too slowly to the ball. *Cause:* The student is not anticipating the ball. *Correction:* Use longer steps when you are farther from the ball and smaller steps as you get closer to the ball for optimal positioning. *Cue:* Long steps for distance or short steps if you are close.
- The student does not square the shoulders to the net after the strike. *Cause:* Student is not returning to the ready position. *Correction:* Prompt the student.
- The student's timing for opening the racket and rotating the shoulder to the net is incorrect. *Cause:* The student's response to the incoming ball is slow. *Correction:* Have the feeder toss the ball to the right and to the left, and have the receiver immediately call out *right shoulder* or *left shoulder* based on direction of the ball. Then, have the feeder randomly toss to the right or left so the receiver does not know which will be next.

TASK 11: FOREHAND FOLLOW-THROUGH

PURPOSE

Following is the purpose of the task as related to aspects of skilled performance.

Technique: In this task, students learn to finish a forehand stroke with proper follow-through.

DESCRIPTION

The follow-through is a very natural movement that aids in aiming the ball and controlling the stroke. The follow-through is executed from low to high (from the contact point at waist level to above the opposite shoulder). The head of the racket should be behind the shoulder pointing downward at the end of the stroke (see figure).

Students are in pairs, and one student is on each side of the court. The feeder holds the ball and stands on center of the service line. The partner with the racket stands on the three-quarter court line. Students begin from the ready position. After contact is made, the receiver focuses on following through long and high into the back. Students repeat this 10 times before changing roles.

EQUIPMENT

One ball and one racket per pair of students

CRITICAL ELEMENTS AND CUES

Technique

- Assume the ready position. *Cue:* Ready position.
- Contact the ball at waist level. *Cue:* Move quickly to the ball.

- Swing low to high. *Cue:* Low to high.
- Above the shoulder. *Cue:* Swing above the shoulder.
- Square the shoulders at the end of the stroke. *Cue:* Square up.
- Finish with the proper follow-through. *Cue:* Drop the head of the racket behind your shoulder at follow through.
- Make a long follow through after contact with the ball. *Cue:* Swing long to finish.

COMMON ERRORS, CAUSES, AND CORRECTIONS

- The student's follow-through goes upward or above the head rather than diagonally to the opposite shoulder. *Cause:* The student lacks mastery of the drive. *Correction:* Have the student practice the follow-through in a controlled setting. Feed balls such that the student must take 1 to 2 steps inside the court (short feeds).
- The student's follow-through goes upward or above the head rather than diagonally to the opposite shoulder. *Cause:* The student does not properly use footwork and weight shifting. *Correction:* Have the student return to previous tasks to develop footwork, body positioning, and weight shifting.
- The student has an interrupted follow-through, without flow. *Cause:* The student uses improper footwork and positioning to the ball. *Correction:* Emphasize either short steps to the ball if close to it or longer steps if further away. The student's ability to perfom task 10 should be reevaluated because they are not ready to perform task 11. They should return to practice task 10.
- The student makes contact above waist level. *Cause:* The student uses improper footwork and positioning to the ball. *Correction:* Toss the ball to the receiver who stops the ball with their non-dominant hand, they should let it bounce, and then strike it as a forehand. Stopping the ball with the non-dominant hand helps creates awareness of the contact zone.
- The student's weight does not shift forward. *Cause:* The student is not leaning into the shot. *Correction:* Lean into the stroke.
- The student does not rotate back to the squared position to the net. *Cause:* The student may be forget to be square. *Correction:* Prompt with cues such as "square up."

TASK 12: READY POSITION TO BACKHAND POSITION

PURPOSE

Following are the purposes of the task as related to aspects of skilled performance.

- Technique: In this task, students learn the positioning of their bodies relative to the incoming ball so they can perform a two-handed backhand stroke from a ready position.
- Technique: Students learn the Continental grip for the two-handed backhand stroke.
- Agility: Students promptly change their grip and turn the proper shoulder to the incoming ball.

DESCRIPTION

First, teach the Continental backhand grip. This grip can be performed with one or two hands, but we use two hands To demonstrate the Continental backhand grip, hold the racket with two hands on the handle. The nondominant hand is on top; the hands are touching one another but not overlapping. The dominant hand is in the Eastern grip. Slide the nondominant hand down from near the strings to the handle and grip so that both hands are in Eastern grip. Then, rotate your palm on the upper right slant bevel, 45 degrees clockwise from the Full Eastern. This makes the racket face tend to tilt upward. Step forward with the dominant foot to the hand rotation, and move the racket to the contact position (strings facing the net) as you rotate the dominant hand on the handle. You are now using the Continental grip with the dominant hand with the strings facing the net.

To teach the ready position place students in pairs, and one student is on each side of the court. Students first practice the movement from the ready position to the backhand position and change the grip without a ball. It is a difficult step for beginners, so it should be isolated.

Then, the feeder stands at the center about halfway between the baseline and the net with the ball. The receiver stands on the baseline on the other side of the net in the ready position with the racket. Next perform the movement with the ball tossed from one student to the other. As the ball is tossed, the receiver moves to the proper position with the shoulder to the net and returns the ball over the net. The feeder catches the ball. Students should repeat this 10 times before changing roles.

EQUIPMENT

One ball and one racket per pair of students

CRITICAL ELEMENTS AND CUES (SEE FIGURE)

Technique

- Assume the ready position: The feet are a little wider than the shoulders, your knees are bent, and your weight is slightly forward on the balls of your feet. The arms are bent, and the hands are on the racket. *Cue:* Ready position.
- Turn to the backhand position. *Cue:* Backhand position.
- On contact, the racket shoulder should point toward the net and the racket foot should be slightly in front of the other foot (for right-handers). *Cue:* Racket shoulder should point toward the net.
- Step forward diagonally with the lead foot with the shoulder to the net. *Cue:* Step to net.
- Make gentle hits. *Cue:* Gentle hits.
- Use the Continental grip. *Cue:* Continental grip.
- Call out *change* when you see the ball move over the net to prompt you to change your grip and assume a straight racket face (strings facing the net). *Cue:* Chase.

COMMON ERRORS, CAUSES, AND CORRECTIONS

- The student does not hold the racket correctly. *Cause:* The student lacks mastery of racket handling. *Correction:* Reteach the Continental grip.
- The student's grip is incorrect or the student doesn't change the grip. *Cause:* The student is used to the Eastern grip and doesn't attend to the grip change. *Correction:* Demonstrate how the striking hand should change on the handle. Have the student practice the change 20 times without a ball and without movement. Then, have the student perform repetitions of the stationary backhand stroke (change from a squared ready position to a side backhand stroke position and change the grip).
- The student's timing for opening the racket and rotating the shoulder to the net is incorrect. *Cause:* The task is occurring too quickly. *Correction:* Encourage getting to the ball quickly or use a slower ball.
- The student moves too slowly to the ball. *Cause:* The student is not anticipating where the ball will be. *Correction:* Track the ball and use longer steps when you are farther from the ball and smaller steps as you get closer to the ball for optimal positioning.

TASK 13: BACKHAND FOLLOW-THROUGH

PURPOSE

Following is the purpose of the task as related to aspects of skilled performance.

Technique: In this task, students learn to finish a backhand stroke with proper follow-through.

DESCRIPTION

Students are in pairs, and one student is on each side of the court. The feeder holds the ball and stands on the center of the service line. The partner with the racket stands on the three-quarter court line. Students begin from the ready position and rotate their hand from the Eastern to the Continental grip. After contact is made, the receiver focuses on following through long and high into the back. Students repeat this 10 times before changing roles.

EQUIPMENT

One ball and one racket per pair of students

CRITICAL ELEMENTS AND CUES (SEE FIGURE)

Technique

- Assume the ready position. *Cue:* Ready position.
- Change to the Continental grip. *Cue:* Rotate your hand to the Continental grip.

- Contact the ball at waist level. *Cue:* Hit at the hip.
- Swing low to high. *Cue:* Swing low to high.
- Swing above the shoulder. *Cue:* Swing over the shoulder.
- Square the shoulders at the end of the stroke. *Cue:* Square up.
- Finish with the proper follow-through. *Cue:* Try to touch the net with back of the hand as you swing.
- The elbows are high at the end of the follow-through. *Cue:* Keep the elbows high.

COMMON ERRORS, CAUSES, AND CORRECTIONS

- The student's follow-through goes upward. *Cause:* Incomplete swing. *Correction:* Finish with the back of your hand facing the net with good extension of the arm.
- Poor fluency in the shot. *Cause:* The student is rushed to perform and cannot connect all the component of the shot. *Correction:* Use slower balls and prompt students to be ready.
- The student makes contact above waist level. *Cause:* The student uses improper footwork and positioning to the ball. *Correction:* Use longer steps when you are farther from the ball and smaller steps as you get closer to the ball for optimal positioning.
- The student's weight does not shift forward. *Cause:* The student is not leaning into the shot. *Correction:* Prompt the student to lean into the shot with weight moving to their front foot.
- The student does not rotate back to the squared position to the net. *Cause:* The student may be forget to be square. *Correction:* Prompt the student to be square.

TASK 14: FAST FEET WEIGHT SHIFT PRACTICE

PURPOSE

Following is the purpose of the task as related to aspects of skilled performance.

Technique: In this task, students learn to make a proper follow-through on both sides of the body while shifting the weight forward into the shot and then return promptly to the ready position.

DESCRIPTION

Students are in pairs, and one student is on each side of the court. The feeder stands on the center of the service line. The partner with the racket stands on the three-quarter court line. Place a cone in the center of the court 3 to 4 steps in front of the baseline on the receiver's side. From a ready position, the receiver responds to an incoming ball by moving into contact position. Once contact is made, the student follows through and steps into the court, circles the cone, and runs backward to the center mark, reassuming the ready position. The feeder should alternate between tossing balls to the left and right sides.

Students switch roles after tosses shots.

EQUIPMENT

Four balls, one racket, and one cone per pair of students

CRITICAL ELEMENTS AND CUES

Technique

- Assume the ready position. *Cue:* Ready position.
- Use the proper grip on both sides. *Cue:* Proper grip.
- Contact the ball at waist level. *Cue:* Contact at hip.
- Swing low to high. *Cue:* Low to high.
- Shift the weight forward. *Cue:* Lean forward as you hit.
- Rotate your waist. *Cue:* Rotate your waist.
- Use fast footwork forward and backward, and face the net. *Cue:* Fast feet.
- Use a long follow-through after the ball. *Cue:* Swing long to follow through.

COMMON ERRORS, CAUSES, AND CORRECTIONS

- The student's follow-through goes upward or there is no follow-through. *Cause:* Incomplete swing. *Correction:* On the forehand, finish up and over your shoulder. On the backhand finish with the back of your hand facing the net with good extension of the arm.
- The student's weight remains on the back leg. *Cause:* The student is not leaning into the shot. *Correction:* Prompt the student to lean into the shot with weight moving to their front foot.
- The student does not rotate back to the squared position to the net. *Cause:* The student may be forget to be square. *Correction:* Prompt the student to be square.
- The student's grip is incorrect. *Cause:* The student is not anticipating the ball and this the change of grip. *Correction:* The student can call out the grip to make as the ball is sent to them.

TASK 15: PARTNER TOSS DECISION GAME

PURPOSE

Following are the purposes of the task as related to aspects of skilled performance.

- Technique: In this task, students learn to move from the ready position to the forehand and backhand positions.
- Tactic: Students begin to develop tactical thinking and aim the ball to an open area on the court. The receiver must decide where to move.
- Agility: Students learn to identify the direction of the incoming ball and quickly respond to it. Students practice fast lateral movement from one spot to another.
- Fair play: Students learn to challenge their partners within the limits of the game.

DESCRIPTION

Students are in pairs, and one student is on each side of the court. The feeder stands at the center about halfway between the baseline and the net. The receiver stands on center of the baseline. The feeder alternately feeds the ball to forehand and to backhand (or two tosses to each side before alternating to the other side). This will help students more efficiently shift between forehand and backhand positions and develop control over varied movements and demands. Next, the feeder randomly tosses the ball to either the left or the right, and the receiver must move from the ready position to either the forehand or the backhand position. As the receiver develops greater competence, the feeder can toss the ball wider or farther from the student to encourage more movement to the ball.

This is a difficult task that requires students to demonstrate technique and efficient movement on the court. Expect some regression in performance for the previously mastered critical elements due to task demands. If an error occurs repeatedly, revert back to previous tasks or use correction tasks to isolate the practice for several trials; then return to the current task.

EQUIPMENT

One ball and one racket per pair of students

CRITICAL ELEMENTS AND CUES

Technique

- Assume the ready position. *Cue:* Ready position.
- Move into the contact position: Turn the shoulder to the net (left for forehand, right for backhand for right-handers; opposite for left-handers). Step forward, and ensure that the strings face the net. *Cue:* Shoulder faces the net; strings face the net.
- Make gentle hits. *Cue:* Hit gently.
- Rotate your waist. *Cue:* Rotate your waist.
- Swing low to high (when playing on the full court). *Cue:* Low to high.
- Use fast footwork forward and backward, and face the net. *Cue:* Fast feet.
- Use a long follow-through after the ball (when playing on the full court). *Cue:* Swing long.
- Finish above the shoulder. *Cue:* Finish up and over your shoulder.
- Shift the weight forward. *Cue:* Lean into the shot.
- Call out *bounce* when you are in position before the ball bounces. *Cue:* Call *bounce*.

COMMON ERRORS, CAUSES, AND CORRECTIONS

- The student's grip is incorrect. *Cause:* The student is not habitually using the correct grip. *Correction:* It is a problem at this stage to continue to have this error. Have the student perform at least 30 strikes using the proper grip without attending to any other critical elements such as distance, target, or height.
- The student's follow-through goes upward or there is no follow-through. *Cause:* Incomplete swing. *Correction:* On the forehand, finish up and over your shoulder. One the backhand finish with the back of your hand facing the net with good extension of the arm.
- The student's weight remains on the back leg. *Cause:* The student is not leaning into the shot. *Correction:* Prompt the student to lean into the shot with weight moving to their front foot.
- The student does not rotate back to the squared position to the net. *Cause:* The student may be forget to be square. *Correction:* Prompt the student to be square.

TASK 16: PARTNER TOSS DECISION GAME MODIFICATION

PURPOSE

Following are the purposes of the task as related to aspects of skilled performance.

- Technique: In this task, students learn to move from the ready position to the forehand and backhand positions.
- Tactic: Students begin to develop tactical thinking and aim the ball to an open area on the court.
- Agility: Students learn to identify the direction of the incoming ball and quickly respond to it. Students practice fast lateral movement from one spot to another.
- Fair play: Students learn to challenge their partners within the limits of the game.

DESCRIPTION

Students are in pairs, and one student is on each side of the court. Six circles are drawn with chalk equally spaced in two rows (see figure in task 4). Each circle about the size of a regular hula hoop (approximately 39 inches [100 centimeters]). The feeder stands at the center about halfway between the baseline and the net. The receiver stands on center of the baseline. If the feeder has difficulties aiming and reaching the proper circles, he or she can take 2 to 3 steps into the court. This task extends the previous tasks and combines it with the circles used in the fast feet game. The feeder begins in the middle of their side of the court about 4 feet (1.2 meters) back from the net. The feeder underhand tosses the ball upward so that it flies 1 to 2 feet (0.3 to 0.6 meters) over the net and lands in one of the circles. The student must move behind the circle in order to return the ball. Each time the student with the racket starts in the ready position in the middle of the baseline. The feeder should use all the circles, but should toss to them in a random order. The balls should always be tossed in an arch to give the receiver time to move into position.

EQUIPMENT

One ball and one racket per pair of students, chalk

CRITICAL ELEMENTS AND CUES

Technique

- Assume the ready position. *Cue:* Ready position.
- Move into the contact position: Turn the shoulder to the net, step forward, and ensure that the strings face the net. *Cue:* Fast feet.
- Turn the shoulder to the net (left for forehand, right for backhand for right-handers; opposite for left-handers). *Cue:* Shoulder to net.
- Make gentle hits. *Cue:* Hit gently.
- Call out *bounce* when you are in position before the ball bounces. *Cue:* Call *bounce*.
- Contact the ball in front of the front foot at waist level. *Cue:* Contact at hip level.

COMMON ERRORS, CAUSES, AND CORRECTIONS

- The student's grip is incorrect. *Cause:* The student is not anticipating the ball and this the change of grip. *Correction:* The student can call out the grip to make as the ball is sent to them.
- The feeder tosses in expected pattern. *Cause:* The feeder is not following directions about tossing randomly. *Correction:* Prompt the feeder.
- The feeder does not use all circles on the court to move the receiver. *Cause:* Lack of experience using different patterns. *Correction:* Have the feeder try to deceive the student by tossing the ball in an unexpected direction (but not more than 4 to 5 steps

from the receiver's position) or toss the ball to the circle that is the farthest from the student.

- The feeder tosses flat balls that the receiver cannot reach. *Cause:* The student is enthusiastic and wants to win. *Correction:* The student should perform a rainbow toss (i.e., an arched toss) with appropriate power.

TASK 17: FOREHAND TO FOREHAND CONTINUOUS GAME A

PURPOSE

Following are the purposes of the task as related to aspects of skilled performance.

- Technique: In this task, students learn to repeatedly move from the ready position to the forehand position. They also learn to aim the ball to the forehand side of their opponent.
- Tactic: Students maintain continuous play with an opponent.
- Agility: Students promptly place themselves in relation to the ball to complete a forehand stroke.

DESCRIPTION

Students are in pairs, and one student is on each side of the court. Both students have rackets. Six circles are drawn with chalk equally spaced in two rows. Each circle about the size of a regular hula hoop (approximately 39 inches [100 centimeters]). One student makes an underhand serve. The receiver, who is on the center of the baseline in the ready position, moves to the ball to make a forehand shot. Students attempt to maintain the rally with forehand shots. Thus, the only circles that can be used are those positioned on the forehand side of the student. When errors occur, restart the play with an underhand serve. If students fail to rally, have them begin at the left corner (for right-handed students); this ensures that all balls arrive to the forehand side.

EQUIPMENT

One ball and two rackets per pair of students, chalk to draw circles

CRITICAL ELEMENTS AND CUES

Technique

- Assume the ready position. *Cue:* Ready position.
- Make correct contact, that is one foot in front, shoulder to the net (left for forehand, right for backhand for right-handers; opposite for left-handers), strings facing the net, and contact made at waist level. *Cue:* Shoulder faces net, strings face net.
- Use the Eastern grip. *Cue:* Eastern grip.
- Call out *bounce* when you are in position before the ball bounces. *Cue:* Call *bounce*.

COMMON ERRORS, CAUSES, AND CORRECTIONS

- The student's wrist is turned too far toward the upper side of the handle. *Cause:* The grip is incorrect. *Correction:* Draw an imaginary diagonal line on the palm to help the student visualize the placement of the hand on the racket. Have the student perform at least 30 strikes using the proper grip without attending to any other critical elements such as distance, target, or height.
- The student opens the index finger so it is along the handle. *Cause:* The student uses the finger for additional support on contact with the ball. *Correction:* Draw an imaginary diagonal line on the palm to help the student visualize the placement of the hand on the racket. Have the student perform at least 30 strikes using the proper grip without attending to any other critical elements such as distance, target, or height.

- The student's racket face is open on contact. *Cause:* When you hit a tennis ball the stringbed is supposed to be either at a right angle to the ground, or facing slightly downward. *Correction:* Have the student call out *waist* when the racket is at waist level before the strike and *shoulder* when the racket is at shoulder level for the finish.
- The student makes inaccurate shots (too long, too strong, or outside the designated forehand area). *Cause:* The student lacks ability. *Correction:* Place two cones within the designated hitting area and ask the student to aim the ball so it bounces between the cones (if the student's balls go out-of-bounds) or before the cones (if the student's balls go too far or outside the end lines).
- The students cannot maintain continuous play. *Cause:* The students do not make controlled and accurate strikes. *Correction:* Ask students to aim the balls so they bounce halfway between the net and the opponent's location.
- The student uses improper footwork to get to the ball *Cause:* The student is too slow to move. *Correction:* Use longer steps when you are farther from the ball and smaller steps as you get closer to the ball for optimal positioning.
- The student is forced to use a backhand strike. *Cause:* Students use slow footwork and proper positioning. *Correction:* Have the student practice moving diagonally backward from the ready position and opening to a forehand strike.

TASK 18: FOREHAND TO FOREHAND AIMING GAME A

PURPOSE

Following are the purposes of the task as related to aspects of skilled performance.
- Technique: In this task, students learn to repeatedly move from the ready position to the forehand position but under more challenging conditions than previously. They also refine their aiming of the ball to a specific area on the other side of the court.
- Tactic: Students maintain continuous play with an opponent.
- Agility: Students promptly place themselves in relation to the ball to complete a forehand stroke.

DESCRIPTION

Six circles are drawn with chalk equally spaced in two rows. Each circle about the size of a regular hula hoop (approximately 39 inches [100 centimeters]). Students are in pairs, and one student is on each side of the court. Both students have rackets. One student makes an underhand serve. The receiver, who is on the center of the baseline in the ready position, moves to the ball to make a forehand shot into one of the six circles. The server can call out the number of the circle they are aiming at as a prompt for the partner. Students attempt to maintain the rally with forehand shots. Thus, only the circles that are positioned on the forehand side of the student can be used. When errors occur, restart the play with an underhand serve.

EQUIPMENT

One ball and two rackets per pair of students and chalk to draw circles

CRITICAL ELEMENTS AND CUES

Technique
- Assume the ready position. *Cue:* Ready position.
- Ensure correct contact – one foot in front, shoulder to the net, strings facing the net, contact made at waist level. *Cue:* Shoulder and strings to the net.
- Use the Eastern grip. *Cue:* Eastern grip.

Agility

- Call out *bounce* when you are in position before the ball bounces. *Cue:* Call *bounce*.
- Quickly return to the ready position. *Cue:* Return to ready position.

COMMON ERRORS, CAUSES, AND CORRECTIONS

- There is a delayed positioning of forehand. *Cause:* The wrist might be turning the racket upward just before impact. *Correction:* Grab the handle more tightly just as the swing is started, this will help to prevent the wrist from turning.
- The student's wrist is turned too far toward the upper side of the handle. *Cause:* The grip is incorrect. *Correction:* Draw an imaginary diagonal line on the palm to help the student visualize the placement of the hand on the racket. Have the student perform at least 30 strikes using the proper grip without attending to any other critical elements such as distance, target, or height
- The student opens the index finger so it is along the handle. *Cause:* The student uses the finger for additional support on contact with the ball. *Correction:* Draw an imaginary diagonal line on the palm to help the student visualize the placement of the hand on the racket. Have the student perform at least 30 strikes using the proper grip without attending to any other critical elements such as distance, target, or height.
- The student's racket face is open on contact. *Cause:* The set up for the swing is incorrect. *Correction:* Tilt the face of the racket down on the backswing. The racket face naturally opens up (tilts upward) as it is swung forward. Students need to start their forehand swing with the racket facing somewhat downward in order for it to end up at vertical as it meets the ball. Have students hold the racket face vertical at the point where you normally meet the ball, then, without turning your wrist, pull the racket back to your normal backswing position. It should face somewhat downward, and that's the angle they want at the start of each swing.
- The student makes inaccurate shots (too long or strong or outside the designated forehand area). *Cause:* The ball is being hit too hard. *Correction:* Students should hit the ball with less force.
- The student remains in an open stance on the shot. *Cause:* The student is not moving to the forearm shot position. *Correction:* Prompt the student to move.
- The student uses improper footwork to get to the ball. *Cause:* The student is not proactive in moving toward the spot. *Correction:* Use longer steps when you are farther from the ball and smaller steps as you get closer to the ball for optimal positioning.
- The student has to use a backhand strike. *Cause:* The student is out of position when making the shot and is not proactive in moving toward the spot. *Correction:* Use longer steps when you are farther from the ball and smaller steps as you get closer to the ball for optimal positioning.

TASK 19: BACKHAND TO BACKHAND CONTINUOUS GAME A

PURPOSE

Following are the purposes of the task as related to aspects of skilled performance.

- Technique: In this task, students learn to repeatedly move from the ready position to the backhand position. They also learn to aim the ball to the backhand side of the opponent.

DESCRIPTION

Six circles are drawn with chalk equally spaced in two rows (see figure in task 4). Each circle about the size of a regular hula hoop (approximately 39 inches [100 centimeters]). Students are in pairs, and one student is on each side of the court. Both students have rackets. One student makes an underhand serve. The receiver, who is on the center of the baseline in the ready position, moves to the ball to make a backhand shot. Students attempt to maintain the rally with backhand shots. Thus, the only circles that can be used are those positioned on the backhand side of the student. When errors occur, restart the play with an underhand serve. If students fail to rally, have them begin at the right corner (for right-handed students); this ensures that all balls arrive to the correct side of the other half of court.

EQUIPMENT

One ball and two rackets per pair of students and chalk to draw circles

CRITICAL ELEMENTS AND CUES

Technique

- Assume the ready position. *Cue:* Ready position.
- Make proper contact with the ball – one foot in front, shoulder to the net, strings facing the net, and contact made at waist level. *Cue:* Shoulder and strings face the net.
- Use the Continental, two-handed backhand grip. *Cue:* Continental grip-two hands.
- Call out *bounce* when you are in position before the ball bounces. *Cue:* Call out *bounce*. Quickly return to the ready position. *Cue:* Ready position.

COMMON ERRORS, CAUSES, AND CORRECTIONS

- Student has delayed positioning for backhand. *Cause:* The student is not setting up the stroke well to ensure they have time to make it. *Correction:* The student could practice getting in position for the backhand from 10-20 practices of having the ball tossed to them.
- The student's racket face is open on contact. *Cause:* The student is using the Eastern grip instead of the Continental grip. *Correction:* Prompt the student to change grip.
- The student's racket face is open on contact. *Cause:* The student doesn't use the correct footwork, the timing of which results in late arrival to the ball and contact made at lower than knee level. *Correction:* Have the student practice a quick approach to the ball and contact it at waist level while calling out *waist*.
- The student makes inaccurate shots (too long or short, too strong, or outside the designated backhand area). *Cause:* The student lacks ability. *Correction:* Place two cones within the designated hitting area and ask the student to aim the ball so it bounces between the cones (if the student's balls go out-of-bounds) or before the cones (if the student's balls go too far or outside the end lines).
- The student cannot maintain continuous play. *Cause:* The student does not make controlled and accurate strikes. *Correction:* Ask students to aim the ball so that they bounce halfway between the net and the opponent's location.
- The student remains in a side stance (shoulder to the net) on the strike and does not rotate back to a squared position. *Cause:* The student is likely forgetting to square up. *Correction:* Prompt the student with the cue, *square up*.
- The student uses improper footwork to get to the ball. *Cause:* At this stage it usually means the student is not moving soon enough and being proactive in attacking the oncoming ball. *Correction:* Be proactive, move sooner, and use longer steps when you are farther from the ball and smaller steps as you get closer to the ball for optimal positioning
- The student is forced to use a forehand strike. *Cause:* The student is using slow footwork and proper positioning. *Correction:* Have the student practice moving diagonally backward from the ready position to the backhand position.

TASK 20: FOREHAND TO BACKHAND CONTINUOUS GAME

PURPOSE

Following are the purposes of the task as related to aspects of skilled performance.

- Technique: In this task, students learn to repeatedly move from the ready position to the backhand or forehand position. Students develop accuracy by aiming their shots to specific areas of the court.
- Tactic: Students maintain continuous play with an opponent.
- Agility: Students develop fluent lateral, forward, and backward movements on the court to maintain the rally.

DESCRIPTION

Students are in pairs, and one student is on each side of the court. Both students have rackets. One student is designated to use forehand shots and the other backhand shots. The game starts with one student making an underhand serve. The receiver, who is on the center of the baseline in the ready position, moves to the ball to make their shot. Students attempt to maintain the rally except one student uses only forehand strokes and the other uses only backhand strokes. This requires students to move quickly and adjust their positions on the court to use the assigned strike, and it also requires them to aim the ball toward the proper area for the opponent to execute the assigned strike. Explain that the racket face should be turned toward the other player at contact. For cross-court shots, the racket face should be 45 degrees to the net on contact. When hitting down the line, the racket fact should be parallel to the net on contact. For opposite cross-court shots, the shoulders should be squared to the other player (a slightly open stance), and contact should occur beside the body with the racket head slightly behind the handle. Beginners can perform the task on a short court, and intermediate and advanced students can use the full court.

EQUIPMENT

One ball and two rackets per pair of students

CRITICAL ELEMENTS AND CUES

Technique

- Assume the ready position. *Cue:* Ready position.
- Make proper contact with the ball — one foot in front, shoulder to the net, strings facing the net, and contact made at waist level. *Cue:* Shoulder and strings face the net.
- Use the proper grip based on the assigned shot. *Cue:* Eastern or Continental.
- Ensure proper positioning of the racket face on contact. *Cue:* Grip strings; face target.

Agility

- Quickly return to the ready position. *Cue:* Ready position.

COMMON ERRORS, CAUSES, AND CORRECTIONS

Many errors or consistent errors of the same kind are being made. *Cause:* The progression to this task has been too fast for the student or the performance . *Correction:* At this level of play significant or recurring errors are difficult to address. We recommend returning to earlier tasks 17-20 (or even earlier tasks) to correct errors. It is a mistake at this stage of learning for students who are making errors to progress. It is developmentally appropriate to return to the tasks they can perform well and move forward from there.

TASK 21: PROGRESSIVE FRIEND-RIVAL RALLY–
INTERMEDIATE OR FULL COURT

PURPOSE

Following are the purposes of the task as related to aspects of skilled performance.

- Technique: In this task, students maintain a rally using forehand and backhand strokes.
- Tactic: Students rally using both ground strokes and play to win points.
- Fair play: Students differentiate between the friendly phase, in which students make comfortable shots to the opponent, and the rival phase, in which shots are made to win the point.

DESCRIPTION

Draw six circles on each side of the court with chalk equally spaced in two rows. Each circle about the size of a regular hula hoop (approximately 39 inches [100 centimeters]). Students are in pairs, and one student is on each side of the court. Beginning students play on three-quarters of the court (intermediate) and stand on the service line, and advanced students play on the full court and stand on the baseline. One student makes underhand toss to begin the rally. Students begin by completing two passes in the friendly phase of the rally before moving on to the rival phase. In the next rally, students add one additional pass to the friendly phase. In the rival phase, students attempt to earn points by placing shots are in the court that are not returned. Encourage students to hit to open spots on the opponent's court (using the circles on the ground). There is no pause between the friend and rival phases. If students make an error during the friendly phase, they restart the rally. Students earn one point for a complete friendly play, one point for winning the rally (i.e., a shot that is not returned successfully), and two points for an ace shot (a strike made to an open area that cannot be returned).

EQUIPMENT

One ball and two rackets per pair of students, chalk for drawing circles

CRITICAL ELEMENTS AND CUES

Technique

- Assume the ready position. *Cue:* Ready position.
- Use the proper grip. *Cue:* Use the correct grip.
- Quickly approach the incoming ball. *Cue:* Move quickly.
- Aim to the designated area on the opponent's court. *Cue:* Hit to the open space.
- Quickly return to the baseline. *Cue:* Return to the baseline.

Tactic

- Play to win in the rival phase of the game. *Cue:* Get ready to place the shot to win.

COMMON ERRORS, CAUSES, AND CORRECTIONS

- Many errors or consistent errors of the same kind are being made. *Cause:* The progression to this task has been too fast for the student or the performance. *Correction:* At this level of play significant or recurring errors are difficult to address. We recommend returning to earlier tasks 17-20 (or even earlier tasks) to correct errors. It is a mistake at this stage of learning for students who are making errors to progress. It is developmentally appropriate to return to the tasks they can perform well and move forward from there.
- The student makes the wrong shot. *Cause:* The student makes an error in judgment regarding the destination of the incoming ball. *Correction:* Have the student return to decision-making tasks for additional practice in fast recognition of the ball's direction.

- The student makes the wrong shot. *Cause:* The student avoids using the weaker stroke. *Correction:* Have the student practice the forehand or backhand stroke (whichever needs improvement).
- The student continues to play friendly in the rival phase of the game. *Cause:* The student is unable to accurately aim the ball to open spaces, or the student lacks proper decision-making regarding ball placement. *Correction:* Have the student identify open areas on the other side of the court and call out the target prior to the strike (e.g., right, back left), or place soft cones or poly spots on the court for the student to use as targets (each correct shot earns two points).
- The student uses difficult-to-return shots in the friendly phase of the game. *Cause:* The student is excited and wants to win. *Correction:* Make the friendly segment longer. Ask the student to make shots that the opponent can reach in three or fewer steps.

TASK 22: FOREHAND TO FOREHAND CONTINUOUS GAME B– INTERMEDIATE OR FULL COURT

PURPOSE

Following is the purpose of the task as related to aspects of skilled performance.

Technique: In this task, students learn the backswing for the forehand drive and refine the forehand drive and placement of the ball.

DESCRIPTION

The task introduces the backswing, which allows for longer shots to accommodate full-court play. To prepare for a forehand drive, students move from the ready position to a backswing position. Students step forward diagonally, stagger the feet, put the weight on the back foot, and turn the shoulder to the net. Students make a semicircle with the racket so the head points toward the wall behind them and the handle points toward the net. The racket is at waist level and parallel to the ground. As the ball approaches, the students move the racket forward to make contact and continue low to high for a proper follow-through.

Students are in pairs, and one student is on each side of the court. Both students have rackets. Students start playing using a three-quarters court (intermediate). The play begins with a self-toss and hit. When the ball bounces on the student's side of the court, the student calls out *bounce* while in a proper backswing position with one shoulder to the net. If the students cannot rally, have them stand at the back-left corner (for right-handed students; reverse this for left-handed students) of the court so the ball can be returned with the forehand drive. Once students achieve 30 points, have them play on the full court. A point is scored when the ball cross the net each time.

EQUIPMENT

One ball and two rackets per pair of students

CRITICAL ELEMENTS AND CUES

Technique

- Assume the ready position. *Cue:* Ready position.
- Use proper contact – one foot in front, shoulder to the net, strings facing the net, contact made at waist level. *Cue:* Shoulder and strings face the net.
- Use the Eastern grip. *Cue:* Eastern grip.
- Call out *bounce* when you are in position before the ball bounces. *Cue:* Call *bounce*.
- Step into the ball. *Cue:* Step toward the ball.
- Point the racket toward the wall behind you. *Cue:* Point.
- Create a full backswing. *Cue:* Swing back.

COMMON ERRORS, CAUSES, AND CORRECTIONS

- Many errors or consistent errors of the same kind are being made. *Cause:* The progression to this task has been too fast for the student or the performance . *Correction:* At this level of play significant or recurring errors are difficult to address. We recommend returning to earlier tasks 17-20 (or even earlier tasks) to correct errors. It is a mistake at this stage of learning for students who are making errors to progress. It is developmentally appropriate to return to the tasks they can perform well and move forward from there.

- The student runs laterally on the baseline rather than into the court. *Cause:* The student is not moving to the ball but waiting for it to come to them. *Correction:* Move off the baseline and toward the ball.

- The student has a short backswing. *Cause:* The student is using the earlier technique and has not incorporated the longer backswing. Improper backswing. *Correction:* Revert to feeding the balls by hand. For each hit, have the student call out the size of backswing performed (long, or short).

TASK 23: BACKHAND TO BACKHAND CONTINUOUS GAME B– INTERMEDIATE OR FULL COURT

PURPOSE

Following are the purposes of the task as related to aspects of skilled performance.

Technique: In this task, students learn the backswing for the backhand stroke and refine the backhand stroke and placement of the ball.

DESCRIPTION

Students are in pairs, and one student is on each side of the court. Both students have rackets. Students use a three-quarters court. The play begins with a self-toss and hit. The receiver moves from the ready position to the backswing position. As the student performs the semicircle, he or she rotates the grip (of the hitting hand only) from Eastern to Continental. When the ball bounces on the student's side of the court, the student calls out *bounce* while in a proper backswing position with one shoulder to the net. If the students cannot rally, have them stand at the back-right corner (for right-handed students; reverse this for left-handed students) of the court so the ball can be returned with the backhand drive. Once students achieve 30 points, have them play on the full court. A point is scored when the ball cross the net each time

EQUIPMENT

One ball and two rackets per pair of students

CRITICAL ELEMENTS AND CUES

Technique

- Assume the ready position. *Cue:* Ready position.
- Use proper contact – one foot in front, shoulder to the net, strings facing the net, contact made at waist level. *Cue:* Shoulder and strings face the net.
- Use the Continental two-handed grip. *Cue:* Continental grip.
- Call out *bounce* when you are in position before the ball bounces. *Cue:* Call *bounce*.
- Step into the ball. *Cue:* Step to the ball.
- Point the racket behind you. *Cue:* Point the racket behind you.
- Create a full backswing. *Cue:* Swing back.

COMMON ERRORS, CAUSES, AND CORRECTIONS

- Many errors or consistent errors of the same kind are being made. *Cause:* The progression to this task has been too fast for the student or the performance . *Correction:* At this level of play significant or recurring errors are difficult to address. We recommend returning to earlier tasks 17-20 (or even earlier tasks) to correct errors. It is a mistake at this stage of learning for students who are making errors to progress. It is developmentally appropriate to return to the tasks they can perform well and move forward from there.

- The student uses the incorrect grip or doesn't change the grip (if the student does not change grip, you will see a break in the wrist). *Cause:* The Continental two handed grip uses the Continental grip for the dominant hand and an Eastern forehand grip for the non-dominant hand. *Correction:* Prompt students to move to the Continental grip.

- The student's racket head is tilted down (head lower than the handle) or up (head higher than the handle) on the backswing. *Cause:* The student doesn't understand the position. *Correction:* Have the student practice using hand tosses from the partner to allow enough time to prepare the backswing. Have the student say *freeze* once the racket is correctly placed. You can also have the student imagine that there is a tray of eggs on the racket frame at the end of the backswing; the student must keep the racket head level so the eggs will not slide down.

- The student's racket face is open on contact. *Cause:* The student makes contact with the ball lower than knee level, which is often related to timing because of improper footwork and a thus a delayed approach to the ball. *Correction:* Have the student imitate the vertical movement of the ball with the knees before and after the bounce. The student bends down when the ball approaches the ground for the first bounce and then quickly rises as the ball begins to elevate from the ground. The student tries to catch the ball at waist level. The student first completes this without a racket; then the student uses a racket to complete the stroke.

- The student runs laterally on the baseline rather than into the court. *Cause:* The student is not moving to the ball but waiting for it to come to them. *Correction:* Move off the baseline and toward the ball

- The student has a short backswing. *Cause:* The student has improper backswing. *Correction:* Revert to feeding the balls by hand. For each hit, have the student call out the size of backswing performed (long, short).

TASK 24: FOREHAND TO FOREHAND AIMING GAME B

PURPOSE

Following are the purposes of the task as related to aspects of skilled performance.

- Technique: In this task, students learn to repeatedly move from the ready position to the forehand position in more demanding conditions that in previous tasks. They also learn to perform a full backswing and hit the ball at a specific target.
- Tactic: Students maintain continuous play with an opponent.
- Agility: Students promptly place themselves in relation to the ball to complete a forehand stroke.

DESCRIPTION

Three circles are drawn with chalk equally spaced in parallel to the baseline. Each circle about the size of a regular hula hoop (approximately 39 inches [100 centimeters]). Students are in pairs, and one student is on each side of the full court. Both students have rackets. This is similar to the forehand to forehand aiming game A (task 18) but there are now only the three circles parallel to the baseline. The students attempt to land the ball into one of three circles.

EQUIPMENT

One ball and two rackets per pair of students and chalk to draw the circles

CRITICAL ELEMENTS AND CUES

Technique

- Assume the ready position. *Cue:* Ready position.
- Ensure correct contact – one foot in front, shoulder to the net, strings facing the net, contact made at waist level. *Cue:* Shoulder and strings to the net.
- Use the Eastern grip. *Cue:* Eastern grip.
- Quickly return to the ready position. *Cue:* Return to ready position.
- Step into the ball. *Cue:* Move to the ball.
- Point the racket behind you. *Cue:* Point the racket behind you.
- Create a full backswing. *Cue:* Swing back.

COMMON ERRORS, CAUSES, AND CORRECTIONS

- Many errors or consistent errors of the same kind are being made. *Cause:* The progression to this task has been too fast for the student or the performance . *Correction:* At this level of play significant or recurring errors are difficult to address. We recommend returning to earlier tasks 17-20 (or even earlier tasks) to correct errors. It is a mistake at this stage of learning for students who are making errors to progress. It is developmentally appropriate to return to the tasks they can perform well and move forward from there.
- The student runs laterally on the baseline rather than into the court. *Cause:* The student is not moving to the ball but waiting for it to come to them. *Correction:* Move off the baseline and toward the ball
- The student has a short backswing. *Cause:* The student has improper backswing. *Correction:* Revert to feeding the balls by hand. For each hit, have the student call out the size of backswing performed (long, short).
- The student makes inaccurate shots (too long or short, too strong, or outside the designated forehand area). *Cause:* The ball is being hit too hard. *Correction:* Prompt the students to hit more lightly with less force.
- The students cannot maintain continuous play. *Cause:* The students do not make controlled and accurate strikes. *Correction:* Ask students to aim the balls so they bounce halfway between the net and the opponent's location.
- The student remains in an open stance on the shot (does not shift from a squared position to or does not move from perpendicular back to a squared position). *Cause:* The student is not moving to the forearm shot position. *Correction:* Prompt the student to move.
- The student uses improper footwork to get to the ball. *Cause:* At this stage it usually means the student is not moving soon enough and being proactive in attacking the oncoming ball. *Correction:* Be proactive, move sooner, and use longer steps when you are farther from the ball and smaller steps as you get closer to the ball for optimal positioning.
- The student has to use a backhand strike. *Cause:* The student is out of position when making the shot and is not proactive in moving toward the spot. *Correction:* Use longer steps when you are farther from the ball and smaller steps as you get closer to the ball for optimal positioning.

TASK 25: BACKHAND TO BACKHAND AIMING GAME

PURPOSE

Following are the purposes of the task as related to aspects of skilled performance.

- Technique: In this task, students learn to repeatedly move from the ready position to the backhand position. Students also learn how to perform a full shot and hit the ball at a target.
- Tactic: Students maintain continuous play with an opponent.
- Agility: Students promptly place themselves in relation to the ball to complete a backhand stroke.

DESCRIPTION

Three circles are drawn with chalk equally spaced in parallel to the baseline. Each circle about the size of a regular hula hoop (approximately 39 inches [100 centimeters]). Students are in pairs, and one student is on each side of the court. Both students have rackets. This is the same general purpose as the forehand to forehand aiming game because the targets are three circles drawn parallel to the baseline. Here the focus is on the backhand and not the forehand. The students attempt to land the ball into one of three circles arranged along the baseline. Award one point for each returned shot.

EQUIPMENT

One ball and two rackets per pair of students, chalk to draw the circles

CRITICAL ELEMENTS AND CUES

Technique

- Assume the ready position. *Cue:* Ready position.
- Use the Continental, two-handed backhand grip. *Cue:* Focus on the grip.
- Step into the ball. *Cue:* Step into the ball.
- Point the racket toward the wall behind you. *Cue:* Point the racket behind you.
- Create a full backswing. *Cue:* Swing back.

COMMON ERRORS, CAUSES, AND CORRECTIONS

- Students use delayed positioning for backhand. *Cause:* The student is not setting up the stroke well to ensure they have time to make it. *Correction:* The student could practice getting in position for the backhand from 10-20 practices of having the ball tossed to them.
- The student runs laterally on the baseline rather than into the court. *Cause:* The student is not moving to the ball but waiting for it to come to them. *Correction:* Move off the baseline and toward the ball.
- The student's racket face is open on contact. *Cause:* Grip of striking hand is Eastern. *Correction:* See previous tasks for error correction.
- The student's racket face is open on contact. *Cause:* The student doesn't use the correct footwork, which results in late arrival to the ball and contact made at lower than knee level. *Correction:* Have the student practice a quick approach to the ball and contact it at waist level while calling out *waist*.
- The student's racket head is tilted down (head lower than the handle) or up (head higher than the handle) on the backswing. *Cause:* The student doesn't understand the position. *Correction:* Have the student practice using hand tosses from the partner to allow enough time to prepare the backswing. Have the student say *freeze* once the racket is correctly placed. You can also have the student imagine that there is a tray of eggs on the racket frame at the end of the backswing; the student must keep the racket head level so the eggs will not slide down.
- The student has a short backswing. *Cause:* The student is not remembering to use a full backswing. *Correction:* Prompt the student with the cue *swing back*.

- The student makes inaccurate shots (too long, too strong, or outside the designated forehand area). *Cause:* The student lacks ability. *Correction:* Place two cones within the designated hitting area and ask the student to aim the ball so it bounces between the cones (if the student's balls go out-of-bounds) or before the cones (if the student's balls go too far or outside the end lines).
- The students has to use a forehand strike. *Cause:* Becasue of slow footwork and the student finishes out of position to strike. *Correction:* Have the student practice moving diagonally backward from the ready position to the backhand position.

TASK 26: BEANBAG VOLLEY IN THE SERVICE BOX

PURPOSE

Following is the purpose of the task as related to aspects of skilled performance.
    Technique: In this task, students learn to volley using a beanbag.

DESCRIPTION

A volley is any shot that is hit before the ball bounces. Students hold the racket firmly in the path of a ball like a stop sign; there is no backswing.

Students are in pairs, and one student is on each side of the court. Have students hold their rackets out so they touch they net and then take one step backward. One student tosses the beanbag over the net on a flat flight path. The receiver uses the nonracket hand to trap the beanbag on the strings of the racket, holds it for a moment, and tosses it back. The partner then traps the beanbag, holds it for a moment, and tosses it back. Students make 20 traps each.

This task emphasizes that the volley is a block rather than a hit; catching the beanbag changes the perception of the object. The problem of quickly looking up toward a target is eliminated.

- *Extension 1.* As students advance, have them toss the beanbag farther away from the center so they have to run to the bag to trap it before it falls.
- *Extension 2.* Repeat the task with a ball instead of a beanbag.

EQUIPMENT

One beanbag, one ball (for the extension), and two rackets per pair of students

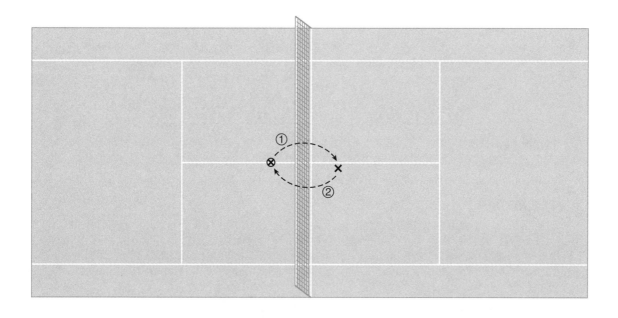

CRITICAL ELEMENTS AND CUES

Technique

- Use the Continental grip for medium-height balls and the Eastern grip for high balls. *Cue:* Eastern grip high, Continental grip low.
- Place the racket in front of the body at a 45-degree angle and tilt the head forward. *Cue:* Racket at 45 degrees.
- Hold the wrist firm. *Cue:* Firm wrist.
- Turn slightly sideways to the target before trapping the beanbag. *Cue:* Turn slightly.
- Contact the beanbag in front of the body. Block the beanbag; do not hit it. *Cue:* Block, do not hit the bean bag.
- Forward movement after blocking. *Cue:* Step forward after blocking, come forward.
- Choke up on the racket to gain control if needed. *Cue:* Choke up.
- On the Continental grip, the nondominant hand remains on the neck of the racket for support. *Cue:* Use Continental grip.
- Catch the beanbag above the height of the net; do not allow the beanbag to drop below this height. *Cue:* Catch the bean bag above the net.

COMMON ERRORS, CAUSES, AND CORRECTIONS

- The student moves laterally instead of forward. *Cause:* The student uses the wrong footwork on the volley stroke. *Correction:* Have the student take two steps forward after the catch or touch the net after the catch (with the hand or the racket).
- The student allows the beanbag to drop below the height of the net. *Cause:* The student does not move to the beanbag on the volley and bean bag falls too low. *Correction:* Have the student step toward the bean bag sooner.
- The student uses the incorrect grip. *Cause:* The students are not using the Continental grip for medium-height balls or the Eastern grip for high balls. *Correction:* Have 10-15 hand tosses of the bean bags to high positions and 10-15 to lower positions to allow students to practice the correct grip.
- The racket face is open and the racket is tilted down. *Cause:* The student doesn't understand the technique. *Correction:* Have the student practice without a racket and use a forward movement to catch the beanbag. The student should catch the beanbag with the palm completely flat and facing the net, imitating the racket position.

TASK 27: VOLLEY GAME IN THE SERVICE BOX

PURPOSE

Following is the purpose of the task as related to aspects of skilled performance.
Technique: In this task, students learn to volley a tennis ball.

DESCRIPTION

Students are in pairs, and one student is on each side of the court. Have students hold their rackets out so they touch the net and then take one step backward. Students stand in the ready position. One student underhand tosses the ball to the partner, who begins moving forward to the ball and opening the racket forward to block it. Students should contact medium-height balls with a straight racket (strings parallel to the net) and low balls (below net height) using a Continental grip with an open racket face to elevate the ball above the net.

- *Extension 1.* Students use only forehand volleys and then use only backhand volleys.
- *Extension 2.* Students alternate between forehand and backhand volleys.
- *Extension 3.* Students make volleys only above the net height.
- *Extension 4.* Set a goal for the number of volleys (e.g., 5, 10, 15).

EQUIPMENT

One ball and two rackets per pair of students

CRITICAL ELEMENTS AND CUES

Technique

- Use the Continental grip for medium-height balls and the Eastern grip for high balls. *Cue:* Eastern grip high, Continental grip low.
- Place the racket in front of the body at a 45-degree angle and tilt the head forward. *Cue:* Racket at 45 degrees.
- Hold the wrist firm. *Cue:* Firm wrist.
- Turn slightly sideways to the target before trapping the beanbag. *Cue:* Turn slightly.

COMMON ERRORS, CAUSES, AND CORRECTIONS

- The student swings to hit the ball. *Cause:* The student attempts to hit a volley using a backswing rather than moving forward to the incoming ball. *Correction:* Have the student practice either the forehand or backhand volley. Stand right behind the student and place your racket in a volley position. The student's backswing will hit your racket and make a sound. Instruct the student to avoid touching your racket.
- The student's wrist is soft. *Cause:* The student lacks arm strength. *Correction:* Have the student practice switching from soft to firm grip at least 20 times. You can also feed the student strong and precise balls to the volley position so the student has opportunities to practice holding the racket firmly on the volley.
- The student is too slow to get to the ball. *Cause:* The student is not anticipating the shot. *Correction:* Prompt the student to anticipate where the ball will be.
- The student uses the incorrect grip—most commonly the Continental grip. *Cause:* The student's timing for releasing the hitting hand is incorrect. *Correction:* Have the student practice only backhand volley strikes off a tossed ball and call out *two* on contact to verify that he or she has both hands on the racket. The student can progress to hitting the balls to the student so the student can apply stronger shots.
- The student allows the ball to drop below the height of the net. *Cause:* The student does not move to the ball on the volley and bean bag falls too low. *Correction:* Have the student step toward the ball sooner.

TASK 28: BASELINE VOLLEY FRIEND-RIVAL GAME

PURPOSE

Following are the purposes of the task as related to aspects of skilled performance.

- Technique: In this task, students learn to volley balls hit from the baseline while improving their ability to aim the ball to a target.
- Agility: Students respond quickly to the incoming ball in a volley position.
- Fair play: Students practice playing cooperatively with an opponent and maintain a rally of at least three shots.

DESCRIPTION

Students are in pairs, and one student is on each side of the court. One student begins the game with a forehand shot from the baseline. The partner is in a volley position. Students begin with two consecutive friendly volley shots, and then they begin playing to score points; one point for each ball across the net. After three points, they switch roles. In the next rally, students add one additional pass to the friendly phase of the volley. This game develops reactions, footwork, control, and the very important habit of moving forward to receive a volley.

EQUIPMENT

One ball and two rackets per pair of students

CRITICAL ELEMENTS AND CUES

Technique

- Assume the ready position with the racket out in front of the body. *Cue:* Ready position.
- Use the Continental grip for medium-height balls and the Eastern grip for high balls. *Cue:* Eastern grip high, Continental grip low.
- Place the racket in front of the body at a 45-degree angle and tilt the head forward. *Cue:* Racket at 45 degrees.
- Hold the wrist firm. *Cue:* Firm wrist.
- Turn slightly sideways to the target. *Cue:* Turn slightly.
- Contact the ball in front of the body. Block the ball; do not hit it. *Cue:* Block don't hit.
- Use forward rather than lateral movement. *Cue:* Move to the ball.

COMMON ERRORS, CAUSES, AND CORRECTIONS

- The student's wrist is soft. *Cause:* The student lacks arm strength. *Correction:* Have the student practice switching from soft to firm grip at least 20 times. You can also feed the student strong and precise balls to the volley position so the student has opportunities to practice holding the racket firmly on the volley.
- The student is too slow to get to the ball. *Cause:* The student is not anticipating the shot. *Correction:* Prompt the student to anticipate where the ball will be.
- The student uses the incorrect grip-most commonly the Continental grip. *Cause:* The student's timing for releasing the hitting hand is incorrect. *Correction:* Have the student practice only backhand volley strikes off a tossed ball and call out *two* on contact to verify that he or she has both hands on the racket. The student can progress to hitting the balls to the student so the student can apply stronger shots.
- The student allows the ball to drop below the height of the net. *Cause:* The student does not move to the ball on the volley and ball falls too low. *Correction:* Have the student step toward the ball sooner.
- The students cannot complete the friendly segment of the rally due to inaccurate shots. *Cause:* The students cannot aim or they have improper technique on the shots. *Correction:* Instruct the baseline student to aim toward the body of the volley student. Instruct the volley student to volley the ball to the service line or beyond it (anywhere between the service line and baseline). Remind students to use proper techniques as required.

TASK 29: SERVE: TOSS THE BALL

PURPOSE

Following is the purpose of the task as related to aspects of skilled performance.

Technique: In this task, students learn to make self-tosses for a serve.

DESCRIPTION

Students stand on the service line in a staggered stance facing the net. First, the students toss the ball upward with the nondominant hand slightly above the height of a racket that is extended above the head. The wrist should not snap on the toss. Second, students repeat this practice while focusing on complete flexion in the shoulder and extension in elbow. Third, students begin the toss from the inside of the thigh. Finally, they follow-through with the nondominant hand by keep lifting the arm up following the ball. Students move to the subsequent step after making 10 correct tosses.

EQUIPMENT

One ball and one racket per student

CRITICAL ELEMENTS AND CUES

Technique

- Grasp the ball with the tips of the spread fingers. *Cue:* Use the tips of your fingers.
- Extend the elbow. *Cue:* Extend the elbow.
- Begin the toss from the inner thigh. *Cue:* Toss from the inner thigh.
- Follow-through with the nondominant hand by keep lifting the arm up following the ball (do not snap the toss). *Cue:* Follow the ball.

COMMON ERRORS, CAUSES, AND CORRECTIONS

- The ball spins too much. *Cause:* The ball rolls over the palm. *Correction:* Have the student grasp the ball with the tips of the fingers and then focus on pushing the ball up from the tips of the fingers.
- The toss is too high or too low. *Cause:* The student does not regulate the power of the toss. *Correction:* Have the student practice the task next to a wall or fence. Mark the desired height on the wall or fence so the student has a visual reference. Award the student one point each time the toss is at the correct height.
- The toss is too far to the side. *Cause:* The student does not begin the toss from the inner thigh. *Correction:* Have the student touch the inner thigh with the nondominant hand holding the ball and call *ready*.
- There is no shoulder extension during the toss. *Cause:* The student makes the tossing movement from the elbow, rather than the shoulder. *Correction:* Have students perform the toss one in front of the other following the ball each time keeping the arm up high each time for a 2 seconds.

TASK 30: SERVE: TOSS THE BALL WITH ACCURATE PLACEMENT

PURPOSE

Following is the purpose of the task as related to aspects of skilled performance.

Technique: In this task, students learn to make accurate self-tosses for a serve.

DESCRIPTION

Students stands on the service line and face the net. This task extends the third phase of task 29. Have students imagine a clock; the head is at 12 o'clock and the feet are at 6 o'clock. Have students extend their rackets and place them where the right hand is straight at the 1 o'clock area out in front of the body. (Use the 11 o'clock position with the left hand for left-handed students.) Then have students place the rackets on that spot on the ground. Students toss the ball with the nondominant hand so it bounces on the racket. Have the students try to achieve 10 hits on the racket.

EQUIPMENT
One ball and one racket per student

CRITICAL ELEMENTS AND CUES

Technique
- Grasp the ball with the tips of the spread fingers. *Cue:* Use spread fingers to hold the ball.
- Extend the elbow. *Cue:* Extend the elbow.
- Begin the toss from the inner thigh. *Cue:* Start at the inner thigh.
- Aim the ball to the 1 o'clock position (if you are right-handed) or the 11 o'clock position (if you are left-handed). *Cue:* Where are you aiming?

COMMON ERRORS, CAUSES, AND CORRECTIONS
- The ball spins too much. *Cause:* The ball is being turned (spun) of the tips of the fingers. *Correction:* Have the student toss to low and then larger heights without spinning the ball too much.
- The toss is too high or too low. *Cause:* The student is not experienced enough with the toss. *Correction:* More trials are needed to refine the toss. Have the student toss and focus just on the height.
- Toss is too far to the side. *Cause:* The student is not experienced enough with the toss. *Correction:* More trials are needed to refine the toss. Have the student toss and focus just on the placement.
- The student makes inaccurate tosses. *Cause:* The student lacks control over the toss with the nondominant hand. *Correction:* Move the student to the fence or the wall. Have the student toss the ball and trap it against the fence or wall with the racket so the student can see if the toss is in the correct position.

TASK 31: SERVE: GRIP, CONTACT, AND FOLLOW THROUGH SHORT COURT

PURPOSE
Following is the purpose of the task as related to aspects of skilled performance.

Technique: In this task, students learn the proper grip, contact, and follow-through for the serve.

DESCRIPTION
Students stand on the service line (i.e., using the short court) and hold the racket in the Continental grip (the hand is placed on top of the racket when the racket is perpendicular to the net). The fingers are spread (but the index finger is not completely open) and the hand is at the bottom of the handle. If the grip is correct, the racket frame will face the net when the racket is extended above the head with the arm straight in the 1 o'clock position (left-handed students use the 11 o'clock position). Teach the students to pronate the wrist so the racket opens and the strings face the net to contact the ball. Pronation is critical because it gives the serve power and speed. Contact should be made out in front of the body.

Progress through the task in two phases. First, have students toss the ball to 1'clock when the racket is in position. When the ball is close to the racket, students should pronate the wrist for contact. The students should make contact with the strings but not hit the ball. Second, have students toss the ball, pronate for contact, and follow through naturally high to low diagonally, finishing the stroke on top of the thigh of the nonhitting side at the same time they should shift the weight onto their front foot. Contact should be made at the highest level possible at 1 o'clock in front of the body. Students should try to make 10 accurate tosses to 1 o'clock with contact and then do 10 serves from the right and 10 from the left to the diagonal service box. Students should focus on grip and pronation.

EQUIPMENT

One ball and one racket per student

CRITICAL ELEMENTS AND CUES

Technique

- Toss the ball toward 1 o'clock. The ball should go toward the racket. *Cue:* 1 o'clock.
- Follow through on the toss. *Cue:* Swing high to low diagonally.
- Follow through to the opposite thigh. *Cue:* Finish the stroke on top of the thigh.
- Maintain the proper grip. *Cue:* Continental grip.
- Shift the weight forward to make contact: *Cue:* Shift forward.
- Reach and make proper contact. *Cue:* Contact high.

COMMON ERRORS, CAUSES, AND CORRECTIONS

- The student's toss and contact are inaccurate. *Cause:* The student is not experienced enough with the toss. *Correction:* More trials are needed to refine the toss. Have the student toss and focus just on the placement.
- The student's follow through is incorrect. *Cause:* The student applies too much force to the swing and doesn't shift the weight forward. *Correction:* On the follow through, have the student place the racket on the opposite thigh and say *check*. Have the student step forward with the back foot after the follow through.
- The student uses the incorrect grip (Eastern instead of Continental) and there is no pronation. *Cause:* The student got used to Eastern grip, which allows for easier direct contact with the ball above the head. *Correction:* Have the student stand next to a fence or wall with the racket in Continental grip and the racket frame pointing toward the fence or wall. The student tosses the ball and performs pronation to trap the ball between the strings and the fence or wall.

TASK 32: SERVE–HALF SWING

PURPOSE

Following is the purpose of the task as related to aspects of skilled performance.
Technique: In this task, students learn to extend the service stroke to a half swing.

DESCRIPTION

This is a demanding task. The serve motion is complex and uses two hands; therefore, it requires some practice without the ball for mastery. Students stand on the service line with the shoulders almost perpendicular to the net, feet in staggered position creating an imaginary line of a 45 and 135 degree angle (left box, right box, respectively) to the service box to where the ball will be served. The student's tossing hand is close to the inner thigh. There is a 90-degree bend in the elbow of the hitting hand, which is elevated at shoulder height so the racket frame is facing the net. Students then follow this sequence of steps:

1. Drop the racket to the back. The frame touches the back.
2. Reach for contact at 1 o'clock while rotating the shoulders to a squared position to the net.
3. Pronate, contact, and follow through to the opposite thigh.

4. Students should alternate practice trials from the right and left sides of the court. Have students perform 20 trials of each item.

Use the following points of emphasis to refine technique.

- Students practice the three-phase movement without a racket while holding a ball in the hitting hand. Students complete the motion and throw the ball as far as possible to the backcourt on the other side of the net.
- Students practice dropping the racket to the back.
- Students practice quick pronation.
- Students practice contact in front of the body.
- Students practice contact at 1 o'clock (11 o'clock).
- Students practice contact at the highest point.
- Students practice proper follow-through.

Most ball placement and contact errors should be practiced and refined next to a fence or wall, where students can visualize the correct positioning by trapping the ball.

EQUIPMENT

One ball and one racket per student

CRITICAL ELEMENTS AND CUES

Technique

- Use the Continental grip. *Cue:* Continental grip.
- Toss the ball toward 1 o'clock. The ball should go toward the racket. *Cue:* 1 o'clock.
- Reach and make contact high. *Cue:* Contact high.
- Contact the ball in front the body. *Cue:* Contact in front.
- Follow through to the opposite thigh. *Cue:* Follow through to thigh.
- Rotate the shoulders. *Cue:* Rotate shoulders.
- Pronate. *Cue:* Pronate.
- Keep the elbow high. *Cue:* Elbow high.

COMMON ERRORS, CAUSES, AND CORRECTIONS

- The student's toss and contact are inaccurate. *Cause:* The student is not experienced enough with the toss. *Correction:* More trials are needed to refine the toss. Have the student toss and focus just on the placement.

- The student's follow through is incorrect. *Cause:* The student's placement is incorrect or the student uses improper follow-through technique. *Correction:* Have the student show you where the follow through should finish (opposite thigh) then have them practice without a ball to finish there.

- The student's stance is incorrect prior to serving. *Cause:* The student has not practiced the stance enough. *Correction:* Have the student draw an imaginary line that passes through the toes of both feet and extends to the target box for the serve. The student should draw the imaginary line with the racket held in a serve grip. Alternately, you can mark proper foot placement on the floor.

- The student uses the incorrect grip (Eastern instead of Continental) and there is no pronation. *Cause:* Using the incorrect grip eliminates pronation. *Correction:* Have the student practice snapping the hand (without a racket) 20 times. The student can also practice the snap against the fence or wall without a ball. The student begins with the racket frame against the fence or wall and quickly pronates so the racket strings hit the fence or wall.

- There is no shoulder rotation. *Cause:* The student does not shift the weight forward. *Correction:* Be sure the student's shoulders are squared to the net after contact. You can also have the student step in diagonally toward the target box immediately after the serve. Alternately, you can place one cone three steps into the court and have the student hit the serve, fall forward, circle the cone, and return to the baseline.

- The ball is contacted too low. *Cause:* This is a timing issue and is related to contacting the ball at the top of the toss. *Correction:* More trials are needed to refine the contact. Have the student toss and focus on the contact.

TASK 33: HALF SERVE AND PLAY ON THE INTERMEDIATE COURT

PURPOSE

Following are the purposes of the task as related to aspects of skilled performance.

- Technique: In this task, students learn to use the half serve in a game.
- Tactic: Students target the serve to a designated box.

DESCRIPTION

Students are in pairs, and one student is on each side of the court. The server is on the three-quarters line with a ball. The partner is on baseline in the middle of the corresponding service box. The server makes a half serve to begin the rally. If the first serve is in, the server gets two points. (If the student misses the first serve, he or she makes a second serve.) Students switch roles after a student has served for five consecutive points. Students should begin serving from the right and then alternate after each point played. Award bonus points for specific critical elements (e.g., high contact, contact in front of the body, accurate toss, proper follow-through).

EQUIPMENT

One racket per student; one ball per pair of students

CRITICAL ELEMENTS AND CUES

Technique

- Use the Continental grip when serving. *Cue:* Use Continental grip.
- Toss the ball toward 1 o'clock. The ball should go toward the racket. *Cue:* 1 o'clock.

- Reach and make contact high. *Cue:* Contact high.
- Contact the ball in front the body. *Cue:* Contact in front.
- Follow through to the opposite thigh. *Cue:* Follow through to thigh.
- Rotate the shoulders. *Cue:* Rotate shoulders.
- Pronate. *Cue:* Pronate.
- Keep the elbow high. *Cue:* Elbow high.

COMMON ERRORS, CAUSES, AND CORRECTIONS

- The student's toss and contact are inaccurate. *Cause:* The student is not experienced enough with the toss. *Correction:* More trials are needed to refine the toss. Have the student toss and focus just on the placement.
- The student's follow through is incorrect. *Cause:* The student's placement is incorrect or the student uses improper follow-through technique. *Correction:* Have the student show you where the follow through should finish (opposite thigh) then have them practice without a ball to finish there.
- The student's stance is incorrect prior to serving. *Cause:* The student has not practiced the stance enough. *Correction:* Have the student draw an imaginary line that passes through the toes of both feet and extends to the target box for the serve. The student should draw the imaginary line with the racket held in a serve grip. Alternately, you can mark proper foot placement on the floor.
- The student uses the incorrect grip (Eastern instead of Continental) and there is no pronation. *Cause:* Using the incorrect grip eliminates pronation. *Correction:* Have the student practice snapping the hand (without a racket) 20 times. The student can also practice the snap against the fence or wall without a ball. The student begins with the racket frame against the fence or wall and quickly pronates so the racket strings hit the fence or wall.
- There is no shoulder rotation. *Cause:* The student does not shift the weight forward. *Correction:* Be sure the student's shoulders are squared to the net after contact. You can also have the student step in diagonally toward the target box immediately after the serve. Alternately, you can place one cone three steps into the court and have the student hit the serve, fall forward, circle the cone, and return to the baseline.

TASK 34: SERVE: FULL STROKE-ON THE FULL COURT

PURPOSE
Following are the purposes of the task as related to aspects of skilled performance.

Technique: In this task, students practice the full serve on a full court, and practice aiming the serve to the appropriate box.

DESCRIPTION
Students are in pairs, and one student is on each side of the court. The server is on the baseline close to the center. The server stands with the shoulders almost perpendicular to the net, feet in staggered position creating an imaginary line of a 45 and 135 degree angle (left box, right box, respectively) to the service box to where the ball will be served. The receiver is on the baseline in the middle of the corresponding service box. The server's tossing hand is close to the inner thigh. There is a 90-degree bend in the elbow of the hitting hand, which is elevated at shoulder height so the racket frame is facing the net. Students then follow this sequence of steps:

1. Students assume the same court position described in the half swing (task 32). Again, students practice without a ball before hitting live balls. Teach the motion in the following steps:

- Hold the racket in the Continental grip with the nondominant hand grasping the ball and slightly supporting the racket underneath the neck. Make a toss from the inner thigh.
- Repeat step 1 and add the hand motion: The nondominant hand tosses while the hitting hand swings down, back, and up with elbow flexed until the frame is touching the back. The knees are bent.
- Complete the two previous steps and continue to swing the racket to contact point (reach up) and follow through.
- Complete the follow-through and shift the back foot forward (weight shift).

2. Once student have mastered this, they can move to executing the full motion with balls. Students should practice each step 10 times and then add the next step. Students should practice 15 serves from each side.

EQUIPMENT

One ball and one racket per student

CRITICAL ELEMENTS AND CUES

Technique

- Use the Continental grip when serving. *Cue:* Use Continental grip.
- Toss the ball toward 1 o'clock. The ball should go toward the racket. *Cue:* 1 o'clock.
- Reach and make contact high. *Cue:* Contact high.
- Contact the ball in front the body. *Cue:* Contact in front.
- Follow through to the opposite thigh. *Cue:* Follow through to thigh.
- Rotate the shoulders. *Cue:* Rotate shoulders.
- Pronate. *Cue:* Pronate.
- Keep the elbow high. *Cue:* Elbow high.
- Hit diagonally to the opposite box. *Cue:* Hit cross court.
- Step forward after the shot. *Cue:* Step forward following the shot.

COMMON ERRORS, CAUSES, AND CORRECTIONS

- The student's toss and contact are inaccurate. *Cause:* The student is not experienced enough with the toss. *Correction:* More trials are needed to refine the toss. Have the student toss and focus just on the placement.

- The student's follow through is incorrect. *Cause:* The student's placement is incorrect or the student uses improper follow-through technique. *Correction:* Have the student show you where the follow through should finish (opposite thigh) then have them practice without a ball to finish there.

- The student's stance is incorrect prior to serving. *Cause:* The student has not practiced the stance enough. *Correction:* Have the student draw an imaginary line that passes through the toes of both feet and extends to the target box for the serve. The student should draw the imaginary line with the racket held in a serve grip. Alternately, you can mark proper foot placement on the floor.

- The student uses the incorrect grip (Eastern instead of Continental) and there is no pronation. *Cause:* Using the incorrect grip eliminates pronation. *Correction:* Have the student practice snapping the hand (without a racket) 20 times. The student can also practice the snap against the fence or wall without a ball. The student begins with the racket frame against the fence or wall and quickly pronates so the racket strings hit the fence or wall.

- There is no shoulder rotation. *Cause:* The student does not shift the weight forward. *Correction:* Be sure the student's shoulders are squared to the net after contact. You can also have the student step in diagonally toward the target box immediately after the serve. Alternately, you can place one cone three steps into the court and have the student hit the serve, fall forward, circle the cone, and return to the baseline.

- The contact point on the racket is incorrect –this is called a rainbow hit. *Cause:* The student is not experienced enough with the toss. *Correction:* More trials are needed to practice appropriate contact.

- The student serves the ball to the wrong box. *Cause:* The student is not experienced in placing the serve. *Correction:* More trials are needed to practice appropriate placement.

TASK 35: SERVICE: FULL-STROKE REFINEMENTS

PURPOSE

Following are the purposes of the task as related to aspects of skilled performance.

Technique: In this task, students practice the full serve on the full court and practice aiming the serve to the appropriate box.

DESCRIPTION

Students are in pairs, and one student is on each side of the court. The server is on the baseline close to the center. The receiver is on the baseline in the middle of the corresponding service box. Due to the complexity of the serve, which involves a chain of synchronized actions with two hands, you will need to work on refinements once students start using the full stroke. You should focus on one critical element at a time. Allow at least 15 trials per service side once you refine a specific element. Elements that may deteriorate and pose challenges for students when hitting the full serve include the toss (too high, too low, to the right, to the left), late contact (above or behind the head instead of in front of the back), low contact, grip, follow-through, and contact below the ball (instead of on top). Award one point each time students properly place the ball on the other side and one point when they demonstrate the proper critical element.

EQUIPMENT

One ball and one racket per student

CRITICAL ELEMENTS AND CUES

Technique

- Use the Continental grip when serving. *Cue:* Use Continental grip.
- Toss the ball toward 1 o'clock. The ball should go toward the racket. *Cue:* 1 o'clock.
- Reach and make contact high. *Cue:* Contact high.
- Contact the ball in front the body. *Cue:* Contact in front.
- Follow through to the opposite thigh. *Cue:* Follow through to thigh.
- Rotate the shoulders. *Cue:* Rotate shoulders.
- Pronate. *Cue:* Pronate.
- Keep the elbow high. *Cue:* Elbow high.
- Hit diagonally to the opposite box. *Cue:* Hit cross court.
- Step forward after the shot. *Cue:* Step forward following the shot.

COMMON ERRORS, CAUSES, AND CORRECTIONS

- The student's toss and contact are inaccurate. *Cause:* The student is not experienced enough with the toss. *Correction:* More trials are needed to refine the toss. Have the student toss and focus just on the placement.
- The student's follow through is incorrect. *Cause:* The student's placement is incorrect or the student uses improper follow-through technique. *Correction:* Have the student show you where the follow through should finish (opposite thigh) then have them practice without a ball to finish there.
- The student's stance is incorrect prior to serving. *Cause:* The student has not practiced the stance enough. *Correction:* Have the student draw an imaginary line that passes through the toes of both feet and extends to the target box for the serve. The student should draw the imaginary line with the racket held in a serve grip. Alternately, you can mark proper foot placement on the floor.
- The student uses the incorrect grip (Eastern instead of Continental) and there is no pronation. *Cause:* Using the incorrect grip eliminates pronation. *Correction:* Have the student practice snapping the hand (without a racket) 20 times. The student can also practice the snap against the fence or wall without a ball. The student begins with the racket frame against the fence or wall and quickly pronates so the racket strings hit the fence or wall.
- There is no shoulder rotation. *Cause:* The student does not shift the weight forward. *Correction:* Be sure the student's shoulders are squared to the net after contact. You can also have the student step in diagonally toward the target box immediately after the serve. Alternately, you can place one cone three steps into the court and have the student hit the serve, fall forward, circle the cone, and return to the baseline.
- The contact point on the racket is incorrect; this is called a rainbow hit. *Cause:* The student is not experienced enough with the toss. *Correction:* More trials are needed to practice appropriate contact.
- The student serves the ball to the wrong box. *Cause:* The student is not experienced in placing the serve. *Correction:* More trials are needed to practice appropriate placement.

TASK 36: FRIEND-RIVAL GAME WITH SERVE

PURPOSE

Following are the purposes of the task as related to aspects of skilled performance.

- Technique: In this task, students apply the serve in a game.
- Tactic: Students practice a serve that will catch the opponent off balance at the start of the rally.

DESCRIPTION

Students are in pairs, and one student is on each side of the court. The server is on the baseline close to the center. The receiver is on the baseline in the middle of the corresponding service box. One student begins the game with a serve. Students can play a friendly phase or can play for the point immediately following the serve.

EQUIPMENT

One ball and two rackets per pair of students

CRITICAL ELEMENTS AND CUES

Technique

- Use the Continental grip when serving. *Cue:* Use Continental grip.
- Toss the ball toward 1 o'clock. The ball should go toward the racket. *Cue:* 1 o'clock.
- Reach and make contact high. *Cue:* Contact high.
- Contact the ball in front the body. *Cue:* Contact in front.
- Follow through to the opposite thigh. *Cue:* Follow through to thigh.
- Rotate the shoulders. *Cue:* Rotate shoulders.
- Pronate. *Cue:* Pronate.
- Keep the elbow high. *Cue:* Elbow high.
- Hit diagonally to the opposite box. *Cue:* Hit cross court.
- Aim to place the ball away from your opponent causing them to move to it. *Cue:* Place the ball away from them.

COMMON ERRORS, CAUSES, AND CORRECTIONS

- The student's toss and contact are inaccurate. *Cause:* The student is not experienced enough with the toss. *Correction:* More trials are needed to refine the toss. Have the student toss and focus just on the placement.
- The student's follow through is incorrect. *Cause:* The student's placement is incorrect or the student uses improper follow-through technique. *Correction:* Have the student show you where the follow through should finish (opposite thigh) then have them practice without a ball to finish there.
- The student's stance is incorrect prior to serving. *Cause:* The student has not practiced the stance enough. *Correction:* Have the student draw an imaginary line that passes through the toes of both feet and extends to the target box for the serve. The student should draw the imaginary line with the racket held in a serve grip. Alternately, you can mark proper foot placement on the floor.
- The student uses the incorrect grip (Eastern instead of Continental) and there is no pronation. *Cause:* Using the incorrect grip eliminates pronation. *Correction:* Have the student practice snapping the hand (without a racket) 20 times. The student can also practice the snap against the fence or wall without a ball. The student begins with the racket frame against the fence or wall and quickly pronates so the racket strings hit the fence or wall.
- There is no shoulder rotation. *Cause:* The student does not shift the weight forward. *Correction:* Be sure the student's shoulders are squared to the net after contact. You

can also have the student step in diagonally toward the target box immediately after the serve. Alternately, you can place one cone three steps into the court and have the student hit the serve, fall forward, circle the cone, and return to the baseline.

- The contact point on the racket is incorrect; this is called a rainbow hit. *Cause:* The student is not experienced enough with the toss. *Correction:* More trials are needed to practice appropriate contact.

- The student serves the ball to the wrong box. *Cause:* The student is not experienced in placing the serve. *Correction:* More trials are needed to practice appropriate placement.

- The student serves an easy, comfortable ball to the receiver. *Cause:* The student cannot properly aim the serve. *Correction:* Have the student practice aiming the serve to different areas in the box. Mark each area with a cone or an empty ball can and challenge the server to hit the target. Assign a point value to each target (use more points for harder targets).

- The student serves an easy, comfortable ball to the receiver. *Cause:* The student doesn't understand the advantages of the serve to win the point. *Correction:* Demonstrate (or show videos on) how the court opens when a server places the ball away from the receiver; this leads to an open court and a quick finish. Award additional points for winning the point with the serve only, and award five points for an ace serve (one the student cannot return).

TASK 37: FRIEND-RIVAL APPLICATION GAMES

PURPOSE

Following are the purposes of the task as related to aspects of skilled performance.

- In this task, students apply specific techniques and tactics in friend-rival games.
- Fair play: Students differentiate between the friendly phase and the rival phase of the game.

DESCRIPTION

Students are in pairs, and one student is on each side of the court. Each student stands with a racket on the end line (i.e., service line, intermediate court, or baseline) of their court based on their play level (beginner, intermediate, advanced). One player begins the rally by executing an underhand toss or an underhand stroke. Determine the number of passes students will make before shifting to the rival portion of the game, in which students play competitively. If students fail to maintain the required rally or demonstrate the required element, students restart from the beginning. Otherwise, there is no pause between the friend and rival phases. Typically, the consecutive friend segment of the game is used to encourage proper performance of specific techniques and tactics just learned. For example, you can ask for at least two proper follow-throughs before the rival play begins. Points are as awarded as follows: one point for completed friendly play, one point for the student who wins the rally, and two points for an ace shot.

Game Variations

The following game variations are identified by letters in the content maps:

1. Ready to side position. Students must move from the ready position to the side position on each shot made in the friendly rally. If students fail to demonstrate this element, the rally restarts. Determine how many consecutive shots students must make prior to beginning rival play. The technical element is required during the friendly segment and is recommended during the rival play.

2. Forehand and backhand shots. Students must complete four consecutive forehand and backhand shots in the friendly rally. Designate one student to hit forehand shots and the other to hit backhand shots. Then students reverse roles after every rally.

3. Grip (progressive rally). Students complete one shot using the proper grip before moving on to rival play. In the next rally, students add one shot (up to four shots) to the friendly segment. Proper grip must be used in each consecutive shot. If the friend rally is unsuccessful (students fail to demonstrate the proper grip or there is a failed shot), players restart.

4. Follow-through. Students must complete two consecutive shots with follow-through before moving on to rival play.

5. Two shots. Students must complete two consecutive shots before they can shift to rally play.

6. Two shots with weight shift. Students must perform two shots with proper forward weight shift. If students fail to demonstrate this, the rally restarts. You can change the number of required shots or make this a progressive game.

7. Baseline and volley. In this rival game one student plays from the baseline and the other plays from the volley position. After a point is won, players switch positions.

8. Aim. Players must aim the ball to particular areas (e.g., left corner, back right court) during the friend rally. Determine how many shots students must make before rival play begins (e.g., two shots per team, two shots for each player).

EQUIPMENT

One ball and two rackets per pair of students

COMMON ERRORS, CAUSES, AND CORRECTIONS

- Students need time to adjust to these games. However, if many errors or consistent errors of the same kind are being made. *Cause:* The progression to any of task has been too fast for the student or the performance . *Correction:* At this level of play significant or recurring errors are difficult to address. We recommend returning to earlier tasks to correct errors depending on the error. It is a mistake at this stage of learning for students who are making errors to progress. It is developmentally appropriate to return to the tasks they can perform well and move forward from there.

- The student continues to play friendly in the rival phase of the game. *Cause:* The student is unable to accurately aim the ball to open spaces, or the student lacks proper decision-making regarding ball placement. *Correction:* Have the student identify open areas on the other side of the court and call out the target prior to the strike (e.g., right, back left), or place soft cones or poly spots on the court for the students to use as targets (each correct shot earns two points).

- The student uses difficult shots during the friend rally. *Cause:* The student is excited and wants to win. *Correction:* Make the friendly segment longer. Ask the student to make shots that the opponent can reach in three or fewer steps.

Chapter 12

Softball (Kickball)

Baseball evolved in the United States more than 100 years ago, and since then it has grown in popularity around the world. Softball initially grew out of baseball as a version of the sport that could be played indoors. Softball has also grown in popularity, and it is played by young and old alike across a lifespan. Because of the safety and field limitations relevant to school environments, softball is often used in physical education curricula instead of baseball. One criticism of the inclusion of softball in physical education is the perceived lack of moderate to vigorous physical activity (MVPA) that is recommended for youth in physical education. Our approach to softball takes this into consideration and is designed to go toward meeting the MVPA recommendations. Due to the use of batting equipment and the technical demands of batting and fielding in softball, we believe the use of a kickball is a more appropriate introduction to softball at the elementary and even early middle school levels. Kickball can be used to teach many of the offensive and defensive strategies of softball so students will have knowledge that can be transferred to softball when they are older. Many of the early kickball tasks are repeated in the early softball tasks; the only difference is the use of a bat and type of ball. You should also consider whether to use softball or Wiffle ball equipment when first teaching softball techniques to older students. For safety reasons, we recommend beginning with Wiffle ball equipment and transitioning to softball equipment in high school. You must make decisions about appropriate equipment based on space, safety, and your students' skill levels.

OUR PEDAGOGICAL APPROACH TO SOFTBALL AND KICKBALL

Softball and kickball are field sports. In this chapter, each task we use to teach these sports builds on the previous tasks. Our focus is on developing skillful performance and game sense through tasks and instructional sequences that teach softball techniques and quickly use these skills in modified games. We first focus on kickball for beginning students; then, we introduce softball. We initially use modified 1v1, 2v2, 3v3, and 4v4 games; 6v6 games are used in more advanced settings.

The rules are modified in the following three ways:

1. There is no pitcher or catcher at the early levels. Including a pitcher limits the extent to which you can control each task and game. Using a stationary, controlled start helps to ensure a focus on batting and kicking and allows fielding to occur in a manner that maximizes physical activity and safety in small-sides games with shorter dimensions. In addition, you should never serve as the pitcher because it limits your ability to monitor all activities for safety, skill development, outcomes, and tactical learning. Using a catcher can pose a significant safety concern and should be avoided. Students can collide, and most physical education programs do not have catching gear that is safe and sanitary. Although all developmental tasks can be done without a pitcher, we recognize that many programs will want to use a pitcher. We recommend that you not use one until students learn all fundamental fielding hitting tactics. In our program, a pitcher is not included until level 3.

2. In kickball, balls are not thrown at runners. Throwing balls at base runners does not transfer to softball, but throwing to and running toward a base a runner is advancing to are paramount critical tactics. Throwing a ball at a runner can hurt or knock over the runner, and some students are fearful of being hit and will not run aggressively to the base.

3. Double bases are used in many tasks for safety. Double bases are used at first base and home plate because we emphasize running hard to and running through these bases. A double base allows the runner to do this without colliding with an infielder who is trying to throw hard to the base or is running fast to the base in an attempt to get the runner out.

As students learn to play these games, you will learn to better identify errors. There are three ways you can respond to these errors: (a) provide feedback to correct errors while keeping the task the same, (b) modify the task to make it easier, or (c) to return to an earlier task and then come back to the game. For example, if you observe that, despite your prompts, the students are not checking runners on second base before making the out at first base, you could take the students back to the task in which they learned this tactic. If you observe that students are not running through first base, you could revisit a task that highlighted this critical element to allow for more practice before returning to the game. Students often know what they are supposed to do, but they cannot apply their knowledge; therefore, revisiting earlier tasks is often more effective than simply providing feedback.

Modifications to Address Individual Needs of Students

For students with disabilities, appropriate modifications to activities depend on the nature of the disability. To modify softball instruction for students with visual impairments, adopt rules and equipment from beep baseball, such as (a) substitute the softball for either a beep baseball or beep kickball (for younger kids), (b) use sound devices or clapping peers or paraprofessionals to signify base location or throwing targets, or (c) use tactile modeling when demonstrating the proper form for complex skills, such as swinging a bat or throwing a ball. Tactile modeling is a demonstration of an activity that is presented to students by touch, rather than using sight. Lastly, use tactile mapping, or three-dimensional figures of the playing area, to show students where different playing surface elements are (e.g., bases, batter) prior to gameplay.

For students with autism spectrum disorders, modify softball instruction by providing one-to-one instruction in isolated areas that provide quiet and calm environments for learning. You can also place colored tape on the handle of the bat and poly spots in the batter box to indicate where the student should be gripping the bat and standing.

Little modifications are necessary to include students who use wheelchairs. Play the game on a hard surface, such as in the gymnasium or on an outdoor basketball court, rather than a field for mobility purposes. Other than that, students who use wheelchairs can participate fully with traditional softball rules.

For individuals with cerebral palsy, one concern may be the weight of the bat and you should have several bat sizes and weights available for students to choose from. Students who have restricted movement of an upper limb (e.g., arm) because of their disability may need accommodations on defense. Those students may benefit from rule modifications where they have extra time to transfer the ball from the glove to a throwing motion. These, and all modifications, should be discussed with students prior to implementation in gameplay.

Organization

Divide the class into groups of 6 or 8 students, and assign each group its own infield area. You should also consider using the sport education curriculum discussed in chapter 3. In all classes there will be variety in students' abilities and needs; we recommend that you try to develop groups of students that have similar skill levels.

Space

Often, the availability of a softball field with a dirt infield is a limiting factor when including softball in a curriculum. While a softball field can be used, the tasks in this chapter are designed in a way that they can be performed in a variety of spaces, including a large gym, an outdoor space with a wall, a large grassy area, or a paved area large enough for throwing and catching. Using several modified infield areas results in increased practice and recommended MVPA. When several fields are needed, an effective formation to place them in is a diamond with the home bases in the center. This allows you to easily monitor and move between groups. While an official softball field is 60 feet (18.3 m) between bases, this may not be appropriate for all students. Recommended sizes are included in some of the task descriptions.

Equipment Needed

For kickball at level 1, we recommend using a firm foam ball with a skin coating rather than a traditional playground ball. The foam ball is easier to grip and bounces less. The ball should be small enough that the student can throw it with one hand; it must fit in the hand when the student tightly grips it. The ball should also be large enough that a student can safely make contact with the foot when kicking it. We recommend that you provide several size choices based on your students' needs and abilities. For bases, poly spots (especially with elementary students), rubber bases, or regular bases can be used. If using poly spots, use different colors for inside bases for the defense and the outside bases for the offense.

At level 2, we recommend starting with similar foam balls that are 9 to 12 inches (22.8 to 30.5 centimeters) in circumference. The coated foam ball is safer, and it can be used indoors with or without fielder's gloves. While the size of the bats used is a teacher's discretion, we recommend plastic fat bats for middle school students. The wider and shorter the bat is, the easier it will be for students to contact the ball.

For level 3 students, use a coated foam ball that is the size of a softball and a narrower bat. If desired, level 3 students can use plastic softball-sized training balls. These balls have a variable flight pattern and are much more challenging to field and throw.

We recommend that a variety of bat choices should be available to accommodate all levels of performance. For safety reasons, we never recommend the use of metal or wood bats or regulation softballs. These tasks do not require fielding gloves, but they can be used at levels 2 and 3 if plastic softball-sized training balls are used.

CONTENT MAP STRUCTURE

Figure 12.1 is a content map that illustrates the flow and connectedness of all of the tasks used to develop skillful performance and game sense in softball and kickball. It is divided into three levels, and each level has a separate content map that includes the application games used to refine the techniques and tactics in that level. The focus of level 1 (see figure 12.2) is teaching basic softball tactics through kickball. Level 1 tasks are appropriate for upper elementary and middle school students. In level 2 (see figure 12.3), we begin to introduce softball-related techniques. These tasks are similar to those in level 1, but they include a bat and use a different ball. Level 3 (see figure 12.4) builds on the previous techniques and focuses on their application in tactical settings. Pitching and hitting a pitched ball are also addressed in level 3, but these do not have to be included in the unit; hitting a ball off a tee is a suitable alternative.

In the content maps, we have numbered the tasks. These numbers are used to cross reference tasks descriptions in the body of the chapter with the content maps. The task numbers should not be interpreted as the order in which they should

Combined Softball and Kickball Content Map:
Tasks only

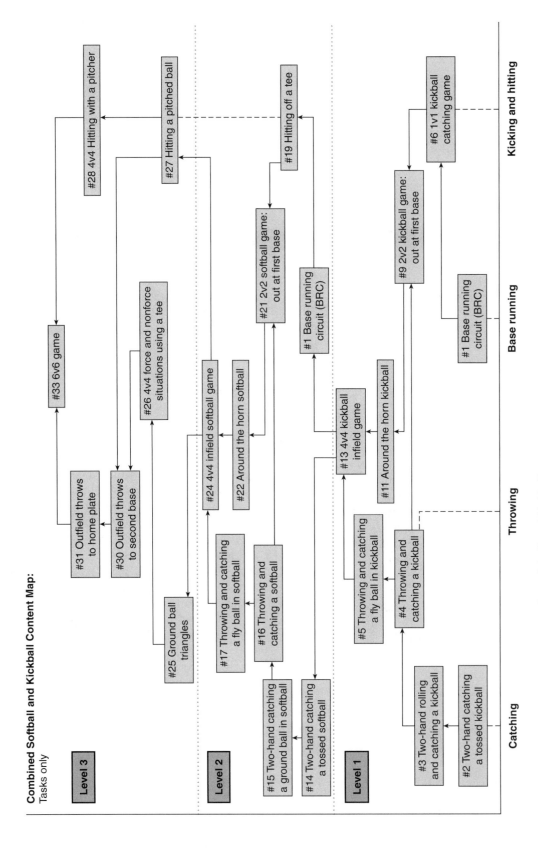

Figure 12.1 Combined content map for softball and kickball.

Level 1 Softball and Kickball Content Map:
Application games

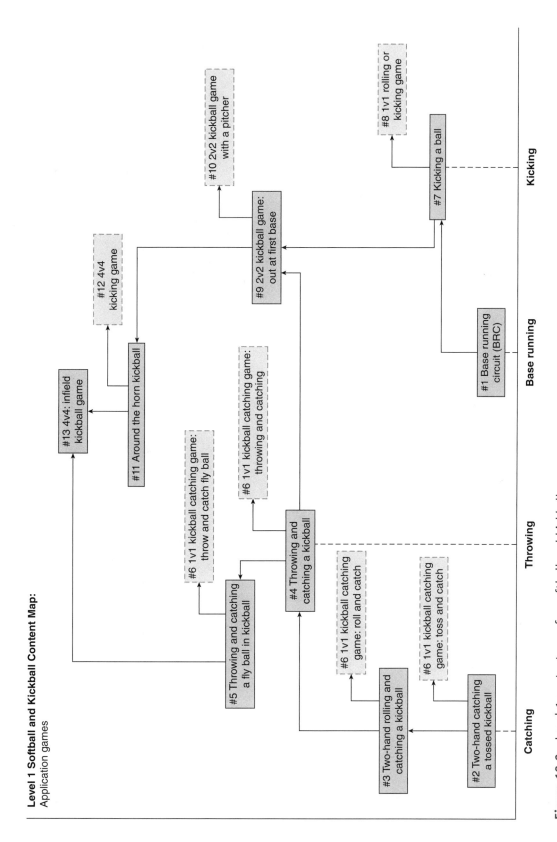

Figure 12.2 Level 1 content map for softball and kickball.

Level 2 Kickball and Softball Content Map:
Application games

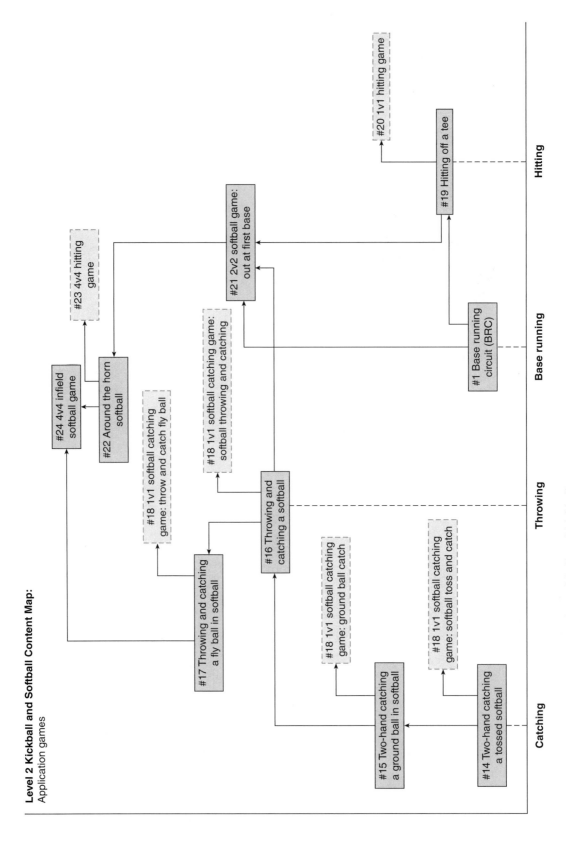

Figure 12.3 Level 2 content map for softball and kickball.

Level 3 Softball and Kickball Content Map:
Application games

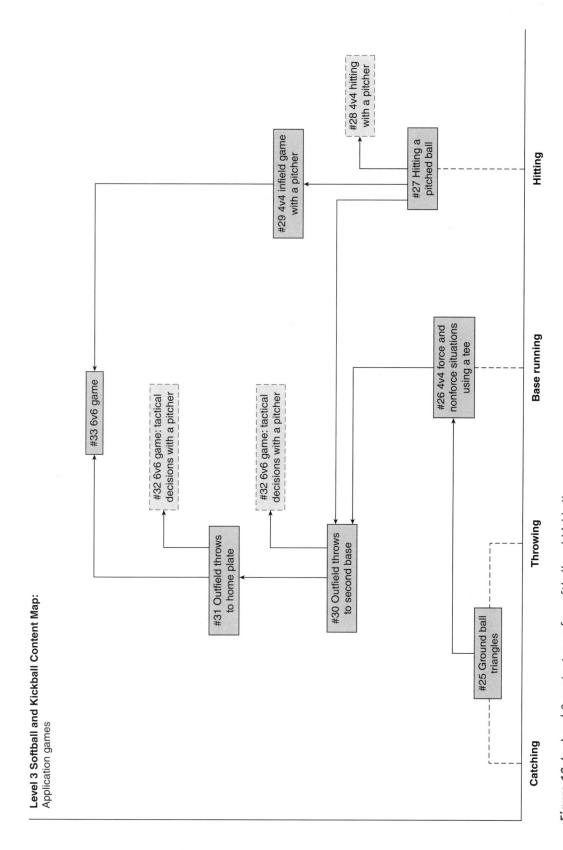

Figure 12.4 Level 3 content map for softball and kickball.

be taught. It is important that tasks are taught and progressed from simpler to more complex forms which is shown in the upward progress of the task sequence on the content map. This is particularly necessary before tasks are combined. For instance in Softball (Kickball) whether you teach throwing and catching first or kicking, the progressions of both need to be taught before they are combined in task 9.

STRUCTURE OF THE LESSONS

The following is a sample daily lesson structure for a 50-minute secondary softball lesson.

Warm-up (5 to 6 minutes)

Application game: 1v1 softball catching game: ground ball (5 minutes)

Informing task: base running circuit, part 2 (6 minutes)

Informing task: throwing and catching a softball (7 minutes)

Application game: 1v1 softball catching game: throw and catch (6 minutes)

Informing task: throwing and catching a fly ball in softball (7 minutes)

Application game: 1v1 softball catching game: throw and catch a fly ball (7 minutes)

Closure (3 minutes)

Warm-up

Elementary School

We use the warm-up to increase the heart rate and body temperature and facilitate blood flow to the muscles that will be used during the activity. This contributes to the amount of MVPA. In the warm-up, students practice and refine base running strategies. You should begin to teach the warm-up on the first day of the unit and add tasks until students can perform the whole circuit. You can have the whole class perform the warm-up, although this is not recommended. If using the entire class, you would need to allow more time for the warm-up and have the class performing various parts at the same time. We strongly recommend that students be divided into groups that use separate infields for the warm-up. This would allow the warm-up be done in an efficient manner and allow for multiple opportunities for students to run the bases. You should lead the warm-up

until students learn the entire progression; then, you can use task cards as prompts at each base. Once students have learned the warm-up, it should not last more than 5 to 7 minutes.

The Base Running Circuit (BRC)

The BRC is taught on day 1 using a field with 45 feet (13.7 meters) between bases and is described in detail in task 1. The BRC is made up of the following five progressions. Follow the timing instructions indicated in task 1. If the students are higher-performing or your groups are larger, subsequent runners can start when the first runner is halfway down the baseline, and the second progression can begin once half the students are through first base.

1. **Part 1: home plate to first base.** Students run through first base, break down the steps by taking smaller steps after touching the base, and turn in foul territory to return to the base.

2. **Part 2: first base to third base.** Students create a rounded pathway while running from first base through second base to third base.

3. **Part 3: third base to home plate.** Starting at third base, students run through home without slowing down until after they touch home plate.

4. **Part 4: home plate to second base and second to home.** The students run a rounded pathway while rounding first or third base.

5. **Part 5: home plate to home plate.** Students run all the way around the bases by creating a circle out of the infield instead of a square.

You can also implement higher-order tactics during each part. For example, when teaching part 3, you can introduce the concept of tagging up. This is done by having the runner leave the base a couple of steps, act as if they are watching a fly ball being caught and then going back to tag the base and then running home.

Secondary School

We recommend that secondary students use the BRC warm-up described in the elementary warm-up (see task 1 for details) but with larger field dimensions (up to 60 feet [18.3 m]) if possible. You can also implement higher-order tactics during each part. For example, when teaching level 3, you can address decision-making about whether to run home depending on where a ball is hit in the infield.

We also recommend that a throwing task be added to the warm-up starting on day 5. Partners throw the ball back and forth. After two throws, students move back two steps. This continues until the partners reach the distance you determine (we recommend not more than 60 feet [18.3 meters]).

BLOCK PLAN

The introductory block plan (see table 12.1) is designed for beginners in fourth and fifth grades. (It can be used in third grade if the teacher feels the students' catching, throwing, and kicking techniques are developed enough.)

Although longer units are always preferred, we recognize that there are time limitations at the elementary level; therefore, the elementary unit is five days for the initial grade in which it is taught. The unit can also be taught across two grades.

The secondary block plan (see table 12.2) is designed for students in middle and high school. It assumes that students were taught the level 1 techniques at the elementary level. If this is not the case, the block plans can be merged. Kickball can be used in the secondary block plan if necessary. Because middle and high school physical education programs have different requirements, these units should *not* be taught in fewer than 10 days. These units are adjusted for 10-, 15-, and 20-day programs, although we recommend units of 20 or more days.

Table 12.1   Elementary Kickball Block Plan: Five-Day Unit

This is an example of a beginning block plan for elementary students that uses the kickball tasks shown in the level 1 content map. You can use this as a template for developing an appropriate block plan for beginning students to learn basic kickball techniques that can later be applied to a softball unit. If you are teaching a longer unit, or if the unit will be continued next year, you can spread out the tasks and include a larger kickball game in the later stages. Your decisions about what tasks to include will depend on your students and their levels of experience.

Lesson 1	Lesson 2	Lesson 3	Lesson 4	Lesson 5
Warm-up • Teach the warm-up	**Warm-up** • BRC parts 1-2	**Warm-up** • BRC parts 1-3	**Warm-up** • BRC parts 1-4	**Warm-up** • BRC parts 1-5
Introductory application game None	**Introductory application game** **(6)** 1v1 kickball catching game (toss and catch)	**Introductory application game** **(6)** 1v1 kickball catching game (throw and catch)	**Introductory application game** **(8)** 1v1 rolling or kicking game	**Introductory application game** **(10)** 2v2 kickball game with a pitcher
Content development • **(1)** BRC parts 1-2 • **(2)** Two-hand catching a tossed kickball	**Content development** • **(1)** BRC part 3 • **(3)** Two-hand rolling and catching a kickball • **(6)** 1v1 kickball catching game (roll and catch) • **(4)** Throwing and catching a kickball	**Content development** • **(1)** BRC part 4 • **(5)** Throwing and catching a fly ball in kickball • **(6)** 1v1 kickball catching game (throwing and catching a fly ball) • **(7)** Kicking a ball	**Content development** • **(1)** BRC part 5 • Review previous tasks as needed • **(9)** 2v2 kickball game: out at first base	**Content development** • **(11)** Around the horn kickball • **(12)** 4v4 kicking game
Closing application game • **(6)** 1v1 kickball catching game (toss and catch)	**Closing application game** • **(6)** 1v1 kickball catching game (throwing and catching)	**Closing application game** • **(8)** 1v1 rolling or kicking game	**Closing application game** • **(10)** 2v2 kickball game with a pitcher	**Closing application game** • **(13)** 4v4 infield kickball game

Table 12.2 Secondary Softball Block Plans: 10-, 15-, and 20-Day Units

This block plan incorporates 10-, 15-, and 20-day units. The last two days of the 10-day block plan, the last three days of the 15-day block plan, and the last five days of the 20-day block plan are game days and are described at the end of the block plan. The first eight days of the block plan are the same for all units. If you need to begin with a kickball unit (level 1 tasks), use the elementary block plan to start the unit.

Lesson 1 of all block plans	Lesson 2 of all block plans	Lesson 3 of all block plans	Lesson 4 of all block plans	Lesson 5 of all block plans
Warm-up • Teach the warm-up	**Warm-up** • BRC part 1	**Warm-up** • BRC parts 1-2	**Warm-up** • BRC parts 1-3	**Warm up** • BRC parts 1-5 and throwing progression
Introductory application game None	**Introductory application game** • **(18)** 1v1 softball catching game (ground ball catch)	**Introductory application game** • **(18)** 1v1 softball catching game (fly ball throw and catch)	**Introductory application game** • **(20)** 1v1 hitting game	**Introductory application game** • **(20)** 1v1 hitting game
Content development • **(1)** BRC part 1 • **(14)** Two-hand catching a tossed softball • **(18)** 1v1 softball catching game (two-hand toss and catch) • **(15)** Two-hand catching a ground ball in softball	**Content development** • **(1)** BRC part 2 • **(16)** Throwing and catching a softball • **(18)** 1v1 softball catching game (overhead throw and catch) • **(17)** Throwing and catching a fly ball in softball	**Content development** • **(1)** BRC part 3 • **(19)** Hitting off a tee	**Content development** • **(1)** BRC part 4 • Review throwing tasks as needed • **(21)** 2v2 softball game: out at first base	**Content development** • **(1)** BRC part 5 • Review task 21 • **(22)** Around the horn softball
Closing application game • **(18)** 1v1 softball catching game (ground ball catch)	**Closing application game** • **(18)** 1v1 softball catching game (fly ball throw and catch)	**Closing application game** • **(20)** 1v1 hitting game	**Closing application game** • **(20)** 1v1 hitting game	**Closing application game** • **(23)** 4v4 hitting game

Lesson 6 of all block plans	Lesson 7 of all block plans	Lesson 8 of all block plans (last instructional day of 10-day block plan)	Lesson 9 of 15- and 20-day block plans (See table 12.3 for lesson 9 for 10-day plan.)	Lesson 10 of 15- and 20-day block plans (See table 12.3 for lesson 10 for 10-day plan.)
Warm-up • Same as day 5	**Warm-up** • Same as day 5	**Warm-up** • Same as day 5	**Warm-up** • Same as day 5	**Warm-up** • Same as day 5
Introductory application game • **(23)** 4v4 hitting game	**Introductory application game** • **(23)** 4v4 hitting game	**Introductory application game** • None	**Introductory application game** • None	**Introductory application game** • **(28)** 4v4 Hitting with a pitcher
Content development • Review any previous tasks as needed	**Content development** • **(24)** 4v4 infield softball game	**Content development** • **(24)** 4v4 infield softball game	**Content development** • **(25)** Ground ball triangles • **(27)** Hitting a pitched ball	**Content development** • **(26)** 4v4 force and nonforce situations using a tee
Closing application game • **(23)** 4v4 hitting game	**Closing application game** • None	**Closing application game** • None	**Closing application game** • **(28)** 4v4 hitting with a pitcher	**Closing application game** • **(28)** 4v4 hitting with a pitcher

(continued)

Lesson 11 of 15- and 20-day block plans	Lesson 12 of 15- and 20-day block plans (last instructional day of 15-day plan)	Lesson 13 of 20-day block plan (See table 12.4 for lesson 13 for 15-day plan.)	Lesson 14 of 20-day block plan (See table 12.4 for lesson 14 for 15-day plan.)	Lesson 15 of 20-day block plan (See table 12.4 for lesson 15 for 15-day plan.)
Warm-up • Same as day 5	**Warm-up** • Same as day 5	**Warm-up** • Same as day 5	**Warm-up** • Same as day 5	**Warm-up** • Same as day 5

Introductory application game
• **(28)** 4v4 hitting with a pitcher
	Introductory application game
	• If a 15 day unit then:
	  • **(33)** 6v6 game (practice)
	• If a 20 day unit then:
	  • **(29)** 4v4 Infield game with a pitcher
		Introductory application game
		• **(32)** 6v6 game: tactical decisions with a pitcher (task 30)
			Introductory application game
			• **(32)** 6v6 game: tactical decisions with a pitcher (task 31)
				Introductory application game
				None

Content development • **(29)** 4v4 Infield game with a pitcher	**Content development** • If a 15 day unit then do practice 6v6 games all period • If 20 day unit then • **(30)** Outfield throws to second base	**Content development** • **(31)** Outfield throws to home plate	**Content development** • Review tasks as needed	**Content development** • **(33)** 6v6 games (practice)

Closing application game
• If a 15 day unit then:
  • **(33)** 6v6 game (practice)
• If a 20 day unit then:
  • **(29)** 4v4 infield game with a pitcher
	Closing application game
	• 20 day unit only:
	  • **(32)** 6v6 game: tactical decisions with a pitcher (task 30)
		Closing application game
		• **(32)** 6v6 game: tactical decisions with a pitcher (task 31)
			Closing application game
			• **(33)** 6v6 game (practice)
				Closing application game
				None

Lesson 16 of 20-day block plan	Lesson 17 of 20-day block plan	Lesson 18 of 20-day block plan	Lesson 19 of 20-day block plan	Lesson 20 of 20-day block plan
Warm-up • Same as day 5	**Warm-up** • Same as day 5	**Warm-up** • Same as day 5	**Warm-up** • Same as day 5	**Warm-up** • Same as day 5
Fixed-time 6v6 games against different opponents (non-exclusionary round-robin tournament) Encourage the use of specific skills. Award an extra point to the score for demonstration of these skills. We recommend at least two games per lesson.	**Fixed-time 6v6 games against different opponents (non-exclusionary round-robin tournament)** Encourage the use of specific skills. Award an extra point to the score for demonstration of these skills. We recommend at least two games per lesson.	**Fixed-time 6v6 games against different opponents (non-exclusionary round-robin tournament)** Encourage the use of specific skills. Award an extra point to the score for demonstration of these skills. We recommend at least two games per lesson.	**Fixed-time 6v6 games against different opponents (non-exclusionary round-robin tournament)** Encourage the use of specific skills. Award an extra point to the score for demonstration of these skills. We recommend at least two games per lesson.	**Fixed-time 6v6 games against different opponents (non-exclusionary round-robin tournament)** Encourage the use of specific skills. Award an extra point to the score for demonstration of these skills. We recommend at least two games per lesson.

Table 12.3 10-Day Block Plan Game Days

Lesson 9 of 10-day block plan	Lesson 10 of 10-day block plan
Warm-up • Same as day 5	**Warm-up** • Same as day 5
Fixed-time 4v4 infield games against different opponents (nonexclusionary round-robin tournament) Encourage the use of specific skills. Award an extra point to the score for demonstration of these skills. We recommend at least two games per lesson.	**Fixed-time 4v4 infield games against different opponents (nonexclusionary round-robin tournament)** Encourage the use of specific skills. Award an extra point to the score for demonstration of these skills. We recommend at least two games per lesson.

Table 12.4 15-Day Block Plan Game Days

Lesson 13 of 15-day block plan	Lesson 14 of 15-day block plan	Lesson 15 of 15-day block plan
Warm-up • Same as day 5	**Warm-up** • Same as day 5	**Warm-up** • Same as day 5
Fixed-time 6v6 games against different opponents (nonexclusionary round-robin tournament) Encourage the use of specific skills. Award an extra point to the score for demonstration of these skills. We recommend at least two games per lesson.	**Fixed-time 6v6 games against different opponents (nonexclusionary round-robin tournament)** Encourage the use of specific skills. Award an extra point to the score for demonstration of these skills. We recommend at least two games per lesson.	**Fixed-time 6v6 games against different opponents (nonexclusionary round-robin tournament)** Encourage the use of specific skills. Award an extra point to the score for demonstration of these skills. We recommend at least two games per lesson.

SHAPE AMERICA'S GRADE-LEVEL OUTCOMES FOR K-12 PHYSICAL EDUCATION

In table 12.5, we identify key grade-level outcomes for softball for 3rd grade through 8th grade. These are linked to specific tasks on the content maps that are appropriate for teaching the skill and assessing the outcome.

Table 12.5 Grade-Level Outcomes for Softball and Kickball

Outcome	Description	Content map focus and tasks
S1.E13.3	Throws underhand to a partner or target with reasonable accuracy.	Level 1, task 2
S1.E14.4a	Throws overhand using a mature pattern in nondynamic environments (closed skills).	Level 1, task 4
S1.E14.4b	Throws overhand to a partner or at a target with accuracy at a reasonable distance.	Level 1, task 5
S1.E16.4	Catches a thrown ball above the head, at chest or waist level, and below the waist using a mature pattern in a nondynamic environment (closed skills).	Level 1, task 4
S1.E16.5c	Catches with reasonable accuracy in dynamic, small-sided practice tasks.	Level 1, task 9
S1.E25.4	Strikes an object with a long-handled implement (e.g., hockey stick, bat, golf club), while demonstrating 3 of the 5 critical elements of a mature pattern for the implement (grip, stance, body orientation, swing plane and follow-through).	Level 2, task 19
S1.M2.6	Throws with a mature pattern for distance or power appropriate to the practice task (e.g., distance = outfield to home plate; power = 2nd base to 1st base).	Level 2, tasks 17, 24 Level 3, tasks 30, 32
S1.M2.7	Throws with a mature pattern for distance or power appropriate to the activity in a dynamic environment.	Level 2, tasks 17, 24 Level 3, tasks 25-26
S1.M2.8	Throws with a mature pattern for distance or power appropriate to the activity during small-sided game play.	Level 2, tasks 17, 21 Level 3, tasks 25-26
S1.M21.6	Catches, with a mature pattern, from different trajectories using a variety of objects in a varying practice tasks.	Level 2, task 15 Level 3, tasks 25-26
S2.M10.8	Identifies sacrifice situations and attempt[s] to advance a teammate.	Level 2, task 21 Level 3, task 26
S2.M11.7	Selects the correct defensive play based on the situation (e.g., number of outs).	Level 2, tasks 22-23 Level 3, tasks 30, 31, 33

TASK 1: BASE RUNNING CIRCUIT (BRC)

PURPOSE

Following are the purposes of the task as related to aspects of skilled performance.

- Technique: In this task, students learn the basics of base running.
- Tactic: Students learn to run bases, which leads to run-scoring opportunities.
- Agility: Students learn to change directions smoothly and quickly when rounding bases.
- Communication: Students encourage each other to run hard and use the appropriate tactics.

DESCRIPTION

Set up an infield that includes home plate and first, second, and third bases; poly spots can be used to mark the bases. There should be 30 to 60 feet (9.1 to 18.3 meters) between bases (depending on available space and ability). If possible, arrange multiple infields. Have students complete the following activities:

- **Part 1: home plate to first base.** Students line up at home plate. The first student runs through first base, slows down by breaking down the steps (taking smaller steps) after touching the base, turns in foul territory, and jogs back to home plate and stands at the end of the line. Once the first runner reaches first base, the second runner begins. Students continue the task until everyone has completed it a designated number of times.

- **Part 2: first base to third base:** Students line up in the foul territory side of first base. The first runner stands on the base and runs in a rounded pathway from first base through second base to third base. The student should not slow down while rounding second base. The student then holds third base. When the first runner is on third base, the second student in line begins. The first student then jogs to the end of the line at first base. Students continue the task until everyone has completed it a designated number of times.

- **Part 3: third base to home plate:** Students line up in the foul territory side of third base. The first runner stands on the base and then runs to home plate. The runner crosses the plate without stopping and then returns to the end of the line at third base. After the first student crosses home plate, the second student runs from third to home. Students continue the task until everyone has completed it a designated number of times.

- **Part 4: home plate to second base and second to home.** Students line up behind home plate. The first runner stands on the base and runs in a rounded pathway from home through second base. The student should not slow down while rounding first base. The student then holds second base. When the first student is rounding first, the next student in line steps onto the plate. When the first runner is on second base, then second student begins. The first student stands near centerfield. Once half the runners have made it to second base, the first runner runs from second base through third base to home plate. Students continue the task until everyone has completed it a designated number of times.

- **Part 5: home plate to home plate.** Students line up behind home plate. The first runner stands on home plate, runs toward first base, and continues running around the bases ending at home plate. As the first runner is rounding second base, the second student in line steps to the plate and begins running. Students continue the task until everyone has completed it a designated number of times.

EQUIPMENT

Four bases or poly spots per infield

CRITICAL ELEMENTS AND CUES

Technique: Part 1

- Do not slow down as you approach first base. *Cue:* Run through first base.
- After crossing first base, slow down by stomping the feet into the ground. *Cue:* Break down steps.
- As you slow down, turn toward foul territory (right) and return to the base. *Cue:* Turn right and return.

Technique: Part 2

- As you approach second base, swing out slightly toward the outfield and round the base in an arc as you continue toward third base. *Cue:* Round the base.
- As you approach third base, slow down and stop on the base. *Cue:* Hold the base.

Technique: Part 3

- As you approach home plate, run through the plate without stopping. *Cue:* Run through the plate.

Technique: Part 4

- As you approach first base, swing out into foul territory to create an arc as you round first base and continue toward second base. *Cue:* Round the base.
- As you approach second base, slow down and stop on the base. *Cue:* Hold the base.
- After half the runners reach second base, run from second base, round third, and run through home. *Cues:* Round third; run through home.

Technique: Part 5

- As you approach first base, swing out into foul territory to create an arc as you round first base and continue toward second base. *Cue:* Round the base.
- Stay wide and run in a circle as you round second and third bases and head toward home. *Cues:* Make a circle; run fast, all the way home.

Tactic

- The ability to run bases effectively opens up opportunities to score runs.

Agility

- Use proper running form. Run as hard as you can to and around the bases.

Communication

- Encourage other students to run as fast as they can by clapping and cheering.
- Encourage other students to run through first and run through home.
- Encourage other students to hold second and hold third when applicable.

COMMON ERRORS, CAUSES, AND CORRECTIONS

- The student slows down before touching first base or home plate. *Cause:* The student thinks he or she is running to the bases and not through the base. *Correction:* Remind the student to run all the way past the base by running hard.
- The student slows down when rounding any base. *Cause:* The student's pathway is direct to the base instead of circular. *Correction:* Have the runner slow down and focus on making the circle.

TASK 2: TWO-HAND CATCHING A TOSSED KICKBALL

PURPOSE

Following are the purposes of the task as related to aspects of skilled performance.

- Technique: In this task, students learn the basic techniques of catching a kickball from a toss.
- Fair play: Students toss the ball to the partner at chest height.
- Communication: Students hold their hands out to indicate readiness to receive the toss.

DESCRIPTION

Students pair up and stand 10 to 15 feet (3 to 4.6 meters) apart. One student has a ball and, on your signal, the students continuously toss the kickball back and forth using the two-handed underhand toss and catch techniques. If students need motivation, have pairs count how many passes and catches they can make in a row or within a designated time.

EQUIPMENT

One ball per pair of students

CRITICAL ELEMENTS AND CUES

Technique: Two-Handed Underhand Toss

- Place both hands on the side of the ball with the fingers and thumbs spread. *Cue:* Fingers spread.
- Start with the ball close to the knees. *Cue:* Ball at your knees.
- Look at the receiver's hands. *Cue:* Eyes on target.
- Step toward the receiver with one leg (either leg is alright since this is a two handed toss). *Cue:* Step to receiver.
- Move the ball away from the knees by swaying the arms, rocking the wrists, and extending the elbows at the same time. *Cue:* All together.
- As the arms extend, rock the wrists and follow through just below chest height. *Cue:* Use your wrists.
- Toss the ball to the partner with gentle force and with an arc. *Cue:* Like a rainbow.

Technique: Two-Handed Catch

- Look at the ball as it comes into the hands. *Cue:* Eyes on ball.
- Catch with two hands. *Cue:* Two hands.
- Step toward the ball as it comes toward you. *Cue:* Step to ball.
- As the ball contacts the hands, pull the ball into the body. *Cue:* Absorb the ball.
- End with the ball close to the body and the elbows flexed. *Cue:* Bring it in.

Fair Play

- Pass the ball directly toward the receiver's chest.
- The pass must have enough force to get to the receiver but still be gentle and have an arc.
- Do not toss the ball higher than the receiver's head.

Communication

- When you are ready to receive a toss, place both hands in the target area with the fingers spread and the palms out. *Cue:* Big target.

COMMON ERRORS, CAUSES, AND CORRECTIONS

- The receiver does not follow the ball into the hands. *Cause:* The student looks at the passer or turns the head. *Correction:* Remind the student to keep the eyes on the ball.
- The ball is away from the body on the catch. *Cause:* The receiver does not absorb the ball into the body. *Correction:* Have the student exaggerate the elbow flex and end with the elbows almost out to the side.
- The ball does not make it to the receiver. *Cause:* The passer does not step toward the receiver. *Correction:* Place a poly spot in front of the passer and have the student step over it when making the pass.
- The ball does not make it to the receiver. *Cause:* The arms are not extended quickly at release. *Correction:* Tell student to reach towards the receiver as they release the ball.
- The toss does not arrive at the receiver's hands. *Cause:* The passer is not looking at the receiver's hands. *Correction:* Have the receiver hold up a number of fingers, and ask the tosser to speak the number.
- The toss does not arrive at the receiver's hands. *Cause:* The passer does not have the strength to get the pass there. *Correction:* Move the partners closer together.
- The toss is too hard. *Cause:* The passer doesn't take into consideration the catching ability of the partner. *Correction:* Remind the student to toss gently.
- The toss is too high or too low. *Cause:* The release point is too early or too late. *Correction:* Remind the student to toss like a rainbow and toss at head height.

TASK 3: TWO-HAND ROLLING AND CATCHING A KICKBALL

PURPOSE

Following are the purposes of the task as related to aspects of skilled performance.

- Technique: In this task, students learn the basic technique of catching a rolling kickball.
- Fair play: Students roll the ball toward the partner's feet without bouncing.
- Communication: Students hold their hands out to indicate readiness to receive the ball.

DESCRIPTION

Students pair up and stand 10 to 15 feet (3 to 4.6 meters) apart. One student has a ball and, on your signal, rolls the ball toward the partner. The partner bends down and catches the ball by scooping it up to the belly area. The receiver then rolls the kickball back to the partner, who catches it the same way. The students continue this for a designated time. If students need motivation, have pairs count how many rolls and catches they can make in a row or within a designated time.

EQUIPMENT

One ball per pair of students

CRITICAL ELEMENTS AND CUES

Technique: Roll

- Place the ball in the dominant hand on the same-side hip with the fingers spread on the back of the ball. *Cue:* Fingers spread.
- Look at the receiver's feet. *Cue:* Eyes on target.
- Step with the foot opposite the dominant hand. *Cue:* Step to receiver.
- As the arms come through on the rolling action, release the ball at ground level so that it stays close to the ground. *Cue:* On the ground.
- The dominant hand follows the path of the ball on the follow-through. *Cue:* Follow the ball.

Technique: Catch a Rolled Ball

- Stand with the knees bent, bend at the waist, and put the arms out in front of the body. *Cue:* Get low and ready.
- Look at the ball as it comes into the hands. *Cue:* Eyes on ball.
- Catch the ball with two hands. *Cue:* Two hands.
- Step toward the ball as it is coming toward you. *Cue:* Step to the ball.
- As the ball contacts the hands, scoop the ball into the belly area. *Cue:* Scoop the ball.
- End with the ball close to the belly with the elbows flexed. *Cue:* Bring it in.

Fair Play

- Roll the ball directly toward the receiver's feet.
- Roll the ball with enough force that is gets to the receiver. The roll should be gentle and the ball should not bounce.

Communication

- When you are ready to receive the ball, place the hands in the target area with the fingers spread and the palms out. *Cue:* Big target.

COMMON ERRORS, CAUSES, AND CORRECTIONS

- The receiver does not follow the ball to the hands. *Cause:* The student looks at the passer or turns the head. *Correction:* Remind the student to keep the eyes on the ball.
- The ball is away from the body on the catch. *Cause:* The receiver does not absorb the ball into the body. *Correction:* Have the student exaggerate the elbow flex and end with the elbows almost out to the side.
- The ball does not make it to the receiver. *Cause:* The roller does not step toward the receiver. *Correction:* Place a poly spot in front of the roller and have the student step over it when making the pass.
- The ball does not arrive at the receiver's hands. *Cause:* The roller is not looking at the receiver's hands. *Correction:* Have the receiver hold up a number of fingers, and ask the roller to speak the number.
- The ball does not arrive at the receiver's hands. *Cause:* The roller does not have the strength to get the pass there. *Correction:* Move the partners closer together.
- The roll is too hard. *Cause:* The roller doesn't take into consideration the catching ability of the partner. *Correction:* Remind the roller to roll gently.

TASK 4: THROWING AND CATCHING A KICKBALL

PURPOSE

Following are the purposes of the task as related to aspects of skilled performance.

- Technique: In this task, students learn the basic technique of catching a kickball with two hands from a one-handed throw.
- Fair play: Students gently throw the ball to the partner's hands at chest height.
- Communication: Students hold their hands out to indicate readiness to receive the ball.

DESCRIPTION

Students pair up and stand 10 to 15 feet (3 to 4.6 meters) apart. One student has a ball and, on your signal, throws the ball overhand to the partner. The partner catches the ball and then throws it back. Students continue for a designated time. If students need motivation, have pairs count how many throws and catches they can make in a row or within a designated time.

EQUIPMENT

One ball per pair of students

CRITICAL ELEMENTS AND CUES

Technique: One-Handed Throw

- Place the throwing hand on the back of the ball with the fingers and thumbs spread. *Cue:* Fingers spread on back.
- Start with the ball close to the chest. *Cue:* Ball at your chest.
- Look at the receiver's hands. *Cue:* Eyes on target.
- Step toward the receiver with the leg opposite the throwing hand. *Cue:* Step to receiver.
- While stepping toward the target, move the ball back with the throwing arm while raising the nonthrowing arm towards the receiver. *Cue:* Make a T.
- Once the arm is back, rotate the hips while bringing the ball forward. *Cue:* Rotate and throw.
- On the release, follow through to the opposite hip. *Cue:* Follow through.

Technique: Two-Handed Catch

- Look at the ball as it comes into the hands. *Cue:* Eyes on ball.
- Catch with two hands. *Cue:* Two hands.
- Step toward the ball as it comes toward you. *Cue:* Step to ball.
- As the ball contacts the hands, pull the ball into the body. *Cue:* Absorb the ball.
- End with the ball close to the body and the elbows flexed. *Cue:* Bring it in.

Fair Play

- Pass the ball directly toward the receiver's chest.
- The pass must have enough force to get to the receiver but still be gentle and have an arc.
- Do not throw the ball higher than the receiver's head.

Communication

- When you are ready to receive the ball, place both hands in the target area with the fingers spread and the palms out. *Cue:* Big target.

COMMON ERRORS, CAUSES, AND CORRECTIONS

- The receiver does not follow the ball into the hands. *Cause:* The student looks at the passer or turns the head. *Correction:* Remind the student to keep the eyes on the ball.
- The ball does not make it to the receiver. *Cause:* The passer does not step toward the receiver. *Correction:* Place a poly spot in front of the passer and have the student step over it when making the pass.
- The ball does not make it to the receiver. *Cause:* The student does not point the nonthrowing hand toward the receiver. *Correction:* Remind the student to make a T with both arms.
- The ball does not arrive at the receiver's hands. *Cause:* The passer is not looking at the receiver's hands. *Correction:* Have the receiver hold up a number of fingers, and ask the passer to speak the number.
- The ball does not arrive at the receiver's hands. *Cause:* The passer does not have the strength to get the pass there. *Correction:* Move the partners closer together.
- The throw is too hard. *Cause:* The passer doesn't take into consideration the catching ability of the partner. *Correction:* Remind the student to throw gently.
- The throw is too high or too low. *Cause:* The release point is too early or too late. *Correction:* Remind the student to release the ball out in front of the body at head height.

TASK 5: THROWING AND CATCHING A FLY BALL IN KICKBALL

PURPOSE

Following are the purposes of the task as related to aspects of skilled performance.

- Technique: In this task, students learn the basic technique of catching a fly ball using a kickball.
- Fair play: Students gently throw the ball to the partner so it can be caught above the head.
- Communication: Students call out *mine* to indicate possession of the ball.

DESCRIPTION

Students pair up and stand 15 to 20 feet (4.6 to 6.1 meters) apart. One student has a ball and, on your signal, throws a fly ball overhand to the partner. The partner moves to catch the ball above the head and then throws a fly ball back to the partner. Students continue for a designated time. If students need motivation, have pairs count how many throws and catches they can make in a row or within a designated time. As an extension, when students are comfortable catching the fly ball, have the receiver throw the ball to the partner as if the ball was being returned to the infield. The partner needs to call out *right here* to indicate where the throw should go.

EQUIPMENT

One ball per pair of students

CRITICAL ELEMENTS AND CUES

Technique: One-Handed Throw

- Place the throwing hand on the back of the ball with the fingers and thumbs spread. *Cue:* Fingers spread on back.
- Start with the ball close to the chest. *Cue:* Ball at your chest.
- Look at the receiver's hands. *Cue:* Eyes on target.
- Take two steps forward and then throw. *Cue:* Two steps.
- Lean back as you step with the opposite foot while creating the T. *Cue:* Lean back.
- Release the ball above the head as the throwing arm is moving up. *Cue:* High release.
- On the release, follow through to the opposite hip. *Cue:* Follow through.

Technique: Catch a Fly Ball

- Take one step back, adjust to the ball, and run in if needed. *Cue:* Adjust to the ball.
- Catch the ball above the head just in front of the body. *Cue:* Ball out front.
- Catch the ball with both hands. *Cue:* Two hands.

Fair Play

- Throw the ball high and toward the receiver so the receiver does not have to take more than 2 to 3 steps to catch it.

Communication

- When you are ready to receive the fly ball, call out *mine* to indicate that you will catch it. *Cue:* Call *mine*.
- In the extension, call out *right here* to indicate where your partner should throw the ball from the outfield.

COMMON ERRORS, CAUSES, AND CORRECTIONS

- The receiver does not follow the ball into the hands. *Cause:* The student looks at the passer or turns the head. *Correction:* Remind the student to keep the eyes on the ball.

- The ball does not arrive at the receiver's hands. *Cause:* The passer is not looking at the receiver's hands. *Correction:* Have the receiver hold up a number of fingers, and ask the passer to speak the number.
- The ball does not arrive at the receiver's hands. *Cause:* The passer does not have the strength to get the pass there. *Correction:* Move the partners closer together.
- The throw is too high and does not make it to the receiver. *Cause:* The passer releases the ball too early. *Correction:* Remind the student to release the ball above the head.
- The throw is too low. *Cause:* The release point is too late. *Correction:* Remind the student to release the ball above the head.

TASK 6: 1V1 KICKBALL CATCHING GAME

PURPOSE

Following are the purposes of the task as related to aspects of skilled performance.

- Technique: In this task, students apply the techniques learned in tasks 2 through 5 in a game-like setting.
- Fair play: Students apply the fair play components of tasks 2 through 5 in a game-like setting.
- Communication: Students apply the communication methods used in tasks 2 through 5 in a game-like setting.

DESCRIPTION

Set two poly spots 5 to 10 feet (1.5 to 3 meters) apart. Then make two rows of 5 to 7 poly spots each as shown in the figure. Each subsequent pair of poly spots is 3 feet (0.9 meters) farther apart than the previous pair.

Students pair up and stand across from each other on the first set of poly spots. One student has a ball and throws it to the partner using the assigned throw. The partner catches the ball using the assigned catch and then throws it back. After both students have successfully thrown and caught the ball, the pair can move to the next set of poly spots and repeat the task. Students progress until one of the following occurs: the throw does not reach the partner, the partner does not catch the ball using the assigned technique or drops the ball, or students successfully toss and catch from all spots and complete the task. If students make an error, they restart at the beginning and try again.

The following are the types of throws and catches you can assign for each game:

- Two-hand toss and catch (task 2)
- Rolled ball and catch off the ground (task 3)
- Overhead throw and catch (task 4)
- Fly ball throw and catch (task 5)

EQUIPMENT

One ball and 12 to 16 poly spots (or floor tape) per pair of students

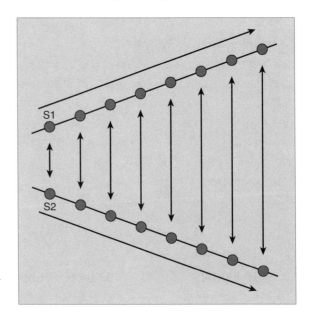

CRITICAL ELEMENTS AND CUES

This application game is used to apply learned techniques in a game situation. Apply all critical elements and cues for the techniques being emphasized after learning the techniques from tasks 2 through 5 as indicated on the level 1 content map.

COMMON ERRORS, CAUSES, AND CORRECTIONS

Look for the errors addressed in tasks 2 through 5 and provide corrections during the appropriate application game (see level 1 content map).

TASK 7: KICKING A BALL

PURPOSE

Following is the purpose of the task as related to aspects of skilled performance.
　　Technique: In this task, students learn the proper way to kick a rolling ball.

DESCRIPTION

Divide students into groups of three. One student is the kicker, one is the pitcher, and the other is the fielder. The kicker stands 8 to 10 feet (2.4 to 3 meters) behind a poly spot that is 20 feet (6.1 meters) in front of the pitcher. The fielder stands 20 feet (6.1 meters) behind the pitcher. The pitcher rolls a kickball toward the poly spot, and the kicker runs up to kick the ball as it crosses the poly spot. The fielder or pitcher attempts to catch the kicked ball. Once the ball is retrieved, the kicker becomes the fielder, the fielder becomes the pitcher, and the pitcher becomes the kicker. Students continue playing and rotating for a designated time or number of rotations. As an extension, if the kicks consistently get to the fielder, have the fielder get the ball back to the infield by throwing it to the pitcher.

EQUIPMENT

One ball and one poly spot per three students

CRITICAL ELEMENTS AND CUES

Technique

- Place the nonkicking foot even with or slightly behind the side of the ball. *Cue:* Step next to the ball.
- Strike the ball with the instep of the foot. *Cue:* Kick with shoelaces.
- After kicking the ball, follow through with the kicking leg slightly across the midline. *Cue:* Follow through.

COMMON ERRORS, CAUSES, AND CORRECTIONS

- The student kicks the ball with the toes. *Cause:* The toes are not pointed down at contact. *Correction:* Have the student practice contacting a stationary ball with the instep (shoelaces).

TASK 8: 1V1 ROLLING OR KICKING GAME

PURPOSE

Following are the purposes of the task as related to aspects of skilled performance.

- Technique: In this task, students roll or kick a ball in a straight line, catch a rolling ball, and run to first base.
- Tactic: Students run to get the runner out at first base.
- Agility: Students quickly move from kicking to running toward first base.
- Communication: Defensive students put an arm up to indicate that they are ready to begin.

DESCRIPTION

Designate a 75-foot (22.9-m) by 30-foot (9.1-m) playing area with four cones (teacher can use larger or smaller dimensions if necessary). Place one red poly spot at one end to serve as home base and a green poly spot for the fielder 75 feet (22.9 m) in front of the home base. Place two poly spots halfway between the home base and fielding poly spots about 3 to 5 feet (0.9 to 1.5 meters) apart. The red poly spot to the right of the home base should be the home base poly spot, and the green poly spot should be the fielding poly spot. Students are in pairs. One student is the kicker and stands at home base with a ball sitting on home base. The other student is the fielder and stands on the farthest poly spot (see figure). The kicker kicks the ball on the ground within the boundaries formed by the cones and then runs to the middle poly spot on their right. The fielder fields the ball and runs to the other middle poly spot. Whoever reaches their spot first gets the point. After each turn, students switch roles. Play continues for a set number of trials. If students have trouble kicking the ball, have them roll the ball instead of kicking it. Both students must run straight to the assigned poly spot to avoid a collision. If students need motivation, have the fielder earn a point each time the ball is kicked in the air instead of on the ground. As an extension, set the fielder's base poly spot 3 to 5 feet (.9 to 1.5 m) to the side of the kicker's home base poly spot. In this extension after the kicker kicks the ball, the kicker runs to the middle poly spot, turns around, and runs back to the home base (see figure). After fielding the ball, the fielder runs to the poly spot that has been moved next to home base and tries to beat the runner there.

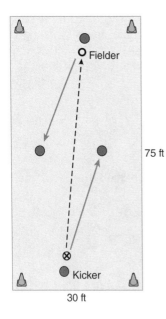 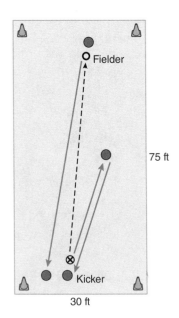

EQUIPMENT

One ball, four cones, and four poly spots (2 red and 2 green) per pair of students

CRITICAL ELEMENTS AND CUES

Technique: Offense

- The kicker runs up to the stationary ball. *Cue:* Approach the ball.
- Place the nonkicking foot even with or slightly behind the side of the ball. *Cue:* Step next to the ball.
- Strike the ball with the instep of the foot. *Cue:* Kick with shoelaces.
- After kicking the ball, follow through with the kicking leg slightly across the midline. *Cue:* Follow through.

Technique: Defense

- Step toward the ball as it comes toward you. *Cue:* Step to ball.
- Look at the ball as it comes into the hands. *Cue:* Eyes on ball.
- Catch with two hands. *Cue:* Two hands.
- As the ball contacts the hands, pull the ball into the body. *Cue:* Absorb the ball.
- End with the ball close to the body and the elbows flexed. *Cue:* Bring it in.
- Tell students to make sure and catch the ball before running to the base. *Cue:* Catch and run.

Tactic

- As soon as you catch the ball, immediately run to try to get to the middle base before the runner to cause the runner to be out.

Agility

- After kicking the ball the student must quickly begin running to the first base.
- The defender must move to the ball and quickly run to the base.
- In the extension, the kicker must quickly turn and run back to the home base.

Communication

- The defense puts an arm up to indicate readiness to begin.

COMMON ERRORS, CAUSES, AND CORRECTIONS

- The student kicks the ball into the air. *Cause:* The student is stepping too far away from the ball or is kicking with the toes. *Correction:* Remind the student to step next to the ball and kick with the instep (or shoelaces).
- The ball goes between the defender's legs. *Cause:* The defender tries to run before fielding. *Correction:* Remind the student to catch the ball first and then run.
- The runner takes too long to turn around during the extension. *Cause:* The student is overrunning the base or tries to hold the base. *Correction:* Tell students to break down their steps before touching the base so they can stop and turn.

TASK 9: 2V2 KICKBALL GAME: OUT AT FIRST BASE

PURPOSE

Following are the purposes of the task as related to aspects of skilled performance.

- Technique: In this task, students apply throwing, catching, kicking, and base running techniques.
- Tactic: Students get the out at first base after a kick with no one on base.
- Agility: Students make quick movements to get to the ball and run through first base.
- Fair play: Students settle safe or out disputes by playing by rock, paper, scissors.
- Communication: Defenders raise a hand when they are ready. Infielders communicate about who is covering first base.

DESCRIPTION

Divide groups of four students into two teams. This game is played on the right half of the infield (the dividing line runs between home and second base) with four poly spots used as bases. The bases are set up 45 feet (13.7 meters) apart. One poly spot serves as home plate, one poly spot serves as second base, and two poly spots are set next to each other 3 feet apart and serve as first bases (see figure). The home plate, second base, and inside first base should be the color red and the outside first base poly spot is the color blue. On offense, both students have a ball and one student is a kicker and one is an on-deck kicker. On defense, one student is a first-base player and the other is a second-base player. The kicker starts on home plate and kicks the ball on the ground and between first and second bases. Anything left of second base or right of first base is a foul ball. If a foul ball occurs, the kicker loses the turn and must go get the ball, and the on-deck kicker is up. If the kicker puts the ball in play on the ground, he or she sprints through first base. The defense makes a play at first base to attempt to get the kicker out. The defense can perform a throw-and-catch force-out at first, tag first base directly, or tag the runner. The defense makes the play on the inside red first base poly spot to avoid collisions while the offensive runner runs through the outside blue poly spot (first base) and then returns home whether safe or out (see figure). If the kicker kicks the ball in the air, the kicker is out and the on-deck kicker is up. Each kicker kicks two times; then the offense and defense switch roles. Defensive players switch positions after each inning. The offense gets a point for being safe, and the defense gets a point for making a force-out. Play continues for a designated number of innings.

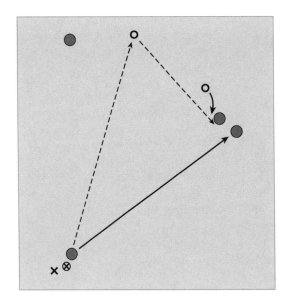

EQUIPMENT

Two balls and four poly spots (3 red and 1 blue) per four students

CRITICAL ELEMENTS AND CUES

Technique

- Students apply critical elements and cues from the previously learned techniques of throwing from task 4, catching a rolling ball from task 3, kicking from task 7, and running to first base from task 1.

Tactic

- If the ball comes to the first-base player, he or she catches the ball and runs to the base to force the out or tags the runner with the ball before the runner gets to first base.
- If the ball goes to the second-base player, the first-base player goes to first base to receive a throw from the second-base player.
- If the ball goes between the two fielders and is caught by the first-base player, the second-base player runs to first to cover the base and receive a throw from the first-base player.

Agility

- Quickly get away from home plate after kicking the ball.
- Quickly move to the side to catch a ground ball.

Fair Play

- If a dispute arises, resolve it by playing rock, paper, scissors.

Communication

- The defense raises a hand to indicate readiness to begin.
- When the second-base player catches the ball, the first-base player covers the base and shouts *one, one, one* to the fielder to throw the ball to first base.
- The first-base player shouts *help* when fielding a ball away from first base, which indicates that the second-base person needs to cover first base.
- When fielding the ball close to the bag, the first-base player says *mine* and tags the runner or bag.

COMMON ERRORS, CAUSES, AND CORRECTIONS

- The offensive student slows down before getting to first base. *Cause:* The student thinks she or he is already out. *Correction:* Tell the student not to slow down and to run through first base.
- The offensive student slows down before getting to first base. *Cause:* The student is watching the ball. *Correction:* Remind the student not to watch the ball.
- The defense makes a wild throw to first base. *Cause:* The second-base player rushes the throw to first. *Correction:* Have offensive student kick the ball without running until the defense is consistent in throwing to the first base.

TASK 10: 2V2 KICKBALL GAME WITH A PITCHER

PURPOSE

Following are the purposes of the task as related to aspects of skilled performance.

- Technique: In this task, students kick a rolled ball and roll (pitch) a ball.
- Tactic: Students run or throw to get the runner out at first base.
- Agility: Students quickly move from kicking to running toward first base.
- Communication: Defensive students put an arm up to indicate that they are ready to begin.

DESCRIPTION

Divide groups of four students into two teams. This game is played on the right half of the infield (the dividing line runs between home and second base) with five poly spots. The bases are set up 45 feet (13.7 meters) apart. One poly spot serves as home plate, one poly spot serves as second base, one poly spots marks the pitcher's spot where the ball is rolled from, and two poly spots are set next to each other 3 feet apart and serve as first bases. The home plate, second base, pitcher's spot, and inside first base should be the color red and the outside first base poly spot is the color blue. On offense, one student has a ball and rolls the ball (pitcher), and one student is a kicker. On defense, one student is a first-base player, and one is the second base player. The kicker stands behind home plate and kicks the rolled ball on the ground and between first and second bases. Anything left of second base or right of first base is a foul ball. If a foul ball occurs, the kicker loses the turn and must go get the ball, and the pitcher then becomes the next kicker while the kicker becomes the next pitcher. If the kicker puts the ball in play on the ground, he sprints through first base. The pitcher does not try to field the kicked ball, only the two defenders can field the ball. The defense makes a play at first base to attempt to get the kicker out. The defense can perform a throw-and-catch force-out at first, tag first base directly, or tag the runner. The defense makes the play on the inside first base red poly spot to avoid collisions while the offensive runner runs through the outside blue poly spot (first base), and then becomes the next pitcher whether safe or out. If the kicker kicks the ball in the air, the kicker is out and the pitcher is up. Each kicker kicks two times; then the offense and defense switch roles.

Defensive players switch positions after each inning. The offense gets a point for being safe, and the defense gets a point for making a force-out. Play continues for a designated number of innings. The defenders raise their arm after to play to indicate that they are ready for the next play. If students need motivation when pitching, award one point to the defense if the pitch bounces more than two times on its path toward the kicker.

EQUIPMENT

One ball and five poly spots (4 red and 1 blue) per 4 students

CRITICAL ELEMENTS AND CUES

Technique:

- Students apply critical elements and cues from the previously learned techniques of rolling and catching a rolling ball from task 3, throwing from task 4, kicking from task 7 and running to first base from task 1.

Tactic

- After a ball is put into play by a kick, the defense tries to get the runner out at first base.

Agility

- Kicker must quickly get into a run after kicking the ball.

Communication

- The defense puts an arm up to indicate readiness to begin.

COMMON ERRORS, CAUSES, AND CORRECTIONS

- The ball bounces too much. *Cause:* The pitcher releases the ball too high or too soon. *Correction:* Remind the pitcher to bend the knees and release the ball closer to the ground and past the hip.
- The ball rolls too far to the left or right of the plate. *Cause:* The pitcher turns the shoulders so that they are not square to the target and does not step in line with the target. *Correction:* Remind the student to keep the shoulders square, step to the target, and step toward the plate.
- The kicker misses the ball. *Cause:* The student is not looking at the ball or starts to run before kicking. *Correction:* Have the student practice a stationary kick (with no pitcher).
- The kick is weak. *Cause:* The student kicks with the toes, the shin, or the bottom of the foot. *Correction:* Put a sticker on the student's foot near the instep (shoelaces) to indicate where the student should kick contact the ball.

TASK 11: AROUND THE HORN KICKBALL

PURPOSE

Following are the purposes of the task as related to aspects of skilled performance.

- Technique: In this task, students learn to throw to bases and catch while standing on the base.
- Tactic: Students throw to the nearest base that a runner is advancing toward in an attempt to get the runner out.
- Fair play: Students settle disputes amicably and promote a safe and fair playing environment.

DESCRIPTION

Set up enough infield diamonds with all four bases 45 feet (13.7 meters) apart to accommodate groups of eight students (teachers can expand this distance out to 60 feet [18.3

meters] as needed). Divide each group of eight students into two teams of four. The four defensive students set up at first, second, and third bases and at shortstop. Set the kickball on home base. There are base runners on first and second base, and there is one kicker and one on-deck kicker. The kicker kicks the ball on the ground and runs to first and stays there. The runner on first advances to second and stays there, and the runner on second goes through third and jogs home to become the next on-deck kicker. The fielders attempt to catch the kicked ground ball and then either run to or throw to the nearest base ahead of the approaching runner in an attempt to force an out. Regardless of whether the runner is safe or out, base runners always reset to runners on first and second. Each kicker kicks one time. After all four players kick, the offense and defense switch roles. After both teams have kicked once, that ends an inning. After each inning, the defense rotates (third base to shortstop, shortstop to second base, second base to first base, and first base to third base). The game ends when all students play each defensive position (4 innings). After a foul ball, the kicker goes to first base, the first-base runner goes to second base, the second-base runner becomes the on-deck kicker, and the on-deck kicker is up. The defense gets a point for each successful force-out, and the offense get a point for each safe runner. As an extension, when the kicker kicks the ball the runners all advance to home plate and the kicker runs out a complete home run (run through all bases). While the offensive students are running the bases, the defense makes the force-out at third base and turns a triple play, third to second to first. Whoever finishes first (the home run or the triple play) gets the point. After the play is complete, the offensive students and defensive students reset and the next kicker goes. Each offensive team member kicks one time and then the defense and offense switch roles. The game ends when all students play each defensive position (four innings).

EQUIPMENT

One ball and four bases per eight students

CRITICAL ELEMENTS AND CUES

Technique

- Students apply critical elements and cues from the previously learned techniques of throwing and catching from task 4, kicking from task 7 and running the bases from task 1.

Tactic

- When fielding the ball, you must recognize where the runners are on the base paths and then decide which you can get the ball to ahead of the runner.
- When doing the extension triple play, the ball comes from the third-base player to second base and the second-base person covers second on the backside of the base. Then the second-base person throws to first.

Fair Play

- Offense and defense should not interfere with each other.
- Settle disputes with rock, paper, scissors.

COMMON ERRORS, CAUSES, AND CORRECTIONS

- The wrong fielder tries to cover second base. *Cause:* Fielders are unaware who covers second base in different situations. *Correction:* Tell the defense that the second-base person covers second when the ball is on the left side of the infield and the shortstop covers it when the ball is on the right side.
- During the extension of the task, the runner shuffles the feet and slows down at bases. *Cause:* The runner does not run the bases in a circular pattern or is afraid to miss the base. *Correction:* Stop the game and have students run the bases at half speed and focus on making the infield a circle.

TASK 12: 4V4 KICKING GAME

PURPOSE

Following are the purposes of the task as related to aspects of skilled performance.

- Technique: In this task, students learn about force-outs and non-force-outs with a full infield and various defensive situations (e.g., runners on different bases in different situations).
- Tactic: Students need to get the lead runner out, try to kick behind runners, and know when to run, stay on the base, or tag up.

DESCRIPTION

Set up enough infield diamonds with all four bases 45 feet (13.7 meters) apart to accommodate groups of eight students (teachers can expand this distance out to 60 feet (18.3 meters) as needed. An additional base is set up to the right side of first base. The extra base to the right of first base is the one the kicker runs through, and the base to the left is the one the infielders use to force an out. Divide each group of eight students into two teams of four. The four defensive students set up at first, second, and third bases and at shortstop. The ball is placed on the home base for the kicker to kick. After kicking the ball, the kicker runs out the play. This means that after the kick, the kicker runs to the furthest base they can obtain without getting out. Once at that base, the kicker stays on that base and this creates either a force-out or non-force-out situation for that base runner and the defenders. If the runner is either on first base or all of the bases behind the base that the runner is on are all occupied this creates a force-out situation for the runners and the defenders. This means that when the ball is kicked each base runner must try to advance to the next base and the defense tries to get the ball to the base ahead of a runner to create an out. In this force-out situation, all the defenders need to do is to get the ball to the base a base runner is attempting to get to and touch it to create an out (all plays at first base are considered force-out situations since the kicker must run to first base after the kick). If the runner is on a base and the base immediately behind that base is open (doesn't have a runner on it) then that creates a non-force-out situation. This means that the base runner does not need to run to the next base when the ball is kicked unless the base runner thinks he can get to the base without being touched with the ball. In non-force-out situations, the base runner must be touched with the ball while off the base to be called out. All kicks must be on the ground; a fly ball is an out. The defense makes the out accordingly depending on the runner's situation by either being in possession of the ball when they touch a base being approached by a runner or touching the runner when running in a force-out situation or by touching the runner with the ball in a non-force-out situation. While the defense is attempting to get runners out, outs do not accumulate so the kickers on each team kick one time before the offense and defense switch roles. After each team has kicked, that marks the end of an inning. The offense gets a point for a run scored, and the defense does not score points. After each inning, the defense rotates (third base to shortstop, shortstop to second base, second base to first base, and first base to third base). The game ends when all students have played each defensive position (four innings). If students need motivation, award defensive bonus points for getting lead runners out and offensive bonus points for kicking behind runners (e.g., kicking to the right side when a runner is on second base).

EQUIPMENT

One ball and five bases per eight students

CRITICAL ELEMENTS AND CUES

Technique

- Students apply critical elements and cues from the previously learned techniques of throwing and catching from task 4, kicking from task 7 and running the bases from task 1 in a game situation.

Tactic

- Always get the lead out if possible. The lead out is the furthest runner on the bases.
- When a runner is on second base, kick behind this player to move him or her to third base and put the player in a scoring position.
- If you are in a force situation, the runner has to run when the ball is kicked.
- When you are in a nonforce situation, the runner should run when the defender cannot tag you with the ball (e.g., kicking behind the runner). It is important to teach this decision-making process.

COMMON ERRORS, CAUSES, AND CORRECTIONS

- The runner does not run during a force situation. *Cause:* The student lacks knowledge or is confused. *Correction:* Remind the students ahead of time that it is a force situation and what they should do when the ball is kicked.
- A runner makes the incorrect running decision in a non-force situation. *Cause:* The student lacks knowledge or is confused. *Correction:* Remind the students ahead of time that it is a non-force-out situation and what they should do with the ball is kicked.
- The defense does not get the lead out and eliminates the force. *Cause:* The runner behind the lead runner is forced out (e.g., with runners on first and second, the defense makes the force-out at first and then tries to make a force-out at third; however, the force-out at third has been eliminated and that runner must be tagged out). *Correction:* The defense tries to get the lead runner in a force-out situation because if the defense forces out a lagging runner or a runner behind, then it is harder to get the lead runner. This is because the situation is no longer a force situation and the only way to get the lead runner out is by being tagged out. Use freeze replay and show the class when improper plays are made. For example, when the defense forces a runner on first out at second and then tags the runner at second running to third out (because the force was eliminated), freeze the class have them do it again. Point out that it would have been better to get the out at third and then at second so the force was not eliminated.

TASK 13: 4V4 INFIELD KICKBALL GAME

PURPOSE

Following are the purposes of the task as related to aspects of skilled performance.

- Technique: In this task, students apply the learned techniques of throwing, catching, kicking, and base running in a game situation.
- Tactic: Students apply learned tactics of force-outs and non-force-outs in a game situation.

DESCRIPTION

Set up enough infield diamonds with all four bases 45 feet (13.7 meters) apart to accommodate groups of eight students (teachers can expand this distance out to 60 feet [18.3 meters] as needed). Divide each group of eight students into two teams of four. An additional base is set up to the right side of first base. The extra base to the right of first base is the one the kicker runs through, and the base to the left is the one the infielders use to force an out. This task is done exactly as task 12 except for one difference. In this game the offensive teams stays up to bat until three outs are made (all kicks start with a stationary ball and the kicked ball must be on the ground; a fly ball is an out). After the third out the offense and defense change roles. The offense gets a point for a run scored, and the defense does not score points. This game continues until a designated number of innings have been played. As an extension, if you have higher-performing students who are successful at getting runners out, a fifth player can be added to both teams and have students kick a rolling pitch. This fifth player fulfills the role of catcher while the team is on defense and as the pitcher when the team is on offense. Having the pitcher come from the offensive team will encourage the pitcher to make a quality rolling pitch. Rotate pitchers each inning to allow everyone an opportunity to pitch. If the offense kicks the ball toward the pitcher, the pitcher does not make a play on the ball and if the ball does not get past the pitcher, the player is automatically out. Set up an additional base or poly spot next to home plate for the catcher to use. The defense can make a play at home plate by throwing to the catcher. If the throw gets to home plate before the offensive runner does, the runner is out regardless of whether the catcher catches the ball.

EQUIPMENT

One ball and five bases per eight students

CRITICAL ELEMENTS AND CUES

Technique

- Students apply critical elements and cues from the previously learned techniques of throwing and catching from task 4, kicking from task 7, and running the bases from task 1 in a game situation.

Tactic

- Always get the lead out if possible. The lead out is the furthest runner on the bases.
- When a runner is on second base, kick behind this player to move him or her to third base and put the player in a scoring position.
- If you are in a force situation, the runner has to run when the ball is kicked.
- When you are in a non-force situation, the runner should run when the defender cannot tag you with the ball (e.g., kicking behind the runner). It is important to teach this decision-making process.

COMMON ERRORS, CAUSES, AND CORRECTIONS

- The runner does not run during a force situation. *Cause:* The student lacks knowledge or is confused. *Correction:* Remind the students ahead of time that it is a force situation and what they should do when the ball is kicked.
- A runner makes the incorrect running decision in a non-force situation. *Cause:* The student lacks knowledge or is confused. *Correction:* Remind the students ahead of time that it is a non-force-out situation and what they should do with the ball is kicked.
- The defense does not get the lead out and eliminates the force. *Cause:* The runner behind the lead runner is forced out (e.g., with runners on first and second, the defense makes the force-out at first and then tries to make a force-out at third; however, the force-out at third has been eliminated and that runner must be tagged out). *Correction:* The defense tries to get the lead runner in a force-out situation because if the defense forces out a lagging runner or a runner behind, then it is harder to get the lead runner. This is because the situation is no longer a force situation and the only way to get the lead runner out is by being tagged out. Use freeze replay and show the class when improper plays are made. For example, when the defense forces a runner on first out at second and then tags the runner at second running to third out (because the force was eliminated), freeze the class have them do it again. Point out that it would have been better to get the out at third and then at second so the force was not eliminated.

TASK 14: TWO-HAND CATCHING A TOSSED SOFTBALL

PURPOSE

Following are the purposes of the task as related to aspects of skilled performance.

- Technique: In this task, students learn the basic technique of catching a softball from a toss.
- Fair play: Students toss the ball to the partner's hands at chest height.
- Communication: Students hold the hands out to indicate readiness to receive the toss.

DESCRIPTION

Students pair up and stand 10 to 15 feet (3 to 4.6 meters) apart. One student has a ball and, on your signal, tosses the ball underhand to the partner. The partner makes a two-handed catch (see figure) and then tosses the ball back. Students continue for a designated time. If students need motivation, have pairs count how many tosses and catches they can make in a row or within a designated time.

EQUIPMENT

One ball per pair of students

CRITICAL ELEMENTS AND CUES

Technique: One-Handed Underhand Toss

- Place one hand on the ball with fingers and thumbs spread. *Cue:* Fingers spread.
- Start with the ball close to the knees. *Cue:* Ball at your knees.
- Look at the receiver's hands. *Cue:* Eyes on target.
- Step toward the receiver with the leg opposite the tossing hand. *Cue:* Step to receiver.
- Move the ball away from the knees by swaying the arm, rocking the wrist, and extending the elbow at the same time. *Cue:* All together.
- As the arms extend, rock the wrists and follow through just below chest height. *Cue:* Use your wrists.
- Toss the ball to the partner with gentle force and with an arc. *Cue:* Like a rainbow.

Technique: Two-Handed Catch (see figure)

- Look at the ball as it comes into the hands. *Cue:* Eyes on ball.
- Catch with two hands. *Cue:* Two hands.
- Step toward the ball as it comes toward you. *Cue:* Step to ball.
- As the ball contacts the hands, pull the ball into the body. *Cue:* Absorb the ball.
- End with the ball close to the body and the elbows flexed. *Cue:* Bring it in.

Fair Play

- Toss the ball directly toward the receiver's chest.
- The toss must have enough force to get to the receiver but still be gentle and have an arc.
- Toss the ball so it does not go too high above the receiver's head.

Communication

- When you are ready to receive a toss, place both hands in the target area with the fingers spread and the palms out. *Cue:* Big target.

COMMON ERRORS, CAUSES, AND CORRECTIONS

- The receiver does not follow the ball into the hands. *Cause:* The student looks at the passer or turns the head. *Correction:* Remind the student to keep the eyes on the ball.
- The toss does not arrive at the receiver's hands. *Cause:* The passer is not looking at the receiver's hands. *Correction:* Have the receiver hold up a number of fingers, and ask the tosser to speak the number.
- The toss does not arrive at the receiver's hands. *Cause:* The passer does not have the strength to get the pass there. *Correction:* Move the partners closer together.

TASK 15: TWO-HAND CATCHING A GROUND BALL IN SOFTBALL

PURPOSE

Following are the purposes of the task as related to aspects of skilled performance.

- Technique: In this task, students learn the basic technique of catching a rolling softball.
- Fair play: Students roll the ball toward the partner's feet.
- Communication: Students hold the hands out to indicate readiness to receive the ball.

DESCRIPTION

Students pair up and stand 10 to 15 feet (3 to 4.6 meters) apart. One student has a ball and, on your signal, rolls the ball toward the partner. The partner bends down and catches the rolling ball with both hands and brings the ball up to the belly area. The receiver then rolls the ball back to the partner, who catches it the same way. The students continue this for a designated time. If students need motivation, have pairs count how many rolls and catches they can make in a row or within a designated time.

EQUIPMENT

One ball per pair of students

CRITICAL ELEMENTS AND CUES

Technique: Roll

- Place the ball in the dominant hand on the same-side hip with the fingers spread on the back of the ball. *Cue:* Fingers spread.
- Look at the receiver's feet. *Cue:* Eyes on target.
- Step with the foot opposite the dominant hand. *Cue:* Step to receiver.
- Swing the dominant hand back and keep the shoulders square to target and the knees bent. *Cues:* Bend your knees; face the target.
- As the arms come through on the rolling action, release the ball at ground level so that it stays close to the ground. *Cue:* On the ground.
- The dominant hand follows the path of the ball on the follow-through. *Cue:* Follow the ball.

Technique: Catch a Rolled Ball

- Stand with the knees bent, bend at the waist, and put the arms out in front of the body. *Cue:* Get low and ready.
- Step toward the ball as it comes toward you. Cue: Step to ball.
- Touch the heels of your hands with the throwing hand on top and the non-throwing hand on the bottom. Spread the fingers of both the lower (nonthrowing) hand and the top (throwing) hand so they are open. *Cue:* Gator hands.
- Look at the ball as it comes into the hands. *Cue:* Eyes on ball.
- As the ball contacts the hands, bring the ball up to the belly area. *Cue:* Bring it up.
- End with the ball to the belly with the elbows flexed. *Cue:* Bring it in.

Fair Play

- Roll the ball directly toward the receiver's feet.
- Roll the ball with enough force that is gets to the receiver. The roll should be gentle and the ball should not bounce.

Communication

- When you are ready to receive the ball, place the hands in the target area with the fingers spread and the palms out. *Cue:* Big target.

COMMON ERRORS, CAUSES, AND CORRECTIONS

- The receiver does not follow the ball to the hands. *Cause:* The student looks at the thrower or turns the head. *Correction:* Remind the student to keep the eyes on the ball.
- The ball rolls under the hands and the receiver misses it. Cause: The receiver moves the hands up too early before catching the ball when trying to bring the ball up and into the belly in order to toss the ball back. *Correction:* Field the ball first.

TASK 16: THROWING AND CATCHING A SOFTBALL

PURPOSE

Following are the purposes of the task as related to aspects of skilled performance.

- Technique: In this task, students learn the basic technique of catching a softball from a throw.
- Fair play: Students gently throw the ball to the partner's hands at chest height.
- Communication: Students hold their hands out to indicate readiness to receive the ball.

DESCRIPTION

Students pair up and stand 10 to 15 feet (3 to 4.6 meters) apart. One student has a softball and, on your signal, throws the ball overhand to the partner (see figure). The partner catches the ball and then throws it back. Students continue for a designated time. If students need motivation, have pairs count how many throws and catches they can make in a row or within a designated time.

EQUIPMENT

One ball per pair of students

CRITICAL ELEMENTS AND CUES

Technique: One-Handed Overhead Throw

- Place four fingers of the throwing hand on the ball with the thumb on the other side of the ball in opposition. *Cue:* Claw.
- Start with the ball close to the chest. *Cue:* Ball at your chest.

- Look at the receiver's hands. *Cue:* Eyes on target.
- Step toward the receiver with leg opposite the throwing hand. *Cue:* Step to receiver.
- While stepping toward the target, move the throwing arm back at shoulder lever with the elbow bent approximately at a 90 degree angle and the ball up. *Cue:* Make an L.
- As the throwing arm goes back, the non-throwing arm needs to come up to shoulder level in the direction of the target. *Cue:* Point.
- Once the arm is back, rotate the hips while bringing the ball forward. *Cue:* Rotate and throw.
- On the release, follow through to the opposite hip. *Cue:* Follow through.

Technique: Two-Handed Catch

- Look at the ball as it comes into the hands. *Cue:* Eyes on ball.
- Catch with two hands. *Cue:* Two hands.
- Step toward the ball as it comes toward you. *Cue:* Step to ball.
- As the ball contacts the hands, pull the ball into the body. *Cue:* Absorb the ball.
- End with the ball close to the body and the elbows flexed. *Cue:* Bring it in.

Fair Play

- Toss the ball directly toward the receiver's chest.
- The toss must have enough force to get to the receiver but still be gentle and have an arc.
- Do not toss the ball higher than the receiver's head.

Communication

- When you are ready to receive a toss, place both hands in the target area with the fingers spread and the palms out. *Cue:* Big target.

COMMON ERRORS, CAUSES, AND CORRECTIONS

- The ball does not make it to the receiver. *Cause:* The passer does not step toward the receiver. *Correction:* Place a poly spot in front of the passer and have the student step over it when making the pass.
- The ball does not make it directly to the receiver. *Cause:* The student does not point the nonthrowing hand toward the receiver. *Correction:* Remind the student to point toward the target.
- The receiver does not follow the ball into the hands. *Cause:* The student looks at the passer or turns the head. *Correction:* Remind the student to keep the eyes on the ball.

TASK 17: THROWING AND CATCHING A FLY BALL IN SOFTBALL

PURPOSE

Following are the purposes of the task as related to aspects of skilled performance.

- Technique: In this task, students learn the basic technique of catching a fly ball using a softball.
- Fair play: Students gently throw the ball to the partner so it can be caught above the head.
- Communication: Students call out *mine* to indicate possession of the ball.

DESCRIPTION

Students pair up and stand 15 to 20 feet (4.6 to 6.1 meters) apart. One student has a ball and, on your signal, throws a fly ball overhand to the partner. The partner moves to catch the ball above the head and then throws a fly ball back to the partner. Students continue for a designated time. If students need motivation, have pairs count how many throws and catches they can make in a row or within a designated time. As an extension, when students are comfortable catching the fly ball, have the receiver throw the ball to the partner as if the ball was being returned to the infield. The partner needs to call out *right here* to indicate where the throw should go.

EQUIPMENT

One ball per pair of students

CRITICAL ELEMENTS AND CUES

Technique: One-Handed Overhead Throw

- Place four fingers of the throwing hand on the ball with the thumb on the other side of the ball in opposition. *Cue:* Claw.
- Start with the ball close to the chest. *Cue:* Ball at your chest.
- Look at the receiver's hands. *Cue:* Eyes on target.
- Step toward the receiver with leg opposite the throwing hand. *Cue:* Step to receiver.
- While stepping toward the target, move the throwing arm back at shoulder lever with the elbow bent approximately at a 90 degree angle and the ball up. *Cue:* Make an L.
- As the throwing arm goes back, the non-throwing arm needs to come up to shoulder level in the direction of the throw. *Cue:* Point.
- Once the arm is back, rotate the hips while bringing the ball forward. *Cue:* Rotate and throw.
- Release the ball above the head as the throwing arm is moving up. *Cue:* High release.
- On the release, follow through to the opposite hip. *Cue:* Follow through.

Technique: Catch a Fly Ball

- Take one step back, adjust to the ball, and run in if needed. *Cue:* Adjust to the ball.
- Catch the ball above the head just in front of the body. *Cue:* Ball out front.
- Catch the ball with both hands. *Cue:* Two hands.

Fair Play

- Throw the ball high and toward the receiver so the receiver does not have to take more than 2 to 3 steps to catch it.

Communication

- When you are ready to receive the fly ball, call out *mine* to indicate that you will catch it. *Cue:* Call *mine.*
- In the extension, call out *right here* to indicate where your partner should throw the ball from the outfield.

COMMON ERRORS, CAUSES, AND CORRECTIONS

- The ball does not make it to the receiver. *Cause:* The passer does not step toward the receiver. *Correction:* Place a poly spot in front of the passer and have the student step over it when making the pass.
- The ball goes over the fielder's head. *Cause:* The fielder takes steps in before going backward. *Correction:* Remind the student to step back first.

TASK 18: 1V1 SOFTBALL CATCHING GAME

PURPOSE

Following are the purposes of the task as related to aspects of skilled performance.

- Technique: In this task, students apply the techniques learned in tasks 14 through 17 in a game-like setting.
- Fair play: Students apply the fair play components of tasks 14 through 17 in a game-like setting.
- Communication: Students apply the communication methods used in tasks 14 through 17 in a game-like setting.

DESCRIPTION

Set two poly spots 5 to 10 feet (1.5 to 3 meters) apart. Then make two rows of 5 to 7 poly spots each. Each subsequent pair of poly spots is 3 feet (0.9 meters) farther apart than the previous pair. Students pair up, and students stand across from each other on the first set of poly spots. One student has a ball and throws it to the partner using the assigned throw. The partner catches the ball using the assigned catch and then throws it back. After both students have successfully thrown and caught the ball, the pair can move to the next set of poly spots and repeat the task. Student progress until one of the following occurs: the throw does not reach the partner, the partner does not catch the ball using the assigned technique or drops the ball, or students successfully toss and catch from all spots and complete the task. If students make an error, they restart at the beginning and try again.

The following are the types of throws and catches you can assign for each game:

- Two-hand toss and catch (task 14).
- Rolled ball and catch off the ground (task 15).
- Overhead throw and catch (task 16).
- Fly ball throw and catch (task 17).

EQUIPMENT

One ball and 12 to 16 poly spots (or floor tape) per pair of students

CRITICAL ELEMENTS AND CUES

Apply all skills and cues from tasks 14 through 17.

COMMON ERRORS, CAUSES, AND CORRECTIONS

Look for the errors addressed in tasks 14 through 17 and provide corrections.

TASK 19: HITTING OFF A TEE

PURPOSE

Following is the purpose of the task as related to aspects of skilled performance.

Technique: In this task, students learn the basic technique of striking a ball off a tee with a bat.

DESCRIPTION

Students pair up and share a batting tee station that consist of a tee and three poly spots. The poly spots are placed on the ground on the side of the tee that the batter will stand. Two red poly spots are placed next to the tee and are set should width apart while the green poly spot is set approximately 1 foot (30 cm) towards the wall that has a target attached (e.g. hula hoop, picture, etc.). The tee height should be even with the belt line of the student, and it should be an arm's length away from the belly button. It should be placed so the barrel of the bat meets the ball when it is extended. One student has a half-inflated beach ball and a bat. The beach ball makes the task easier, reduces recoil off the wall, and reduces shagging time. It also makes the task safer. If you want to use a softball-sized ball, we recommend a foam ball to reduce recoil and make the task safer.

The partner places the ball on the tee and helps shag the ball. The student with the bat checks the area to be sure that the partner and other students are not in the flight path of the ball or the swing plane of the bat. Once all is clear, the student starts with the feet on the red poly spots, steps onto the green spot with the front foot, and hits the ball off the tee toward a target on the wall. The student takes five swings; then students switch roles. Students continue the task for a designated time. If students need motivation, have pairs count how many times the ball hits a target. As an extension, have the partner two-hand underhand soft toss the beach ball from the side instead of using the tee.

EQUIPMENT

One ball, one bat, one tee, two red poly spots, and one green poly spot and a wall target per pair of students

CRITICAL ELEMENTS AND CUES

Technique: Batting Stance

- The feet are shoulder-width apart and the shoulders are parallel to the tee. *Cue:* Feet shoulder width apart.
- The hands grip the bat just above the knob, and the dominant hand is above the nondominant hand. *Cue:* Two hands on bat.
- The position of the hands and elbows form an upside down V with the hands at the apex of the V and the elbows the open part of the V. *Cue:* Upside down V.
- Hold the handle of the bat at ear height and with the barrel pointing up at approximately a 45 degree angle. *Cue:* Hands at your ear, bat up.

Technique: Swinging Motion (see figure)

- Step with the foot opposite the dominant hand. *Cue:* Step.
- Rotate the hips and shoulders. *Cue:* Rotate hips.
- Extend the arms and take the knob of the bat towards the ball. *Cue:* Knob to the ball.
- Strike the ball with the barrel of the bat. *Cue:* Bat on ball.
- Follow through with bat ending at the nondominant shoulder. *Cue:* Follow through hard.
- The belly should face the target after the swing. *Cue:* Belly to target.

COMMON ERRORS, CAUSES, AND CORRECTIONS

- The student hits the tee instead of the ball. *Cause:* The student steps away from the target line, lifts the head, or drops the hands. *Correction:* Remind the student to step to the target, keep the eyes on the ball, and swing the hands toward the ball.
- The student consistently hits ground balls instead of line drives. *Cause:* The student strikes top half of the ball. *Correction:* Remind the student to hit the middle of the ball.
- The student consistently hits ground balls instead of line drives. *Cause:* The student is too far away from the ball. *Correction:* Reposition the student correctly.

TASK 20: 1V1 HITTING GAME

PURPOSE

Following are the purposes of the task as related to aspects of skilled performance.

- Technique: In this task, students hit a ball on the ground in a straight line, catch a ground ball, and run to first base.
- Tactic: Students run to get the runner out at first base.
- Agility: Students quickly move from hitting to running toward first base.
- Communication: Defensive students put an arm up to indicate that they are ready to begin.

DESCRIPTION

Designate a 75-foot (22.9-meter) by 30-foot (9.1-meter) playing area with four cones (teacher can use larger or smaller dimensions if necessary). Place one red poly spot at one end to serve as home base and a green poly spot for the fielder 75-feet in front of the home base. Place two poly spots halfway between the home base and fielding poly sports about 3 to 5 feet (0.9 to 1.5 meters) apart. The poly spot to the right of the home base should be red like the home base poly spot and the other poly spot should be green like the fielding poly spot.

Students are in pairs. One student is the hitter and stands at home base. The other student is the fielder and stands on the farthest poly spot. The hitter hits the ball off a tee onto the ground within the boundaries of the cones and then runs to the middle poly spot on their right. The fielder fields the ball and runs to the other middle poly spot. Whoever reaches their spot first gets the point. After each turn, students switch roles. Play continues for a set number of trials. Both students must run straight to the assigned poly spot to avoid a collision. If the students need motivation, have the fielder earn a point each time the ball is hit in the air instead of on the ground. As an extension, set the fielder's middle poly spot 3 to 5 feet to the left side of the hitter's base poly spot. The hitter then runs to the middle poly spot, turns around, and runs back to the home base. After fielding the ball, the fielder runs to the green poly spot that has been moved next to home base and tries to beat the runner there.

EQUIPMENT

One ball, one bat, one tee, four cones, and four poly spots (2 red and 2 green) per pair of students

CRITICAL ELEMENTS AND CUES

Technique: Defense

- Look at the ball as it comes into the hands. *Cue:* Eyes on ball.
- Catch with two hands. *Cue:* Two hands.
- Step toward the ball as it comes toward you. *Cue:* Step to ball.
- As the ball contacts the hands, pull the ball into the body. *Cue:* Absorb the ball.
- End with the ball close to the body and the elbows flexed. *Cue:* Bring it in.
- Catch the ball before running to the base. *Cue:* Catch then run.

Technique: Offense

- Apply hitting critical elements and cues from task 19.
- After hitting the ball, the batter must bend their knees and place the bat onto the ground without dropping or throwing it. They are not to run with the bat towards the base. *Cue:* Set the bat down.

Tactic

- As soon as you catch the ball, immediately run to try to get to the middle base before the runner to cause the runner to be out.

Agility

- The defender must move to the ball and quickly run to the base.
- In the extension, the kicker must quickly change directions after running to the first base to run back to home base.

Communication

- The defense puts an arm up to indicate readiness to begin.

COMMON ERRORS, CAUSES, AND CORRECTIONS

- The student strikes the tee and not the ball. *Cause:* The student does not step straight ahead. *Correction:* Remind the student to step to the target.
- The student strikes the tee and not the ball. *Cause:* The student is not looking at the ball. *Correction:* Remind the student to keep the eyes on the ball.
- The ball goes between the defender's legs. *Cause:* The defender is trying to run before fielding the ball. *Correction:* Remind the student to catch the ball first and then run.
- The runner takes too long to turn around during the extension. *Cause:* The student is overrunning the base or tries to hold the base. *Correction:* Set up an infield and have all students run from first to second base (mimic the base running circuit). Tell students to break down their steps before touching the base so they can stop. Then return to the extension task.

TASK 21: 2V2 SOFTBALL GAME: OUT AT FIRST BASE

PURPOSE

Following are the purposes of the task as related to aspects of skilled performance.

- Technique: In this task, students apply throwing, catching, striking, and base running techniques.
- Tactic: Students get the out at first base after a kick with no one on base.
- Agility: Students make quick movements to get to the ball and run through first base.
- Fair Play: Students settle safe or out disputes by playing by rock, paper, scissors.
- Communication: Defenders raise a hand when they are ready. Infielders communicate about who is covering first base.

DESCRIPTION

Divide groups of four students into two teams. This game is played on the right half of the infield (the dividing line runs between home and second base) with four poly spots used as bases. The bases are set up 45 feet (13.7 meters) apart. One poly spot serves as home plate, one poly spot serves as second base, and two poly spots are set next to each other 3 feet apart and serve as first bases. The home plate, second base, and inside first base should be the color red and the outside first base poly spot is the color blue. On offense, one student is a hitter and one is an on-deck hitter. On defense, one student is a first-base player and the other is a second-base player. The hitter starts with the softball on a tee at home plate and hits it on the ground in between first and second bases. Anything left of second base or right of first base is a foul ball. If a foul ball occurs, the hitter loses the turn and must go get the ball; then the on-deck hitter is up. If the hitter puts the ball in play on the ground, he or she sprints through first base. The defense makes a play at first base in an attempt to get the hitter out. The defense can perform a throw-and-catch force-out at first, tag first base directly, or tag the runner. If the hitter hits the ball in the air, the hitter is out and the on-deck hitter is up. Each hitter hits two times; then the offense and defense switch roles. Defensive players switch positions after each inning. The offense gets a point for being safe, and the defense gets a point for making a force-out. Play continues for a designated number of innings. The offense runs through the outside poly spot and the defense makes the play on the inside poly spot to avoid collisions. The offensive runner runs through first base and returns home whether safe or out.

EQUIPMENT

One ball, one bat, one tee, and four poly spots (3 red and 1 blue) per four students

CRITICAL ELEMENTS AND CUES

Technique

- Apply the critical elements and cues from the previously learned techniques of throwing and catching in task 16, striking in task 19 and ground-ball catching in task 15 and base running techniques in task 1.

Tactic

- If the ball comes to the first-base player, he or she catches the ball and runs to the base to force the out or tags the runner with the ball before the runner gets to first base.
- If the ball goes to the second-base player, the first-base player goes to first base to receive a throw from the second-base player.
- If the ball goes between the two fielders and is caught by the first-base player, the second-base player runs to first to cover the base and receive a throw from the first-base player.

Agility

- Quickly get away from home plate after hitting the ball.
- Quickly move to the side to catch a ground ball.

Fair Play

- If a dispute arises, resolve it by playing rock, paper, scissors.

Communication

- The defense raises a hand when they are ready.
- When the second-base player catches the ball, the first-base player covers the base and shouts *one, one, one* to the fielder to throw the ball to first base.
- The first-base player shouts *help* when fielding a ball away from first base, which indicates that the second-base person needs to cover first base.
- When fielding the ball close to the bag, the first-base player says *mine* and tags the runner or bag.

COMMON ERRORS, CAUSES, AND CORRECTIONS

- The offensive student slows down before getting to first base. *Cause:* The student thinks he or she is already out. *Correction:* Tell the student not to slow down.
- The offensive student slows down before getting to first base. *Cause:* The student is watching the ball. *Correction:* Remind the student not to watch the ball.
- The defense makes a wild throw to first base. *Cause:* The second-base player rushes the throw to first. *Correction:* Have the batter hit the ball without running until the defense is consistent.

TASK 22: AROUND THE HORN SOFTBALL

PURPOSE

Following are the purposes of the task as related to aspects of skilled performance.

- Technique: In this task, students learn to throw to bases and catch while standing on the base.
- Tactic: Students throw to the nearest base that a runner is advancing toward in an attempt to get the runner out.
- Fair play: Students settle disputes amicably and promote a safe and fair playing environment.

DESCRIPTION

Set up enough infield diamonds with all four bases 45 feet (13.7 meters) apart to accommodate groups of eight students (teachers can expand this distance out to 60 feet (18.3 meters) as needed). Divide groups of eight students into two teams. The four defensive students set up at first, second, and third bases and at shortstop. Set the softball on a tee at home plate. There are base runners on first and second base, and there is one hitter and one on-deck hitter. The hitter hits the ball on the ground and runs to first and stays there. The runner on first advances to second and stays there, and the runner on second goes through third and jogs home to become the next on-deck hitter. The fielders attempt to catch the hit ground ball and then either run to or throw to the nearest base ahead of the approaching runner in an attempt to force an out. Regardless of whether the runner is safe or out, base runners always reset to runners on first and second. Each hitter hits one time. After all four hitters hit, the offense and defense switch roles. After both teams have hit once, the inning is over. After each inning, the defense rotates (third base to shortstop, shortstop to second base, second base to first base, and first base to third base). The game ends when all students play each defensive position (4 innings).

After a foul ball, the hitter goes to first base, the first-base runner goes to second base, the second-base runner becomes the on-deck hitter, and the on-deck hitter is up. The defense gets a point for each successful force-out, and the offense get a point for each safe runner. As an extension, when the hitter hits the ball the runners all advance to home plate and the hitter runs out a complete home run (run through all bases). While the offensive students are running the bases, the defense makes the force-out at third and turns a triple play, by throwing from third to second to first. Whoever finishes first (the home run or the triple play) gets the point. After the play is complete, the offensive students and defensive students reset and the next batter hits. Each team member hits one time and then the defense and offense switch roles. The game ends when all students play each defensive position.

EQUIPMENT

Four balls, one bat, one tee, and four bases per eight students

CRITICAL ELEMENTS AND CUES

Technique

- Apply the critical elements and cues from the previously learned techniques of throwing and catching in task 16, striking in task 19 and ground-ball catching in task 15 and base running techniques in task 1.

Tactic

- When fielding the ball, you must recognize where the runners are on the base paths and then decide which you can get the ball to ahead of the runner.
- When doing the extension triple play, the ball comes from the third-base player to second base, and the second-base person covers second on the backside of the base. Then the second-base person throws to first.

Fair Play

- Offense and defense should not interfere with each other.
- Settle disputes with rock, paper, scissors.

COMMON ERRORS, CAUSES, AND CORRECTIONS

- The wrong fielder tries to cover second base. *Cause:* Fielders are unaware who covers second base in different situations. *Correction:* Tell the defense that the second-base person covers second when the ball is on the left side of the infield and the shortstop covers it when the ball is on the right side.
- The second-base player goes to the front of the base and interferes with the runner. *Cause:* The student does not realize where the base runner is. *Correction:* Tell the student to go to the backside of the base toward the outfield.
- During the extension of the task, the runner shuffles the feet and slows down at bases. *Cause:* The runner does not run the bases in a circular pattern or is afraid to miss the base. *Correction:* Stop the game and have the students run the bases at half speed and focus on making the infield a circle.

TASK 23: 4V4 HITTING GAME

PURPOSE

Following are the purposes of the task as related to aspects of skilled performance.

- Technique: In this task, students learn about force-outs and non-force-outs with a full infield and various defensive situations (e.g., runners on different bases in different situations).
- Tactic: Students need to get the lead runner out, try to hit behind runners, and know when to run, stay on the base or tag up.

DESCRIPTION

Set up enough infield diamonds with all four bases 45 feet (13.7 meters) apart to accommodate groups of eight students (teachers can expand this distance out to 60 feet [18.3 meters] as needed). An additional base is set up to the right side of first base. The extra base on the right of first base is the one the hitter runs through, and the base to the left is the one the infielders use to force an out. Divide groups of eight into two teams. The four defensive students set up at first, second, and third bases and at shortstop. After hitting the ball off a tee, the hitter runs out the play. This means that after the hit, the hitter runs to the furthest base they can obtain without getting out. Once at that base, the hitter stays on that base, and this creates either a force-out or non-force-out situation for that base runner and the defenders. If the runner is either on first base or all of the bases behind the base have a runner on, this creates a force-out situation for the runners and the defenders. This means that when the ball is hit each base runner must try to advance to the next base, and the defense tries to get the ball to the base ahead of a runner to create an out. In this force-out situation, all the defenders need to do is to get the ball to the base a base runner is attempting to get to and touch it to create an out (all plays at first base are considered force-out situations since the hitter must run to first base after the hit). If the runner is on a base and the base immediately behind that base is open (doesn't have a runner on it) then that creates a non-force-out situation. This means that the base runner does not need to run to the next base when the ball is hit unless the base runner thinks she can get to the base without being touched with the ball. In force-out situations, the base runner must be touched with the ball while off the base to be called out. All hits must be on the ground; a fly ball is an out. The defense makes the out accordingly depending on the runner's situation by either being in possession of the ball when they touch a base being approached by a runner or touching the runner with the ball when running towards a base in a force-out situation or by touching the runner with the ball in a non-force-out situation. While the defense is attempting to get runners out, outs do not accumulate so the hitters on each team hit one time before the offense and defense switch roles. After each team has hit, that marks the end of an inning. The offense gets a point for a run scored, and the defense does not score points. After each inning, the defense rotates (third base to shortstop, shortstop to second base, second base to first base, and first base to third base). The game ends when all students have played each defensive position (four innings). If students need motivation, award defensive bonus points for getting lead runners out and offensive bonus points for hitting behind runners (e.g., hitting to the right side when a runner is on second base).

EQUIPMENT

One ball, one bat, one tee, and five bases per eight students

CRITICAL ELEMENTS AND CUES

Technique

- Apply the critical elements and cues from the previously learned techniques of throwing and catching in task 16, striking in task 19 and ground-ball catching in task 15 and base running techniques in task 1.

Tactic

- Always get the lead runner out if possible.
- When a runner is on second base, hit behind this player to move him or her to third base and put the player in a scoring position.
- If you are in a force situation, you have to run.
- When you are in a non-force situation, you should run when the defender cannot tag you with the ball (e.g., hitting behind the runner), but you can run whenever you please. It is important to teach this decision-making process.

COMMON ERRORS, CAUSES, AND CORRECTIONS

- The runner does not run during a force situation. *Cause:* The student lacks knowledge or is confused. *Correction:* Remind the students ahead of time of options in force-out situations.

- A runner makes the incorrect running decision in a non-force situation. *Cause:* The student lacks knowledge or is confused. *Correction:* Remind the students ahead of time of the options in non-force-out situations.

- The defense does not get the lead out and eliminates the force. *Cause:* The runner behind the lead runner is forced out (e.g., with runners on first and second, the defense makes the force-out at first and then tries to make a force-out at third; however, the force-out at third has been eliminated and that runner must be tagged out). *Correction:* The defense has to get the lead runner in a force-out situation because if the defense gets a lagging runner (runner behind the front base runner) out, then it is harder to get the lead runner out. This is because the situation is no longer a force situation and the only way to get the lead runner out is by tagging them out. Use freeze replay and show the class when improper plays are made. For example, when the defense forces a runner on first out at second and then tags out the runner at second running to third (because the force was eliminated), freeze the class have them do it again. Point out that it would have been better to get the out at third and then at second so the force was not eliminated.

TASK 24: 4V4 INFIELD SOFTBALL GAME

PURPOSE

Following are the purposes of the task as related to aspects of skilled performance.

- Technique: Students apply learned techniques of throwing, catch, striking, catching ground balls and base running in a game situation.

- Tactic: Students will apply learned tactics of force-outs and non-force-outs in a game situation.

DESCRIPTION

Set up enough infield diamonds with all four bases 45 feet (13.7 meters) apart to accommodate groups of eight students (teachers can expand this distance out to 60 feet [18.3 meters] as needed). Divide each group of eight students into two teams of four. An additional base is set up to the right side of first base. The extra base to the right of first base is the one the kicker runs through, and the base to the left is the one the infielders use to force an out. This task is done exactly as task 23 except for one difference. In this game the offensive teams stays up to bat until three outs are made (all batting attempts start with a ball on a tee and the hit ball must be on the ground; a fly ball is an out). After the third out, the offense and defense change roles. The offense gets a point for a run scored, and the defense does not score points. This game continues until a designated number of innings have been played. As an extension, if you have higher-performing students that are successful at getting runners out on the bases, a catcher can be added (no pitcher is added since hitting a pitched ball has not yet been taught). The catcher must come from the offensive team. Set up an additional base or poly spot next to home plate for the catcher to use. The defense can make a play at home plate by throwing to the offensive team's catcher. If the throw beats the offensive runner, the runner is out regardless of whether the catcher catches the ball.

EQUIPMENT

One ball, one bat, one tee, and six bases per eight students

CRITICAL ELEMENTS AND CUES

Technique

- Apply the critical elements and cues from the previously learned techniques of throwing and catching in task 16, striking in task 19 and ground-ball catching in task 15 and base running techniques in task 1 and 23 in a game situation.

Tactic

- Apply the tactics learned in task 23
- Always get the lead runner out if possible.
- When a runner is on second base, hit behind this player to move him or her to third base and put the player in a scoring position.
- If you are in a force situation, you have to run.
- When you are in a non-force situation, you should run when the defender cannot tag you with the ball (e.g., hitting behind the runner), but you can run whenever you please. It is important to teach this decision-making process.

COMMON ERRORS, CAUSES, AND CORRECTIONS

- The runner does not run during a force situation. *Cause:* The student lacks knowledge or is confused. *Correction:* Remind the students ahead of time of options in force-out situations.
- A runner makes the incorrect running decision in a non-force situation. *Cause:* The student lacks knowledge or is confused. *Correction:* Remind the students ahead of time of the options in non-force-out situations.
- The defense does not get the lead out and eliminates the force. *Cause:* The runner behind the lead runner is forced out (e.g., with runners on first and second, the defense makes the force-out at first and then tries to make a force-out at third; however, the force-out at third has been eliminated and that runner must be tagged out). *Correction:* The defense has to get the lead runner in a force-out situation because if the defense gets a lagging runner (runner behind the front base runner) out, then it is harder to get the lead runner out. This is because the situation is no longer a force situation and the only way to get the lead runner out is by tagging them out. Use freeze replay and show the class when improper plays are made. For example, when the defense forces a runner on first out at second and then tags out the runner at second running to third (because the force was eliminated), freeze the class have them do it again. Point out that it would have been better to get the out at third and then at second so the force was not eliminated.

TASK 25: GROUND BALL TRIANGLES

PURPOSE

Following are the purposes of the task as related to aspects of skilled performance.

- Technique: In this task, students learn to field a ground ball.
- Agility: Students move left and right while maintaining proper field positions.

DESCRIPTION

Designate a 15-foot by 15-foot (4.5-meter) playing area with cones. Divide students into groups of three. While this task can be done without softball gloves, it is recommended that each students use a glove when doing this task. One student is a fielder and stands on a poly spot, and the other two students each has a ball and stand 10 feet apart from each other facing the fielder on a line that is 5 to 10 feet (1.5 to 3 meters) from the fielder (see figure). The student to the left of the fielder slowly rolls a ground ball to the left side of the fielder. The fielder moves to the left to get in front of the ball then fields the ball and throws it back to the roller. The second student to the right then slowly rolls a ball straight ahead, which forces the fielder to move to the right side to get in front of the ball and then fields the ball and throws the ball back to the roller. This continues for a designated time. Then, students rotate as follows: left-side roller to fielder, fielder to right-side roller, right-side roller to left-side roller. If students need motivation, award five points to the team for every five trials they complete. As an extension, increase the speed of the roll and increase the distance to the fielder, which makes throwing more difficult and increases aerobic activity. Shorten the distance to make fielding more difficult.

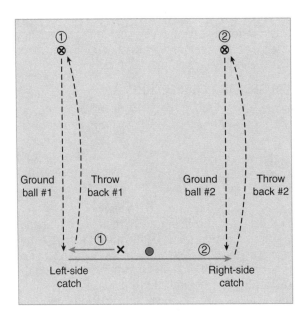

EQUIPMENT

Two balls, four cones, 3 gloves (recommended), and one poly spot per three students

CRITICAL ELEMENTS AND CUES

Technique: Fielding

- Do not stand up when moving to the side. *Cue:* Stay low.
- When moving to the backhand side (right-side for right-handed students and left-side for left-handed students), keep your non-throwing hand or glove down, and have the glove hand cross over to the throwing side to field the ball in front of the glove-hand leg while staying low. *Cue:* Low and across.
- When moving to the front hand side (left-side for right-handed students and right-side for left-handed students), extend your glove out and down to field the ball in front of the glove-hand leg while staying low. *Cue:* Glove down and out.
- After fielding the ball, bring the ball up, and set the feet to throw it without standing straight up. *Cue:* Ball up, set and throw.

Technique: One-Handed Overhead Throw

- When throwing the ball back to the roller, apply the throwing cues learned in task 16.

Agility

- Change directions after fielding the ball. Move from side to side so the ball doesn't get past you.

COMMON ERRORS, CAUSES, AND CORRECTIONS

- The fielder stands up before moving to the left or right. *Cause:* The student thinks this results in quicker movement. *Correction:* Have students slow down the rolls, and remind the fielder to stay down.
- When moving to either the glove hand side the student fields the ball out to the side of the body or when moving to the non-glove-hand side the student fields the ball by reaching across the body and turning the hand so that the thumb is down even though he is fast enough to get in front of the ball. *Cause:* The student misunderstands the point of the task. The student should always try to get in front of the ball. *Correction:* Slow down the roll or shorten the distance. Remind the student to get in front of the ball.

TASK 26: 4V4 FORCE AND NONFORCE SITUATIONS USING A TEE

PURPOSE

Following are the purposes of the task as related to aspects of skilled performance.

- Tactic: When batting, students learn where to try and hit the ball in force-out and non-force-out in various situations with a full infield. Infielders learn where to throw the ball in various defensive situations (e.g., runners on different bases in different situations).

DESCRIPTION

Set up the infield with an additional base to the right of first base. Divide groups of eight into two teams. Use runners on various bases to demonstrate situations and tactical decisions. To begin, place a runner on second base. The offense must try to hit a ball off a tee to the right side of the infield in order to move the runner to third base. After hitting, the hitter runs to first base and the runner on second runs to third (since the ball was hit toward the first base side of the infield). If the ball is fielded, the ball is to thrown to first base to force the out. The hitter then goes to second to become the next runner, and the runner that went to third goes back to home plate and waits in line to bat. After everyone has had a chance to run from second base, the offense and defense switch roles.

- *Extension 1.* With the runner on second, have the hitter hit the ball to the left side (shortstop side). While this is not what the hitter would want to do, this will happen in a game. The infielder that catches the ball will then look at the runner back on second base before throwing to first base. This forces the runner on second to stay on while the throw is made to first. The rotation is the same.
- *Extension 2.* Put a runner on first base. Regardless of where the ball is hit, as long as it is on the ground, the runner has to run to second base. The defender then needs to throw to second base to get the lead runner out, or, if they do not think they can get the ball to second in time to get the out, throw to first to get the batter out.

EQUIPMENT

One ball, one bat, one tee, four gloves (if used), and five bases per each group of eight

CRITICAL ELEMENTS AND CUES

Tactic

- When you are batting with a runner on second, try to hit the ball behind the runner (on the right side) to advance the runner to third. *Cue:* Hit behind the runner.
- Remind students that in a force-out situation with runners on first, first and second, or loaded bases all base runners need to run if the ball is hit on the ground.
- In force-out situations, the defense needs to get the lead runner. *Cue:* Get the lead runner.
- In the extension, when fielding a ground ball hit ahead of the runner on second base in a non-force-out situation, look at the runner before throwing to first base. *Cue:* Look the runner back.

COMMON ERRORS, CAUSES, AND CORRECTIONS

- Students make incorrect decisions. *Cause:* Students are confused as to the base running situation. *Correction:* Stop play and let the defense know what the decision should have been. Freeze replay is a good technique here: Freeze the students, discuss the situation, and ask them to replay it correctly.

TASK 27: HITTING A PITCHED BALL

PURPOSE

Following are the purposes of the task as related to aspects of skilled performance.

- Technique: In this task, students learn the basic technique of hitting a ball with a bat from a pitcher and the basic techniques of pitching.
- Fair play: Students make pitches that can be hit. All students help gather hit balls.

DESCRIPTION

Students pair up and share a station. One student is on a poly spot that is designated as the pitcher's mound and has 5 to 10 Wiffle balls in a bucket. The other student has a bat and is approximately 30 to 50 feet (9.1 to 15.2 meters) away (depending on space and skill level). If possible, have a wall or net available for the batter to hit toward. (This makes ball retrieval easier.) The student with the bat checks the area to be sure the partner and other students are not in the flight path of the ball or the swing plane of the bat. Once all is clear, the students start. Each student takes five swings or throws five pitches, and then the students switch. Both students pick up the Wiffle balls before switching. The task continues for a designated time. If students need motivation, have pairs count how many times a ball hits a target that is hanging on the wall. As an extension, place 2 to 4 poly spots on the ground as a strike zone. Encourage the pitcher to pitch to multiple spots within the strike zone.

EQUIPMENT

Wiffle balls (as can be divided evenly among the class—the more the better), one bat, and 3 to 5 poly spots per pair of students and targets for the wall

CRITICAL ELEMENTS AND CUES

Technique: Hitting

See teaching points for task 19.

- Do not swing until you see the ball start to drop from the top of the arc. *Cue:* See it drop.

Technique: Pitching (see figure)

- Place the ball in the dominant hand on same-side hip. *Cue:* Ball at hip.
- Step with the opposite foot. *Cue:* Step in opposition.
- Swing the hand back and keep the shoulders square to the target. *Cue:* Swing back, shoulders square.
- Release the ball past the hip. *Cue:* Release at hip.
- The ball should move in an arc. It should not go higher than 3 feet (0.9 meters) above the batter's head. *Cue:* Make a rainbow.
- The ball should land 1 to 2 feet (0.3 to 0.6 meters) behind home plate. *Cue:* Hit the target.

Fair Play

- Pitch balls that can be hit by the batter.
- Work with your partner to gather the balls between turns.

COMMON ERRORS, CAUSES, AND CORRECTIONS

- The student misses the ball. *Cause:* The batter swings too soon. *Correction:* Have the student wait to swing until the ball starts to descend from the peak of the arc.
- The student hits the ball, so it goes foul on the side they are standing. *Cause:* The student swings too early. *Correction:* Have the student wait on the ball to drop a little bit more before swinging.
- The student hits the ball, so it goes foul on the side they are standing. *Cause:* The student steps toward third base when they swing. *Correction:* Place a poly spot of the ground in front of the front foot towards the pitcher and tell the student to step to the poly spot when swinging.
- The batter does not step when swinging. *Cause:* The batter forgets to step with the front leg. *Correction:* Place a poly spot of the ground in front of the front foot and tell the student to step to the poly spot when swinging.
- The ball lands short. *Cause:* The pitcher releases the ball too late or the pitcher is not strong enough to pitch the ball all the way to the plate. *Correction:* Have the pitcher release the ball sooner, or bring the pitcher in closer.
- The ball lands too deep. *Cause:* There is not enough height on the ball, the release is too early, or the pitcher puts too much power into the pitch. *Correction:* Have the student add more height or release the ball later. Put targets on the ground for the pitcher to hit.

TASK 28: 4V4 HITTING WITH A PITCHER

PURPOSE

Following are the purposes of the task as related to aspects of skilled performance.

- Technique: In this task students pitch, hit a pitched ball, catch and throw a hit ball, and run to first base.
- Tactic: Students attempt to get the runner out at first base.
- Agility: Students quickly move from hitting to running toward first base.
- Communication: Defensive students put an arm up to indicate that they are ready to begin.

DESCRIPTION

Set up enough infield diamonds with all four bases 45 feet (13.7 meters) apart to accommodate groups of eight students (teachers can expand this distance out to 60 feet [18.3 meters] as needed). An additional base is set up to the right side of first base. The extra base on the right of first base is the one the hitter runs through, and the base to the left is the one the infielders use to force an out. Divide groups of eight into two teams. The four defensive students set up at first, second, and third bases and at shortstop. Three of the four offensive batters are at the plate with one ready to hit and the other two in line waiting their turn. The fourth offensive student serves as the pitcher. After hitting the pitched ball, the hitter runs to first base. The ball must be hit along the ground to be in play, if a fly ball is hit, it is an out. The defenders field the ball and throw to first base in an attempt to get the batter out. The offensive rotation is that the hitter becomes the pitcher, the pitcher gets in the back of the batting line and the next student in line becomes the next batter. After all students have batted one time, the two groups switch and the defense comes in to bat. Each time the team moves to the defense the defenders switch positions (first to third, third to short stop, short stop to second, and second to first). For motivation, award one point to the offense for each time the hitter beats the throw to first and one point to the defense each time they get the batter out at first. The play needs to last until every student has played each defensive position (4 innings) or for a designated time.

EQUIPMENT

One ball, one bat, five bases and gloves (if used) per groups of eight students

CRITICAL ELEMENTS AND CUES

Technique

- Apply the critical elements and cues from the previously learned techniques of fielding in task 25, pitching and hitting in task 27 and base running techniques in task 1.

Tactic

- Apply the critical elements and cues from task 26 (force-out and non-force-out situations).

Agility

- Quickly get into your run after hitting the ball.

Communication

- The defense puts an arm up to indicate that they are ready to begin.

COMMON ERRORS, CAUSES, AND CORRECTIONS

- Look for common errors, causes and corrections of previous tasks 25 (fielding) and task 27 (hitting and pitching).

TASK 29: 4V4 INFIELD GAME WITH A PITCHER

PURPOSE

Following are the purposes of the task as related to aspects of skilled performance.

- Technique: In this task, students apply hitting, catching, throwing, and base running techniques in a game-like setting.
- Tactic: Students need to get the lead runner out, try to hit behind runners, and know when to run, stay on the base or tag up.

DESCRIPTION

Set up enough infield diamonds with all four bases 45 feet (13.7 meters) apart to accommodate groups of eight students (teachers can expand this distance out to 60 feet [18.3 meters] as needed). Divide each group of eight students into two teams of four. An additional base is set up to the right side of first base. The extra base to the right of first base is the one the kicker runs through, and the base to the left is the one the infielders use to force an out. This task is done exactly as task 28 except for the following differences. In this game the offensive teams stays up to bat until three outs are made (all batting attempts at against a pitched ball and the hit ball must be on the ground; a fly ball is an out), hitters stay on base until they are gotten out and the pitcher pitches the entire inning (not rotated out until the next inning). After the third out the offense and defense change roles. The offense gets a point for a run scored, and the defense does not score points. This game continues until a designated number of innings have been played. As an extension, if you have higher-performing students that are successful at getting runners out on the bases, a catcher can be added. The catcher must come from the offensive team. Set up an additional base next to home plate for the catcher to use. The defense can make a play at home plate by throwing to the offensive team's catcher. If the throw beats the offensive runner, the runner is out regardless of whether the catcher catches the ball. If students need motivation, award defensive bonus points for getting lead runners out and offensive bonus points for hitting behind runners (e.g., hitting to the right side when a runner is on second base).

EQUIPMENT

One ball, one bat, gloves (if used) and six bases per eight students

CRITICAL ELEMENTS AND CUES

Technique

- Apply the critical elements and cues from the previously learned techniques of fielding in task 25, pitching and hitting in task 27, and base running techniques in task 1.

Tactic

- Apply the critical elements and cues from task 26 (force-out and non-force-out situations).

COMMON ERRORS, CAUSES, AND CORRECTIONS

- Look for common errors, causes and corrections of previous tasks 25 (fielding), task 26 (force-out and non-force-out situations), and task 27 (hitting and pitching).

TASK 30: OUTFIELD THROWS TO SECOND BASE

PURPOSE

Following are the purposes of the task as related to aspects of skilled performance.

- Technique: In this task, students learn to throw the ball from the outfield.
- Tactic: Students throw the ball to second base to keep the batter from advancing.

DESCRIPTION

Divide groups of eight students into two teams. This game is played on the right half of the infield (the dividing line runs between home and second base) with three bases (home, first and second). The bases are set up 45 feet (13.7 meters) apart (teachers can expand this distance out to 60 feet [18.3 meters] as needed). On offense, one student is a hitter and the other students are in a line waiting their turn to hit. On defense, three students are in the infield (first, second and short stop) and the fourth is in right field. The batter hits the ball off a tee toward the right side into the outfield. As the ball goes to the right side of the field, the shortstop moves to cover second base while the second-base person moves into right field in a line between the outfielder and second base and the first base-person covers first base. The second–base person becomes what is called the cutoff person. This role will be explained in task 31. The outfielder throws the ball directly to second base. Each batter hits and runs through first as the throw goes to second base. Afterward, the batter returns to home. Each batter gets one at-bat; then the defense and the offense switch roles. Each time a team moves back to defense, the players switch roles by rotating first base to right field, right field to short stop, short stop to second base, and second base to first base. If students need motivation, award a point to the offense if the ball is hit to the outfield. As an extension, move the outfielder to left field and have the student hit to the left side of the outfield. The shortstop then moves toward the outfielder and becomes the relay or cutoff person while the second-base person covers second and the ball is thrown to second base (not to the cutoff person).

EQUIPMENT

One ball, one bat, one tee, four bases per eight students.

CRITICAL ELEMENTS AND CUES

Technique

- Apply the critical elements and cues from the previously learned techniques of throwing and catching in task 17, hitting in task 19, and base running techniques in task 1.

Tactic

- When a ball is hit to the outfield, an out cannot be made at first base so the outfielder should throw directly to the next open base to keep the runner from advancing.

COMMON ERRORS, CAUSES, AND CORRECTIONS

- Outfielder cannot get the ball to second base. *Cause:* The outfielder is not strong enough to get the ball to second base. *Correction:* Explain the role of the cutoff person and have the outfielder throw to the cutoff student and then have the cutoff student throw to second base.

TASK 31: OUTFIELD THROWS TO HOME PLATE

PURPOSE

Following are the purposes of the task as related to aspects of skilled performance.

- Technique: In this task, students learn to throw the ball from the outfield.
- Tactic: Students throw the ball to the cutoff person, who then relays the ball to home plate to keep the runner from advancing to home or to get the runner out at home.

DESCRIPTION

Set up enough infield diamonds with all four bases 45 feet (13.7 meters) apart to accommodate groups of eight students (teachers can expand this distance out to 60 feet [18.3 meters] as needed). Set up a double base for home, one to be used by the runner and the other by the catcher. Divide each group of twelve students into two teams of six. The defense consists of a catcher, a short stop, second base and first base and two outfielders (left center and right center) while the offense provides the hitters. Start each at bat with a runner on second base. The batter hits the ball off a tee toward the right side of the outfield. As the ball goes to the right side of the field, the runner on second runs towards third and then runs towards home plate. The shortstop covers second base while the second-base person moves toward the outfielder and becomes a cutoff person. The outfielder throws to the cutoff person who then relays the ball by throwing it to the catcher at home plate. Each batter hits and runs through first regardless of what the outfielder does with the ball. Afterward the play is over, the batter goes to second base to become the next runner, and the runner that came home waits in line to hit. Each batter gets one at-bat; then the defense and offense switch roles. Each time a team moves back to defense, the players switch roles by rotating catcher to first base, first to second, second to short stop, short stop to left field, left field to right field and right field to catcher. If students need motivation, award a point to the offense if the ball is hit to the outfield. As an extension, have the student hit to the left side of the outfield. The shortstop then moves toward the outfielder and becomes the cutoff person while the second-base person covers second and the ball is thrown to the cutoff person, who relays it to home plate.

EQUIPMENT

One ball, one bat, one tee, gloves (if used) and five bases per twelve students

CRITICAL ELEMENTS AND CUES

Technique

- Apply the critical elements and cues from the previously learned techniques of throwing and catching in task 17, hitting in task 19, and base running techniques in task 1.

Tactic

- When a ball is hit to the outfield and a runner is trying to run home for a score, the outfielder must throw to the cutoff person so a shorter and stronger throw can be made to home base.

COMMON ERRORS, CAUSES, AND CORRECTIONS

- The outfielder doesn't throw to the cutoff student. *Cause:* The outfielder tries to throw home. *Correction:* Stop play and let the outfielder know what the decision should have been. Freeze replay is a good technique here: Freeze the students, discuss the situation, and ask them to replay it correctly.

TASK 32: 6V6 GAME: TACTICAL DECISIONS WITH A PITCHER

PURPOSE

Following are the purposes of the task as related to aspects of skilled performance.

- Technique: In this task, students applying throwing, catching, hitting, pitching and base running techniques taught in previous softball tasks.
- Tactic: Students make the correct tactical decisions based on the offensive situations.

DESCRIPTION

This application game is used to apply the tactics learned in tasks 30 (outfield throws to second base) and task 31 (outfield throws to home plate). Set up enough infield diamonds with all four bases 45 feet (13.7 meters) apart to accommodate groups of eight students (teachers can expand this distance out to 60 feet [18.3 meters] as needed). Set up double bases for first and home, one to be use by the runner and the other by the fielder. Divide each group of twelve students into two teams of six. The defense consists of the full infield (four) and two outfielders (left center and right center) while the offense provides the pitcher, catcher, and hitters. The defense applies the appropriate tactical techniques for throwing to second base or first base when used with task 30. The defense earns a point each time the infielders get the runner out at first or the outfielders correctly get the ball to second base and keeps the hitter from advancing to second. The offense must hit the ball past the pitcher and if the ball is hit towards the pitcher, the pitcher does not make a play on the ball, only the defense can make a play on the ball. The defense must make the appropriate decision of where to throw the ball based on the base runner situation. If a runner is running towards home plate, the defense does not make a play at home plate by throwing to the catcher. When this application game is used with task 31, the game is played the same except now if the runner is advancing towards home plate, the defense can throw to home plate to get the runner out. If the throw beats the offensive runner, then the runner is out regardless of whether the catcher catches the ball. In both versions of this game, the offense does not score because the emphasis is on the defense making the correct tactical decisions. The offense bats until three outs are made which motivates them to hit the ball effectively so they can stay at bat. The offensive pitcher pitches for the entire inning and then rotates to being a batter in the next inning. After a runner is out, the runner returns to home plate and for the task 31 application game the returning runner becomes the next catcher (catcher rotates through the batters).

EQUIPMENT

One ball, one bat, gloves (if used), and six bases per 12 students

CRITICAL ELEMENTS AND CUES

Technique

- Apply the critical elements and cues from the previously learned techniques of throwing and catching in task 17, hitting in task 19, and base running techniques in task 1.

Tactic

- See tactical points for tasks 30 and 31.

COMMON ERRORS, CAUSES, AND CORRECTIONS

- Students make incorrect decisions. *Cause:* Students are confused about the base running situation. *Correction:* Stop play and let the defense know what the decision should have been. Freeze replay is a good technique here: Freeze the students, discuss the situation, and ask them to replay it correctly.
- The outfielder doesn't throw to the cutoff student. *Cause:* The outfielder tries to throw home. *Correction:* Stop play and let the outfielder know what the decision should have been. Freeze replay is a good technique here.

TASK 33: 6V6 GAME

PURPOSE

Following are the purposes of the task as related to aspects of skilled performance.

- Technique: In this task, students apply throwing, catching, hitting, and base running techniques taught in the softball tasks.
- Tactic: Students make the correct tactical decisions based on the offensive situations.

DESCRIPTION

This is the culminating game for the softball unit and is used to apply the techniques and tactics learned in the previous tasks. Set up enough infield diamonds with all four bases 45 feet (13.7 meters) apart to accommodate groups of eight students (teachers can expand this distance out to 60 feet [18.3 meters] as needed). Set up double bases for first and home, one to be used by the runner and the other by the fielder. Divide each group of twelve students into two teams of six. The defense consists of the full infield (four) and two outfielders (left center and right center) while the offense provides the pitcher, catcher and hitters. As before, the pitcher pitches for the entire inning and rotates to a hitter in the next inning. The catcher is always the hitter that was either the runner that got out or the hitter that was not successful. The offense bats until three outs are made. Strikes have not been used thus far in the unit as the focus has been on participation and learning. As the teacher you can decide if or how to apply restrictions to the number of hitting attempts each batter is allowed. If these restrictions are applied, we urge that a batter who does not make contact with the ball is not counted as an out. This will encourage full effort and allow for more play development. As an extension, you can add a third outfielder.

EQUIPMENT

One ball, one bat, gloves (if used), and six bases per 12 students

CRITICAL ELEMENTS AND CUES

Apply all previous softball skills and cues.

COMMON ERRORS, CAUSES, AND CORRECTIONS

Look for all previously discussed softball errors and provide corrections.

References

Preface

Castelli, D. M., & Williams, L. (2007). Health-related fitness and physical education teachers' content knowledge. *Journal of Teaching in Physical Education, 26*, 2-19.

Kim, I., Ward, P., Li, W., Stuhr, P., & Lorson, K. (2010). *Content knowledge on basketball as a function of playing and coaching experience*. Paper presented at the Ohio Association for Health, Physical Education, Recreation, and Dance (OAHPERD), Columbus, Ohio.

Launder, A., & Piltz, W. (2013). *Play practice: Engaging and developing skilled players from beginner to elite*. Champaign, IL: Human Kinetics.

Li, W., Ward, P., & Lehwald, H. (2013). *Basketball content knowledge: Playing, coaching, and teaching experience*. Paper presented at the American Alliance for Health, Physical Education, Recreation, and Dance Convention, Charlotte, North Carolina.

Stuhr, P. T., Lee, Y. S., Ressler, J., Rodrigues-Neto, M., Zhang, P., & Ward, P. (2007). *The relationship between prior soccer experience and current soccer content knowledge*. Paper presented at the annual conference of the Ohio Association for Health, Physical Education and Recreation.

Chapter 1

Ball, D. L., Thames, M. H., & Phelps, G. (2008). Content knowledge for teaching: What makes it special? *Journal of Teacher Education, 59,* 389-407.

Ericsson, K. A. (2008). Deliberate practice and the acquisition and maintenance of expert performance: A general overview. *Academic Emergency Medicine, 15,* 988-994.

Ericsson, K. A., Krampe, R. T., & Tesch-Römer, C. (1993). The role of deliberate practice in the acquisition of expert performance. *Psychological Review, 100,* 363-406.

Gov.UK, (2013). National curriculum in England: PE programmes of study. Retrieved from: https://www.gov.uk/government/publications/national-curriculum-in-england-physicaleducation programmes-of-study.

Griffey, D., & Housner, L. (2007). *Designing effective instructional tasks for physical education and sports*. Champaign, IL: Human Kinetics.

Hill, H., Ball, D. L., & Schilling, S. (2008). Unpacking "pedagogical content knowledge": Conceptualizing and measuring teachers' topic-specific knowledge of students. *Journal for Research in Mathematics Education, 39*(4), 372-400.

Kim, I., Lee, Y. S., Ward, P., & Li, W. (2015). A critical examination of content knowledge courses in physical education teacher education programs. *Journal of Teaching in Physical Education, 34,* 59-75.

Schempp, P. G., Manross, D., Tan, S. K. S., & Fincher, M. D. (1998). Subject expertise and teachers' knowledge. *Journal of Teaching in Physical Education, 17,* 342-356.

SHAPE America – Society of Health and Physical Educators. (2013). *Grade-level outcomes for K-12 physical education*. Reston, VA: Author.

SHAPE America – Society of Health and Physical Educators. (2017). 2017 National Standards for Initial Physical Education Teacher Education. Retrieved from: http://www.shapeamerica.org/accreditation/upload/2017-SHAPE-America-Initial-PETE-Standards-and-Components.pdf

Shulman, L. S. (1987). Knowledge and teaching: Foundations of the new reform. *Harvard Educational Review, 57,* 1-22.

Siedentop, D. (2002). Content knowledge for physical education. *Journal of Teaching in Physical Education, 21,* 368-377.

Siedentop, D., & Eldar, E. (1989). Expertise, experience and effectiveness. *Journal of Teaching in Physical Education, 8,* 254-260.

Siedentop, D., Hastie, P. A., & van der Mars, H. (2011). *Complete guide to sport education* (2nd ed.). Champaign, IL: Human Kinetics.

Sinelnikov, O., Kim, I., Ward, P., Curtner-Smith, M., & Li, W. (2016). Changing beginning teachers' content knowledge and its effect on student learning. *Physical Education and Sport Pedagogy, 21,* 425-440.

Tsangaridou, N. (2009). Preparation of teachers for teaching physical education in schools: Research on teachers' reflections, beliefs and knowledge. In L. Housner, M. Metzler, P. Schempp, & T. Templin (Eds.), *Historic traditions and future directions of research on teaching and teacher education in physical education* (pp. 373-382). Morgantown, WV: Fitness Information Technology.

Wang, X.Z., Housner, L., Ji, L., Torsney, C. & Mao, F. (2011). Reform of physical education in China. *International Sport Studies, 33* (1), 11-27.

Ward, P. (2009) Content matters: Knowledge that alters teaching. In L. Housner, M. Metzler, P. Schempp, & T. Templin (Eds.), *Historic traditions and future directions of research on teaching and teacher education in physical education* (pp. 345-356). Morgantown, WV: Fitness Information Technology.

Ward, P., & Ayvazo, S. (2016). Pedagogical content knowledge: Conceptions and findings in physical education. *Journal of Teaching in Physical Education, 35,* 194-207.

Ward, P., Kim, I., Ko, B., & Li, W. (2015). Effects of improving teachers' content knowledge on teaching and student learning in physical education. *Research Quarterly for Exercise and Sport, 86,* 130-139.

Ward, P., & Lee, M.A. (2005). Peer assisted learning in physical education: A review of theory and research. *Journal of Teaching Physical Education, 24,* 205-225.

Ward, P., Li, W., Kim, I & Lee Y-S. (2012). Content knowledge courses in physical education programs in South Korea and Ohio. *International Journal of Human Movement Science, 6,* 107-120.

Ward, P., & O'Sullivan, M. (2006). The contexts of urban settings. *Journal of Teaching Physical Education, 25,* 348-363.

Chapter 2

Alexander, K. (1982). *Behavior Analysis of Tasks and Accountability in Physical Education,* doctoral dissertation, The Ohio State University, 1982, Dissertations Abstracts International 43: 3257A.

Ayvazo, S., & Ward, P. (2011). Pedagogical content knowledge of experienced teachers in physical education: Functional analysis of adaptations. *Research Quarterly for Exercise and Sport, 82,* 675-684.

Brophy, J. (1991). Conclusion. In J. Brophy (Ed.), Advances in research on teaching (Vol. 2, pp. 349-364). Greenwich, CT: JAI Press.

Chen, A. (2004). Learning the skill theme approach: Salient and problematic aspects of pedagogical content knowledge. *Education, 124,* 194-212.

Doyle, W. (1986). Classroom Organization and Management, in M.C. Wittrock (ed.) *Handbook of Research on Teaching,* 3rd ed., pp. 392–431. New York: Macmillan.

Launder, A., & Piltz, W. (2013). *Play practice: Engaging and developing skilled players from beginner to elite.* Champaign, IL: Human Kinetics.

Rink, J. (2014). *Teaching physical education for learning* (7th ed.). Boston, MA: McGraw-Hill.

Siedentop, D., Hastie, P. A., & van der Mars, H. (2011). *Complete guide to sport education* (2nd ed.). Champaign, IL: Human Kinetics.

Siedentop, D., & Tannehill, D. (2000). *Developing teaching skills in physical education.* Mountain View, CA: Mayfield.

Ward, P., Ayvazo, S., & Lehwald, H. (2014). Using knowledge packets in teacher education to develop pedagogical content knowledge. *Journal of Physical Education, Health, Recreation and Dance, 85*(6), 38-43.

Ward, P., Kim, I., Ko, B., & Li, W. (2015). Effects of improving teachers' content knowledge on teaching and student learning in physical education. *Research Quarterly for Exercise and Sport, 86,* 130-139.

Ward, P., Lehwald, H., & Lee, Y. S. (2015). Content maps: A teaching and assessment tool for content knowledge. *Journal of Physical Education, Health, Recreation and Dance, 86*(5), 46-54.

Chapter 3

Ayvazo, S., & Ward, P. (2011). Pedagogical content knowledge of experienced teachers in physical education: Functional analysis of adaptations. *Research Quarterly for Exercise and Sport, 82,* 675-684.

Griffey, D., & Housner, L. (2007). *Designing effective instructional tasks for physical education and sports.* Champaign, IL: Human Kinetics.

Launder, A., & Piltz, W. (2013). *Play practice: Engaging and developing skilled players from beginner to elite.* Champaign, IL: Human Kinetics.

Rink, J. (2004). It's OK to be a beginner. *Journal of Physical Education, Recreation & Dance, 75,* 31-34.

Siedentop, D., Hastie, P. A., & van der Mars, H. (2011). *Complete guide to sport education* (2nd ed.). Champaign, IL: Human Kinetics.

Ward, P. (2009). Content matters: Knowledge that alters teaching. In L. Housner, M. Metzler, P. Schempp, & T. Templin (Eds.), *Historic traditions and future directions of research on teaching and teacher education in physical education* (pp. 345-356). Morgantown, WV: Fitness Information Technology.

Ward, P. (2013). The role of content knowledge in conceptions of teaching effectiveness in physical education. *Research Quarterly for Exercise and Sport, 84,* 431-440.

Ward, P., Ayvazo, S., & Lehwald, H. (2014). Using knowledge packets in teacher education to develop pedagogical content knowledge. *Journal of Physical Education, Health, Recreation and Dance, 85*(6), 38-43.

Chapter 4

Gallahue, D., Ozman, J., & Goodway, J. (2012) *Understanding motor development: Infants, children, adolescents, adults.* New York: McGraw Hill.

Chapter 8

Bailey, R., Hillman, C., Arent, S., & Petipas, A. (2013). Physical activity: An underestimated investment in human capital? *Journal of Physical Activity and Health, 10,* 289-308.

Physical Activity Council. (2016). *Physical Activity Council 2016 participation report.* Retrieved from http://www.physicalactivitycouncil.com/pdfs/current.pdf

Rikard, G. L., & Baneville, D. (2006). High school student attitudes about physical education. *Sport Education and Society, 11,* 385-400.

Chapter 9

Launder, A., & Piltz, W. (2013). *Play practice: Engaging and developing skilled players from beginner to elite.* Champaign, IL: Human Kinetics.

About the Authors

Dr. Phillip Ward is a professor of physical education teacher education in the department of human sciences at The Ohio State University. Dr. Ward is passionate about physical education and teacher education. He is director of the Learning to Teach Physical Education Research Program (https://u.osu.edu/ltpe), which develops pedagogical content knowledge for teaching physical education. Dr. Ward has authored or coauthored more than 100 research papers and book chapters and has presented over 150 papers at international, national, and state conferences. He has served as an invited lecturer at 22 universities worldwide, including Belgium, China, Israel, and Japan, as well as at 16 international conferences. In 2014, he received the SHAPE America Curriculum and Instruction Honor Award. In 2015, he received the American Educational Research Association (AERA) Research on Learning and Instruction in Physical Education Outstanding Scholar Award. He is a fellow of the National Academy of Kinesiology and a research fellow of SHAPE America.

Dr. Harry Lehwald is a senior lecturer of physical education teacher education in the department of human sciences at The Ohio State University. He and the other faculty at The Ohio State University were awarded the 2014 Physical Education Teacher Education Honor Award from the National Association for Sport and Physical Education (NASPE). In addition to his teaching, he has provided in-service teacher training and presented workshops and research on the topic of content knowledge at state and national conferences, as well as in Russia. He is a member of the Learning to Teach Physical Education Research Program at The Ohio State University. He has also coauthored several articles dealing with content knowledge and pedagogical content knowledge. He served on South Carolina's elementary physical education assessment writing team. Prior to his time in higher education, he taught and coached in public schools for 11 years and coached track and field and cross country at the collegiate level for 13 years, winning two Coach of the Year awards.

About the Contributors

Dr. Shiri Ayvazo is with the department of special education at David Yellin College in Jerusalem, Israel. She holds a doctoral degree in physical education teacher education from The Ohio State University. She has expertise in physical education, special education, and teacher education. Her content expertise is in tennis.

Chris Bell is with The Ohio State University. She holds a master's degree in teacher education from The Ohio State University. She is a former elementary school physical education teacher and teacher educator. In both roles, she has been recognized for her expertise. Her content expertise is in elementary physical education and gymnastics.

Dr. Ali Brian is with the department of physical education at University of South Carolina in Columbia, South Carolina. She holds a doctoral degree in physical education teacher education from The Ohio State University. She has expertise in physical education and motor development. Her content expertise is in softball.

Dr. Insook Kim is with the school of teaching, learning, and curriculum studies at Kent State University in Kent, Ohio. She holds a doctoral degree in physical education teacher education from The Ohio State University. She has expertise in physical education and physical education teacher education. Her content expertise is in badminton.

Dr. Yun Soo Lee is with the department of special education at Dankook University in Yongin-si, South Korea. He holds a doctoral degree in physical education teacher education from The Ohio State University. He has expertise in physical education and physical education teacher education.

Dr. Kevin Lorson is with the department of kinesiology and health at Wright State University in Dayton, Ohio. He holds a doctoral degree in physical education teacher education from The Ohio State University. He has expertise in physical education and physical education teacher education. His content expertise is in flag football.

Dr. Jim Ressler is with the department of kinesiology and physical education at the University of Northern Illinois in DeKalb, Illinois. He holds a doctoral degree in physical education teacher education from The Ohio State University. He has expertise in physical education and physical education teacher education. His content expertise is in basketball.

Dr. Deb Sazama is with the department of exercise and sport science at the University of Wisconsin at La Crosse. She holds a doctoral degree in curriculum and instruction from the University of Northern Iowa. She has expertise in physical education teacher education. Her content expertise is in volleyball.

Bobbie Siedentop is with The Ohio State University. She holds a master's degree in physical education from The Ohio State University. She is a former elementary school physical teacher and teacher educator. In both roles, she has been recognized for her expertise. Her content expertise is in elementary physical education and locomotion.

Dr. Adrian Turner is with the school of human movement and leisure studies at Bowling Green State University in Bowling Green, Ohio. He holds a doctoral degree in teaching and teacher education from the University of North Carolina at Greensboro. He has expertise in physical education and physical education teacher education. His content expertise is in soccer.

About SHAPE America

SHAPE America – Society of Health and Physical Educators is committed to ensuring that all children have the opportunity to lead healthy, physically active lives. As the nation's largest membership organization of health and physical

education professionals, SHAPE America works with its 50 state affiliates and is a founding partner of national initiatives including the Presidential Youth Fitness Program, Active Schools and the Jump Rope for Heart and Hoops for Heart programs.

Since its founding in 1885, the organization has defined excellence in physical education, most recently creating *National Standards & Grade-Level Outcomes for K-12 Physical Education* (2014), National Standards for Initial Physical Education Teacher Education (2016), National Standards for Health Education Teacher Education (2017) and *National Standards for Sport Coaches* (2006). Also, SHAPE America participated as a member of the Joint Committee on National Health Education Standards, which published *National Health Education Standards, Second Edition: Achieving Excellence* (2007). Our programs, products and services provide the leadership, professional development and advocacy that support health and physical educators at every level, from preschool through university graduate programs.

The SHAPE America website, www.shapeamerica.org, holds a treasure trove of free resources for health and physical educators, adapted physical education teachers, teacher trainers and coaches, including activity calendars, curriculum resources, tools and templates, assessments and more. Visit www.shapeamerica.org and search for Teacher's Toolbox.

Every spring, SHAPE America hosts its National Convention & Expo, the premier national professional-development event for health and physical educators.

Advocacy is an essential element in the fulfillment of our mission. By speaking out for the school health and physical education professions, SHAPE America strives to make an impact on the national policy landscape.

Our Vision: A nation in which all children are prepared to lead healthy, physically active lives.

Our Mission: To advance professional practice and promote research related to health and physical education, physical activity, dance and sport.

Our Commitment: 50 Million Strong by 2029

Approximately 50 million students are enrolled currently in America's elementary and secondary schools (grades pre-K to 12). SHAPE America wants to ensure that by the time today's preschoolers graduate from high school in 2029, all of America's young people are empowered to lead healthy and active lives through effective health and physical education programs. To learn more about 50 Million Strong by 2029, visit www. shapeamerica.org.

With one step, you'll join a national movement.

Membership will advance your career — and connect you to a national movement of educators who are preparing students to lead healthy, physically active lives.

Joining SHAPE America Is Your First Step Toward:

- **Improving your instructional practices.** Membership is your direct connection to the classroom resources, webinars, workshops, books, and all the professional development you need. **Members save up to 30%!**

- **Staying current on trends in education.** We will deliver the news to you through our weekly e-newsletter *Et Cetera,* our quarterly member newsletter *Momentum,* and peer-reviewed journals such as *Strategies: A Journal for Physical and Sport Educators,* the *American Journal of Health Education, Journal of Physical Education, Recreation & Dance,* and *Research Quarterly for Exercise and Sport.*

- **Earning recognition for you and your program.** Showcase your school's achievements and gain funding through grant and award opportunities.

- **Growing your professional network.** Whether it's a face-to-face event or online through the member-exclusive community—*Exchange*—you'll gain access to a diverse group of peers who can help you respond to daily challenges.

Join Today. shapeamerica.org/membership